CW00705458

THE

PUBLICATIONS

OF THE

PIPE ROLL SOCIETY

NEW SERIES – VOLUME LXI

The White Book, p. 1: a copy of a bull of Alexander III, 28 July 1171 (**1**)

THE WHITE BOOK
(LIBER ALBUS)
OF SOUTHWELL

VOLUME I

EDITED BY

MICHAEL JONES,
JULIA BARROW, DAVID CROOK
AND TREVOR FOULDS

WITH CONTRIBUTIONS FROM

NEIL BETTRIDGE, JEAN CAMERON,
PAUL CAVILL AND TERESA WEBBER

PRINTED FOR THE PIPE ROLL SOCIETY BY
THE BOYDELL PRESS
2018

First published 2018

A Pipe Roll Society publication
published by The Boydell Press
an imprint of Boydell & Brewer Ltd
PO Box 9, Woodbridge, Suffolk IP12 3DF, UK
and of Boydell & Brewer Inc.
668 Mt Hope Avenue, Rochester, NY 14620-2731, USA

website: www.boydellandbrewer.com

ISBN 978-0-901134-67-7

A CIP catalogue record for this book is available
from the British Library

The publisher has no responsibility for the continued existence or
accuracy of URLs for external or third-party internet websites referred to
in this book, and does not guarantee that any content on such websites is,
or will remain, accurate or appropriate

This publication is printed on acid-free paper

Typeset by Word and Page, Chester, UK

Printed and bound in Great Britain by
TJ International Ltd, Padstow, Cornwall

*In memory of
Sir Frank Stenton (1880–1967),
whose family was long connected with
Southwell Minster,
medieval historian, university administrator
and benefactor,
on the fiftieth anniversary of his death*

CONTENTS

THE WHITE BOOK OF SOUTHWELL

ILLUSTRATIONS

Other than frontispieces, illustrations are placed after the Introduction

The editors and publishers are grateful to all the institutions and persons listed for permission to reproduce the materials in which they hold copyright. Every effort has been made to trace the copyright holders; apologies are offered for any omission, and the publishers will be pleased to add any necessary acknowledgement in subsequent editions.

GENERAL EDITORS' PREFACE

2017 marked the fiftieth anniversary of the death of Sir Frank Stenton, to whose memory this edition is dedicated. Sir Frank is one of the greatest historians of the Danelaw and of England in the two centuries either side of the Norman Conquest, and was one of the foremost supporters of the Pipe Roll Society in the first half-century of its existence. The Pipe Roll Society Council wished to mark his contribution by supporting an edition of the White Book, the main surviving cartulary of Southwell Minster, the collegiate church in the town in which Sir Frank was educated and whose history he wrote. This is a manuscript which contains numerous copies of government records, the originals of which are to be found at The National Archives; it throws considerable light on landholding practices and patterns of religious observance over four centuries. It forms a worthy addition to the publications of the Society.

It is an enormous pleasure to record our thanks to the editors of this volume, led by Professor Michael Jones. Their expertise, knowledge and willingness to discuss editorial matters patiently and frankly have been remarkable. The edition is testament to this. We also particularly wish to offer our thanks to the officers and council of both the Stenton Fund and the Lincoln Record Society for awarding grants to ensure this edition can be published together as two volumes.

Paul Dryburgh, The National Archives
Louise Wilkinson, Christ Church University, Canterbury
February 2018

CO-ORDINATING EDITOR'S PREFACE

Shortly before I retired in 2002 from an academic career as a historian of medieval France, my colleague John Beckett, thinking that I might have some spare time and knowing that I would be living in the small rural village of Norwell in central Nottinghamshire, asked if I would like to contribute an entry on its parish church to the Southwell Diocesan Advisory Council (DAC) Churches website. This ambitious project, then in its early days, aimed to make available on the internet an account of every Anglican church in the diocese of Southwell (now Southwell and Nottingham). Such accounts were to cover not only the history of individual churches but also their archaeology and their material remains, reflecting parochial life and religious practice over the centuries. They were also to provide a standardised inventory of the architectural and other riches (stained glass, monuments, bells and other fittings) represented by these buildings, many of which have medieval origins.

Attracted by the suggestion, but also pointing out that Norwell was then one of four parishes (with Caunton, Cromwell and Ossington) in a joint benefice, rather unwisely I said that I would form a small team to work on all four churches simultaneously, not realising the amount of time needed to produce even one entry. It was while undertaking the necessary research that I first became fully aware of the significance of the White Book of Southwell for the medieval history of several of the chosen churches, most notably for Norwell itself. Already held by the collegiate minster church of St Mary's, Southwell, by the time of Domesday Book (1086), most of Norwell parish remained in the hands of two (from *c.* 1200, three) canons or prebendaries of St Mary's until the old Chapter was abolished in 1840. Indeed, even after this had occurred, because the Ecclesiastical Commissioners for England assumed the Chapter's rights as landlords, most land and many houses in Norwell parish remained under church control until as late as 1952, an astonishing record of tenurial continuity from Anglo-Saxon times to the near-present.

Much of the medieval evidence for how this affected Norwell is fortuitously preserved in the *Liber Albus*, White Book, of Southwell. A substantial manuscript of nearly 500 pages, containing 620 individual documents, this is a major medieval cartulary. It contains copies of the principal privileges granted to and enjoyed by the Chapter of St Mary's, as well as the title deeds of the properties acquired by the Chapter or individual prebendaries between the early twelfth century and the end of the Middle Ages. Its contents will be described in more detail in the Introduction that follows. Here it is only necessary to note that discovering its riches, and aware that it had been exploited by historians of Nottinghamshire since the days of Dr Robert Thoroton in the later seventeenth century but never edited in full, I decided that it would be a service to remedy this scholarly oversight. Appreciating the scale of the project and the variety of material contained in the White Book, it was clear to me that the edition should be a collaborative venture. I thus invited several colleagues to join me in preparing the present edition, and to make accessible to a much wider public a key source not only for the history of the minster itself, but one which also throws considerable light on wider social and economic issues affecting developments within Nottinghamshire in the Middle Ages.

Thus in 2007, with the encouragement of the then Dean, Dr John Guille, and Chapter of Southwell, to whom the White Book belongs, and with the cooperation of Mark Dorrington (then Principal Archivist, Nottinghamshire Archives) responsible for curating the White Book on behalf of the Chapter, an editorial team under my chairmanship was formed. Its main task was to prepare a definitive text and the necessary scholarly annotation. The principal members were Dr (now Professor) Julia Barrow (University of Nottingham, now University of Leeds), Dr David Crook (formerly Assistant Keeper, The National Archives), Dr Trevor Foulds (then Leisure Services, City of Nottingham) and myself. Neil Bettridge (then Nottinghamshire Archives), who had been contracted to catalogue the records of the Chapter deposited at Nottinghamshire Archives, also helpfully transcribed an important section of text. Dr Nicholas Bennett (Canon Librarian, Cathedral Library, Lincoln) kindly photographed a number of original Southwell charters now to be found in Lincolnshire Archives. We also invited Dr Teresa Webber (Trinity College, Cambridge) to examine the palaeography and structure of the manuscript, and Dr Paul Cavill (English Place-Name Society, University of Nottingham), assisted by Mrs Jean Cameron (formerly University of Nottingham), agreed to help with place-names. Among those offering general counsel during our regular editorial meetings, Dr Alison McHardy (University of Nottingham) has contributed much sound advice as well as providing information on particular *acta* and individual clergy.

We are also grateful for general support from many others during the course of the project, thanks being noted at appropriate places, but here we must especially thank Professors Richard Sharpe and Nicholas Vincent for providing material and advice on the *acta* of Henry I and Henry II in advance of their publication, and Professor Philip Dixon, Charles Leggatt, Richard Jarvis and Nigel Coates, then acting dean of Southwell, for help with obtaining suitable illustrative material. Thanks are also due to copyright holders for permission to reproduce material in their possession: The British Library Board, The National Archives, Lincolnshire Archives, the Trustees of the Savile Estate, and, above, all Dean Nicola Sullivan and the Chapter of Southwell, owners of the White Book, and Ruth Imeson and her colleagues at Nottinghamshire Archives, who curate it on behalf of the Dean and Chapter. Sue Sinclair kindly drew two maps. While in preparing this edition for publication by the Pipe Roll Society, we are extremely indebted to its current Chairman, Dr David Crook, and general editors, Dr Paul Dryburgh and Prof. Louise Wilkinson, for advice and encouragement. Dr Dryburgh, ably assisted and abetted by Dr Crook, has been particularly helpful in the final revision of the indices. As the general co-ordinator of the project, can I finally add my own very sincere thanks to my co-editors and to other colleagues, old friends and new, for their hard work and uncomplaining and enthusiastic cooperation over the ten years and more it has taken us to complete the edition, very much a team effort, though for whatever shortcomings it may still have, I am happy to take responsibility.

The edition is dedicated to the memory of Sir Frank Stenton, whose family was long associated with the legal affairs of the Chapter, who himself wrote about the Minster's history, encouraged study of the White Book, and was buried in the graveyard of the prebendal church at Halloughton, just outside Southwell, where Lady Stenton later joined him.

Michael Jones
Norwell
Candlemas 2018

ABBREVIATED REFERENCES

AALT
Anglo American Legal Tradition, http://aalt.law.uh.edu/ AALT.html Documents from Medieval and Early Modern England from The National Archives, Kew

Alexander, 'Patronage Deferred'
Jennifer S. Alexander, 'A Case of Patronage Deferred: the Chancel of Bunny Church, Nottinghamshire and Its Patrons', *TTS* 100 (1996), 61–75

Alumni Oxonienses
Joseph Foster, *Alumni Oxonienses, 1500–1714*, 4 vols (Oxford, 1891–2); *Alumni Oxonienses, 1715–1886*, 4 vols (Oxford, 1887–8)

Barraclough, *Papal Notaries*
Geoffrey Barraclough, *Papal Notaries and the Papal Curia: a Calendar and a Study of a Formularium Notariorum Curie from the Early Years of the Fourteenth Century* (London, 1934)

Barrow, 'Cathedral Communities'
Julia Barrow, 'English Cathedral Communities and Reform in the Late Tenth and Eleventh Century', *Anglo-Norman Durham 1093–1193*, ed. D. Rollason, M. Harvey and M. Prestwich (Woodbridge, 1994), 25–39

Barrow, 'Appendix I'
Julia Barrow, 'Appendix I: The Constitution of Hereford Cathedral in the Thirteenth Century', in *Hereford Cathedral: A History*, ed. G. Aylmer and J. Tiller (London and Rio Grande, 2000), 633–6

Barrow, 'Statutes'
Julia Barrow, 'The Statutes of St Davids Cathedral', *St David of Wales: Cult, Church and Nation*, ed. J. Wyn Evans and Jonathan M. Wooding (Woodbridge, 2007), 317–29

Barrow, *The Clergy*
Julia Barrow, *The Clergy in the Medieval World: Secular Clerics, Their Families and Careers in North-Western Europe, c. 800–c. 1200* (Cambridge, 2015)

Beaumont, *Chapter*
R. M. Beaumont, *The Chapter of Southwell Minster: A Story of 1,000 Years* (1956), 3rd edn (Dorchester, 1978); 4th edn (Derby, 1994)

BI
York, Borthwick Institute for Archives

BI, Reg. Wills
Register of Wills

BL
London, The British Library

Blyth
The Cartulary of Blyth Priory, ed. R. T. Timson, 2 vols (London: HMSO, Historical Manuscripts Commission, JP 17 and Thoroton Society, RS, XXVII and XXVIII, 1973)

BM Catalogue of Seals
W. de G. Birch, *Catalogue of Seals ... in the British Museum*, 6 vols (London, 1887–1900)

BMF
Richard T. W. McDermid, *Beverley Minster Fasti* (YAS, Record Series CXLIX, 1993)

Book of Fees
Liber Feodorum. The Book of Fees commonly called Testa de Nevill, 3 vols (London: HMSO, 1920–31)

Brand, 'Oldcotes'   P. A. Brand, 'Oldcotes v. d'Arcy', *Medieval Legal*
                           Records edited in memory of C. A. F. Meekings, ed. R. F.
                           Hunnisett and J. B. Post (London: HMSO, 1978), 64–113
Bresslau, *Handbuch*   Harry Bresslau, *Handbuch der Urkundenlehre für*
                           Deutschland und Italien, 2 vols and index, 2nd edn
                           (Leipzig, 1912–60)
Brett, *English Church*   Martin Brett, *The English Church under Henry I*
                           (Oxford, 1975)
Brown, *Newark*   Cornelius Brown, *A History of Newark-on-Trent*, 2 vols
                           (Newark 1904), reprinted (Nottingham, 1995)
BRUC   Alfred B. Emden, *A Biographical Register of the Uni-*
                           versity of Cambridge to AD 1500 (Oxford, 1963)
BRUO   Alfred B. Emden, *A Biographical Register of the Uni-*
                           versity of Oxford to AD 1500, 3 vols (Oxford, 1957–9); *A*
                           Biographical Register ... AD 1501–1540 (Oxford, 1974)
Cal. Inq. Misc.   *Calendar of Inquisitions Miscellaneous, Chancery,*
                           preserved in the Public Record Office, 7 vols (London:
                           HMSO, 1916–68)
Cal. Scrope   *A Calendar of the Register of Richard Scrope, Arch-*
                           bishop of York, 1398–1405, ed. Robert N. Swanson
                           (York: Borthwick Texts and Calendars nos 8, 1981 and
                           11, 1985)
Cal. Waldby   *A Calendar of the Register of Robert Waldby, Arch-*
                           bishop of York, 1397, ed. David M. Smith (York: Borth-
                           wick Texts and Calendars no. 2, 1974)
Cameron, 'Bunny'   Alan Cameron, 'Bunny's First Vicarage', *TTS* 86 (1982),
                           62–72
Carter, 'Fledborough'   W. F. Carter and R. F. Wilkinson, 'The Fledborough
                           Family of Lisures', *TTS* 44 (1940), 14–34
Carter, 'Lisures'   W. F. Carter and R. F. Wilkinson, 'Notes on the Family
                           of Lisures', *YAJ* 35 (1943), 183–200
Cart. Treas. York   *The Cartulary of the Treasurer of York Minster and*
                           related documents, ed. Janet E. Burton (Borthwick Texts
                           and Calendars, Records of the Northern Province, 5,
                           1978)
CChR   *Calendar of Charter Rolls, 1226–1516*, 6 vols (London:
                           HMSO, 1903–27)
CCR   *Calendar of the Close Rolls preserved in the Public*
                           Record Office, 62 vols (London: HMSO, 1892–1963)
CFR   *Calendar of Fine Rolls of the Reign of Henry III, 1216–*
                           1272, eds Paul Dryburgh and Beth Hartland, technical
                           eds Arianna Ciula, Tamara Lopez, Jose Miguel Vieira,
                           3 vols (Woodbridge, 2007–11); also available online at
                           www.finerollshenry3.org.uk
Chancellor's Roll   *The Chancellor's Roll for the Eighth Year of King*
                           Richard the First, Michaelmas 1196, ed. D. M. Stenton
                           (London: PRS 45, ns 7, 1930)
Chantry Certificates   *The Chantry Certificate Rolls for the County of Notting-*
                           ham and *The Certificates of the Chantry Commissioners*
                           for the College of Southwell in 1546 and 1548, with an
                           Introduction and Notes, ed. A. Hamilton Thompson

	(Nottingham, 1914) (previously printed in *TTS* 15 (1911), 15–62; 16 (1912), 91–133; 17 (1913), 59–119; 18 (1914), 83–184)
Chaplais, *English Royal Documents*	
	Pierre Chaplais, *English Royal Documents, King John–Henry VI 1199–1461* (Oxford, 1971)
Cheney, *Bishops' Chanceries*	C. R. Cheney, *English Bishops' Chanceries 1100–1250* (Manchester, 1950)
Cheney and Cheney	C. R. Cheney and Mary G. Cheney, *The Letters of Pope Innocent III (1198–1216) concerning England and Wales. A Calendar with an Appendix of Texts* (Oxford, 1967)
Chron. Majora	Matthew Paris, *Chronica Majora*, ed. H. R. Luard, 7 vols (London: Rolls Series, 1872–83)
CIPM	*Calendar of Inquisitions Post Mortem and other analogous documents in the Public Record Office, Henry III–Henry V*, 20 vols (London: HMSO, 1904–95); 6 vols, *1422–47* (Woodbridge, 2002–9)
Clay, *Early Yorkshire Families*	
	Sir Charles Clay, *Early Yorkshire Families, with Illustrative Documents*, ed. Diana E. Greenway (YAS, Record Series CXXXV, 1973)
Close Rolls	*Close Rolls of the Reign of Henry III*, 14 vols (London: HMSO, 1902–38)
Colchester, *Wells*	L. S. Colchester, *Wells Cathedral Fabric Accounts 1390–1600* (Wells, 1983)
Colvin, 'Origin of Chantries'	Howard Colvin, 'The Origins of Chantries', *Journal of Medieval History* 26 (2000), 163–73
Complete Peerage	*The Complete Peerage* by G. E. Cokayne, revised edn by V. Gibbs, H. A. Doubleday, Lord Howard de Walden, G. H. White and R. S. Lee, 13 vols in 14 (London, 1910–59)
CPL	*Calendar of Entries in the Papal Registers relating to Great Britain and Ireland. Papal Letters*, 20 vols (London: HMSO and Dublin: Irish Manuscripts Commission, 1893–2005)
CPP	*Calendar of Entries in the Papal Registers relating to Great Britain and Ireland. Petitions to the Pope* (London: HMSO, 1896)
CPR	*Calendar of the Patent Rolls preserved in the Public Record Office*, 73 vols (London: HMSO, 1891–1982)
Crook, 'Spigurnels'	David Crook, 'The Spigurnels of Skegby', *NMS* 21 (1977), 50–70
Crook, 'Struggle'	David Crook, 'The Struggle over Forest Boundaries in Nottinghamshire, 1218–1227', *TTS* 83 (1979), 35–45
Crook, *General Eyre*	David Crook, *Records of the General Eyre, 1194–1348* (London: Public Record Office Handbooks 20, 1982)
Crook, 'Establishment'	David Crook, 'The Establishment of the Derbyshire County Court, 1256', *Derbyshire Archaeological Journal*, CIII (1983), 98–106
Crook, 'Robin Hood'	David Crook, 'The Sheriff of Nottingham and Robin Hood: the Genesis of the Legend?', *Thirteenth Century*

England II: Proceedings of the Newcastle upon Tyne
Conference 1987, ed. P. R. Coss and S. D. Lloyd (Woodbridge, 1988), 59–69

Crook, 'Archbishopric'   David Crook, 'The Archbishopric of York and the
Boundaries of the Forest in Nottinghamshire in the
Twelfth Century', *Law and Government in Medieval
England and Normandy: Essays in Honour of Sir James
Holt*, ed. G. Garnett and J. Hudson (Cambridge, 1994),
325–40

Crook, 'A Dying Queen'   David Crook, 'A Dying Queen and a Declining Knight:
Sir Richard de Weston of Weston, Nottinghamshire (d.
1301) and His Family', *Recognitions: Essays presented
to Edmund Fryde*, ed. C. Richmond and I. Harvey
(Aberystwyth, 1996), 89–124

Crook, 'Dynastic Conflict'   David Crook, 'Dynastic Conflict in Thirteenth-Century
Laxton', *Thirteenth Century England XI*, ed. Björn
Weiler, Janet Burton, Phillipp Schofield and Karen
Stöber (Woodbridge, 2007), 193–214

Crook, 'Robert of Lexington'   David Crook, 'Robert of Lexington, Chief Justice of the
Bench, 1236–44', *Laws, Lawyers and Texts: Studies in
Medieval Legal History in Honour of Paul Brand*, ed.
Susanne Jenks, Jonathan Rose and Christopher Whittick
(Leiden and Boston, 2012), 149–75

Crook, 'Anatomy of a knightly homicide'
David Crook, 'The Anatomy of a Knightly Homicide in
Rural Nottinghamshire, 1295', *NMS* 57 (2013), 69–88

CRR   *Curia Regis Rolls of the Reigns of Richard I, John and
Henry III preserved in the Public Record Office*, 17 vols
(London: HMSO, 1922–92)

CYS   Canterbury and York Society

Dale   *The Cartulary of Dale Abbey*, ed. Avrom Saltman (London: HMSO, Historical Manuscripts Commission, JP
with Derbyshire Record Society, 11, 1967)

Darley   *The Cartulary of Darley Abbey*, ed. Reginald R. Dar-
lington, 2 vols (Kendal, 1945)

Davis, *Cartularies*   G. R. C. Davis, *Medieval Cartularies of Great Britain
and Ireland*, revised by Claire Breay, Julian Harrison
and David M. Smith (London: The British Library,
2010)

DB   Domesday Book

Denton and Dooley   J. H. Denton and J. P. Dooley, *Representatives of the
Lower Clergy in Parliament 1295–1340* (Woodbridge,
1987)

De Ville, 'Deyvilles'   Oscar de Ville, 'The Deyvilles and the Genesis of the
Robin Hood Legend', *NMS* 43 (1999), 90–109

De Ville, 'John Deyville'   Oscar de Ville, 'John Deyville: a Neglected Rebel',
Northern History 34 (1998), 17–40

Dickinson, *Southwell*   William Rastall Dickinson, *The History and Antiquities of the Town of Southwell* (1787), new edn (1819),
reprinted (Nottingham, 1996)

Dimock, 'Architectural History'
James F. Dimock, 'Architectural History of Southwell Minster', *Reports and Papers read at the Meetings of the Architectural Societies of the Diocese of Lincoln, County of York, Archdeaconry of Northampton, County of Bedford, Diocese of Worcester, County of Leicester and Town of Sheffield during the year MDCCCCLXIX* (Lincoln, 1869), 39–56

Dimock, *History*
James F. Dimock, *History of the Collegiate Church and Town of Southwell; with a Descriptive Account of the Church* (Southwell, 1875)

Dixon, 'Vicars Choral'
Philip Dixon, 'The Vicars Choral at Ripon, Beverley and Southwell', *Vicars Choral at English Cathedrals. Cantate Domino: History, Architecture and Archaeology*, ed. Richard Hall and David Stocker (Oxford, 2005), 138–46

Dobson, 'Later Middle Ages'
R. Barrie Dobson, 'The Later Middle Ages, 1215–1500', in Gerald Aylmer and R. J. Cant, *A History of York Minster* (Oxford, 1977), 44–109

Dobson, 'Residentiary Canons'
R. Barrie Dobson, 'The Residentiary Canons of York in the Fifteenth Century', *Journal of Ecclesiastical History* 30 (1979), 145–73

Documents Newark
Documents relating to the Manor and Soke of Newark-on-Trent, ed. M. W. Barley, TS, Record Series XVI (1955)

Domesday People
K. S. B. Keats-Rohan, *Domesday People. A Prosopography of Persons occurring in English Documents 1066–1166, I, Domesday Book* (Woodbridge, 1999)

Dukery Records
The Dukery Records, being notes and memoranda illustrative of Nottinghamshire Ancient History, collected during many years by Robert White, of Worksop, Privately printed for subscribers (Worksop, 1904)

Dyer, 'Sheepcotes'
Christopher Dyer, 'Sheepcotes: Evidence for Medieval Sheepfarming', *Medieval Archaeology* 39 (1995), 136–64

Edwards, *Secular Cathedrals*
Kathleen Edwards, *The English Secular Cathedrals*, 2nd edn (Manchester, 1967)

EEA
English Episcopal Acta

EEA, Lincoln 1067–1185
English Episcopal Acta I, *Lincoln 1067–1185*, ed. David M. Smith (Oxford, 1980)

EEA, York 1070–1154
English Episcopal Acta 5, *York 1070–1154*, ed. Janet E. Burton (Oxford, 1988)

EEA, York 1154–1181
English Episcopal Acta, 20, *York 1154–1181*, ed. Marie Lovatt (London, 2000)

EEA, York 1189–1212
English Episcopal Acta, 27, *York 1189–1212*, ed. Marie Lovatt (London, 2004)

EHR
English Historical Review

English Lawsuits
English Lawsuits from William I to Richard I, vol. 1, *William I to Stephen (nos 1–346)*, ed. R. C. Van Caenegem (London: Selden Society 106, 1990)

EPNS
English Place-Name Society

Everson and Stocker, 'Archaeology of Episcopal Reform'
: Paul Everson and David Stocker, 'The Archaeology of Episcopal Reform: Greater Churches in York Diocese in the 11th Century', *The Archaeology of the Eleventh Century. Continuities and Transformations*, ed. Dawn Hadley and Christopher Dyer (London 2016), 177–202

EYC
: *Early Yorkshire Charters*, vols i–iii, ed. W. Farrer (Edinburgh 1914–16); vols iv–xii, ed. C. T. Clay (YAS, Record Series, extra series, 1935–65)

Eyton, *Itinerary*
: R. W. Eyton, *The Court, Household and Itinerary of King Henry II* (Dorchester, 1878)

Excerpta e rot. fin.
: *Excerpta e rotulis finium in turri Londinensi asservatis. Henrico Tertio Rege A.D. 1216–1272*, ed. C. Roberts, 2 vols (London: Record Commission, 1835–6)

Fasti Parochiales
: *Fasti Parochiales*, i & ii, eds A. Hamilton Thompson & C. T. Clay; iii, ed. N. A. H. Lawrance; iv, eds Nora K. M. Gurney & Sir Charles Clay (YAS, Record Series, LXXXV, 1933, CVII, 1943, CXXIX, 1967 and CXXXIII, 1971)

Fasti 1066–1300
: John Le Neve, *Fasti Ecclesiae Anglicanae 1066–1300*, compiled by Diana E. Greenway et al., 11 vols (London, 1968–2011)

Fasti 1300–1541
: John Le Neve, *Fasti Ecclesiae Anglicanae, 1300–1541*, compiled by J. M. Horn et al., 12 vols (London, 1962–7)

Fasti 1541–1857
: John Le Neve, *Fasti Ecclesiae Anglicanae, 1541–1857*, compiled by J. M. Horn et al., 11 vols (London, 1969–2004)

Fasti Dunelm.
: *Fasti Dunelmenses: a Record of the Beneficed Clergy of the Diocese of Durham*, ed. D. S. Boutflower (SS 139, 1926)

Fasti Ebor.
: W. H. Dixon, *Fasti Eboracenses: the Lives of the Archbishops of York*, ed. James Raine, vol. 1 (London, 1863)

Feet of Fines, Yorks. 1327–1347
: *Feet of Fines for the County of York from 1327 to 1347, 1–20 Edward III*, ed. W. Paley Baildon (YAS, Record Series XLII, 1910)

Feudal Aids
: *Inquisitions and Assessments relating to Feudal Aids; with other analogous documents preserved in the Public Record Office*, 6 vols (London: HMSO, 1899–1920)

Foedera (O)
: *Foedera, conventiones, litterae, etc.*, ed. Thomas Rymer et al., 20 vols (London, 1704–35)

Foedera (RC)
: Thomas Rymer, *Foedera, conventiones, litterae, etc.*, ed. J. Caley et al. for the Record Commission, 4 vols in seven (London, 1816–69)

Foulds, 'Lenton Priory'
: Trevor Foulds, 'The Foundation of Lenton Priory and a Reconstruction of Its Lost Cartulary', *TTS* 92 (1988), 34–42

Foulds, 'Siege of Nottingham'
: Trevor Foulds, 'The Siege of Nottingham Castle in 1194', *TTS* 95 (1991), 20–8

Foulds, '*In medio chori*'   Trevor Foulds, '*In medio chori*: the Tomb of Thomas of
                              Corbridge, Archbishop of York, in Southwell Minster',
                              Journal of the British Archaeological Association 167
                              (2014), 109–23

Godfrey, *Bingham*   John T. Godfrey, *Notes on the Churches of Nottingham-
                              shire: Hundred of Bingham* (London, 1907)

Hamilton Thompson, *TTS* 15 (1911)

                              A. Hamilton Thompson, 'The Certificates of the Chantry
                              Commissioners for the College of Southwell in 1546 and
                              1548, with an Introduction and Notes', *TTS* 15 (1911),
                              15–62 [reprinted in *The Chantry Certificate Rolls for
                              the County of Nottingham* and *The Certificates of the
                              Chantry Commissioners for the College of Southwell in
                              1546 and 1548, with an Introduction and Notes*, ed. A.
                              Hamilton Thompson (Nottingham, 1914)]

Hamilton Thompson, *Visitations*

                              'Documents relating to Diocesan and Provincial
                              Visitations from the Registers of Henry Bowet, Lord
                              Archbishop of York 7 Oct. 1407–20 Oct. 1423, and John
                              Kempe, Cardinal-Priest of Santa Balbina, Lord Arch-
                              bishop of York, 20 July 1425–1 July 1452', *Miscellanea*
                              II (SS, 1916), 131–302

Hardstaff   R. E. Hardstaff, *The Southwell Domesday Survey 1086
                              AD. A Reconstruction of Farm and Domestic Life on the
                              Manor of Southwell* (Southwell: Southwell and District
                              Local History Society, 2003)

HBC, ed. Fryde   *Handbook of British Chronology*, 3rd edn, ed. E. B.
                              Fryde, D. E. Greenway and I. Porter (London: Royal
                              Historical Society, Guides and Handbooks 2, 1986)

Hemingway   Guy Hemingway, 'A History of Norwell', typescript
                              1983 [copy at Nottinghamshire Archives]

Heslop, 'English Seals'   T. A. Heslop, 'English Seals from the Mid Ninth
                              Century to 1100', *Journal of the British Archaeological
                              Association* CXXXIII (1980), 1–16

Historians of York   *The Historians of the Church of York and Its Archbish-
                              ops*, ed. James Raine, 3 vols (London: Rolls Series,
                              1879–94)

HMC   Historical Manuscripts Commission

HMSO   Her/His Majesty's Stationery Office

Hodgson, *Thomas II*   W. E. Hodgson, *The Life of Thomas II, Archbishop
                              of York and his connection with Southwell Minster.
                              An essay for the Eight Hundredth Anniversary of the
                              Consecration to be held at Southwell on June 29th 1909*
                              (Nottingham, 1909)

House of Commons, 1386–1421

                              J. S. Roskell, Linda Clark and Carole Rawcliffe, *The
                              House of Commons 1386–1421*, 4 vols (Stroud, 1992)

HRH, i   *The Heads of Religious Houses: England and Wales
                              940–1216*, ed. Dom David Knowles, C. N. L. Brooke
                              and Vera London (Cambridge, 1972)

HRH, ii

The Heads of Religious Houses: England and Wales
1216–1377, ed. David M. Smith and Vera C. M. London
(Cambridge, 2001)

Hugh the Chanter

Hugh the Chanter, The History of the Church of York
1066–1127, ed. and trans. C. Johnson, M. Brett, C. N. L.
Brooke and M. Winterbottom (Oxford, 1990)

Image, Text and Church

Image, Text and Church, 1380–1600; essays for Margaret Aston, eds Linda Clark, Maureen Jurkowski and
Colin Richmond (Toronto: Pontifical Institute of Mediaeval Studies, 2009)

IPM Notts. 1279–1321

Abstracts of the Inquisitiones Post Mortem relating to
Nottinghamshire, Henry III, Edward I and Edward II,
1279–1321, ed. John Standish, TS, Record Series IV
(1914)

IPM Notts. 1321–1350

Abstracts of the Inquisitiones Post Mortem relating to
Nottinghamshire, Edward II and Edward III, 1321–1350,
ed. T. M. Blagg, TS, Record Series VI (1939)

IPM Notts. 1350–1388

Abstracts of the Inquisitiones Post Mortem relating to
Nottinghamshire, Part I, Edward III and Richard II,
1350–1388, ed. K. S. S. Train, TS, Record Series XII
(1949)

IPM Notts. 1388–1436

Abstracts of the Inquisitiones Post Mortem relating
to Nottinghamshire, Part II, Richard II–Henry VI,
1388–1436, ed. K. S. S. Train, TS, Record Series XII
(1951)

IPM Notts. 1436–1485

Abstracts of the Inquisitiones Post Mortem relating to
Nottinghamshire, Henry VI–Richard III, 1436–1485, ed.
M. A. Renshaw, TS, Record Series XVII (1956)

Jeayes, Derbyshire Charters

I. H. Jeayes, Descriptive Catalogue of Derbyshire
Charters in Public and Private Libraries and Muniment
Rooms (London, 1906)

JEPNS

Journal of the English Place-Name Society

JL

Regesta pontificum romanorum ad annum 1198, ed. P.
Jaffé, revised edition by S. Loewenfeld and others, 2
vols (Leipzig, 1885–8; reprint Graz, 1956)

Jones, 'Significance'

Michael Jones, 'The Enduring Significance of the 956
AD Southwell Charter: Change and Continuity on the
Prebendal Estates of Norwell, Nottinghamshire', TTS 111
(2007), 63–72

Jones, 'Master Vacarius'

Michael Jones, 'Master Vacarius, Civil Lawyer, Canon
of Southwell and Parson of Norwell, Nottinghamshire',
NMS 53 (2009), 1–20

Jones, Norwell Buildings

Michael Jones, Norwell Buildings, Norwell Heritage
Booklet 1 (Nottingham, 2009)

Jones, Norwell Farms

Michael Jones, Norwell Farms, Norwell Heritage Booklet 5 (Nottingham, 2009)

Jones, Willoughby by Norwell Michael and Elizabeth Jones, Willoughby by Norwell
Deserted Village, Norwell Heritage Booklet 6 (Notting-
ham, 2012)

Jones, Norwell Church

Michael and Elizabeth Jones, Norwell Church &
Chapel, Norwell Heritage Booklet 7 (Nottingham, 2013)

JP   Joint Publication
Ker and Piper   N. R. Ker and A. J. Piper, *Medieval Manuscripts in British Libraries*, IV, *Paisley–York* (Oxford, 1992)
Kirkby's Inquest   *The Survey of the County of York taken by John de Kirkby, commonly called Kirkby's Inquest; also Inquisitions of the Knights' Fees, the Nomina villarum for Yorkshire, and an appendix of illustrative documents*, ed. R. H. Skaife (SS 49, 1867)
LA   Lincolnshire Archives
Landon, *Itinerary*   Lionel Landon, *The Itinerary of King Richard I* (London: PRS 51, 1935)
Latham, *Word-List*   R. E. Latham, *Revised Medieval Latin Word-List from British and Irish Sources* (London: British Academy, 1965)
Le Neve   John Le Neve, *Fasti Ecclesiae Anglicanae*, corrected and continued by T. Duffus Hardy, 3 vols (Oxford, 1854)
Lincs. Domesday   *The Lincolnshire Domesday and the Lindsey Survey*, ed. C. W. Foster (LRS 19, 1924)
List & Indexes, IX   PRO Lists and Indexes, IX: *List of Sheriffs for England and Wales to 1831* (London, 1898)
LRS   Lincoln Record Society
McHardy, 'Haxey's Case'   A. K. McHardy, 'Haxey's Case 1397: the Petition and Petitioner Reconsidered', *The Age of Richard II*, ed. James L. Gillespie (Stroud, 1997), 93–114
McHardy, 'John Scarle'   A. K. McHardy, 'John Scarle: Ambition and Politics in the Late Medieval Church', *Image, Text and Church, 1380–1600; essays for Margaret Aston*, ed. Linda Clark, Maureen Jurkowski and Colin Richmond (Toronto: Pontifical Institute of Mediaeval Studies, 2009), 68–93
McNeill, 'Chronology'   J. McNeill, 'The Chronology of the Choir of Southwell Minster', *Southwell and Nottinghamshire: Medieval Art, Architecture and Industry*, ed. J. S. Alexander, British Archaeological Association Conference Transactions 21 (1998), 24–32
Marcombe, *Leper Knights*   David Marcombe, *Leper Knights: The Order of St Lazarus of Jerusalem in England, c. 1150–1544* (Woodbridge, 2003)
Marritt, 'Secular Cathedrals' Stephen Marritt, 'Secular Cathedrals and the Anglo-Norman Aristocracy', in *Cathedrals, Communities and Conflict in the Anglo-Norman World*, eds Paul Dalton, Charles Insley and Louise J. Wilkinson (Woodbridge, 2011), 151–67
Meekings   C. A. F. Meekings, 'Robert of Nottingham, Justice of the Bench, 1244–6', *BIHR* 41 (1968), 132–8 [reprinted in his *Studies in Thirteenth Century Justice and Administration*, ed. R. F. Hunnisett and D. Crook (London, 1981)]
Mems. Beverley   *Memorials of Beverley Minster: The Chapter Act Book of the Collegiate Church of S. John of Beverley, A.D. 1286–1347*, ed. A. F. Leach, 2 vols (SS 98, 1898 and 108, 1903)

Mems. Ripon	*Memorials of the Church of SS. Peter and Wilfrid, Ripon*, ed. J. T. Fowler, 4 vols (SS 74, 1882; 78, 1886; 81, 1888; 115, 1908)
Migne, *PL*	J-P. Migne, *Patrologiae cursus completus, series Latina*, 221 vols (Paris, 1844–64)
Mon. Ang.	Sir William Dugdale and Roger Dodsworth, *Monasticon Anglicanum*, eds J. Caley, H. Ellis and B. Bandinel, 6 vols in 8 (London, 1817–30, reprinted 1846)
Moor	Rev. Charles Moor, *Knights of Edward I*, 5 vols (Harleian Society, LXXX, LXXXI, LXXXII, LXXXIII and LXXXIV, 1928–32)
Mowbray Charters	*Charters of the Honour of Mowbray 1107–1191*, ed. D. E. Greenway (London: British Academy, Records of Social and Economic History, new series, i, 1972)
NA	Nottinghamshire Archives
Newstead	*Newstead Priory Cartulary, 1344 and Other Archives*, translated Valerie W. Walker, ed. Duncan Gray, TS, Record Series VIII (1940)
Nicholl, *Thurstan*	Donald Nicholl, *Thurstan, Archbishop of Canterbury (1114–1140)* (York, 1964)
North, 'Legerwite'	Tim North, 'Legerwite in the Thirteenth and Fourteenth Centuries', *Past and Present* 111 (1986), 3–16
NMS	*Nottingham Medieval Studies*
NUM	Department of Manuscripts and Special Collections, University of Nottingham
ODNB	*The Oxford Dictionary of National Biography*, ed. H. C. G. Matthew and B. Harrison, 60 vols (Oxford, 2004) (also the on-line version at http://www.oxforddnb.com)
Ottey, *Southwell Minster*	John L. Ottey, *The Story of Southwell Minster, A History* (Nottingham, 2005)
Patent Rolls	*Patent Rolls 1216–32*, 2 vols (London: HMSO, 1901–3)
Payling, *Political Society*	S. J. Payling, *Political Society in Lancastrian England. The Greater Gentry of Nottinghamshire* (Oxford, 1991)
PCC	Kew, The National Archives (formerly Somerset House), Prerogative Court of Canterbury, Registers of Wills
Phillips, *Edward II*	Seymour Phillips, *Edward II* (New Haven and London, 2010)
Placita de Quo Warranto	*Placita de Quo Warranto temporibus Ed. I, II, III in curia recepta scaccarii Westm. asservata*, ed. W. Illingworth (London: Record Commission, 1818)
Plumpton Correspondence	*Plumpton Correspondence*, ed. T. Stapleton (London: Camden Society, 1839)
PN Nt	J. E. B. Gover, Allen Mawer and F. M. Stenton, *The Place-Names of Nottinghamshire*, EPNS 17 (Cambridge, 1940)
Pontefract cartulary	*The Chartulary of St John of Pontefract*, ed. R. Holmes, 2 vols (YAS, Record Series XXV, 1899 and XXX, 1902)
Potthast	Augustus Potthast, *Registrum pontificum romanorum (1198–1304)*, 2 vols (Berlin, 1873–5; reprinted Graz, 1957)

PR | *Pipe Roll* ... published by the Pipe Roll Society (London 1884–)
PRO | London, Public Record Office (now TNA, Kew)
PROME | *The Parliament Rolls of Medieval England 1275–1504*, ed. Chris Given-Wilson et al. (Leicester, 2005)
PRS | Pipe Roll Society
PUE | Walther Holzmann, *Papsturkunden in England*, 3 vols (Abhandlungen der Gesellschaft der Wissenschaften zu Göttingen phil.-hist. Kl. N. f. 25, 1930–1, 3 Folge 14–15, 1935–6 and 3 Folge 33, 1952)
Purvis, *Notarial Signs* | Canon J. S. Purvis, *Notarial Signs from the York Archiepiscopal Records* (London and New York, 1957)
Raine, 'Fabric Rolls' | J. Raine, 'The Fabric Rolls of York Minster', SS 35 (1859), 1–120
Rastall | See Dickinson
Red Book | *The Red Book of the Exchequer*, ed. H. Hall, 3 vols (London: Rolls Series, 1896)
Reeves, 'Cathedral Deans' | Albert Compton Reeves, 'Cathedral Deans and Lancastrian Kings', *Medieval Prosopography*, 27 (2012), 130–43
Reeves, *Lancastrian Englishmen* | Albert Compton Reeves, *Lancastrian Englishmen* (Washington DC, 1981)
Reg. Antiq. | *The Registrum Antiquissimum of the Cathedral of Lincoln*, ed. C. W. Foster and Kathleen Major, 10 vols + two vols of plates (LRS 27–9, 32, 34, 41–2, 46, 51, 62, 67–8, 1931–73)
Reg. Laurence Booth | BI, Reg. 22, Laurence Booth, abp of York 1476–80
Reg. William Booth | BI, Reg. 20, William Booth, abp of York, 1452–64
Reg. Bowet | BI, Reg. 17, Henry Bowet, abp of York 1407–23
Reg. Burghersh | *The Registers of Henry Burghersh*, ed. Nicholas Bennett, 3 vols to date (LRS 87, 1999, 90, 2003, 101, 2011)
Reg. Chedworth | LA, Episcopal Reg. XX, John Chedworth, b. of Lincoln 1452–71
Reg. Chichele | *Register of Henry Chichele, Archbishop of Canterbury 1414–1443*, ed. E. F. Jacob, 4 vols (Oxford, 1943–7)
Reg. Cobham | *The Register of Thomas Cobham, Bishop of Worcester, 1317–1327*, ed. E. H. Pearce (Worcester Historical Society 40, 1930)
Reg. Corbridge | *The Register of Thomas of Corbridge, Lord Archbishop of York, 1300–1304*, ed. W. Brown and A. H. Thompson, 2 vols (SS 138, 1925 and 141, 1928)
Reg. Fleming | *The Register of Richard Fleming, Bishop of Lincoln 1420–1431*, ed. Nicholas Bennett, 2 vols (CYS 73, 1984, 99, 2009)
Reg. Fordham | Cambridge University Library, EDR, G/1/3, Register of John Fordham, b. of Ely 1388–1426
Reg. Giffard | *The Register of Walter Giffard, Lord Archbishop of York, 1266–1279*, ed. W. Brown (SS 109, 1904)
Reg. Gray | *The Register, or Rolls, of Walter Gray, Lord Archbishop of York with Appendices of Illustrative Documents*, ed. James Raine (SS 56, 1870)

Reg. Greenfield	*The Register of William Greenfield, Lord Archbishop of York, 1306–1315*, ed. W. Brown and A. H. Thompson, 5 vols (SS 145, 149, 151–3, 1931–40)
Reg. Honorius IV	*Les registres (Recueil des bulles) d'Honorius IV. Publiés d'après le manuscrit des archives du Vatican*, ed. M. Prou (Athens: École française d'Athènes, 1888)
Reg. Jean XXII	*Lettres communes analysées d'après les registres dits d'Avignon et du Vatican*, ed. Guillaume Mollat et al. 17 vols (Paris, 1904–46)
Reg. Kempe	BI, Reg. 19, John Kempe, abp of York 1426–52
Reg. Melton	*The Register of William Melton, Lord Archbishop of York, 1317–1340*, ed. Rosalind M. T. Hill, David Robinson, Reginald Brocklesby and T. S. B. Timmins, 5 vols (CYS LXX, LXXI, LXXVI, LXXXV, XCIII, 1977–2002)
Reg. Alexander Neville	BI, Reg. 12, Alexander Neville, abp of York 1374–88
Reg. George Neville	BI, Reg. 21, George Neville, abp of York 1464–76
Reg. Newark	*The Register of Henry of Newark, Lord Archbishop of York, 1296–1299*, ed. W. Brown (SS 128, 1916)
Reg. Nicolas IV	*Les registres de Nicolas IV*, ed. Ernest Langlois, 2 vols (Paris, 1905)
Reg. Romeyn, i	*The Register of John Le Romeyn, Lord Archbishop of York, 1286–1296*, Part I, ed. W. Brown (SS 123, 1913)
Reg. Romeyn, ii	*The Register of John Le Romeyn, Lord Archbishop of York, 1286–1296*, Part II, ed. W. Brown (SS 128, 1916)
Reg. Rotherham	BI, Regs 23 and 24, Thomas Rotherham, abp of York 1480–1500
Reg. Rotherham	*The Register of Thomas Rotherham, Archbishop of York, 1480–1500*, i, ed. E. E. Barker (CYS 69, 1976) [= fols. 1r–289v of BI, Reg. 23]
Reg. Savage	BI, Reg. 25, Thomas Savage, abp of York 1501–7
Reg. sede vacante	BI, Reg. 5A, York vacancy 1405–8
Reg. Stretton i	*The Registers or Act Books of the Bishops of Coventry and Lichfield. Book 5, being the Second Register of Bishop Robert de Stretton, A.D. 1360–1385: an abstract of the contents*, ed. R. A. Wilson (Stafford: William Salt Archaeological Society, new series 8, 1905)
Reg. Stretton ii	*The Registers or Act Books of the Bishops of Coventry and Lichfield. Book 4, being the Register of the Guardians of the Spiritualities during the Vacancy of the See, and the First Register of Bishop Robert de Stretton, 1358–1385: an abstract of the contents*, ed. R. A. Wilson (Stafford: William Salt Archaeological Society, new series, 10, part 2, 1907)
Reg. Sudbury	*Registrum Simonis de Subiria diocesis Londoniensis, A.D. 1362–1375*, ed. R. C. Fowler and C. Jenkins, 2 vols (CYS 34, 38, 1927–38)
Reg. Sutton	*The Rolls and Register of Bishop Oliver Sutton 1280–1299*, ed. Rosalind M. T. Hill, 8 vols (LRS 39, 43, 48, 52, 60, 64, 69 and 72, 1948–86)

Reg. Thoresby	BI, Reg. 11, John Thoresby, abp of York 1353–73
Reg. Wakering	Norwich and Norfolk Record Office, Reg/4/8, John Wakering, b. of Norwich 1416–25
Reg. Welton	*The Register of Gilbert Welton, Bishop of Carlisle 1353–1362*, ed. R. L. Storey (CYS 88, 1999)
Reg. Wickwane	*The Register of William Wickwane, Lord Archbishop of York 1279–1285*, ed. William Brown (SS 114, 1907)
Reg. Zouche	BI, Reg. 10, William Zouche, abp of York 1342–52
Reynolds, *Wells Cathedral*	H. E. Reynolds, *Wells Cathedral: Its Foundation, Constitutional History and Statutes* (Leeds, 1881)
Rogers, *Southwell Minster*	Alan Rogers, *Southwell Minster after the Civil Wars* (Nottingham: Department of Adult Education, University of Nottingham, 1974)
Rolls, ed. Stenton	*Rolls of the Justices in Eyre for Lincolnshire (1218–19) and Worcestershire (1221)*, ed. D. M. Stenton (Selden Society LIII, 1934)
Rot. Cancellarii	*Rotuli Cancellarii, vel Antigraphum magni rotuli pipae de tertio anni regis Johannis*, ed. J. Hunter (London: Record Commission, 1833)
Rot. Chartarum	*Rotuli Chartarum in Turri Londinensi asservati*, ed. T. D. Hardy (London: Record Commission, 1837)
Rot. Cur. Reg.	*Rotuli Curiae Regis. Rolls and Records of the Court held before the King's Justiciars or Justices*, ed. Sir Francis Palgrave, 2 vols (London: Record Commission, 1835)
Rot. Litt. Pat.	*Rotuli Litterarum Patentium in Turri Londinensi asservati*, ed. T. D. Hardy (London: Record Commission, 1835)
Rot. Orig.	*Rotulorum Originalium in Curia Scaccarii Abbreviatio*, vol. 2 (London: Record Commission, 1810)
RRAN	*Regesta Regum Anglo-Normannorum*, ed. H. W. C. Davis, C. Johnson, H. A. Cronne and R. H. C. Davis, 4 vols (Oxford, 1913–69)
Rufford	*Rufford Charters*, ed. C. J. Holdsworth, 4 vols (TS, Record Series XXIX, XXX, XXXII, XXXIV, 1972–81)
Salzman, *Building*	L. F. Salzman, *Building in England down to 1540. A Documentary History* (Oxford 1967, corrected reprint of 1952 edn)
Sanders, *English Baronies*	I. J. Sanders, *English Baronies: a Study of Their Origin and Descent 1086–1327* (Oxford, 1960)
Sayers, *Papal Judges*	Jane E. Sayers, *Papal Judges Delegate in the Province of Canterbury 1198–1254. A Study in Ecclesiastical Jurisdiction and Administration* (Oxford, 1971)
SC	Southwell Chapter Muniments, NA
Selby Coucher	*The Coucher Book of Selby*, ed. J. T. Fowler, 2 vols (YAS, Record Series 10, 1891 and 13, 1893)
Sharpe, *Acta Henry I*	*The Letters and Charters of King Henry I (1100–1135)*, ed. Richard Sharpe et al. (Oxford, forthcoming)
Sharpe, 'Address and Delivery'	
	Richard Sharpe, 'Address and Delivery in Anglo-Norman Royal Charters', *Charters and Charter Scholarship*

	in Britain and Ireland, ed. Marie Therese Flanagan and Judith A. Green (Basingstoke, 2005), 32–52
Sherwood Book	*The Sherwood Forest Book*, ed. Helen E. Boulton (TS, Record Series XXIII, 1965)
Somerset Wills 1383–1501	*Somerset Medieval Wills 1383–1501*, ed. F. W. Weaver (Somerset Record Society, vol. 16, 1901); also available in Microprint edition, Gloucester: Alan Sutton 1983)
SS	The Surtees Society
Statutes, ed. Bradshaw and Wordsworth	
	Statutes of Lincoln Cathedral, ed. Henry Bradshaw and Christopher Wordsworth, 2 vols in 3 parts (Cambridge, 1892–7)
Stenton, *Danelaw Charters*	*Documents illustrative of the Social and Economic History of the Danelaw, from various collections*, ed. F. M. Stenton (London: British Academy, 1920)
Stenton, *Gilbertine Charters*	*Transcripts of Charters relating to the Gilbertine Houses of Sixle, Ormsby, Catley, Bullington and Alvingham, edited with a translation from the King's Remembrancer's Memoranda Rolls nos 183, 185 and 187*, ed. F. M. Stenton (LRS 18, 1922)
Sullivan, 'Waddington'	Matthew Sullivan, 'The Author of the *Manuel des Péchés*', *Notes and Queries* 236 (1991), 155–7
Sullivan, 'Textual History'	Matthew Sullivan, 'A Brief Textual History of the *Manuel des Péchés*', *Neuphilologische Mitteilungen* 93 (1992), 337–46
Summers 1988	Norman Summers, *A Prospect of Southwell*, revised edn (Southwell, 1988)
Test. Ebor.	*Testamenta Eboracensia, or Wills Registered at York … from the Year MCCC downwards*, eds James Raine and J. W. Clay, 6 vols (SS 4, 30, 45, 53, 79 and 106, 1864–1902)
Thoroton	Robert Thoroton, *The Antiquities of Nottinghamshire* (1677), edited and enlarged by John Throsby, 3 vols (1790–6), reprinted (Nottingham, 1972), with introduction by M. W. Barley and K. S. S. Train
Thurgarton	*The Thurgarton Cartulary*, ed. Trevor Foulds (Stamford, 1994)
Tillmann	Helene Tillmann, *Die Päpstlichen Legaten in England bis zur Beendigung der Legation Gualas (1218)* (Bonn, 1926)
Torre	BI, Torre MSS
Tout, *Chapters*	Thomas Frederick Tout, *Chapters in the Administrative History of Mediaeval England*, 6 vols (Manchester, 1920–33)
TNA	Kew, The National Archives of the United Kingdom
Train, *Clergy of N. Notts.*	K. S. S. Train, *Lists of the Clergy of North Nottinghamshire*, TS, Record Series XX (1961)
TS	Thoroton Society of Nottinghamshire
TTS	*Transactions of the Thoroton Society*
Valor Eccl.	*Valor Ecclesiasticus temp. Henr. VIII*, ed. J. Caley, 6

	vols (London: Record Commission, 1810–34)
VCH	*The Victoria County History*
Venn	J. Venn and J. A. Venn, *Alumni Cantabrigiensis*, 10 vols (Cambridge, 1922–54)
Vincent, *Acta Henry II*	*The Letters and Charters of King Henry II (1154–1189)*, ed. Nicholas Vincent et al. (Oxford, forthcoming)
Visitations	*Visitations and Memorials of Southwell Minster*, ed. A. F. Leach (London: Camden Society, new series XLVIII, 1891)
Walker, 'Yorkshire Risings'	Simon Walker, 'The Yorkshire Risings of 1405: Texts and Contexts', in his collected essays, *Political Culture in Later Medieval England*, ed. Michael Braddick (Manchester, 2006), 223–44
Wilkinson, 'Fledborough'	R. F. Wilkinson, 'Fledborough Church', *TTS* xx (1940), 1–13
Wollaton Manuscripts	*The Wollaton Medieval Manuscripts. Texts, Owners and Readers*, ed. Ralph Hanna and Thorlac Turville-Petre (York, 2010)
Woodman, *Charters*	*Charters of Northern Houses*, ed. D. A. Woodman (Oxford for The British Academy, 2012)
Wright, *Church and Crown*	J. Robert Wright, *The Church and the English Crown 1305–1334* (Toronto: Pontifical Institute of Mediaeval Studies, 1980)
YAJ	*Yorkshire Archaeological Journal*
YAS	Yorkshire Archaeological Society
Yeatman, *Feudal History of the County of Derby*	
	John Pym Yeatman et al., *The Feudal History of the County of Derby*, 6 vols (London, 1886–1907), i
York Fasti	C. T. Clay, *York Minster Fasti, being notes on the Dignitaries, Archdeacons and Prebendaries in the Church of York prior to the year 1307*, 2 vols (YAS, Record Series CXXIII and CXXIV, 1957–8)
Yorkshire Assize Rolls	*Three Yorkshire Assize Rolls for the Reigns of King John and King Henry III*, ed. C. Clay (YAS, Record Series 44, 1911)
Yorkshire Inquisitions, ed. Brown	
	Yorkshire Inquisitions of the Reigns of Henry III and Edward I, ed. W. Brown, vol. 1 (YAS, Record Series 12, 1891–2)
Yorkshire Lay Subsidy	*Yorkshire Lay Subsidy, being a Ninth collected 25 Edward I (1297)*, ed. W. Brown (YAS, Record Series 16, 1894)

OTHER ABBREVIATIONS

abp/s	archbishop/s
Add.	Additional
adm.	admitted
archdcn/s	archdeacon/s
archdcnry	archdeaconry
app.	appointed
b.	bishop
c.	century
c.	*circa*/about
cal.	calendar/ed
can.	canon
Cantab.	Cambridge
Ch.	charter
cnry	canonry
coll.	collated
cons.	consecrated
d.	died
da.	daughter
el.	elected
esp.	especially
exp.	expectative
f./ff.	folio/s
fl.	flourished
gtd	granted
inst.	instituted
Mr	Master
MS/MSS	manuscript/s
n	note
no./nos	number/s
Oxon.	Oxford
pd.	printed
pr.	proved
preb.	prebend
prob.	probably
reg.	register
resig.	resigned
ser.	series
temp.	in time of
trans.	translated, in translation
vac.	vacated

INTRODUCTION

The Manuscript of the White Book (Liber Albus) of Southwell

The *Liber Albus* or White Book of Southwell is currently deposited with other Southwell Minster Chapter records in Nottinghamshire Archives.[1] It is 'a folio volume of 487 pages of parchment with a few additional interleaved insertions, bound in thick boards of oak with a white vellum covering, from which it derives its name'.[2] A collection of copies of the privileges, title deeds and other records relating to the medieval collegiate church of St Mary, Southwell, the Chapter which governed it and the administration of its estates, and internal documentary evidence as well as palaeography (both discussed in more detail below) suggest that this cartulary was begun around 1347. Entries continued to be intermittently copied into it until the later fifteenth century, possibly even into the early sixteenth century. After the Reformation a few further documents were added, notably three letters of *c.* 1546 from the Court of Augmentations, one of 1582 and a final one of 1609. Marginalia and other annotations show that the White Book remained of importance in the administration of the Chapter's affairs until at least the eighteenth century. It was even produced in legal cases in the 1830s. In its present form, measuring 325 x 215 mm, it appears to have been bound around 1500.[3]

In total, the cartulary contains 620 individual items according to the numbering scheme introduced by W. A. James, then Minster librarian, in the 1920s to distinguish its contents unambiguously. This numeration has been used in this edition, with individual items being referred to in the form White Book (or WB) **I** or simply by the number in bold.[4] While the majority of the documents it contains, notably many of its medieval charters, are relatively short, some are of substantial length.[5] They range in date from *c.* 1100 to 1460, with a few outliers as mentioned above.[6] The opening section

---

[1] Nottinghamshire Archives (NA), SC/7/1/1.

[2] *Visitations*, lxvii; cf. the *Magnum Registrum Album* of York or the White Book of Peterborough for similar nomenclature. As currently numbered in an Arabic sequence the volume appears to contain 476 pages, but a page was missed out after p. 182 (now numbered in pencil p. 182a) and following p. 333 ten pages are duplicated as pp. 324–33 before the sequence resumes at p. 334. The duplicated pages have also been numbered 333a–333j in pencil in a modern hand and we retain that sequence in our edition. Two inserted documents occur between pp. 27 and 28 of the Arabic sequence, and have been numbered 28a and 28b in pencil, while an inserted original notarial instrument (**158**) was already bound into the volume when it was paginated and occurs as p. 85.

[3] cf. Davis, *Cartularies*, 184, no. 912, which provides a succinct description.

[4] James numbered from **I–617A**, the other duplicates being **128A** (an entry unaccountably omitted from the main sequence by James) and **148A** which we have distinguished from **148**.

[5] The longest is **377**, proceedings in the court of Mr Robert de Wolvendon, prebendary of Norwell Overhall, 30 August 1406.

[6] A writ charter of Henry I, 1100 x 1107 (**148**) and some well-known letters issued by the Chapter of St Peter's, York relating to their privileges, traditionally dated 1106 (**27**, **28**) are the earliest documents recorded.

of the volume consists of copies of papal bulls from Alexander III (1171) to Urban VI (1379).[7] There are royal charters, letters and orders from many English medieval kings from the reign of Henry I onwards, together with transcripts of proceedings in royal courts, *Quo warranto* inquiries and so on. Charters or statutes issued by several archbishops of York relating to the rights of the Chapter at Southwell, to those of individual canons (later usually called prebendaries, and sixteen in number by 1291) and to the parishes where the Chapter held lands or controlled the livings, constitute an important proportion of the documents. The bulk of them relate to lands which the prebendaries of Southwell held as individuals or in common as members of the Chapter.

Particularly prominent are deeds relating to land and other property which had been given for the establishment of chantries from *c.* 1230 onwards. These were mainly founded either in memory of particular canons or of laymen prominent in the service of the archbishop of York in his manor at Southwell. Numerous deeds relating to lands acquired by the Chapter to maintain the Vicars Choral or the chantry priests are also present. These estates were widely scattered through Nottinghamshire but especially along the Vale of Trent, while a few documents relate to lands and the important living of Barnburgh in South Yorkshire, to the alien priory of West Ravendale in Lincolnshire and even to properties in Leicestershire which came into the hands of the Chapter. The White Book thus furnishes valuable evidence not simply for ecclesiastical history (organisation and personnel of the Chapter; pastoral care; spiritual life; relations with other religious institutions, including the minsters at Beverley and Ripon as well as with St Peter's, York) but for broader social and economic developments in medieval Nottinghamshire. Because of the piecemeal way in which lands were acquired or mentioned and the incomplete record of them that is found in the White Book, however, a full account of the estates owned by the Chapter and their financial worth in the Middle Ages cannot be easily written from the surviving evidence.[8]

Naturally the White Book covers relations between the Chapter and the higher social levels of county society (notably knights and gentry) but it also covers the Chapter's relations with the townspeople of Southwell and, to a lesser degree, Newark, and with the peasantry of the prebendal and other parishes which formed the ecclesiastical Liberty or Peculiar of Southwell. Originating in two grants made by the Anglo-Saxon kings Ead-

---

[7] Several bulls have been redated in comparison with the list given in *Visitations*, ci.

[8] The *taxatio* of 1291 shows that the total annual income enjoyed by the sixteen prebendaries was around £275 (Dickinson, *Southwell*, 119–20) and the total value of the college as £342 13s 4d (*Visitations*, lxvi), while the *Valor Ecclesiasticus* of 1535 and two surveys of 1546 and 1548 at the time of the dissolution of the chantries, show that the prebendaries had by then a joint income just under £300 p.a., the Vicars Choral around £125 p.a., that about £16 was received annually for Pentecostal processions, a common fund produced about £50 p.a. and there were other small sources of income (Dickinson, *Southwell*, 113; Ottey, *Southwell Minster*, 29–40), giving a total net value for the college of £463 10s 7½d and gross value of £691 7s 9d (*Visitations*, lxvi), putting it 'in the second rank, as compared with the great cathedrals and great abbeys, but equally distinctly to be classed among the greater and not among the lesser ecclesiastical foundations.' (ibid., lxvii).

wig and Edgar to Archbishop Oscytel of York in the mid-tenth century,[9] the franchise that these charters created, eventually extending into twenty-eight parishes, retained its separate court and jurisdiction (e.g., for proving wills) until its abolition in the mid-nineteenth century.[10] A considerable number of documents (terriers, rentals, estate surveys and court proceedings) shed useful light on agricultural practices and questions of demography in the wake of the Black Death.[11] In addition to 'historical' material, the White Book furnishes a remarkable (and surprisingly little investigated) amount of onomastic and linguistic evidence for personal-, place- and field-names, with documents making use of three languages: medieval Latin, Anglo-Norman French and Middle English.[12]

Structure (Teresa Webber)

The White Book has a complex physical structure. It is comprised of twenty-six parchment quires of varying numbers of leaves, which bear witness in various ways to the stages by which its component elements were produced, brought together and supplemented over the course of the fourteenth and fifteenth centuries. A single sequence of foliation in Roman numerals was added to the leaves of quires 1–23 probably during the second quarter of the fifteenth century, since it is absent from quires 24–6, which contain the hands only of scribes active after that date. A leaf was subsequently lost between the current pp. 22 and 23, resulting in the loss of text from item **36**, after which a second sequence of foliation was supplied in Arabic numerals, incorporating quires 24–6. Sometime later, a number of other (presumably blank) leaves were excised.

Quires 1–3 (pp. 1–64, **1**–**137** [**12**–**13**, **42**, **45**, **55**–**6**, **59**, **60**, **81**, **83**, **89**, **109**–**10**, **133**–**4** and **138**–**41** are later additions]) represent the first stage of compilation: a cartulary written by a single scribe (Scribe 1; **Plate 1**) and datable on palaeographical grounds to the fourteenth century and on internal evidence to 1347 at the earliest (see **36**). Leaf-signatures were supplied to the first half of each of these quires to ensure the correct sequence of leaves. Little attempt was made to update the cartulary during the fourteenth century, other than the addition of two entries by Scribe 2 on p. 5 (**12**–**13**), in or after 1379 (see **12**).

The cartulary was significantly amplified during the second quarter of the fifteenth century, when Scribe 4 (**Plate 1**) not only supplied entries both on slips and spaces left blank in the original quires but also oversaw the production of an additional twelve quires: quires 4–15, pp. 65–292, **142**–**387** (**158**, **186**, **207**, **213**–**14**, **223**–**44**, **344**–**5**, **355**–**7** and **388**–**9** are later additions),

---

[9] Woodman, *Charters*, nos 2 and 3 for the most recent edition of these important documents, together with extended commentary.
[10] In 2010–11, Neil Bettridge completed a full catalogue of all the Chapter's records that had been recently deposited in NA, in the series SC. A large proportion of original wills from the Peculiar between 1506 and 1841, with their supporting probate inventories and administration bonds, are separately listed in the series PR/SW, or survive as register copies in DD/PR/SR (from 1567–1858) or in the Chapter registers (SC/2/1/1 et seq.) which begin in 1469.
[11] See, for example, the notes to **110**, **171**, **207**, **223**, **377**, **382**, **384**, **388**, **577**.
[12] *EPNS Notts.* made only very limited use of the White Book; see further below, pp. cvi–cxiii.

and supplied running titles and headings.[13] A note in his hand on p. 205 (at the end of **348**, within quire 12), which refers to a copy of the same text in the original cartulary (**106**, p. 46) as being 'above, on folio 24' (*Ista quidem carta scribitur superius xxiiii folio*), confirms that all of these quires were intended from the outset to accompany the cartulary. They were designed to accommodate additions, with leaves originally left blank at the end of quires 6, 11, 12 and 15. The remains of a sequence of quire signatures comprising both letters of the alphabet and numbers still visible in quires 5, 6, 9, 10 and 11 indicates that quires 5 and 6 (pp. 81–115) were originally intended to follow quires 7–11 (pp. 116–202): the former are labelled 'f' and 'g', and numbered 6–7, while quires 9–11 are labelled 'C'–'E' and are numbered 3–5.[14] Scribe 4 and other scribes subsequently supplemented the compilation in a more intermittent fashion with entries added in the spaces left blank in these and the original three quires.

It was probably also as part of this same programme of amplification during the second quarter of the fifteenth century that quires 16–23 (pp. 293–428, **390–582** [**417–20, 505–49, 569–77** and **583–8** are additions]) were incorporated. These form a discrete unit with their own numerical sequence of quire signatures (1–7, on the first leaf of each quire), and contain records concerning Southwell's chantries. They were produced by a single scribe (Scribe 3; **Plate 2**) in or not long after 1398 (see **582**), to judge from the character of his handwriting, but were subsequently amplified by Scribe 4, who inserted two additional sub-gatherings (pp. 369–76 and pp. 377–90) into quire 21, as well as making other additions to this series of quires. It seems likely that the sequence of foliation in Roman numerals that runs throughout quires 1–23 was also supplied around this time, but not before the order of leaves of quire 11 had been altered, with pp. 191–4, originally the outer bifolium of the quire (to judge from the presence of a quire signature on p. 191), being moved to the centre of the quire. It is tempting to speculate that all this activity corresponded with the period when William Duffield, treasurer of York, was prebendary of Norwell Overhall (1432–50, 1451–3) and, as other evidence in the White Book shows, working to remedy defects in the Chapter's administration of its estates, and thus that it may have been undertaken at his initiative.

At least two further phases of amplification took place in the later fifteenth century. Quire 24 (pp. 429–48, **589–613**) was added some time during the second half of the fifteenth century and contains entries supplementing the section on the chantries. These were begun by Scribe 6 and later supplemented by Scribe 7 (**Plate 3**) and other scribes. Scribe 6 (or another very similar hand or hands) and Scribe 7 also inserted entries in blank spaces elsewhere in the volume, with Scribe 7 additionally supplying headings to existing entries. It is unclear when Scribe 5 supplied **388** (a revised extent of 1433) or when one or two other scribes (who were working after Scribe

---

[13] The latest datable entry in the hand of scribe 4 is **340**, a copy of a document of 1427. Entries comprising documents dated to 1433 (**388**) and later are in the hands of subsequent scribes.
[14] The signatures in quire 11 are on p. 191, now the first page of the bifolium at the centre of the quire, but which originally formed the outermost bifolium. Signatures are no longer visible in quires 7–8 but they can be assumed to have been A and B, and 1–2.

4 but before Scribe 7) supplied **213A–F** and **223–4**. **389** and **577** (the work of Scribe 8), **345** (in a very similar hand) and **587** were also added at some point during the mid or later fifteenth century, but these additions can be dated no more closely than this.

Quires 25 and 26 (pp. 449–76, **614–17**) contain the hands only of two sixteenth-century scribes who wrote **614–16** and **617** respectively. In the late sixteenth and early seventeenth centuries, John Lee added two further entries (**612–13**) and John Martiall another six (**45**, **141**, **186**, **344**, and **594–5**) to earlier quires in the volume. Lee identifies himself as registrar to the Chapter, and other evidence shows that Martiall held the same office. A second sequence of foliation, in Arabic numerals, was supplied after the White Book had achieved its present form, either during the sixteenth century or perhaps as late as the seventeenth, when copious marginal annotations were made.

The White Book also contains two original single sheet documents, **60** (p. 28b, dated 1333) and **158** (p. 85, 5 July 1345), neither was numbered in the original sequence of foliation in Roman numerals, but **158** was included within the subsequent sequence in Arabic numerals. This is insufficient evidence, however, from which to infer the date at which each was incorporated within the compilation.

The original cartulary and the enlarged compilation assembled during the second quarter of the fifteenth century may have been protected only with a parchment wrapper until the current binding of tawed skin over oak boards was added, perhaps as early as *c*. 1500. A bifolium of very stout parchment now acting as front endleaves and displaying signs of wear may once have acted as a wrapper but it displays no evidence to indicate its association with the White Book prior to the current binding. The same is true of a very similar bifolium that now forms the rear endleaves.

Palaeography (Teresa Webber)

The White Book is the work of more than eight medieval scribes, some of whose hands are not readily distinguishable and who wrote only a few entries. Three scribes (scribes 1, 3 and 4) contributed the bulk of the entries, each working independently during the mid or second half of the fourteenth century, the turn of the fourteenth/fifteenth centuries, and the second quarter of the fifteenth century respectively. None of these scribes can be identified by name, as is also the case for all the other medieval scribes, with the exception of the public notary, John de Tyverington, who wrote an original instrument of 1345 which was subsequently bound into the cartulary (**158**).

Scribe 1 was responsible for the oldest part of the White Book, the cartulary, which he produced in or after 1347 (the latest dated or datable document that he copied is **108**, letters patent of Edward III of 30 July 1347), while additions by scribe 4 on p. 48 include a document of 1349 (**110**). He wrote: **1–11** (pp. 1–5), **14–41** (pp. 6–24), **43–4** (p. 25), **46–54** (pp. 26–7), **57–8** (p. 28), **61–80** (pp. 29–37), **82** (p. 38), **84–8** (pp. 39–40), **90–103** (pp. 41–4), **105–8** (pp. 46–8); **111–32** (pp. 49–59), **136–7** (p. 61). He wrote in *littera textualis*, a formal book script, rather than in cursive handwriting, a variety of which was used by all subsequent scribes in the White Book. He also supplied rubrics in the same script (in red) for almost every entry up to and including **113** (p. 50), and was also presumably responsible for applying a stroke of the same red ink to highlight *litterae notabiliores* in each entry as far as **114**. It is impossible to know whether the decorated initials that introduce each of his entries (blue with red pen-flourishing) were also his work. Coloured rubrics and initials are not found elsewhere in the White Book.

Scribe 2 inserted two entries (**12–13**) in a blank space on p. 5. He wrote in or after 1379 (the date of **12**), but no later than the early fifteenth century, to judge from the character of his handwriting. He wrote in the native English cursive script, Anglicana, with no intrusion of letter forms from the continental cursive first introduced to England in the 1370s (subsequently known as Secretary).

Scribe 3 was responsible for quires 16–23, which concern Southwell's chantries. He produced these quires in or after 1398, his final entry (**582**) being dated 14 May 1398. His activity certainly preceded that of Scribe 4, and is unlikely to have been much later than the turn of the fourteenth/fifteenth centuries, to judge from his handwriting. Like Scribe 2 he wrote in Anglicana without incorporating any variant forms from the Secretary script (variants that increasingly became part of the graphic repertoire of English scribes during the fifteenth century). He wrote **390–416** (pp. 293–308); **421–504** (pp. 313–63); **550–68** (pp. 397–406); **578–82** (pp. 421–4).

Scribe 4 played a major role in bringing together and supplementing all the various component elements of the White Book (other than the final three quires), and subsequently making further additions, inserting entries in blank spaces he himself had left, and supplying headings to his own and others' earlier work. This activity is broadly datable on internal evidence to the second quarter of the fifteenth century (**340**, a document of 1427, is the latest datable document that he transcribed). He wrote a 'mixed hand', in which both Anglicana and Secretary forms are deployed, and which exhibits a considerable degree of variation both within and between stints, at first sight sometimes giving the impression of a different hand at work. It is not possible always to distinguish between the different layers of his activity. His entries are therefore presented here as a single sequence, but are punctuated to indicate evident breaks in the sequence of copying. He wrote: **42** (p. 24); **55–6** (p. 27); **59** (p. 28a: *per archiepiscopum* in heading perhaps added later by the same scribe); **81** (p. 37); **83** (p. 38); **89** (p. 40a); **104** (p. 45); **109–10** (p. 48); **133–4** (p. 60); **142–7** (pp. 65–75); **148** (p. 76); **148a** (p. 76); **149–57** (pp. 77–84); **159–84** (pp. 86–101); **185** (p. 116); **187–90** (pp. 117–18); **191–3** (pp. 118–19); **194–9** (pp. 120–1); **200–1** (pp. 121–2: **201** perhaps added later); **202–4** (p. 123); **205** (p. 124); **206** (p. 124); **208–12** (pp. 126–30); **215–16** (p. 134); **217** (pp. 134–5); **218–22** (pp. 136–9); **225–343** (pp. 144–82, 182a–92); **346–54** (pp. 203–13); **358–87** (pp. 225–84); **417–20** (pp. 309–10); **505–25** (pp. 365–75: **521** on p. 372 has a different appearance but may be an addition in the same hand); **526** (p. 375); **569–76** (pp. 407–12); **583–4** (pp. 425–6).

An unidentified hand of similar character and date to that of Scribe 4, but not certainly identifiable as that scribe, wrote **138–9** (pp. 61–2), and another very similar hand wrote **140** (p. 63). A more readily distinguishable 'mixed hand', that of Scribe 5, who was probably also active during the second quarter or middle of the fifteenth century, supplied **388** (pp. 289–90), a document of 1433. Two further sets of entries were also supplied by one or two otherwise unidentified scribes, certainly working after Scribe 4 but before the late fifteenth-century activity of Scribe 7: **213A–F** (pp. 131–3), and **223–4** (pp. 140–3), these last two entries being copies of documents datable to 1445 and 1443 x 1445 respectively.

The later fifteenth century witnessed further scribal activity. Scribe 6, at work in or after 1460 (the date of **593**), wrote a Secretary hand and supplied a series of entries to a new quire, quire 24. He wrote **589–93** (pp. 429–30). A very similar hand, but not certainly identifiable as that of Scribe 6 wrote **355–7** (pp. 214–17), and another very similar hand wrote **527–41** (pp. 377–84) and **605–10** (pp. 439–40).

Scribe 7 wrote a distinctive late fifteenth-century Anglicana, strongly influenced by the features of style of Secretary. His activity went beyond adding further entries to include the addition of headings to existing entries. He wrote: **207** (p. 125); **214** (p. 133); heading for **355** (p. 214); heading for **527** (p. 377); **542–9** (pp. 392–5); **585** (p. 426); **588** (p. 428); **596–604** (pp. 435–8).

Another mid or late fifteenth-century scribe, Scribe 8, wrote **389** (p. 291) and **577** (pp. 413–15); **345** (pp. 200–2) is in a very similar hand. Another fifteenth-century scribe wrote **587** (p. 428), but the scrappiness of the writing precludes identification. The chronology of all these additions in relation to the activity of Scribes 6 and 7 is uncertain. A document of 1475, **617** (pp. 474–5), may have been written as early as the late fifteenth century, but the hand of the scribe (otherwise not found in the White Book) could well date from the sixteenth century. Another unidentified sixteenth-century scribe wrote **614–16** (pp. 451–2). Two certainly post-Dissolution scribes who made additions to the White Book are identifiable as John Lee and John Martiall, both registrars to the Chapter. Lee wrote **612–13** (pp. 443–5) and Martiall wrote **45** (p. 25); **141** (p. 64); **186** (p. 116); **344** (pp. 193–4); **594–5** (pp. 431–4).

Diplomatic and seals

The usual style adopted by the Chapter in its formal documents was 'the Chapter of the church (or collegiate church) of St Mary, Southwell', sometimes with the addition 'diocese of York'. In its communications with others, it used a number of forms as was common practice and followed well-established diplomatic rules formally acquired by most clerks who had responsibility for drawing up documents. The conventions used were partly dependent on the status of the addressee, partly influenced by current scribal fashions, partly by the preferences of the individual clerks who wrote the documents. From the evidence in the White Book, it seems that none of the diplomatic forms used at Southwell for Chapter business were truly exceptional. A brief summary of preferences will be useful, however, especially since it is clear that the periods in which some scribal forms were employed appear limited. Such indications may thus eventually serve to identify individual clerks whose work is represented in the White Book, although currently they largely remain anonymous.

Four main forms were used for the *inscriptio* and address over the period for which the White Book provides evidence of the Chapter issuing its own charters. The earliest protocol, from shortly after 1200, was the rather peremptory 'The Chapter of St Mary's, Southwell, to all who see or hear these letters, greetings'.[15] The word of greeting, *salutem*, might be qualified by 'greetings in the name of the author of salvation'.[16] Around 1300, this form was most frequently used when the Chapter was communicating with its own members or those dependent on its favours in some way, a vicar or someone receiving a small grant or lease.[17] In letters of 1332 threatening the prior and convent of Sixhills with excommunication for failure to pay a pension, it was clearly used with a touch of sarcasm: *Capitulum ... priori et conventus de Sixhill id quod meruerint non salutem* (**584**). No later usages have been noted.

The most common address in formal letters between the early thirteenth century and the mid-fifteenth was a general one to 'all Christians' or 'all sons of Mother Church' – in the form *Universis Christi fidelibus* or *Universis sancte matris ecclesie filiis* – 'who might see or hear the letters'. As in the *Capitulum* form above, the greeting was normally qualified with a short pious injunction like *salutem in domino sempiternam*,[18] *salutem in omnium salvatore*,[19] *eternam in domino salutem*[20] or, more rarely, *salutem in eo qui est omnium vera salvus*.[21] For a period in the mid-thirteenth century, another frequently used form of address was *Omnibus Christi fidelibus*, 'To all the faithful in Christ', usually with the short greeting *salutem in domino*. But since that form is restricted to a period of about twenty-five years at most it suggests that this may have been the scribal preference of one clerk rather than a general practice at Southwell.[22]

Another form used fairly commonly was a general notification, *Noverint universi* ... Such letters usually relayed information about what the Chapter had done or was proposing to do. Examples from the mid-thirteenth to the early fifteenth century are to be found in the White Book.[23] A variant on this form is *Sciant presentes et futuri*, 'Be it known ...', used in a document of 1361 (**298**). But the most exceptional form is the self-effacing one used in a document of 1250 x 1270, *Humile capitulum beate Marie Suellensis omnibus hanc presentem cartam intuentibus vel audientibus salutem in omnium salvatore* (**133**), which is not replicated elsewhere in the White Book.

As far as dating practice is concerned, documents issued in the name of the Chapter use a range of methods and calendars. Some, especially early documents down to the mid-thirteenth century, may not be dated at all.[24]

---

[15] 'Capitulum ecclesie beate Marie de Suthwell' omnibus has litteras visuris vel audituris salutem' (**431**, *c.* 1220, and cf. **434**, *c.* 1220 and **433**, *c.* 1244).

[16] 'salutem in salutis auctore' (**225**, pre-1230; **73**, 1318).

[17] cf. **187**, 1295; **188**, 1297; **189**, 1318, **190**, 1297.

[18] cf. **408**, pre-1230, **285**, 1268, **45**, 1295, **262**, *c.* 1300, **259**, 1322.

[19] **82**, 1301, **297**, 1311; cf. **577**, 1413, 'littere sive transumptum ... in omni salvatore' and **593**, 1460, 'salutem in eo qui est omnium vera salvus'.

[20] **296**, 1287, **317**, 1288, **279**, 1296, **316**, 1322, **268**, 1324, **311**, 1366.

[21] **223**, 1445.

[22] **427**, *c.* 1244, **263**, 1248–61, **409**, *c.* 1249, **410**, 1249–67, **394**, *c.* 1249, **260**, 1250–60.

[23] **218**, 1238, **103**, 1259, **315**, 1273, **299**, 1373, **498**, 1395, **587**, 1421.

[24] **119**, 1191–6, **129**, before 1 May 1200; **222**, late 12th–early 13th century; **225**, before 28 May 1230; **232**, 1230–50; **394**, 1241–9, **408**, 1218–29, **409**, *c.* 1249, **410**, 1249–67, **427**, *c.* 1244, **431**, *c.* 1220, **433**, *c.* 1244, **434**, *c.* 1220, **507**, 1230 or earlier, **526**, 1191–1205. Sometimes,

Where they are, the year is usually expressed as the year of grace or year of our Lord (*anno domini*). In early documents the year date may be all that is given.[25] Elsewhere there is sometimes an added note 'according to the Church in England', but no examples have been found in documents issued in the name of the Chapter. Some documents announce the month as well as the year.[26] From the mid-thirteenth century the most usual forms provide precise dating to the day of issue by reference to a relevant feast day,[27] or by giving the day and month according to the Roman calendar.[28] In fourteenth- and fifteenth-century documents, there is a tendency to use – either as an additional detail or standing alone – the king's regnal year for the year date, together with the day and month, without reference to feast days though these are still occasionally used.[29] Naturally letters (or public instruments) drawn up on behalf of the Chapter by accredited notaries use a full panoply of dating formulae, including papal regnal year, year of grace and the indiction.[30] The beginning of the year in medieval England was normally Lady Day (25 March).

The Chapter certainly possessed a common seal by the mid-twelfth century (**Plate 5a–c**). Among the earliest surviving impressions is that affixed to a notification of various grants to Rufford abbey which has been assigned date limits of 1146–56. This seal has been described by Holdsworth as 'Oval, pinkish wax, lower two thirds only remains, c. 1.6 inches x 2.3 inches. The Virgin seated with the Child in her lap ... Very worn, legend illegible.'[31] Another near contemporary but sharper impression survives on a further notification for Rufford, dated 1146–66.[32] Together, as well as a clearer image of the Virgin and Child on this latter example, they provide the legend +SIGILLUM SANCTE MARIE DE SUWELLA. This is confirmed by later

---

of course, as probably in the case of **409**, **410** and **417**, all mid 13th century, the absence of a date is the result of abbreviation by a copyist. Among the latest undated documents are **126**, after 27 January 1257, and **133**, 1250–before 1270. 'The Laudable Customs' (**151**) are also unfortunately undated.

[25] **218**, 1238; **316**, 1322, for a late example.

[26] **315**, October 1273, for an early example.

[27] **104**, Thursday after St Matthew the Apostle, 23 September 1260, **80**, All Saints, 1 November 1263, and **30**, feast of Oswald, king and martyr, 5 August 1266, for three early examples.

[28] **103**, Pridie Id. Oct. i.e. 14 October 1259, and **124**, VI Kal. Feb., i.e. 27 January 1259, for two early examples. The latest usage of the Roman calendar appears to be **213E**, 1352.

[29] Year of grace and regnal year: **223**, 1445. **233**, 1308, for an early example of the regnal year alone.

[30] **500**, 1395, **577**, 1413.

[31] *Rufford*, 325 note (after the original, BL, Harley Charters 83 D 2), and cf. *BM Catalogue of Seals*, no. 4058.

[32] *Rufford*, 180, the original is now NA, DD/SR 102/13, 68 x 40 mm, damaged, with most of the legend lost. Holdsworth describes it as: 'Pointed oval, natural varnished brown, c. 3 inches x 1.6. inches. The Virgin seated with the Child upon her lap. She is very tall, her head-dress coming through the band in which the inscription is to just below the cross. The first finger and thumb of her right hand are cupped level with the child's head: her left hand is held with palm flat pointing upwards. The child has a head-dress on, and holds his right hand up in blessing (?), and his left may support it (as in *BM Catalogue of Seals*, no. 4058) or merely rest on his lap... Although damaged this is a fine impression and provides more of the details than any other example in the collection. The lower third is better preserved in 963.'

impressions, several of which, clearly from the same seal matrix, survive on other Rufford charters before 1200.[33] The Chapter seal was also affixed to other Rufford charters but the impressions have either now been lost or the cartulary copies fail to make mention of them.[34]

After 1200, the use of the seal by the Chapter is frequently referred to in the White Book. It is normally, but not invariably, announced, usually in the form 'under our common seal', or simply 'under our seal' or by 'the attachment of our seal'.[35] Few later impressions of it have survived; none have come to light between *c.* 1200 and the end of the Middle Ages. But no fewer than seven impressions, all dating to 1539 or 1540, survive (**Plate 5d**). One example is appended to the deed of surrender by the Chapter to Henry VIII on 17 November 1540,[36] the first of what proved to be several unsuccessful attempts to abolish the Chapter between then and its actual abolition three centuries later in 1841. The seal was also attached in confirmation to deeds of surrender of their manors and other properties by individual prebendaries in 1540. At least five such deeds have survived bearing both the Chapter's seal and that of a named prebendary.[37] The Chapter's seal had also been used a year earlier to confirm a similar but collective surrender of property, including their 'capital house', by the chantry priests.[38] As Leach commented about the Chapter's main deed of surrender, 'the seal seems to be of a date not later than the first half of the 12th century'.[39] The design is

[33] *Rufford*, 246, 1175–1200, after NA, DD/SR 102/134, 68 x 40 mm, a fine impression with an almost complete legend; 166, 1180–1200, after DD/SR 102/7, 68 x 38 mm, damaged, with only about half the impression surviving; 180, 1180–1200, after DD/SR 102/29, a fair impression, but most of the legend on left destroyed; 963, 1180–1200, after DD/SR 102/140, a good impression, almost complete legend.

[34] *Rufford*, 167, 1194–7, after BL, Harley Charter 112 I 12, seal lost; 179, 1146–56, a notification by the Chapter, but details on sealing not stated.

[35] 'sigillum nostrum commune' (**221**, 1369; **223**, 1445); 'sigillum capituli nostri' (**103**, 1259); 'commune sigillum ecclesie Suwell'' (**192**, 1257); 'sigillum nostrum apposuimus/appensum' (**40**, 1295; **225**, before May 1230; **213E**, 1352). For letters lacking an announcement of the seal, see **187**, 1295, **188**, 1297, **190**, 1297, **198**, 1296, all relating to business between the Chapter and individual prebendaries.

[36] TNA, E 322/218, sealed on tongue, impression damaged at bottom, green wax.

[37] TNA, E 328/80 (15 August 1540, Richard Deane, prebendary of Halloughton, 68 x 42 mm, good impression), 81 (8 November 1540, Thomas Whyte, prebendary of Normanton, damaged impression, only 42 x 55 mm), 82 (12 August 1540, Thomas Marsar, prebendary of North Leverton, 68 x 42 mm, fair impression), 83 (12 October 1540, John Oliver, prebendary of Norwell Overhall, damaged, only 45 x 42 mm), and 88 (John Fitzherbert, prebendary of Oxton II, damaged). That of John Adams, Sacrista prebend, 12 August 1540 (ibid., 85) lacks a seal. All were issued in the Chapter House, appended on tongues, in green wax, in most cases now brown, complete impressions measuring approximately 68 x 42 mm.

[38] TNA, E 328/79, 12 August 1539, sealed on ten tongues. The Chapter seal is appended on tongue 1, tongues 3, 4 and 9 bear impressions of one seal, and 5–8 and 10 two impressions each of the signet seals of the thirteen chantry priests. Tongue 2 has an impression of a small, slightly oval seal 22 x 20 mm bearing a ?pelican in its piety and with a largely illegible legend which may be an impression of the communal seal for the Chantry Priests or the small seal ordered for Chapter use by Archbishop Le Romeyn in 1294, both hitherto unknown.

[39] *Visitations*, caption to frontispiece. He even suggested it dated to 'the time of Ealdred, archbishop of York, 1061–75 [*recte* 1069]', though stylistically this seems unlikely as is shown by comparison with the examples of institutional seals discussed by Heslop, 'English Seals'.

clearly identical with that of the matrix that produced surviving impressions on Rufford charters from before 1200. This suggests that, remarkably, the same matrix had served unaltered for at least 400 years.[40] It was finally 'broken up by the Chapter in 1588, to invalidate some deeds fraudulently sealed with it' and a new seal was made.[41]

In statutes issued in January 1294 after a visitation, Archbishop John Le Romeyn instructed that the Chapter's great seal was to be kept under the seals of three canons, and that a 'small one for citations' should similarly be kept under the seal of a single canon, clearly to avoid similar fraudulent usage.[42] Whether this small seal was ever made is doubtful since no evidence has been found in later medieval statutes or in the White Book or elsewhere for its existence.

Individual prebendaries, as noted above with regard to the deeds of surrender to Henry VIII, had their own seals which were sometimes used by them for Chapter business. The Chapter also expected lesser clergy to have their own seals. In 1318, for example, the Chapter ordered the vicar of Bleasby to cite Robert de la Cressoner to appear before them to answer various charges, instructing him, as proof of the citation, to remit it to them with *sigillo vestro pendente* (**189**). The Vicars Choral also had a common seal.[43] In 1261 it was announced in letters issued by them on behalf of Richard of Sutton, canon, when promising to pray for him (**58**).[44] Thoroton also records having seen an original charter issued by the Vicars Choral in 1262 to which they had affixed their own common seal (*Commune sigillum Vicariorum Suwell*) before that of the Chapter.[45] Interestingly it too is a deed relating to Richard of Sutton but is apparently now lost, and no other impressions of such a seal have been discovered.[46] Nevertheless the Vicars Choral continued to use a common seal as they did in giving a procuration to one of their number in 1367.[47] An indenture drawn up in 1474 and issued in their name

---

[40] Although thus very venerable, it pales before that of Wilton abbey's conventual seal in the later Middle Ages which originated as the seal of Edith, half-sister of Edward the Martyr and Ethelred the Unready who died in 984 (Heslop, 'English Seals', 4 citing F. Douce, 'Some remarks on the Original Seal belonging to the Abbey of Wilton', *Archaeologia*, 18 (1817), 40–50).

[41] *Visitations*, lxxi.

[42] **114**, 'Item sigillum magnum sub sigillis trium Canonicorum, et parvum ad citaciones, sub sigillo unius canonici habeantur'.

[43] Summers 1988, 24 categorically denies that they did so, and is followed by Dixon, 'Vicars Choral', 144.

[44] 'Et ut hec nostra concessio robur perpetue firmitatis optineat presenti scripto sigillum nostrum communie una cum sigillo capituli Suthwell' ecclesie appponi fecimus'.

[45] Thoroton, iii, 156, then in the hands of William Scrimshire, esquire, of Bathley. Throughout we have used the enlarged edition of Thoroton, *The Antiquities of Nottinghamshire (1677)* by John Throsby (3 vols, 1790–6), in the reprint edited by M. W. Barley and K. S. S. Train (1972), which clearly distinguishes between Thoroton's original text and Throsby's additions.

[46] The charter confirmed a grant by Sutton to his chamberlain, Hugh de Mortun, of a messuage in Bathley and other lands in Bathley, North Muskham and Holme, from which a rent of 10 shillings per annum was to be paid to the Vicars Choral. Hugh may be identified as Hugh, son of Elias de Morton (**511**), who witnesses a number of other mid 13th-century charters (cf. **396**, **402**, **512**, **530**). There also seems to have been an elder Hugh, father of Roger of Morton (cf. **392**, **511–13**), though it is unlikely he was still alive in 1262.

[47] Borthwick Institute, Reg. 11, f. 269ʳ, procuration to Walter de Ulseby, 'In cuius rei testi-

(Appendix A, **AII**) is sealed with a small, round seal (23 mm diameter), with a damaged legend from which some have read the letters VIC suggesting that it might be a surviving example of the vicars' communal seal. After close inspection by the present editors, and after consultation with several leading sigillographers, we have concluded that it is much more likely be a personal seal, possibly of an individual vicar choral or of someone sealing on behalf of Marjorie Hare, the other party to the indenture.[48]

Subsidiary documents: original charters

There are a few hints in the White Book about archival practice at Southwell in the Middle Ages. A note by the Chapter about the duties of the chaplain of South Wheatley was ordered to be placed in the treasury for safe-keeping (**526**, pre-1250). In 1328 it was stated that rolls relating to proceedings in the Southwell frankpledge court were to be kept in the treasury and details entered in a register (**153**).[49] An indenture relating to the chantry of St John the Baptist was to be placed in a chantry chest (*in cuius cantarie pixide*) in 1341 (**583**). The original of **105**, a charter of Henry III (1257) was also in a casket or chest (*In xviii peixide*) when copied by Scribe 1 a few years later. The Chapter was able to locate some of its original documents when required to do so, as it did on one occasion in 1344.[50] But there are also indications that there were serious gaps in the collection available in the Minster's archives around the time the decision was taken to compile the White Book. At the start of *Quo warranto* proceedings between 1329 and 1333 (**14–16, 145–7**), perhaps the main incentive for the Chapter to put its records into some kind of order shortly afterwards, specific reference was made in a petition from the canons to a notorious recent robbery of letters and muniments that would have assisted their case, beseeching the king not to allow this to lead to their disinheritance, and suggesting archival security had been lax.[51]

In the next few years copies of some key documents appear to have been acquired from York, possibly from Beverley Minster and Ripon, too, for the purpose of establishing Southwell's privileges.[52] A few references to documents being sent to Southwell for safe-keeping in the early fourteenth century have been discovered.[53] A set of statutes agreed in Chapter in 1329

monium sigillum nostrum communem presentibus est appensum', 10 May 1367.

[48] For further details see note to Appendix A, **AII**.

[49] As compilation of the White Book only began in 1347 (see above, p. xxxiii), it is clearly not the register in question here, but the White Book was certainly later used for summary entries of frankpledge proceedings at Southwell (**154–84**), and is itself called a register (**358**).

[50] **108**, when some of Southwell's original papal bulls were apparently displayed along with other records.

[51] Petition to Edward III from Henry de Edwinstowe and other canons (**147**) '... eyant regard qe toutez lour lettres et autres munimentz depar quelx ils se poent aver eyde furent enportez qant lesglise estoit derobbe come conu chose est a toute le paiis issint qe la dit eglise ne soit disherite'.

[52] See note to **28**.

[53] An unnamed correspondent of Archbishop Greenfield, *c.* 1309, informed him, 'La bosoingne entre vous e Thomas de Beleuwe est escheuie, kar il ad enseele lescrit qi est doublee, dunt sire Robert ad lun ... e ioe lautre pour mettre en garde en la Tresorie de Suwelle' (*Reg. Greenfield*, i, no. 496).

(but not recorded in the White Book) made provision for three chests with locks to be kept, though where they were to be stored is not stated, most likely in the treasury where the deeds of chantries like St John the Baptist were certainly being preserved around this date. One chest was to be used for muniments and money, suggesting that the number of documents was still relatively modest,[54] though the numbers would certainly have expanded considerably in the later Middle Ages as evidence from the White Book shows. Their fate, especially once they had been entered into the cartulary, is uncertain. It was not unusual for original charters to be neglected, discarded or even destroyed once cartulary copies had been made.

Later upheavals at the time of the Reformation or a century later during the Civil Wars and Commonwealth period, when the Minster was put to secular use, almost certainly resulted in the further dispersal or destruction of surviving medieval charters. Anecdotal evidence at the time of the Restoration recalled some records being destroyed around 1650.[55] It is also indicative that, while he cites the White Book, the first major Nottinghamshire antiquary, Dr Robert Thoroton, does not mention other manuscript material relating to the Chapter at Southwell, apart from a 'Lib. mag. pen Capital de Southwell',[56] though he does cite some charters relating to the town of Southwell then in private hands.[57] Nevertheless the originals of some documents that were copied into the White Book have survived to the present. They form part of a small collection of medieval charters, most of which have an evident connection with Southwell Minster, that was acquired in the mid-nineteenth century by a member of the Cragg family of Threckingham House, Billingborough, Lincolnshire. Their immediate provenance is unknown though it is probable that they were still preserved in or near Southwell when acquired. They are currently deposited in Lincolnshire Archives and have been collated with the White Book copies in this edition.[58]

Attention can also be drawn to another clutch of twenty-four original charters, dating between *c.* 1268 and 1435, now in the British Library, some of which may once have formed part of the Chapter's archive. They chiefly relate to property acquired in the town of Southwell by John of Southwell, a king's clerk, either side of 1300.[59] He did not, as far as can be established, have any official position in the Minster during his own lifetime, although he would have been familiar with other royal clerks who did hold prebends.

---

[54] *Visitations*, 215–16. The second chest was for jewels and relics and the third for books held in common only to be lent out on security.

[55] Rogers, *Southwell Minster*, 16–17, citing the Visitation record of 1662 that 'writings were plundered in the rebellion; part of them were detained by Mr William Clay ... [who] refused to deliver them', but warning against exaggerating the damage caused to the fabric and muniments during the Civil War and the Interregnum.

[56] See below p. xlix–li.

[57] See further next paragraph.

[58] LA, Cragg MSS 3 and 4; see **214, 279, 294, 453, 460**, and Appendix A, **AI, A5, AII**.

[59] BL, Add. Charters 27458–27479 and 36459. For a grant by Southwell to the Minster see **405** (1296); he was also a witness on other occasions between *c.* 1280 and 1302 (**426, 429, 438, 439**). With his wife Alice, Southwell agreed a final concord with Hugh, son of Maurice *de Gardino* and his wife, Juecta, for the purchase of a toft and its appurtenances in Southwell for £10 in November 1302 (TNA, CP 25/1/183, no. 1). See the note to **426** for further details on his career.

These charters, because of the subsequent descent of the properties concerned, may have come to the Chapter at the end of the Middle Ages. Some
certainly passed into the hands of clerks and chaplains attached to the Minster
after Southwell's death. They may have left some of the properties mentioned to augment chantries or for other endowments in later generations.
So far it has proved difficult to locate the exact position in the town of the
tenements in question or to correlate the information they contain with that
found in the White Book charters relating to Southwell. None are copied
into the White Book, though many individuals named in them do occur
in its pages. Some of these charters have early endorsements for archival
purposes. At least three of them, together with two others that do not appear
to have survived, were in the hands of a descendant of John of Southwell
in the mid-seventeenth century when seen by Robert Thoroton.[60] To date,
no clear link between them and other charters once known to have been
in the Chapter's hands has been established though it might be suspected.

Other cartulary material

Two parchment gatherings, each now in a modern binding, contain material
closely associated with the White Book. One has been given the modern title,
'Second Cartulary of the Collegiate Church'.[61] It is a large quarto, 235 x 275
mm, rebound in a hard cover in 1973, consisting of nineteen folios including
the original parchment cover labelled *Registrum eccl[es]ie Southwell.*[62]
Twenty-nine documents are transcribed in full, of which twenty occur dis-
persed through the White Book, though not in the same order as found here.
   The date range for the documents is *c.* 1223–1543, the last being Henry
VIII's letters for the Chapter of 4 June 1543 which provides a *terminus a quo*
for the compilation of this collection of charters.[63] They are a very eclectic
choice. Why they were selected for copying is not immediately evident since
there does not seem to be any obvious connecting link between them. Why
others were omitted remains mysterious when their content appears to be
of similar relevance to that of documents that were included in the White
Book. Completed after Henry VIII had revoked his earlier decision in 1540
to abolish the Chapter, it is likely that continuing uncertainties threatening
the privileges and properties owned by the Chapter at the end of his reign
and the start of that of Edward VI, when the Court of Augmentations was
stripping away most of the Minster's other assets, provided an incentive for
compiling this small cartulary.[64]

---

[60] Thoroton, iii, 83–6 for the Southwell family. He cites specifically BL, Add. Charters
27466, 27469 and 27474 (at pp. 83–4) then 'Autogr. penes Rob. Southwell, Equ. Aurat.', as
well as two now apparently lost charters of Peter, son of Mr Gilbert of Eaton, of 1293 and
1311 then in the same collection.
[61] NA, SC/7/1/5.
[62] Xerox copies of this small volume and an extensive catalogue of contents were made
by NA prior to its return from the Church Commissioners of England to Southwell Minster
Library in May 1972 (NA/DD SP 69/1).
[63] The 1543 document is in a different, later, hand from the rest of the transcripts.
[64] The actions of the Court of Augmentations with regard to Southwell are revealed by the
letters of Sir Edward North to the Dean and Chapter (**614–16**).

Table 1
Correlation between charters in the 'Second Cartulary of the Collegiate Church' and the White Book

SC/7/1/5	White Book	SC/7/1/5	White Book	SC/7/1/5	White Book
f. 2^r	214	f. 7^r	57	f. 13^r	556
f. 3^r	97	f. 7^v	74	f. 13^{r-v}	564
f. 3^{r-v}	115	f. 7^v	18	f. 13^v	571
f. 3^v	Appendix A, A3	ff. 7^v–8^v	Appendix A, A13	f. 14^{r-v}	72
f. 4^{r-v}	Appendix A, A8	f. 9^r	497	ff. 14^v–15^v	Appendix A, A6
ff. 4^v–5^v	Appendix A, A10	ff. 9^v–10^r	456	f. 15^v	cf. 587
f. 5^v	Appendix A, A9	ff. 10^{r-v}	455	ff. 16^r–18^v	Appendix A, A12
f. 6^r	34	ff. 11^{r-v}	414	f. 19^r	Appendix A, A14
f. 6^{r-v}	41	ff. 12^{r-v}	579		
f. 6^v	55	ff. 12^v–13^r	449		

The second volume, also repaired in 1973, is a small cartulary of St Mary's chantry, titled *Munimenta Cantarie beate Marie*.[65] The modern cover measures 265 x 210 mm, with the original parchment sheets being 255 x 195 mm. Foliated in an early modern hand, which now starts at folio 5 and ends at folio 22^v, it thus contains eighteen folios of which the last is badly rubbed. As it currently stands, the first entry begins in the middle of another copy of White Book **485**. There follow further transcriptions of **486–521**, with some very minor differences in order to that in the White Book. The date range for the documents included is *c.* 1180–1395. It can be deduced that the missing folios 1–4 almost certainly contained copies of White Book **464–84**, the other, earliest, items contained in the section devoted to St Mary's chantry, ranging in date from the late thirteenth century to 1364. This small cartulary is in a single hand, probably of the first half of the fifteenth century. It is not identifiable with any of the scribes of the White Book. The heading in the upper margin of f. 1 (*Munimenta Cantarie beate Marie*), however, resembles the hand of Scribe 4 of the White Book, and may perhaps have been supplied by him. As with the 'Second cartulary', we can only speculate for the moment on the purpose of producing this duplicate copy of the charters relating to Gunthorpe's chantry (**464–504**) and part of the White Book relating to lights at various altars (**504–21**). Was it a draft of material intended for the White Book, or copies made after entries already in the White Book? Because its sheets are a different size from those in the White Book, it was clearly not a quire intended initially for insertion into that manuscript. A modern typescript calendar of the documents was produced by the Rev. E. H. R. Wood.[66]

[65] NA, SC/7/1/7.
[66] NA, SC/7/1/8.

Historical Usage

The manuscript evidence

The White Book, as already briefly noted, continued to be used for administrative purposes until at least the early eighteenth century and was produced in evidence in cases before the Exchequer and Chancery as late as the 1830s. In addition to marginal and other comments added in early modern hands,[67] its value as a source of reference for the affairs of the Chapter is also highlighted by the provision of indexes and the transcription of portions of the White Book for use in the eighteenth century. The earliest index currently surviving appears to be an 'Abstract of the principal Matters contained in the Registrum Album of the Church of Southwell, Notts.'[68] A draft version of this Abstract is also preserved in BL, Add. MS 24817.[69] Its compiler, towards the middle or later part of the eighteenth century, completes the title with the statement: 'the first Column denotes the Pages of the Book, the second the Date of the Deed'. The summaries of each document it lists are precise, the dating evidence is carefully presented and in some cases a fairly full paraphrase or even some verbatim translation of parts of the original is provided, for example, in the sections relating to Norwell Overhall prebend. Among other early modern copies of documents from the White Book revealing further consultation, there are transcripts of some relating to Sutton's Chantry and its lands (cf. **61–72**) also dating from the early eighteenth century.[70]

As a legal record, the White Book was produced in evidence in cases concerning the Chapter in the Exchequer on 30 September 1833 and in Chancery on 4 April 1838.[71] That relating to the Exchequer proceedings consists of a manuscript note reading:

> In the Exchequer/[72] Between Henry Becher Esquire Plaintiff/ and/ The Reverend William Claye and others/ Defendants/ 30th September 1833. At the execution of a commission in the

---

[67] Where significant, these have been noted in this edition.

[68] NA, SC/7/1/2, concluding with full transcripts of the letters of Sir Edward North from the Court of Augmentations (pp. 121–4 = **614–16**).

[69] Purchased from C. Devon Esq. in 1862, but without other evidence of provenance. Some of its sheets have been bound in an incorrect order; a few are of a different size to the main text. Like NA, SC/7/1/2, it begins with Pope Alexander III's bull of 1171 (**1**) and ends on f. 48ᵛ with Archbishop Sandys's licence of 1582 allowing the inhabitants of Halam to bury their dead in the churchyard of their chapel rather than bringing them to Southwell (**613**). Then follows on ff. 49ʳ–50ʳ a copy of **151**, the 'Laudable Customs' of St Peter's, York (*c.* 1106), followed on ff. 51ʳ–56ᵛ by brief extracts from various documents relating to Norwell, others of which had already been included on ff. 22ʳ–35ʳ (= White Book, pp. 245–91, **373–89**). On ff. 51ʳ–53ʳ, which are only half the size of the other sheets in the manuscript, these extracts are taken from White Book, pp. 241–4 (= parts of **373**) and on ff. 54ʳ–56ᵛ they are taken from pp. 206–40 but again concentrate on the Norwell entries (**358–72**). The revised edition of Davis, *Medieval Cartularies*, 184 incorrectly continues to call BL, Add. MS 24817 a copy of the White Book.

[70] NA, DDM/53/1 and 2.

[71] Information written on two separate preliminary parchment sheets (folios A and B) inserted before the medieval folios of the White Book were bound in their current form in the sixteenth century as notes on f. Bᵛ in a 16th- /17th-hand indicate.

[72] Slashes indicate the end of lines.

examination of witnesses in this cause this parchment Book was shown to George Hodgkinson Barrow a witness sworn and examined and by him deponed unto at the time of his examination on the complainants behalf, Before us/ Wm Hurst, W. Carsham, G^{eo}. Freeth.

That relating to the case in Chancery is a notice stamped in at right-angles showing that the Chapter, as complainants, were proceeding against Paul Beilby, Lawley Thompson Beilby, Richard Lawley Thompson and Sir Francis Lawley,[73] defendants, and that again 'this Book was produced and shown to George Hodgkinson Barrow a witness sworn and examined … [before] J. Mee, Wm Haines and Walter Hall Cappel'.

In the mid-nineteenth century, Rev. J. F. Dimock, one of the last Vicars Choral at Southwell who was also the last to be presented by the Chapter to its richest living, the rectory of Barnburgh (Yorks. W.R.), produced what is usually referred to as a translation of the White Book.[74] However his work included some calendaring or paraphrasing besides verbatim translation of items in the White Book.[75] Neverthless it was the fullest set of extracts from the volume surviving to that date, and a copy was made by (or for) the Yorkshire antiquary, James Raine, senior.[76] Raine's copy was later presented to the first bishop of Southwell, Dr George Ridding (1884–1904). In May 1928 it was deposited in the Minster Library. It is now kept at Nottinghamshire Archives.[77]

In 1891, A. F. Leach's *Visitations and Memorials of Southwell Minster* brought the Minster's medieval and early modern records, previously largely the preserve of local antiquaries and historians, to the attention of a much wider readership. His introduction provided the fullest account of the Minster's institutional development since the twelfth century that has yet been produced. While chiefly editing visitation records from a register for the seventy years or so before the Reformation,[78] Leach also printed a few key medieval texts from the White Book which had not been previously edited or had been poorly reproduced (see further below). As he noted, 'There are a great many more which might be printed with advantage, but the White Book really requires a separate volume to do justice to its contents.'[79]

---

[73] The traditional absence of punctuation in legal documents makes these identifications problematic.

[74] *Visitations*, c. Among his still valuable works are Dimock, 'Architectural History' and Dimock, *History.*

[75] NA, SC/7/1/3–4, apparently Canon Raine's copy of Dimock's work, now bound in two volumes, vol. 1, 159 folios, consisting of White Book, pp. 1–228, and vol. 2, foliated 160–353 = White Book, pp. 229–475, with an index of names (ff. 306–53). We have not been able to discover whether an original or other copies of Dimock's work now survive (cf. next note).

[76] We are grateful to Kirsty McHugh, archivist, Yorkshire Archaeological Society, Leeds, for searching the Society's collections for possible correspondence between Raine and Dimock, but none came to light.

[77] NA, SC/7/1/3 and 4.

[78] Now NA, SC/2/1/1, for the period 1469–1547.

[79] *Visitations*, lxix note a. He continued: 'I have only printed the earliest document in it [= **151**], one which shows the position of the church as a parish as well as collegiate church [= **221**], and the pre-Reformation Statutes [**113**, **114 et al.**], which were very inaccurately printed by Dickinson, and with many lacunæ.'

A generation later, guided by Professor Frank Stenton, W. A. James, later librarian at the Minster,[80] began a complete transcription of the White Book. He started on 12 September 1925 and by 12 April 1926 he had a full typescript transcript.[81] He then almost immediately produced a revised version, finished on 11 January 1929.[82] Finally, he began to type out a further, third, clean version which he eventually completed over ten years later on 26 November 1939. This he had 'read down', that is, corrected, by 26 January 1940.[83] Three versions of James's work of transcription thus now survive in typescript copies among the Chapter records deposited in Nottinghamshire Archives and in the Minster Library. Photocopies of these have also been made over the years.[84]

Besides his labours transcribing the White Book, James was also very active in compiling indexes to assist those using his transcriptions. These also now survive in multiple copies either with the Chapter's records in Nottinghamshire Archives or at Southwell. Among them are hand-written notebooks briefly summarising contents in page order,[85] and a 'Calendar of all the Clergy mentioned in the White Book, together with other entries to the same in other books'.[86] He also made notes on chantries, chantry priests and Vicars Choral, using the White Book and other records,[87] and on prebends and prebendaries which are a valuable source of additional information.[88] In parallel with this work, James had also transcribed (and partially translated) the two small cartularies, described above, that duplicate material in the White Book[89] as well as copying the charters he thought relevant to

---

[80] Doris Stenton, 'Frank Merry Stenton 1880–1967', *Proceedings of the British Academy*, 54 (1968), 315–423, at p. 379, describes how the Stentons became acquainted with 'a pleasant eccentric Londoner called Ashley James' who at the age of 50 had 'retired to live in one of the prebendal houses at Southwell', and how they taught him to read 'old documents'. The copies of the transcripts and other notes made by James from the White Book, which the Stentons once owned, are now largely to be found among the Chapter records deposited at NA (cf. notes 86 and 90 below). We are grateful to Sally Kent, Reading Room Assistant, Museum of English Rural Life and Special Collections Service, University of Reading, for checking that there do not appear to be significant further copies now among White Book material in the Stenton Papers deposited there.

[81] NA, SC/11/4/17 and 18.

[82] NA, SC/11/4 19 (= WB, pp. 1–167) and 20 (= pp. 168–475), typescript, heavily corrected in ink. There is a note in Vol. 1 that he started indexing this version on 8 September 1928 and finished this task on 15 November 1929.

[83] Southwell, Minster Library, typescript now bound in four volumes, with some additional notes and commentary on individual chantries, as 12/3 (WB, **1–141**, with an English summary of **450–80**), 11/3 (WB, **142–343**), 17/3 (WB, **344–420**) and 16/3 (WB, **421–617**).

[84] The editors are grateful to the late Brian Whitehouse, Minster librarian, for generously providing a complete photocopy of James's third transcript as this edition of the White Book took shape, and to Mrs Christine Whitehouse, former librarian, for additional help.

[85] NA, SC/11/4/21.

[86] NA, SC/7/1/22, completed on 12 September 1938, with the bookplate of the Stentons. There is a bound photocopy of this in Southwell, Minster Library, 14/3.

[87] NA, SC/11/4/40–2.

[88] Southwell, Minster Library, 3/2. Other aids in that library include James's indexes to Places (16/11) and Laymen (17/2) mentioned in the White Book, and a list correlating the information it gives on dates (17/1).

[89] Cf. above **pp.** xliv–xlv.

the Minster's history in Captain William Cragg's collection.[90] This work has proved helpful to the present editorial team even where we provide different readings or dating of texts, or suggest alternative identifications of individuals mentioned.

The printed evidence

Perhaps not surprisingly, the first printed evidence for exploitation of the White Book by antiquarians and historians comes from that Golden Age of Sir William Dugdale and his friends, among whom was numbered Dr Robert Thoroton.[91] Documents relating to the collegiate church of Southwell were published in the third volume of the first edition of Dugdale's *Monasticon Anglicanum*, issued in 1673.[92] Ten of them were taken 'Ex registro albo penès Canonicos de Suthwell', the rest from inspeximuses found in the Patent Rolls, apart from Elizabeth I's statutes of 1585. Now usually cited after the enlarged edition of the early nineteenth century, in fact the selection of documents relating to Southwell in *Monasticon Anglicanum* remained little changed in successive versions after that first appearing in 1673.[93] In 1677, the White Book was naturally exploited more extensively in Thoroton's *Antiquities of Nottinghamshire*.[94]

Dugdale had visited Southwell in early September 1641 to 'draw and record the tombs and monuments' with William Sedgwick, a genealogist and arms painter, because of their fear that, like others throughout the country, these 'were at very grave risk of being destroyed by civil war'.[95]

---

[90] NA, SC/11/4/82, 'Copy of Some Manuscripts in the possession of Captain William A. Cragg of Threckingham House, Billingborough, Lincolnshire, lent to me to copy in August 1925. Finished copying 29th August 1925', with the bookplate of Frank and Doris Stenton.

[91] cf. Thoroton, i (v–xi) for a useful summary of Thoroton's career by Barley and Train, which was re-published with some minor corrections as 'Robert Thoroton' in *English County Historians. First Series*, ed. Jack Simmons (Wakefield, 1978), 22–43. For a brief modern summary see Myles Thoroton Hildyard, 'Thoroton, Robert (1623–1678), antiquary', *ODNB online*: http://www.oxforddnb.com/view/article/27371?docPos=1 (accessed 13 December 2016).

[92] *Monasticon Anglicanum*, ed. Roger Dodsworth and William Dugdale, 3 vols (London, 1655–73), iii, part 2, 10–26. We have usually used the revised 19th-century edition, cited as *Mon. Ang.*

[93] *Mon. Ang.*, VI, ii, 1313–23. The main difference, apart from the more generous typographical lay-out, is not an increase in the number of edited documents in 1830 but that the engravings of Southwell between pp. 1312 and 1313, an external view from the north-west and an internal one of the crossing, were etched in 1814 while the 1673 edition contained views of the Minster from the north-east corner and the other from the north-west engraved by Wenceslaus Hollar in 1672. This latter shows the Booth Chantry in place towards the west end of the southern side of the nave.

[94] Particularly, of course, for the account of Southwell (Thoroton, iii, 71–86), though Dickinson expressed some surprise that Thoroton and others had not made even greater use of the White Book (Dickinson, *Southwell* (1819), 117 note). Thoroton also cites a 'Lib. mag. pen. Capit. de Southwell' on at least two occasions (pp. 71, 82) which contained copies of some key documents and was made after the issue of Elizabeth's statutes of 1585. We have failed to identify this, since none of the surviving copies of collections of statutes which we have seen match Thoroton's description.

[95] Foulds, '*In medio chori*', 112.

It may have been on this occasion that he first became aware of the White Book, though it is doubtful, given the shortness of his stay and the urgency of the task he had in hand, that he had time to transcribe any of it during this visit. Although the proof is lacking, it is not an unreasonable assumption that Dugdale only later learnt of the White Book from Thoroton.[96] It was Dugdale himself, according to Thoroton, who encouraged him to begin his *Antiquities* and the work was dedicated to the great antiquary.[97] It followed in essentials the model provided by Dugdale in the greatest of early county histories to be published, *The Antiquities of Warwick, illustrated; from Records, Leiger-Books, Manuscripts, Charters, Evidences, Tombes and Armes: beautified with Maps, Prospects and Portraictures* (1655).[98] Possibly known to one another already at that period, the two men had certainly been acquainted since Dugdale's visitation of Nottinghamshire as Norroy King of Arms which began in 1662, because Thoroton helped to certify some of the genealogies that were presented, evidence for his already long-standing passion for local history to which Dugdale clearly had given purpose and direction.[99] Gervase Pigot of Thrumpton Hall, Barton-in-Fabis, who shared an interest in the history of other local gentry families, was another mutual friend who also encouraged him.[100] Certainly by 1667, if not much earlier, Thoroton was seriously at work accumulating more notes for his book.

Thanks to his many acquaintances as well as his standing as a country doctor and gentleman, Thoroton was frequently able to borrow original manuscripts to work on in the privacy of his own study.[101] Among them was 'our Chapter booke', almost certainly the White Book, for the return of which Francis Leeke, prebendary of Woodborough, asked in a letter sent on 10 April 1667, surviving in a collection of notes made by or for Thoroton.[102] Among these notes, there are also transcriptions of nine items from the White Book

---

[96] They may well have met at Gervase Pigot's house at Barton-in-Fabis in April 1666; Dugdale later stayed for at least a night with Thoroton at Car Colston on 14 July 1670, and he noted in his diary for 28 November 1678 'Dr Thoroton dyed' (*Life, Diary and Correspondence of Sir William Dugdale*, ed. William Hamper (London, 1827), 122, 132 and 140).

[97] Thoroton, i, vii, 'Epistle dedicatory'.

[98] William Lambarde, *Perambulation of Kent* (1576), Richard Carew, *Survey of Cornwall* (1602) and Sampson Erdeswicke, *Survey of Staffordshire* (incomplete and unpublished at his death in 1603) had provided earlier examples, but it was Dugdale who fully developed the form.

[99] Barley and Train, in Thoroton, vi–vii.

[100] cf. note 96 above.

[101] Barley and Train, in Thoroton, vii–viii, provide a good account of some of his sources.

[102] Ibid., viii, citing Nottingham Public Library M493 f. 24ᵛ. This and a similar manuscript are now NA, M 493 and 494, and contain miscellaneous notes made by and for Thoroton, and other relevant material, now bound in order to reflect their usage in the first edition of his *Antiquities*. Many of the notes, tricks of arms and drawings of now lost stained glass, were made on the dorse of letters written to Thoroton in his professional capacity as a doctor to save the expense of new paper. Most of the letter from Leeke to Thoroton is lost, apart from the last paragraph: 'This messenger comes to fetch our Chapter booke, pray returne it by him, and you shal contand it and him that ys your humble servant, Francis Leek, Good Friday (i.e. 5 April) 1667', with the note 'sent 10 April', together with the address and the remains of a small seal in red wax closing it. On the reverse are notes towards a genealogy of the family of Rempston.

by a professional copyist for Thoroton's use, including three papal bulls, three royal letters, two charters issued by Archbishop John Le Romeyn and one of Robert Malluvel for the foundation of Rampton prebend.[103]

Since the publication of the *Antiquities of Nottinghamshire* in 1677 the White Book has been cited by most subsequent generations of Nottinghamshire's historians. Some naturally did look again at the original manuscript, but most have either simply paraphrased or more blatantly plagiarised Thoroton's references, often without acknowledgement. A century later, just before John Throsby completed his revised edition of the *Antiquities* (1790–6), William Rastall Dickinson translated some documents from the White Book and edited others in his *History of the Antiquities of the Town and Church of Southwell*. This first appeared in 1787, was revised and re-issued on several occasions in the next few years, and was last re-published by Dickinson himself in 1819. It is this edition, most recently reprinted in 1996, that is now most frequently cited.[104] Dickinson's shortcomings as an editor of texts were noted by some, including A. F. Leach, but like Thoroton before him, he has also been plundered by later writers, while the major part of the White Book has remained unedited to the present.

Survey of Contents

Papal documents in the White Book

The White Book of Southwell contains fifteen papal documents, three of them in duplicate (**1–13**, **48**, **83**, **356**, **359** and **522**, of which **2** is duplicated in **8**, **12** in **359** and **83** in **522**). There are three documents from the pontificate of Alexander III (1159–81: **1**, **4**, **46**), seven issued by Innocent III (1198–1216: **3**, **5**, **6**, **9–11**, and **83/522**), two by Urban IV (1261–4: **2/8** and **7**), one by Nicholas IV (1288–92: **13**), one by Urban VI (1378–89: **12/359**) and one by Martin V (1417–31: **356**). Of the fifteen documents, one is a privilege (**1**), six are confirmations (**2**, **3**, **7**, **9**, **46**, **83**), seven are mandates (**4–6**, **10–12**, **356**), of which four were addressed to papal judges-delegate (**5**, **6**, **10**, **11**), and there is also a grant of remission from penance (**13**).

The form of papal privileges became established over the eleventh and early twelfth centuries, though many features had become fixed much earlier.[105] The evolution process was complete well before 28 July 1171, when Alexander III issued his solemn privilege for Southwell confirming its rights, including the maintenance of peace in its cemetery, its right to hold

---

[103] NA, M 494 ff. 105ʳ–108ʳ, 'Ex libro quodam inter Monumenta venerabilium virorum dominorum Capituli Collegiatae Ecclesiae Beatae Maria Virginis de Southwell in Comitatu Nottingham remanente extractum fuit et est prout sequitur, videlicet ...'. The items transcribed are WB, **1**, **4**, **17**, **18**, **33**, **41**, **46**, **57** and **74**. For some unknown reason, **46**, a bull of Alexander III, begins *Urbanus episcopus servus servorum Dei ...*, but is otherwise a fairly accurate transcript of the WB text.

[104] Dickinson, *Southwell* (London, 1819), reprinted with a preface by Barbara I. Wilson, for Nottinghamshire County Council Leisure Services (Bristol, 1996). For his life and work see Adrian Henstock, 'Dickinson, William (*bap.* 1756, *d.* 1822), antiquary and political manager', *ODNB online*: http://www.oxforddnb.com/view/article/7608?docPos=9 (accessed 13 December 2016).

[105] Bresslau, *Handbuch*, i, 79–80.

Pentecostal processions for all the faithful in Nottinghamshire, and the right of its canons to have a year's prebendal income paid after their deaths to clear debts and make charitable bequests (I). The document opens with the pope's name, his title ('bishop') and the humility formula 'servant of the servants of God', used by all popes from the time of Gregory I (590–604): 'Alexander episcopus servus servorum Dei'. There follows a specific address, naming the beneficiaries and terming them 'beloved sons' ('dilectis filiis canonicis ecclesie sancte Marie de Suwell' tam presentibus quam futuris canonice substituendis'), and then, as standard in privileges, no greeting but instead the phrase 'IN PERPETUUM'. On the original document, these two words would have been written in *elongata* script and the cartulary copyist employed majuscules to represent this. Next comes an arenga, a general moral statement appropriate to the occasion, in this case saying that Alexander has been given rule (*regimen*) of all churches to provide for their well-being and advancement. The arenga brings in a number of key words that popes liked to associate with their office – *regimen* (rule), *studium* (zeal), *solicitudo* (care) and *vigilare* (to be watchful). It also displays another standard feature of papal charters, the use of the *cursus* or rhythmic prose. Thus this arenga closes with the *cursus velox*: 'fuérimus diligéntes'. With the word *Eapropter* opening the next sentence the draftsman moves to the dispositive part of the privilege, and since it is a grant the main verb is *annuimus* ('we grant'), backed up by *suscipimus* ('we receive': Alexander was taking the canons into papal protection) and *communimus* ('we confirm'). This part of the disposition ends with the *cursus tardus* ('illibáta permáneant'), while the disposition as a whole ends with the *velox* ('capítuli distribuátur'). Following the dispositive clauses comes a negative sanction in which Alexander decrees that no one should disturb the grant ('Decernimus ergo ut nulli omnino hominum liceat … perturbare') and that if anyone does so he should be excommunicated, a clause opening 'Si qua igitur' (sentences starting with two monosyllables were favoured by papal draftsmen because they sounded more solemn). A positive sanction comes next, blessing those maintaining the grant. An *apprecatio* comes next, the word AMEN in majuscules representing the *elongata* of the original,[106] and finally comes the date, with statement of place (here Tusculum, one of the favourite papal retreats from Rome in the hot summer months), the name of the datary, the day of the month in classical Roman form ('quinto kalendas Augusti'), the indiction, the incarnation year and Alexander's pontifical year. The original would have been sealed with a lead *bulla* on silk threads.

Although privileges were much more complex in form than other papal documents, several of their features, notably the *intitulatio*, the address and the use of the *cursus* are standard in other papal acts and arengae and sanction clauses are also normal in letters of grace, the form of document in which popes most often issued grants and confirmations from the twelfth century onwards. Over the course of the twelfth century a clear division began to be made

---

[106] In the original the AMEN would have been written threefold, but the copyist presumably omitted the repetitions, and he also appears to have omitted the rota, subscriptions and monogram that would have occupied some of the space between the main text of the document and the dating clause.

between letters of grace, sealed on silk threads, and letters of justice, sealed on hemp cords.[107] A mandate issued by Alexander III to order the archdeacon of Nottingham and all clergy in the shire to render Southwell its ancient rights (**4**), is a letter of justice, though in effect it provides confirmation for the solemn privilege: it was issued almost a fortnight before the privilege, suggesting that the proctor sent by Southwell to the curia stayed in Tusculum for at least two weeks while obtaining both documents. After the standard papal *intitulatio* and an address describing the archdeacon and other Nottinghamshire clergy as 'beloved sons' the mandate has a greeting standard in papal letters: 'salutem et apostolicam benedictionem' ('greeting and apostolic blessing'). There is then a *narratio* in which Alexander reflects that he has been promoted to his office to preserve the rights of churches with attentive care ('solicitudo'). As normal in papal mandates, the verb used to express command is *mandamus* and the document winds up with a clause promising punishment if the address-ees disobey. Finally comes the date, which in papal letters of Alexander III consisted simply of the place and the day of the month ('Datum Tusculani idus Iulii').[108] The third charter of Alexander III in the White Book is a confirmation for one of the Southwell canons, Roger, brother of Martin de Capella (**46**). This has an arenga which is a variant of one of the most popular forms used by the papal chancery: 'Iustis petentium desideriis facilem nos convenit impartiri consensum et vota que a rationis tramite non discordant effectu sunt prosequente complenda'. The confirmation is expressed with the standard phrase 'auctoritate apostolica confirmamus et presentis scripti patrocinio communimus', and there is a sanction clause frequently found in papal acts: 'Si quis autem hoc attemptare presumpserit indignationem omnipotentis Dei et beatorum Petri et Pauli apostolorum se noverit incursurum'.

Among Innocent III's seven acts are four mandates delegating the hearing of cases to papal judges-delegate (**5**, **6**, **10**, **11**). These cases had been brought to the papal curia by Southwell and, as normal in such circumstances, the task of investigating the complaints was delegated to locally-based judges who would act on papal authority.[109] Normally two or three ecclesiastics of some standing would be appointed, sometimes bishops, more often heads of religious houses, archdeacons and cathedral dignitaries, and often also learned clergy (*magistri*). The judges appointed by Innocent in these four cases included the archbishop of York, the abbots of Rufford and Welbeck, the priors of Newstead, Worksop and Shelford, the archdeacon of North-ampton, a canon of Lincoln and the otherwise unknown Master Richard de Vasselo. Innocent's mandates present statements about the complaints followed by instructions to the judges, with the verb *mandamus* conveying the injunction, and then a clause specifying that if it is not possible for all (or both) the judges appointed to hear the case it will be sufficient for two out of the three or one out of the two to carry out the task. The wording is almost identical across all four mandates and that of **10** will suffice as an example: 'Quod si non omnes hiis exequendis potueritis interesse duo vestrum ea nichilominus exequuntur'.

---

[107] Bresslau, *Handbuch*, ii, 589.
[108] Bresslau, *Handbuch*, ii, 472: from 1188 onwards papal letters included the pontifical year.
[109] Sayers, *Papal Judges*.

Innocent III's three confirmations in the White Book include one for Archbishop Geoffrey of York (**9**) and two for Southwell (**3, 83**). In form they closely resemble Alexander III's confirmation (**46**, discussed above), and the arenga in **9** is close in wording to that of **46**: 'Iustis petentium desideriis dignum est nos facilem prebere consensum et vota que a rationis tramite non discordant effectu prosequente complere'. The two confirmations for Southwell have the same arenga: 'Solet annuere sedes apostolica piis votis et honestis petentium precibus favorem benevolum impartiri'. Although Southwell was keen to obtain documents from Innocent III, it did not bother to have them registered.

Of the acts issued by subsequent popes contained in the White Book, two are confirmations issued by Urban IV on 28 October 1261 (**2, 7**), two are mandates (**12, 356**) issued respectively by Urban VI in 1379 and Martin V in 1429 ordering a local ecclesiastic (in each case the then prior of Thurgarton) to carry out an investigation of claims being made by Southwell, and one (**13**) is an indulgence granting remission from penance for one year and forty days for all those visiting Southwell Minster on feasts of the Virgin and during the eight days following each feast, issued by Pope Nicholas IV in 1290. The only one of these documents that appears to have been registered is Nicholas IV's indulgence.[110] One of Urban IV's confirmations (**2**) has an arenga with the same wording as **9** (discussed above), while the other has 'Cum a nobis petitur quod iustum est et honestum, tam equitatis quam ordo exegit rationis ut id per solicitudinem officii nostri ad debitum perducat effectum'. Much more elaborate is the arenga praising the Virgin Mary in Nicholas IV's indulgence: 'Virga venustissima et omnium virtutum floribus insignita virgo dei genitrix gloriosa, cuius pulcritudinem sol et luna mirantur, cuius precibus iuvatur populus Cristianus florem preciosissimum inmercessibilem et eternum dominum nostrum Cristum ineffabili sancti spiritus coniunxione produxit ob cuius reverentiam loca eiusdem virginis [vocabulo] insignita sunt et Cristi fidelibus merito veneranda ut eius piis et adiuti suffragiis [eterne] retributionis premium consequi mereamur'. This contains a quotation from a prayer in honour of the Virgin that forms part of the Advent liturgy ('... Ave venustissima/ Ave virga Jesse data ...'),[111] and another from a chant in honour of St Agnes ('cuius pulchritudinem sol et luna mirantur').[112] It was apparently newly introduced into the papal chancery in Nicholas' pontificate, and was often used by him in indulgences for churches dedicated to the Virgin.[113] It was widely used by popes and bishops

---

[110] *Reg. Nicolas IV*, i, 411, no. 2348, in a group of four indulgences with the same wording (nos 2347–50).

[111] Prosper Guéranger, *L'année liturgique* (Le Mans, 1841), 437.

[112] Antiphon for feast of St Agnes, occurring in many manuscripts between the late tenth and the sixteenth century: *Cantus: A Database for Latin Ecclesiastical Chant*, at http://cantusdatabase.org/text-search?string=sol+luna+mirantur , consulted 13 August 2015.

[113] *Reg. Nicolas IV*, nos 947, 1050–1, 1507–9, 1639–40, 1692, 1732–3, 1822–3, 1900, 1960, 2063, 2347–50, 2520–3, 2558–65, 2630, 2641–6, 2728, 2809, 2832–3, 2836, 3058, 3065, 3074–5, 3253–60, 3298–9, 3348, 3449, 3665, 3687, 3737, 3751, 3753, 3946–7, 3961, 4155–7, 4569, 4623–5, 4989–90, 5023, 5036, 5052, 5105–6, 5126, 5328, 5371–2, 5408, 5520–3, 5550, 5704, 5815, 5831, 5999, 6353, 6430, 6486–7, 6579, 6589, 6598, 6781, 6872–9; see also *Initienverzeichnis zu August Potthast, Regesta Pontificum Romanorum (1198–1304)*, MGH (Munich, 1978), s.v. virga venustissima et, virgo venustissima, virgo venustissima etc.

in the fourteenth century.[114]

Charters issued by kings

The White Book contains some forty-seven charters issued by English kings, some of which occur only as texts cited in full in charters of inspeximus and therefore do not appear as separate items in the cartulary.[115] The sequence of royal charters begins with Henry I and ends with Henry VI: within this span, John and Henry V are the only rulers who do not feature. Richard II tops the list with eight charters, Edward III is not far behind with seven, and Henry III is next with six. Five charters of Henry I are preserved in the White Book, one of which (contained in **27**, an inspeximus of Henry III) is a charter of liberties for York, which survives in other copies elsewhere as well; it is somewhat unusual in form and may be a later concoction. The other four (**17**, **18**, **21** and a charter preserved in **148**) are all more easily acceptable. They are writ charters,[116] and are all addressed to the members of the shire court of Nottinghamshire, and, in the case of **21**, also Derbyshire, understandable since the sheriffdoms of Nottinghamshire and Derbyshire were normally held by the same man. Down to the early 1170s, royal grants and confirmations were often issued in the form of orders addressed to the court of the shire where the rights or property were situated to entrust the court with the task of ensuring that the beneficiary could hold what was being granted freely.[117] By contrast, the charter of liberties for York has a

---

114 The opening seventeen words are included in a curial formulary of the very early fourteenth century: Barraclough, *Papal Notaries*, 214, no. 276. Pope John XXII used this arenga in full in indulgences issued in 1326 and 1327: *Römische Quellen zur Konstanzer Bistumsgeschichte zur Zeit der Päpste in Avignon*, ed. Karl Rieder (Innsbruck, 1908), 207, no. 738; *Annals de Montserrat (1258–1485)*, ed. Benet Ribas i Calaf (Montserrat, 1997), 164–5; Clement VII used it in 1384 (Étienne-Nicolas Villette, *Histoire de l'image miraculeuse de Notre-Dame de Liesse* (Laon, 1769), 28–30. This arenga was also frequently used in collective indulgences issued by groups of bishops, for example one for Padua in 1299 (Francesco Scipione Dondi dall'Orologio, *Dissertazioni sopra l'istoria ecclesiastica di Padova* (Padua, 1815), 73), one issued at Carpentras in 1313 by seventeen archbishops and bishops, headed by Archbishop Raymond of Adrianople (Hippolyte Delehaye, 'Les lettres d'indulgence collectives', *Analecta Bollandiana*, 44 (1926), 342–79, at 359–60), one issued for St Mary of Guadalupe in 1326 (Peter Linehan, 'The Beginnings of Santa María de Guadalupe and the Direction of Fourteenth-Century Castile', in Peter Linehan, *Past and Present in Medieval Spain* (Aldershot, 1992), ch. XII (285–304), at 304), and one issued by a group including Bishop John of Langres in 1350 (Patrick Arabeyre, 'La lactation de Saint-Bernard à Châtillon-sur-Seine: Données et problèmes', in *Vie et légendes de Saint-Bernard de Clairvaux: Création, diffusion, reception (XIIe–XXe siècles)*, ed. Patrick Arabeyre, Jacques Berlioz and Philippe Poirrier (Saint-Nicolas-lès-Cîteaux, 1997), 173–97, at 191–2).

115 The charters are as follows: Henry I: **17**, **18**, **21** (with duplicate at **26**), a charter cited in **27**, a charter cited in **148**; Stephen: **22**; Henry II: **19**, **47**, **48**, **144**, and possibly **25** (but see Richard I); Richard I: **20** and possibly **25**; Henry III: **23**, **24**, **27**, **105**, **106**, **361**; Edward I: **61**, **66**, **107**, **209**, **349**; Edward II: **185** and a charter cited in **208**; Edward III: **36**, **116**, a charter cited in **130**, a charter cited in **147**, **213B**, **346**, **347**; Richard II: **148**, **148A**, **149**, **150**, a charter cited in **171**, **354**, **503**, **582**; Henry IV: **380** and a charter cited in **380**; Henry VI: **214**, **345**, **355**, **594** and a charter cited in **594**.

116 Sharpe, 'Address and Delivery', 32–3 for definition.

117 Ibid., 33–45. Uniquely the two counties also shared a joint county court until 1256

general address opening *archiepiscopis, episcopis, abbatibus, consulibus, proceribus et universis fidelibus Francis et Anglis tocius Anglie*, an early and imprecise version of the general address *archiepiscopis, episcopis, abbatibus, comitibus, vicecomitibus, baronibus et omnibus fidelibus* (or variants thereon) that started to appear between 1106 and 1110 and that came to be associated with notifications rather than injunctions.[118]

Two of the four Henry I charters addressed to the shire court confirm manorial or honorial customs within Nottinghamshire to archbishops of York (**21** for Archbishop Thomas II, probably issued in 1109, and the Henry I charter for Archbishop Gerard 1100 x 1107 that is quoted in full in **148**), while the other two (**17–18** of 1119 x 1133) confirm grants by Archbishop Thurstan of churches to form prebends at Southwell. Henry I was keen to confirm grants of parish churches as prebends to major churches: he hoped in this way to extend the range of patronage available to his own clerks, since he could appoint them in episcopal vacancies and otherwise could persuade his bishops to collate royal clerks at least some of the time.[119] In this way the drop in royal patronage that was occurring during his reign as many former royal minsters were being converted into Benedictine and Augustinian priories could be partly compensated for.[120] The protocol of **17–18**, **21** and the charter for Gerard conforms to the normal pattern of Henry's *acta*: a very simple *intitulatio* ('Henricus rex Anglorum'), an address to members of the shire court and the simple greeting *salutem*. Three of the charters have a notification, *Sciatis* (**17**, **18**, **21**), and this is followed by an injunction, usually including the verb *precipio*. The charters end with very short witness lists and the place of issue (Winchester for **17–18**, Dover for **21**).

The only surviving charter of Stephen resembles those of Henry I in form (**22**): it deals with a topic that features frequently in subsequent royal acts for Southwell, the canons' rights to woodland or to property lying in the royal forest. Five acts of Henry II are preserved in the White Book (**19**, with a second copy as **142**, **25**, **47**, **48**, **144**). Nos **19** and **144** are addressed to Ranulf fitz Ingelram, sheriff of Nottingham, and order him to ensure that the canons are not troubled with keeping the ways (**19**, **25**) and can enjoy their rights (**144**). Nos **47** and **48** are addressed to the bailiffs of the archbishop of York at Southwell, ordering them first to deliver liberties to a royal clerk for whom Henry is seeking a prebend (**47**) and then to protect his rights (**48**). In form Henry II's acts for Southwell are similar to those of his predecessors. Nos **19**, **47**, **48** and **144** were all issued before May 1172, when *dei gratia* was added to the royal style.[121] No. **25**, attributed to 'H. dei gratia rex Anglorum' in the White Book, and in most respects a close copy of **19**, Henry II's charter of privileges for Southwell, must be later than May

(Crook, 'Establishment').

[118] Ibid., 46, on origins; see Chaplais, *English Royal Documents*, 6–7, and 13–14 for the development of charters as opposed to letters under Richard I.
[119] Barrow, *The Clergy*, 263; Marritt, 'Secular Cathedrals', 161–2.
[120] Barrow, *The Clergy*, 96, 108–11.
[121] Chaplais, *English Royal Documents*, 13; Nicholas Vincent, 'Regional Variations in the Charters of King Henry II (1154–89)', in *Charters and Charter Scholarship in Britain and Ireland*, ed. Marie Therese Flanagan and Judith A. Green (Basingstoke, 2005), 70–106 at 74–5.

1172, and the 'Randulf', sheriff of Nottingham, to whom it is addressed may be in fact Ralph Murdac, sheriff in the 1180s. It was witnessed by 'H. Cant'', who cannot be an archbishop of Canterbury or a royal chancellor, since the only H. who fits either of these positions, Hubert Walter (archbishop of Canterbury 1193–1205 and chancellor in the early years of John's reign), did not acquire them until well after Henry II's death. It is possible that H. Cant' might be Herbert le Poer, archdeacon of Canterbury 1175–94 and later bishop of Salisbury.[122] The canons of Southwell obtained a charter from Richard I in December 1189 (**20**) confirming their right to hold their lands free of forest law. This charter, written in the plural of majesty that Richard I introduced into English royal charters, has a general address (*archiepiscopis, episcopis, abbatibus, comitibus, baronibus, iusticiariis, vicecomitibus et omnibus forestariis et ballivis et fidelibus suis*), and a dating clause stating the day of the month and regnal year and stating that it was given by the hand of William, bishop-elect of Ely, Richard's chancellor.[123]

The division of chancery acts into formal charters and letters developed further under John, when the letters themselves were separated into letters patent and letters close, and these innovations are visible in the six Henry III charters preserved in the White Book. Two of these are charters of inspeximus (**23, 27**), three of them are confirmations (**105, 106, 361**) and one is a pardon (**24**). Charters of inspeximus, that is, charters quoting a whole charter in full in order to confirm it, had been used by bishops in England since the later twelfth century, but were new to royal Chancery practice in the thirteenth century. One of the inspeximus charters displays the new general address that from John's reign had begun to be used in letters patent and writs patent: 'omnibus ad quos presentes litere pervenerint';[124] the pardon (**24**), which describes itself as 'literas … patentes' in its text but which was enrolled among the letters close, was addressed to all the king's bailiffs and faithful men. The other Henry III charters all have full general addresses appropriate to charters, of the kind noted for **20** above. Dating clauses (with place, day of the month and regnal year) had become standard under John, being built into the end of the witness clause in letters and forming a separate clause in charters, opening by saying who had acted as datary ('Datum per X'). After 1238 Henry III took over the role of datary ('Datum per manum nostram' [**27, 105, 361**]).

Edward I's charters (**61, 66, 107**, a charter cited within **209**, and **349**) are similar in form to Henry III's and the main innovation from this reign observable in the White Book is the appearance of the licence of mortmain (**61**), now required as a result of Edward's mortmain legislation (1279, 1290) by those churches trying to acquire new property. Licences in mortmain occur several times among later medieval royal charters preserved in the White Book (**36** of Edward III; the Edward III charter cited in **140**; **503** of Richard II). Charters of inspeximus remain frequent, and in a note at the end of **148**, an inspeximus issued by Richard II in 1381, we learn that five

---

[122] *Fasti 1066–1300*, ii, 14.
[123] Chaplais, *English Royal Documents*, 13 on Richard's use of the plural of majesty and the form of address in charters; 14–15 on dating clauses in Richard's documents.
[124] Chaplais, *English Royal Documents*, 19.

marks were paid into the hanaper, the chest in which charters were kept in the Chancery until payment was forthcoming; the note also preserves the name of the clerk responsible, Horbury.[125] Southwell was evidently prepared to pay large sums for royal charters: charters of inspeximus were valuable because they provided authorised copies of older charters that might be worn or might subsequently be lost. An increasing number of royal acts in the fourteenth and fifteenth centuries are addressed to royal justices (the charter of Edward III cited within **147**; **347** of Edward III; **149** of Richard II and a mandate of Henry VI cited within **594**), and give some idea of the expansion of administration in the later Middle Ages, though many types of royal document of more ephemeral character are not represented in the pages of the White Book.[126]

Episcopal charters

The White Book contains thirty-six *acta* issued by archbishops of York, who were the patrons of Southwell as well as the diocesans, and six *acta* issued by bishops of other sees. Episcopal *acta* are frequent in cartularies, but the fact that Southwell was a collegiate church in archiepiscopal patron-age influenced the types of episcopal charters that it received. Licences to appropriate parish churches, institutions of vicars and indulgences – all types of episcopal *acta* not infrequently occurring in monastic cartularies – do not feature in the White Book.[127] Here, episcopal *acta* are grants, confirmations (usually of single specified grants, not general confirmations), ordinances establishing prebends, statutes, letters of attorney and mandates.[128]

Of the *acta* issued by archbishops of York and preserved in the White Book, five are from the twelfth century and one from the cusp of the twelfth and thirteenth centuries (**29, 34, 49, 55, 206** and **523**); fourteen are from the thirteenth century (**32, 41, 57, 59, 97, 100, 102, 109, 114, 115, 215, 430, 459, 460**) and thirteen from the fourteenth century (**108, 110, 113, 202–5, 208, 209** (both contained in charters of vidimus), **216, 217, 354** and **369**). From the fifteenth century we have only two letters of John Kempe (**207, 344**) and there is an outlier from the post-Reformation period, **613** issued by Edwyn Sandys. The archbishops best represented are Walter de Gray (**32, 97, 100, 102, 430, 459, 460**), John Le Romeyn (**41, 57, 59, 114, 115**), Thomas Corbridge (**113, 202–4, 209**) and William Melton (**205, 208, 216, 217**). Taken as a group, the sequence provides quite a good overview of developments in English episcopal diplomatic across the Middle Ages and into the early modern period. The earliest actum is **206**, a short charter of Archbishop Thomas II (1109–14), asking inhabitants of Nottinghamshire to give alms to Southwell to assist its rebuilding, and allowing them to make their Pentecostal procession there rather than to York. Thomas' *intitulatio* (probably cropped by the copyist) runs simply 'Thomas dei gratia'; the

---

125 Chaplais, *English Royal Documents*, 22 on the hanaper.
126 For some idea of the range, see Chaplais, *English Royal Documents*, 23–45.
127 However, **97** is a grant by Archbishop Walter de Gray of a church to Southwell Chapter to be converted to the uses of the common fund, and is therefore close to a licence to appropriate.
128 For different types of episcopal *acta*, see introductions to volumes of *EEA*, and also Cheney, *Bishops' Chanceries*, 57–8, 70. For statutes, see pp. lxii–lxiv below.

address is 'omnibus parochianis suis de Notinghamscira'; the greeting is 'salutem et dei benedictionem'. The verb used to make the request is 'Precamur' ('we beseech'), and the document closes with a farewell ('Valete'). The awkward transition from third person *suis* in the address to first person plural in the dispositive clause is normal in episcopal *acta* of the first half of the twelfth century, and is noticeable also in Archbishop Thurstan's *acta* (1119–40: **34**, **49**), the first of which switches from third person to a mixture of first person plural ('apposuimus') and singular ('manerii mei'), while the other moves from 'suis' to 'me dedisse'. Thurstan's *intitulatio* in both acts is 'Turstinus dei gratia Ebor' archiepiscopus' and the addresses in both open 'omnibus successoribus suis', though in **49** the address goes on to add 'et omnibus hominibus suis de Notinghamsire, clericis et laicis, Francis et Anglis'; in both acts the greeting is simply 'salutem'. Both charters show some influence from royal writs, especially **49** with its mention of men of a shire and reference to French and English.[129] Thurstan moves straight from the greeting into the disposition in **34** but in **49** the transition is made with a notification, 'Sciatis'. There is no concluding clause in **34**, but **49** closes with a witness list.

Only one charter of Archbishop Roger of Pont-l'Évêque (1154–81) is preserved in the White Book (**55**). Here too the *intitulatio* is 'R. dei gratia Ebor' archiepiscopus', Roger's standard *intitulatio* before he became papal legate in 1164.[130] The address is a specific one, to the Dean and Chapter of York Minster and to Southwell Chapter. Again, the greeting is simply *salutem*, which Roger used in over three-quarters of his *acta*,[131] and the transition to the disposition is effected with a one-word notification, 'Sciatis'. Reflecting a normal usage in royal writs, Roger orders ('Quare volumus et precipimus') that the grantee be allowed to hold the property freely.[132] The document closes with a witness list. The similarity of this charter to royal writs may be explained by its probable place of issue, an assembly held by Henry II in Normandy in April 1162.[133] Archbishop Geoffrey (1189–1212) issued at least five charters for Southwell, but the texts of only two of these survive.[134] These two *acta* display features typical of later twelfth-century English episcopal *acta*: consistent use of the first person plural, a more ecclesiastical phraseology in greetings and notifications, and witness lists consisting of clerics of the episcopal household. Geoffrey's standard *intitulatio*, 'G. / Galfridus dei gratia Ebor' archiepiscopus et Anglie primas' occurs in both;[135] unusually for the 1190s, this clause comes ahead of the general address, 'omnibus sancte matris ecclesie filiis ad quos littere iste pervenerint' in **21** and 'omnibus has literas visuris vel audituris' in **523**.[136] Many of Geoffrey's

---

[129] See Sharpe, 'Address and Delivery', 46–9 on combinations of local and general elements in addresses in royal writs of this period.

[130] *EEA York 1154–1181*, lviii.

[131] Ibid., lix.

[132] Injunction clauses such as this occur only twice in Roger's *acta*: ibid., lxi.

[133] See also below, p. lxi–lxii, for discussion of other episcopal *acta* issued at this meeting.

[134] *EEA York 1189–1212*, nos 63–7; 64, 65 and 67 are missing but are mentioned in other sources.

[135] Ibid., cxv.

[136] The address in WB **523**, a type less often used by Geoffrey, is paralleled in *EEA York*

acta contain corroborations, and the one in **523**, opening with an imitation of papal diplomatic ('Ut autem') and mentioning Geoffrey's seal, is typical.[137]

Walter de Gray's *acta* (1215–55) open with the address, usually 'Omnibus Christi fidelibus ad quos presens scriptum pervenerit' (**32**, **97**, **430**, **460**), though with some variation; **100**, addressed to the justices of the King's Bench, runs 'viris venerabilibus et amicis in Christo dilectissimis iusticiis domini regis de banco'. Walter's *intitulatio* is normally similar to Geoffrey's, save in **102**, which omits the primatial title, and his greeting in *acta* with general addresses is always 'salutem in domino'; by contrast, the greeting for the king's justices in **100** is 'salutem et sinceram in domino dilectionem'. There is more variation in the notification, though 'Noverit universitas vestra' (**97**, **102**) and 'Noveritis quod' (**100**, **460**) seem to be preferred. Walter's *acta* usually have corroborations, two of them opening 'Ut autem' and all of them making some use of the past participle 'ratus'. The methods used by Walter's clerks to close his *acta* show variation, not surprisingly given the length of his pontificate and the fact that it straddled the period in which English episcopal charters finally routinely began to include dating clauses. Three of his *acta* in the White Book are dated (**102**, **459–60**), all with mention of place, day and month in Roman style (e.g. 'septimo idus Octobris' in **460**), and Walter's pontifical year. Two of the dated *acta* are also witnessed (**459**, **460**), and two other acts also have witness lists (**97**, **430**); in all cases the witness list comes last. The letter to the king's justices ends 'Valete' (**100**).

Of the five *acta* of Archbishop John Le Romeyn (1286–96) in the White Book, four are ordinances concerning prebends (**41**, **57**, **59** and **115**) and the fifth (**114**) is a set of statutes. The ordinances all open with general addresses, 'Universis (or 'Omnibus' in **59**) sancte matris ecclesie filiis ad quorum notitiam pervenerit hec scriptura'; John's *intitulatio* is 'Johannes permissione divina Ebor' archiepiscopus, Anglie primas' (in **41** the primatial title is omitted), and the greeting usually mentions the embraces of the Saviour ('salutem in sanctis/ sanctissimis/ sinceris amplexibus salvatoris' in **41**, **57**, **59**). The greeting in the statutes (**114**) is 'salutem, gratiam et benedictionem' and in **115** the greeting is replaced by an appeal to memory 'subscripta ad perpetuam memoriam eorundem'. Three of the ordinances (**41**, **57**, **59**) have arengae stressing the need to care for the praise of the Saviour, to promote worship or to ensure that Vicars Choral are provided for, and all four ordinances have corroborations opening 'In cuius rei testimonium' and commenting on the sealing; **59** also notes that the charter was issued as a chirograph ('hoc scriptum bipartitum'). Typically for episcopal *acta* of the late thirteenth century, there are no witness lists and the documents close with dating clauses giving place of issue, day of the month in Roman form and the year of grace, together with (in **57**, **59**, **114**, **115**) the pontifical year.

Henry Newark's short pontificate (1296–9) provided two *acta* for the White Book (**109**, **215**), both letters addressed to the Chapter of Southwell, one citing them to appear in his court (**109**) and the other ordering them to sequestrate prebendal income from one of their colleagues (**215**). These have a similar *intitulatio* to that of John Le Romeyn, and, as letters, they

1189–1212, no. 51 for Nostell priory.
[137] Ibid., cxix.

close with 'Valete' and a date. The five *acta* of Thomas Corbridge (1300–4) recorded in the White Book (**113**, **202–4**, **209**) consist of four letters and a set of statutes (**113**). Thomas' *intitulatio* is in the form established by his two immediate predecessors (it is however omitted, probably by copyists, from **202** and also from **209**, which is preserved within a document issued by Thomas' official). **113** and **202–4** are all addressed to Southwell Chapter and **209** to his official, and the greeting in all cases is 'salutem, gratiam et benedictionem'. Nos **113** and **202–4** have a farewell ('Valete') and all five *acta* close with a date stating place of issue, day and month in Roman form and year of pontificate. The four *acta* issued by William Melton (1316–40) for Southwell (**205**, **208**, **216**, **217**) are close in form to Thomas Corbridge's. William de Zouche (1342–52) issued two letters dimissory to Southwell (**108**, **110**), both opening 'Universis sancte matris ecclesie filiis'. Only **108** contains an *intitulatio*, and this is similar in type to that of Romeyn, Newark and Corbridge. The greeting in **108** is the same as John Le Romeyn's in **59**. Both **108** and **110** have dating clauses giving place of issue, day of the month in modern form, incarnation year and pontifical year. The sole *actum* (**369**) of John Thoresby (1352–73) occurring in the White Book is close in form to those of his immediate predecessors, the main changes being the addition of 'et apostolice sedis legatus' to the *intitulatio* and a switch to 'salutem in domino sempiternam' for the greeting. That of Robert Waldby (1396–9) (**354**) shows similar features to the *acta* of Zouche and Thoresby.

John Kempe, archbishop of York 1425–52, was also a cardinal, so his *intitulatio* in **207** (cropped in **344**) runs 'Johannes miseratione divina sacrosancte Romane ecclesie titulo sancte Balbine presbiter cardinalis, Ebor' archiepiscopus, Anglie primas et apostolice sedis legatus'; this is preceded by the address 'Omnibus Christi fidelibus ad quos presentes litere pervenerint'. **344**, an ordinance, opens with an invocation 'In dei nomine, amen' before the address 'Universis sancte matris ecclesie filiis ad quos presentes litere pervenerint'. While **344** opts for the same greeting ('sincere embraces') as **59**, **207** has 'salutem in domino et fidem indubiam presentibus adhibere'. The language of Edwyn Sandys' charter of 1582 (**613**) is medieval in form, the only innovation being the adding of 'et metropolitanus' to the *intitulatio*.

Of the six *acta* issued by bishops other than archbishops of York, three (**50–2**) are confirmations of a grant made by Archbishop Roger of York to form a prebend at Southwell for one of Henry II's clerks (**55**): all four charters appear to have been issued together, in April 1162, at an assembly held by Henry II in Normandy. Rotrou, bishop of Évreux, Robert Chesney, bishop of Lincoln and Froger, bishop of Sées all issued confirmations of Roger's grant. The phrasing of all three confirmations is similar; indeed the wording of Robert's and Froger's charters is almost identical, while Rotrou's only deviates from theirs by providing a more elaborate warranty clause. All three open with a similar *intitulatio* (e.g. 'Robertus dei gratia Linc' episcopus' in **51**); there follows the general address 'omnibus sancte matris ecclesie filiis' (to which Robert and Froger add 'ad quos carta ista pervenerit'), and then the greeting 'salutem'. In all cases the notification is 'Noverit universitas vestra'. All three charters are fairly typical of mid-twelfth-century episcopal diplomatic: the general address was still normally being placed after the *intitulatio*. The remaining episcopal *acta* in the White

Book are two charters issued by Bishop Oliver Sutton of Lincoln in 1287/8 (**64**, **68**) and one *actum* of Gilbert of Welton, bishop of Carlisle (1352–62) and a former canon of Southwell, issued in 1359 (**227**). In **64**, Oliver grants property in North Muskham to Master Henry of Newark as prebendary of North Muskham in a tersely worded document opening 'Sciant presentes et futuri'. This opening, common in conveyances issued by laymen, was relatively little used by bishops. Oliver's other *actum*, **68**, is a letter addressed to two of his clerks committing to them the induction of Master Henry of Newark into full seisin of the property granted in **64**. This is a more typically worded episcopal charter opening with the *intitulatio* 'Oliverus permissione divina Lincoln' episcopus'; the address terms his clerks 'sons in Christ' and the greeting is the papal 'salutem, gratiam et benedictionem'. The letter closes with the corroboration 'In cuius rei testimonium has literas nostras patentes signari fecimus signo nostro'. Gilbert of Welton's charter (**227**) is in fact two *acta*, a notification of a grant of property in Sturton le Steeple and a letter of attorney to ensure delivery of seisin. As in **64**, the grant opens simply 'Sciant presentes et futuri'. In both documents, Gilbert is 'permissione divina Karliolensis episcopus'. Gilbert's grant also contains a witness list, rare in episcopal *acta* in the later Middle Ages except in the case of grants of land (as here).

Statutes

The White Book contains three sets of statutes for the Chapter of Southwell Minster issued by archbishops of York between 1225 and 1302 (**102**, **113**, **114**) and a confirmation of the first of these made by the canons of Southwell in 1260 that in fact makes significant additions (**104**). Three further sets of statutes from the thirteenth and fourteenth centuries, issued by the canons between 1248 and 1335, survive in a collection of Southwell statutes compiled in the reign of Elizabeth I.[138] Put together, the documents form a sequence with layers of accretions and refinements, illuminating the changing preoccupations of the Chapter and the archbishops over the period. In producing a large number of sets of statutes in this era Southwell was by no means unusual: the thirteenth century was a peak period for legislation and for the compilation of regulations throughout Western Christendom, and all English secular cathedrals and many secular collegiate churches documented their existing regulations and issued new ones.[139] Some of the inspiration for this came from the Fourth Lateran Council of 1215, but the groundwork had been laid in a number of episcopal *acta* of the later twelfth centuries establishing common funds for major churches and laying down rules for distribution of payment from these, together with rules for the behaviour of minor clergy attached to cathedrals and collegiate churches.[140]

---

[138] *Visitations*, 205–9 (1248), 215–16 (1329), 216 (1335), and see **201**n for comment on transmission.

[139] For discussion, see Edwards, *Secular Cathedrals*, 22–7, and Barrow, 'Statutes', 316–29; most of the cathedral statutes are published in *Statutes*, ed. Bradshaw and Wordsworth; for the medieval statutes of Salisbury cathedral see *Vetus Registrum Sarisberiense*, ed. W. H. R. Jones, 2 vols, Rolls Series (London, 1883–4).

[140] cf. discussion in Barrow, 'Appendix I', 633–6.

Archbishop Roger of Pont-l'Évêque's foundation charter for his chapel of St Mary and Holy Angels in York could well have been a starting-point for chapter statutes in the archdiocese of York.[141]

The full flowering of chapter statutes in the archdiocese of York began in the 1220s under Archbishop Walter de Gray. The Chapter of York Minster drew up statutes about residentiary canons in 1221, about Vicars Choral in 1250 and further statutes in the 1290s and 1325, as well as compiling a set of customs about liturgical observance, the roles of dignitaries and the process of installation at some point in the later thirteenth century.[142] Archbishops John Le Romeyn, Thomas Corbridge and William Greenfield issued ordinances for Beverley Minster in 1290, 1302 and 1307; of these, Romeyn's and Greenfield's texts deal with residence, while Corbridge, though ranging more widely, concentrated on liturgical observance.[143] Ripon was slower to acquire statutes, but Corbridge issued a set in 1303 and Archbishop William Melton in 1332.[144] At Southwell, Archbishop Walter de Gray's act of 1221 granting Rolleston church to the common fund (**97**) formed the starting point for the sequence of statutes, creating the groundwork for his 1225 statutes (**102**), which mention the Rolleston grant and which regulate the management of the common fund and payments to be made from it. All resident canons and any visiting canons attending Matins on feasts of nine lessons should have 3d and on double feast days 6d each; Gray further defined residence as three months in the year, either as one continuous block or in two parts, allowing those canons absent to study theology to count as resident and permitting brief leave of absence for canons with urgent business. Gray's statutes were issued in the form of a charter, in the first person plural, and used the verb *ordinare* ('to ordain'). On Monday 30 March 1248 the Chapter issued statutes for themselves, in the form of a document in the third person, with the regulatory phrases being expressed as 'ordinatum fuit et statutum'. This document, not preserved in the White Book, is a much longer text than Gray's, and the main target seems to have been the Vicars Choral of Southwell, whose behaviour, especially in choir, had evidently given grounds for concern. The canons also regulated how the warden of the fabric should render accounts and tried to control the operation of grammar schools within canons' prebends.[145] Next in the sequence comes a confirmation of Walter de Gray's 1225 statutes made by the Chapter on 22 September 1260 (**104**), with fuller commentary on the points Gray had made to provide more careful definition of where and for how long in the year students should study to count as resident, and a fuller explanation of the other permissible reasons for absence, as well as extra regulations for the warden of the fabric. New to the statutes was a regulation allowing a share in the distribution of commons to be paid to the estates of recently deceased residentiaries. Like the 1248 statutes this document is in the third person,

---

[141] *EEA York 1154–1181*, no. 129 of 1173/4 x 1181, probably 1177 x 1181.

[142] *Statutes*, ed. Bradshaw and Wordsworth, ii, part 2, 90–135.

[143] *Mems. Beverley*, i, 190–2, 192–4; ii, 161–3, 166–9, 181–4.

[144] *Mems. Ripon*, ii, 44–6, 109–11; subsequent statutes were issued in 1401 (iv, 141–6) and 1439 (ii, 147–51).

[145] *Visitations*, 205–9.

but it avoids legislative verbs such as *statuere* and *ordinare*, preferring to say that the canons were confirming Gray's *ordinatio* and using the verb *intelligere* (*intelligentes*) to introduce the definitions. The canons say they agreed (*consensuerunt*) the item about payments of commons to deceased canons. It appears that in 1260 the canons were being careful not to tread on the archbishop's toes. In January 1294 Archbishop John le Romeyn held a visitation of Southwell that evidently uncovered a number of failings in the way in which services were held, together with the behaviour of the minor clergy inside and outside choir and the canons' management of their concerns, especially the upkeep of houses held by absentee canons. His resulting statutes (**114** of 12–13 January 1294) open with the statement that he had reformed ('reformavimus') what he had learned was worthy of correction; the verbs *mandare*, *precipere*, *velle* and *statuere* also occur in the text. Several of the points that he noted were also picked up in Archbishop Thomas Corbridge's statutes of 4 June 1302 (**113**), arising out of a visitation held in February 1301. Reform makes an appearance here too ('duximus reformanda' at the start) but with frequent use of *statuere* in several of the clauses. Later in the fourteenth century, on 22 September 1329, the canons drew up a memorandum regulating the election of wardens of the commons, the control of keys to the three chests containing the Chapter's muniments and other treasures,[146] and they followed this on 14 October with a further memorandum ordaining that all canons should hold their prebends for a year before being allowed to participate in the Chapter's decisions, and also making further regulations for Chapter business.[147] These memoranda, which are not recorded in the White Book, open with 'Memorandum quod' and are written in the third person, with full lists of all the canons present on each occasion. For these documents, the canons were happy to use legislative verbs such as *ordinare* and *statuere*. In their choice of subjects on which to legislate and also in their use of language the archbishops of York and the canons of Southwell were conforming to general practice within the thirteenth- and fourteenth-century English church.

Legal records

Eyres of Justices of the Forest

During the twelfth century and the first quarter of the thirteenth the Southwell estate was included in the royal forest of Nottinghamshire and so was subject, like the whole of the rest of the county north and west of the Trent, to the visits of forest justices to hold forest eyres in the county.[148] Individual clergy were subject to forest law just as individual laymen were, a point clarified in 1176 by an agreement between Henry II and the pope. It was therefore possible for Master Vacarius, the Italian civil lawyer who was prebendary of Norwell Overhall, to have a financial penalty imposed on him by the forest justices in 1185, while on an earlier occasion, in 1167, his men in Norwell

---

[146] *Visitations*, 215–16.
[147] *Visitations*, 216.
[148] For what follows, see Crook, 'Archbishopric', 325–40.

were similarly dealt with.[149] The church of Southwell was however the only body or individual in the county that can be shown to have attempted to free itself from the forest laws during the period before the implementation of the boundary clauses of the Charter of the Forest of 1217 and 1225 led to the disafforestation of the eastern and northern areas of the county in the latter year, the new boundaries being confirmed with slight amendment in 1227. The disafforestation was confirmed in a royal charter of 1232, which was, as might have been expected, recorded in the White Book (**106**).

Chronologically, the first reference to the forest occurs in a charter of King Stephen, made on a visit to York at an unknown date during his reign, which ordered that the canons of Southwell should have possession of their prebendal woods and enjoy them as in the time of Henry I, and forbidding his foresters from taking or selling anything from them (**22**). If the reference to the position under Henry I is true, the canons had some exemption from the forest laws in the earlier days of the forest of Nottinghamshire. For the period after 1154 there is much more material in the White Book. It contains a copy of an inquiry concerning the liberties of the archbishop of York in the Nottinghamshire forest in the reign of Henry II, made sometime between 1154 and 1166 before the earl of Leicester and the bishops of Durham and Lincoln (**23**). It is an early date for a document of this kind, and since the earliest version of the text dates from 1271 its authenticity must be in some doubt, but a brief reference to the activities of the earl and the two bishops is made in the next, less problematic, document concerning the forest, which also refers to related charters said to be in the church of York. This is the charter of 9 December 1189, issued by Richard I at Dover to his illegitimate half-brother Geoffrey, recently elected archbishop of York, just before he departed on crusade (**20**). It granted disafforestation of all the lands of the archbishopric of York in Nottinghamshire, whether in demesne or on any of the prebendal estates. The terms of this charter did not hold good in the later years of King Richard or in the reign of King John, because in 1198 and 1209 the archbishop and the canons respectively were subject to heavy penalties, but these were the last such recorded before the disafforestation of 1225.

Individual prebendaries and others on the Southwell estate however continued after 1225 to be liable for trespasses committed within the forest. In 1319 William of Bevercotes, prebendary of Rampton, was in prison at Nottingham for a trespass in Sherwood Forest before being released to mainpernors who would ensure his appearance before justices of the forest at Nottingham to stand to right concerning it.[150] In 1331–3 a number of men from Southwell, Halam and Edingley were bailed after being in Nottingham gaol awaiting trial in the forthcoming forest eyre, eventually held in 1334.[151] The church of Southwell itself seems on several occasions to have been accused of usurping jurisdiction over pleas of the vert. In the forest eyre of 1287, Archbishop Le Romeyn was accused of having held pleas of trespasses of the vert in woods within the forest bounds and within the regard in his court of Southwell. His attorney, Hugh of Stapleford, denied

---

[149] *PR 13 Henry II*, 138; *31 Henry II*, 114; *32 Henry II*, 105.
[150] *CCR 1318–23*, 159.
[151] *CCR 1330–3*, 249, 257, 484, 503.

any offence, pleading that similar pleas had been held there in the times of Archbishops William Wickwane (1279–85), Walter Giffard (1266–79) and Godfrey Ludham (1258–65); that under Henry II the lands of the archbishop in Nottinghamshire, both in demesnes and prebends, had been disafforested; and that this had been confirmed by King Richard's charter of 9 December 1189 (**20**). The assertion was made that all the archbishops since Walter de Gray (1215–55), who had drawn (*attraxit*) those pleas to his court of Southwell, had exercised the right to hold them, and the question eventually turned on whether Archbishop Geoffrey, Richard's half-brother and the recipient of that charter, had died seised of the right to hear them. A jury of the king's ministers of Sherwood Forest swore that they did not know the answer, so the case was referred to the king in the next parliament after his return to England.[152] The issue seems not to have been resolved then because later, in 1308, the archbishop's wood within the forest was taken into the king's hand because his bailiffs had held pleas of the vert in his court of Southwell outside the forest.[153] It is possible that Gray sought to appropriate the right to protect the vert outside the forest bounds on his estate once royal control was removed from the area in 1225, but no formal justification for doing so has been recorded in the White Book, so this can only be speculation. In 1355 the archbishop's park of Hexgreave, said to be 'within the bounds of the forest', was taken into the king's hands for a forest trespass until his trespass was pardoned by the king.[154] In fact the area which included Hexgreave park had by then been outside the forest for 130 years, so it is difficult to interpret the significance of this incident.

The church of Southwell and the itinerant and central courts of common law

The Chapter seems never to have been corporately involved as a litigant at common law, whether as plaintiff or defendant, because it did not appear as such in the records of the royal courts of the Common Bench, the King's Bench or the eyres for common pleas. There were occasional cases in which an individual prebendary attempted to defend what he regarded as his prebendal property. For example, in 1223 Master Walter de Taney, prebendary of Norwell Palishall, proceeded by writ of entry in the Common Bench against Walter Malet over half a carucate of land in Willoughby by Norwell. Canon Wischard, Taney's predecessor, had demised it to Walter Malet's father Robert without the assent of the Chapter. Walter's son Alan answered for his father, saying that Walter had demised all his property to him because he was old and impotent and he could not see or hear, and it was in his custody. This was confirmed by the testimony of many, so the case against Walter could not proceed, and if he wished to take proceedings against Alan Malet, who now held the property, Taney would have to obtain

---

[152] TNA, E 32/127, rot. 14d; *Sherwood Book*, 183–5.

[153] *CCR 1307–13*, 70. The wood in question must have been that of Blidworth, still within the forest boundary after the disafforestation of 1225, and temporarily taken into the king's hands during the Nottinghamshire forest eyre of 1239 because of damage by the canons (i.e. the prebendaries) of Oxton (**24**).

[154] *CCR 1354–60*, 113, 288.

another writ.[155] In the 1280 Nottinghamshire eyre six canons: Master John Clarell, Master Henry of Skipton, Master Nicholas of Welles, Nicholas de Knoville, Master John of Penistone and Master Benedict of Halur (i.e. Halam), were joint defendants in a case brought by Nicholas de Grey, keeper of the land and heir of Aucher de Freschville, as to why they had brought a suit over the advowson of the church of Bunny in court Christian. The sheriff reported that he was unable to distrain them because they were clerks and had no lay fee. In a neighbouring entry Robert son of Walter of Strelley's charter to the church of Southwell and Master William de Clifford, canon, of four selions of land containing three rods in Oxton next to the south of Master William's court (*curia*) there, was enrolled in full.[156] In the 1280 and 1329 eyre rolls and in feet of fines there are several cases involving property in the town of Southwell without reference to the Minster.[157]

In the 1329 Nottinghamshire eyre for common pleas, the Chapter of Southwell appointed two attorneys (John Buk' and Thomas of Ashbourne junior) to act for them 'in all pleas and plaints by them or against them moved or to be moved against anyone and to prosecute and defend its liberties claimed'. The Chapter of York, several Yorkshire monastic houses, and Worksop priory, Thurgarton priory, Shelford priory, Rufford abbey and Newstead priory also made similar appointments. Alone among the canons, John of Thoresby, prebendary of Norwell Overhall, appointed an attorney of his own.[158] The only canon involved in a civil case in the eyre was William of Newark, prebendary of North Muskham, and then as a defendant. The details give an interesting insight into some of the privileges claimed by individual canons in the parishes in which their prebends lay. Roger Deyncourt brought a writ of trespass against William for allegedly destroying crops worth 100s in North Muskham by pasturing his cattle. Newark, through his attorney Nicholas Bernak, claimed that he was the intermediate lord (*dominus medietatis*) of North Muskham by reason of his Southwell prebend, and was throughout the year entitled to pasture one free bull and one free boar to graze on grass wherever it grew; and also to have a horse or mare graze on the grass in a meadow called the Holmede from the feast of the Invention of the Holy Cross (3 May) until the removal of the hay (*usque asportatione fenorum*). He claimed that his predecessors as prebendaries had exercised these rights from time immemorial. A jury was summoned to adjudicate on Saturday after the feast of St Agatha (10 February 1330), at which date Deyncourt withdrew his writ and was in mercy.[159]

---

[155] *CRR*, XI, no. 1187.
[156] TNA, JUST 1/664, rot. 22 [AALT, http://aalt.law.uh.edu/AALT4/JUST1/JUST1no664/aJUST1no664fronts/IMG_3741.htm].
[157] For example, JUST 1/664, rot. 4 [AALT, http://aalt.law.uh.edu/AALT4/JUST1/JUST1no664/aJUST1no664fronts/IMG_3704.htm].
[158] TNA, JUST 1/685, attorneys rots 1 [AALT, http://aalt.law.uh.edu/AALT4/JUST1/JUST1no685/aJUST1no685fronts/IMG_6439.htm]; 1d [AALT, http://aalt.law.uh.edu/AALT4/JUST1/JUST1no685/bJUST1no685dorses/IMG_6708.htm; http://aalt.law.uh.edu/AALT4/JUST1/JUST1no685/bJUST1no685dorses/IMG_6709.htm].
[159] TNA, JUST 1/685, rot. 38d [AALT, http://aalt.law.uh.edu/AALT4/JUST1/JUST1no685/bJUST1no685dorses/IMG_6553.htm].

Jurisdictional immunity from royal eyre courts

When claims of jurisdictional privileges were made by Nottinghamshire lords in the 1329 eyre for common pleas in the county, the Chapter claimed, through the presentments made by the jury representing the wapentake of Thurgarton and Lythe, that 'in each eyre of the justices the justices itinerant are accustomed to sit in the south doorway of the church of Southwell and there determine the pleas of the eyre concerning all the tenants of the Chapter, and to answer before the justices by twelve jurors and not otherwise' (**14, 145, 147**). There are no surviving Nottinghamshire eyre rolls before those of the eyre of 1280–1, but the roll of that eyre made up for the chief justice, John de Vaux, includes a single rotulus of 'Pleas of the liberty of the canons of Southwell held at the south door of the church of St Mary of Southwell on Sunday one month after Easter before John de Vaux and Master Thomas de Sodyngton, justices itinerant, in the ninth year of King Edward, son of King Henry [11 May 1281]'. The face of the membrane carries the civil pleas, followed by the lists of the financial penalties imposed, while the dorse carries the crown pleas and the names of the twelve jurors.[160] The contents of the membrane are given in full below in Appendix A, **A2**. There is however evidence of two earlier separate Southwell eyre sessions, in the form of three feet of fines made in the Nottinghamshire-Derbyshire eyres of 1219 and 1236. Two related fines made 'in the king's court at Southwell' on 23 May 1219 show that a separate Southwell session of the eyre, which had begun at Nottingham on 18 February 1219, was held at that date. Similarly, a fine dated 14 October 1236 was made at Southwell in the eyre that began at Nottingham on 24 September that year.[161] The implication must be that such sessions took place in all the Nottinghamshire eyres between 1219 and 1280, although there are no surviving records for those held in 1226, 1232, 1240, 1245, 1252, 1257 and 1268. The eyre of 1329 was the last to be held in the county and, despite the assertion made during it of the right to have such a session, its voluminous records show that none was held on that occasion.[162] Also, the crown pleas held in Thurgarton wapentake show no evidence of crown pleas on Southwell estates, nor was there a presenting jury to represent them. The only direct involvement in criminal justice occurred when a female thief, Alice of Kynelferie, who confessed to stealing goods worth 10s, took sanctuary in the church of Southwell and abjured the realm.[163]

---

[160] TNA, JUST 1/669, rot. 16; Crook, *General Eyre*, 150.

[161] TNA, CP 25/1/182/3, nos 12 and 13 [AALT, http://aalt.law.uh.edu/AALT2/CP25no1/CP25_1_182/IMG_0076.htm; http://aalt.law.uh.edu/AALT2/CP25no1/CP25_1_182/IMG_0077.htm]; CP 25/1/182/7/237 [AALT, http://aalt.law.uh.edu/AALT2/CP25no1/CP25_1_182/IMG_0339.htm]; Crook, *General Eyre*, 75, 96; *Rolls*, ed. Stenton, xl, xlvi. The fines successively involved: Roger of Sowerby, canon of Southwell, over land in Muskham and Carlton, which he claimed versus Adam son of Albert as part of his prebend of South Muskham; a similar case but against Henry Gernun; and Roger parson of Beckingham, canon of Southwell, over land in Beckingham which he claimed belonged to his church in free alms, versus William son of Adam.

[162] Crook, *General Eyre*, 185–6.

[163] TNA, JUST 1/686, rot. 42d [AALT, http://aalt.law.uh.edu/AALT4/JUST1/JUST1no686/bJUST1no686dorses/IMG_7042.htm].

Quo warranto and jurisdiction over the Southwell estate

In the 1329 Nottinghamshire eyre a great deal of effort was expended in examining the legal basis of the privileges of the bigger estates in the county, among which the property of the church of Southwell, and especially those parts of it in the hands of its prebendaries, were prominent. The material concerning the liberty was recorded at great length in the cartulary, with a great deal of repetition when the same material was exemplified for subsequent proceedings at which the suits progressed. A crucial point proved to be the need to clarify whether the prebendaries held their prebends in common as a Chapter or in severalty. After being granted a licence to imparl, the canons considered the question and decided in favour of the latter (**14**, at the top of WB, p. 8 (pp. 16–17 of our edition); and **147**, near top of p. 71 (p. 160) (**Plate 4**)).[164]

The question arose with reference to the issue as to whether views of frankpledge pertained to the Chapter or to the individual prebendaries. The presenting jurors of the wapentake of Thurgarton and Lythe stated that the Chapter of Southwell had view of frankpledge of all their tenants in Southwell, Norwell, South Muskham, North Muskham, Caunton, Oxton, Calverton, Woodborough, Cropwell Bishop, Blidworth, Halloughton, Beckingham, Dunham, Halam, Edingley and Normanton. The king's attorney in the eyre, William of Deanham, disputed some of the details on the basis of what had been claimed in the eyre of 1280, after which the case was initially adjourned to the Derbyshire eyre of 1281 for judgment before being referred to the King's Bench (**145**). There the justices considered a petition to the king by some of the canons, led by Henry of Edwinstowe and Robert of Woodhouse, in 1331, claiming their own rights to view of frankpledge in their prebends. The subsequent proceedings in the King's Bench confirmed the rights of the prebendaries through a jury verdict (**147**), and an inspeximus of the proceedings was issued by the king in 1333 (**14**). Another case was brought in the eyre by Deanham, against the Chapter's claim by prescription to hold view of frankpledge of its tenants in fifteen places, and the right to hold the pleas of its tenants in the eyres of the king's justices. The views of Beckingham and Dunham were confirmed as a result of a fine of 40s, but the remainder were also referred to the King's Bench (**145**). No subsequent proceedings in this case have been identified. The right of Robert of Woodhouse, prebendary of Norwell Palishall, to free warren in Norwell and Norwell Woodhouse, was also challenged by Deanham in the eyre, but his right was confirmed because of a charter of Edward II (of 1310) granting it

---

[164] 'Quesitus est ab eisdem canonicis ob quam causam venire fecerunt hic processum predictum et si dictum capitulum libertates superdictas simul cum canonicis predictis in communi teneant vel non et dictum est eis quod ulterius ostendant curie qualiter et quo modo illis libertatibus utuntur etc. Qui quidem canonici petunt inde licenciam loquendi etc. et habita inde deliberacione dicunt quod ipsi canonici sunt prebendarii ecclesie predicte et faciunt capitulum et quod tenent prebendas suas separatim et quod idem capitulum tenet aliquas libertates libertatum predictarum in terris tenementis et feodis ad illud spectantibus per se et quilibet canonicorum predictorum per se aliquas libertates earumdem libertatum et feodis prebendarum suarum ecclesie predicte.'

to him and its subsequent confirmation by Edward III in 1330 (**15**).[165] Finally, Deanham challenged John of Thoresby, prebendary of Norwell Overhall, over his claims to a warren, market, fair, breaches of the assize of bread and ale and judgment of pillory and tumbrill in Norwell. The first three were covered by a charter of Henry III in 1256 to his predecessor John Clarell (**361**), while the latter two were claimed by long and uninterrupted use.[166] Because the market had fallen into disuse and offenders against the assize had been punished by amercement rather than corporal punishment, they were taken into the king's hand, but then restored for a fine of one mark (**16**).

Views of frankpledge and the courts of the Chapter and the canons

The White Book records material showing that at least some of the individual prebendaries held views of frankpledge for their prebends, but under the supervision of the Chapter court, presided over by the steward of the Southwell estate, which was able to overturn 'errors of judgments' (*errores judiciorum*). There was sometimes competition from the sheriff in the wapentake courts as regards frankpledge. This is indicated by a writ of Richard II in 1381, issued at the request of three prebendaries, to uphold their privilege to take views of frankpledge of their own men, and ordering the sheriff to cease citing them before his court of Thurgarton and Lythe (**150**). As well as impinging on the jurisdiction of the liberty-holder, holding views would deprive him of valuable income. At the same time, the sheriff was sent another writ ordering him to respect all the privileges granted to the canons by the king's predecessors (**148A**), and the justices of weights and measures were told to allow the canons their established rights of assizes of bread, wine and ale in all the prebendal villages (**149**).

The views of frankpledge were in fact full-blown manorial courts, dealing with the whole range of manorial court business, much of it relating to succession to land. The most detailed material is to be found in the distinct sequence of proceedings held at Norwell in the early fifteenth century (**373, 377, 381–6**), but most of the court entries are in an earlier run of entries from 1327 to 1411 (**152–84**). The point is clarified by the wording of the heading of **155**: 'view of frankpledge with the court of the said Chapter…'. Nevertheless, nineteen of the thirty-three headings of the extracts from the main sequence of court records describe the sessions as views of frankpledge (**155, 159–60, 164–5, 167–8, 170–8, 180, 183–4**), although only one, two or three of these entries include any business relating to the administration of frankpledge (**155, possibly 159, 160**); the first consists entirely of frankpledge business, the latter two include only the names of men who failed to attend. It is interesting that the first two are almost the only recorded sessions held at the fixed times of the year for the holding of views of frankpledge, just after Easter and Michaelmas, being just after Michaelmas in October 1344 and after Easter in April 1346; nearly all the others are at other times. Four court sessions of 1409, 1411 and 1412 recorded in the section of Norwell entries later in the volume are also called views of frankpledge, and took

---

[165] *CChR*, ii, 137.
[166] *CChR*, i, 454.

place shortly after Michaelmas or Easter in those years (**381–2**, **385–6**), but a fifth was held nearly a month after Easter in 1412 (**384**).

The main sequence of entries relating to the sessions of the Southwell courts is preceded by a list of the customs of inheritance and succession to holdings on the Chapter lands, whose date is unknown but is likely to be no earlier than 1411, when the sequence of illustrative cases comes to an end (**151**). It specified that each tenant was obliged to attend the court at least twice a year, for the views of frankpledge held after Michaelmas and after Easter, on pain of amercement, and no essoins (excuses for non-attendance) were allowed. Each unfree tenant (*nativus*) owed regular suit once every three weeks; was bound to pay a heriot of 5s 4d to succeed to his holding after the death of his predecessor; pay the same amount to marry a daughter; and the same for letherwyte if she had been deflowered before marriage. A widow could inherit her husband's holding for life, also for 5s 4d, with other provisions in the event of re-marriage. If a tenant died having only daughters, the youngest of them would inherit the holding for a heriot of 5s 4d; if she then married without licence, merchet was payable at the same amount; and if she died her husband could only retain the tenement with the licence of the court. As a general rule, a free man could not inherit an unfree tenement without the leave of the court. No unfree man holding by copyhold for a term of years or for life could alienate it without the court's licence, nor alienate part of it outside the jurisdiction of the court without its agreement. Any tenant wasting, selling or causing damage during his term would be prosecuted by a writ of waste. Many of these customs and penalties are also mentioned in the inquisitions concerning the obligations of the bondmen of the prebendary of Norwell Overhall (**376**).

The main sequence of entries that follow the list of inheritance customs give many examples of particular decisions in the courts, overwhelmingly that of the Chapter (**152–7**, **159–60**, **164–84**), which are full of interesting detail. They are arranged in date order, and run from 1327 to 1411. Three entries alone record hearings at sessions of a prebendal court, that of Oxton (**161–3**). The Chapter court's claim to the right to overturn errors in the prebendal courts is specified in its list of customs (**151**, final paragraph).[167] The process is illustrated by a long entry recorded at the Oxton court in 1327, concerning land in Calverton (**152–3**). However, on occasion appeal could be made to the court of the Chapter of York (**158**) or directly to the archbishop (**157**). The latter entry also includes the full texts of two letters issued by the Chapter ordering the restoration of a tenant to his holding, and several other entries also quote documents in full. No. **157** also includes two letters issued by the Chapter in 1317; **171** two Halam deeds made in the Chapter court and of a royal writ of Richard II; **174** an indenture relating to Edingley. Among the Norwell documents later in the volume are an inquisition into the commoning of sheep in Carlton on Trent (**381**); a deed issued by a

---

[167] 'si error aliquis sive difficultas aliqua inveniatur sive assignetur in aliquo placito infra curiam alicuius prebende capituli predicti per favorem senascalli ignoranciam vel aliquam aliam causam in favorem alterius partis, ad sectam partis que prosequi voluerit ad capitulum predictum placitum illud debet removeri a curia predicta, in curiam capituli, et terminari per inquisicionem capiendam de magis discrecioribus tocius jurisdiccionis capituli'.

canon and an inquisition at Norwell Woodhouse into the alienation of lands in 1359 (**382**); two Norwell deeds of 1349, one of 1352 and another of 1388 (**385**); and another Norwell deed of 1337 (**386**). Several include lists of jurors or panels from which jurors were to be selected (**157, 171**), or give lists of persons who failed to attend sessions (**155, 159, 160**). It is noteworthy that one of the Chapter court's suitors who failed to attend the post-Easter view of 1346 was none other than the royal justice Sir Richard de Willoughby, a former chief justice of the King's Bench, along with three other knights (**159**). Another knight, Sir John Zouch, described elsewhere as the lord of Kirklington (**178**), was obliged to attend the Easter and Michaelmas views of the prebend of Norwell Palishall (**377**, top of p. 386).

A little important similar material exists elsewhere. In Nottinghamshire Archives a collection of rotuli, now filed together, record the sessions of the views of frankpledge held by the Chapter of Southwell between 1355 and 1369 (rots 1–2), 1388 and 1392 (rot. 3), 1409 and 1410 (rot. 4d), 1412 and 1413 (rot. 4), 1418 (rot. 6), and between 1421 and 1424 (rot. 5).[168] None of the sessions or cases recorded in the White Book also appear in the roll, with the possible exception of one where the membrane of the roll is very damaged.[169] The most consistent contents of the court's proceedings in this roll include the names of those fined for 'default', usually 2d each, probably for failing to attend the view, and lists of brewers fined for breaches of the assize of ale. There are a number of entries recording the election of a taster of ales (*attastator cervisie*) and his swearing in; there are also frequent records of the transfer of holdings between individuals or the confirmation of an existing tenure, which began with the appearance of an individual concerned and his swearing of faith (*fecit fidem*) to the Chapter. Occasional entries of plaints concerning debt brought by the debtor and settled before the court also occur. The court also dealt with the results of minor affrays between individuals and sometimes involving minor injuries. At least one deed is recorded. The general character of the material in the roll suggests, as indeed do the entries in the White Book, that both the Chapter and the individual prebendaries used their claims to hold views of frankpledge independently of the sheriff, which enabled them to hold what were in effect manorial courts. These brought in a moderate income not only for frankpledge defaults but also for breaches of the assize of ale and other general business typical of the courts of the lay lords of manors, while also regulating the succession to tenements which produced numerous fines.

The Chapter and its Administration

As noted in the discussion of episcopal charters and archiepiscopal statutes for Southwell, the White Book contains some evidence on how the Chapter, 'the greatest of the medieval collegiate foundations of England',[170] was to be

---

[168] NA, DD SP 4/o/1, formerly Ecclesiastical Commissioners, Court Rolls 62/4, which was transferred to Nottinghamshire Archives in 1959 together with some later court documents relating to the Southwell estate. It is prefaced by a small membrane giving a list of vicars choral of Southwell at an unknown date.

[169] NA, DD SP 4/o/1, rot. 4d; cf. **183, 373** (p. 363) and **377** (p. 382) for Henry Shepherd.

[170] Hamilton Thompson, *TTS* 15 (1911), 63–4.

organised and its functioning. These documents were used by A. F. Leach in the most detailed treatment of those topics, which was supplemented some twenty years later by A. Hamilton Thompson, accounts from which most recent discussions ultimately derive.[171] There can be no question of covering the same ground in similar detail here. Our aim is simply to outline some characteristics of the Chapter and its organisation, especially where our analysis modifies or augments that of those two scholars. Subsequent sections will then survey the development of the prebendal system at Southwell and the foundation of chantries, with particular reference to the prebendaries themselves, chantry priests and Vicars Choral and, finally, a survey in a little more detail on how the fabric was maintained.

Pope Alexander III's bull in 1171 confirming that the canons and church of St Mary's were to enjoy the same privileges as those enjoyed by St Peter's, York (1), together with other twelfth-century charters confirming or augmenting the privileges or liberties enjoyed by the Chapter or by individual prebendaries, issued by Henry I and his successors or by the archbishops of York, ensured that the Chapter enjoyed considerable freedom to run its own affairs. It had almost unfettered jurisdictional powers within the Liberty or Peculiar of Southwell, an area extending eventually to cover twenty-eight parishes in Nottinghamshire.[172] Most of the evidence for the structure of the Chapter and the nature of its administration has to be deduced incidentally, however, or by comparison with what is known about how St Peter's and the other great collegiate churches of York archdiocese, Beverley and Ripon, most notably, were organised rather than from documents clearly setting out a formal constitution, whether found in the White Book or elsewhere.

As will be shown in more detail below in discussing the prebends and prebendaries (pp. lxxix–lxxxi), the Chapter at Southwell had first assumed the form in which it appears in the White Book towards the end of the Anglo-Saxon period and in the years immediately after 1066. Domesday Book (1086) shows the Minster possessed as prebends some estates in Cropwell Bishop and Woodborough,[173] and in the period either side of the Conquest it would seem that seven or eight prebends, consisting of lands and rents in parishes of the Peculiar, were established to maintain individual canons. These were then passed to their successors in office and were held, as the *Quo warranto* investigations early in the reign of Edward III showed, not communally by the Chapter but severally by each prebendary (147). The number of prebends continued to expand through the twelfth century until there were fourteen shortly after 1200, finally increased to sixteen in 1290–1, at which number they remained for the rest of the Middle Ages and beyond, forming the full Chapter. The *capitulum* at Southwell is first mentioned just before 1150 when Gilbert de Gant wrote to it on behalf of Rufford abbey (1146 x 1150) and the Chapter itself issued a notification, also on behalf of

---

[171] *Visitations*, xvii–lxvii; Hamilton Thompson, *TTS* 15 (1911), 15–62; Beaumont, *Chapter*; Ottey, *Southwell Minster*.
[172] Hamilton Thompson, *TTS 15* (1911), 68, states the Chapter 'possessed complete temporal and spiritual jurisdiction within the parishes and manors which made up the liberty of Southwell'.
[173] Barrow, *The Clergy*, 297.

Rufford, to which the Chapter seal was attached (1146 x 1156), though it had probably enjoyed a formal existence for some years previously, hidden from us by lack of surviving documents.[174]

When similar developments occurred at York, Beverley and Ripon after the Conquest, the chapters there appointed one of their number to act as head, a dean at York, a provost at Beverley, the prebendary of Stanwick as *rector chori* at Ripon. Appointments were also made to other offices, dignities, like that of precentor (especially responsible for organising divine services and singing), treasurer and chancellor. Southwell was very reluctant to follow this path. Although Archbishops Cynesige and Ealdred had encouraged the canons at Southwell to adopt a communal life and by the mid-twelfth century their use of a corporate seal (above p. xxxix) is evidence for them acting in common,[175] as is the presence of several canons as witnesses on occasions when the seal was affixed, no chapter dignitaries are mentioned either by name or by office in the twelfth century, nor were any subsequently endowed (with the exception of the sacrist). The only apparent twelfth-century exception, Gilbert the precentor (**34**), who owned a house in Southwell in Henry I's reign, had been precentor of York rather than at Southwell since at least 1093.

Shortly after 1200 nineteen charters in the White Book are witnessed by Hugh, usually styled 'the dean', on five occasions as 'Hugh the dean of Southwell' and twice as 'Sir Hugh the dean of Southwell' (*domino Hugone decano de Suthwell'*). The date range for the majority of these charters (**14**) is between 1219 and May 1230, by which date Hugh was dead, but a few of them could have been issued by 1210 or earlier (**234, 241, 242, 252**), one (if as seems most probable he was also known as Hugh of Pickering), certainly pre-1200 where he occurs as 'Hugh of Pikering dean' (**521**). In all except this last charter and one other (**510**), he is named as the first or only witness. His name thus precedes that of other canons, even those with university degrees (*magistri*) and important posts in royal or archiepiscopal service. In some charters he is noted as enjoying or sharing the status of canon with fellow witnesses (for example, **225**). In **408**, a confirmation by the Chapter of a grant of land in Southwell for maintaining two candles on the feasts of St Catherine and St Nicholas issued in 1218 or 1219, 'Hugh the dean' heads perhaps the most impressive witness list of Minster clergy for any medieval Southwell charter, naming six other canons in addition and fifteen chaplains as well as at least four prominent local laymen.

It was on the basis of such evidence that Leach stated categorically that there was 'a space of perhaps ten or twenty years ... during which the White Book certainly shows something like a head of the Chapter in the shape of a dean',[176] but it was an experiment that ceased on Hugh's death.[177] Ham-

---

[174] *Rufford*, 325 (Chapter) and 718 (Gant).

[175] *Rufford*, 338, for a charter of 1165 x 1196 drawn up in the Chapter at Southwell in the presence of at least six canons, and another, 246, 1175 x 1200, given under the Chapter's seal in the presence of at least four canons, five chaplains, four deacons and other clerics.

[176] *Visitations*, xxxv, with a long development of his argument, xxxvi–xxxvii.

[177] Ibid., xxxvii, 'a curious exception on an exception, the solitary and short-lived monarchical excrescence in the thousand-year republican life of the head-less chapter of Southwell'.

ilton Thompson was not convinced and argued that Hugh was probably a rural dean appointed by the archbishop in connexion with his Liberty of Southwell.[178] Canon Ottey, supporting this suggestion, has pointed to two further pieces of evidence for this conclusion. First, there is a later document (**433**, *c.* 1244) witnessed by 'Richard the dean of Southwell' (to which we can add **513**, 1248 x 1249, witnessed by 'Richard the dean of Christianity of Southwell', *Ricardo decano Christianitas Suthwell'*). This demonstrates that the post of rural dean of Southwell certainly existed for a period with the implication that Hugh was not the only holder of it. Secondly, the fact that Hugh the dean was also parson of Bilsthorpe, a living which was not within the Peculiar of Southwell, although not far away from the Minster, may explain why he was considered a suitable candidate to be rural dean, allowing him to take precedence over fellow-canons.[179] Yet since, as Ottey also notes, Archbishop Gray was a disciplinarian and some other great churches were appointing chapter deans in this period,[180] the possibility of Hugh holding this post briefly at Southwell cannot be entirely eliminated: indeed his prominent position in witness lists suggests that he was acting as Chapter dean, ranking above fellow canons, rather than as a rural dean, who normally ranked beneath canons of a community.[181]

Whatever the case, thereafter there is no suggestion of the Chapter being led by a dean. As explained in more detail below (p. lxxix), by the later thirteenth century, for some purposes the prebendaries of Normanton, Norwell Overhall and Norwell Palishall shared responsibility for Chapter affairs. Later the senior residentiary canon sometimes made decisions on behalf of his confrères,[182] many of whom were absentees. Normally after 1300, there should have been two or three residentiaries in Southwell at the same time if the archiepiscopal statutes were followed. By default, when there was no residentiary present at all, decisions had to be taken by churchwardens, usually recruited from the Vicars Choral,[183] though there remained occasions when plenary sessions of the Chapter were held at which decisions were taken collectively or by a majority vote.[184] A dean is not mentioned again until after Henry VIII re-established the Chapter in 1543 following its abolition in 1540.[185] Once more the post failed to become a permanent one; indeed it may never have been formally established.

As far as other offices are concerned, in his statutes of 1302 Archbishop Corbridge assumed that there would be a precentor, with a deputy, at South-

---

[178] Hamilton Thompson, *TTS 15* (1911), 68.
[179] Ottey, *Southwell Minster*, 34.
[180] Ibid., 33–4, citing the appointment of a dean at Exeter in 1225 and Archbishop Gray's decision in 1230 to make the prebendary of Stanwick permanent head of the Chapter at Ripon (cf. *Reg. Gray*, 2–3).
[181] For a charter of William of Newton 'dictus nepos decani' see **276**.
[182] cf. *Visitations*, xxxvii–xxxviii.
[183] Ibid., xlvii–xlviii.
[184] Letters from the Chapter and various canons, serving as a small formulary (**187–201**), are particularly informative about the conduct of Chapter business around 1300.
[185] See the letters of Sir Edward North of the Court of Augmentations to the 'dean and chapter' or 'dean and prebendaries' of Southwell in 1546 (**614–16**). Henry VIII's letters of 1543 simply re-established the Chapter without any mention of a dean (Appendix A, **A13**).

well (**113**). Hamilton Thompson suggests that the precentor may have been linked to one of the Oxton prebends,[186] but he was not able to provide a reference and the White Book certainly does not confirm this. It is clear that a precentor (or even two joint precentors) were assumed to function in the choir in the later Middle Ages. In 1475 it was reported that chantry priests were failing to follow the precentor when chanting, while in 1478 no precentor was present on either side of the choir as they were supposed to be.[187] Lack of other references suggests that the post was not held in such high esteem as it was elsewhere.

At Southwell the role of the treasurer was from around the Conquest played by the sacrist who had his own prebend, although many of his duties were fairly menial and some sacrists may have deputed them. Archbishop John Le Romeyn in 1294 ordered the sacrist to sleep in the church and 'according to the clock, ring the hours' (**114**).[188] He made payments on behalf of the Chapter under supervision but the common fund established by the mid-thirteenth century had its own wardens (p. lxxxi). In the visitation records surviving from 1469 onwards, the sacrist was criticised on several occasions for venial failures such as providing sour wine or stale bread, and failing to sleep in the church, lead the singing or ring bells at the appropriate time.[189]

The role taken by the chancellor at York and elsewhere, especially his responsibility for education of both clergy and laity, was taken at Southwell by the prebendary of Normanton. His jurisdiction in this matter also spread beyond the Peculiar and may even have extended to the whole of Nottinghamshire. A note added in the late fifteenth century to an accord of 1238 (**218**) over presentation of a suitable clerk to instruct boys in grammar at Newark, for instance, claims that collation of masters to all grammar schools in the archdeaconry of Nottingham belonged solely to him 'as chancellor of the said church' [of Southwell], a unique description in the White Book. Some prebendaries of Normanton certainly exercised their rights as patrons, as in December 1475 when John Barre was admitted as master of Southwell Grammar School by the Chapter on the presentation of John Danvers, prebendary, who in 1477 replaced a negligent master of Nottingham Grammar School by a more suitable candidate.[190] Leach even goes so far as to say 'the *Magister Scolarum* was the earliest dignitary' of the collegiate church on the basis of this note, but the absence of any other references to a chancellor in late medieval Southwell suggests Leach's view is incorrect.[191]

---

[186] Hamilton Thompson, *TTS 15* (1911), 75; his argument was chiefly based on general analogies about dignitaries in the other great collegiate churches of the archdiocese of York and the fact that by the 1540s the two Oxton prebendaries were resident and one of them could have acted as precentor or *rector chori*.

[187] *Visitations*, 24 and 34.

[188] If sacrists did follow this injunction, it is not known where they slept in the church. As later visitation records show, most probably preferred living in the medieval predecessor of Sacrista Prebend house as fellow canons did.

[189] *Visitations*, 22, 32–4, 42, 43, 45, 52, 54, 67, 85.

[190] *Visitations*, 29–31. W. A. James, *An Account of the Grammar and Song Schools of the Collegiate Church of Blessed Mary the Virgin of Southwell in the County of Nottingham* (Lincoln, 1927) provides a well-documented account of the Minster's schools.

[191] cf. *Visitations*, xli–xlii, and the note to **218** for further comment.

It is clear from this short discussion of dignitaries within the medieval Chapter that there was not much emphasis on individual offices and the rewards that they might bring. What mattered most was appointment to one of the sixteen prebends, where there was a clear gradation between the richest and poorest prebends, leading to many unseemly internal scrambles for more lucrative ones when vacancies occurred. There is also evidence that men who had received expectative canonries from the pope (or from the king during archiepiscopal vacancies) sometimes moved to Southwell where they hoped eventually to succeed to a prebend.[192] Here some took part in chapter business while awaiting installation as prebendaries, or remained after their hopes had been disappointed by other nominations. So in addition to the sixteen prebendaries, their sixteen Vicars Choral (below pp. lxxxi–lxxxiv), and the thirteen chantry priests serving altars established between c. 1230 and 1478 (pp. lxxxiv–cii), the collegiate church in the later Middle Ages also furnished employment for other clerics, usually in minor orders, as well as for laity with secular tasks like the vergers.

In running the Chapter's court, for example, there is mention of a bailiff (or steward), a sub-bailiff, a clerk and a bedel (**157, 176, 178, 181, 233, 413**). Keepers of the common fund and keepers (or wardens) of the fabric might be chosen from Minster personnel, from prebendaries or chaplains, but also from inhabitants of the town (cf. below pp. civ–cvi). The *rector scolarum*, the school master of Southwell, was always a cleric though, as the case of Mr William of Nottingham in the mid-thirteenth century shows (**420**), he might be in minor orders and thus able to marry. In conjunction with the precentor, he would teach the choristers sufficient Latin for them to accompany the Vicars Choral when singing the main daily offices and the chantry priests during the many sung requiem masses which benefactors demanded. As a result, overall the Minster community in the fifteenth century probably employed sixty or more men in a wide range of duties, and a few women to do laundry and repair clerical clothing,[193] without mentioning the small body of craftsmen who were more or less permanently employed in maintaining and repairing the building. Evidence from the visitation returns from 1469 onwards shows a fair proportion of them from prebendaries down to acolytes infringing statutes intended to maintain good order in all manner of ways.[194] We can only speculate whether stronger direction and control by a dean would have made much difference to how most members of the collegiate church of St Mary's, Southwell behaved in the years before the Reformation!

The Prebends

At the moment Southwell's architectural jewel, the Chapter House, was being completed at the end of the thirteenth century, the full complement of sixteen prebends in the medieval Chapter was reached when Archbishop

---

[192] Appendix C lists most of those who received expectatives but failed to make good their claims.

[193] **393**, mid 13th century, mentions a toft once owned by Matilda the laundress.

[194] *Visitations*, I–95.

Le Romeyn decided in 1290 to erect the church of Eaton as a prebend (57) and in the following year to separate North Leverton from Beckingham to create the last prebend (41, 42). The White Book also provides evidence for the establishment of five other prebends after 1100: Dunham (18, 1119 x 1133), Beckingham, with North Leverton (34, 1119 x 1133), Halloughton (47, 48, 50–3, 55, 56, c. 1162), Norwell Tertia Pars (29, 1191 x 1194), Rampton (74, 77–9, before 1197, the only prebend known to have been founded by lay patrons rather than by the archbishops), while the division of 'Muskham', resulted in the separation of a new South Muskham prebend from North Muskham (c. 1204).[195] This leaves the origins of the other eight prebends which formed the full medieval Chapter unresolved, a matter which has much exercised generations of historians of the Minster.[196]

Although the clergy attached to it had probably enjoyed certain privileges in common from a very early date (analogies are often drawn with the Anglo-Saxon minsters at Beverley and Ripon where initial endowments of seven prebends are sometimes alleged), most available evidence now points to the mid and later eleventh century as a critical period in the organisation of the collegiate church and its prebends in the form in which they were to survive until its dissolution in 1841. That is with the canons (prebendaries) serving the Minster also having pastoral responsibilities for churches in the rural parishes from which most of their individual incomes derived and where they also usually possessed rural manor houses and estates, as the White Book abundantly illustrates.

This form of organisation was also encouraged by the late Anglo-Saxon archbishops of York. Both Cynesige (1050–61) and Ealdred (1061–9) were deeply influenced by continental ideas on reforming secular clergy by encouraging celibacy and establishing a communal life for those serving great churches.[197] At Southwell they did this by providing a refectory and other facilities for clergy to live in common and by augmenting the Minster's endowments. They encouraged comparable reforms at their other great churches like Beverley and Stow in Lindsey, and even seem to have developed an architectural model for these churches, rebuilt as Southwell seems to have been in this period.[198] A twelfth-century history of the archbishops of York reports that Ealdred bought with his own private means estates that were then handed over to the collegiate church at Southwell.[199] The early Anglo-Norman archbishops, Thomas of Bayeux (1070–1100), Gerard (1100–8) and Thomas II (1108–14), who may well have established some of

---

[195] EEA York 1189–1212, nos 13–14 and cf. 525n.

[196] cf. Visitations, xxv–xxvii; Hamilton Thompson, TTS 15 (1911), 66–75. See Ottey, Southwell Minster, 16–17; Jones, 'Enduring Significance', 63–72 and 'Master Vacarius', 1–20 for recent summaries.

[197] cf. Barrow, 'Cathedral Communities', 34.

[198] Everson and Stocker, 'The Archaeology of Episcopal Reform', 177–202. We are very grateful to the authors for sharing their findings with us in advance of publication.

[199] Raine, Historians, ii, 353, 'Terras multas de suo proprio emit et eas ecclesiis suis adiecit et de quibusdam prebendas apud Suthwellam fecit'. Sharpe (Acta Henry I), headnote to Henry I's acts for Southwell, judges this source 'unreliable' and is very doubtful that Archbishop Ealdred 'was adding prebends at Southwell a generation before they were created in his own church at York', preferring to see them established by the first Anglo-Norman archbishops.

the earliest prebends, certainly enjoyed visiting their manor at Southwell, partly because of its convenient geographical position on the route south and partly because it was a more comfortable (and often safer) place for them to stay than York itself. They were thus also able to exercise close oversight of the Minster's affairs.[200] In these circumstances, it can be presumed that whatever remoter origins the prebendal system may have had at Southwell, this period either side of the Conquest was critical for its full development here in what Hamilton Thompson called 'the greatest of the medieval collegiate foundations of England' after the secular cathedrals.[201]

The evidence of Domesday (1086) supports this suggestion: it indicates that prebends had been established by then in a number of villages around Southwell. These included Norwell (where two prebends, Overhall and Palishall, were formed at an early point), Woodborough and Cropwell Bishop (later to be linked with Oxton to form two prebends, Oxton I and Oxton II), probably too at (North) Muskham called a 'berewick' of the manor of Southwell in 1086. No prebend was created for the town of Southwell, but that of Normanton (whose holder subsequently presented to the vicarage of Southwell and would come to share administration in the thirteenth century of the common tithes for the Minster with the prebendaries of Norwell Overhall and Norwell Palishall, **30, 371**, 1266) may also have come into existence around this time. Finally, to account for the full Chapter of sixteen prebendaries in the Minster, the sacrist, who held 'a dignity or office executed in the church',[202] was also given prebendal status at an early date though he did not have responsibility for a rural parish church, unlike his confrères, being supported by oblations from the Minster rather than by rural estates.[203] He was expected to be permanently in residence, and indeed, to sleep in the church.[204] The White Book contains documents that refer to all sixteen of the prebends. The most extensive are those which relate to Norwell Overhall, which was perhaps used to exemplify a full range of the different types of administrative documents required for a prebendal estate, form letters or models which could be applied if necessary to other prebends by its compilers (cf. **360–89**).

The Prebendaries

Although it appears that some prebends had already been established at Southwell by or shortly after Domesday, for much of the period down to 1200, except for a few rare instances, it is not possible to link known canons with particular prebends. Among the earliest who can be so linked is Roger de Capella, a king's clerk, who was appointed as the first prebendary of Halloughton *c*. 1162 (cf. **46–8**). Another was the celebrated Italian lawyer and administrator, Master Vacarius. He passed from the service of Archbishop Theobald of Canterbury (d. 1161) to that of Archbishop Roger of

---

[200] Archbishop Gerard is reported to have died in his garden at Southwell.
[201] Hamilton Thompson, *TTS* 15 (1911), 63.
[202] *Visitations*, xxvi.
[203] Hamilton Thompson, *TTS* 15 (1911), 70–1, 75.
[204] Ibid., 70.

Pont l'Évêque of York and was, by 1166, prebendary of Norwell Overhall, a post he held until his death around 1200.[205] Shortly before 1200, the prebendary of Woodborough was Geoffrey of Dorchester (**521**); Mr Thomas *de Disce* (?Dishforth, Yorks) became the first prebendary of South Muskham *c.* 1204,[206] while Eustace de Fauconberg, named bishop of London in 1221, had previously held the prebend of Rampton[207] and his contemporary Alan de Ripon held that of Norwell Overhall in which he was succeeded in May 1214 by Robert of Laxton (usually styled Lexington in the White Book), later one of Henry III's principal judges (**435, 436**).[208] Indeed, from the early thirteenth century onwards, it is possible to trace, often in considerable detail, the very varied careers of those who received prebends at Southwell.

This is not the place to examine that theme in detail, though it can be noted that from the earliest point that evidence becomes available, from just after the mid-twelfth century at Southwell, royal and archiepiscopal service was frequently rewarded by the grant of a prebend. Increasingly during the course of the thirteenth and for much of the fourteenth century, papal favour also often resulted in appointments, or the expectation of appointment, at Southwell when vacancies occurred in the Chapter. Evidence from the White Book and elsewhere reveals that competition for appointment was often intense and that many legal disputes arose, some of them very long-running, especially between 'natives' appointed by king or archbishop and 'foreigners' named by the pope. As Richard Helmholz has remarked, 'The canon law attached to [prebends] became complex enough that a commentator described litigation arising from prebendal rights as "a source of income, a cause for sin and a source of shame"'.[209]

Already at the end of the twelfth century a sizeable contingent of Italians held prebends at Southwell, and foreigners would continue to be appointed for the rest of the Middle Ages, though their numbers tended to diminish after 1350.[210] More usually, those holding prebends at Southwell were rising civil servants and administrators favoured by the king or archbishop. The majority also held their Southwell prebends (most of which produced only modest financial rewards in comparison with some elsewhere) in plurality with prebends in other cathedral or collegiate churches. The most ambitious and able could thus collect significant numbers of prebends, sometimes reaching into double figures.[211] This also posed the problem of residence as already noted above (p. lxii–lxiv). In the summary *Fasti* which form Appendix C of this edition, some of the major appointments enjoyed else-

---

[205] Jones, 'Master Vacarius', 3–4.

[206] *EEA York 1189–1212*, nos 13–14.

[207] *EEA York 1189–1212*, no. 64.

[208] Laxton was appointed by King John in 1214 (*Rot. Litt. Pat.*, I, pars i, 115b) though this grant may not have been immediately effective.

[209] Richard H. Helmholz, *The Canon Law and Ecclesiastical Jurisdiction from 597 to the 1640s (The Oxford History of the Laws of England*, gen. ed. Sir John Baker), vol. 1 (Oxford, 2004), 217–18 citing Albericus de Rosate (d. 1354).

[210] Appendix C for details.

[211] *Visitations*, l–li cites as a notorious example William of Wykeham, who in addition to his prebend of Dunham, held ten other prebends as well as various other dignities in 1366, which provided him with an annual income of £866.

where by Southwell prebendaries are listed but no attempt has been made to provide comprehensive biographies. A full prosopographic study of the prebendaries of Southwell thus remains a *desideratum* for which the White Book provides much incidental evidence.

The Vicars Choral

The Vicars Choral were the work-horses who, in the later Middle Ages, performed the major purpose of the Minster, 'mynystringe of the most blessed sacraments, and for to have all dyvine service there dayleye songe and sayde'.[212] Probably already in the twelfth century, and certainly by the early thirteenth, many canons were frequent absentees, with important responsibilities beyond Southwell in archiepiscopal, royal or papal service. To carry out their duties locally, especially in the daily recitation of the offices, it became usual for them to appoint fully ordained priests to act as their vicars at Southwell as they also did for their prebendal churches. Initially the vicars were paid by their own prebendaries, but later a common fund was also established and other endowments for their maintenance acquired. A number of vicars probably occur as chaplains or clerks witnessing charters in the White Book from around 1200 onwards.[213] Those responsible for singing the mass soon became known as Vicars Choral, one deputising for each prebendary. By the mid-thirteenth century statutes were drawn up to regulate their conduct and duties.[214]

One of the earliest mentions of the Vicars Choral at Southwell is in a charter of 1241 x 1247 where they were charged by William of Widdington, the archbishop's steward, with singing his obit (**415**). In 1261 they promised to say a prayer for Canon Richard of Sutton on days when masses for the dead were celebrated for brothers and benefactors (**58**). From 1248 a canon or vicar was to be associated with the warden of the fabric in hearing and auditing accounts.[215] By then a common fund was also in place since another elected warden (*custos communiae*) was to divide 'all the goods and legacies bequeathed to the brotherhood of the church of Southwell equally amongst them'. Each vicar was to be bound

> by his corporal oath that whatever shall come to his hands either for an annual, or for a trental, or for any legacy left to the said brotherhood of the said church, or from any income which has been customarily regarded as belonging to the petty commons of the vicars, he will faithfully and without any deduction hand over to the aforesaid warden, to be distributed equally among the vicars

---

[212] *Visitations*, lvi, citing the chantry certificates of 1546; see also Hamilton Thompson, *TTS* 15 (1911), 75–9.
[213] cf. **408**, 1218 x 1229, where seven canons and no fewer than fifteen chaplains witness, or **414**, *c.* 1248–9.
[214] *Visitations*, 205–9, statutes drawn up by the Chapter in 1248, absent from the White Book (cf. above pp. lxii–lxiv).
[215] Ibid., p. lxiii.

on pain of a fine of two shillings.[216] The vicars also accompanied or depu-
tised for prebendaries carrying out visitations of prebendal churches and
chapels attached to the commons, and received fixed stipends. As already
noted above, by 1260 the Vicars Choral of Southwell possessed a common
seal though they were never formally incorporated.[217]

With the growth in their numbers (the full complement of sixteen Vicars
Choral was reached after the erection of North Leverton as a prebend in
1291), both Archbishops Le Romeyn and Corbridge felt it necessary to issue
further statutes regulating the stipends and duties of the Vicars Choral. In
1294 Le Romeyn decreed that each of them should receive £3 a year (**114**),
apparently an increase on their previous stipend, 'to relieve the vicars,
who had been too much burdened owing to the two vicars of the two new
prebends [Eaton and North Leverton] sharing in the oblations and obits'.[218]
Le Romeyn's statutes also include clauses relating to the ill-discipline of
Vicars Choral both with regard to unseemly behaviour during divine service,
such as laughing and talking in the choir, as well as moral failings like allowing the presence of women who were not relatives in their houses. Those
prebendaries who failed to pay their vicars were to be strongly disciplined,
though Corbridge in 1302 had to issue a further stern warning about arrears
'lest for want of them neglecting the divine service to which they are daily
bound, and in which they ought to be vigilant and assiduous, and to your
own and the church's scandal, they be compelled to rove about the country,
as they used to do, and so provoke an outcry'.[219]

The phrase 'roving about ... as they used to do' suggests that by 1302 the
Vicars Choral were living communally but the location of their residence
has been a matter of some debate, before it was replaced by a new lodging
on a new site in 1379. Dickinson (1787) asserted confidently that from an
early point the Vicars Choral did live communally, alleging the existence of
lodgings and ancillary rooms in a building standing well to the east of the
Minster beyond Potwell dyke in Easthorpe. This site has not been located
nor does he give a specific reference to any documentary source.[220] It was
probably the 'manse heretofore built for [their] habitation' referred to in a
petition from Richard of Chesterfield, prebendary of Norwell Overhall, to
Alexander Neville, archbishop of York, requesting permission to construct
a new lodging within the north-eastern corner of the churchyard next to the
now-lost manse of the prebend of Beckingham in 1379.[221] The former lodging,
according to Chesterfield's petition, was 'situated at a great distance [from
the Minster], the road between muddy and deep', and the building itself had
'fallen into such ruin that for a long time the vicars would not live in it, but
lived by themselves scattered about the town in hired lodgings "whereby
divine worship in the church is minished, occasions of insolence are given,

[216] Ibid., 206–7.
[217] p. xli.
[218] *Visitations*, lviii, after **114**.
[219] Ibid., after **113**.
[220] Summers 1988, 57.
[221] Appendix A, **A4**. The statement by Summers 1988 (69 n. 1) that 'The original [of the petition] is in the White Book' is incorrect in every respect.

popular obloquy is engendered, and scandals and dangers to souls arise"'.[222] Between Corbridge's comment in 1302 suggesting that the Vicars Choral had then ceased 'to rove about the country' and 1379 when plans for the new lodging were made, Archbishop Melton had also concerned himself with the housing and discipline of the Vicars Choral just as he also grappled with the problem of absentee canons and the duties of residentiaries.[223] In 1336 he began acquiring tenements in Southwell for a communal residence for the Vicars Choral, perhaps an earlier admission of the poor state of the old lodgings mentioned in 1379.[224] On 17 February 1337 he handed over two messuages and a croft in 'Prest gate' (?modern Church Street) to the Vicars Choral, all sixteen of whom (very unusually) are mentioned by name.[225] It is unclear from surviving evidence why this site turned out to be inadequate and was superseded by Chesterfield's new college.

The area which was chosen for it, after careful examination by the official of York and the prior of Thurgarton, in consultation with local witnesses, was an irregular rhomboid measuring over 200 feet along its north and south sides, 146 feet on the west and 100 feet on the east, a space marginally larger than that of the present Vicars' Court which later occupied the same site.[226] On this a rectangular building with lodgings on the west, north and south sides and a hall on the east was constructed, following closely the model of contemporary colleges at Oxford and Cambridge. Access to the quadrangle was through a gateway on the west side as it is to Vicars' Court.[227] A watercolour of the western façade made *c.* 1774 by S. H. Grimm (**Plate 11**), shortly before its demolition to make way for an enlarged Vicars' Court,[228] shows it as 'a large building with a stone ground floor, and a timber-framed first floor. The roof trusses are crown posts and the framing seems very suitable for the late 14th century.'[229] Construction thus probably began shortly after it was authorised in 1380, though it may have taken some time, perhaps several years, to complete. Although its foundation deed is not found in the White Book, this shows that the endowment was also placed on a more secure footing by Chesterfield and his fellow Norwell prebendary William

[222] *Visitations*, lix for this translation.

[223] In 1332 Melton decreed that canons should reside for twelve weeks a year at Ripon as they did at Southwell and Beverley (*Mems. Ripon*, ii, 111).

[224] *IPM Notts. 1321–50*, 176–7, inquiry at Southwell as to the harm to be caused if two messuages and 2½ acres of land were to be assigned for a house for the vicars, 28 November 1336.

[225] *Reg. Melton*, v, no. 482.

[226] NA, DDM 105/44, a 19th-century translation of Appendix A, **A4**, '... in a corner of the said cemetery contiguous to the Manse belonging to the Prebend of Bekyngham on the east side of the said church which we then caused to be faithfully measured which said place from the corner of the Manse aforesaid on the west side thereof to the wall of the cemetery opposite inclusively towards the north contains according to true measurement 146 feet in breadth and from the said corner next the wall of the said Manse towards the east to an entrance to the cemetery contains in length 211 feet and in breadth at the east end of the said place 100 feet and on the other side of the said place on the north as the wall of the cemetery extends contains 206 feet'; cf. Summers 1988, 57.

[227] Summers 1988, 57–9 provides a good brief architectural and historical account.

[228] Summers 1988, 59–68.

[229] Dixon, 'Vicars Choral', 144–5, with a reproduction of Grimm's view (BL, Add. MS 15544, f. 174), also in Summers 1988, Plate XL.

of Gunthorpe in 1392, when a long list of properties in the town of Southwell and many surrounding parishes were assigned for the upkeep of the Vicars Choral (**612**).[230] The document recording this is dated at Southwell on 27 September 1392 and it was witnessed by a very distinguished gathering of local gentry, perhaps on the occasion marking the formal completion of the college.

The endowment was further augmented in 1439 when Henry VI sanctioned the appropriation of the alien priory of West Ravendale (Lincs.) for the maintenance of the lesser clergy serving the Minster (**214**), an arrangement which Cardinal-Archbishop Kempe confirmed in 1452.[231] Furthermore, between 1459 and 1461, Archbishop William Booth added the advowson of Kneesall church to the patronage enjoyed by the Vicars Choral and drew up further regulations to govern their conduct.[232] A few other small gifts were also made to the Chapter for the Vicars Choral in the mid-fifteenth century (**591**, **592**), while their income was further boosted by income from coalpits and other property in south Yorkshire later in the century.[233] The *Valor Ecclesiasticus* shows that by 1535 each vicar received a stipend of £4.

The Chantries

The fashion for establishing chantries, 'essentially an endowment for the performance of masses and other works of charity for the benefit of the souls of specified persons',[234] began in England as it did on the continent in the late twelfth century.[235] The White Book contains documents relating to the foundation and endowment of ten chantries between the first half of the thirteenth century and the beginning of the fifteenth. These will be discussed in more detail here in their presumed order of foundation.[236] Another was founded by Robert Oxton, before *c.* 1408, for which no documents occur in the White Book, but which is known from other records, including the *Valor Ecclesiaticus* (1535), when it was worth £5 13s 1d, and two estimates of £5 in 1546 and 1548 at the time of the dissolution of the chantries.[237] Likewise, Archbishops William and Laurence Booth were responsible for the foundation of two chantries, associated with the Booth mortuary chapel, which also survived to the dissolution, but for which the White Book offers no information.[238] Fabric accounts from 1429–30 reveal the presence of a

---

[230] This does not mention the land and weir at Kelham given in 1363 to the Vicars Choral by Robert of Edwinstowe, prebendary of Woodborough (*IPM Notts. 1350–1436*, 18–19).

[231] NA, SC/7/1/5 f. 4. Accounts for the Chapter's administration of West Ravendale in 1453–7, 1491–2, 1493–4 and 1522–4 survive in NA, SC 5/3/1.

[232] Appendix A, **A10**. Accounts of 1482–4 for Kneesall church survive in NA, SC5/7/1.

[233] Appendix A, **A11**.

[234] Howard Colvin, 'The Origins of Chantries', *Journal of Medieval History*, 26 (2000), 163–73 at 164.

[235] David Crouch, 'The Origin of Chantries: Some Further Anglo-Norman Evidence', *Journal of Medieval History*, 27 (2001), 159–80 is an important critique of Colvin's views but also confirms that the 1170s and 1180s were critical in the evolution of the chantry.

[236] Hamilton Thompson, *TTS* 15 (1911), 79–87 adopts a similar chronological schema, but the evidence of the White Book has led us to different conclusions as will become clear.

[237] Hamilton Thompson, *TTS* 15 (1911), 92, 114–15; Ottey, *Southwell Minster*, 38.

[238] Foulds, '*In medio chori*', 110–11.

number of other altars in the Minster dedicated to St Anthony, St Catherine, St Laurence and St Margaret, one to St Leonard which is called a chantry and a 'new' chantry in the cemetery but little further has been discovered about any of them.[239] In endowing the tenth chantry mentioned in the White Book in 1415, but in a document that is not found in it, Thomas Haxey, prebendary of Rampton, refers to the 'new building' which he himself had provided and endowed for the priests to live in.[240] This Chantry Priests' House stood in the north-west corner of the churchyard where modern Church Street meets Westgate. S. H. Grimm painted a watercolour of it, viewed from the south-east, c. 1774. It was finally demolished to be replaced by a new Grammar School building in 1819 that now acts as the Minster Visitors' Centre (**Plates 12 and 13**).[241]

The Chantry of St Stephen, founded in memory of Andrew the bailiff

Andrew the bailiff of the archbishop of York at Southwell[242] sold a toft and croft that he had bought from William son and heir of Richard of Edingley and his wife between 1226 and 1230 (**413**). He may be the same as Andrew the chaplain who witnessed Henry son of Thomas de Rolleston releasing all his claims on the advowson of Rolleston to the Chapter on 3 April 1221 (**98**). As 'magistro Andrea tunc seneschalco' he witnessed a grant of lands by Agnes daughter of Hugh Lumbard at Rolleston c. 1220 x 1230 (**509**) and another of land in the soke of Southwell as 'magistro Andrea tunc ballivo de Suthwell' in a charter for which the date limits 1224 x 1228 have been assigned (**563**). The title 'magister' suggests that he was probably an early graduate of Oxford or Cambridge, perhaps sent to study at a university after joining the household of an archbishop.[243] He appears to have died between 1226 and 1228 (**564**), perhaps as early as 1226 when William of Widdington was appointed seneschal of the archbishop. In **564**, the Chapter paid forty marks to Robert de Screwen, clerk, to acquire various lands in Halam and Edingley for the maintenance of the chaplain celebrating for the soul of Andrew 'quondam ballivi Suthwell', making this the first known chantry founded at Southwell, of which the altar may have been in the east aisle of the north transept.[244]

---

[239] NA, SC/5/2/2. A chantry dedicated to St Vincent is mentioned in 1308 (*Reg. Greenfield*, i, no. 76) when John de Swyna, vicar, was collated. It was perhaps later absorbed into the parish altar (cf. **138**), since nothing further has been found relating to this chantry.

[240] Appendix A, **A6** after NA, SC/7/1/5 ff. 14ᵛ–15ᵛ, 20 July 1415, 'quodam manso quondam vocato saynt Mary place ex parte occidentali ecclesie collegiate predicte situato per me prefatum Thomam de novo edificato'.

[241] Summers 1988, 4, 24, 65, 73 and Plate VI after BL, Add. MS 15544 f. 172, also reproduced in Chapman, 'Chantry House', 16, with Richard Ingleman's plan of 1818, now NA, Accession MS 7521.

[242] 'Andreas baillivus domini Walteri Ebor' archiepiscopi de Suthwell' ...'.

[243] A clerk named Andrew who appears in one of Archbishop Geoffrey's charters of 1198 x 1205, at the end of a long list of witnesses, could be the future bailiff early in his career (*EEA York 1189–1212*, no. 26), but Andrew the chaplain who received custody and administration of all the goods of the hospital of Alverton, Northallerton, on 6 May 1227 (*Reg. Gray*, 77–8 no. CCCXXXVI) seems unlikely to be our Andrew.

[244] Hamilton Thompson, *TTS* 15 (1911), 83; Ottey, *Southwell Minster*, 37. As Leach (*Visi-*

The remaining deeds in the White Book in which Andrew's name is mentioned all refer to the acquisition of further properties for the endowment of the chantry of St Stephen, a process which (unusually when compared with other chantry endowments at Southwell) continued for some decades after his death, or concern their subsequent administration. Thus after 1282 Sybil, widow of an important local knight, Robert de Burstall, confirmed a grant formerly made by William de Tolney, 1245 x 1257 (**556, 559**) of two bovates of land at South Muskham and South (i.e. Little) Carlton for maintaining the chaplain. Previously, but after 1254, Thomas son of Thomas of Muskham quitclaimed the Chapter for a tenement in Holme which his aunt, Emma, had previously granted to them before 1237 (**573**, and cf. **571, 572**). In the later thirteenth century, this tenement was apparently producing an annual rent of 16s (**574**). By 1373 the chantry was worth £3 12s, with rents being drawn from tenements in Holme, South Muskham, Little Carlton, Halam and Edingley; it also possessed a house (*mansus*) in Southwell, where the chaplain may have lived (**577**) before the Chantry Priests' House was built around 1400. At the dissolution in 1548 the chantry was valued at £5 19s.[245]

The Chantries of St Thomas, founded by Robert of Laxton

Robert of Laxton, the leading member of a local gentry family from Laxton which particularly distinguished itself in his generation by also producing a bishop of Lincoln, the head of the Cistercian order and a steward of Henry III's household, was named as a prebendary of Southwell by King John on 25 May 1214.[246] From then until his death in 1250 he held the prebend of Norwell Overhall, where he proved to be an energetic landlord.[247] He was frequently active in the Chapter's affairs for much of the period to *c.* 1230 as several charters in the White Book which he witnessed show.[248] He also began to make small benefactions to the Chapter.[249] As he rose in Henry III's service, however, becoming the senior justice of the Common Bench between 1236 and 1244, Laxton was absent from Southwell and his manor at Laxton Moorhouse nearly all the time from about 1220 until his retirement (1244), except probably during the court vacations, especially the long summer vacation. After his retirement from royal service, in his last years he once again returned to play his part in Chapter business.[250] It is indicative of this life-long personal attachment to Southwell that between 1241 and 1243 Laxton made arrangements for the establishment of an impressive chantry in the Minster to be served by two priests, two deacons and two sub-deacons in honour of St Thomas the Martyr (**455**).

---

tations, lxii) pointed out, the establishment of chantries at Southwell lagged a little behind some other great churches where the practice had begun *c.* 1180.

[245] Details for values in 1546 and 1548 for this and other chantries are derived from the relevant 'Chantry Certificates' edited by Hamilton Thompson and are not further referenced here.

[246] *Rot. Litt. Pat.* I, 115b.

[247] cf. **430, 432, 434–6**.

[248] cf. **76, 89, 92, 225, 308, 507, 508**, all dated before May 1230.

[249] cf. **506**, two bovates of land at Laxton to furnish a rent of 2 lbs of wax for two candles daily at the mass of the Blessed Virgin Mary (before May 1230).

[250] cf. **427, 578–80**.

Even prior to this, there is other evidence suggesting that Robert of Laxton was already an enthusiastic supporter of the cult of Becket since he had also made provision for another chaplain to serve an altar in a chapel dedicated to Thomas the Martyr in the town of Southwell (**456**). He endowed this chantry with an income of 64s annual rent from lands in Newton and Saxondale. The chapel would appear to be that already in existence around 1200,[251] which stood near the point where modern King Street runs into the Burgage.[252] However, if this were indeed so, the chantry itself was apparently later transferred to the Minster since a jury in 1373 declared categorically *quod tres cantarie perpetue fundate sunt in capella sancti Thome martiris in ecclesia collegiata predicta*, and distinguished carefully between the endowment for the two chaplains and this other endowment with lands in Newton (**577**).[253] The Chantry certificates of 1546 state that this latter chantry was by then known as that of St Thomas the Apostle, but at the dissolution in 1548 it was again listed as a chantry of St Thomas the Martyr, worth £5 12s 4d.[254]

The main endowment for Robert of Laxton's principal chantry of St Thomas the Martyr in the Minster consisted of the advowson of the church of Barnburgh (Yorks. W.R.) and lands nearby which he had acquired from Henry de Neufmarché (**450–5**). In addition to maintaining the two chaplains, two deacons and two sub-deacons, the endowment was also to provide 6s 8d annually for maintenance of lights and ornaments, to furnish 27 lbs of wax for a candle to burn at all masses and 13 lbs of wax for two candles to burn continually on the feasts of the passion (29 December) and translation (7 July) of St Thomas the Martyr (**455**). On 9 October 1241, Archbishop Gray, with the assent of the Chapter, decreed that when a vacancy occurred in the church of Barnburgh, the Chapter should present a suitable candidate to him or his successors to be canonically appointed (**460**; **Plate 6**), an arrangement that was to endure until the abolition of the Chapter in 1841. The rector of Barnburgh was to pay the Chapter twenty-three marks (£15 6s 8d) a year for the maintenance of the chaplains, deacons and sub-deacons serving in the chantry. Their duties included prayers for King John, Brian de Lisle and Robert of Laxton's parents, brothers and sister.[255] Initially this certainly meant a considerable diminution of the rector's own income, since an inquisition found that the church at Barnburgh, in Laxton's presentation, was worth forty marks (£27 13s 4d) in common years (**462**). But since the parish lay within the south Yorkshire coalfield and coal was increasingly mined in the surrounding

---

[251] One of the earliest mentions of this chapel is in **525** (early 13th century) when 10d was given for purchasing oil for lamps burning there. Sometime before 1249, William of Widdington granted to John Muskyng a burgage plot and four shops (*seldas*) standing to the north of the chapel of Blessed Thomas the Martyr which he had bought from Henry the chaplain (**419**).

[252] We are grateful to Ellis Morgan and the Digging the Burgage team for help with this location.

[253] By then it was also receiving a small rent from Laxton Moorhouse (15s) and was valued at £4 1s 3d.

[254] Hamilton Thompson, *TTS 15* (1911), 79–80; Ottey, *Southwell Minster*, 36.

[255] On 29 January 1242 Archbishop Gray confirmed the grant of a toft and land at Barnburgh, together with the advowson (**459, plate 7**).

area in the later Middle Ages,[256] his income from tithes grew markedly, so that the living at Barnburgh was for long the richest in the Chapter's gift.[257]

After the initial endowment, the White Book records one further small benefaction. This was a grant by William Browning, chaplain of the chantry of St John the Apostle (Evangelist), of a toft with its buildings in Easthorpe towards the end of the thirteenth century, at the instance of his friend, Sir Simon Brainde, chaplain of St Thomas the Martyr (**457**).[258] The 1373 inquiry simply notes that the rector was responsible for paying twelve marks (£8) a year to maintain the two chantries, while the income from this Easthorpe toft seems by then to have been absorbed into that of the third chantry of St Thomas the Martyr since a rent of 10d was due from Sybil Browning (**577**). The *Valor Ecclesiasticus* estimated the combined worth of the two chantries of St Thomas at £9 12s 11d, which had fallen to £8 6s 8d by 1546, but £8 16s 8d in 1548 when each chaplain was to get £4 8s 4d.

The Chantry of St John the Evangelist, founded by Henry of Nottingham

Henry of Nottingham was certainly a canon of Southwell by 1219.[259] He occurs as a witness to at least a dozen charters found in the White Book over a period of some twenty-five years, and can be presumed to have been resident in Southwell for much of this period, holding the rich prebend of Normanton. He was dead by 7 May 1245,[260] having founded towards the end of his life a chantry in honour of St John the Evangelist before the altar of which he was buried.[261] This probably lay on the north side of the nave immediately west of the north porch.[262] To maintain it, he gave a cottage and lands in Carlton on Trent worth 53s 4d in rental value (**500**).

Shortly after his death, this chantry seems to have been augmented by his close friend and colleague at Southwell for many years, Robert of Laxton, so that there would be two priests serving the altar (**584**). The main additional endowment came in the form of an annual payment of ten marks by the prior and Gilbertine convent of Sixhills near Market Rasen, Lincs. This pension was made up in part of revenue from lands or rents which Robert of Laxton had acquired in Kesteven and Lindsey and given to the priory for that purpose (**578**). Laxton also made another grant directly to the Minster of additional rents, totalling two marks (26s 8d), on lands in Warsop and

---

[256] cf. the indenture by which Thomas Fitzwilliam of Aldwark (York) allowed the Vicars Choral of Southwell to enter when necessary *Elcokepitte* in neighbouring Rawmarsh to extract coal (LA, Cragg MS 3/13, 21 May 1482; Appendix B, **B102**).
[257] cf. above p. xlvii.
[258] cf. **458**, another charter of donation by William Browning, confirming **457**, but with reference to the chaplain serving the altar as Sir Simon of Farnsfield. To be distinguished from Simon Brainde, he occurs in a number of other charters, one possibly as early as *c.* 1244 (**433**), though he in turn must be distinguished from a lay namesake (**99, 401**).
[259] *Book of Fees*, 287.
[260] TNA, CP 25/1/182/9, no. 305.
[261] He needs to be distinguished from a contemporary of the same name, Henry of Nottingham, parson of Rothwell, who held a prebend in Pontefract Castle, dead by September 1241 (*CCR 1237–42*, 329; *CPR 1232–47*, 258) with whom he has been confused by the editor of the *Pontefract Cartulary*.
[262] Hamilton Thompson, *TTS* 15 (1911), 82; Ottey, *Southwell Minster*, 37.

Carlton on Trent, Notts., to increase the endowment of the chantry (**579, 580**). This should have ensured a combined annual income of at least £9 19s 8d. But it proved difficult to collect all the rents in later years. In 1332, for example, the Chapter had to threaten the prior and convent of Sixhills with excommunication for failure to pay their share (**584**). By 1373 the income only amounted to £5 6s 8d, six marks (£4) from the Sixhills rent, 20s from tenements in Warsop and 6s 8d from Willoughby by Norwell (**577**). In 1395 the Chapter decided to use Henry of Nottingham's initial endowment amounting to 53s 4d, which was now deemed insufficient to sustain a chaplain, to augment the chantry which William of Gunthorpe was then founding in honour of the Virgin (**500**), thus leaving only one priest to serve the altar of St John the Evangelist. At the dissolution in 1548, his annual income was £5 15s, while he also held the position of parish vicar of Southwell (for which he received £1 from the prebendary of Normanton). The chantry altar was probably still in the north aisle of the nave.[263]

The Chantry of St Nicholas, founded by William of Widdington

William of Widdington probably came from Widdington, a settlement in the parish of Little Ouseburn eight miles north-west of York.[264] His first dated appearance would seem to be on 3 April 1226 when he was the first witness to the quitclaim made at Knaresborough (Yorks.) by Richard of Lotherton to Walter Gray, archbishop of York.[265] Widdington was an important official of Archbishop Gray. He acted as one of Gray's justices in the liberty of Hexham along with William Brito and Geoffrey de Bocland before 14 January 1228 (**414**n) and also in that office with the same men in the years 1229, 1235 and 1237.[266] Probably before 23 May 1228 and certainly by 1237, Widdington was Archbishop Gray's seneschal, an office he held until his death.[267] He was also termed a knight (**420**) but he was not returned as such in the surviving evidence.[268]

On 25 May 1226 Archbishop Gray granted in hereditary fee to Widdington two and three-quarter roods of land with two burgages in *Brikelawe*, probably Brinklow in Warwickshire, that Samson of Cornwall (*Sanson Cornubien'*) had sold to Gray, for which Widdington was to perform the services of the fifteenth part of one knight's fee to Nigel de Mowbray.[269] Widdington also

---

263 Hamilton Thompson, *TTS 15* (1911), 81–2.

264 Sullivan, 'Waddington', 155 argues that he took his name from Waddington, Lancs., but all the early forms of it are variants of Widdington and a Yorkshire origin makes his employment in the service of the archbishop of York much more comprehensible.

265 *Reg. Gray*, 221n. He may have witnessed the confirmation of a grant to York Minster by Hugh, son of Hugh of Leathley as early as 1221–2 (ibid., 143n).

266 *Reg. Gray*, 228, 235, 248. William Brito was married to Eva, the sister of Archbishop Gray, and Gray made grants to his nephew William, son of William Brito, at Southwell on 17 September 1235 (*Reg. Gray*, 227, 248).

267 *Reg. Gray*, 232n, 251–3, 257, 286, 290. Perhaps Widdington succeeded William de Schegenes (Skegness, Lincs.) seneschal on 3 September 1220 (*Reg. Gray*, 137), or it may have been Andrew the bailiff (above pp. lxxxv–lxxxvi).

268 *Reg. Gray*, 266n, 285.

269 *Reg. Gray*, 223. Gray had granted to Samson of Cornwall land in Hexham on 15 September 1225 (*Reg. Gray*, 222).

received further patronage from Archbishop Gray. He was granted custody of the land of Alexander of Hilton in Swine until his heir came of age on 27 March 1237.[270] He also obtained the marriage of the heir Thomas of Rigsby to his niece the unnamed daughter of Simon of Grimblethorpe on 28 April 1245.[271]

Although a secular serving Archbishop Gray as seneschal and a justice, Widdington was seemingly a man of some learning. He wrote, in French, a practical handbook on confession which gained a considerable readership (*Le Manuel des Péchés*).[272] It was later translated by Robert Mannyng of Bourne (d. 1338) and incorporated in his own work on confession under the title of *Handlyng Synne*.[273] A copy of Widdington's book was inventoried as among the possessions of the parish altar of St Vincent in Southwell Minster in an indenture dated 6 August 1369 (**221**).[274]

---

[270] *Reg. Gray*, 253. Alexander held of the archbishop of York in Swine and Winestead, wapentake of Holderness (Yorks.), for one knight's fee. He also held one toft for a rent of 12d per annum in Warkworth (*Werkwrth*), Northumberland, and he had been collector of scutage for Northumberland in 1235 (*Book of Fees*, 553, 1123). On 28 April 1245 Gray granted to his nephew, Walter, the land Alexander held of him but this may only have applied to Winestead as there is no record of Widdington's surrender of Swine (*Reg. Gray*, 256). Alexander's heir was Robert who had come of age by early December 1256 (*CFR 1256–57*, no. 161, translating TNA, C 60/54, m. 12); *Kirkby's Inquest*, 305, 389). The nuns of Swine complained of the nuisances perpetrated against them by Robert and his servants in 1268 (*Reg. Giffard*, 148).

[271] *Reg. Gray*, 255. On the same day Thomas of Rigsby's lands had been granted to Walter of Lowdham (*Ludham*). Thomas was the son of Gilbert of Rigsby who held one fee of the archbishop of York in Lincolnshire in 1212 (*Book of Fees*, 162). Gilbert was probably descended from Gilbert I, son of Herbert I of Rigsby, who made a grant to Greenfield priory *c.* 1150, witnessed by the Chapter of Southwell and Robert de Bella Aqua, and who held two fees of the archbishop of York in 1166 (Stenton, *Gilbertine Charters*, 79; Stenton, *Danelaw Documents*, xli–xlii, 76–85; *Red Book*, 414). In 1195 Gilbert held the church of Alford (Lincs.), was patron of Leake church (Lincs.) in 1217, and in 1205–6 he was a pledger of Thomas of Moulton (*Feet of Fines Henry II* (PRS), 54; *Rot. Litt. Pat.*, 64; *Rot. de Fin.*, 369, 424). Gilbert was dead by 7 June 1232 when Elizabeth his widow made a final concord with the prior of Freiston (Lincs.) concerning land in Freiston (TNA, CP 25/1/182/5). In 1242–3 Thomas of Rigsby held Rigsby, Ailsby, Tothby, Alford, Well, Sutton le Marsh and Lissington (*Book of Fees*, 1059; *Lincolnshire Domesday*, lxviii). His son or grandson, Thomas, made homage for these lands including land in Rolleston next Southwell for the fourth part of one fee to Archbishop Henry of Newark on 19 November 1298 (*Reg. Romeyn*, ii, 264). Ralph his son did homage for these lands in 1326, and his son, Thomas, in 1332 but with no mention of the land in Rolleston (*Kirkby's Inquest*, 392n, 393n).

[272] Sullivan, 'Waddington', 155, noting that the early manuscripts of the *Manuel* attribute authorship to William of Widdington. The now-common attribution to William of Waddington derives from the nineteenth-century editor of the English translation F. J. Furnivall: see next note. Sullivan, 'Textual History', for surviving manuscripts and structure of the work, while for recent discussion see also *Wollaton Manuscripts*, 68–71, 73–5.

[273] *Roberd of Brunne's Handlyng Synne with the French Treatise on which it is founded Le Manuel des Pechiez by William of Waddington*, ed. F. J. Furnivall (1862), though modern scholars are highly critical of Furnivall's work: J. Hughes, 'The Administration of Confession in the Diocese of York in the Fourteenth Century', *Studies in Clergy and Ministry in Medieval England*, ed. D. M. Smith (York, 1991), 90–2; Raymond G. Biggar, 'Mannyng, Robert (*d.* in or after 1338)', *ODNB online*: http://www.oxforddnb.com/view/article/17986 (accessed 13 December 2016).

[274] *unus liber qui vocatur manuele peche lingua Gallica conscriptus* (cf. also *Visitations,*

The last mention of Widdington was on 13 November 1248 when he witnessed a charter of Archbishop Gray.[275] He was still alive in 1249 (**414**) but may have died that year, and certainly by 16 March 1253 when Robert de Ripariis and Richard de Boyville witnessed as seneschals of Archbishop Gray.[276] Widdington's executors were Henry de Mora, canon of Southwell, Roger of Widdington, William of Thornton and John of Barnetby (**397**). The relationship between Widdington and Roger of Widdington is unknown. This is also the case with Andrew of Widdington, who had one toft, three bovates of land and six messuages in Misson by means of his wife Alice and held of William Clarel with whom Andrew and Alice made a final concord on 13 October 1245.[277] It is not clear if William of Widdington had married, and if he had, he may have been childless. His niece was the daughter of Simon of Grimblethorpe, who was married to Clemencia so that Clemencia was Widdington's sister. Simon and Clemencia confirmed Widdington's grants to Southwell and **412** mentions the heirs of Clemencia which would suggest that any residual rights in the lands and properties granted were hers as an heir of Widdington. Since John, son of Benedict of Barnetby, probably Barnetby le Wold (Lincs.), and his wife Agnes confirmed Widdington's grants in an almost identical charter to that of Simon of Grimblethorpe and Clemencia (**415, 416**), this would suggest that Agnes was also an heir of Widdington, perhaps another sister.[278]

As Archbishop Gray's seneschal Widdington was probably familiar with the archiepiscopal lands and properties in Nottinghamshire but he appears to have had no interest in Southwell until 22 May 1226 when Archbishop Gray granted to him a half carucate of land in Southwell for the service of a fifteenth part of a knight's fee which Robert de Landa (**396**) had quitclaimed to the archbishop. A further grant was made by Gray on 14 August 1227 of fifty acres of waste in the manor of Southwell in *Hingewethdal* between *Hespedik* and *Newedik* and a little toft in Easthorpe called *Goldegrene* for a rent of 2s per annum.[279] The last grant made by Archbishop Gray to him on 21 February 1235 was of three bovates of land in Morton that had been held by Geoffrey of Desborough (*Deresbur'*) until forfeited by him for

---

198); Sullivan, 'Waddington', 156 n. 10 suggests this manuscript may now be Cambridge, St John's College, MS 167 which, as a signature on f. 157ʳ shows, was in the hands of John Strelley of Linby in the mid fifteenth century.

[275] *Reg. Gray*, 291. William de Shendon and Reginald of Stowe, canons of Southwell, also witnessed.

[276] *Reg. Gray*, 272n (Robert de Ripariis and Richard de Boyville *senescallis nostris*), 291 (Robert de Riperiis then seneschal and Richard de Boyvill *senescallo ejusdem domini de hospitio*).

[277] TNA, CP 25/1/182/9, no. 121. William Clarel must have been related to John Clarell canon of Southwell and prebendary of Norwell I. On 3 November 1282 Alice, widow of Andrew de Wydington, by her attorney her son Edmund, made a final concord with William son of Saer of Sutton in Holderness concerning the manor of Misson, and Robert, Thomas and Edmund, sons of Andrew of Widdington, and Alice, daughter of Robert of Mattersey, put in their claims (TNA, CP 25/1/183/15, no. 65).

[278] Although Archbishop Gray granted in hereditary fee to Widdington the land and burgages in Brinklow, there is no record in Gray's register of it passing to his male or female heirs.

[279] *Reg. Gray*, 223, 226.

having committed homicide. In addition to the land there was pasture called *Bredemede* which lay on the road or stream (*ductum*) from Halloughton (*Haluton*), a toft in Southwell called *Sabinetoft* (**395**) situated next to land sometime of Roger of Laneham, clerk (**396, 400**), and which abutted on the road towards Easthorpe, for which the rent was 2s per annum for the three bovates and pasture and 12½d for the toft.[280]

Widdington used the lands and properties of these grants by Gray to found his chantry. In addition he made five other purchases of land: two tofts in Southwell from Roger the scribe, one of which was held of the treasurer of York (**392**), two furlongs of land in Southwell from William son of Nicholas de Grauntcurt (**398**), the meadow called *Turneholme* in Southwell and land in Halam from Roger of Laneham, clerk (**400**), two acres of land in Southwell from Hugh son of William the plumber (**402**) which mentions the land of Robert the preacher (*sermonitoris*, probably the *sarmoner* of **414**), and a toft and croft from Andrew, bailiff of Southwell (**413**).[281] In the foundation deed of the chantry *c.* 1248–9 (**414**) Widdington stated that he had acquired one and a half acres of meadow in Beckingham from Richard, rector of Egmanton, but there is no evidence for this.[282] The meadow, however, would appear to be that of **403–4**. After Widdington's death his chantry attracted only two further grants: a plot of land in Southwell (**397**) and one and a half acres of meadow in Beckingham (**403**).

Widdington's chantry is rather unusual in two respects. It was initially founded at the altar of St Nicholas within the chapel of ease in the fields of Easthorpe (*Estethorppefeldis*) dedicated to St Mary Magdalene and only after Widdington's death was it to be transferred to the altar of St Nicholas in Southwell Minster, probably located in the east aisle of the north transept.[283] It was also unusual in that the chantry priest could sing or read the mass 'as the Lord shall inspire him to the greater excitement of the devotion of those hearing him' (*quandoque cantando quandoque legendo secundum quod ei dominus inspirabit ad devocionem audientum magis excitandam*).

There is little evidence for Widdington's chantry in the late medieval period. In 1373 it was said to have an income of £6 8s, most of it derived from rents on properties in the town of Southwell, of which there seem to have been at least twenty, and lands in Halam and Morton (**577**). Among those owing rents to the chantry were the prior of Thurgarton (10s 10d), the

---

[280] *Reg. Gray*, 244–5. Geoffrey of Desborough held in Fiskerton and Morton. He married Golderon (Juliana), daughter of Osbert of Morton and Potterhanworth. Geoffrey was dead by 1234. His son Hugh would appear to have recovered the land, or some of it, by 1248 (*Thurgarton*, 75n, 78n, 100, 102n). For *Bredemede* (*Braidemare, Braithemare, Braithemere*) in Fiskerton, see *Thurgarton*, 94–6, 102n, 108–9.

[281] On 20 October 1230 William of Rotherfield, treasurer of York, made a final concord with William of Rolleston and Lecia his wife for seven bovates of land and a messuage with garden in Southwell, ratified by letters patent of Archbishop Gray dated 2 October 1230. The treasurer surrendered the land in Southwell in 1547 (*Cart. Treas. York*, xi, 77; nos 40, 97–8).

[282] Richard of Sherburn (*Syrebur'*), instituted to Egmanton 9 June 1244 (*Reg. Gray*, 93–4). Richard de Schyreburne was still alive on 30 November 1270 to agree with the patron of Egmanton, Cecilia de Meynill, concerning her oratory, although she had presented Geoffrey, son of John de Caturco, to Egmanton on 26 September 1269 (*Reg. Giffard*, 91, 247).

[283] Hamilton Thompson, *TTS 15* (1911), 82–3.

Vicars Choral (1s 10d) and the vicars of Morton (8d) and Rolleston (6d). By 1513 the chapel of ease of Halam had been united to the chantry to be served by the chantry priest.[284] In 1546 the income of the chantry was £5 17s 10½d and, in 1548, £5 16s 10½d besides 8s 4½d paid out to 'divers persons'. The last chantry priest was Thomas Palmere.

The Chantry of St Peter, founded in memory of Richard of Sutton

Richard of Sutton was collated to the prebend of 'Caunton and Muskham' (i.e. Great or North Muskham) on 14 September 1241 which Henry of Laxton had resigned.[285] He occurs fairly frequently as a witness to charters found in the White Book for over twenty-five years, and among other livings he was presented to the church of Warsop in 1245 by John of Laxton, and shortly afterwards became vicar of Thorpe by Newark.[286] By May 1257 he was also a canon of Lincoln,[287] eventually holding the prebend of Nassington, almost certainly because of the patronage of Henry of Laxton, now bishop of Lincoln, of whom he was later an executor.[288] By 1260, reflecting on his mortality, he agreed with the Vicars Choral at Southwell that

> daily for ever when the mass for the dead is celebrated in their church for the brethren and benefactors of the church, a special prayer shall be said for the said Richard, and another prayer for the souls of Robert of Sutton his father and Alice his wife; also that they will find for ever for the soul of the said Richard, one wax taper, to burn at the mass of the blessed Virgin (**58**).[289]

Mention of Richard's parents, Robert and Alice, raises a number of issues of Sutton family history. In the most recent authoritative account of their genealogy, Christopher Holdsworth states that Robert, father of Richard the canon, was a son of Rowland of Sutton and his wife Elizabeth, sister of the five Laxton brothers (Robert, John, Henry, Stephen and Peter). This Robert of Sutton's eldest brother was, in all probability, William (born *c*. 1218, died 1268), whose succession continued in the male line for many generations.[290]

---

[284] In 1535 the value was £5 19s 10½d (*Visitations*, 180; *Valor Ecclesiasticus* 5, 197). In 1546 Halam chapel was worth £1 16s per annum for 'c howselinge people' (i.e. the number of those taking the Eucharist) and described as 'somtyme covered with leade called halum chapell' (Hamilton Thompson, *TTS* 15 (1911), 111).

[285] *Reg. Giffard*, 84 no. CCCXVII. In accepting, he was obliged to pay an annual life pension of fifty marks at Easter to Adinulf, nephew of Pope Gregory IX, a sum still being paid many years after Sutton's own death.

[286] *Reg. Giffard*, 85; *Reg. Gray*, 95, 96.

[287] cf. *CPR 1247–58*, 556 (24 May 1257), licence as canon of Lincoln for him to hunt, with his own dogs, hare, fox, cat, badger and squirrel in the forests of Nottinghamshire and Northamptonshire.

[288] *Fasti 1066–1300*, iii, 90; *Reg. Antiquissimum*, ii, no. 402. For charters witnessed by Richard of Sutton as canon of Lincoln, probably at Lincoln, see *Reg. Antiquissimum*, ii, nos 629 and 630 (both 1254 x 1258). Between May 1260 and October 1262, he also bought the house at Lincoln formerly owned by a fellow canon, Mr Odo of Kilkenny, for 100 marks (ibid., ix, no. 2551).

[289] cf. *Visitations*, lx.

[290] *Rufford*, i, cix–x, and table, cxi.

Thus Robert himself would likely have been born a year or two later, but if he was, he could not have fathered Richard the canon appointed in 1241 who was clearly an adult. Thoroton, basing himself on this entry in the White Book (**58**), was aware of the difficulty without resolving the problem definitively: 'Richard de Sutton, canon of Southwell ... was son of Robert de Sutton, and Alice his wife ... but I find it was another elder Robert, and Alice'.[291] Holdsworth, curiously without making the connection, provides evidence for a possible solution since he notes that Rowland of Sutton had a brother called Robert, though stating that he 'died overseas, presumably before Richard [another brother of Rowland] fined for their father's land in 1200'.[292] Can we accept that this earlier Robert, probably an elder brother of Richard and Rowland, before his premature death, had already married Alice and left a young son, Richard the future canon? We suggest he did; but if this is not the case, the problem of placing the canon's parents firmly in the Sutton genealogy remains since Richard was clearly not a son of Robert, son of Rowland.[293]

In the event Richard died (around 6 August 1268)[294] before he could make final arrangements for the foundation of his chantry.[295] Indications of his intent to do so are provided by the actions of his executor Arnold of Caunton. Arnold acquired first, at the cost of £100, rents to the value of £3 6s 8d in the township of Holme by Sutton from Sir Philip de Pawnton (**62**, *c.* 1270 x before 21 September 1273). He then transferred these to Richard's cousin,[296] Mr Oliver Sutton, also a canon of Lincoln, then dean, to complete the endowment of the chantry in memory of Richard (**63**). It was through Oliver's energy and perseverance that the foundation was eventually successfully made, though the process took several more years to achieve. A critical point was passed when Edward I granted a licence on 1 October 1283 to Oliver, now bishop of Lincoln (1280–99), to amortise lands in North Muskham and Holme to endow the chaplaincy at Southwell (**61**).

The final stage came between 1287 and 1290 when Oliver Sutton transferred to Henry of Newark, prebendary of North Muskham, all the lands and rents which had been acquired for the chantry (**64**), and Henry agreed that he and his successors as prebendaries would pay six marks a year to Southwell for the chaplain (**72**, November 1288). Philip de Pawnton, still active, signified his assent (**65**) as did Robert, heir of Arnold of Caunton

---

[291] Thoroton, iii, 108.

[292] *Rufford*, i, cviii citing *PR 2 John*, 19 and Thoroton (orig. edn), 359–60 'referring to the Newstead cartulary'.

[293] This Robert was old enough to accompany Henry III to France in 1242 (*CPR 1232–47*, 296, 337). To confuse matters still further, by letters issued at Bordeaux on 15 April 1243, Robert son of Richard of Sutton was exempted from being put on assizes, juries or recognisances or from being appointed coroner (ibid., 373).

[294] *Reg. Giffard*, 84–5.

[295] An annual payment of 12d was owing to the choir boys of Lincoln from the obit of Richard in the fourteenth century (*Reg. Antiquissimum*, ii, 488), where the list containing this information is dated *c.* 1330, though it includes the names of some canons like Henry of Edwinstowe or bishops like Henry Burghersh and Richard de Stretton who died several years later.

[296] If we accept that Richard's father was indeed a brother of Rowland of Sutton.

(**70**) and on 17 August 1290, Edward I confirmed Oliver's grant to Henry of Newark (**66**).

In 1373, attributing the foundation to Richard of Sutton, an inquisition found that the income was indeed six marks and that this was owing from the prebendary of North Muskham who possessed the lands attached to the chantry (**577**). The location of the altar is uncertain though it may have been at the east end of the north aisle in the choir.[297] On the eve of the dissolution, the chantry priest also administered the chapel of ease at Morton, receiving £5 16s 8d for his duties at the chantry and chapel of ease in 1548.

The Chantry of St John the Baptist, founded by Henry le Vavassour

Henry le Vavassour,[298] prebendary of Norwell Palishall by 23 July 1257 (**192**) until shortly before 13 September 1280,[299] founded his chantry in honour of St John the Baptist at some point before the summer of 1275.[300] The White Book contains twenty-five deeds relating to the properties with which it was endowed.

Henry was a younger son of Sir Robert (II) le Vavasor of Shipley (Derbys.), who had acted as under-sheriff of Nottinghamshire and Derbyshire in 1236 and sheriff between 1246 and 1255.[301] As Holdsworth pointed out in a valuable account of the family,[302] according to the Register of Beauvale,[303] an ancestor, Sir Robert had been enfeoffed with the manor of Shipley by Robert of Muskham. This Sir Robert may be identical with Robert (I) le Vavasor, lord of Shipley, a vassal of Hugh of Muskham, in the mid-twelfth century.[304] Robert (I) was still alive in 1176–7, when he paid 100s for his wife's inheritance,[305] but died shortly afterwards leaving his son William (I) as his heir.[306] In turn William (I) le Vavasor of Shipley was succeeded (after 1206) by his son Robert (II), the later under-sheriff and sheriff. In 1242–3 Robert (II) 'was returned as holding two thirds of a knight's fee, with Nicholas fitz John of Heanor, in Shipley of Hugh fitz Ralf, i.e. the then tenant of the Muskham honour'.[307] Earlier, in 1239, Archbishop Gray confirmed a grant by Hugh fitz Ralf, as patron, and Hugh of Cressy, as rector, of Greasley (Notts.), permitting Robert (II) and his heirs to have a chantry at Hempshill (in Nuthall, Notts.).[308] By his wife, apparently a daughter of Richard de Riboeuf of Bilborough (Notts.), Robert (II) certainly had three,

---

[297] Hamilton Thompson, *TTS 15* (1911), 81; cf. *Visitations*, 98 and 143; Ottey, *Southwell Minster*, 37.

[298] His name is given in several different forms in the White Book, the most common being Vavas(s)ur or Vavas(s)our.

[299] *Reg. Wickwane*, 10 no. 36.

[300] The traditional date of foundation is claimed as 1271, but the main endowment of the chantry dates from 1275 (**421**).

[301] *Lists & Indexes*, IX, 102.

[302] *Rufford*, i, cxvi.

[303] BL, Add. MS 6060, f. 28.

[304] *Rufford*, 386, 734.

[305] *PR 23 Henry II*, 61.

[306] *Rufford*, 313, 383, 387–8.

[307] Ibid., i, cxvii after *Book of Fees*, 983.

[308] *Reg. Gray*, 84.

and probably four, sons and at least two daughters by the time of his death in early 1257.[309]

His eldest son, William (II) seems to have been dead by 1263, leaving two daughters Elizabeth and Annora, as his heirs, both then under age.[310] Elizabeth married Robert (I) of Strelley (d. 1284),[311] and they were the progenitors of a line of Strelleys who continued to hold Shipley into the fifteenth century.[312] The other known sons of Robert (II) all followed clerical careers. John, probably the second son, was presented to the church of *Leyk* (Leake, Notts.) in 1239 by the prior and convent of Repton, and in 1252, after a dispute, he was instituted to the church of Selston (Notts.).[313] By then Leake had passed into the hands of his, presumably younger, brother Henry, instituted on 24 May 1250 again at the presentation of Repton priory.[314] Henry is mentioned here for the first time but not yet as a canon of Southwell. Finally, as Holdsworth suggested,[315] a Mr Robert le Vavasor, rector of the church of Bilborough, granted leave to study for two years in 1269,[316] is likely from his name and the Vavasor interest in Bilborough to have been a fourth son of Robert (II).

Henry le Vavassour does not appear to have acquired other livings apart from Leake and his prebend at Southwell but he resided and played an active role in the administration of the Chapter. In 1266, for example, along with Mr Henry of Skipton, prebendary of Normanton (1255–86), and Mr John Clarell, prebendary of Norwell Overhall (1256–95), the three prebendaries drew up an agreement whereby they and their succesors in those prebends were to collect and administer the common tithe of Southwell on behalf of the Chapter, an arrangement that endured until its abolition in 1841 (**30, 371**). In the previous year Henry had been on a commission to investigate the misdemeanours of a vicar, Mr John of Hockerton (**191**). But he himself was in trouble in 1275 when, along with his fellow Norwell prebendary, John Clarell, he was accused of emparking land there without permission.[317] Otherwise, most of what is known about him is derived from the charters relating to his chantry. These show him accumulating lands and rents by the early 1270s, which would be used to endow the chantry, that he eventually handed over to the Chapter (**449**), though in a document sadly bereft of any further personal details on his reasons for founding the chantry or on the names of those for whom he wished prayers to be said, apart from the souls of himself and his successors as prebendaries of Norwell Palishall.

Many of the rents he acquired were due on various properties in Southwell itself. In a charter of 1275, John of Glentham transferred to Le Vavassour

---

[309] Johanna, who married Patrick de Saucheverell of Boulton, and was a widow by 1255 (*Dale*, 75) and an unnamed daughter who married Alexander of Wansley and was in dispute over the church of Selston in 1289 (*Reg. Romeyn*, i, 310).

[310] *CCR 1256–9*, 314, 487; *Dale*, 163.

[311] See **351** for an agreement between Mr William of Clifford, prebendary of Oxton II, and Sir Robert of Strelley over a disputed lake and fishery at Oxton in 1280.

[312] *Feudal Aids*, i, 263, 300.

[313] *Reg. Gray*, 84, 111.

[314] Ibid., 109.

[315] *Rufford*, i, cxviii.

[316] *Reg. Giffard*, 3.

[317] *Rot. Hund.*, ii, 311.

his rights over some fourteen rents, assigned on various tofts and land, totalling £1 13s 5d in annual revenue, and more than six bovates of land together with at least eleven separate tofts (**421**),[318] but with the obligation on Le Vavassour to pay 12s in rents to other parties already assigned on these properties. Another charter shows him exercising rights of wardship and marriage and acquiring a further bovate of land in Southwell but one already charged with an annual rent of 2s (**424**). Also in 1275, which seems to have been a critical year in the establishment of the chantry, Le Vavassour acquired a toft and lands in Edingley for which a rent of 6d was initially owing that was to be increased to 100s after sixteen years, suggesting that it was an estate of some size (**441**).[319] His other main acquisition outside Southwell was of a messuage and thirty acres of land in Norwell and Norwell Woodhouse, or rather its re-acquisition since the land forming this tenement had been granted around 1244 by one of Le Vavassour's predecessors as prebendary of Norwell Palishall, Walter de Taney, to his own brother, Robert de Taney (**425**). It was Alice, Robert de Taney's daughter, who had ceded it to Le Vavassour at a token rent of one halfpenny by March 1273 (**428**). Her grant was later confirmed by her own daughter Agnes after Le Vavassour's death (**426**). There was however some resistance to it from other members of Alice's family; by 1284 agreement had been reached that the disputed property, consisting of a toft, croft, twelve acres of arable and three acres of meadow, owed an annual rent of 20s to the Chapter towards the expenses of the chaplain of Le Vavassour's chantry.[320] In the same year, the family of Edingley which had agreed to the cession of the toft in Edingley in 1275, released any claims to the 100s rent that it was to bear after sixteen years in return for an unspecified sum of money, thus removing an important charge on that particular estate (**443**).

Only one other small addition to the original endowment in the years following Le Vavassour's death is recorded in the White Book, when *c.* 1302, John Scot of Southwell, chaplain, who also occurs in some other Southwell town charters of the period, gave to the Chapter half a toft in Easthorpe that he had bought to augment Le Vavassour's chantry (**438**). It seems to have had an annual income of nearly £4 at this point, but this would certainly have been augmented by additional revenues from Edingley. This was apparently sufficient for a chapel to be constructed in the western part of the south aisle of the nave.[321] By 1373 the chantry was said to be worth £3 19s 2d, when rents of 20s from Norwell, 6s 8d from Henry Marshall of Norwell, 3s from a place in Norwell Woodhouse, 13s 4d from a pasture in Edingley, 3s from the toft in Easthorpe and 10s 2d from the fabric clearly derived from some of the initial endowment (**577**). Two further rents of 8s 6d from John of Wainfleet and 6s 5d from a tenement once occupied by Richard de Wylyghby also probably derived from the Southwell properties

---

[318] The acreage of a bovate fluctuated according to the quality of the land and local custom, but may be assumed to be between 20 and 30 acres in extent.

[319] By agreement with Robert, son of Gerald of Edingley.

[320] See also **429** and note for the release by Robert fitz Ingelram of Oldcotes, another of Robert de Taney's heirs.

[321] Hamilton Thompson, *TTS 15* (1911), 89–91; Ottey, *Southwell Minster*, 25, 37.

acquired by Le Vavassour, but it is not clear how rents of 3s 8d from Mr Robert Tanour, 12d from Sibyl Browning, 2s from the chantry of St Nicholas, 12d from the chantry of St Thomas and 2d from Isabella de Cromwell related to earlier endowments. Under Archbishops William Booth (1452–64) and Laurence Booth (1476–80) the chapel was rebuilt and enlarged.[322] At the end of the Middle Ages (if not previously) the priest serving the altar of St John the Baptist also acted as curate of Halloughton. In 1535 the chantry was listed as being worth £6 10s 6½d,[323] and at the dissolution in 1548 at £4 17s 6d, with an additional allowance of £1 8s for Halloughton, giving a total value of £6 5s 6d.

The Chantry of St Mary, founded by William of Gunthorpe

William of Gunthorpe is first mentioned as rector of Langar *c.* 1360.[324] By 1362 he also occurs as a king's clerk, and in 1363 as king's cofferer,[325] becoming keeper of the wardrobe from 1366–8 and then treasurer of Calais from 1368–73.[326] From 1373–87 his remaining years in royal service were as a secondary baron of the Exchequer; in 1385 he had been one of the receivers of a parliamentary grant. As a modestly successful career civil servant, he was naturally rewarded by the Crown with various ecclesiastical livings.

He was first named to an expectative canonry at Southwell on 22 April 1363, when he already held the church of *Esenden* [Essendine, Hertfordshire (Lincoln diocese)],[327] but he is not mentioned as a prebendary until June 1380 when he held Norwell Palishall.[328] From this point until his death, almost certainly in September 1400, now largely retired from his obligations at Westminster, Gunthorpe played an active role in the administration at Southwell, where his financial expertise was of particular value for resolving some economic and organisational difficulties facing the Chapter. His role in placing the finances of the Vicars Choral on a firmer footing is mentioned elsewhere.[329] His contacts with Westminster were also of value for promoting both his own interests as prebendary of Norwell Palishall,[330] and in obtaining royal consent for the establishment of his chantry, which necessitated some re-arrangement of earlier provisions for chantries. He also took an active part in the running of his prebendal estate at Norwell to the end of his life.[331] Among other livings which he had acquired were

[322] Hamilton Thompson, *TTS 15* (1911), 87–92; Foulds, '*In medio chori*', 110–11.

[323] *Valor Ecclesiasticus*, v, 197.

[324] Godfrey, *Bingham*, 289.

[325] *CPR 1361–4*, 53; *CPP*, i, 415.

[326] His accounts for May 1371–July 1372 have survived: Manchester, John Rylands University Library, MS Latin 240, edited by Édouard Perroy, *Compte de William de Gunthorp, trésorier de Calais, 1371–1372* (Arras, 1959).

[327] *CPP*, i, 415.

[328] *CPR 1377–81*, 521.

[329] Above, pp. lxxxiii–lxxxiv.

[330] Shortly after Norwell Palishall came into his hands, he requested an exemplification of Edward III's confirmation in 1330 of Edward II's charter of 1310 granting William Melton and his successors at Palishall rights of free warren in Norwell and Norwell Woodhouse (*CPR 1381–5*, 63).

[331] His last known act was to invest his servant, John Wedonne, with a messuage there on

the prebends of Weighton (York) and Grantham South (Salisbury)[332] while for a period he was also parson of Fakenham (Norwich). When he died, he was buried at Southwell and left at least two manuscripts to the Chapter, an erased inscription in one providing the probable date of his death as well as some hint of his intellectual interests.[333]

Initially, Gunthorpe promoted an earlier chantry of St Mary at Southwell served by a chaplain attached to St Helen's, South Wheatley (or his nominated deputy).[334] Since the time of the Black Death the chaplain had celebrated daily a sung mass in the Minster but found mounting financial difficulties in maintaining the chantry so Gunthorpe added six marks annual rent (£4) to its endowment from lands he had acquired in Sutton and Carlton on Trent to the 40s assigned from the annual rent owing by the prior and convent of Sixhills for the chantry (**577**).[335] Later, Gunthorpe, with the consent of the rest of the Chapter, decided that an entirely new foundation was preferable, partly using resources that had come into his own hands as prebendary of Norwell Palishall, partly by diverting other endowments, to create a viable chantry in changed economic circumstances. By 1390, through a series of land transactions, he had acquired any remaining interests from the heirs of Robert of Woodhouse, prebendary of Norwell Palishall (1317–46) and his successors to various lands and tenements at Sutton and Carlton on Trent (**475–95**). Then, following a licence to alienate in mortmain granted by

12 June 1400 (LA, Cragg MS 3/29).

[332] *Reg. Scrope*, no. 20; *Fasti 1300–1541*, iii, 54 (Grantham South), vi, 88 (Weighton, held from 1368–1400).

[333] Cambridge, St John's College, MS A.4, containing Guido de Baysio, *Apparatus libri sexti decretalium*, the text of the sixth book of the Decretals and two further commentaries on it, originally four volumes, now bound in one, early 14th century, finely written and ornamented in England. At the end there is an erased inscription which appears to read: *Sextus liber decretalium legatus Capitulo de Suthwell per dominum Willelmum de Gunthorp canonicum eiusdem ecclesie et prebendarium alterius prebendarius de Northwell' vocatur Palishall ad remanendum in libraria eiusdem ecclesie ibidem perpetuo per ... Qui quidem dominus Willelmus obiit xix mensis Septembris apud Suthwell' anno domini millesimo ccccᵐᵒ Qui alienavit anathema sit.* The other manuscript is Cambridge, Gonville & Caius, MS 449/390, late 14th century, also finely written in England, an interesting miscellany of historical materials including the chronicle of Martinus Polonus, lists of popes, emperors and kings of Britain and Anglo-Saxon England, a genealogy of the kings of England to Richard II, a chronicle tracing the descent of Richard II from Rollo, duke of Normandy, documents relating to the history and administration of York Minster, a short history of Beverley, a copy of the treaty of Brétigny (1360), and Thomas de Swinburne's account of his journey to Jerusalem in 1392–3. On f. 169b is the fifteenth-century inscription: *Legato capitulo de Suthwell per d. Will. de Gunthorp, qui alienaverit anathema sit.* We are grateful to Kathryn McKee (St John's) and Mark Statham (Caius) for help identifying these manuscripts.

[334] The Chapter had enjoyed the advowson of South Wheatley since 1205 (**83, 523**) and an obligation of the rectory there to furnish three candles for the mass of the Blessed Virgin Mary at Southwell had been established at much the same period (**525, 526**).

[335] This information comes at the end of the March 1373 inquisition into the value of the chantries when Gunthorpe himself would still have been in Calais. However, if it was part of the original return, it suggests he was already in possession of a prebend, though it seems more probable that the information (like Gunthorpe's augmentation of the original chantry of St Mary) was added at some point after 1373 and before the recitation of the inquisition by the Chapter on 1 September 1413 (see **577n**).

Richard II on 12 July 1395 (**503**), on 20 July Gunthorpe transferred these properties to the Chapter (**496–8**), having previously obtained the consent of the capital lord of the lands in question, Bertram de Mountbourcher (**499**).[336] Formal proceedings were completed in September 1395 when Gunthorpe set out in very considerable detail what he expected of the chaplain, how he was to be remunerated, what was to happen if he were unable to carry out his duties, and, most importantly, for whom he was to pray (**502**).[337] The altar was sited in the chapel of St Mary on the north side of the Minster.[338] For its part, the Chapter on 22 September 1395 also fulsomely recognised the endowment by Gunthorpe and sanctioned the augmentation of its income by appropriating the endowment once made for his chantry by Henry of Nottingham (**500**). In 1535 the chantry of St Mary was worth £6 3s 11½d[339] and at the dissolution £6 0s 7d.

The Chantry of St John the Baptist, founded by Thomas Haxey

Thomas Haxey, prebendary of Rampton from 1388–1425, made a modestly successful career as a king's clerk from 1382. Probably originally from Haxey in the Isle of Axholme (Lincs.), he was early rewarded with prebends at Lichfield, Lincoln and Salisbury as well as at Southwell in addition to other benefices, among them holding the church of Laxton from 1393 to 1408.[340] He achieved a brief national fame in 1397 when, as one of the clerical proctors in parliament, he presented a petition which asked for a reduction in the costs of the king's household and of the number of bishops and ladies at court among other things. When Richard II discovered who had brought this bill before the Commons, he was incensed 'not least because this controversial proposal had originated with a long-standing royal servant, and the Lords then declared, retrospectively, that it was treasonable to call for reform of the king's household'. Haxey was condemned as a traitor on 7 February 1397, but fortunately for him, although benefit of clergy had been abolished for treason, Thomas Arundel, archbishop of Canterbury (from whom Haxey had received his two earliest benefices when Arundel was bishop of Ely), 'swiftly claimed custody of him as a criminous clerk'. Eventually, on 27 May 1397, at the request of 'the bishops and multitude of ladies' in the king's household, Haxey was pardoned,[341] and he was able to resume both his benefices and

---

[336] The grant included three messuages, eighty-three acres of arable, fifteen and a half acres of meadow, twenty acres of pasture, a fishery on the Trent, 4s in rent and various bondmen and bondwomen living in North Carlton (Carlton on Trent) and Sutton on Trent.

[337] His father and mother, Henry of Nottingham (cf. pp. lxxxvi–lxxxix), Edward III, Queen Philippa and their children, Thomas Percy, bishop of Norwich (1355–69), John of Rolleston, and Hamo of Barsham as well as for his own soul.

[338] 'in subvencionem sustentacionis unius capellani idonei et honesti qui cotidie celebrabit missam de beate Marie cum nota in capella beate Marie ex parte boriali predicte ecclesie Suthwell' situata' (**502**); cf. Hamilton Thompson, *TTS 15* (1911), 84–5.

[339] *Valor Ecclesiasticus*, v, 197.

[340] This account draws heavily on work by Alison McHardy, usefully summarised in her *ODNB* article on Haxey as ecclesiastic and administrator: A. K. McHardy, 'Haxey, Thomas (*d.* 1425), ecclesiastic and administrator', *ODNB online*: http://www.oxforddnb.com/view/article/12702 (accessed 11 August 2014).

[341] *CPR 1396–9*, 141.

career in royal service, still acting as late as 1412 as a king's clerk. Perhaps not surprisingly after this traumatic incident, from 1397 the focus of Haxey's attention tended to turn northwards away from Westminster. He was frequently resident at Rampton and in Southwell, where for many years he played (as described more fully below) an active part in the Chapter's affairs. In 1419 he exchanged his Salisbury prebend for one at Ripon, later also exchanged for one at Beverley in 1423. From 1405 he additionally held the prebend of Barnby (York) and after 1408 spent periods as residentiary at York, becoming treasurer in December 1418. He was 'perhaps the most active residentiary at York in the years immediately before his death' in January 1425 when he was still treasurer.[342] He was buried in York Minster leaving much of his residual wealth to the fabric or other members of the York clergy after establishing a chantry and considerable personal outlay on building works, including the re-leading of the Minster library roof.[343]

Apart from his occasional appearance as a witness (**502**, 1395), or presence in a prebendal court (**377**, 30 August 1406),[344] Haxey is most evident in the White Book as a benefactor of St Mary's, Southwell. For instance, on 16 August 1407, at Southwell, he granted a messuage and toft in the town to the fabric (**343**), the reversion of the lease of which he had acquired two months earlier (**342**). Other evidence shows him active in the local property market, mainly in acquiring real estate for his subsequent benefactions,[345] of which the most important was to undertake the building of a house for all the ten chantry priests to hold in common.[346] This was built on a rectangular, courtyard plan rather like an Oxbridge college and largely in imitation of the house for the Vicars Choral erected some twenty years earlier, with a great hall on the west side and small rooms for priests occupying much of the rest of the building (**Plates 12 and 13**). It was sited in the north-west corner of the Minster yard and survived until 1819, although after the Reformation, with the abolition of the chantries, 'it was let piecemeal to various people'.[347]

Haxey's endowment for his chantry and the Chantry Priests' House eventually consisted of at least six messuages, twelve tofts, 360 acres of arable, sixty-six acres of pasture, six acres of woods and a rent of 19s 4d derived from properties in Beckingham, North Muskham, Bathley, Holme, Bole,

---

[342] Dobson, 'Later Middle Ages', 105.

[343] BI, Reg. Wills 1, ff. 219ʳ–220ᵛ for his will, 29 September 1424, proved 23 January 1425.

[344] When assisting Robert de Wolvendon at Norwell Overhall.

[345] NA, Newark Borough Deeds, T 157 (F 22), grant by Ralph Lude, son and heir of Thomas Lude of Little Marlow, Bucks., to Thomas Haxey, canon, of all the lands and services he possessed in North and South Muskham, South (Little) Carlton, Bathley, Holme and North and South Clifton, at Bathley, 1 June 1409. See also **355n.** for Thomas Lude's landed interests.

[346] Including one endowed by Haxey himself (cf. above p. lxxxv). Chapman, 'Chantry House', 17 gives, but without reference, the date 1385 for its construction.

[347] *Visitations*, lxiii. As late as 1574 provision was made for the lessee of the west part of the house 'to allow "Sir Francis Hall and Sir Richard Harryson", sometime chauntrie priests to enjoy their several chambers therein for their lives' (ibid.). Hall was apparently 69 years old and Harryson 77, but being 'unlerned' they had not been able to obtain any new office after the dissolution. For the Chantry Priests' House, see also above p. lxxxv. It was replaced by what Leach called 'a hideous red-brick building', which still stands and is now occupied by offices and the Minster Centre.

Southwell and Normanton (all Notts.) and Burton upon Trent (Staffs.).[348] Earlier arrangements for payment of some of this, a rent of 9s 10d derived from properties in Normanton, are illustrated in **596–604**, while the 1415 endowment seems to have included the 120 acres of arable and seven of meadow in North and South Muskham, South (Little) Carlton, Bathley, Holme, North and South Clifton, acquired in 1409 (cf. **355**).[349] Some of this benefaction too was later used to bolster the endowment of the Vicars Choral, a matter which had deeply concerned Haxey and one of his colleagues at Westminster and Southwell, William of Gunthorpe, prebendary of Norwell Palishall.[350] On 24 November 1415, Haxey issued at Southwell another charter granting a further two messuages, six tofts, 160 acres of arable, thirty acres of meadow, six woods and 13s 4d in rents on properties in Beckingham and Normanton to the Chapter (**141**). As a result of these very generous benefactions culminating in 1415, Haxey's chantry, sometimes called the Morrow Mass chantry,[351] which probably shared a chapel with Le Vavassour's chantry also dedicated to St John the Baptist, was one of the richest in 1548 when it was said to be worth £8 1s 9d, while that of Haxey's benefaction to the ten chantry priests was stated to be £6 8s 8d.

Chantry priests

A few names of priests serving individual chantries are known (especially in the period leading up to the dissolution). Only a handful occur in the White Book. Among the earliest is Thomas de la Barre, who was probably the first priest to serve Henry of Nottingham's chantry (**579**). He also witnessed a number of charters in the mid-thirteenth century.[352] One of his successors at St John the Evangelist's chantry, William Browning, occurs as a benefactor 1280 x 1296 (**457**). William of Earlshaw was serving the altar of St Nicholas around 1300 (**560**) and one of his successors in 1325 was Henry Ketill who held a number of other posts (**404**), while in turn at the beginning of the fifteenth century William Ketill held the same chantry (**173, 176–8**). William of Farndon was the perpetual chaplain of St Stephen's chantry before 1286 (**574**) and a successor in 1437–8 was Thomas son of Robert Barber (**542, 543**). Simon Brainde possibly served as chantry priest for one of the altars dedicated to St Thomas the Martyr 1280 x 1286 (**457**) and his successor was Simon of Farnsfield (**458**). From evidence not found in the White Book, it is known that John Sampson, priest and perpetual beneficiary of the altar of St Mary Magdalene, founded by Robert Oxton, petitioned for an increase of income on 23 October 1427, following an order from Pope Martin V in March 1427 to the treasurer of Lincoln to investigate the need for such increases for chaplains serving the chantries at Southwell, a reminder that most of them lived on very small stipends.[353] The White Book provides little evidence of them receiving promotion.

---

[348] Appendix A, **A6**. Although in Notts., Bole was a prebend of York Minster.
[349] cf. note 345 above for the acquisition of this land.
[350] See further above, p. lxxxiv.
[351] One said for those going on a journey that day (Hamilton Thompson, *TTS 15* (1911), 86).
[352] Among them **394, 397, 433** and **513**.
[353] *CPL*, vii, 545, 569.

The Fabric

The White Book is unusual in that it contains a section for the fabric (**225–343**).[354] The fabric came to hold lands and property in Sturton le Steeple, Willoughby in Norwell parish, Rolleston, Upton, Normanton, Kirklington, Halam, Flintham and Eaton, and in Southwell and its sub-settlement of Easthorpe.

Twelve charters can be securely dated to before the death of Hugh the dean, which had occurred by 28 May 1230 (**234, 237–42, 252, 274, 307–9** and probably **276**). On 23 November 1233 Archbishop Walter Gray had issued his indulgence of twenty days to raise money for the fabric 'lately begun': he also issued similar indulgences to York (1227), Beverley (1232) and Ripon (1233).[355] The twelve charters would appear to show that the preparation of the canons – probably indicated by Gray's statute of 20 April 1225 (**102**) – and local community, appeal for funds and the decision to build the new east end of the Minster had been taken before 1230, perhaps in the period 1225–7 (**Plate 14**). Building began shortly afterwards and it was certainly in progress by April 1233. The build began with the new extreme east wall, progressed westwards and was continuous with a short pause probably to allow for the demolition of the old Romanesque east end.[356] By about 1241 the build was sufficiently advanced to contain the altar dedicated to St Thomas Becket for the chantry founded by Robert of Laxton which was located in the 'new work' (**455–6**: *in capella beati Thome martiris in novo opere*). Another statute for Southwell issued by Gray in 1248 would indicate that the new east end of the Minster was now fit for purpose if not completed (**104**).

The funding for the building of the new Chapter House in progress on 25 January 1288 was largely achieved in house by a fixed subsidy levied on the prebends with seemingly little in the way of appeal for funds to the wider community.[357] Apart from the Chapter House, the only significant thirteenth-century new build was the chantry of St John the Baptist founded by Henry le Vavassour (dead by 13 September 1280) and probably funded entirely by him. The chantry was built off the south aisle of the nave immediately behind (east of) the south-west tower and was the length of two bays. It was embellished, perhaps refurbished and extended, in the fifteenth century by Archbishops William Booth (1452–64) and especially his half-brother Laurence Booth (1476–80) for the chantries dedicated to the Virgin Mary and St Cuthbert founded by Laurence, and as a mausoleum for the tombs of both archbishops. The chapel was demolished in 1784.[358] Beyond this there was no significant new build or alteration to the extant Romanesque and thirteenth-century fabric, though work on the towers seems to have been in hand in 1320 when permission was given to two proctors to seek alms

---

[354] No. **225** appears to be placed under the wrong heading and thus seemingly nothing to do with the fabric. The wardens of the fabric had failed to burn a torch at the altar of St Peter or St Leonard in 1478 (*Visitations*, 35).

[355] *Reg. Gray*, 64–5: *cum igitur facultates ecclesie Suwell' ad incepte dudum fabrice consummationem non sufficiant ...*

[356] McNeill, 'Chronology', 24–32.

[357] *Reg. Romeyn*, i, 370–1.

[358] Foulds, '*In medio chori*', 110–11.

throughout the province of York for a year for this purpose.[359] The pulpitum was constructed in the fourteenth century, the large window inserted in the Romanesque west front was probably done in the mid-fifteenth century, and the lowering of the roof levels may have occurred at this time.[360]

In addition there is the rare survival of three fifteenth-century fabric accounts. Only two of these accounts for the years 1428–9 and 1429–30 are legible, whereas the text of the account for the year 28 October 1438–9 is very faint and largely illegible.[361] In these accounts all the lands and properties recorded in the White Book can be identified with some certainty but there is no mention of the land and meadow in Rolleston or the land in Flintham. By the fifteenth century all the fabric lands and properties were leased and supplied an annual income of £8 2s 9d in 1428–9 and £8 3s 7d in 1429–30. Additional income for the fabric was obtained from altarage, oblations, sale of hay crops, sale of hempen cloth (a very unusual source of income), bequests from five wills, procurations donated by the *questores* of the archdeacons of Cleveland and York, and the sale of some surplus stock. The total income, before expenses, was thus £18 0s 7d in 1428–9 and £26 14s 2¼d in 1429–30. These figures are low when compared with the income received by the fabric at Ripon: for the six surviving fabric accounts for the period 1408 to 1426 from Ripon the average annual income is £52.[362]

Archbishop Gray's statute of 1248 (**104**) has the first mention of the office of warden of the fabric (*custos fabrice ecclesie*). It required that the warden was to prepare his account annually and once a year present it to the two canons residentiary. Gray also ordained that another canon or vicar was to be associated with the warden to oversee his account. In 1260 the same arrangement was confirmed except that the colleague was to be a chaplain. The origins of the fabric and its officers may often have arisen because of major building work, yet thereafter the fabric fund was primarily applied to the physical upkeep and maintenance of the extant fabric on a regular basis for minor building work and repairs. Although there were wide variations in detail, this remit encompassed the repair and maintenance of internal fittings and fixtures to include, among other things, statues, images, cleaning the fabric inside and out, even livery for choristers at Ripon and Beverley, and clocks and organs which were becoming more prevalent in the greater churches such as Southwell from the fourteenth century onwards.[363]

From what meagre evidence is available the wardens of the fabric at Southwell were chaplains or Vicars Choral. Thomas de Helyton and Robert de Wycthon, who reported to the Chapter after they had made an inquisition concerning the vacant vicarage of South Muskham dated 24 July 1295,

---

[359] *Reg. Melton*, v, no. 83, 9 July 1320, licence to Robert de Sprotborough and Elias de Lumby (previously a proctor at Beverley between 1306 and 1313), proctors for the fabric, notwithstanding the archbishop's previous inhibition.

[360] Summers 1988, 42–3.

[361] NA, SC/5/2/1–3.

[362] Accounts for 1408–9, £27 16s 8½d; 1416–17, £39 9s 6¼d; 1418–19, £45 11s 4d; 1419–20, £54 15s 4½d; 1424–5, £74 5s 0½d; 1425–6, £73 14s 11¾d (*Mems. Ripon*, ii, 135, 141, 142, 144, 150, 155).

[363] Trevor Foulds, 'Pigeons in the Bell Tower: Three Fifteenth-Century Fabric Accounts of Southwell Minster' (in preparation).

described themselves as wardens of the fabric and of the commons (**40**: *commune canonicorum et fabrice ecclesie supradicte custodes*). Helyton is otherwise unknown but Wycthon was described as a chaplain in 1288 and 1308 (**233, 317**). Henry de Ketell and Robert of Morton were addressed as wardens of the fabric in a release and quitclaim dated 3 August 1322 (**258**). Described as priests the Chapter leased to Morton and Ketell land and meadow in Easthorpe in 1325, and Ketell was chaplain of St Nicholas' chantry in 1324, and perhaps rector of South Wheatley in 1345 (**268, 404** (*capellano et ministro altare beati Nicholai*), **519**). The headings of the three surviving fifteenth-century fabric accounts do not record the status of the named wardens of the fabric. In 1428 Robert Sampson and John Chetill had only just been appointed as wardens: Sampson was a chaplain in 1395 and a vicar choral in 1414 (**357, 498**). With some four months before the end of his term as one of the wardens of the fabric, Chetill was appointed one of the wardens of the commons from 10 June 1430 to 27 May 1431 and named in the heading of the commons account after Walter Lanley the other warden.[364] Unfortunately one of the names of the wardens of the fabric in 1438 cannot be read with certainty apart from his Christian name which was perhaps Anthony, and the other was Thomas Kirk, but they are not mentioned in any other evidence. It is possible, but not certain, that Thomas Urkyll and Richard Rooper, Vicars Choral, mentioned in a licence 'to newly found and build' the old chapel of St Katherine, Westhorpe, on 1 October 1481, were wardens of the fabric.[365] Both men were Vicars Choral in 1473, wardens of the Chapter in 1476, wardens of the church (*gardianis ecclesie collegiate*) in 1479, and Urkyll was described as a chaplain in 1475.[366] Rooper or Roper remained a vicar choral in 1486 and by 1491 he was the parish vicar of Southwell, an office he held when he made his will on 20 July 1499.[367]

Although there may have been slight changes over time, there is nothing unusual about the number or status of the wardens of the fabric at Southwell: there were usually two holders of the office and they were not canons. At Exeter the office of warden of the works (*custos operis*) is first mentioned in 1204 but its origins were probably twelfth century. For the period 1299 to 1353 there was only one warden who held office for a number of years but the status only of John de Schyrford (chaplain) is given.[368] From the first complete extant fabric account for York of 1415 there were two wardens of the fabric to 1432 and thereafter to 1538 only one warden. For the years 1415, 1418–19 and 1421, the second warden was termed the *contrarotularius*, that is, to keep a check on his colleague (and *vice versa*) as in Gray's ordinations for

364 NA, SC/5/1/1.
365 BI, Reg. 23, f. 204ᵛ. *Reg. Rotherham*, 193 (no. 1557) erroneously gives f. 205ᵛ.
366 *Visitations*, 99, 100, 168, 169.
367 *Visitations*, 104, 109.
368 A. M. Erskine, 'The Accounts of the Fabric of Exeter Cathedral, 1279–1353', *Devon and Cornwall Record Society*, 24 (1981), xi–xiv, 8, 17, 72, 213, 259, 278. Although there is a gap in the accounts from 1329 to 1340, the wardens were: Dom Robert de Asperton (about sixteen years), John de Schyreford, chaplain (about twelve years), Peter de Castro (about six years), W. de Haselholte (about eight years), Thomas Canyng. The only exception was for the year 1299–1300 with two: Dom Robert de Asperton and Master Roger the mason, wardens of the new work.

Southwell.[369] At Ripon there were two wardens of the fabric (1354–1532) who were often chaplains, and who served for a number of years.[370] At Lichfield, from probably before 1272, there were two wardens, and at Wells usually only one but two for 1457–8 with no indication of the status of the wardens given in the headings of the surviving accounts.[371]

Although men might serve as wardens of the fabric for a number of years consecutively, by the fifteenth century it was common practice for them to be appointed annually by the Chapter. For example, Richard Pomerey was sworn warden of the fabric at Wells for the first time on 1 October 1488 by the Dean and Chapter and he was subsequently re-appointed at Chapter meetings held on 8 September 1490 and 30 September 1491 even though at this latter date he was not actually present. He served at least until 1506 or beyond so that for about twenty years or more he remained warden of the fabric elected annually.[372] The annual appointment of wardens of the fabric at Southwell is not mentioned but it is likely, as elsewhere, that this was so as the wardens of the commons, at their annual account, were to surrender their keys to the two canons residentiary and then the canons residentiary would decide whether to re-appoint them as wardens or to appoint others to succeed them.[373] At Wells another official, John Waryn (canon in 1390–1), was appointed at the audit before the Dean and Chapter on 5 November 1369 to supervise John Hulle, warden of the works and fabric, and attend to the fabric accounts.[374] It was also common practice for the wardens of the fabric to have a spending limit imposed on them above which they had to apply to the Chapter to spend more and they could not themselves initiate any new building work without Chapter authority. If they exceeded the limits they were subject to disciplinary action. Richard Pomerey at Wells felt it necessary (or was denounced) to come before the Chapter on 25 July 1501 as 'he had unjustly and badly abused his office'. He confessed that he had taken down the great bell from the south-west tower (*de turri australi ecclesie*) to be re-cast without the consent or authority of the Chapter, for which offence he was pardoned but fined five marks.[375] No such misdemeanours are recorded at Southwell in the fragmentary surviving evidence.

Minor Place-Names in the White Book

The White Book provides a great deal of information about the ecclesiastical rights, dues, lands and personnel of Southwell and its vicinity. It also records, in the vernacular, the names of many land-features, plots and places in the area. These have been relatively little studied. *The Place-Names of Nottinghamshire* (PN Nt) in the English Place-Name Survey used a range

---

[369] Raine, 'Fabric Rolls', 1–120.

[370] *Mems. Ripon*, ii, 88–196.

[371] No medieval fabric accounts survive for Lichfield (http://www.british-history.ac.uk/vch/staffs/vol3/pp140–166); Colchester, *Wells*, 3–41.

[372] Reynolds, *Wells Cathedral*, 173, 180, 183; Colchester, *Wells*, 21 (1492–3), 28 (1500–1), 35 (1505–6). Similarly at Salisbury after 1440 (Edwards, *Secular Cathedrals*, 231).

[373] *Visitations*, 205.

[374] Reynolds, *Wells Cathedral*, 116, 197.

[375] Ibid., 203.

of names from the cartulary, but in 1940 the focus of the county editors was on recording and analysing major settlement names and excerpting from documents that gave mainly national coverage, and their work on the White Book was not systematic.[376] In recent years, Jean Cameron and Paul Cavill have analysed and published parish surveys, which use material from the White Book among other sources; and Michael Jones has collected the material extensively in his work on Norwell.[377]

The parish names of the Peculiar of Southwell are treated in PN Nt and the White Book material makes no major revision of the etymologies necessary. It is to be noted, however, that the White Book contains a wider range of spellings than those represented in PN Nt. The spellings in the White Book for Blidworth are listed below in the order: spelling, date of document, number of document.

Blidewarda 1271 (**23**, x2)
Blideword' (p)[378] a.1249 (**514**)
Blideworth' (p) 1268 (**284**), (p) late 13 (**286**), (p) late 13 (**289**),
   (p) *c.* 1241–9 (**394**)
Blithworth 1333 (14), 1331 (**147**), 1346 (**162**), (p) 1321 (**353**)
Blithworth' (p) mid13 (**291**)
Blitheworth 1333 (**14**, x2), 1301 (**349**)
Blithewortgh 1333 (**14**, x3)
Bliyeword' (p) 1275 (**421**)
Blidworth 1321 (**353**)

This series of spellings has -*i*- in the first element: most of the other WB spellings have -*y*-. Not one of these precise spellings occurs in the listing in PN Nt 115. One of the peculiarities here, in *Bliyeword'*, suggests that the scribe was unfamiliar with þ in his exemplar and replaced it with *y* (a mistake perpetuated in the present-day designation 'Ye olde ...').

Minor names – that is, names of land-features, plots, streams, paths, buildings, enclosures, hills and so on – reveal much about the language used by ordinary people, about the topography, flora and fauna, agricultural practices and ownership of the land. These aspects will be briefly analysed below, principally with the aim of throwing light on the configuration and use of the land, but with a secondary aim of providing a gloss on some of the naming elements that would otherwise be obscure. In what follows, the names are discussed giving the spelling as it occurs in the document, a gloss

---

[376] J. E. B. Gover, Allen Mawer and F. M. Stenton, *The Place-Names of Nottinghamshire*, English Place-Name Society 17 (Cambridge, 1940); hereafter PN Nt. This gap in widely-available place-name scholarship on minor names (much excellent work is being done by local historians) is being addressed by Rebecca Gregory, currently a research student at the University of Nottingham, working on the minor names of Thurgarton Wapentake.

[377] Jean Cameron, 'Minor Names of Caunton, Nottinghamshire', *JEPNS* 38 (2006), 37–42; 'Minor Names of Norwell, Nottinghamshire', *JEPNS* 37 (2005), 53–8; with Paul Cavill, 'Kelham, Thurgarton Wapentake, Nottinghamshire', *JEPNS* 44 (2012), 66–72; 'Carlton on Trent', *JEPNS* 39 (2007), 145–9; 'Lowdham, Thurgarton Wapentake, Nottinghamshire', *JEPNS* 41 (2009), 49–56; with Paul Cavill and Richard Jones, 'Upton, Thurgarton Wapentake, Nottinghamshire', *JEPNS* 40 (2008), 23–34.

[378] (p) = a personal name, e.g. William de *Blitheworth*.

in inverted commas, the parish or locality in which the name occurs and the number of the document. Name elements are given in bold.[379]

Language

Minor names in the White Book reinforce the notion that Nottinghamshire was strongly influenced by speakers of Scandinavian languages. How that influence came about, and how great a number of Scandinavian settlers there were in the area following the establishment of the Danelaw before the Norman Conquest, is still hotly debated; but that there was a significant influence is clear enough.[380] Name elements of Scandinavian origin include the following:

1 **vangr** (Old Norse; ME *wang, wong*) 'piece of enclosed land'
  Goswong', OE **gōs** 'goose', Holme **62, 63**
  Longbuskwong', ON **lang** 'long', **buskr** 'bush, thicket', Norwell **375**
  Newcrosse wong', ME 'new cross', Norwell **375**
  Oatewong, OE **āte** 'oats', Norwell **375**
  Polewong', OE **pōl** 'pond, pool', Norwell **375**
  Nabwong', ON **nabbi** 'knoll', Norwell **375**
  Hallewonge, OE **hall** 'hall', Norwell **388**
  Redwonge, OE **hrēod** 'reed', Southwell **279**
  le Vinerwong, ME **viner** 'vineyard', Sutton **473, 474**

By far the largest concentration of these names is in Norwell (not all of which are listed here), and in the 1406 document **375**. One name in Southwell from the early thirteenth century, *Redwong*, appears in 1296 as *le Redewang'* (**276**).

2. **eng** 'meadow, pasture' is distributed quite widely and includes the following:
  Tweryng', ON **þverr** 'lying across', Beckingham **403**
  Damfesteyng', OE ***damm** 'dam' + OE **fæst** 'rampart', Caunton **379**
  Wrongeng', OE **wrang** 'crooked', Holme **63**

---

[379] As is the common practice among toponymists, A. H. Smith, *English Place-Name Elements*, 2 vols, EPNS 25–6 (Cambridge, 1956) has been used. This normalises elements to the language of literary Old Norse-Icelandic. Old Danish was, however, the major influence on the names in the White Book; work on Old Danish toponyms continues. Elements are generally etymologised, and the abbreviation OE (Old English) does not mean the particular name dates from Anglo-Saxon times; the date of the name can be checked by referring to the document number and the main text. Elements that do not occur outside toponymy are asterisked. Work continues also on the vocabulary of English place-names, David Parsons, with Tania Styles and Carole Hough, *The Vocabulary of English Place-Names* (Nottingham: Centre for English Name-Studies and English Place-Name Society, 1997–), Fascicle 1, *Á–BOX*; 2, *BRACE–CÆSTER*; 3, *CEAFOR–COCKPIT*. Further explanation of minor names comes from John Field, *English Field-Names: A Dictionary* (Newton Abbot, 1972).

[380] For the most comprehensive treatment of the place-name evidence, see Lesley Abrams and David N. Parsons, 'Place-names and the History of Scandinavian Settlement in England', in J. Hines, A. Lane and M. Redknap, eds, *Land, Sea and Home: Proceedings of a Conference on Viking-Period Settlement, at Cardiff, July 2001* (Leeds, 2004), 379–431. For a summary of the history of the debate, see Matthew Townend, 'Scandinavian Place-names in England', in Jayne Carroll and David Parsons, eds, *Perceptions of Place: Twenty-First-Century Interpretations of English Place-Name Studies* (Nottingham, 2013).

Prestereng', OE **prēost** (genitive plural *prēosta*) 'priest', Normanton
    541
Southyng', OE **sūð** 'south', Norwell **387**
Longbuskenge, ON **lang** 'long', **buskr** 'bush, thicket' (cf. *Longbusk-
    wong* above), Norwell **388**
Northyng', OE **norð** 'north', Norwell **375, 377**
Rilandynge, ME **ryland** 'rye fields', Norwell **388**
Gret enge, OE **grēat** 'wide', Upton **303**
Overpresting', OE **uferra** 'higher' + **prēost** 'priest', Upton **540**

3. **holmr** 'raised ground in marsh, water meadow'
Halumholme, p.n. Halam, Halam **281**
le Milne Holme, OE **myln** 'mill', Holme **63** (see also (*le*) *Mylneholm*,
    Southwell **266, 305**)
Roholme, possibly OE **rūh** 'rough', Norwell **378**
Halleholme, OE **hall** 'hall', Norwell **375**
Holmis, *lez Holme*, 'the holmes', Southwell **269, 549**
Ryholm, OE **ryge** 'rye', Sutton **474, 492**
Burneholme, OE **burna** 'stream', Upton **541**[381]

4. **vrá** 'corner of land'.
(*le*) *Cocstretewroe*, possibly OE **cocc** 'woodcock' + **strǣt** 'street',
    Normanton **539**[382]
Swynstihewro, OE **swīn** 'pig' + **stigu** 'sty', Normanton **536** (variants
    539, 541)
Swynshaghwroo, OE **swīn** 'pig' + **haga** 'enclosure', Norwell **388**
Cattewroe, OE **catt** 'wild cat', Upton **450**

5. **bekkr** 'stream'
Mykelbek', ON **mikill** 'big', Caunton **379**
le Bek', Norwell **388**
Fulwudebec', OE **fūl** 'foul, muddy' + **wudu** 'wood', Rolleston **136**
Mortonbek', p.n. Morton (OE **mōr** 'wasteland' + **tūn** 'farm'), Southwell
    266

Less commonly occurring elements of Scandinavian origin include **kjarr**
'brushwood marsh' (*Le Karre*, Norwell **388**; *Nunnekere*, OE **nunne** 'nun',
Sherwood Forest **106**), **kirkja** 'church' (*Kyrkbrigg'*, *le Kyrkbrygg*, Caunton
377, 378; *le Kyrkecrofte*, Southwell **264**), **toft** 'building plot' (*le Halletoft*,
OE **hall** 'hall', Eaton **60**), **þveit** 'clearing' (*Mekilthueyt*, ON **mikill** 'big',
Southwell **518**), **konungr** 'king' (*Coningeswath* and variants, ON **vað** 'ford',
Sherwood Forest **23, 106, 349**; *Conyngeslound'*, ON **lundr** 'grove', Sutton
492), ***hvin** 'gorse, whin' (*Whynnylandes* Southwell **542, 543**).
    These elements entered the ordinary vocabulary and Scandinavian pro-
nunciations were heard quite generally. In Edingley, *Holgatebusk* **172, 173**,
and elsewhere, the **busk** 'bush, thicket' element may be Scandinavian or it
may be a Scandinavianised pronunciation of OE **busc** (pronounced 'bush').

---

[381] PN Nt 276 notes '**burna** has only been noted in *Kettleburne* 1609 [in Nottinghamshire]'.
This name antedates that significantly.
[382] This might possibly be a variant of ***cocc-scīete** 'place where woodcock fly, or where
nets are stretched to catch woodcock'.

In Sherwood Forest, an area with clear Scandinavian names, *Raynwathforth* 'Rainworth ford' **349**, has been partially Scandinavianised by the pronunciation of the English element **worð** 'enclosure' as if it were ON **vað** 'ford', and the English element **ford** appears in the northern form *forth* (EPNE **I** 180). By contrast, Southwell has an early (mid-thirteenth century, **518**) Scandinavian name *Mekilberk*, ON **mikill** 'big' + **birki** 'birch tree', later adapted to a more English pronunciation, *Mekillberch* (mid-fourteenth century, **519**), with OE **birce** (pronounced 'birch'). Many of these elements also occur in the major names, and the Scandinavian influence on nomenclature is undeniable.

Flora

A wide range of flora is found in the minor names. The following list does not contain every example, but a representative sample.

OE **æppel** 'apple': *Appulton' wong'* (**æppel-tūn** 'apple orchard') Norwell **375**

OE **æspe** 'aspen': *Espes, Espis* Southwell **399, 414, 518, 519**

OE **āte** 'oats': *Oatewong* Norwell **375**

OE **birce**, ON **birki** 'birch tree': *Mekilberk'*, *Mekillberch'* Southwell **518, 519**

OE **docce** 'dock, water-lily': *Dokedyc* Carlton **39** (OE **dīc** 'ditch, dyke'); *Dockyland* Southwell **266, 269**

ME **flagge** 'reed, rush': *le Flagges* Norwell **388**

ME **hilder-tre** 'elder-tree': *le Hildetrestubbe* (OE **stubb** 'tree-stump') Holme **575**

OE **hrēod** 'reed': *Redegate* (probably ON **gata** 'road, way') Norwell South Field **388**; *le Redewang'*, *Redwonge* (ON **vangr** 'an enclosed piece of land') Southwell **276, 279**

ON ***hvin** 'whin, gorse': *Whynnylandes* Southwell **542, 543**

OE **līn** 'flax': *Lynelandes* Holme **575**

OE **pese** 'pease': *Peseland'* Holme **575**, *Peselandtoung'* (OE **tunge**, ON **tunga** 'a tongue of land') Holme **575**

OE **ryge** 'rye': *Rilands* Norwell **388**; *Ryland'* Southwell **266, 269**; *Rilandynge* (ON **eng** 'meadow') Norwell **388**; *Ryholm* (ON **holmr** 'raised land in marsh') Sutton on Trent **474, 492**

OE **salh** 'willow, sallow': *Selegh'* Sherwood Forest **106**

OE **secg** 'sedge': *Seggesdale, Seggisdale* Rolleston **237, 238, 239, 240, 241**

OE **þorn** 'thorn': OE **þyrne**, ON **þyrnir** 'thorn bush': *Thyrin* Caunton **379**; *Marthorn'*, *Merthorne* (OE **mere** 'pool, lake') Halam **281, 317, 516**; *le Haggethorn'* (OE **hagu-þorn** 'hawthorn, white thorn') Normanton **534**, *Thirneclive, Tirneclive* (OE **clif** 'cliff, bank') Willoughby in Walesby **234, 235, 236**

OE ***wilig** 'willow', *Willowedale, Willwedale* Morton **512, 513**; *le Wilewes, Willowes* Barnby in the Willows **14, 147, 228**

The list above is remarkable for the fact that it contains relatively few elements that we would think of as crops (apples, oats, flax, pease and rye), and these are predominantly hardy crops. There are several mills recorded in the names, however (*Estmilne*, OE **ēast** 'east', *le Milne Holme*, Holme **62**, **63**; *Mylnefeld'*, ME **feld** 'field', *le Mylnehill'*, *Milnecroft'*, *Milnedam'*, *Milnefurlonge*, Norwell **375**, **387**, **388**; *le Mylnefurlong'*, *le Milne dale*, Caunton **378**, **379**; *le Mylneholm'*, ON **holmr** 'raised land in marsh', *le Milnegate*, Southwell **266**, **305**, **612**).

Other elements reinforce the picture of rather poor arable land: the flora represented in these thirteenth- to fifteenth-century names are plants and trees that are suited to damp land or are found on rough ground. Many names containing the elements OE **dīc**/ON **dík** 'ditch, dyke' (*Longedyke*, Norwell **388**; *Bukhildyk'*, *Bukhildyke*, OE **bucc** 'male deer' + **hyll** 'hill', Southwell **518**, **519**; *Bikeresdich*, ON **bý** 'village' + **kjarr** 'brushwood marsh',[383] Sherwood Forest **106**); OE **mōr**, here most likely 'wet wasteland' (*Aldemore*, OE **ald** 'old', Ordsall **60**; *Fowreacremore*, 'four-acre', *Longemor* OE **long** 'long', *le Morefeld'*, OE **feld** 'open land', all Norwell **388**; *le Mikelmore*, ON **mikill** 'big', Eaton **60**; *le Morehill'*, Southwell **537**, **538**, **605**); OE **sīc**/ON **sík** 'stream, drainage channel' (*Frithsyk'*, *Frythsyke*, OE **fyrhð** 'scrubland', Southwell **266**, **549**; *Hokertonsyke*, *Hokyrtonsyke*, p.n. Hockerton, Normanton **549**; *Northwell'syke*, p.n. Norwell, Caunton **379**); alongside *le Merche*, OE **mersc** 'marsh', Sturton le Steeple **233**, and *Flasshefurlonge*, ME **flasshe** 'marsh' + **furlang** 'strip in the common field', Norwell **388**. There are also wells, meres and pools.

Fauna

The following is a list of the fauna found in minor names:

OE **amore** 'bunting': *Amerlandes* Southwell **136**

OE **bucc** 'male deer': *Buchill'*, *(le) Bukhill'*, *Bukhyull'* (OE **hyll** 'hill') Southwell **372**, **512**, **513**, **514**, **518**, **519**, *Bukhildyk'*, *Bukhildyke* (OE **dīc**, ON **dík** 'ditch, dyke') Southwell **518**, **519**; *Bukfordhagh'* (OE **ford** 'ford' + **haga** 'enclosure') Norwell **388**

OE **bulloc** 'young male steer, bullock': *Bullakhagh*, *Bullakhaw* (OE **haga** 'enclosure') Norwell **388**

ME **catel** 'cattle': *Catelcroftewonge* (OE **croft** 'small enclosure', ON **vangr** 'enclosed piece of land') Norwell **375**

OE **catt** 'wild cat': *Cattewroe* (ON **vrá** 'corner of land'), *Catwrofurlonge* (OE **furlang** 'a strip of land') Upton **540**, **549**

OE **cocc** 'woodcock': *le Cocstretewroe* (OE **strǣt** 'paved road, street' + ON **vrá** 'corner of land') Normanton **539**

OE **cū** 'cow': *ye Cowpasture* Norwell **375**

OE **gōs** 'goose': *Goswong'* (ON **vangr** 'enclosed piece of land') Holme **62**, **63**

OE **henn** 'hen, water-hen': *Henbek'*, *Hennebeke* (ON **bekkr** 'stream') Southwell **392**, **395**

OE **heorde-wīc** 'cattle farm': *Herdewik*, *Herdewyk'* Sherwood Forest **106**

---

[383] This is the uncertain etymology proposed in PN Nt 2; more plausible is OE **bīcere** 'beekeeper', thus meaning 'bee-keeper's dyke', and referring to a significant agricultural worker.

OE **hors** 'horse': *le Horsgres* (OE **gærs** 'grass') Holme **63**; *Horspole, Horspoole* Southwell **597, 598, 599, 600, 612**
ME **paddok** 'frog': *Paddokpro* (possibly ON **vrá** 'corner of land', with *p* for OE, ME wynn which looks like a *p*), *Padoc Pit, Padokpitt* (OE **pytt** 'pit, hollow') Rolleston **238, 239**
OE **scēap** 'sheep': ?*Schecotezerde* (OE **cot** 'cottage, shed' + **geard** 'yard') Norwell **375**
OE **swīn** 'pig': *Swyneshede* (OE **hēafod** 'headland') Caunton **378, 379**; *Swynestrehit* (possibly OE **strǣt** 'paved road, street') Southwell **518**; *Swynestyche* (OE **stycce** 'piece of land') Southwell **519**; *Swynesty-hyrne* (OE **stigu** 'sty' + **hyrne** 'angle, corner'), *Swynsteghwro, Swyn-steghwroe, Swynstihewro* (+ ON **vrá** 'corner of land') Upton **536, 539, 541, 549**; *Swynhaw* (OE **haga** 'enclosure'), *Swynshaghwroo* (+ ON **vrá** 'corner of land') Norwell **375, 388**

This list suggests limited resources for pastoral farming. There are cows and cattle, bullocks and livestock, horses, geese and possibly sheep, but the names indicate a predominance of pigs and deer. The deer were hunted, the pigs were grazed on the woodland mast. A range of names reinforces the importance of woodland, and its clearance: *le Ryddyng', le Ryddynges*, OE ***ryding** 'clearing', **373, 375, 377**; *Lowriddynge, Medilriddyng'* and *Netheriddynge* **388**, all in Norwell; *le Stokkes*, OE **stocc** 'tree stump', Caunton **373**; *Prestestubbyng'*, OE **prēost** 'priest' + **stubbing** 'clearing', Edingley **174**. These names are augmented by a large number of toponyms containing OE **lēah** 'grove, clearing'. *Neubotle, Neubotull', Nuebotle*, OE **nīwe** 'new' + **botl** 'dwelling, house', Caunton **379**, represents expansion of the settlement, possibly on land newly cleared.

Other names

Document **223** contains a remarkable concentration of names containing the ME element **thing** 'property' and a personal name: *Beregething', Beregethyng', Danyelthing', Daunserthing', Skynnerthing', Skynnerthyng', Symkynsonthing', Symkynsonthyng', Wallerthing', Wallerthyng* in North Muskham; *Hansonthing', Hansonthyng', Sowterhtyng'* (*sic*), *Sowterthyng'*, in Bathley; and *Grayvethyng', Gybsonthyng'*, in Holme. The personal names are interesting, containing probably surnames from forenames (Daniel, Hanson, Symkynson, Gybson), surnames from occupational terms (Dauncer 'dancer', Skinner 'worker in fur', Waller 'wall-builder'? and Souter, OE **sūtere** 'shoemaker'). Some of these people are mentioned in other documents in the cartulary (for example, Hansons are mentioned in **182** as well as in **223**; John Grafe **378** and William Graue **547** are also mentioned). There are several names formed rather similarly with Old French **place** 'open space in a town': *Jordanplace, Mathewplace, Mathew place, Pekeplace, Wardplace*, all in Norwell **373, 377**.

Norwell had an enclosed plot (ON **vangr**) for its gallows and another plot for burial: *Galowtrewong'*, OE **galg-trēow** 'gallows-tree' is a division in Norwell's North Field, and nearby is *Dedmans wong'*, OE **dēad-mann** 'a corpse', **375**. In **388**, a reference to *Dedmangrave* in the same area of Norwell may refer to a trench for bodies, OE **grǣf** 'trench, grave'. Medieval people were not squeamish about death. They did, however, appear to be wary of water monsters: *Thirsele*, *Yhirsely*, *Yirsley*, between Edingley and Halam **441**, **445**, **446**, most likely represents OE **þyrs** 'giant, water monster' with OE **lēah** 'clearing, grove', a haunted and forbidding place.

It has not been possible here to give a complete analysis of the minor names found in the White Book. This treatment has necessarily been very selective; and of course the White Book itself is selective in a different way, in that it only records materials and names of relevance to Southwell. Nevertheless, this is a unique collection of early names, and it has shown something of the limited range of land configurations, crops and vegetation, animals, and agricultural and domestic uses of the land and its products that formed the medieval estates of St Mary's, Southwell.

Editorial methods

The scale of the White Book, the variety of its contents, the number of different scribes who helped to create it and the long chronological period it covers have provided several problems for its modern editors. In principle, we have tried to reproduce as closely as possible the form of the text as it appears in the volume. However, in order to aid comprehension and readability, some editorial interventions are inevitable, and absolute consistency impracticable and unrealistic. For example, in names of persons or places the initial letters have been capitalised as standard, but in titles (archbishop, bishop ...) and dates of feasts, lower case is normally used apart from capitalisation of the saint's name.[384] If proper/place-names end with an abbreviation sign, these too have been reproduced as written (e.g. Suthwell', Cromwell', Osmundtorp'). Punctuation has been introduced in most documents, e.g. commas to separate names in witness lists, or to make the text more reader-friendly by splitting up clauses, very long sentences or lists of adjectives (like *libere*, *quiete*, *pacifice*, *integre et ...*). In some longer documents, paragraphs and (in a few instances, numbering) have been used to assist comprehension and facilitate reference.

In our transcriptions, v = consonant; u = vowel; i = i and j in Latin (but capital J has normally been used in proper names like *Johannes*). In numbers, what the scribe has written, usually in Roman numerals, has been preserved; where Arabic numerals occur, it is because they do so in the text. In references to money, we have standardised abbreviated £ s d references in the text, following the number in the form xx l xi s viii d. Where *denarius* is written in full, this has been retained. In added editorial material the abbreviations £ s d are used (with twelve (old) pennies to the shilling and twenty shillings (240d) to the pound sterling). Interlineations have been signified in the form \ ... /. If contemporary, this has not usually been commented upon, although if it is later, a footnote or textual reference might be given. Square brackets [...] have been used to indicate editorial interference, whether the addition of a letter or word. In editing early royal or episcopal charters, we have followed some but not all conventions adopted by major modern projects supported by the British Academy like the *English Episcopal Acta* series

---

[384] Among exceptions are Easter and Pentecost.

and the *Acta* of the Anglo-Norman kings Henry I and Henry II currently in progress. Variant readings and comments on other textual matters are normally supplied (with a numerical sequence [1, 2, 3,] etc.) printed immediately after the document concerned. An exception has been made with regard to some major legal documents, where the copies in the White Book have been collated with those enrolled in royal records, and where because of the number of textual variants and the length of the documents, this textual annotation has been supplied in footnote form on relevant pages rather than collectively at the end.[385]

Similarly where original charters or other important contemporary copies survive (especially among the Crown's archives), the copies in the White Book have been collated with them. In the case of originals, the text they supply has been followed, with significant variants in the White Book indicated, likewise where other copies appear to provide better readings. In a few cases, we have even been able to complete a partial entry in the White Book by consulting such additional material. Nevertheless it remains true that for the majority of entries the eccentricities of the different medieval clerks who contributed to compiling the White Book have been allowed to emerge from their individual, sometimes very idiosyncratic, handling of Latin.

Finally, it can be noted that in presenting the documents, we have largely followed the practices adopted by previous recent editors of medieval cartularies, particularly of Nottinghamshire's cartularies like those of Rufford abbey and the priories of Blyth and Thurgarton. Each entry is numbered, and introduced by a short precis of its content and date. Square brackets have been used in giving approximate dates, or their limits, for undated charters. Then follows the text, followed by the textual notes,[386] a separate mention of relevant marginalia, discussion of any dating issues, and a note on earlier editions. Places and persons mentioned are also identified where possible, and some commentary on content or other aspects of the document concerned may be offered. No attempt has been made to be comprehensive in these miscellaneous notes, many of which could easily be expanded. That, however, would be an unwarrantable exploitation of the generosity of our patron, the Pipe Roll Society, which has already indulged us to the extent of issuing this edition in two volumes.

---

[385] Following a convention still used by lawyers, only minimal punctuation has been introduced into some of these legal documents like the Quo warranto proceedings (**14–16**, **145–7**).
[386] Apparatus appears at the end of each text, except **14–16** and **145–7**, which have footnotes for each page of text.

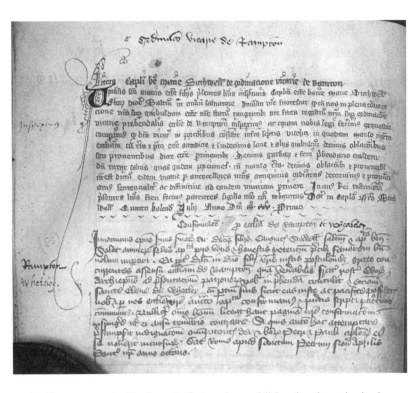

1. Scribe 1, upper half of p. 38 (**82**) and an addition by the principal supplementing scribe, Scribe 4 (**83**), reduced (for discussion see pp. xxxiii, xxxv–xxxvi) © The Dean and Chapter of Southwell Minster

2. Scribe 3's first entry, p. 293, lines 2–9 (**390**), reduced (for discussion see pp. xxxiv, xxxvi) © The Dean and Chapter of Southwell Minster

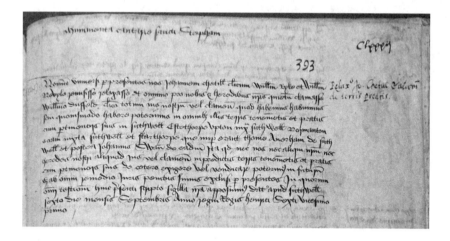

3. Scribe 7: p. 393, lines 1–13 (**545**), and heading in the upper margin, which is also in his hand, reduced (for discussion see pp. xxxiv, xxxv, xxxvii)
© The Dean and Chapter of Southwell Minster

4. Middle p. 71 (**147**), where a hand drawn in the margin, probably in the fifteenth century, points out that the canons, pleading before the justices in eyre in 1331, claimed after discussion among themselves that they held their prebends separately and not in common.
© The Dean and Chapter of Southwell Minster

5a–d. Impressions of the Chapter's seal: a, b and c, three late twelfth-century impressions attached to Rufford abbey charters (Nottinghamshire Archives, DDSR 102 nos 29, 134 and 140, published by kind permission of the Trustees of the Savile Estate); an impression of 1540 when Henry VIII suppressed the Chapter, The National Archives, E 328/80 (by permission; for description and discussion see pp. xxxix–xli)

6. Archbishop Walter Gray's ordinance concerning the patronage of the church of Barnburgh, given to the Chapter of Southwell by Mr Robert of Laxton, Oxton, 9 October 1241 (Lincolnshire Archives, Cragg MS 4/36; see **460**)

7. Second version of Archbishop Walter Gray's ordinance concerning the patronage of Barnburgh church, London, 29 January 1242 (Lincolnshire Archives, Cragg MS 4/20 (formerly 21); see Appendix A, A1)

8. Lease by the Chapter of Southwell to Sir Henry of Staythorpe, his sister and brother, of four acres of land in Southwell, 3 September 1296 (Lincolnshire Archives, Cragg MS 3/19; see 279)

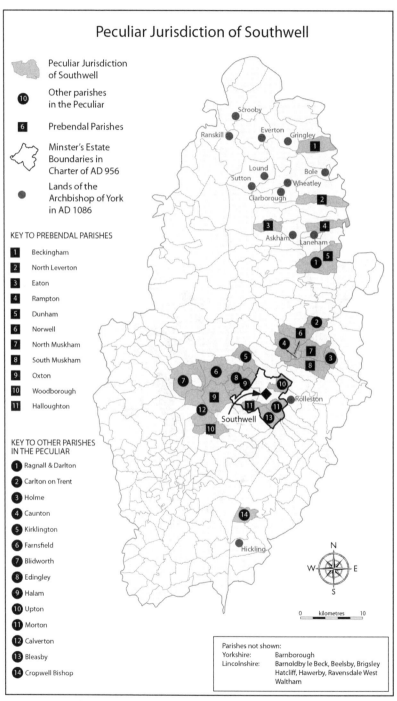

Peculiar Jurisdiction of Southwell

Peculiar Jurisdiction of Southwell

10 — Other parishes in the Peculiar

6 — Prebendal Parishes

Minster's Estate Boundaries in Charter of AD 956

Lands of the Archbishop of York in AD 1086

KEY TO PREBENDAL PARISHES

1 Beckingham
2 North Leverton
3 Eaton
4 Rampton
5 Dunham
6 Norwell
7 North Muskham
8 South Muskham
9 Oxton
10 Woodborough
11 Halloughton

KEY TO OTHER PARISHES IN THE PECULIAR

1 Ragnall & Darlton
2 Carlton on Trent
3 Holme
4 Caunton
5 Kirklington
6 Farnsfield
7 Blidworth
8 Edingley
9 Halam
10 Upton
11 Morton
12 Calverton
13 Bleasby
14 Cropwell Bishop

Scrooby
Ranskill Everton Gringley
Lound Bole
Sutton Wheatley
Clarborough
Askham Laneham
Rolleston
Southwell
Hickling

N
W — E
S

0 kilometres 10

Parishes not shown:
Yorkshire: Barnborough
Lincolnshire: Barnoldby le Beck, Beelsby, Brigsley
                Hatcliff, Hawerby, Ravensdale West
                Waltham

9. The Peculiar Jurisdiction of Southwell and the estates of the Archbishop of York in Nottinghamshire in the Middle Ages. © Sue Sinclair

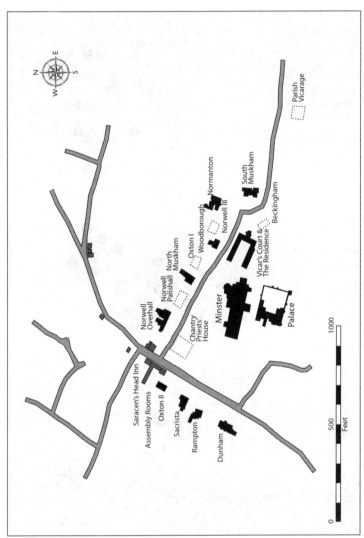

10. The Prebendage, Southwell, showing the principal medieval buildings surrounding the Minster. © Sue Sinclair

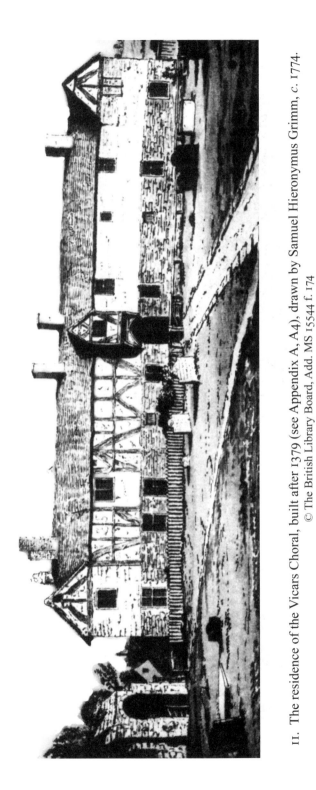

11. The residence of the Vicars Choral, built after 1379 (see Appendix A, A4), drawn by Samuel Hieronymus Grimm, *c.* 1774.

12. The college of the chantry priests, built after 1415 (see Appendix A, A6), drawn by Samuel Hieronymus Grimm, c. 1774. © The British Library Board, Add. MS 15544 f. 172

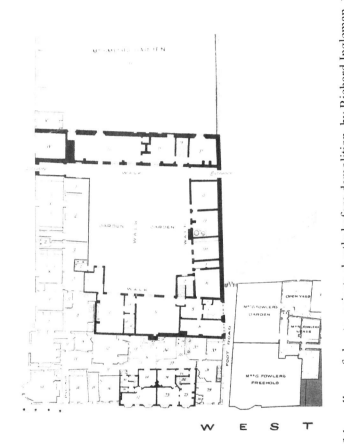

13. Plan of the college of chantry priests shortly before demolition, by Richard Ingleman, 1818 (Nottinghamshire Archives, MS Accession 7251)

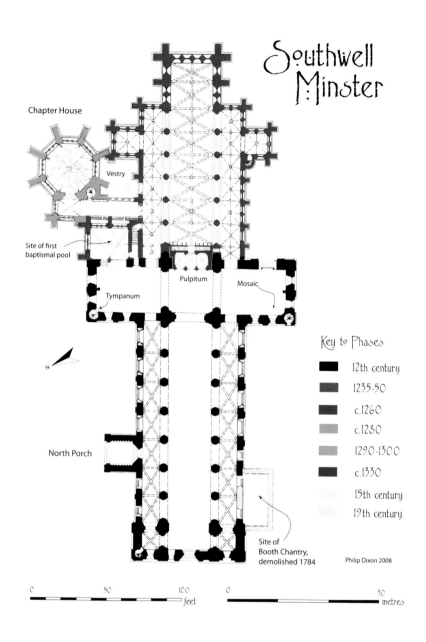

Chapter House

Vestry

Site of first
baptismal pool

Pulpitum

Mosaic

Tympanum

Key to Phases

■ 12th century
■ 1235-50
■ c.1260
■ c.1280
■ 1290-1300
■ c.1330
  15th century
  19th century

North Porch

Site of
Booth Chantry,
demolished 1784

Philip Dixon 2008

Southwell Minster

N

0   50   100
feet

0   50
metres

14. Plan of the Minster, showing the main phases of construction
© Philip Dixon

THE WHITE BOOK OF SOUTHWELL

Nottinghamshire Archives, SC/7/1/1

As currently bound, there are two preliminary parchment sheets (A, B) before the first folio of the White Book, containing information on its display in legal proceedings in cases concerning the Chapter before the Exchequer on 30 September 1833 (B[r]) and Chancery on 4 April 1838 (A[v]), together with some sixteenth–seventeenth-century notes (B[v]); see also **Introduction**, pp. xlvi–xlvii.

PAPAL LETTERS, 1–13

1   *Pope Alexander III takes the canons and church of St Mary, South-well, into the protection of St Peter and himself and confirms that the church is to have the same privileges as the church of York has had from ancient times and which have been confirmed by kings of England in various charters, threatening with excommunication any parishioners who damage lands and houses of the Chapter; any who commit violence in the cemetery or who take things from houses will incur ecclesiastical sanction; no one who commits such offences and is condemned by the Chapter will be pardoned without its licence; all prebendal churches and what is held in common [by the Chapter] shall be free from any interference by the Archbishop or Chapter of York in accordance with earlier grants of privilege; also, following earlier practice, the clergy and laity of Nottinghamshire are permitted to process peacefully to the church at Pentecost to receive the Chrism from the deans of the county; also in accord with ancient custom, whenever any canon of the church dies or changes his style of life, with the advice of the Chapter, a year of his income shall be distributed for the good of his soul or to pay his debts; stern admonitions against any who infringe these rights are threatened*
Tusculum, 28 July 1171

Bulla Alexandri [pape][1] de libertatibus et consuetudinibus capituli p. 1
ecclesie beate Marie Suthwellie

Alexander episcopus servus servorum Dei dilectis filiis canonicis ecclesie sancte Marie de Suwell' tam presentibus quam futuris canonice substitutis IN PERPETUUM. Ad hoc sumus ad universarum ecclesiarum regimen licet insufficientibus meritis superna providentia deputati, ut singularum commodis et profectibus propensiori studio debeamus intendere et pro ipsarum statu in pigra solicitudine vigilare ne a superno patre familias negligentie[2] merito possimus redargui, si circa ecclesiarum regimen minus, quod absit, fuerimus diligentes. Ea propter dilecti in domino filii vestris iustis

postulationibus clementer annuimus, et prefatam ecclesiam sancte Marie in
\qua/ divino estis obsequio mancipati sub beati Petri et nostra protectione
suscipimus et presentis scripti privilegio communimus. Statuentes ut
quascumque possessiones quecumque bona eadem ecclesia in presentiarum
iuste et canonice possidet aut in futurum concessione pontificum, largitione
regum vel principum, oblatione fidelium seu aliis iustis modis prestante
domino poterit adipisci firma vobis vestrisque successoribus et illibata
permaneant. Preterea antiquas libertatum consuetudines illas videlicet
quas Eboracensis ecclesia ab antiquo habuisse et adhuc habere dinoscitur[3]
sicut eas vobis et ecclesie vestre archiepiscopi, capitulum Ebor' et
illustres Anglorum reges pia et rationabili providentia indulserunt, et
suis scriptis autenticis confirmarunt auctoritate duximus apostolica
confirmandas sub interminatione anathematis infringere aut contra eas in
aliquo temeraria presumptione venire. Ad hec adicientes statuimus ut si
aliquis parochianorum vobis in terris vel domibus aut rebus aliis ad vestram
ecclesiam pertinentibus violentiam seu ruinam irrogare presumpserit
liceat nobis in eum absque alicuius contradictione excommunicationis
sententiam promulgare.[4] Ceterum si quis parochianorum vestrorum vel
etiam parochianorum Ebor' ecclesie infra cimiterium ecclesie vestre in
aliquem violentes manus iniecerit aut ipsum inde vel a domibus vestris
violenter extraxerit seu contra pacem ecclesie in eisdem indultum censura
ecclesiastica cohercere. Prohibemus insuper ut qui a vobis sicut dictum
est pro suis excessibus et iniuriis ecclesie vestre et vobis illatis vinculo
fuerint interdicti vel anathematis innodati nulli facultas vel licentia pateat
eis absolutionis beneficium exhibere nisi prius super hiis inde a vobis
interdicti vel excommunicati sunt congrue vobis et ecclesie vestre fuerit
satisfactum. Nichilominus etiam presentis scripti decreto sanctimus ut
ecclesie prebendarum et communionis[5] ab omni iure et consuetudine
episcopali libere sint penitus et immunes et in eisdem ecclesiis vobis liceat
vicarios idoneos[6] absque aliqua contradictione instituere sicut Eboracenses
archiepiscopi et capitulum id vobis et predecessoribus vestris permisisse
noscuntur et in presentiarum in ecclesia Ebor' et vestra pacifice observantur.
Preterea quemadmodum ab eisdem archiepiscopis vobis concessum est
et longa consuetudine observatum statuimus ut tam clerici quam laici[7]
comitatus de Notingham syre in Pentecosten ad ecclesiam vestram cum
sollempni processione accedant et annis singulis ibidem iuxta antiquam
et rationabilem ipsius ecclesie consuetudinem synodus celebretur et illuc
crisma per decanos illius comitatus ab Eboracensi ecclesie deferatur per
alias inde ecclesias distribuendum. Illud etiam sicut antiqua et rationabili
consuetudine noscitur observatum et inconcussum de cetero manere
censemus quod videlicet cum aliquis canonicorum vestrorum decesserit vel
habitum et vitam mutaverit redditus qui ad ipsum eodem anno spectarent
pro anima eius aut etiam solutione debitorum suorum cum consilio capituli
distribuatur. Decernimus ergo ut nulli omnino hominum liceat memoratam
ecclesiam temere perturbare, aut eius possessiones auferre, vel ablatas
retinere, minuere seu quibuslibet vexationibus fatigare sed omnia integra
conserventur eorum pro quorum gubernatione aut sustentatione concessa
sunt usibus omnimodis profutura salva sedis apostolice auctoritate et
Eboracen' archiepiscopi canonica iustitia et debita reverentia. Si qua igitur

in futurum ecclesiastica secularisve persona hanc nostre constitutionis paginam sciens contra eam temere venire temptaverit secundo tertiove commonita nisi reatum suum digna satisfactione correxerit[8] potestatis honorisque sui dignitate careat ream que se divino iudicio existere de perpetrata iniquitate cognoscat et a sanctissimo corpore et sanguine Dei et domini redemptoris nostri Jesu Cristi aliena fiat atque in extremo examine districte ultioni subiaceat. Cunctis autem eidem loco sua iura servantibus sit pax domini nostri Jesu Cristi quatinus et hic fructum[9] bone actionis percipiant et apud districtum iudicem premia eterne pacis inveniant. AMEN. | Datum Tusculani per manum Gratiani sancte Romane ecclesie p. 2 subdiaconi et notarii quinto kalendas Augusti indictione iiii incarnationis dominice anno m° c° lxx° i° pontificatus vero domini Alexandri pape[10] tertii anno duodecimo.

[1] *pape* erased   [2] MS *necligentie*   [3] MS *denoscitur*   [4] *promulgare* rewritten by same scribe over an erasure   [5] MS *comunionis*   [6] MS *ydoneos*   [7] MS *layci*   [8] MS *corexerit*   [9] MS *futurum*   [10] *pape* has been erased

Margin   As noted in the **Introduction**, pp. xxxiii, xxxv, in the White Book pp. 1–61 (**1–137**) rubrics and texts are all in the same 14th-c. hand (= Scribe 1), unless otherwise mentioned. Here several brief headings, some now illegible, have been added in an early modern hand (or hands) in the right margin: *(1160) Ric. i; possessiones; Libertates; Exemptio prebendalibus . . . synodalis ; Annis.*

Note   Several later medieval and early modern copies of this bull survive, all after **1**, among them one found in Thoroton's notes (NA, M 494, f. 105r–v; see also **Introduction**, p. li). Pd. in *Mon. Ang.*, vi, pt iii, 1313 (iii) and Migne, *PL*, 200, 731–2; mentioned in *PUE*, ii, 108 = JL 11899.

2   *Urban IV confirms the liberties and immunities of the Chapter of the church of Southwell*   Viterbo, 28 October 1261

Urbanus episcopus servus servorum dei dilectis filiis capitulo ecclesie Suwellen' \Eboracen'/ dyocesis salutem et apostolicam benedictionem. Justis petentium desideriis dignum est nos facilem prebere consensum et vota que a rationis tramite non discordant effectu prosequente complere. Eapropter dilecti in domino[1] vestris iustis postulationibus grato concurrentes assensu omnes libertates et immunitates a Romanis pontificibus predecessoribus nostris vobis vel ecclesie vestre concessas necnon libertates et exemptiones secularium exactionum a regibus et principibus ac aliis Cristi fidelibus rationabiliter vobis ac ecclesie predicte indultas sicut eas iuste et pacifice optinetis vobis et per vos eidem ecclesie auctoritate apostolica confirmamus et presentis scripti patrocinio communimus. Nulli ergo omnino homini liceat hanc paginam nostre confirmationis infringere vel ei ausu temerario contraire. Si quis autem hoc attemptare presumpserit indignationem omnipotentis Dei et beatorum Petri et Pauli apostolorum eius se noverit incursurum. Datum Viterbii quinto kalendas Novembris pontificatus nostri anno primo.

[1] MS omits *filii*

Margin   *Confirmatio libertatum et immunitat' Urban .3. 1185* (16th–17th c.)

Date In spite of the marginal note this must be a bull of Urban IV, who was at Viterbo in October and also in November 1261; Urban III was at Verona for all of 1186, including October. We have used the standard lists of papal bulls (Jaffé and Potthast) and calendars of papal records to establish papal movements here and elsewhere.

Note Repeated with only small textual variants as **8** below. This bull is not listed in Potthast.

3 *Innocent III confirms Alexander III's bull (1) granting various privileges to the canons of St Mary's, Southwell*

Lateran Palace, Rome, 13 March 1202

Innocentius episcopus servus servorum Dei dilectis filiis canonicis sancte Marie de Suwell' salutem et apostolicam benedictionem. Solet annuere sedes apostolica piis votis et honestis petentium precibus favorem benivolum impertiri. Eapropter, dilecti in domino filii vestri iustis postulationibus grato concurrentes assensu, libertates et immunitates ecclesie vestre a bone memorie Alexandro papa predecessore nostro concessas, sicut in eius privilegio continetur, ratas precipimus et inviolabiliter observari et eas autoritate apostolica confirmamus et presentis scripti patrocinio communimus. Nulli ergo omnino homini licitum sit[1] hanc nostre paginam confirmationis infringere vel ei ausu temerario contraire. Siquis autem hoc attemptare presumpserit, indignationem omnipotentis Dei et beatorum Petri et Pauli apostolorum eius se noverit incursurum. Datum Laterani, iii idus Martii pontificatus nostri anno quinto.

[1] *Sic* for *liceat*

Margin *Confirmatio similis Innocent III 1202* (16ᵗʰ–17ᵗʰ c.)

Note Cal. in Cheney and Cheney, no. 395, and pd. p. 229 (with omissions). Not listed in Potthast.

4 *Alexander III informs the archdeacon, rural dean and other clergy of Nottinghamshire that they should render to the church of Southwell, for which he is making suitable provision, any customary dues and particularly to respect its ancient rights with regard to the Pentecostal procession, warning the archdeacon and his officials not to infringe these rights on pretext of carrying out visitations* Tusculum, 15 July [1171]

Alexander episcopus servus servorum Dei dilectis filiis archidiacono decano et ceteris clericis de Notingham[s]yra salutem et apostolicam benedictionem. Cum suscepti regiminis et caritatis offici[o][1] promovemur pro ecclesiarum statu satagere singulis Dei ecclesiis dignitates et iura sua attenta solicitudine conservare, inde est quod nos ecclesie de Suwell' in iure et dignitate sua providere volentes, universitati vestre per apostolica scripta percipiendo mandamus quatinus eidem ecclesie debitum et consuetum honorem et reverentiam impendatis quam antecessores nostri et nos ipsi ei hactenus exhibuisse noscimini et eiusdem ecclesie iura et antiquas libertates consuetudines in crismate ab Eboracen' ecclesia ante Pasca ad antedictam ecclesiam per vos, filii, decano[2] deferendo et inde per alias ecclesias et monasteria[3] illius archidiaconatus more solito distribuendo et ad annuam synodum statuto tempore et ad processionem in Pentecosten sollempniter de more conveniendo et in aliis illesas et integras conserveris.

Tibi vero, archidiacone, auctoritate apostolica prohibemus ne tu vel officiales clerici tui ecclesias seu clericos eiusdem archidiaconatus sub pretextu visitationis aut frequentie[4] capitulorum conventus indebite gravare temptetis ne magna et sumptuosa comitiva vobis faciatis de paupertate clericorum per suas ecclesias preparari nec ab eisdem clericis in debitum pretium pro | redimendis hospitiis contra sanctorum patrum statuta ac antecessorum vestrorum consuetudinem exigatis. Set secundum loci facultatem ubi ratio postulaverit ita receptionem vestram moderari curetis quod visitatio vestra magis eis grata esse debeat quam dampnosa. Clericis quoque predictis discretos et honestos decanos providere studeatis qui eos videantur conversatione et moribus informare et qui non tam commodum temporaliter quam morum correctionem et profectum exigant animarum. Provideatis autem attentius ut ita preceptum nostrum in hac parte exequi videamini quod nulla exinde ad verbum vos ad nos debeat perferri querela. Quia si nobis in hoc inobedientes fueritis inobedientiam vestram auctore divino dure animadversionis curabimus verbere castigare. Datum Tusculani idus Julii.

p. 3

[1] The final letter has been erased   [2] MS *decretali* after correction from *dec--*   [3] MS *monasterea*   [4] MS *freqhentie*

Margin   *Alexander the 4th 1254*   *Synodus* (16th–17th c.)

Note   Also copied for Thoroton (NA, M 494, f. 105v–106r). Pd. in *Mon. Ang.*, vi, iii, 1314 (iv) and Migne, *PL*, 200, 731–2, mentioned in *PUE*, ii, 108 = JL 11898, 15 July [1171]. Since **1** and **4** were issued within a fortnight of each other, this suggests that a representative of the Chapter had been sent to Rome to collect bulls (cf. **Introduction**, p. liii).

5   *Innocent III delegates [Geoffrey], archbishop of York, the prior of Newstead (Notts.) and Mr Richard de Vassel to investigate a complaint of the canons of Southwell (who had previously appealed unsuccessfully to the archbishop of Canterbury), that the canons of Launde (Leics.) were in arrears with a rent of 20s because the villeins* (coloni) *holding the lands were arguing in court that they were not customarily obliged to pay*
Lateran, [Rome], 11 May [1200]

Innocentius episcopus servus servorum Dei venerabili fratri Eboracen' archiepiscopo et dilectis filiis priori de Novo Loco et magistro Ricardo de Vasselo[1] salutem et apostolicam benedictionem. Porrectam nobis dilectorum filiorum fratrum de Suwell' recepimus questionem, quod[2] canonici de Landa quandam ipsorum terram pro viginti solidis annuis detinerent, quoniam coloni terre ipsius eos coram tam dictis fratribus arguerunt inde de terra eadem debitam custodiam non gerebant. Canonici ad venerabilem fratrem nostrum Cantuariensem archiepiscopum frustratorie appellarunt, qui causam quibusdam commisit[3] fine[4] debito terminandam. Delegati vero canonicorum contumacia deprehensa in custodiam terre prescripte capitulum induxerunt, set canonici cum priore suo in terram nichilominus irruentes, post appellationem ad nos igitur[5] nullus premittere debeat ultionem. Discretioni vestre per apostolica scripta mandamus quatinus canonicos memoratos ad satisfactionem de dampnis et iniuriis nominato capitulo interrogatis[6] congruam exhibendam monitione premissa per censuram ecclesiasticam, appellatione remota, prout iustum fuerit compellatis, nullis literis veritati et iustitie preiudicantibus a sede apostolica impetratis. Quod si omnes hiis exequendis nequiveritis interesse tu frater archiepiscope cum eorum altero ea nichilominus exequaris. Datum Lateran' v idus Maii pontificatus nostri anno tertio.

[1] Cheney and Cheney, 216, no. 232 suggest *Basselo*, commenting reading is doubtful; comparisons with other capital Bs and Vs by Scribe 1 clearly indicates V is correct   [2] Cheneys suggest followed by *cum*   [3] and state that this MS reads *comisit*   [4] MS *sine*   [5] Cheneys note MS 'reads *g[i] nullus promittere debeant ultionem*; probably some words are missing and the rest corrupt'   [6] Cheneys read *irrogatis*

Margin   *Terra capituli quam valoris in Landa 20s* (16th–17th c.)

Note   Pd. in Cheney and Cheney, 216, no. 232, 11 May 1200 (with omissions), but not in Potthast. Geoffrey Plantagenet, archbishop of York (1189–1212); Aldred, prior of Newstead (c. 1186–before 1215) and Walkelin, prior of Launde (c. 1186–1201/2), *HRH*, i, 169–70, 177; Richard de Vasselo does not occur in *Fasti 1066–1300*, nor in Emden. The Chapter's case against Launde is not mentioned in Sayers, *Papal Judges*.

6   *Innocent III delegates [William], subdean [of Lincoln], the archdeacon of Northampton and Mr Walter Blund, canon of Lincoln, to investigate claims by the canons of Southwell that many of their possessions in the dioceses of York and Lincoln are being unjustly occupied by clerics and laymen who refuse to acknowledge the rights of the canons*
                                     St Peter's, Rome, 6 April 1205

Innocentius episcopus servus servorum Dei dilectis filiis subdecano, archidiacono Norhanton', et magistro Waltero Blundo canonico Lincolnien' salutem et apostolicam benedictionem. Ex parte dilectorum filiorum canonicorum Suwellensium nos accepisse noscatis[1] quod cum plures possessiones habeant et prebendas, quidam viri religiosi et alii tam clerici quam laici Eboracensis et Lincolniensis diocesum plura beneficia que ad dictas prebendas et possessiones pertinere noscuntur contra iustitiam detinent occupata. Quo circa discretioni vestre per apostolica scripta mandamus quatinus detentores ipsos, ut beneficia ipsa cum satisfactione congrua subtractorum restituant conquerentibus ut tenentur, monitione premissa, per censuram ecclesiasticam appellatione remota cogatis, nullis literis veritati et iustitie preiudicantibus si que apparuerint a sede apostolica impetrate.[2] Quod si non omnes hiis exequendis potueritis interesse duo vestrum ea nichilominus exequantur. Datum Rome apud Sanctum Petrum, octavo idus Aprilis pontificatus nostri anno octavo.

[1] MS *noscaris*   [2] MS *impetrare*

Margin   *Contra detentoris possessiones* (16th–17th c.)

Note   Cal. in Cheney and Cheney, 102 no. 613, and pd. p. 245 (with omissions); not in Potthast. William of Bramfield, subdean of Lincoln, c. 1200–25 September 1205; Mr Walter Blund, senior, prebendary of Louth by 1183/4, dead by February 1208 (*Fasti*

1066–1300, i, 80, 84). The archdeacon of Northampton is probably Mr Robert de Man-
ecestre (= Mancetter, Warwicks., or Manchester, Lancs.), in office before 25 June 1206,
and as R. archdeacon mentioned in papal letters of 24 April 1205 (ibid., 31 and Cheney
and Cheney, no. 472).

7 *Urban IV, in response to a petition from the Chapter, confirms to it
the donation by Ralph son of Odo, a layman, of his right of patronage
over the church of Bunny (Notts.)* Viterbo, 28 October 1261

Urbanus episcopus servus servorum Dei dilectis filiis capitulo ecclesie
Suwellen' Eboracen' diocesis salutem et apostolicam benedictionem.
Cum a nobis petitur quod iustum est et honestum tam equitatis quam
ordo exigit rationis ut id per solicitudinem officii nostri ad debitum
perducat effectum. Exhibita nobis siquidem vestra petitio continebat
quod quondam Radulfus filius Odonis laicus Eboracen' dyocesis ius
patronatus quod ipse tunc in ecclesia de Boneya eiusdem dyocesis
optinebat de assensu dyocesani loci vobis pia et provida liberalitate
donavit prout in patentibus literis confectis inde plenius contineri. Nos
itaque vestris supplicationibus inclinati quod ab | eodem Radulpho super   p. 4
hoc pie et provide factum est ratum et firmum[1] habentes id auctoritate
apostolica confirmamus et presentis scripti patrocinio communimus.
Nulli ergo omnino homini liceat hanc paginam nostre confirmationis
infringere vel ei ausu temerario contraire. Si quid autem hoc attemptare
presumpserit indignationem omnipotentis dei et beatorum Petri et Pauli
apostolorum eius se noverit incursurum. Datum Viterbii v kalendas
Novembris pontificatus nostri anno primo.

[1] MS *futurum*, but note above in rather later hand saying *firmum*

Margin *Boney advo[catio]* (16th–17th c.)

Note Not in Potthast; for another bull of Urban IV in favour of Southwell on this day,
see **2**, repeated in **8**. Below this item the following papal documents and the ones on p. 5
have large cross-marks across them; this makes several words hard to read, especially in
the two final items on p. 5. It is not clear when Ralph son of Odo made his donation. At
Domesday, Ralph FitzHubert held the manor of Bunny, and in Henry I's reign his son
Odo held 'much land hereabouts' (Thoroton, i, 85; *Domesday People*, 340). If Ralph the
donor were this Odo's son, his grant would have been made in the mid or later twelfth
century. Unfortunately it conflicted with an earlier gift by Odo of Bunny who, shortly
after its foundation 1102 × 1108, granted two-thirds of his demesne tithes to Lenton priory.
This led to uncertainty in determining which lands in Bunny owed tithe to Lenton and
which to Southwell (Thoroton, i, 86), as well as over who possessed the advowson, as
the Chapter's petition to Urban IV to confirm their rights over presentation to Bunny
shows. Over the next eighty years or so, there were frequent disputes between the
Chapter, the priory of Lenton and the lay lord of the manor of Bunny over presentation,
before the Chapter accepted the sale by Robert of Woodhouse, prebendary of Norwell
Palishall (who had been instituted as vicar of Bunny after buying out the rights to the
advowson of the lay lord in 1312), of the reversion to Thomas de Ferrars in 1342 for an
endowment he wished to make at the Augustinian priory of Ulverscroft in Charnwood
forest (diocese of Lincoln), to which the advowson was transferred in 1345. After that
the priory exercised patronage until the Reformation despite some challenges. Some
aspects of this convoluted history were first highlighted by Thoroton (i, 90 citing Pl. de
Banc. Trin 5 E. 1, rot. 24, f. 36 = TNA, CP 40/20, rot. 24, AALT, http://aalt.law.uh.edu/

E1/CP40no20/aCP40no20fronts/IMG_5259.htm; http://aalt.law.uh.edu/E1/CP40no20/ aCP40no20fronts/IMG_5260.htm), when in the 1270s the Chapter challenged the claims of Richard de Grey, as keeper of the land and heir of Aucher de Freschville, late lord of Bunny, but are best teased out in Cameron, 'Bunny's First Vicarage', 62–72. It includes the Chapter's nomination of a champion to defend their claims in a trial by battle in 1292 which he seems to have lost (ibid., 64, citing *Reg. Le Romeyn*, no. 921 and TNA, JUST 1/1092, rot. 3), though Cameron was unaware of this papal bull. A separate inquiry by the archdeacon of Nottingham in May 1270, following the nomination of Mr Peter of Radnor to the living by the Chapter, had resulted in a return that confirmed that Aucher de Freschville's 'ancestors had possessed the advowson, and that Southwell's interest was confined to a portion of the income from the commoning of the church valued at £10' (ibid., 64 citing *Reg. Giffard*, nos 228, 235 and 245), though, as noted, this did not prevent many further legal proceedings. Alexander, 'A Case of Patronage Deferred', 72–3, argues that Robert of Woodhouse began to rebuild the chancel of Bunny church, probably in advance of his own burial there, but by 1342 had decided to found a house for the Austin friars at Stamford where he was later buried, so that the expense of finishing the rebuilding fell on Ulverscroft priory and its vicar.

8   A second version of **2**, with minimal scribal differences.

Margin   *Confirmacio libertatem* (16th–17th c.)

9   *Innocent III confirms to Geoffrey, archbishop of York the lands that were granted to his church in Nottinghamshire by his late brother, Richard I, king of England*   Lateran, [Rome], 8 November 1206

Bulla[1] confirmationis terre archiepiscopi in Notyngham schira

Innocentius episcopus servus servorum Dei venerabili fratri G. Eboracen' archiepiscopo salutem et apostolicam benedictionem. Justis petentium desideriis dignum est nos facilem prebere consensum et vota[2] que a rationis tramite non discordant effectu prosequente complere. Ea propter venerabilis in Cristo frater tuis iustis postulationibus grato concurrentes assensu libertates et immunitates[3] ab inclite recordationis R. illustri Anglorum rege super terris tuis omnibus archiepiscopatus Eboracen'[4] et in Notyngham syre positis, quas ipse rex deforestavit, tibi et successoribus tuis concessas, sicut in eiusdem regis scripto plenius continetur, ac tu eas iuste possides et quiete, auctoritate apostolica confirmamus et presentis scripti patrocinio communimus, statuentes ut nulli omnino hominum liceat hanc paginam nostre confirmationis infringere vel ei ausu temerario contraire. Si quis autem hoc attemptare presumpserit indignationem omnipotentis Dei et beatorum Petri et Pauli apostolorum eius se noverit incursurum. Datum Lateran' vi idus Novembris pontificatus nostri anno nono.

[1] *Bulla* erased; heading in later hand (Scribe 4)   [2] MS *tota*   [3] MS *imminitates*   [4] MS *Eboracey*

Margin   *Confirmacio libertatum* (16th–17th c.)

Note   Cal. in Cheney and Cheney, 120 no. 721; pd. p. 252 (with omissions); not in Potthast. For Richard I's charter, see **20**.

10 *Innocent III delegates to the abbots of Rufford and Welbeck and to the prior of Newstead powers to resolve the dispute between the Chapter of Southwell and the Dean and Chapter of York over the Pentecostal procession, referring to a previous mandate addressed to Robert, abbot of St Mary's, York and others (now lost)* Lateran, Rome, 3 April 1204

Innocentius episcopus servus servorum Dei dilectis filiis de Ruchford et de Wellebec abbatibus et priori de Novo Loco Eboracensis diocesis salutem et apostolicam benedictionem. Ex parte dilectorum filiorum capituli Suwellen' ecclesie nostris auribus est relatum quod cum inter ipsos ex una parte et decanum et capitulum Eboracensis ecclesie ex altera parte super processione iam dicte ecclesie in festivitate Pentecostes debita questio verteretur, idem decanus et capitulum contra Suwellensem ecclesiam, nulla prorsus habita mentione de confirmatione quam eidem ecclesie supra dicta processione apostolica dicitur indulsisse. Literas apostolicas ad dilectum filium abbatem sancte Marie Eboracensis et suos coniudices impetrarunt. Quo circa discretioni vestre per apostolica scripta mandamus quatinus non obstantibus literis in quibus de confirmatione predicta nulla mentio fuit facta, partibus convocatis, audiatis hinc inde proposita et quod canonicum fuerit, appellatione postposita, statuatis, facientes quod decreveritis per censuram ecclesiasticam firmiter observari. Testes autem qui nominati fuerint, si se gratia, odio vel timore subtraxerint simili distinctione, cessante appellatione, cogitatis veritati testimonium perhibere, nullis literis veritati et iustitie preiudicantibus a sede apostolica impetratis. Quod si non omnes hiis exequendis potueritis interesse duo vestrum ea nichilominus exequuntur.[1] Datum Lateran' iii nonas Aprilis pontificatus nostri anno septimo.

[1]MS *exequiunt*

Margin *Commissio cause super processione pentecostes audite et terminata* [*sic*] (16th–17th c.)

Note Cal. in Cheney and Cheney, 90 no. 553 and pd. p. 241 (with omissions). Not in Potthast. The earlier mandate of Innocent III, now lost, addressed to the abbot of St Mary's York and others is calendared at ibid., 86 no. 524. The abbot of Rufford (Notts.) was probably called William; Richard of Southwell, abbot of Welbeck, Notts. (1187–d. by 1223); Aldred, prior of Newstead (c. 1186–before 1215); Robert de Longchamp, abbot of St Mary's, York (1197–1239), *HRH*, i, 84, 141, 177, 198; Simon of Apulia, dean of York (1194–1214), *York Fasti*, i, 1–2.

11 *Innocent III to the abbot of Rufford, the priors of Worksop and Shelford of the diocese of York, relating that the Chapter of Southwell has complained that [Simon], dean and [Hamo], treasurer of York have laid an interdict on the church of Southwell and its churches because of a debt due from [Geoffrey], archbishop of York, ordering them to annul the sentence if it was given after appeal to the apostolic see; otherwise, to relax it on receiving sufficient pledge from the Chapter* St Peter's, Rome, 17 April 1205

Innocentius episcopus servus servorum Dei dilectis filiis abbati de Ruchford et de Wyrkesop et de Sceldford prioribus Eboracensis dyocesis salutem p. 5

et apostolicam benedictionem. Sua nobis dilecti filii capitulum Suwell' significatione monstrarunt quod cum decanus et capitulum Eboracen' super sollempni processione Pentecostes contra privilegium suum eis moverint questionem et idem decanus et thesaurarius Eboracenses litteras accepissent a nobis ut venerabilem fratrem nostrum Eboracensem archiepiscopum ad solutionem cuiusdam pecunie, quam S.[1] clericus sibi deberi proponebat, ab eo per censuram ecclesiasticam appellatione remota compellerent, ipsi, ex eo quod idem archiepiscopus moram fecerat in solvendo, in ecclesiam Suwell' et alias ecclesias pertinentes ad ipsam, licet idem capitulum nec ex fidei[2] iussione nec alio modo ad solutionem ipsius pecunie tenerentur, interdicti sententiam protulerunt. Quo circa discretioni vestre per apostolica scripta mandamus quatinus sententiam illam, si eam post appellationem ad sedem apostolicam legitime interpositam noveritis esse latam, nuntietis sublato appellationis[3] obstaculo non tenere; alioquin sufficienti ab eis cautione recepta super hiis pro quibus eorum est ecclesia interdicta[4] eandem sententiam relaxetis. Quod si non omnes hiis exequendis potueritis interesse duo vestrum ea nichilominus exequuntur. Datum Rome apud Santum Petrum, xv kalendas Maii pontificatus nostri anno octavo.

[1] MS *silicet*; the Cheneys (note below) propose correction to *S.* as initial of name [2] MS *fide* [3] MS *apellationis* [4] MS *antedicta*

Margin *De processione Pentecost* (16th–17th c.)

Note Cal. in Cheney and Cheney, 102 no. 617 and pd. p. 246 (with omissions). Not in Potthast. William, abbot of Rufford; Henry, prior of Worksop (*c.* 1200–*c.* 1214); Alexander, prior of Shelford, Notts. (*c.* 1203–15), *HRH*, i, 183, 191; Simon of Apulia, dean of York (1194–1214); Hamo, treasurer (*c.* 1199–1218), subsequently dean, d. 1220, *York Fasti*, i, 2–3. For other entries concerning the Pentecostal procession see **4, 10** and **206**.

12 *Urban VI delegates the prior of Thurgarton (Notts.) to investigate charges that the Chapter had given away to clergy and laymen for life some of their tithes, rents, lands, vines, houses, meadows, pastures, granges, woods, mills and other rights and goods by written instruments, some for long periods of time, others in perpetuity, at annual rents, to the grave harm of the Chapter, and for which grants some were now seeking papal confirmation. Since this concerns the pope's own interests, the prior is ordered to investigate any such alienations which appear illicit and revoke any written instruments contrary to the interests of the Chapter, threatening any who resist with ecclesiastical censure*

St Peter's, Rome, 1 December 1379

[U][1]rbanus episcopus servus servorum Dei dilecto filio nostro[2] priori de Thurgarton Eboracensis diocesis salutem et apostolicam benedictionem. Ad audientiam nostram pervenit quod tam dilecti filii nostri capituli ecclesie beate Marie de Suthwell' Ebor' diocesis quam predecessores eorum decimas redditus terras vineas possessiones domos casalia prata pascua grangias nemora molendina iura iurisdictiones et quedam alia bona ipsius capituli, datis super hoc literis confectis, ex hoc, puris[3] instrumentis interpositis, iuramentis factis, renuntiationibus et penis adiectis ad gravem ipsius capituli lesionem nonnullis clericis et laicis aliquibus eorum a[d] vitam quibusdam vero ad non modicum tempus et aliis perpetuo ad firmam vel sub censu annuo concesserunt, quorum aliqui dicuntur super hiis confirmationis litteras in forma communi a sede apostolica impetrasse. Quia vero nostrum interest super hoc de oportuno remedio providere, discretioni tue per apostolica scripta mandamus quatinus ea que de bonis ipsius capituli per concessiones huius alienata inveneris illicite vel distracta, non obstantibus literis, instrumentis, iuramentis, renuntiationibus, penis et confirmationibus supradictis ad ius et proprietatem eiusdem capituli legitime revocare procures. Contradictores per censuram ecclesiasticam, appellatione postposita, compescendo. Testes autem qui fuerint nominati, si se gratia, odio vel timore subtraxerint, censura simili, appellatione cessante, compellas veritati testimonium perhibere. Datum Rome apud Sanctum Petrum kalendas Decembris, pontificatus nostri anno secundo.

¹ The initial *U* has been omitted for the rubricator to fill in; this entry and **13** are in a different 14ᵗʰ/15ᵗʰ c. hand (= Scribe 2), from previous entries; subsequently the entry has been crossed out making some readings uncertain ² MS *n.* which has been extended here as *nostro* but it may simply be an initial *n.* (see Note for identity of the prior) ³ Thus in MS; transcript by W. A. James proposes *publicis* which may have been the bull's original wording.

Margin *De bonis ablatis restituendis Bulla* (16ᵗʰ–17ᵗʰ c.); *See p. 225* (pencil, 20ᵗʰ c.)

Date Urban V was in still in Avignon in December 1363, whilst Urban VI was usually based at St Peter's, Rome in late 1379.

Note Repeated at **359**. Robert of Clawson, prior of Thurgarton (1349–79), *Thurgarton*, ccv.

13 *Nicholas IV grants remission of a year and forty days from sins to all those who visit St Mary's, Southwell, built in honour of the Virgin, on her feast days and the eight days following*

Santa Maria Maggiore, Rome, 10 March 1290

Nicholaus¹ episcopus servus servorum Dei universis Cristi fidelibus presentes literas inspecturis salutem et apostolicam benedictionem. Virga venustissima et omnium virtutum floribus insignita virgo dei genitrix gloriosa, cuius pulcritudinem sol et luna mirantur, cuius precibus iuvatur populus cristianus florem preciosissimum inmercessibilem et eternum dominum nostrum Cristum ineffabili sancti spiritus coniunxione produxit ob cuius reverentiam loca eiusdem virginis² [vocabulo] insignita sunt et Cristi fidelibus merito veneranda ut eius piis et adiuti suffragiis [eterne] retributionis premium consequi mereamur. Rogamus itaque universitatem vestram et hortamur in domino in remissionem peccaminum, iniungentes quatinus ad ecclesiam Suthwellen' Eboracensis³ diocesis que sicut asseritur in honorem ipsius Virginis est constructa, imploraturi a domino veniam delictorum cum humilitate spiritus acc[edant?]. Nos enim de omnipotentis dei misericordia et beatorum Petri et Pauli apostolorum eius auctoritate confisi omnibus vere penitentibus et confessis qui eandem ecclesiam devote visitaverint annuatim in singulis eiusdem virginis festivitatibus et per octo dies festivitates ipsas immediate sequentes unum annum et quadraginta dies de iniunctis sibi penitentiis misericorditer relaxamus.

Datum Rome apud sanctam Mariam Maiorem vi idus Martii pontificatus nostri anno tertio.

¹ The initial *N* has been left for the rubricator to fill in   ² Gap about ten letters long; the arenga 'ob cuius ... mereamur' occurs fairly frequently in 14ᵗʰ-c. papal bulls; see **Introduction**, p. liv   ³ MS *Oboracen'*

Margin   *Mandatum de ecclesia Southwell visitanda* (16ᵗʰ–17ᵗʰ c.)

Date   Not in Potthast, but he shows that every bull issued by Nicholas IV between 22 October 1289 and 20 May 1290 (nos 23100, 23823) was issued at Santa Maria Maggiore, Rome.

Note   In same hand as **12**; both have been crossed out with St Andrew's saltires and some words through which the saltires pass have been written over by another hand, making each difficult to read.

Liberties, 14–16

14   *Inspeximus by Edward III, dated at Clarendon (Wilts.) on 26 November 1333, of the record and process of a suit, originating in the eyre of William of Harle and his associates, justices in eyre at Nottingham in 1329, and continued subsequently in the court of King's Bench, between the king and the Chapter and individual canons of Southwell, concerning by what warrant they had claimed certain liberties. The suit was concluded in favour of the Chapter and canons in King's Bench on 26 June 1331*

1329–33

p. 6   **Placita de quo warranto pro libertatibus**

Edwardus Dei gratia rex Anglie dominus Hibernie et dux Aquitani[e]¹ omnibus ad quos presentes littere pervenerint salutem. Inspeximus tenorem recordi et processus loquele que fuit coram nobis per breve nostrum inter nos et capitulum ecclesie beate Marie Suwell' nec non et quosdam canonicos eiusdem ecclesie quam² quidem tenorem coram nobis in cancellaria nostra venire fecimus in hec verba. Placita coram domino rege apud Westm' in termino Pasce anno regni regis Edwardi tercii post conquestum quinto rotulo cxvᵒ. Dominus rex misit iusticiariis suis hic per breve suum clausum quandam peticionem dilectorum clericorum filiorum³ suorum Henrici de Edenestowe et Roberti de Wodhous et aliorum canonicorum ecclesie beate Marie Suthwell'⁴ coram ipso domino⁵ rege et consilio suo exhibitam ac quendam processum de quibusdam libertatibus coram Willelmo de Herle et sociis suis iusticiariis nuper in comitatu Notingham⁶ itinerantibus per capitulum ecclesie de Suthwell'⁷ et canonicos predictos clamatis ac eciam coram eisdem iusticiariis presentatis⁸ per breve predictum iusticiariis suis hic mandans quod inspectis petitione illa et indorsamento facto ad eandem nec non processu predicto finem

¹ These letters patent are enrolled on the patent roll for 7 Edward III, part 2 (C 66/182, mm 8–7), which is here, as 'A', collated with the version in the White Book; see Note for further details.   ² A *quem*   ³ *Sic*; A omits.   ⁴ A *Suwell'*   ⁵ A omits.   ⁶ A *Notingh'*   ⁷ A *Suwell'*   ⁸ A inserts *et*.

ab eisdem canonicis pro libertatibus in predicto processu contentis habendis per plevinam recipiant et ulterius ad finalem discussionem eiusdem negocii procedunt[9] eo non obstante quod libertates ille in aliis itinerantibus iusticiariorum itinerancium in comitatu predicto clamate non extiterunt ac dicto negotio coram eisdem iusticiariis indiscusso pendente de quicquam ab eisdem canonicis seu de capitulo predicto levandis sine ipsos premissa occasione onerandis seu gravandis supersederi faciatis qui quidem peticio et processus sequuntur[10] in hec verba:[11]

A nostre signur[12] le Roy et[13] son conseil monstrent ses clercs Robert de Wodehous Henri de Edenestowe et les autres chanoignes de leglise de Suthwell' en le counte de Notingh' qe come le chapitre de mesme le glise en les terrez et tenementz appurtenaunz a icel et les ditz provenders en lur[14] provendes en meisme le glise ount eu et use daver vewe de fraunc plegge et qantque a vewe apertient et auxint amendes dassise de pain et de cerveise enfreinte de lur[15] tenantz puis temps de memorie et auxint qe en chescun eyre[16] en meisme le counte qe les iustices soleient seer en les eus de leglise et illeoqes terminer lez ples tochaunt la dite eglise et les tenantz dicel et tut soit il qe presente fust[17] en leyre de Notingh' qe le dite chapitre avoit lez dites franchises si ne voleient lez iustices de meisme leiyre[18] a lower au dit chapitre meismes les franchises ne a les chanoignes susditz par ce[19] qils ne clamarent pas si largement en le darrein eyre devant qestoit a qaurante et cink aunz passez dont les ditz chanoignes prient qils puissent aver restitucion de la dite vewe qe ne vaut par an forsqe vii soldz come poet apparer par le transcript'[20] du proces en fait en meisme leyre qe vynt de souz[21] le seas[22] monser William de Herle en chauncellerie et qe ore est attache a ceste peticion ensemblement oue tutes[23] les[24] autres franchises avantdites eaunt regardz qe toutz lor letres et munimentz depar queux ils se poeient aver eide furent enportz qant leglise estoit derobbe com conu[25] chose est a tut le pais issi qe la dite eglise ne soit desherite.

Indorsamentum peticionis predicte talis est. Soit tut cest[26] proces mande devant les iustices le roy a ses pleez tenir assignez oue la peticion et vewes et examinez illeoqes meisme le proces preignent meismes[27] iustices pur les franchises clamez reavoir par plevine fin et outre aillent a finale discussion de la busoigne nient contresteaunt[28] qe les fraunchises ne ount mie este clamez en autres eyres et pendante la busoigne nient termine soit mande a surseer de rien lever charger ou grever par cele[29] enchesoun.

Processus coram Willelmo de Herle sequitur in hec verba. Placita de quo waranto coram Willelmo de Herle et sociis suis iusticiariis domini regis itinerantibus apud Notingh' die lune proxima post festum sancti Martini anno regni regis Edwardi tercii post conquestum[30] tercio rotulo quinto.

---

[9] A *procedant*   [10] A *secuntur*   [11] A inserts *Peticio.*   [12] A *seignur*   [13] A inserts *a.*   [14] A *lour*   [15] A *lour*   [16] A *eire*   [17] A *fut*   [18] A *leyre*   [19] A *pur ceo*   [20] A *transcrit'*   [21] A *desoutz*   [22] A *seal*   [23] A *totes*   [24] A omits.   [25] A *conue*   [26] A *ces*   [27] A inserts *les.*   [28] A *conteesteant*   [29] A *cel*   [30] 13 November 1329. A *a conquestu*

Presentatum est per xii iuratores wapentachii de Thurgarton et de Lyth'[31] quod capitulum de Suthwell' habet visum franciplegii de omnibus tenentibus suis in Suwell'[32] Northwell' Suthmuskham Northmuskham[33] Calneton Oxton Calverton Wodeburgh' Cropil[34] Blitheworth Halghton Bekyngham Dunham Halum Eddynglay[35] et Normanton quo waranto vel a quo tempore ignorant. Et eciam presentant quo[d] in quolibet itinere iusticiariorum etc. iusticiarii itinerantes solebant sedere in ostio australi

p. 7   ecclesie de Suthwell' predicte et ibidem terminare | placita de itinere de omnibus tenentibus dicti capituli et respondere coram iusticiariis per xii et non alibi. Ideo predicte libertates capiantur in manum domini regis. Postea venit predictum capitulum per Thomam de Asseheburn[36] attornatum suum in omnibus placitis et querelis et similiter ad libertates suas calumpniandas etc. Et petit predictum visum per plevinam et habet. Et dicit quod ipsum capitulum a tempore quo non extat memoria habuit predictum visum in predictis villis ut de iure ecclesie sue beate Marie Suwell'[37] etc. Et Willelmus de Denum qui sequitur pro rege dicit quod capitulum predictum ad huiusmodi clamium titulo prescripcionis admitti non debet. Dicit enim quod idem capitulum alias coram J. de Wallibus et sociis suis iusticiariis ultimo itinerantibus hoc[38] tempore regis E. avi domini regis nunc summonitus fuit ad clamium suum proprium ad respondendum predicto E. regi etc. quo waranto clamat emendas assise panis et cervisie etc. in predictis villis de Suwell'[39] Northwell' Northmuskham[40] Suthmuskham Calneton Oxton Calverton Wodeburgh et Blitheworth. Et idem capitulum tunc tamen clamat emendas assise panis et cervisie in predictis villis de Suwell'[41] Northwell' Northmuskham[42] Calneton Oxton Calverton Wodeburgh et Blithewortgh et emendam assise cervisie fracte tamen in Suthmuskham.[43] Et similiter idem capitulum nunc in itinere isto summonitus est ad respondendum etc. quo waranto clamat emendas assise panis et cervisie etc. in predictis villis de Suthwell' Northwell' Northmuskham[44] Suthmuskam Calneton Oxton Calverton' Wodeburgh Cropill'[45] Blithewortgh[46] et Halghton ad quod clamium idem capitulum respondet quo ad Suthmuskham[47] quod ipsum non clamat nisi emendas assise panis et[48] cervisie fracte tamen ibidem. Et quo ad emendas assise panis et cervisie in Crophull' et Halghton nichil clamat ad presens. Unde dicit quod cum idem capitulum coram J. de Wallibus[49] etc. ad breve etc. ad quod tunc summonitum fuit et similiter ad breve ad quod nunc summonitus est etc. non clamat nisi illa que sunt parcelle visus etc. et hoc in quibusdam villis etc. et in quibusdam non unde petit iudicium si predictum capitulum titulo supradicto visum franciplegii etc. in eisdem villis clamare possit vel debeat in hac parte etc. Et capitulum dicit quod ipsum alias in predicto itinere J. de Wallibus[50] etc. non fuit \summonitus ad/ respondendum predicto regi avo etc. quo waranto clamat visum franciplegii vel aliquid aliud in predictis villis de Bekyngham et Dunham

---

[31] A *lith'*   [32] A *Suthwell'*   [33] A *Northmuscam*   [34] A *Crophill'*   [35] A *Edyngley*   [36] A *Assheburn*   [37] A *Suthwell'*   [38] A *hic*   [39] A *Suthwell'* [40] A *Northmuscam*   [41] A *Suthwell'*   [42] A *Northmuscam*   [43] A *Suthmuscam* [44] A *Northmuscam*   [45] A *Crophill'*   [46] A *Blitheworth'*   [47] A *Suthmuscam* [48] A omits *panis et.*   [49] A *Vallibus*   [50] A *Vallibus*

etc. nec aliquid tunc presentatus fuit super ipsum capitulum de aliquibus libertatibus in eisdem villis unde dicit quod de illo ad quod tunc non fuit positum ad respondendum admitti debet ad presens ad clamandum etc. Et dicit quod ipsum capitulum a tempore quo non extat memoria habuit visum franciplegii apud Bekyngham de tenentibus suis ibidem et eciam visum franciplegii apud Dunham de tenentibus[51] ibidem ut de iure ecclesie predicte etc. Et Willelmus de Denum qui sequitur pro rege[52] etc. petit quod inquiratur pro rege si predictum [capitulum] habuit predictum visum in predictis villis de Bekyngham[53] Dunham etc. Et si sit tunc qualiter illis visum[54] est etc. Ideo inquiratur etc. Jure dicunt [*sic*] super sacramentum suum quod predictum capitulum a tempore quo non extat memoria habuit in Bekyngham visum per se de omnibus tenentibus suis ibidem. Et in Dunham visum est per se de omnibus tenentibus suis residentibus ibidem. Et dicunt quod idem capitulum semper usum est illos punire qui deliquerunt contra assisam panis et cervisie etc. per penam pecuniariam et nunquam ponere ipsos ad iudicium corporale. Et iuratores quesitus quantum predicti visus in omnibus villis exceptis Bekyngham et Dunham valent per annum dicunt quod visus de tenentibus suis in Eddynglai[55] Halum[56] Halghton Normanton et Suwell'[57] tentus apud Suwell'[58] valet per annum duos solidos. Et visus de tenentibus in Crophill' Calverton Blithworth[59] et Oxton tentus apud Oxton valet duos solidos per annum. Et visus de tenentibus in Calneton et Northmuscam tentus apud Northmuscam duodecim denarios per annum. Et visus de tenentibus suis in Suthmusham[60] duodecim denarios per annum. Et visus est de[61] Wodeburgh tenentes[62] ibidem per se duodecim denarios per annum. Ideo predicti visus in omnibus predictis villis capiantur in manu domini regis etc. Postea Johannes de Waynflete[63] Petrus de Wiche[64] de eodem comitatu fecerunt \finem/ cum domino rege de quadraginta solidis pro predictis visibus in Bekyngham et Dunham tamen eidem capitulum rehabendis.[65] Ideo predictum capitulum rehabeat visus illos utendi illis modo quo decet etc. Et quo ad visus illos inde sine die salvo iure regis nostri etc. Et modo venit hic coram rege tam predictum capitulum quam canonici predicti per Robertum de Totel attornatum suum et inspectis petitione et processu predictis pro eo quod compertum est quod libertates predicte per capitulum predictum in itinere predicto clamate fuerunt et libertas visus franciplegii in villis de Bekyngham et Dunham eidem capitulo adiudicata fuit et per dictum[66] processum non est compertum quod predicti canonici | aliquam libertatem predictarum in itinere illo clamarunt. Quesitus est ab eisdem canonicis ob quam causam venire fecerunt hic processum predictum et si dictum capitulum libertates superdictas simul cum canonicis predictis in communi teneant vel non et dictum est eis quod ulterius ostendant

p. 8

---

[51] A inserts *suis*.   [52] A omits *pro rege*.   [53] A inserts *et*.   [54] *Recte* usum
[55] A *Edyngley*   [56] A inserts *et*.   [57] A *Suthwell'*   [58] A *Suthwell'*   [59] A
Blitheworth   [60] A *Suthmuscam*   [61] A has *in* instead of *est de*.   [62] A *tenta*
[63] A *Waynflet'*   [64] A *del Wyche*   [65] Next to this sentence a bracket has been
drawn in the margin, against which *Nota libertates de Bekyngham et Dunham* is written
in a 17th-c. hand. See also note 95 below.   [66] A *predictum*

curie qualiter et quo modo illis libertatibus utuntur etc.[67] Qui quidem canonici petunt inde licenciam loquendi etc. et habita inde deliberacione dicunt quod ipsi canonici sunt prebendarii ecclesie predicte et faciunt capitulum et quod tene[n]t prebendas suas separatim[68] et quod idem capitulum tenet aliquas libertates libertatum predictarum in terris tenementis et feodis ad illud spectantibus per se et quilibet canonicorum predictorum per se aliquas libertates earumdem libertatum[69] et feodis prebendarum suarum ecclesie predicte videlicet predictum capitulum visum franciplegii se[70] de omnibus hominibus tenentibus suis et residentibus in feodo suo de Suwell'[71] Halum et Eddynglay[72] tenendum bis per annum. Et quod[73] \in/ quolibet itinere justiciariorum itinerancium in comitatu Notingh' quod justiciarii ibidem itinerantes veniant apud Suwell'[74] audiant et terminent ad ostium ecclesie predicte omnia placita tangencia capitulum canonicos tenentes suos de ecclesia predicta et ministros suos preter placita corone que predicti justiciarii audiant et terminabunt ad domum alicuius canonici extra sanctuarium. Et Robertus de Wodehous unus canonicorum predictorum et prebendarius prebende de Northwell' in ecclesia predicta tenet visum franciplegii et ea que ad visum pertinent de omnibus hominibus tenentibus et residentibus in feodo suo de Northwell' ut de iure ecclesie[75] sue predicte apud Northwell' bis per annum etc. Et Robertus de Notyngham[76] prebendarius prebende de Oxton et Cropil in ecclesia predicta visum franciplegii in ea que ad visum pertinent de omnibus hominibus tenentibus et residentibus suis in Oxton Blythworth[77] Calverton Wodeburgh et Croppill'[78] ut de iure prebende sue.[79] Et Lambertus de Trikyngham prebendarius prebende de Halghton in ecclesia predicta visum franciplegii et ea que ad visum pertinet tenendum ibidem bis per annum ad prebendam suam predictam. Henricus de Edenestowe prebendarius prebende de Oxton et Cropill' in ecclesia predicta visum franciplegii et ea que ad visum pertinent de omnibus hominibus tenentibus et residentibus in feodo suo in Oxton et Blithewortgh[80] Calverton Suthwell' Wodeburth[81] et Cropill'[82] ut de iure prebende sue predicte. Robertus de Bridlyngton[83] prebendarius prebende de Wodeburgh in ecclesia predicta visum franciplegii et ea que ad visum pertinent de omnibus hominibus tenentibus et residentibus in feodo suo in Wodeburgh[84] et Eddynglay[85] ut de iure prebende sue predicte. Willelmus de Barneby prebendarius prebende de Bekyngham in ecclesia predicta visum franciplegii et ea que ad visum pertinent de omnibus tenentibus et residentibus in feodo suo in Suwell'[86] Eddynglay[87] et Bekyngham ut de iure prebende sue predicte.

---

[67] Alongside this sentence in the margin *Preb. faciunt Capitulum* is written in what may be a late 17th-c. cursive hand. [68] *dicunt...separatim* is underlined in a later hand and *prebendarii?Faciunt Capitulum* written in the margin in a mid 16th-c. hand, to which has been added below in a different hand, possibly an imitation of a late medieval cursive hand, *et tenent prebendas suas seperatim.* [69] A inserts *in terris tenementis.* [70] A omits. [71] A *Suthwell'* [72] A *Edyngley* [73] A omits. [74] A *Suthwell'* [75] A *prebende* [76] A *Notingh'* [77] A *Blitheworth* [78] A *Crophill'* [79] A inserts *predicte.* [80] A *Blitheworth* [81] A *Wodeburgh* [82] A *Crophill'* [83] A *Bridelyngton* [84] A *Wodburgh* [85] A *Edyngley* [86] A *Suthwell'* [87] A *Edyngley* [88] A *Newerk*

Willelmus de Newerck[88] prebendarius prebende de Northmuskham[89] in ecclesia predicta visum franciplegii et ea que ad visum[90] pertinent de omnibus hominibus tenentibus et residentibus in feodo suo in Northmuscam Calneton Suthmuskham[91] Normanton iuxta Suwell'[92] ut de iure prebende sue predicte. Thomas de Sancto Albano prebendarius prebende de Dunham in ecclesia predicta visum franciplegii et ea que ad visum pertinent de omnibus hominibus tenentibus et residentibus in feodo suo in Dunham ut de iure prebende sue predicte. Johannes de Sandale prebendarius prebende de Normanton in ecclesia predicta visum franciplegii et ea que ad visum pertinent de omnibus hominibus tenentibus et residentibus in feodo suo in Suwell'[93] et Normanton ut de iure prebende sue predicte. Et sic hactenus illis uti consueverunt et petunt admitti ad libertates illas clamandas et placitandas in forma predicta. Et Adam de Fyncham qui sequitur pro domino rege petit quod ex quo omnes libertates predicte in itinere predicto per predictum capitulum clamate fuerunt et visus franciplegii in predictis villis de Bekyngham et Dunham ibidem dicto capitulo adiudicatus fuit pro ut per predictum processum manifeste liquet et quod libertas aliqua in predicto itinere per canonicos predictos clamata non extitit nec eisdem adiudicata fuit et modo eidem[94] canonici cognoscunt quod ipsi faciant capitulum et quod dictum capitulum aliquas libertates libertatum predictarum scilicet de omnibus tenentibus et residentibus in feodo eiusdem capituli separatim tenet et quilibet canonicorum predictorum per se aliquas libertates libertatum predictarum de omnibus tenentibus et residentibus in feodis illis prebendarum suarum predictarum ut supradictum est separatim tenet et sic illis utantur in contrarium clamii supradicti per predictum[95] capitulum in itinere predicto facti petit quod omnes libertates predicte capiantur in manum domini regis. Ideo omnes libertates predicte capiantur in manu domini regis etc.

Postea dominus rex mandavit breve suum clausum justiciariis suis hic in hec verba: Edwardus Dei gratia rex Anglie et[96] dominus Hibernie et dux Aquitanie dilectis et fidelibus suis Galfredo de[97] Scrop'[98] iusticiario ad placita coram nobis tenenda assignato salutem. Cum nos nuper ad prosecutionem dilectorum clericorum nostrorum Roberti de Wodehous[99] et[100] Henrici de Eddenestowe[101] et aliorum canonicorum ecclesie beate Marie Suwell'[102] in comitatu | Notyngh'[103] per peticionem suam coram nobis et concilio nostro exhibitam nobis suggencium quod capitulum ecclesie illius in terris et tenementis ad idem capitulum spectantibus et eciam prebendarii prebendarum eiusdem ecclesie in prebendis suis usi fuerunt habere visum franciplegii et quicquid ad huiusmodi visum pertinet et emendas assise panis et cervisie de tenentibus suis fracte necnon quasdam libertates alias in eadem petitione contentas et quod iusticiarii nostri nuper itinerantes in eodem comitatu libertates illas eis allocare distulerunt quamquam

p. 9

---

[89] A *Northmuscam*   [90] A *franciplegii* inserted above the line.   [91] A *Suthmuscam*   [92] A *Suthwell'*   [93] A *Suthwell'*   [94] A *iidem*   [95] The two lines *per se...per predictum* are bracketed in the margin with a note *nota*, apparently in the same hand as that referred to in note 65 above.   [96] A omits.   [97] A *le*   [98] A inserts *et sociis suis*   [99] A *Wodhous*   [100] A omits.   [101] A *Edenestowe*   [102] A *Suthwell'*   [103] A *Notingh'*

coram eis quod idem capitulum libertatibus illis usum fuerit presentatum
exititerit peticionem predictam simul cum tenore tocius processus inde
coram prefatis iusticiariis nostris in itinere illo habiti quem coram nobis
in cancellaria nostra venire fecimus nobis[104] miserimus sub pede sigilli
nostri mandantes quod visis et examinatis processu et peticione predictis
finem ab eis per eisdem libertatibus per plevinam rehabendis reciperetis
et ulterius ad finalem discuscionem[105] negocii illius procederetis et iam ex
parte ipsorum clericorum nostrorum accepimus quod predicti prebendarii
et capitulum coram nobis allocuti utrum libertatibus illis in communi an
idem capitulum per se et predicti prebendarii per se usi fuerunt coram nobis
responderunt[106] quod predictum capitulum in terris tenementis et feodis
ad illud spectantibus aliquibus earumdem libertatum per se et quilibet
eorum prebendariorum in terris tenementis et feodis prebendarum suarum
aliquibus predictarum libertatum per se semper hactenus usi fuerint et
sic eis uti et habere clamium et non in communi per quod exitus finalis
inde modo quo predicte libertates in itinere illo fuerunt clamate coram
nobis fieri non potest super quo nobis supplicarunt eis per nos de remedio
provideri. Nos volentes supplicationi ipsorum clericorum nostrorum
pretextu laudabilis obsequii progenitoribus nostris regibus Anglie et
nos[107] per ipsos hactenus impensi quatino[108] bono remedio[109] potuerimus
in hac parte subvenire vobis mandamus quod a quolibet prebendariorum
predictorum pro libertatibus quas iidem prebendarii coram nobis clamare
voluerint in terris et tenementis sive feodis suis prebendarum illarum per
plevinam rehabendam finem per se et a predicto capitulo pro libertatibus
quas coram nobis clamare voluerit in terris tenementis sive feodis ad idem
capitulum spectantibus per plevinam rehabendis finem per se recipiatis
et ulterius ad finalem discussionem inde procedatis non obstante quod
libertates ille in aliis itineribus justiciariorum in eodem comitatu clamate
non extiterunt seu quod idem capitulum libertates predictas[110] in terris
tenementis[111] feodis illorum[112] prebendariorum a possessionibus ipsius
capituli seperatis quod[113] in terris tenementis sive feodis ad predictum
capitulum spectantibus clamat ut predictum est et dicto negotio indiscusso
pendente de quicquam ab eisdem prebendariis seu aliquo eorum sive de
predicto capitulo levandi seu ipsos ea occasione onerandis seu gravandis
supersederi faciatis. Teste me ipso apud Wyndesore xviii die Februarii
anno regni mei[114] quinto.

Et super[115] venit \tam/ capitulum predictum quam canonici predicti per
attornatum suum predictum et petunt libertates predictas per plevinam
rehabendas et quod possint admitti ad libertates suas clamandas et
placitandas iuxta formam brevis predicti et eis conceditur videlicet
capitulum predictum beate Marie Suwell' dat domino regi de fine pro
libertatibus suis rehabendis per plevinam per placitum Roberti Russell'
dimidia marca. Robertus de Wodehous[116] prebendarius prebende de
Northwell' pro eodem per idem placitum xl d. Robertus de Notingh'

[104] A vobis   [105] A discussionem   [106] A responderint   [107] A nobis   [108] A
quatenus   [109] A modo   [110] A inserts tam.   [111] A inserts et.   [112] A
ipsorum   [113] A quam   [114] 18 February 1331. A nostri   [115] A inserts hoc
[116] A Wodhous

prebendarius prebende de Oxton et Croppill'[117] pro eodem per idem placitum xl d. Lambertus de Trikyngham prebendarius prebende de Halghton pro eodem per idem placitum xl d. Henricus de Eddenestowe[118] prebendarius prebende de Oxton et Croppill'[119] pro eodem per idem placitum xl d. Robertus de Bridlyngton[120] prebendarius prebende de Wodeburtgh[121] pro eodem per idem placitum dimidia marca. Willelmus de Barneby prebendarius prebende de Bekyngham pro eodem per idem[122] placitum dimidia marca. William de Newerk prebendarius prebende de Northmuskham pro eodem per idem placitum[123] dimidia marca. Thomas de Sancto Albano prebendarius prebende de Dunham pro eodem per idem placitum dimidia marca. Johannes de Sandale prebendarius prebende de Normanton pro eodem per idem placitum dimidia marca. Clamium capituli[124] et prebendariorum ecclesie[125] Suwell'[126] in comitatu Notingh' ut patet super[127] hac forma. Capitulum ecclesie beate Marie Suthwellie[128] in comitatu Not'[129] clamat habere visum franciplegii et ea que ad visum pertinent de omnibus hominibus[130] tenentibus suis et residentibus in feodo suo[131] Suthwell' Halum et[132] Neuton tenendum per annum bis apud Suwell'.[133] Item clamat habere[134] [visum franciplegii et ea que ad visum pertinet] de omnibus[135] tenentibus suis et residentibus in feodo suo in Eddynglay[136] tenendum bis per annum. Item capitulum clamat quod in quolibet itinere iusticiariorum itinerancium in comitatu Notyngh'[137] quod iusticiarii ibidem itinerantes veniant apud Suwell'[138] audiant et terminent ad ostium predicte ecclesie omnia placita tangencia capitulum canonicos tenentes suos de ecclesia predicta et ministros suos preter placita corone que predicti iusticiarii audient et terminabunt ad domum alicuius canonici extra sanctuarium. Robertus de Wodehous[139] prebendarius prebende de Northwell' in ecclesia beate Marie | de Suwell'[140] clamat habere visum franciplegii et ea que ad visum pertinet[141] de omnibus hominibus tenentibus et residentibus in feodo suo in Norhwell' Wodehous[142] Welegby[143] et[144] Midelthorp'[145] apud Northwell' bis per annum et wayf in eisdem villis ut de iure prebende sue predicte. Robertus de Notingh' prebendarius prebende de Oxton' et Croppill'[146] in ecclesia beate Marie Suwell' clamat habere visum franciplegii et[147] ea que ad visum pertinent de omnibus hominibus tenentibus et residentibus in Oxton Blytheworgh[148] Calverton Wodeburgth'.[149] Clamat eciam habere wayf in terris et feodis suis in eisdem villis[150] de iure prebende sue. Idem clamat habere visum franciplegii et ea quod ad visum pertinet[151] de omnibus hominibus tenentibus et residentibus suis

p. 10

---

[117] A *Crophill'*   [118] A *Edenestowe*   [119] A *Crophull'*   [120] A *Bridelyngton* [121] A *Wodburgh*   [122] A *predictum*   [123] A *placitum predictum*   [124] *Clamium Capituli* written in the margin, in a mid 16ᵗʰ-c. hand.   [125] A inserts *de*.   [126] A *Suthwell'*   [127] A *sub*   [128] A *Suthwell'*   [129] A *Notingh'*   [130] A inserts *et*.   [131] A inserts *in*.   [132] A omits.   [133] A *Suthwell'*   [134] A inserts *visum franciplegii et ea que ad visum pertinent*.   [135] A inserts *hominibus et*.   [136] A *Edyngley*   [137] A *Notingh'*   [138] A *Suthwell'*   [139] A *Wodhous*   [140] A *Suthwell'*   [141] A *pertinent*   [142] A *Northwell' Wodhous*   [143] A *Wyleghby* [144] A omits.   [145] A *Middelthorp'*   [146] A *Crophull'*   [147] From the beginning of page 10 to this point the lines are bracketed in the margin and *Norwell' Oxton* are written in a mid 16ᵗʰ-c. hand, possibly the first one mentioned in note 65.   [148] A *Blitheworth'*   [149] A *Wodburgh'*   [150] A inserts *ut*.   [151] A *pertinent*

in Croppilli[152] et Hickelyng' tenendum bis per annum et wayf in eisdem villis[153] de iure prebende sue predicte. Lambertus de Trikyngham prebendarius prebende de Halgthton in ecclesie beate Marie Suwell' clamat habere[154] in manerio suo de Halghton visum franciplegii et quicquid[155] ad visum pertinet[156] de omnibus hominibus tenentibus et residentibus[157] tenendum ibidem bis per annum et wayf et stray pertinencia ad prebendam suam predictam. Henricus de Edenestowe prebendarius prebende de Oxton et Croppull[158] in ecclesie beate Marie de Suwell'[159] clamat habere visum franciplegii et ea quod ad visum pertinet[160] de omnibus hominibus tenentibus et residentibus in feodo suo in Oxton'[161] Blytheworth'[162] Calverton Suwell'[163] et Wodburgth[164] tenendum bis per annum apud Oxton et wayf in eisdem villis ut de iure prebende sue predicte. Idem clamat habere visum franciplegii et ea quod ad visum pertinet[165] de omnibus hominibus tenentibus suis[166] et residentibus in feodo suo de Croppull'[167] et Hickynglay[168] tenendum bis per annum et wayf in eisdem villis ut de iure prebende sue predicte. Robertus de Bridlyngton'[169] prebendarius prebende de Wodburgh in ecclesia beate Marie de Suwell'[170] clamat habere visum franciplegii et ea que a visum pertinet[171] de omnibus hominibus et[172] tenentibus[173] suis in Wodburgh et Eddynglay[174] tenendum bis per annum. Clamat eciam habere wayf in terris et feodis suis ut de iure prebende sue predicte. Willelmus de Barneby prebendarius prebende de Bekyngham in ecclesia beate Marie de Suwell'[175] clamat habere visum franciplegii et ea que ad visum pertinet[176] de omnibus hominibus tenentibus et residentibus in feodo suo de[177] Suwell'[178] et Eddynglay[179] ut de iure prebende sue[180] apud Suwell'[181] bis per annum. Idem clamat habere visum franciplegii et ea que a visum pertinet[182] de omnibus hominibus tenentibus et residentibus suis in feodo suo de Bekyngham ut de iure prebende sue predicte tenendum apud Bekyngham bis per annum.[183] Willelmus de Newerk prebendarius prebende de Northmuskham[184] in ecclesia beate Marie de Suwell'[185] clamat habere visum franciplegii et ea que ad visum pertinet[186] de omnibus hominibus tenentibus suis[187] et residentibus in feodo suo in Northmuskham[188] Calneton Suthmuskam[189] North Carlton[190]

---

[152] A *Crophill'* [153] A inserts *ut.* [154] Followed by *clamat habere* expunged. [155] *Oxton* is written in this margin at this point, in what may be a 16th- or early 17th-c. hand. Below it *waif et stray ad Halgton'* is written in a different and fainter cursive hand, perhaps of the same period. [156] A *pertinent* [157] A omits *de omnibus… residentibus.* [158] A *Crophull'* [159] A *Suthwell'* [160] A *pertinent* [161] A inserts *et.* [162] A *Blitheworth'* [163] A *Suthwell'* [164] A *Wodburgh* [165] A *pertinent* [166] A omits. [167] A *Crophull'* [168] A *Hickelyng* [169] A *Bride-lyngton'* [170] A *Suthwell'* [171] A *pertinent* [172] A omits. [173] A inserts *et residentibus.* [174] A *Edyngley* [175] A *Suthwell'* [176] A *pertinent* [177] A in [178] A *Suthwell'* [179] A *Edyngley* [180] A inserts *predicte.* [181] A *Suthwell'* [182] A *pertinent* [183] In the margin alongside the whole William of Barnby entry is written *Prebenda de Bekyngham habet visum franciplegii bis in anno tam apud Suthwell' quam apud Bekyngham*, probably in a late 15th- or early 16th-c. hand. [184] A *Northmuscam* [185] A *Suthwell'* [186] A *pertinent* [187] A omits. [188] A *Northmuscam.* In the White Book the place-name is underlined and *Northmuskam* is written in the margin in a mid 16th-c. hand. [189] A *Suthmuscam* [190] A *Carleton*

Normanton iuxta Suthwell tenendum apud Northmuskham[191] bis per annum. Clamat eciam habere wayf in terris et feodis suis in eisdem villis ut de iure prebende sue predicte. Thomas de Sancto Albano prebendarius prebende de Dunham in ecclesia beate Marie de Suwell'[192] clamat habere visum franciplegii et ea que ad visum pertinet[193] de omnibus hominibus tenentibus et residentibus in feodo suo in Dunham Derelton'[194] Wymton et Ragunhull' ut de iure prebende sue predicte tenendum apud Dunham bis per annum.[195] Johannes de Sandale prebendarius prebende de Normanton' in ecclesia beate Marie de Suwell'[196] clamat habere visum franciplegii et ea que ad visum pertinet[197] de omnibus hominibus tenentibus et residentibus in[198] feodo suo in Suwell'[199] et Normanton[200] ut de iure prebende sue predicte tenendum[201] bis per annum apud Suwell'.[202] Et modo scilicet in crastino ascensionis domini venit predictum capitulum per Robertum de Totel attornatum suum et similiter predicti Robertus de Wodhous et alii prebendarii per attornatum suum et dicunt quo ad hoc quod ipsi singillatim clamant habere visum franciplegii de omnibus hominibus tenentibus[203] et residentibus in feodis suis in villis predictis et similiter quo ad libertates quas predicti prebendarii clamant habere wayf et strayt'[204] in predictis villis dicunt quod ipsi et predecessores sui a tempore quo non exta[205] memoria semper hactenus usi fuerunt libertatibus illis in predictis villis ut de iure prebendarum suarum predictarum. Et hoc petunt quod inquiratur per patriam etc. Et Adam de Fyncham qui sequitur pro domino rege similiter. Ideo preceptum est vicecomiti quod venire faciat coram domino rege in crastino sancti Johannis baptiste ubicumque etc. xxiiii tam milites etc. de visum de Suwell'[206] Eddynglay[207] Northwell Oxton Crophill'[208] Wodburgh Halghton Bekyngham et[209] Northmuscham[210] Dunham etc.[211] per quos etc. Et qui capitulum et prebendarios predictos nulla affinitate etc. ad recognoscendum etc. si predicti capitulum et prebendarii separatim usi fuerint libertatibus predictis in forma predicta nec ne. Quia etc. Et quo ad hoc quod predictum capitulum clamat quod in quolibet itinere iusticiariorum itinerancium in comitatu Notingh' iusticiarii itinerantes veniant apud Suwell'[212] et sedeant in ostio ecclesie predicte et ibidem terminent placita etc. Ut predictum est idem capitulum dicit quod semper hactenus a tempore quo non extat memoria | seisitum fuit quod iusticiarii itinerantes venerunt ibidem et sederunt in ostio ecclesie de Suthwell' et ibidem audierunt[213] omnia placita tangencia capitulum canonicos et tenentes suos de ecclesia predicta et ministros suos preter placita corone

p. 11

---

[191] A *Northmuscam* [192] A *Suthwell'* [193] A *pertinent* [194] A *Derleton'*
[195] The whole Thomas of St Albans entry is bracketed in the margin, and *Dunham* is written there in the same 17th-c. hand mentioned in note 65 above. [196] A *Suthwell'*
[197] A *pertinent* [198] A omits. [199] A *Suthwell'* [200] Part of the Sandale entry is bracketed in the margin and *Normanton* is written in what may be a 16th-c. hand.
[201] A omits. [202] A *Suthwell'* [203] A inserts *suis*. [204] A *stray* [205] A *extat*
[206] A *Suthwell'* [207] A *Edyngley* [208] A *Crophull'* [209] A omits. [210] A *Northmuscam et* [211] A omits. [212] A *Suthwell'* [213] A inserts *et terminaverunt.*
A pointing hand is drawn in the margin at this point, the end of the first line of page 11.

que prefati justiciarii audiaverunt[214] et terminaverunt ad domum cuiusdam[215] canonici extra sanctuarium. Et dicunt[216] quod in ultimo itinere iusticiariorum in comitatu predicto ante istud iter iusticiarii itinerantes venerunt ibidem ad predicta placita tenenda et similiter in aliis itineribus precedentibus a tempore predicto. Et de hoc vocant recordum rotulorum eorumdem iusticiariorum itinerancium etc.

Ideo mandatum est thesaurario et camerariis suis quod scrutatis rotulis suis de itineribus suis regem inde certificent ad prefatum terminum etc. ad quem crastinum sancti Johannis baptiste scilicet anno domini regis nunc quinto venit predictus Adam qui sequitur pro domino rege et similiter predictum capitulum Robertus de Wodehous Robertus de Notingh'[217] et omnis et[218] alii prebendarii[219] in ecclesia predicta de Suthwell' et eciam iuratores scilicet Hugo de Normanton' Ricardus Ingram Thomas de Whatton' de Stoke Willelmus de la Basage Henricus Cotel Johannes in le Wilewes[220] Ranulphus de Kylvyngton'[221] Robertus de Whiten'. Hugo de Colston' Radulphus de Bulwell' Radulphus clericus de Langar et Alanus de Raby ad hoc electi et triati. Qui dicunt[222] super sacramentum suum quod capitulum predictum et similiter predictus Robertus de Wodehous et omnes prebendarii predicti et eorum predecessores a tempore quo non extat memoria singillatim usi sunt habere visum franciplegii et ea que ad visum pertinent de omnibus hominibus[223] tenentibus suis et residentibus in feodis ipsorum in villis predictis tenendum bis per annum apud Suthwell' et alibi prout superius clamant etc. Et similiter quod predicti[224] Robertus de Wodehous[225] Robertus de Notingham[226] Lambertus de Trikyngham[227] Henricus de Edenstow[228] et Robertus de Bridlyngton'[229] et predecessores sui prebendarii in ecclesia predicta a tempore quo non extat memoria singillatim usi sunt habere libertatem que dicitur wayff in terris et feodis suis prout superius clamant ut de iure prebendarum suarum predictarum. Et quod[230] predictus Lambertus de Trikyngham et eciam predecessores sui a tempore quo non extat memoria semper usi sunt habere libertatem que dicitur stray in manerio suo de Halghton ut de iure prebende sue predicte. Ideo idem capitulum[231] Robertus de Wodehous[232] et omnis alii prebendarii predicti quo ad libertatem visus franciplegii habendum separatim et similiter predicti Robertus de Wodehous Robertus de Notingh'[233] Lambertus de Trikyngham Henricus de Edennestowe[234] et Robertus de Brydlyngton'[235] prebendarii quo ad libertatem habendi wayff in terris tenementis et feodis suis separatim et predictus Lambertus de Trikyngham quo ad libertatem

[214] A *audierunt*   [215] A *alicuius*   [216] A *dici*   [217] A *Notingham*   [218] A omits. [219] A inserts *predicti*.   [220] A *Wylewes*   [221] A *Kylvynton'*   [222] Between the third line of page 11 and this point *nota* is written in the margin in four places.   [223] A inserts *et*.   [224] A *predictus*   [225] A *Wodhous*; underlined in a later hand in the White Book.   [226] Underlined in a later hand.   [227] Underlined in a later hand.   [228] A *Edenestowe*; underlined in a later hand in the White Book.   [229] A *Bridelyngton'*; underlined in a later hand in the White Book.   [230] *Stray* is written in the margin at this point in the same hand as the second note mentioned in note 155 above.   [231] A *iidem capituli*   [232] A *Wodhous*   [233] A *Notingham*   [234] A *Edenestowe*   [235] A *Bridelyngton'*

habendi stray prout superius separatim clamant et prout per predictam iuratum compertum est inde sine die salvo iure domini regis.[236] Nos autem tenorem recordi et processus predictorum ad requisicionem domini Henrici de Eddenestowe[237] tenore presencium duximus exemplificandum. In cui[238] rei testimonium has litteras nostras fieri fecimus patentes.[239] Teste me ipso[240] apud Clarendon' vicesimo sexto die Novembris[241] anno regni nostri septimo.[242]

Margin Heading in 17th-c. hand; the rest of the marginalia for this item are cited at the appropriate place as signified in the textual notes.

Note The White Book also includes versions of the original enrolment from Harle's plea roll of the eyre, and of the subsequent proceedings from the King's Bench plea roll of Easter term 5 Edward III (1331), for which see **145** and **147**. The details of the case are given in full in the introductions to those entries. As noted above (p. 12 n. 1) these letters patent are enrolled on the patent roll for 7 Edward III, part 2 (TNA, C 66/182, mm. 8–7 = A), which have been collated with the version in the White Book. TNA, C 260/43, no. 32 (formerly C 47/73/1/6) is the Chancery file copy of this enrolment, on the Recorda file for 7 Edward III (1333–4), copied following the issue of a writ of *certiorari* issued by the king at Clarendon on 10 November 1333, ordering the copy when made to be returned into Chancery under the seal of Richard of Willoughby, 'chief justice of the king'. The original letters do not survive. In the patent roll the letters are described in the margin as *Pro Henrico de Edenestowe canonico ecclesie beati Marie Suthwell' et capitulo ac aliis canonicis ecclesie illius. CPR 1330–4*, 485, has a very unsatisfactory brief summary. For letters close, dated at Waltham Holy Cross on 8 October 1333, to the treasurer and barons of the Exchequer to order the sheriff to acquit the Chapter and the individual prebendaries of charges and arrears claimed from them in respect of annual income from view of frankpledge in their manors, see *CCR 1333–7*, 149–51. The nine prebendaries individually mentioned in these proceedings are Robert of Woodhouse (Norwell Palishall, 1317–46), Henry of Edwinstowe (Oxton II, 1327–c. 1350), Robert of Nottingham (Oxton I, 1323–after 1333), Lambert of Threekingham (Halloughton, 1310–31), Robert of Bridlington (Woodborough, by 1329–33), William of Barnby (Beckingham, by 1329–61), William of Newark (North Muskham, 1298–1340), Thomas of St Albans (Dunham, 1312–34) and John of Sandale (Normanton, 1317–after 14 December 1349).

15 *Record of the Quo warranto case brought by the king against Robert of Woodhouse, prebendary of Norwell [Palishall], concerning his free warren in Norwell and Norwell Woodhouse, in the Nottinghamshire eyre which began at Nottingham on 13 November 1329, after a claim made by him in the eyre which was not made within the time limit allowed, as a result of which the warren had been taken into the king's hand in distraint. John of Derby, Robert's general attorney, comes to court and successfully reclaims the liberty. He says that the king had inspected a*

---

[236] A inserts *etc. Judic' nota* is written in the margin in what may be a 17th-c. hand.
[237] A *Edenestowe* [238] A *In cuius etc.* [239] A omits *rei...patentes.* [240] A *Teste Rege* [241] A omits the remainder of the sentence. [242] 26 November 1333. Below the end of the entry the following is inserted in a late 15th- or early 16th-c. hand: *Nota infra folio lxxix quomodo Edwardus tercius scribit mandando iusticiariis quod permittat capiendum etc. canonicos ?ander' super hiis articulis premissi. nota.* The entry referred to is **347** below.

charter of Edward II which granted to William of Melton, prebendary of Norwell [Palishall], and his successors in perpetuity, free warren in all his demesne lands in Norwell and Norwell Woodhouse, not being within the king's forest, so that no one could enter and hunt therein without the permission of the liberty holder, on pain of forfeiting £10 to the king. Woodhouse, described as the king's treasurer [an office he held from 16 September 1329 to 1 December 1330], proffers Edward III's charter, dated at Eltham on 29 January 1330, as his warrant, together with a writ close of the king to the justices, dated at Winchester on 12 March 1330, instructing them to permit him to have his warren, so he goes without day [13 November 1329–after 12 March 1330]

p. 12   **Warenna de prebendarii [*sic*] de Overhall' in Norwell'**

Placita¹ de quo waranto coram Willelmo de Herle et sociis iusticiariis domini regis itinerantibus apud Not' die lune proxima post festum sancti Martini episcopi anno regni regis Edwardi tercii post conquestum tercio   HERLE

Robertus de Wodhous² prebendarius prebende de Northwell' in ecclesia beate Marie de Suwell' clamat habere liberam warennam in omnibus dominicis terris suis de Northwell' et Wodhous³ iuxta Northwell' et quia predicta libertas non fuit clamata tempore limitato libertatum clamandum etc. Ideo predicta libertas capiatur in manu domini regis nomine districcionis etc. Postea Johannes de Darby⁴ generalis attornatus predicti Roberti venit in curia hic et petit predictam libertatem per plevinam. Et habet. Et dicit quod dominus rex nunc inspexit cartam domini Edwardi⁵ nuper regis Anglie patris sui in qua continetur quod idem dominus E. R.⁶ pater etc. concessit et confirmavit dilecto clerico suo Willelmo de Melton prebendario prebende de Northwell in ecclesia beate Marie Suwell'⁷ quod ipse et suscessores⁸ sui prebendarii prebende predicte imperpetuum habeant liberam warennam in omnibus dominicis terris suis de Northwell' et Wodhous iuxta Northwell' que sunt a⁹ prebenda predicta dum tamen terre ille non sunt infra metas foreste regis. Ita quod nullus intret terras illas ad fugandum in eisdem vel ad aliquid capiendum quod ad warennam pertineat sine licencia et voluntate ipsius vel successorum suorum predictorum super forisfacturam regi decem libras etc. Tenorem cuius carte dominus rex nunc per cartam suam ad requisicionem dilecti clerici sui Roberti de Wodhous¹⁰ tesaurarii (*sic*) sui nunc prebendarii prebende de Northwell' duxit exemplificandum etc. Et profert predictam cartam predicti domini regis nunc que hoc idem¹¹ testatur etc. cuius datus est apud Elteham¹² vicesimo nono die Januarii anno regni sui quarto.¹³ Et eo waranto clamat habere liberam warennam predictam etc. Profert eciam breve domini regis nunc iusticiariis suis hic

---

¹ The cartulary copy has been compared with the enrolled version beginning in TNA, JUST 1/687, rot. 15d (= A).   ² A *Wodhouse*   ³ A *Wodhouse*   ⁴ A *Derby*   ⁵ A *E*   ⁶ A *Rex*   ⁷ A *Suthwell'*   ⁸ *Sic*; A *successores*   ⁹ A *de*   ¹⁰ A *Wodehous*   ¹¹ Corrected from *eidem* by erasure.   ¹² A *Eltham*   ¹³ 29 January 1330.

clausum mandans eisdem quod dilectum clericum suum Robertum de Wodhous nunc prebendarium prebende predicte warennam predictam habere permittant iuxta tenorem carte supradicte et eam ei coram ipsis in itinere suo allocent et cuius datus est apud Wyiton[14] xii die Martii anno regni sui iiii[15] et ideo predictus Robertus inde sine die salvo iure regis etc.

Margin Page heading in mid-16th-c. hand.

Note The entry is collated with the text as given in the main plea roll of the chief justice in the eyre, William of Harle, TNA, JUST 1/687, rot. 15d, referred to as 'A' in the notes, printed in *Placita de Quo Warranto*, 636, of which the opening image on the AALT website is http://aalt.law.uh.edu/AALT4/JUST1/JUST1no687/bJUST1no-687dorses/IMG_7264.htm. The plea roll readings are more authoritative than those in the White Book itself. In the Rex roll, JUST 1/684, the entry is found on rot. 16d, but that version has not been collated here. The original charter for the warren, by Edward II to William of Melton, was granted on 9 June 1310 at Kempton: *CChR 1300–26*, 137.

16 *Record of the Quo warranto case brought by the king against John of Thoresby, prebendary of Norwell [Overhall], in the Nottinghamshire eyre which began at Nottingham on 13 November 1329, concerning his claim to liberties in Norwell. He was summoned to answer by what warrant he claims a warren in his demesne lands in Norwell, a market every week on Thursday; a fair every year lasting for three days on the eve, day and morrow of Trinity; correction of breaches of the assize of bread and ale; and judgment of pillory and tumbrel. He claims the warren, market and fair through a charter, dated at Winchester on 24 November 1256 (361), granted by Henry III to Master John Clarell, canon of the prebend of Norwell [Overhall], his predecessor, which he proffers. He claims the other liberties by uninterrupted use from time immemorial by his predecessors. William of Deanham, who sues for the king, seeks an inquiry as to whether Thoresby and his predecessors did use the liberties as he claims, and if so by what right, in what way and from what time. Afterwards twelve jurors say on oath that John Clarell and Thoresby used the warren and the fair from the time the charter was made. As to the market, they say that they had it first from the making of the charter, but afterwards it was disused because nobody came. As to correction of breaches of the assize of bread and ale, they say that they held it from time immemorial until now, and that they punished offenders against the assize by amercements, not corporal punishment. The assize and the market are taken into the king's hand. Afterwards, Thomas of Radcliffe and Adam of Cradley made fine of one mark on John's behalf to have his liberties restored, to use how he pleases, and he goes without day, saving the king's right* [After 13 November 1329]

---

[14] *Sic, recte* Wynton'; A *Wynton'*   [15] 12 March 1330.

Libertates prebendarii de Overhall' in Norwell'

Johannes de Thoresby[1] canonicus Suwell' prebendarius prebende[2] de Northwell' summonitus fuit ad respondendum domino rege de placito quo waranto clamat habere warennam in omnibus dominicis suis in Northwell' in comitatu Not'[3] et mercatum qualibet septima ibidem per diem iovis et unam feriam singulis annis duraturis per tres dies scilicet vigilia et die et in crastino sancte Trinitatis ad emendum[4] assise panis et cervisie fracte et iudicium pillore et[5] tumbrelli etc. Et quo ad omnes libertates predictas preter emendas assise panis et cervisie et pillor' et tumbrell' dicit quod dominus H. quondam rex Anglie proavus domini regis nunc per cartam suam concessit et confirmavit pro se et heredibus suis dilecto clerici suo magistro Johanni Clarell' canonice[6] prebende de Northwell' in ecclesia de Suwell predecessori predicti Johannis quod ipse et successores sui canonici eiusdem prebende imperpetuum habeant liberam warennam in omnibus dominicis terris[7] suis predicte prebende sue de Northwell in comitatu predicto dum tamen terre ille non sunt[8] infra metas foreste regis. Ita quod nullus intret terras illas ad fugandum in eis vel ad aliquid capiendum que ad warennam pertinent[9] sine licencia et voluntate ipsius Johannis vel predictorum successorum suorum super forisfacturam regis decem librarum. Concessit eciam eidem predecessori suo et per eandem cartam confirmavit pro se et heredibus suis quod ipse et predicti successores sui imperpetuum habeant unum mercatum singulis septimanis per diem iovis apud predictam prebendam suam de Norwell. Et quod habeant ibidem unam feriam singulis annis duraturam per tres dies videlicet in vigilia et in die et in crastino sancte Trinitatis nisi mercatum illud et feria sint ad nocumentum mercatorum vicinorum et vicinarum feriarum. Et profert cartam eiusdem Henrici regis[10] proavi etc. que predictas concessiones et confirmationes testatur in forma predicta cuius datus est apud Wynton' vicesimo quarto die Novembris anno regni sui quadragesimo primo.[11] Et eo waranto etc. Et quo ad libertates residuas dicit quod ipse predecessores[12] | sui prebendariis prebende predicte a tempore quo non extat memoria habuerunt huiusmodi emendas de omnibus residentibus in feodo predicte prebende[13] et ratione eiusdem libertatis pillor' et tumbrell' tanquam iudicialia eisdem. Et illis huc usque usi sint[14] sine interupcione. Et eo waranto etc. Et Willelmus de Denum qui sequitur pro rege petit quod inquiratur si predictus Johannes et predecessores sui libertatibus illis usi sint[15] sicut idem Johannes superius clamat et si[16] sic tunc qualiter et quo modo et a qua tempore etc. Ideo inquiratur etc. Postea xii iuratores dicunt super sacramentum suum quod predictus Johannes Clarell' predecessor etc.

p. 13

---

[1] The cartulary copy has been compared with the enrolled version beginning in TNA, JUST 1/687, rot. 21 (= A). The images of the entry on the Anglo-American Legal Tradition website begin with http://aalt.law.uh.edu/AALT4/JUST1/JUST1no687/aJUST1no687f-ronts/IMG_7216.htm   [2] A *de prebenda*   [3] A *Notingh'*   [4] A *et emendas*   [5] A *cum*   [6] *Sic*; A *canonico*   [7] A omits.   [8] A *sint*   [9] A *quod ad warennam pertineat*   [10] A *H. R.*   [11] 24 November 1256, cf. **361**.   [12] A *et omnes predecessores*   [13] A *prebende predicte*   [14] *Sic*; A *sunt*   [15] *Sic*; A *sunt*   [16] Corrected from *sic* by erasure.

et similiter predictus Johannes de Thoresby a tempore confeccionis carte predicte warenna illa huc usque bene usi sunt et similiter predicta feria. Et quo ad mercatum predictum dicunt quod ipsi habuerunt primo virtute confeccionis[17] carte predicte et postea illi abusi sunt eo quod nullus ibi venit. Et quo ad emendas assise panis et cervisie fracte dicunt quod ipsi et predecessores sui a tempore quo non extat memoria[18] emendas illas huc usque habuerunt. Et[19] dicunt quod ipsi et predecessores sui usi sunt punire decelinquentes[20] contra assisam predictam per amerciamenta[21] et non per penam corporalem. Ideo predictum mercatum et emende etc. capiantur in manum domini regis. Postea Thomas de Radclyff[22] Adam de Cradele fecerunt finem cum domino rege pro predicto Johanne de i marca pro libertatibus eidem[23] Johanni rehabendis. Ideo predictus Johannes rehabeat libertates suas predictas et illis utantur modo quo decet. Et quo ad alias libertates predictus Johannes inde sine die salvo iure regis.[24]

Margin   Heading in mid-16th-c. hand, as is **Libertates de Norwell'** in the left margin above the entry in the same hand.

Note   John Thoresby, prebendary of Norwell Overhall (1327/9–33). For Henry III's grants to John Clarell (Norwell Overhall, 1256–95), see **360** and **361**.

ROYAL LETTERS, 17–27

17   *Notification by Henry I to Thurstan, archbishop of York, and all of Nottinghamshire that he has confirmed the archbishop's grant to Southwell, of the churches of [North] Leverton and Beckingham to form a prebend*   Winchester [19 October 1119 × April–May 1133]

Carta regis Henrici de prebenda de Bekingham

Henricus,[1] rex Anglie,[2] archiepiscopo Ebor' et iusticie et vicecomiti et omnibus baronibus \et/ suis fidelibus de Notingham scira, salutem. Sciatis quia[3] concessi pro Dei amore donacionem[4] illam quam Thurstinus, archiepiscopus Ebor' dedit et concessit ecclesie sancte Marie de Suwell' in prebendam, videlicet ecclesiam de manerio suo de Legreton et ecclesiam de manerio suo [de] Bechingeham, sicut idem archiepiscopus predicte ecclesie in prebendam dedit et concessit. Et volo et precipio ut bene et \in/ pace et honorifice teneat. Testibus: Rogero episcopo Sar' et Eustacio filio Johannis apud Wynton'.

[1] In this and **18** and **19**, the king's name is abbreviated to a small H in the main text, with a large rubricated H in the left margin   [2] *sic* here and in following royal charters when the usual royal style at this period was *rex Anglorum*   [3] *sic* for *quod*   [4] MS *donaciacionem*

Date   After Thurstan was consecrated (19 October 1119) and Henry I's last visit to Winchester (April–May 1133); see *EEA York 1070–1154*, no. 65 for comment. In Sharpe, *Acta Henry I*, under Southwell, it is dated 1114–33, but with note 'The lack of names or initials for officers suggests later rather than earlier'.

[17] A *concessionis*   [18] Followed by a space with a red line through it.   [19] A *set*   [20] *Sic*; A *delinquentes*   [21] A *amerciamentam*   [22] A *Radeclif*   [23] Written twice, the first marked with a red mark above the line.   [24] A adds *etc.*

Note   NA, M 494, f. 106ʳ for a copy made for Thoroton. Pd. in *Mon. Ang.* viii, 1314 (vii) after **17**; Dickinson, 183 (after Dugdale); cal. in *RRAN*, ii, no. 1871 (with date range 1114–33); to be published in Sharpe, *Acta Henry I*, under Southwell, after **17** and **33**, where it is copied again with very minor orthographical differences. For Thurstan's charter, see **34**. Roger, bishop of Salisbury (elected 1102, consecrated 1107–39). Eustace FitzJohn (d. 1157), one of the most important servants of Henry I, especially active in northern England from *c.* 1120, where he carried out many judicial inquiries. As Sharpe comments, 'North Leverton and Beckingham appear as berewicks in the archiepiscopal manor of Laneham (Notts) in Domesday Book (*DB*, i. 283a; § 5. 4), but both are now described as manors and both have acquired churches since 1086'.

18   *Notification by Henry I to the archbishop of York, justiciars, sheriffs, barons and his faithful men that he has permitted Thurstan, archbishop of York, to assign to St Mary's, Southwell, for the establishment of a prebend, the church of Dunham which the king had previously given to Thurstan*   Winchester [19 October 1119 × April–May 1133]

Carta regis Henrici de prebenda de Dunham

Henricus, rex Anglie, archiepiscopo Ebor' et iusticie et vicecomiti et omnibus baronibus et fidelibus suis, salutem. Sciatis quia¹ concessi Turstino, archiepiscopo Ebor' ut ponat ad ecclesiam sancte Marie de Suwell' in prebendam ecclesiam de Duneham, quam prius dederam ipsi archiepiscopo. Sicut idem archiepiscopo eam predicte ecclesie concessit et posuit. Et volo et precipio ut bene et in pace et honorifice teneat. Testibus: episcopo Sar' et Eustacio filio Johannis apud Winton'.

¹ MS *sic* for *quod*

Date   See note to **17**; this was probably issued on the same occasion and the witnesses are identical.

Note   Repeated in **31**. A late 15ᵗʰ-c./early 16ᵗʰ-c. copy survives in NA, SC7/1/5, f. 8ᵛ, and one made for Thoroton in NA, M 494, f. 106ᵛ. Pd. in *Mon. Ang.*, viii, 1314 (vi), Dickinson, *Southwell*, 183 (after Dugdale); to be published in Sharpe, *Acta Henry I*, under Southwell; cal. in *RRAN*, ii, no. 1870. Thurstan's charter granting Dunham church does not seem to have survived. Dunham was the king's most valuable manor in Nottinghamshire in 1086 (*DB*, i. 281a; § 1. 1) but it is not clear when Henry I had given the church to the archbishop.

19   *Writ by Henry II to Ranulf the sheriff and his other ministers confirming the privileges and customs of the canons of Southwell as held since the time of his grandfather, Henry I, and warning them not to trouble the canons with keeping the ways or other unjust causes*   Nottingham [September 1155 × August 1158]

Carta regis de libertatibus et consuetudinibus canonicorum Suthwell'

Henricus, rex Anglie¹ et dux Normannie et Aquitanie et comes Andegavie, Randulfo, vicecomiti, et ministris suis, salutem. Precipio quod canonici de Suwell' teneant omnes terras et res et possessiones et tenuras suas cum omnibus libertatibus et liberis et consuetudinibus et pertinenciis suis ita bene et in pace et libere et quiete et juste et honorifice sicut umquam melius et liberius et quietius et honorificentius tenuerunt tempore regis Henrici, avi mei. Et prohibeo quod neque pro custodia viarum[2] neque pro aliqua injusta occasione eos gravetis, neque injuste inplacitum ponatis. Et nisi feceritis, justicia mea faciat fieri. [Teste:] Thoma cancellario apud Notingham.

[1] Sic for *Anglorum*, and likewise *Normannorum*, *Aquitanorum* and *Andegavorum*   [2] *marium* in **25** below, and in an original inspeximus of Richard II and its enrollment according to *Acta Henry II*, ed. Vincent, no. 2520, but clearly *viarum* in the Southwell copies here and at **142** and **144**.

Date   After the promotion of Ranulf fitz Ingelram as sheriff at Michaelmas 1155 (Green, *English Sheriffs to 1154*, 68; *PR 2–4 Henry II*, 38), during the chancellorship of Thomas Becket and before his promotion as archbishop, thus before Henry II's crossing to France in 1158 (*Acta Henry II*, no. 2520 and note).

Note   Pd. in *Mon Ang.*, VI, iii, 1314 (v); see *Acta Henry II*, no. 2520 for full details. For Henry I's charter of privileges see **21**.

20   *Charter of Richard I confirming to the church of York and to his brother, Geoffrey, archbishop-elect, and his successors, that all the lands they hold in Nottinghamshire in demesne and prebends are to be free of forest law as decided before Hugh, bishop of Durham, Robert, bishop of Lincoln and Robert, earl of Leicester, justices of Henry II*
Dover, 9 December 1189

Carta Ricardi regis de quibusdam libertatibus terre domini archiepiscopi

Ricardus, Dei gracia rex Anglie, dux Normannie, comes Andegavie, archiepiscopis, episcopis, abbatibus, comitibus, baronibus, iusticiariis, vicecomitibus et omnibus forestariis et ballivis et fidelibus suis, salutem. Sciatis nos concessisse et presenti carta confirmasse Deo et ecclesie sancti Petri Ebor' et Galfrido, fratri meo, eiusdem ecclesie electo, et successoribus suis quod omnes terre que sunt in Notinghamsyra de archiepiscopatu Ebor' in dominicis quam in prebendis sint deforestate. Ita quod sint quiete de wastis, essartis et placitis forestatis et de omni rewardo quod nullus forestarius nec aliquis ballivorum suorum se quicquam intromittat, sicut disracionatum fuit coram Hugone Dunelmensi et Roberto Lincolniensi episcopis | et Roberto comite Legr', iusticiariis domini regis Henrici,   p. 14 patris nostri, et carte eorundem que sunt in ecclesia Ebor' testantur. Testibus: Hugone Dunelm', Hugone Coventre', Huberto Mar',[1] episcopis, Johanne Marscalle, Willelmo Marescall'. Datum apud Doveriam ix die Decembris per manum Willelmi Elyensis electi, cancellarii nostri, regni nostri anno primo.

[1] A scribal error for *Sar'*, either because in charters 's' occasionally looks like 'm', or because the scribe was looking ahead to the Marshal family members.

Margin   *Prebendarum . . . [two illegible words]* in right margin in late medieval hand.

Note   *Sherwood Book*, 183–4 for another, slightly abbreviated, copy of this charter. It is mentioned in the chronicle of Roger of Howden, who may have been present: *Gesta*

Regis Henrici Benedicti Abbatis, ed. W. Stubbs (London: Rolls Series 1867), ii, 100: *Et idem rex clamavit Deo et Sancto Petro Eboraci, et eidem Gaufrido Eboracensi electo, et omnibus archiepiscopis ei successuris, omnes terras suas et canonicorum suorum, quietas in perpetuum de rewardo foreste, et ab omnibus aliis exigentiis et gravaminibus foreste et forestariorum. Et liberam potestatum dedit ei, et carta sua confirmavit, licentiam capiendi venationem per omnes prebendas suas in Eboraci et Notinham syriis.* The hearing before the three justices of Henry II must have taken place before the death of Robert de Chesney, bishop of Lincoln, on 27 December 1166.

The 1189 witnesses were: Hugh de Puiset, bishop of Durham (1153–95), Hugh de Nonant, bishop of Coventry (1185–98), Hubert Walter, bishop of Salisbury (1189–May 1193, when translated to Canterbury), John the Marshal (d. March 1194) and his half-brother, William Marshal, later earl of Pembroke (d. 1219), the most celebrated of English Marshals. The charter was delivered by the Chancellor, William Longchamp, bishop-elect of Ely since 15 September 1189, who was consecrated on 31 December 1189.

21 *Writ of Henry I to the sheriffs of Nottingham and barons of Nottinghamshire and Derbyshire that he has confirmed to Archbishop Thomas all his customs over his lands, especially those of the church of Southwell, as held in the time of his brother, and ordering justice to be administered in accordance with the rights of the canons of St Peter's [York]*

Nottingham, [?17 October 1109]

Carta regis Henrici de libertatibus et consuetudinibus terre archiepiscopi in Notingham sira

Henricus, rex Anglie, vicecomitibus de Notingham syra et omnibus baronibus suis de Notingham syra et Derbia syra salutem. Sciatis me concecisse[1] Thome archiepiscopo omnes posessiones et consuetudines suas super omnes terras suas quam habet in Notingham syra et maxime super illas que pertinent ad ecclesiam sancte Marie de Suwell', sicut melius tenuit et habuit tempore fratris mei. Et siquis aliquam calumpniam super homines qui in illis terris manent, fecerint, talem rectitudinem qualem canonici sancti Petri facerent talem facient et in tali loco. Et si quis super hoc aliquam iniuriam fecerit, michi emendabit. Testibus: Rogero episcopo Salesbr' et Ranulpho, cancellario, et comite de Mellen apud Notingham.

[1] MS *cocecisse*

Date Probably issued at the time of a well-known council held at Nottingham on 17 October 1109 as a number of other charters with the same witnesses suggest; see *RRAN*, ii, nos 918–23 and Sharpe, *Acta Henry I*, passim.

Note *Acta Henry I* (York 18) for the fullest discussion of the manuscript tradition. This copy and three further ones (**26, 143** and a partial one in **148**) are apparently the earliest now surviving. That in **148** is from a confirmation for Southwell by Richard II, 4 December 1381 (*CPR 1381–5*, 57), which subsequently served for further confirmations by Henry IV, Henry V, Henry VI, Edward IV, Henry VIII and Philip and Mary (details listed in *Acta Henry I*). Previous editions include *Mon. Ang.*, viii, 1314 (no. v) and *CChR*, v, 478–9. Roger, bishop of Salisbury (1102–39); Ranulf, chancellor of Henry I (1107–c. 1 January 1123); Robert de Beaumont, count of Meulan, earl of Leicester (d. 1118).

22 *Writ by King Stephen to William Peveril of Nottingham, the sheriffs and his other ministers of Nottinghamshire ordering that the canons of Southwell should have possession of their prebendal woods and enjoy them as in the time of King Henry, forbidding his foresters from taking or selling anything from them* [York, 1136 × 1154]

Carta regis Henrici¹ de boscis canonicorum ecclesie beate Marie Suthwell'

Stephanus, rex Anglie, Willelmo Peverell de Notingham et vicecomitibus et ministris suis de Notingham syra salutem. Precipio quod canonici sancte Marie de Suwell' habeant in manu sua et propria custodia boscos de prebendis suis et quicquid eis opus fuerit inde capiant et habeant ad aisiamenta sua facienda sicut melius habuerunt tempore regis Henrici. Et prohibete forestariis nostris ne inde capiant vel vendant. Teste: Hugone de Essart' apud Eboracum.

¹ *sic*

Date Limits as assigned in *RRAN*, iii, no. 831 where it is printed in full. Hugh de Essartis was a fairly frequent witness throughout the king's reign.

Note Pd. in Dickinson, *Southwell* (1787), 185 and also (1819), 391.

23 *Inspeximus and confirmation by Henry III of the customs and liberties of the archbishop of York in the forest of Nottinghamshire established following an inquiry at Nottingham before Robert, earl of Leicester [before 27 December 1166, and cited in full], as to the customs in the time of Henry I* Westminster, 15 June 1271

Carta regis Henrici de libertatibus et consuetudinibus domini archiepiscopi de foresta

Henricus, Dei gracia rex Anglie, dominus Hibernie et dux Aquitanie, omnibus¹ ad quos presentes litere pervenerunt² salutem. Inspeximus scripturam de consuetudinibus et libertatibus archiepiscopi Ebor' in Notingham syre in hec verba:

Ranulphus, vicecomes, Hugo de Burrun, Radulphus Asselyn, Robertus de Perer, Radulphus de Anneleya, Galfridus de Leffremunt, Radulphus de Herouvilla, Hugo filius Wulnet, Robertus de Hovringham, Alexander filius Tocthe, Symon filius Ricardi de Muez, Engelramus filius vicecomitis, Hugo filius Rogeri, Willelmus filius Rainerii, Hugo filius Aldridi, Herdwinus, Gaufridus de Stanton'. Isti iuraverunt apud Notingham in presencia Roberti, comitis Leycestrie, qui ex parte regis eis precepit quod veram dicerent de consuetudinibus et libertatibus quas terra archiepiscopi que est in Notynghamsyre et ipse archiepiscopus habuit in eadem syra tempore Henrici senioris et anno et die que ipse Henricus fuit vivus et mortuus. Et postquam iuraverunt et dixerunt quod tota terra archiepiscopi extra forestam erat que intra \sub/scriptos terminos continetur. De sicut Dovrbek' in [cadit]³ Trentam et ex parte superiori ab aqua de Dovrbek' usque in Cuningeswad de sicut via de Blia vadit et tota terra eius que est ultra Cuningeswad et ultra predictam viam que est extra forestam erat usque Bicheresdic. Ita quod nullus forestarius regis ex parte regis se de terra illa intromittebat, set archiepiscopus et homines sui libere et essartabant et faciebant quicquid volebant sicut de sua. Et extra terminos prenominatos in veteri foresta venebatur archiepiscopus per novem dies in anno, scilicet tribus diebus contra natale, tribus diebus contra Pasca, tribus contra Pentecosten per totum nemus de Blidewarda. Et in nemore illo de Blidewarda habeat archiepiscopus et canonici sui et homines sui omnia easiamenta sua sine guasto, et habeat proprios forestarios suos et mel et areas aucipitium et nisorum et pasnagium. Ego Robertus episcopus Lincoln' interfui et sigillo meo signavi. Et ego Hugo episcopus Dunelm' interfui et sigillo meo signavi.

Nos igitur scripturam predictam exemplicari fecimus ad cautelam, volentes quod per ruptas eiusdem scripture archiepiscopo Ebor' qui pro tempore fuerit inde periculum remineat temporibus futuris. In cuius rei testimonium has literas nostras fieri fecimus patentes. Teste me ipso apud Westmonasterium quintodecimo die Junii anno regni nostri quinquegesimo quinto.

¹ *omnes*   ² MS *sic*   ³ Supplied from TNA, C 66/89, m. 13.

Margin   *Nota pro venacione archiepiscopi* in late medieval hand towards bottom left margin.

Date   Before the death of Robert de Chesney, bishop of Lincoln (27 December 1166).

Note   Cal. in *CPR 1266–72*, 541–2 (TNA, C 66/89, m. 13), with six more witnesses, while some of the later witnesses in this list are not in the patent roll version, of which the full Latin text is given in Crook, 'Archbishopric', 339–40.

24   *Letters patent of Henry III pardoning Archbishop William [recte Walter] for waste by his canons at Oxton in the archbishop's wood at Blidworth within the forest of Sherwood which had been taken into the king's hand following the forest eyre in 23 Henry III [1238–9]*
                                                        Windsor, 10 March 1240

p. 15   **Carta r[egis] H[enrici] de perdonacione facta Willelmo archiepiscopo de wasto facto a canonicis Suthwell' in bosco Blytheworh**

Henricus, Dei gracia rex Anglie, dominus Hibernie, dux Normannie et Aquitanie, comes Andegavie, omnibus ballivis suis et fidelibus suis presentes literas inspecturis¹ salutem. Sciatis quod perdonavimus venerabili patri Willelmo, Ebor' archiepiscopo, in perpetuum omne vastum tam vetus quam novum factum a canonicis suis de Oxton in bosco ipsius archiepiscopi de Blytheward', que est infra forestam de Shyrewude, usque ad ultimum iter iusticiariorum nostrorum itinerantium ad placita foreste in comitatu Notingham anno regni nostri vicesimo tercio, pro quo quidem vasto predictus boscus captus fuit in manum nostram quem,² boscum eidem archiepiscopo reddidimus. In cuius rei testimonium has literas nostras patentes fieri fecimus. Teste me ipso apud Wyndesor' decimo die Marcii anno regni nostri vicesimo quarto.

¹ MS *inspecturos*   ² Followed by *et* struck out.

Note   *Close Rolls ii*, 180, with an additional clause after '*reddidimus*': *Et ideo vobis mandamus quod de toto vasto predicto ipsum archiepiscopum quietum esse, et ei talem saisinam habere faciatis de eodem bosco qualem inde habuit antequam captus esset in manum nostram occasione predicta, salvis (*sic*) predictis canonicis solito estoverio suo quod in eo habere debent.* The Sherwood Forest eyre referred to is the one that had been held by Robert de Ros and associates in 1238.

25   *Writ by Henry II to Ranulf the sheriff and his other ministers confirming the privileges and customs of the canons of Southwell as held since the time of his grandfather, Henry I, and warning them not to trouble the canons with keeping the ways or other unjust causes*
Nottingham [September 1155 × August 1158, or after May 1172 × 1189]

Carta r[egis] H[enrici] de libertatibus et consuetudinibus terre canonicorum Suthwell'

Henricus, Dei gratia rex Anglie et dux Normannie et Aquitanie et comes Andegavie, Randulfo, vicecomiti, et ministris suis, salutem. Precipio quod canonici de Suwella teneant omnes terras et res et possessiones et tenuras suas cum omnibus libertatibus et liberis consuetudinibus et pertinenciis suis ita bene et in pace et libere et quiete et juste et honorifice sicut umquam melius et liberius et quietius et honorificentius tenuerunt tempore regis H[enrici], avi mei. Et prohibeo quod neque pro custodia viarum[1] neque pro aliqua alia injusta occasione eos[2] gravetis, neque injuste inplacitum ponatis. Et nisi[3] feceritis, justicia mea faciat fieri. T[este:] H. Cant' apud Notingham.

[1] MS *marium* (cf. **19** textual note 1 above)   [2] MS *eas*   [3] MS *nichil* corrected to *nisi*

Date   See **19** for justification of the date and publication details if this is another version of that charter of Henry II. However if the royal *intitulatio* 'H. dei gratia rex Anglorum' here is correct (i.e. if the copyist did not insert it simply because he was used to it), **25** must be later than May 1172, and the 'Randulf', sheriff of Nottingham, to whom it is addressed may in fact be Ralph Murdac, sheriff in the 1180s. The witness 'H. Cant'', cannot be an archbishop of Canterbury or a royal chancellor, since the only H. who fits either of these positions, Hubert Walter (archbishop of Canterbury 1193–1205 and chancellor in the early years of John's reign), did not acquire them until well after Henry II's death. It is possible he might be Herbert le Poer, archdeacon of Canterbury 1175–94 and later bishop of Salisbury (cf. **Introduction**, p. lvii).

Note   For Henry I's charter of privileges see **21**.

26   *Another copy of **21**, with only minor orthographical differences but with rubric* Carta regis Henrici de libertatibus et consuetudines capituli Suthwell'. *See also **143** and **148***

Note   Sharpe (*Acta Henry I*, York 18) considers this a better copy than **21** for establishing a definitive edition.

27   *Inspeximus and confirmation by Henry III of the purported charter of liberties of Henry I for the church of York confirming its ancient immunities as in the time of King Edward, with further concessions*
Portsmouth, 5 July 1253

Carta regis Henrici de libertatibus et consuetudinibus ecclesie beati Petri Ebor' et ecclesie beate Marie Suthwell' per magnam bullam Alexandri[1]

Henricus, Dei gracia rex Anglie, dominus Hybernie, dux Normannie [et] Aquitanie et comes Andigavie, archiepiscopis, episcopis, abbatibus, prioribus, comitibus, baronibus, iusticiariis, vicecomitibus, prepositis, ministris et omnibus ballivis et fidelibus suis salutem. Inspeximus cartam quam dominus Henricus quondam rex Anglie proavuus noster fecit ecclesie sancti Petri Ebor' in hec verba:

Henricus, rex Anglie, archiepiscopis, episcopis, abbatibus, consulibus, proceribus et universis fidelibus Francis et Anglis tocius Anglie, salutem.

Posessiones et dignitates et libertates et consuetudines quas habuit Ebor[acensis] ecclesia, concedo regia autoritate et presenti carta confirmo sicut hic subscripte sunt sub regibus antiquis, archiepiscopis et quod plerique meminisse possunt Edwardo rege et Aldredo archiepiscopo fuit ecclesie sancti Petri consuetudo egregie libertatis.

Siquis enim quemlibet cuiuscunque facinoris aut flagitii reum et convictum infra atrium ecclesie caperet et retineret universali judicio vi hundreth emendabit. Si vero infra ecclesiam xii hundreth, infra chorum xviii retinencia[2] quousque de singulis sicut de sacrilegiis injuncta in hundreth viii libre continentur.

Quod si aliquis vesano spiritu agitatus, diabolico ausu quemquam capere presumeret in cathedra lapidea iuxta altare quam Angli vocant friðstol, id est cathedra quietudinis vel pacis, huius tam flagitiosi sacrilegii emenda sub nullo iudicio erat sub nullo pecunie numero claudebantur, sed apud Anglos boteles, hoc est sine emenda vocabatur.

Hec emende nichil ad episcopum sed ad canonicos pertinebant. Canonici sancti Petri in hirð, id est domestica vel intrinseca familia appellabatur.

Terra canonicorum proprie mensa sancti Petri.

Denique si quid in ecclesia vel in cimiterio vel in domibus canonicorum vel in terris eorum in iuste agerent, aut ipsi canonici adversus se invicem aut adversus alios aut alii adversus canonicos vel adversus alios forisfactura nulla archiepiscopo sed tota canonicis iudicabatur.

Archiepiscopus autem in rebus canonicorum hoc tantum iuris habebat, quod defuncto canonico ipse aliis prelationes et prebendas prebebat. Nec tamen sine sigillo et assensu decani et capituli.

Si vero archiepiscopus adversus apostolicum vel regem comitteret ad quod redimendum vel pacificandum pecunia opus esset nichil tamen canonici archiepiscopo preter suam voluntatem darent, | et pecunia canonicorum et hominum eorum pro commisso vel debito archiepiscopo nec eciam in manum[3] capientur.

Habebant canonici in domibus et in terris suis soccam et saccam, tol et theam, intol et uuttol et infangenetheof et omnes easdem honoris et libertatis consuetudines quas ipse rex in terris suis habebat et quas archiepiscopus de domino Deo et de rege tenebat.

Hoc eciam et amplius quod nemo de terra canonicorum sancti Petri wayntachmot nec tridingmot nec schiresmot sequebatur, sed calumpnans et calumpniatus ante hostium monasterii sancti Petri rectitudinem recipebat

p. 16

et faciebat. Hoc autem a religiosis principibus et bonis antecessoribus sic provisum est, quatinus canonici placitantes, puls[at]o signo ad horas canonicas cito possint regredi, archepiscopus vero per senescallos suos et milites suos facilius erat predicta placita sequi et tenere.

Si vero aliquis terram sancto Petro daret vel venderet, nemo postea seccam vel saccam, thol aut theam, in illa clamabit, sed easdem consuetudines quas et alia terra sancti Petri ista habebat, tamen amoris et reverencie antecessores nostri huic sancte principis apostolorum ecclesie deferebant.

Quando autem rex congregabat exercitum unus[4] *homo tantum preparabatur de tota terra canonicorum cum vexillo sancti Petri qui, si burgenses in exercitum irent, dux et signifer eos precederent, sine burgensibus vero nec ipse iret.*

Hanc igitur consuetudinem sive dignitatem habent canonici sancti Petri ab antecessoribus regibus, nominatim quoque a rege Edwardo concessam et conformatam, ut nullus de familia regis vel de exercitu eius in propriis domibus canonicorum nec in civitate nec extra hospit[ar]etur.

Ubicunque fit duellum Ebor[aci] iuramenta debent fieri super textum vel super reliquias ecclesie sancti Petri, et facto duello victor arma victi ad ecclesiam sancti Petri offerebat gracias a Deo et sancto Petro pro victoria.

Si canonici vel clerici vel homines eorum clamorem fecerint in placitis regis clamor eorum ante omnem causam terminetur quantum potest terminari servata ecclesie dignitate.

Teste: [T] archiepiscopo, W[illelmo] Giffard', episcopo Winton', R[oberto] Balo', episcopo Lincoln', R[annulfo] Flamb[ard], episcopo Dunelm', W[illelmo], comite Sear',[5] R[adulfo] Basset, G[alfrido] Ridel, F[orne] filio Singulfi apud Winton'.

Nos autem concessionem et confirmacionem predictam ratam habentes et gratam eam pro nobis et heredibus nostris predicte ecclesie concessimus et confirmamus sicut prefata carta ipsius regis Henrici racionabiliter testatur et sicut eadem ecclesia libertatibus in predicta carta contentis huc usque usa est.

Et ad declaracionem quarundam libertatum in eadem carta subquibusdam [*sic*] generalitatibus contentarum et concessionem libertatum uberiorem concedimus decano et capitulo eiusdem ecclesie et hac via confirmamus pro nobis et heredibus nostris quod ipsi decanus et capitulum in perpetuum habeant omnia merciamenta omnium hominum suorum ad ipsos decanum[6] et capitulum et singulos canonicos pertinencium, et fines pro eisdem merciamentis. Ita quod nec nos nec heredes nostros nichil inde pertineat. Sed ipsi decanus et capitulum et canonici recipiant de hominibus suis quicquid recipere debemus pro quocunque delicto seu transgressione amerciati fuerint in curia nostra, sive coram nobis vel baronibus nostris de scaccario sive coram iusticiariis nostris de banco sive coram iusticiariis nostris itinerantibus ad communia placita sive coram iusticiariis nostris assignatis ad quascunque assisas capiendas vel gaiolas deliberandas, sive ad quascunque inquisiciones faciendas, sive eciam inexcitati coram quibuscunque aliis iusticiariis nostris, vicecomitibus, inquisitoribus, prepositis, ballivis seu aliis ministris nostris ad quocunque officium ex parte nostra deputatis. Exceptis iusticiariis nostris et heredum nostrorum ad placita foreste nostre deputatis, salvis nobis et heredibus nostris amerciamentis predictorum decani et capituli de propriis delictis suis ubicunque in curia nostra amerciati fuerint et omnibus aliis finibus quam pro amerciamentis hominum suorum quos ipsi et quicunque homines sui fecerint nobiscum vel coram iusticiariis aliis ballivis nostris. Salvis eciam nobis placitis foreste nostre et omnibus finibus et merciamentis proventuris de ipsis hominibus suis de eadem foresta.

Et quod idem decanus et capitulum in perpetuum habeant omnia catalla et bona quoruncunque hominum suorum ut legatorum,[7] dampnatorum et fugitivorum de quibus posset aliquis questus ad nos pertinere, sive homines illius capituli sive decani sive singularis canonici et eciam animalia in terris suis que vocantur weyf'. Volumus eciam et concedimus pro nobis et heredibus nostris quod iidem decanus et capitulum et singuli canonici atque eorum successores et eorum homines universi et singuli canonici atque eorum successores et eorum homines universi sint quieti in civitate, in burgo, in foris et nundinis, in transitum poncium et maris portuum et in omnibus locis per totam Angliam, Hiberntiam[8] et Walliam et omnes terras et aquas nostras de quolibet theloneo, tallagio, passagio, pedagio, lastagio, stallagio, hidagio, wardagio, operibus et auxiliis castellorum, ruinorum pontium et parcorum, walliarum, fossatorum et vinatiorum.

p. 17 Navigio domini regalium edificacione | et omnimoda operacione et custodia castrorum de omni carreio et sumagio nec eorum carri', carecte aut equi capiantur ad aliqua caragia facienda et quod silve eorum ad predicta opera vel aliqua alia nullo modo capiantur.

Et quod sint quieti de sectis comitatum, hundredorum, wapentagiorum et de omnibus geldis, danegeldis, fengeldis, hornegeldis, forgeldis, penigeldis, thechingpeny, hundredpany, miskemingio, chanagio, chemmagio et herbagio et de vectigalibus et tributis et de exercitu et equitatu et de omni terreno servicio et seculari exaccione, salvo servicio unius signiferi secundum quod continetur in prescripta carta prefatis regis Henrici proavi nostri.

Et similiter quod in perpetuum sint quieti de sectis comitatum, hundredorum, wapentagiorum et thrichmigii et de murdro et latrocinio, escapilio et concelamento et hamsocne, gribruch, bodewite, fichwite, forstallairwite, hengwite et wardpeny et bordwalpeny et omnibus auxiliis vicecomitum et ministrorum suorum et de saccagio et assisis et recognicionibus et inquisicionibus et summonicionibus, nisi pro libertate et negociis ecclesie Ebor' et tunc si sit placitum inter homines predicte ecclesie et canonicos vel inter canonicos per se vel inter homines per se, ex utraqua parte omnes de assisa sint *de libertate predicte ecclesie vel libertate beate Marie Ebor'*. Si illi non sufficiant.

Si vero inter decanum et capitulum vel eorum aliquem canonicos singulos vel eorum homines et aliquem qui non sit de eorum libertate assisa debeat namiari et capi, *medietas assise sit de hominibus libertatis predicte ecclesie et alia medietas de forinsetis et quod* iidem decanus et capitulum habeant curiam suam et iusticiam cum socco et sacca, tol et theam, et infangnesthef et utfangnesthef, flemenfrath, ordel et orest' infra tempus et extra cum omnibus aliis immunitatibus, libertatibus, consuetudinibus et quietanciis suis.

Concedimus eciam pro nobis et heredibus nostris quod si iidem decanus et capitulum et canonici predicti vel eorum homines placitum habeant adversus aliquos vel alii adversus eos vel ipsi ad invicem placitum illud non audiatur nec teneatur alibi quam in hostio predicte ecclesie sancti Petri. Salvis placitis corone nostre que in domo alicuius canonici extra cimiterium audiantur et teneantur, sicut iidem decanus et capitulum usi[9] sunt et eis a predecessoribus nostris regibus Anglie est concessum et quod finitis placitis predictis, habeant iidem decanus et capitulum extractas rotulorum iusticiariorum nostrorum qui placita predicta tenuerint de omnibus amerciamentis hominum suorum sub sigillo eorundem iusticiarorum. Ita quod ipsa amerciamenta vel fines pro merciamentis veniunt in summoni comitatus a scaccario nostro per quod iidem decanus et capitulum et eorum[10]

Homines aliquitenus molestentur, sed licet eisdem decano et capitulo homines suos ad eorundem amercia\men/torum solucionem distringere modo quo viderint meliori.

Nullus eciam vicecomes aut alius ballivus vel ministri nostri terras et libertates earundem decani et capituli ad aliquas districciones faciendas ipsis irrequisitis ingrediatur nec animalia eorum in manum capiantur sed inperpetuum habeant returnum brevium nostrorum de omnibus ipsis et homines suos et eorum terras et tenementa contingentibus.

Et hoc eis pro nobis et heredibus nostris concedimus et carta nostra confirmamus, prohibentes eciam quod nullus vicecomes vel ballivus vel alius minister noster infra terras predictorum decani et capitulum vel ecclesie predicte aliquem hominem capere, lugare, verberare, interficere vel sanguinam fundere seu rapinam vel aliquam violenciam facere presumat; nec nativos nec fugitivos suos vel catalla eorum aliquis detineat, nec eos vel homines eorum pro consuetudine aliqua vel servicio aut exaccione, vel aliqua causa disturbet de rebus suis quas homines eorum affidare poterunt suam esse proprias.

Quare volumus et firmiter precipimus pro nobis et heredibus nostris quod predicti decanus et capitulum et canonici eorum et eorum homines in perpetuum habeant omnes libertates, consuetudines et quietancias predictas sicut predictum est sine impedimento et contradiccione nostri et heredibus nostrorum et omnium ballivorum nostrorum.

Et prohibemus super gravem foristfactam nostram ne quis eos contra easdem libertates in aliquo vexet, disturbet vel inquietet nec eis molestam inferat aut gravamen.

Hiis testibus: venerabili patre Bonifacio Cant' archiepiscopo, Ricardo comite Cornubie, Rogero Bigod comite Northfolk et marscallo Anglie, Johanne de Plessetes comite Warwic', Petro de Sabaud', Johanne filio Galfridi, iusticiario nostro Hibernie, Petro Chaceporth archidiacono Welhensis, magistro Willelmo de Bellemny[11] archidiacono Coventrie, Petro de Rivall', Henrico de Wengham', Ricardo filio Nicholai, Bertramo de Crioyll', Johanne de Grey, Roberto Walerand', Bartholomeo Pecch, Stephano Bautan', Willelmo de Grey, Nicholao de Sancto Mauro et aliis. Datum per manum nostram apud Portesmuth quinto die Julii anno regni nostri tricesimo septimo.

¹ Followed by *Pape* erased; as soon becomes apparent this part of the heading is mis-leading. The clerk highlights some main sections of the two royal charters transcribed here with paragraph marks which have been used to break up the long text. A number of sentences in this document have been underlined by a later medieval hand, signified here by italic script. Apart from one instance on p. 15, none of the underlinings appear to be accompanied by marginal notes   ² MS *sic* for *penitencia*   ³ MS *sic*; other copies read *namium*   ⁴ MS *uunus*   ⁵ MS *sic* for *Warr'*   ⁶ MS *Decanus*   ⁷ MS *sic*; the scribe apparently did not know the Latin word for outlaw   ⁸ MS *sic*   ⁹ After *usi* there is a cross in the text indicating an omission with a corresponding cross in the bottom left margin and four lines of text which are written at the bottom of the page.   ¹⁰ End of omitted lines, and main text resumed.   ¹¹ MS *sic* for *Kellemny*

Margin   In bottom right margin, p. 15, opposite the first underlined sentence, there is an almost illegible phrase in a late medieval hand which may read *Nota bene pro canonicorum jurisdiccio facere archiepiscopus non habet ad ag[..] ... canonicorum. Nota bene hunc libertatem* in left margin, p. 16, immediately after reference to the right of *weyf'*.

Date   Henry I's purported charter would seem to follow, but not necessarily immediately, an inquiry into the immunities of St Peter's, York, held in 1106 (see note below and **28**).

Note   Sharpe, *Acta Henry I*, York 31 (forthcoming), fully discusses the problems connected with Henry I's purported charter confirming the immunities of the church of St Peter's, York, as they were in the days of Edward the Confessor, a text which 'is in no sense a charter but a statement of customs'. He also comments: 'The relationship with [the] inquest at York in 1106 is not so secure that the text can be accepted as having existed so early, but parallels with Domesday Book give weight to the underlying claims'. In this copy the initial of the name of the first witness of Henry I's 'charter' is left blank, where other copies supply *T.*, i.e. Archbishop Thomas II (1108–14); among others named are William Giffard, bishop of Winchester (1100–29), Robert Bloet, bishop of Lincoln (1093–1123), Ranulf Flambard, bishop of Durham (1099–1128), and William II, earl Warenne (d. 1138). For Basset and Ridel, see **28n**. Most of the other attestations of Henry I's charters by Forne, son of Sigulf, of Greystoke (d. 1130) occur post-1120 (*RRAN*, ii, no. 1083 note). Besides the cartulary copy of Henry I's purported charter in the White Book, many other 13ᵗʰ- and 14ᵗʰ-c. copies survive, most notably in the *Magnum Registrum Album* of York Minster, pt. I, f. 92r and pt. II, f. 103r. To preserve its own unique witness, no attempt has been made to collate the White Book text with other copies. Since Dugdale's time, the document has been printed on numerous occasions from different sources (cf. *Mon. Ang*, viii. 1180, no. xxxi) as well as calendared (cf. *RRAN*, ii, no. 1083). Some of the text is also repeated in **28**.

The inspeximus by Henry III was not enrolled, though a 15ᵗʰ-c. copy survives in BL, Cotton Nero D III ff. 44ᵛ–45ʳ. It has usually been cited from an inspeximus of it by Edward I (TNA, C 53/91 no. 31, 20 May 1305 = *CChR 1300–26*, 56–8), subsequently confirmed by virtually every monarch down to Elizabeth I. No attempt has been made to collate or list all these copies here. Among the witnesses of this confirmation, Peter Chaceporc was archdeacon of Wells, keeper of the wardrobe, 1241–54, and treasurer of Lincoln (cf. *Fasti 1066–1300*, vii, 34, 59), and Mr William of Kilkenny, archdeacon of Coventry by 20 January 1238, was promoted bishop of Ely in 1255 (*Fasti 1066–1300*, xi, 30).

28 *Letters of the Chapter of St Peter's, York, to the Chapter at Southwell*
informing it about the liberties and customs of their church (as well as
those of Ripon, Beverley, St Cuthbert's, Durham, and Hexham) as found
by an inquest of 1106 at York   1106

Litera capituli ecclesie beati Petri Ebor' de libertatibus et   p. 18
consuetudinibus eiusdem ecclesie et Suthwell'

Universis matris ecclesie filiis humillime capitulum beati Petri Ebor'
salutem et orationes in domino. Sciant omnes ad quos litere iste pervenerint,[1]
has esse consuetudines et libertates ecclesie beati Petri ab Alestano
rege antiquitus datas, et a successoribus eius reverenter servatas, et
apostolicorum privilegiis confirmatas.

Anno ab incarnacione domini mcvi quando Osbertus[2] fuit primum
vicecomes Eboraci, voluit ipse auferre ecclesie sancti Petri et omni
archiepiscopatui per placita et iniurias [vertere] omnes bonas consuetudines,
quas antiquitus juste tenuerant. Pro quo cum Girardus [archi]episcopus
clamorem fecisset apud regem, misit rex Robertum, episcopum Lincolnie,
et Radulfum Basset et Galfridum Ridel, Ranulfum le Meschin et Petrum
de Valoniis, Eboracum, ut ibi inquirerent, que essent ecclesie beati Petri
consuetudines.

Hi cum comitatum advocassent, coniuraverunt prudentissimos Anglos
illius comitatus per fidem quam regi debeant, quatinus de consuetudinibus
illis verum dicerent. Videlicet Uctreth filium Alwini, Gamellum filium
Swartecol, Gamellum filium Grim, Normannum presbyterum, Willelmum
filium Ulf, Frengerum presbyterum, Uctreth filium Turkilli, Norman filium
Basing', Turstinum filium Turmot', Gamellum filium Ormi, Morcar filium
Ligulf, Ulvet filium Fornonis, hereditario iure lagaman civitatis, quod
latine potest dici legis lator vel iudex, et tunc quibus fuit prefectus qui
coram ita disservit,[3] et Ansketinus de Bolomer, tunc quidem prepositus
de Nortreding, interpres fuit.

Nos omnes recordati testamur quod omnis terra, que ad prebendas
ecclesie Sancti Petri pertinet, est adeo quieta et libera quod nec prepositus
regis nec vic[ecomes][4] nec aliquis alius potest in ea vel rectum habere, vel
namum capere, donec canonicus illius prebende prius fuerit requisitus;
et si canonicus rectum non fecerit, debet requiri decanus, et ipse diem
statuet, ad hostium sancti Petri rectum faciet.

Si quis eciam quemlibet, cuiuscunque facinioris aut flagitii reum et
convictum, infra arctum[5] ecclesie ceperit et retinuerit, universali iudicio
vi hundreth emendabit.

Si vero infra ecclesiam xii hundreth. Infra chorum xviii hundreth.
Penitencia quoque de singulis sicut de sacrilegiis injuncta. In hundreth
sex libre continentur.

Quod si aliquis vesano spiritu agitatus, diabolico ausu quemcunque
capere presumpserit, in cathedra lapidea iuxta altare quod Angli vocant
fritstol, id est cathedra quietudinis vel pacis, huius tam flagisiosi sacrilegii
emendacio sub nullo iudicio est, sub nullo pecunie numero claudetur, sed
apud Anglos botoles, id est sine emenda vocatur.

Hec vero emende nichil ad archiepiscopum sed ad canonicos tantum pertinent.

Canonici sancti Petri in hirth, id [est] domestica vel intrinseca familia appellabantur. Terra canonicorum proprie mensa sancti Petri.

Denique si quid in ecclesia, vel in cimiterio, vel in domibus canonicorum, vel in terris eorum iniuste egerint, aut ipsi canonici adversus invicem aut adversus [se] alios, vel alii adversus canonicos, vel adversus alios, forisfactura nulla archiepiscopo, sed tota canonicis iudicabatur.

Archiepiscopus autem in rebus canonicorum hoc tantum iuris habet, quod defuncto canonico ipse alii prebendam prebet, nec tamen sine consilio et assensu capituli.

Si vero archiepiscopus adversus apostolicum vel regem comiserit, ad quod redimendum vel pacificandum pecunia opus erit, nichil tantum[6] canonici archiepiscopo preter suam voluntatem dabunt; et pecunia canonicorum et hominum eorum pro comissa vel debito archiepiscopo nec in namum[7] capietur.

Habent canonici in domibus et in terris suis socam et saccam, tol et theam, et infangenthef et intol et utol, et omnes easdem honoris et libertatis consuetudines quas ipse rex in terris suis habet, et quas archiepiscopus de domino Deo et de rege tenet. Hoc eciam amplius, quod nemo de terra canonicorum sancti Petri wapentachimot, nec tredincimot, nec siremot sequetur, sed calumpnians et calumpniatus ante hostium monasterii sancti Petri rectitudinem recipiet et faciet. Hoc autem a religiosis[8] principibus et bonis antecessoribus sic provisum est, predicta placita sequi et tenere.

Si vero aliquis terram aliquam[9] sancto Petro dederit vel vendiderit, nemo postea socam vel sacam, tol aut theam in illa clamabit, sed easdem consuetudines quas et alia | terra sancti Petri ista habebit, tantum honoris et reverencie antecessores nostri sancti principis apostolorum ecclesie deferrebant. Postremo ab omni consuetudine et exactione quieta et soluta est terra sancti Petri.

p. 19

Quando autem rex congregabit exercitum unus homo tantum preparabatur de tota terra canonicorum cum vexillo sancti Petri, qui, si burgenses in exercitum ier\i/nt,[10] dux et signifer eos precedet, sine burgensiis[11] vero nec ipse ibit.[12]

Si quis homicida, vel fur, vel criminator, vel exul, fugerit ad ecclesiam sancti Petri, pro defensione vite sue et membrorum suorum, per spacium xxx dierum ibi pacem habebit.

Quod si infra hoc spacium non potuerit pacificare hominem cum illis cum quibus male egerit infra illos xxx dies poterint clerici illum ducere, quocunque malefactor eligerit, usque ad xxx leugas, cum aliquo \signo/[13] pacis ecclesie et reliquiis, et qui fregerit pacem super illos infra predictum spacium reus erit pacis ecclesie fracte, videlicet i hundreth, et hoc modo poterunt illum ducere, illum malefactorem tribus vicibus et reducere.

Si vero aliquis, inter malos existens, consortia illorum vitare voluerit, et ad ecclesiam sancti Petri venerit, volens ibi libencius in pace vivere quam inter criminosos habitare, ex consuetudine ecclesie, quam diu voluerit, ibi in pace esse poterit.

Quod si aliquis ex necessitate urgente inde discedere voluerit, conductu canonicorum cum signo pacis ecclesie, pacifice poterit ire ad vicinam ecclesiam similem libertatem pacis habentem, videlicet ad ecclesiam beati Johannis in Beverlaco, ad ecclesiam beati Wilfridi in Ripun, et beati Cuthberti in Dunelmo, et ad ecclesiam sancti Andree in Hestoldesham. Similem[14] emendacionem pro pace fracta habent prefate ecclesie. Ecclesia vero beati Johannis in Beverlaco miliare unum habet circa se liberum et quietum ab omni regali consuetudine, et ab omni reddicione pecunie, et ab omni gildo, quod regi per universam Angliam persolvitur. A principio illius miliarii usque ad crucem Alestani regis, si quis pacem fregerit, reus erit i hundreth. A cruce Alestani usque ad cimiterium, de iii hundreth. Qui in cimiterio pacem fregerit de vi hundreth. Qui infra ecclesiam de xii hundreth. Qui infra chorum, amissa omni possessione sua, corporis sui subjacebit periculo, absque omni satisfactione nominate[15] pecunie. Simili modo cum eadem libertate miliare suum habet circa se ecclesia beati Wilfridi in Ripum. A cuius principio usque ad cimiterium, pacis violator reus erit de iii hundreth. In cimiterio de vi. In choro ut de aliis prediximus.

Preterea in tribus festivitatibus et in Pentecosten pacem habent omnes ad hec festa venientes a domibus suis eundo et redeundo, et siquis super eos pacem fregerit, reus erit i hundreth. Similiter in festo[16] sancti Johannis baptiste et beati Johannis confessoris, et dedicacionis ecclesie apud Beverlacum, eodem modo, in duobus festivitatibus sancti Wilfridi[17] pacem habent euntes et redeuntes, et qui eam interim fregerit, usque ad miliare veniendo, et a miliari redeundo, reus erit pro pace fracta de i hundreth.

Terra autem illa quam archiepiscopus habet in civitate Eboraci, debet esse tam quieta et libera ad opus archiepiscopi in omnibus consuetudinibus, sicut dominium regis est regi, et si mercatores undicunque venerint, voluerint in terra archiepiscopi hospitari, non debet eos prepositus regis, vel alius, impedire, \et/ si in terra archiepiscopi consuetudinem dederint ministris archiepiscopi, quocunque voluerint debent abire quieti.

Preterea in Walbugath et in Fiskargat cuiuscunque terra sit, tercia pars redditus debet esse archiepiscopi in placitis, et in theloneo et husgable, et in omni consuetudine; et totum bladum delatum de Austriding, et pisces inde delati, debent ibidem in eadem consuetudine vendi, et totum theloneum erit archiepiscopi in Clementesthorp de omnibus navibus que illuc applicuerint, et juxta Clementesthorp inferius quantum terra archiepiscopi durat, ea tota consuetudo piscium archiepiscopi ex ambabus partibus aque.

Preterea in maneria Syreburne debet esse prepositus, qui est ad comitatum et triding et wapentac, et si aliquis de territorio illius manerii ibi fuerit calumpniatus; ipse debet ibi pro eo rectum offerre, et in maneria[18] in consuetudine archiepiscopi rectum facere. Per prepositum illum, et iter illius ad placita; debent homines illius prepositure manere quieti. Respectum autem debet habere iste prepositus, nec sequatur comitatum, nec cetera placita, ex illo die quo primum firmam archiepiscopi parare ceperit, usque viii dies post discessum archiepiscopi, | et si interim, quam p. 20 diu archiepiscopus erit in manerio, de hominibus illius manerii aliqua calumpnia contigerit; per plegium illius prepositi ille qui calumpniatus est debet esse quietus, donec viii dies post discessum archiepiscopi de manerio. Et si prepositus a comitatu vel ceteris placitis defuerit sine occacione, quam evidenter ostendat, prima vice emendabit i bovem, secunda vice v solidos et iiii denarios. Tercia vice dimidium foresfacture, videlicet x horas.

Hanc consuetudinem habet manerium de Beverlaco, quod ei pertinet et cetera maneria totius archiepiscopatus. Et dapifer archiepiscopi, si sit in comitatu, potest acquietare omnes prepositos maneriorum faciendo id, quod facerent prepositi, si adessent.

¹ MS *pervenerunt*   ² MS *Obsertus*   ³ Van Caenegem (139 n. b) states 'The phrase *et tunc . . . disservit* sounds corrupt and could be emended as follows *et tunc quidem fuit praedictus qui coram eis disseruit'*   ⁴ MS rubbed   ⁵ Read *atrium*?   ⁶ *Sic* for *tamen*?   ⁷ *namum* or *namium*, gage, 'from a word akin to German "nehmen", to take, i.e. distress; security taken' (Van Caenegem, 140 n. 10)   ⁸ MS *aregiosis*   ⁹ *aliquam* in left margin with insertion sign   ¹⁰ After *e* struck out   ¹¹ MS *sic* for *burgensibus*   ¹² The text in **27** which duplicates much of **28** to this point breaks off here (see below)   ¹³ *signo* added in margin   ¹⁴ MS *Silmilem*   ¹⁵ Van Caenegem (142 n. f) suggests *numeratae*   ¹⁶ MS *feto*   ¹⁷ MS *Wilfridri*   ¹⁸ MS *manerium*

Margin   The words *et Suthwell'* in the rubric may have been added by a later hand. *Alestanus Rex* in ?16/17ᵗʰ-c. hand in top left margin, and *Nota de consensu Capituli* and *Libertates terrarum ecclesie de Suthwell'* towards bottom (p. 18).

Date   The verdict relating to Ripon (see note below) states that the inquisition took place at York 'on the Tuesday after the feast of the Translation of St Thomas'. This is presumably St Thomas the Apostle, whose translation was celebrated on 3 July, rather than St Thomas Becket, whose translation was celebrated on 7 July, but only instituted in 1220. In 1106 the translation of St Thomas the Apostle fell on a Tuesday, so the Tuesday after would be 10 July 1106.

Note   Pd. first in *Visitations*, 190–6 as an edition of 'perhaps, the most interesting of all the documents in the White Book', with extensive English marginal summary; also in Van Caenegem, *English Lawsuits*, 138–44, no. 172A (with translation). Part of the verdict referring to sanctuary at Ripon, which supplies an exact date of 10 July 1106 (ibid., 172B) is also pd. in *Mems. Ripon*, i, 58–9 and translated also in *Sources for York to AD 1100*, ed. David W. Rollason, Derek Gore and Gillian Fellows-Jensen (York, York Archaeological Trust. The Archaeology of York, vol. 1, 1998), 220–5. The textual history of this document is intimately linked with **27**, and has generated a large critical literature most recently summarised in the commentary in Sharpe, *Acta Henry I*, York, no. 31 (forthcoming), where the passages common to **27** and **28** are helpfully set out in parallel columns, and D. M. Palliser, *Medieval York, 600–1540* (Oxford, 2014), 126–7.

A few main points of the discussion can be very briefly glossed here by considering four key questions: (i) When was the document sent from York to Southwell? (ii) In the form in which it currently survives, when was it compiled? (iii) Was there an inquisition held at York in 1106? (iv) Do some of the claimed privileges go back to the days of King Æthelstan?

With regard to (i), a *terminus ad quem* is provided by its occurrence in what appears to be the earliest part of the White Book to have been compiled, sometime around 1347. Leach (*Visitations*, 190 note) suggested that this letter 'was possibly written to assist the Chapter of Southwell in view of the Quo warranto proceedings of the reign of Edward III', i.e. *c.* 1330–3. Indeed that inquiry may have been the main stimulus for creating the White Book (see **Introduction** for further comment). The date of 1330–3 for composition has been accepted most recently by Woodman (*Charters*, 264). It is worth pointing out, however, that the Quo warranto early in Edward III's reign, though certainly it seems to have been carried out with the greatest thoroughness (cf. **14–16, 145–7**), was not the first time the Chapter needed to defend itself. In 1272, even before the great Quo warranto inquiries launched in Edward I's reign, an inquisition had already considered whether the

Chapter enjoyed the same privileges as those of St Peter's, York (*IPM Notts. 1279–1329*, 130–1 after TNA, C 145/16 (25)) and Archbishop Wickwane was also summoned in a general eyre in 1280 to justify his privileges at Southwell (*Reg. Melton*, v, no. 333 and cf. TNA, JUST 1/670). On both occasions a copy of the '1106' privileges would have been useful to the Chapter.

In answering (ii), there are several hints, providing a *terminus a quo*, in the language of the document that in its surviving form it must have been put together at some point from the late twelfth century onwards even if based on an earlier version. The address *Universis matris ecclesie filiis* (normally *Universis sancte matris ecclesie filiis*), for instance, does occur on some occasions before 1150, but is much more common after the mid-point of the century. Moreover, placing it before the name of the issuer is a feature of the later twelfth century. *Humillime capitulum* suggests that the Chapter has been influenced by the habit bishops had of calling themselves *minister humilis*. This only became fashionable as a result of the example of Thomas Becket. This also hints that the form in which the privileges now survive cannot be much earlier than the later twelfth century, though in both cases, these usages continued into the later Middle Ages.

It is generally accepted, with regard to (iii), that the document does incorporate evidence which derives from a genuine enquiry early in Henry I's reign (the inquisitors, for example, were all active at that point), though the text of their findings has subsequently been reworked (cf. *Sources for York*, 30–1, where reference to the unique copy of this document should be to the White Book of Southwell, not the Great White Book of York). A version of it was certainly known to Richard of Hexham in the mid-twelfth century (cf. *Acta Henry I*, York, no. 31). Other evidence from Ripon and Beverley, which like Southwell also both claimed to enjoy the same privileges as St Peter's, York, suggests further reworking may have occurred at Ripon by 1229 at the latest and at Beverley by the pontificate of Archbishop John Le Romeyn (cf. T. B. Lambert, 'Spiritual Protection and Secular Power: The Evolution of Sanctuary and Legal Privileges in Ripon and Beverley, 900–1300', *Peace and Protection in the Middle Ages*, ed. T. B. Lambert and D. W. Rollason (Durham, 2009), 128–31; Woodman, *Charters*, 215–20, 262–5).

With regard to (iv), Lambert argues strongly for the view that the '1106' privileges can be traced a considerable way back into the Anglo-Saxon period. A case can be made that King Æthelstan may well indeed have made the (now lost) grant or grants from which the privileges claimed at York in 1106 derived. In any event there is a consensus that the '1106' privileges certainly do include pre-1066 material, as arguments advanced by Sharpe further confirm (*Acta Henry I*, York, no. 31). But it is also worth noting, in considering the earliest form in which **28** survives, that King Stephen's reign appears to have been a time when interest in King Æthelstan revived more generally (Susan E. Wilson, 'King Athelstan and St John of Beverley', *Northern History* 40 (2003), 5–23). This would lead eventually at both Beverley and Ripon to the forgery in the early fourteenth century of two remarkable metrical pseudo-charters of privileges attributed to that king (see Woodman, *Charters*, 208–20 and 260–5 for texts and discussion).

Among those involved in the 1106 inquest were: Archbishop Gerard (1101–8), who died in his garden at Southwell; the justices, Robert Bloet, bishop of Lincoln (1093–1123), previously chancellor of William I; Ralph Basset, one of the most famous of the new men allegedly raised from the dust by Henry I; Geoffrey Ridel, drowned in the White Ship disaster of 1120; Ranulf le Meschin, later earl of Chester (d. 1129); Peter de Valognes, probably the lawman of Lincoln mentioned in Domesday Book. The Scandinavian character of the witnesses at York is very evident in their names, some of which also occur in Domesday Book.

The penalties to be exacted for breaching the peace, especially noted in the case of Beverley, accord with principles set out in Domesday Book, where 'payments by six, twelve, or eighteen hundreds at the rate of £8 per hundred' occur (*DB*, i, 280c, 298d, 336c, cited by Sharpe). Anglo-Saxon frithstools (*fritstol*) still survive at Beverley and Hexham. *Infanganthef/infangenetheof* was the right of seizing and beheading or hanging a thief caught red-handed. The three feasts at which pilgrims visiting the churches were to enjoy the benefits of peace are probably St Peter in Cathedra (22 February), St Peter the Apostle (29 June), and St Peter ad Vincula (1 August), according to Van Caenegem.

NORWELL PREBEND, 29

29 *Confirmation by Geoffrey, archbishop of York, to Reginald, nephew of Mr Vacarius, [prebendary of Norwell Overhall], of a moiety of Norwell church that Mr Vacarius granted him, for a rent of half a mark per annum*   [probably at Southwell, 18 August 1191 × 1194]

Galfridus Dei gratia Ebor' archiepiscopus et Anglie primas omnibus sancte matris ecclesie filiis ad quos littere iste pervenerint, salutem et Dei benedictionem. Ad vestram notitiam volumus pervenire quod nos confirmamus Reginaldo, nepoti magistri Vac[ari]e medietatem ecclesie de Northwell', quam ei magister Vac[ari]em[1] concessit sub annua prestatione dimidie marce; quia constitit nobis assentione canonicorum de[2] Suthwell' quoniam predicto ecclesia portionalis est, et predecessores magistri Vac[ari]e eam consueverunt[3] dare ceteris personis. Hiis testibus: magistro Symone de Appulia, Ebor' ecclesie cancellario, abbate de Wellebeck, Alano, canonico de Ripon, magistro Martino Lumbard, Willelmo Muscamp', magistro Rogero, magistro Gilleberto, canonicis de Suthwell', et pluribus aliis.

[1] MS *sic*   [2] MS *le*   [3] MS *consuevit*

Date   *EEA York 1189–1212*, no. 63 notes that it was between Geoffrey's consecration as archbishop and the nomination of Simon de Apulia as dean of York in 1194, and given the witnesses, almost certainly issued at Southwell.

Note   Pd. in *EEA York 1189–1212*, no. 63. It seems clear from this letter and other evidence that this does indeed indicate the formation of the prebend of Norwell Tertia Pars by division of some of the resources of Norwell Overhall which Vacarius held (Jones, 'Master Vacarius'). The abbot of Welbeck was Adam (*HRH*, i, 198). Alan, canon of Ripon, chaplain to Archbishop Geoffrey, later provost of Beverley, occurs frequently in *EEA*. He later seems to have added the prebend of Norwell Palishall to his other offices. Master Roger is identified by Lovatt as Roger of Arundel, rather than as Roger, brother of Master Martin the Lombard (*alias* de Capella), the first prebendary of Halloughton (**46–8**). William of Muskham was a canon from *c.* 1167–84 (*Rufford*, 172), later becoming archdeacon of Derby, dying in 1231. Mr Gilbert of Southwell was a canon from at least 1164–81 (*EEA York, 1154–1181*, no. 6).

COMMON TITHE, 30

30 *Agreement on behalf of the Chapter for the division and administration of the common tithes of the parish of Southwell between Mr Henry of Skipton, [prebendary of Normanton], Mr John Clarell, [prebendary of Norwell Overhall], and Henry Le Vavassour, [prebendary of Norwell Palishall], dividing collection into three separate areas, with provision for these to be mutually exchanged every three years between these prebendaries and their successors*   Southwell, 5 August 1266

Divisio decimarum in parochia Suthwell' inter tres prebendas dicte ecclesie

Omnibus sancte matris ecclesie filiis presens scriptum visuris vel audituris, magistri Henricus de Skypton', Johannes Clarel [et] dominus Henricus le Vavasor', canonici ecclesie de Suthwell' salutem in domino sempiternam. Universitati vestre tenore presencium innotescat quod cum participes essemus consuete decime garbarum et feni quarumdam villarum in parochia de Suthwell' pro porcionibus indivisis, de voluntate et assensu capituli nostri de Suthwell' pro nostra communi utilitate,[1] providimus et ordinavimus pro nobis et successoribus [nostris][2] quod dicte decime in tres viriles[3] porciones dividerentur, et quod quilibet nostrum et successorum nostrorum partem suam inde separatim colligat et recipiat. Quarum una pars est consueta decima campi et prati de Suthwell' cum campis et pratis de Westorp, Wodehous et de Normanton', et alia pars est consueta decimam campi et prati de Estorp cum campis et pratis de Gipismere, Bleseby et Gorton'. [Et] tercia pars est consueta decima campi et prati de Halum cum consuetis decimis de Halhton', Edynglay, Farnesfeld' et Osmuthorp et de Kyrtlington', partibus autem inter nos sorte divisis, remansit pars decimarum predictarum de Suthwell' cum porcionibus suis supradictis, penes magistrum Johannem Clarel, et pars decimarum de Halum cum porcionibus suis penes magistrum Henricum de Skypton', [et] pars decimarum de Estorp cum suis porcionibus memoratis penes dominum Henricum le Vavasour.[4]

Et eisdem successoribus succedent per tres annos proximos continuos in porcione decimarum magistrum Henricum de Skypton' et successoribus eiusdem. Dictus autem dominus Henricus le Vavasour et eiusdem successores tradent magistro Henrico de \Skypton'/ et eiusdem successoribus porcionem suam et succedent per tres annos continuos in porcione magistri Johannis Clarel et successorum eiusdem. Dictus vero magister Henricus de Skypton' et eiusdem successores tradent magistro Johanni et eiusdem successoribus porcionem suam et succedent in porcione dicti domini Henrici le Vavasour et eiusdem successoribus per tres proximos annos sequentes. Quibus elapsis dictus magister Johannes et eiusdem successores dictam porcionem suam tradent domino Henrico le Vavasour et eiusdem successoribus et succedent per tres annos proximos continuos in porcione decimarum magistri Henrici de Skypton' et successorum suorum. Dictus autem dominus Henricus de Skypton' et eiusdem successores tradent dicto magistro Johanni et eiusdem successori[bu]s porcionem suam predictam et succendent (*sic*) in porcione domini Henrici le Vavasour et eiusdem successorum per tres annos proximos sequentes, et ita deinceps imperpetuum modo predicto fient permutacione per solarem circuitum de trennio in trennium in porcionibus supradictis, et istam provisionem seu ordinacionem in singulis articulis in posterum firmiter observandam propriis sacramentis pro nobis et successoribus nostris firmamus. In procuracione cum negociorum ad prebendas nostras spectantium cum necesse fuerit communes esse volumus sicut prius fuimus. In huius rei testimonium sigilla nostra una cum sigillo capituli predicti huic scripto apponi fecimus. Actum in capitulo Suthwell' die sancti Oswaldi regis et martiris, anno domini m° cc° lx° vi. Teste capitulo supradicto.

¹ *voluntate* but cf. **371**   ² Added from **371**   ³ *vitiles* but cf. **371**   ⁴ At this point **371** adds a couple of sentences before resuming more or less verbatim

Margin   Title in same hand as text (Scribe I); *Divisio magne decime inter prebendarios de Normanton 'et Northwell'* in late medieval hand, in left margin, with a late (16/17ᵗʰ-c.) addition *whats called now the Current tythe.*

Note   A slightly augmented version of **30** is found as **371**. Mr Henry of Skipton, a king's clerk and canon of Southwell by 14 May 1255, prebendary of Normanton, dead by 29 December 1286 (*Reg. Romeyn*, i, no. 1032; *Fasti 1066–1300*, vi, 46); Mr John Clarell, nominated to Norwell Overhall by 24 November 1256, died *c.* 1 May 1295 (cf. *Fasti 1066–1300*, vi, 123); Henry Le Vavassour, prebendary of Norwell Palishall by 23 July 1257 (**192**), d. by 13 Sept. 1280 (*Reg. Wickwane*, 10, no. 36), founder of a chantry (**425–49**). By this arrangement the successors of these three prebendaries continued to administer tithes from Southwell parish until the abolition of the Chapter in 1841.

DUNHAM PREBEND, 31–2

p. 21   **31**   *Another copy of 18 with only minimal orthographical differences and a late medieval marginal cross-reference* prius folio vii.

32   *Order of Walter [Gray], archbishop of York, with the assent of the Chapter at Southwell, that whoever holds the prebend of Dunham should pay Norman, son of Guy de Gueleria, canon of Santa Maria in Trastevere, thirty-six marks at the octave of Easter for his lifetime from the fruits of the prebend, and promising not to name anyone to the prebend while Norman lived*   [probably at Southwell, before 1 May 1255]

Litera Walteri archiepiscopi de prebenda de Dunham

Omnibus Christi fidelibus ad quos presens scriptum pervenerit Walterus Dei gratia Ebor' archiepiscopus Anglie primas salutem in domino. Ad universitatis vestre notitiam volumus pervenire nos de communi assensu et unanimi voluntate capituli nostri Suthwell' ecclesie circa prebendam de Dunham ad commodum¹ et utilitatem ecclesie memorate ita ordinasse et firmiter statuisse scilicet² ut quicumque pro tempore canonicus fuerit illius prebende, quamdiu vixerit dominus Normannus filius Guidonis de Gueleria sancte Marie trans Tiberim canonicus, teneatur ei annuatim persolvere triginta sex marcas in octabis Pasce prout in autentico nostro et capituli Suthwell' ei super hoc confectis expressius continetur; de fructibus ipsius prebende sufficienter etiam calverere³ tenetur idem canonicus nobis et capitulo memorato de indempnitate nostra tam quoad⁴ dicte pecunie solutionem quam quoad⁴ penas adiectas et alia onera que nobis et eidem capitulo pro defectu solutionis possint evenire. Statuimus etiam de eiusdem capituli assensu et voluntate quod nec nos nec successores nostri sine onere memorato vivente predicto Normanno dictam prebendam alicui possimus conferre nec capitulum ab antiquo presentatum amittere. Ut autem hec nostra ordinatio firmitatis robur optineat michi posterum presenti scripto tam sigillum nostrum quam sigillum dicti capituli apponi fecimus.

¹ MS *comodum*   ² MS *silicet*   ³ MS *sic*, perhaps a mistake for *solvere?*   ⁴ MS *quo ad*

Date Walter Gray, archbishop of York (1216–1 May 1255); this charter appears to have been given at Southwell since it was authenticated by the Chapter's seal. Norman son of Guy de Gueleria does not appear in the registers of Innocent IV (1243–54) or Alexander IV (1254–61) (pers. comm. Patrick Zutshi). Santa Maria trans Tiberim, otherwise Santa Maria in Trastevere, Rome.

BECKINGHAM PREBEND, 33–6

33 *Another copy of 17 with minimal variants.*

Rubric *Carta regis Henrici de prebenda de Bekingham*

Note NA, M 494, f. 106ᵛ for a copy made for Thoroton.

34 *Notification by Thurstan, archbishop of York, endowing the prebend of Beckingham following the grant of the churches of Beckingham and [North] Leverton by Herbert, together with a house which once belonged to Gilbert the precentor, a tithe on the demesne of his manor in Southwell and a quarter of his corn tithe and three-quarters of all the tithes of his assarts in the demesne of the manor* [19 October 1119 × 1133]

Litera Turstini archiepiscopi de prebenda de Beckingham

Turstinus Dei gratia Ebor' archiepiscopus omnibus successoribus suis salutem. Ut in ecclesia sancte Dei genitricis Marie multiplicius ipsius dei et domini nostri servitium augeretur apposuimus unam ibidem addere prebendam, ipsam quam Herberto donavimus, videlicet ecclesiam de Bekingham et ecclesiam de Lavetona, in Suthwella mansum quod fuit Willeberti cantoris et decimam totius nutrimenti de dominio manerii mei de Suthwell' et quartam partem decime totius bladi mei et tres partes totius decime assartorum meorum que pertinet ad dominium eiusdem manerii.

Date Cal. *EEA York 1070–1154*, no. 65, where dated 19 October 1119–33 and it is explained that the *terminus ad quem* is the latest possible date for Henry I's confirmation of the grant (*RRAN*, ii, no. 1871), issued at Winchester and therefore prior to the king's last departure from England in 1133. Archbishop John Le Romeyn eventually separated North Leverton from this prebend to form a new one in 1292 (*Reg. Romeyn*, ii, 9–12 and **41** below). Gilbert is known as precentor of York Minster in 1093 (Hugh the Chanter, 12), and remained in office under Archbishops Gerard and Thomas II (*Fasti 1066–1300*, vi, 13). His successor does not witness at any date that helps to narrow the possible date-range of this act.

Note NA, SC7/1/5, f. 6ʳ for a late 15ᵗʰ-c. copy. Pd. in *Mon. Ang.*, viii, 1313 (ii).

35 *Grant in hereditary fee by William of Brampton, with the consent of Peter and William, his heirs, to Laurence Southwell, of a half-carucate and three acres of land in Brampton for 3s 4d rent per annum, for which Laurence has performed homage, given 8s 4d, to Agnes, his wife, a gold ring, to Peter, his son 3s, and to William, his other son, 12d* [mid–late 13ᵗʰ century]

Carta Willelmi de Brantuna de[1] terris pertinentibus prebendi de Bekingham

Willelmus de Brantuna omnibus humilibus tam presentibus quam futuris salutem. Sciatis me donasse concessione Petri et Willelmi heredum meorum et presenti carta confirmasse Laurentio Suthwell' dimidiam carucatam terre \et tres acras/ in feodum et hereditatem sibi et heredibus suis tenendam de me et heredibus meis libere et quiete cum libertatibus et consuetudinibus et cum omnibus rebus ad eam pertinentibus in bosco et plano et agris et pratis et aquis et viis et semitis et aliis pertinentiis reddendo michi et heredibus meis singulis annis tres solidos et iiii denarios pro omni servitio quod ad me vel ad heredes meos pertinerit[2] dimidium ad Pentecosten

p. 22 et dimidium | ad festum sancti Martini. De predicta sunt due bovate \et tres acre/ in Bramtuna et due bovate in Miclehil; de duabus bovatis \et iii acris/ de Bramtuna faciet forinsecus servitium quantum ad illas duas bovatas \et iii acras/ pertinerit[2] secundum servitium quod ego facio de feodo meo. De duabus bovatis de Miclehil nullum forinsecus servitium faciet. Pro predicta quoque dimidia carucata terre \et tribus acris/ faciet michi Laurentius homagium et preterea donavit michi octo[3] solidos et iiii denarios[4] et Agneti uxori mee unum anulum aureum et Petro filio iii s[5] et Willelmo altero filio meo xii d. Hiis testibus, Radulfo de Insula, Willelmo de Langathuait, Alano filio Thome, Hugone filio Hugonis, Rainaldo de Insula, Willelmo de Milleorai aliud, Roberto de Scalcebi, Nicholao de Donecastria, Turstino clerico de Suttuna, Willelmo Prat, Ricardo de Buusce, Jordano de Insula, Simone filio Godefridi, Waltero filio Malgeri, Bartholomeo Hausterio, Osberto filio eius, Willelmo de Insula, Edone de Cantalara, Ailsi, Alexandro filio Willelmi, Ricardo de Dunham.

[1] Followed by a small erasure   [2] MS *pertinnerit*   [3] MS *octod'* for *octodecim?*   [4] *octo solidos et iiij d'* over erasure in same 15th-c. hand which has added all the references to the three acres   [5] *iij s* over erasure in same hand as other insertions

Date Laurence Suthwell may be the same as Laurence the chaplain of Southwell living in the mid-thirteenth century (**393–4**). Jordan de Insula held a half fee in Ingham (Lincs.) of the honour of Lancaster in 1242–3. On 1 March 1272 he made a final concord with Andrew of Misson (*Misne*) and Alice, his wife, concerning land in Misson, and Jordan is mentioned in an inquest, dated 1297, held by Robert of Beckingham concerning the tenants of Blyth priory in Billingley (*Book of Fees*, 1075, 1110; *Lincs. Final Concords*, 272; *Blyth*, A 81).

Note Brampton in Torksey parish (Lincs.), seven miles south-east of Beckingham, across the Trent, was held by the bishop of Lincoln (Foster, *Lincs. Domesday*, 48, 243). There were a number of families termed 'de Insula' (L'Isle) and it difficult to distinguish between them. A Jordan de Insula holding in Ingham appears in the early thirteenth century (*Reg. Antiq.*, iv, 37–40). In the late twelfth century William de Insula granted to Blyth priory, with the consent of his wife Cecily, and William, Othuel, Robert and Richard, his sons, the tithes of Appleby and Sawcliff, Lincolnshire (*Blyth*, 290, 357; Foster, *Lincs. Domesday*, xl, 57, 106). Othuel held in Northumberland and Lincolnshire, and a William de Insula was a justice (*Rufford*, 110, 424, 857; *Thurgarton*, 1020, 1025–7, 1042, 1048).

36 *Charter of Edward III confirming, at the request of William, vicar of Beckingham, Alan de Fery and Henry de Fery of Beckingham, his earlier licence of 4 May 1341 for Walter de Fery of Beckingham to give a messuage and various lands for the foundation of a chaplaincy in Beckingham church*   Reading, 20 July 1347

Carta regis de cantaria in Bekyngham

Edwardus[1] Dei gracia rex Anglie et Francie, dominus Hibernie, omnibus ad quos presentes litere pervenerunt,[2] salutem. Supplicarunt nobis Willelmus, vicarius ecclesie de Bekyngham, Alanus de Fery [et] Henricus de Fery[3] de Bekyngham quod cum nos quarto die Maii anno regni nostri Anglie quinto decimo per finem centum solidorum quem Walterus de Fery de Bekyngham fecit nobiscum concessimus et licenciam dedimus pro nobis et heredibus nostris quantum in nobis fuit eidem Waltero quod ipse unum messuagium, unum toftum, quadraginta acras terre, decem acras prati et septem denaratas[4] redditus cum pertinenciis in Bekyngham *in the clay* dare posset et assignare cuidam capellano divina singulis diebus ecclesia de Bekyngham pro salubri statu nostro et ipsius Walteri quam diu[5] vixerimus et pro animabus nostris cum ab hac luce migraverimus et animabus progenitorum nostrorum et antecessorum predicti Walteri et omnium fidelium defunctorum iuxta ordinacionem inde faciendam celebraturo, habendum et tenendum eidem capellano et successoribus suis capellanis divina singulis diebus in ecclesia predicta ut'[6] predictum est celebraturus in perpetuum pro ut in literis nostris patentibus inde confectis plenius continetur, que quidem licencia ipso Waltero superstite debitum non sorciebatur effectum. Idem que Walterus mesuagium, toftum, terram, pratum et redditum predicta in vita sua Hugoni Gerland' de Bekyngham, capellano.[7] Dictus que Hugo prefatis Willelmo, Alano, Henrico et Roberto talem effectum ut ea prefato capellano sibi et successoribus suis in forma predicta possidendum darent et assignarent [et] concesserint, velimus eisdem Willelmo, Alano, Henrico et Roberto concedere quam[8] predicta mesuagium, toftum, terram et pratum et redditum cum pertinenciis prefato capellano dare possint et assignare, habenda et tenenda[9] sibi et successoribus suis in forma predicta in perpetuum. Nos ad concessionem nostram predictam et ad piam ipsorum Willelmi, Alani, Henrici et Roberti intencionem consideracionem habentes ac volentes eo pretextu eorum supplicacioni graciose annuere in hac parte: concessimus pro nobis et heredibus nostris quantum in nobis est eisdem Willelmo, Alano, Henrico et Roberto quod ipsi predicta mesuagium, toftum, terram, pratum et redditum cum pertinenciis dare possint et assignare prefato capellano, habenda et tenenda sibi et successoribus suis capellanis divina singulis diebus pro nostro et liberorum nostrorum ac ipsorum Hugoni, Willelmi, Alani,[10] Henrici et Roberti salubri statum dum vixerimus et pro animabus nostris cum subtracti fuerimus ab hoc mundo necnon pro animabus Johannis Darcy le piere et predicti Walteri ac antecessorum et heredum prefati Hugoni et omnium fidelium defunctorum in ecclesia predicta celebraturus imperpetuum. Et eidem capellano quod ipse mesuagium toftum terram pratum et redditum predictum cum pertinenciis et prefatis Willelmo, Alano, Henrico et Roberto recipere possit et tenere sibi et successoribus suis predictis imperpetuum tenore presencium similiter licenciam dedimus specialem statuto de terris et tenementis ad manum mortuam non ponendum edito non obstante. Nolentes quod iidem Willelmus, Alanus, Henricus et Robertus vel heredes sui aut prefatus capellanus seu successores sui ratione statuti predicti per nos vel heredes nostros inde occasionentur molestentur in aliquo seu graventur salvis tamen capitalibus dominis feodi illius serviciis inde debitis et consuetis. In cuius etc. Teste custode predicto apud Redyng' xx die Julii.

Et memorandum quod predicte prime litere restitute fuerunt in cancellaria regis dicto xx die Julii.

[1] The text breaks off in MS at the point of note 10, because a page has been excised before the MS was paginated or foliated, and the rest of the entry is taken from the original patent roll, TNA, C 66/221, m. 11. The significant variants between the text in the patent roll and the White Book, where both exist, have been noted here, with A denoting variant readings in the patent roll   [2] MS *sic*   [3] A inserts *et Robertus de Parys*   [4] MS *sic* for *denariatas*   [5] A has *dum*   [6] MS *sic*; A has *ut*   [7] This sentence lacks a main verb like *dedit* or *tenet*, but is the same in A   [8] A has *quod ipsi*   [9] A omits *et tenenda*   [10] The text breaks off in MS at this point

Margin   Title in different hand (Scribe 4) from main text; in right margin in text hand *de cantaria de Bekingham*

Note   Cal. in *CPR 1345–8*, 361. The fine of 100s for the licence to alienate in mortmain is printed in *Rot. Orig.*, ii, 150, from TNA, E 371/100, rot. 115.

SOUTH MUSKHAM PREBEND, 37–40

37   *Grant by Hugh, son of Ralph to Southwell, and to the prebend of Mr William of Markham of South Muskham for the souls of himself and Agnes his wife, of one strip of land*   [1228 × 1241]

p. 23   **Carta pertinens ad prebendam de Suthmuscam**

Omnibus sancte matris ecclesie filiis ad quos presens scriptum pervenerit Hugo filius Radulphi salutem. Noverit universitas vestra me dedisse et concessisse et hac presenti carta mea confirmasse Deo et beate Marie de Suthwella et prebende magistri Willelmi de Marcam de Suthmusham pro salute anime mee et Agnetis uxoris mee et antecessorum et successorum meorum in puram et perpetuam elemosinam unam selionem de cultura mea iacentem proximam culture predicti Willelmi versus aquilonem scilicet ad crementum curie sue. Ego vero et heredes me predictam selionem predicte prebende in perpetuum warantizabimus et huic scripto sigillum meum in testimonium apposui. Hiis testibus magistro Willelmo de Tanay, magistro Henrico de Notingham, domino Willelmo de Gressi, domino Radulpho de Trehamton', domino Henrico de Steping' et aliis.

Date   After William of Markham was appointed prebendary of South Muskham and before William de Taney was appointed archdeacon of Nottingham.

Note   Hugh fitz Ralph (**75**), probably dead by 1261, held a knight's fee in Muskham, and he may be the same man who held four carucates for a half-fee in Steeping (Lincs.) of Gant in 1212 (Moor, ii, 53; *Book of Fees*, 162). A William de Cressy was active as a royal judge *c*. 1218–19 in Lincolnshire (*Reg. Antiq.*, ii, nos 194, 214, 258). Ralph de Trehampton had succeeded his father Roger by 1212. In 1242–3 he held a half-fee in Aylesby (Lincs.) of the bishop of Durham and he witnessed until *c*. 1260 (*Book of Fees*, 162, 1019–20, 1080; *Reg. Antiq.*, ii, nos 270, 293, 295; iv, nos 1443, 1445; v, no. 1556n). Henry of Steeping and Robert le Travers held a half-fee in Great Steeping and Gunby (Lincs.) of Hugh Fitz Ralph of Gant in 1242–3, and Henry witnessed at Easter 1249 (*Book of Fees*, 156, 1069; *Reg. Antiq.*, vii, no. 1990).

38   *Quitclaim by William, son of Geoffrey de Bale to Henry, son of Hugh de Pascy, of all his land in South Muskham which he held by custody of Thomas son of Henry de Bale, and the land and meadow that sometime was of Ralph Smethe and that of Richard Tupe, together with Richard and his descendants, to be held of Henry until Thomas comes of age, for which Henry gave William one mark*   [1230 × 1250]

Alia carta pertinens \ad/ eandem prebendam

Omnibus universis[1] visuris vel audituris hoc scriptum Willelmus filius Galfridi de Bale salutem in domino. Noveritis me concessisse quietum clamasse et hoc scripto confirmasse Henrico filio Hugonis de Pascy totam terram cum pertinentiis in Suthmusham que me[2] contigit ratione custodie heredum Thome filii Henrici de Bale, et terram cum prato et pratum quod fuit quondam Radulfi Smethe et terram Ricardi Tupe cum ipso Ricardo et sequela sua tenend' et habend' heredibus suis et assignatis donec heredes dicti Thome ad plenam etatem pervenerit[3] secundum consuetudinem regni. Pro hac dimissione et concessione dedit michi dominus Henricus unam marcam argenti. In huius rei testimonium apposui sigillum meum huic scripto. Hiis testibus Johanne de Burstal', Rogero de Launton', Willelmo de Marcam, Thoma de Seggebroc, Willelmo filio Odonis et aliis.

[1] MS *sic*   [2] MS *sic*   [3] For *pervenerint*

Date   While John de Burstall was active (*Thurgarton*, cxxi–cxxiii).

Note   Is William de Marcam in this charter to be distinguished from a namesake in **37**?

39   *Grant by Henry Gernon of Carlton, to the church of St Wilfrid, South Muskham, for the augmentation of the prebend [of South Muskham], of one toft in Carlton for the service of 6d per annum which his son Robert paid when he held it*   [1228 × 1230]

Alia carta pertinens ad eandem prebendam de Suthmuscham

Omnibus in Cristo fidelibus ad quos presens scriptum pervenerit Henricus Gernon de Carleton salutem in domino. Notum sit vobis quod ego Henricus assensu et voluntate uxoris mee et heredum meorum dedi et concessi et hac presenti carta mea confirmamus Deo et ecclesie beati[1] Wilfridi de Suthmuscham pro anima mea et pro animabus antecessorum et successorum meorum in puram et perpetuam voluntatem et elemosinam ad augmentum prebende toftum unum in Carleton' cum crofto et plateo, situm inter terram Henrici filii Henrici et terram Simonis filii Roberti ab occidentali parte vie, et toftum alium cum crofto ab orientali parte vie exposito predicti tofti, situm inter terram predicti Henrici et terram Suani hominis Thome de Muscham, et pratum unum apud Dokedyc, cum servicio totius predicte terre, scilicet sex denarios, quod Robertus filius meus michi annuatim de terra illa pro omni servitio reddere consuevit dum de me per illud servitium terram predictam tenebat. Ad cuius etiam petitionem terram illam cum servitio in perpetuam elemosinam transtuli ad prebendam et ego et heredes mei warantizabimus[2] predictam terram cum prato et cum servitio Deo et ecclesie beati Wilfridi et predicto magistro Willelmo et suis successoribus in perpetuam elemosinam contra omnes homines. Ut hoc ratum permaneat sigillum meum huic scripto apposui. Hiis testibus Hugone decano de Suthwell', Roberto de Muscham capellano,[3] Willelmo de Roldeston', domino Radulfo de Sersel, Roberto de Muscham, Thoma de Erleshae et multis aliis.

[1] *et ecclesie beati* in later hand over erasure   [2] MS *warantazabimus*   [3] MS *cappellano*

Date   While Mr William of Markham was prebendary of South Muskham and before the death of Hugh the dean (by 28 May 1230, *Reg. Gray*, 35, no. CLXX).

Note   It is not clear why Mr William of Markham is referred to as *predicto*. Perhaps he was originally included in the passage later erased, or perhaps *predicto* is the scribe's error for *prebendario*. Carlton is probably Little or South Carlton where the Gernons held land.

40   *Notification by Thomas de Helyton' and Robert de Wython', wardens of the commons and of the fabric, to the Chapter that, by the Chapter's mandate, they had summoned an inquisition of the prebendal church of South Muskham to inquire into the vacancy of the vicarage. The jury confirmed that there had been no previous appointment, and that if a vicar were to be appointed, Mr John of Penistone should be the patron and make the presentation, that there was no litigation, that the man appointed would not be a co-parson (*personaria), that the vicarage consisted of a toft, that the great and small tithes, oblations and other payments owed to the church were assessed at six marks, except the tithes of sheaves, hay, wool, lambs and geese*   South Muskham, 24 April 1295

Litera ordinationis vicarie de Suthmuscham

Viris venerabilibus et discretis dominis capitulo ecclesie collegiate[1] beate Marie Suthwell' devoti sui Thomas de Helyton' et Robertus de Wython' commune[2] canonicorum et fabrice ecclesie[3] supradicte custodes, salutem et obedientiam et reverenciam cum omni subiectione. Ad mandatum vestrum vocatis coram nobis fidedignioribus de parochia ecclesie prebendalis de Suthmuscham tam clericis quam laycis diligentem fecimus inquisitionem super vacatione vicarie eiusdem, scilicet per dominum Henricum capellanum[4] parochie loci eiusdem, Willelmum Oldeman, Henricum clericum, Robertum Petevin, Ricardum Glade, Robertum de Birton', Matheum in Venella, Gilbertum Derling, Willelmum ad Capud Welle, Henricum de Venella, Henricum Cope, Hugonem filium Henrici, Robertum Gamage iuratos. Dicunt quod nullus antefuerat vicarius aliquo tempore, ut sciant, institutus in eadem, et si de novo debeat ibidem aliquis creari vicarius, magister Johannes de Peniston' est verus patronus et presentare debet eundem. Non est litigiosa, non est personaria. Consistit autem prefata vicaria in uno tofto iacente iuxta plateam Roberti dicti Petit' ex parte boriali[5] et in omnibus decimis maioribus et minoribus, oblationibus et obventionibus, quibuscumque ad dictam ecclesiam spectantibus, que omnia taxantur per estimationem ad sex marcas. Excipiuntur autem | appositione[6] assignata vicarie decima garbarum, feni, lane, agnorum et aucarum. De persona presentata ad eandem dicunt quod est bone conversationis et honeste et abilis ad illud et ad maius beneficium optinendum nec obstat presentanti seu presentato aliquid canonicum quod sciant. In cuius rei testimonium sigilla nostra una cum sigillis aliquorum contestantium presenti inquisitioni[7] sunt appensa. Datum apud Suthmuscham die translacionis sancti Wilfridi Ebor' archiepiscopi anno domini m° cc° nonagesimo quinto.

p. 24

[1] MS *colligiat'* [2] An erasure follows with a line drawn through to prevent extra words from being added [3] MS appears to add Tironian *et* and then strikes it out [4] MS *cappellanum* [5] MS *boreali* [6] MS *apositione* [7] MS corrected from *inquisitioei*

Note The inquest was clearly held on a very auspicious day for the church at South Muskham since it was dedicated to St Wilfrid and 24 April was, as noted, the feast of his translation. Mr John of Penistone, prebendary of South Muskham, had been a canon since 1268 (*Reg. Giffard*, 1 no. 1) but was dead by 2 April 1296 (*CPR 1292–1301*, 186). For his subsequent appointment of a vicar, see **45**. Note that 'geese' are among the items on which tithes were due, perhaps a reference to the hibernating wild geese still to be found in the meadows along the Trent as much as to domesticated geese?

NORTH LEVERTON PREBEND, 41

41 *John [Le Romeyn], archbishop of York, following the submission of William of Rotherfield over the prebend of Beckingham in the church of Southwell of which he was a canon (cf.* **42**)*, and with the assent of the Chapter, ordains that the prebend is to be divided into two equal parts, and that the church of North Leverton over which the archbishop enjoyed rights of patronage and which had previously been part of Beckingham prebend, should be erected into a prebend with its holder having a stall on the north side of the choir [at Southwell] next to that of the Sacrist, with a place in the Chapter House, and that the canon named to the prebend shall have the right to institute a vicar to act for him in the choir like other canons, and that William of Rotherfield shall not suffer any other diminution in his rights as prebendary of Beckingham*
In Chapter at Southwell, 19 October 1291

Litera Johannis Ebor' archiepiscopi de ordinatione unius prebende de Northleverton'

Universis sancte matris ecclesie filiis ad quorum notitiam pervenerit hec[1] scriptura Johannes permissione divina Ebor' archiepiscopus salutem in sanctis amplexibus salvatoris. Acceptum credimus obsequium impendere[2] altissimo creatori dum operam damus sollicitam ad extollend' in nostris ecclesiis laudes eius que congruum profecto augmentum suscipiunt excressente[3] meritorio numero ministrorum ut eo celeberius magnificenter divina quo plures ministri conveniunt in laudibus exsolvendis. Ad gratam itaque et spontaneam submissionem dilecti domini filii Willelmi de Rotherfeld' imprime in nos factam super prebenda de Bekingham in ecclesia nostra de Suthwell' cuius est canonicus in eadem accidente ad hoc capituli eiusdem ecclesie requisito consensu super statu dicte prebende sic duximus ordinandum.

Intendentes placere domino Jhesu Cristo ad eiusdem et gloriose virginis matris sue que prefate ecclesie patrona existit gloriam et honorem de voluntate expresso[4] domini Willelmi de Rotherfeld' canonici et prebendarii prebende de Bekyngham capitulorum cathedralis Ebor' et Suthwell' ecclesiarum nostrarum consensu[5] unanimi concurrente ordinamus et discernimus ordinando quod de prebenda de Bekyngham ecclesie Suthwell predicte quam ex certis considerationibus propter multiplicationem bonis spiritualis auctoritate pontificali in duas equitate dividimus suadente ecclesia de Northleverton que pars prebende de Bekingham in qua ius patronatus habemus notorie dum integra quondam erat esse hactenus consuevit sit perpetuis temporibus de cetero cum suis iuribus et pertinentibus universis prebenda in memorata ecclesia de Suthwell' singularis quam per hanc nostram ordinationem in prebendam eiusdem ecclesie creamus et erigimus singularem ab ecclesia de Bekyngham predicta que similiter[6] semper de cetero manebit eiusdem ecclesie prebendalis totaliter sit divisam per nos et successores nostros successivis temporibus cum eam vacare contigerit conferendam. Sitque hec nova prebenda in se adeo libera deinceps in omnibus sicut dum pars prefate prebende de Bekingham fuerat esse hactenus consuevit ac ipsius prebende canonico stallus in choro ex parte boriali iuxta stallum sacriste et locus in capitulo per capitulum Suthwell' debite assignetur. Ordinamus insuper et decernimus ordinando quod canonicus dictus nove prebende vicarium in dicta ecclesia Suthwell' habeat suo nomine ministrantem dicto capitulo Suthwell' per ipsum canonicum presentandum et per dictum capitulum in choro inibi instituendum sicut de aliis vicar[iis] chori fieri consuevit iuxta morem capituli supradicti cui solvat stipendia annua prout alii dicte ecclesie solvunt canonici consueta.[7] Volumus etiam ordinando quod prefatus dominus Willelmus de Rotherfeld obtentu liberalitatis sue predicte memoratam prebendam de Bekingham ut premittitur nunc divisam habeat et possideat suis temporibus absque diminutione qualibet amodo facienda. In cuius rei testimonium sigillum nostrum una cum predictorum capitulorum sigillis presentibus est appensum. Actum et datum in capitulo Suthwell' xiiij kaln' Novembris anno gratie m° cc° nonagesimo primo.

[1] *hec* seems to have been rewritten in 15th c. [2] MS *inpendere* [3] ? for *excrescente* [4] For *expressa* [5] MS *concensu* [6] MS *siliter* [7] MS *cosueta*

Margin Page heading *Northleverton* (Scribe 4). *De ordinatione prebend' de North-leverton'* (at head of **41**, in hand of main text, Scribe 1).

Note NA, SC7/1/5, f. 6[r–v] for a 15th-c. copy and NA, M 494, f. 106[v]–107[r] for one made for Thoroton. Pd. in *Mon. Ang.*, vi, pt iii, 1314 (viii) and *Reg. Romeyn*, ii, 9–12. William of Rotherfield had been a canon since 1257 (**192**).

BECKINGHAM PREBEND, 42

42 *Notification by William of Rotherfield, canon and prebendary of Beckingham, of his submission to John [Le Romeyn], archbishop of York*   Southwell, 18 October 1291

Pateat universis per presentes quod ego Willelmus de Rotherfelde, canonicus Suwelliensis ecclesie, prebendam meam de Bekyngham in dicta ecclesia et statum eiusdem ad utilitatem ipsius ecclesie et honorem Dei et virginis gloriose matris sue ordinancioni venerabilis patris domini Johannis, Dei gracia Ebor' archiepiscopi, Anglie primatis, pure et absolute submitto. Ratum habitum et firmandum quicquid prefatus ad¹ utilitatem et honorem Dei et gloriose virginis matris sue duxerit ordinandum. In cuius rei testimonium sigillum meum una cum sigillo capituli dicto ecclesie presentibus est appensum. Datum apud Suwell' xv kalendas Novembris anno gracie mᵒ cc nonagesimo primo.

¹ *ad* repeated in MS; this charter has been added in a later hand (Scribe 4), from that normally used in this section of the MS

Margin   *Submissio prebende de Beckingham* in post-1583 hand.

Note   As **41** reveals, the archbishop divided Beckingham prebend on the following day to establish a new prebend at North Leverton, exacting this acknowledgement from Rotherfield in order to avoid future disputes. Rotherfield was dead by 23 June 1292 when Beckingham was assigned to Reginald of St Albans (*Reg. Romeyn*, i, no. 865).

SOUTH MUSKHAM PREBEND, 43–5

43 *Grant by John of Ingham, son of Thomas of Bathley, to Henry de Pascy, his uncle, of all his land in South Muskham that William of Bathley gave to Thomas his father, for 3s rent per annum paid to William of Bathley, chief lord*   [1250 × 1282]

Carta Johannis de Ingham' pertinens ad prebendam de   p. 25
Suthmuscham

Sciant presentes et futuri quod ego Johannes de Ingham, filius Thome de Batheleye, dedi, concessi et hac in presenti carta mea confirmavi Henrico de Pascy, avunculo meo, totam terram meam in Suthmuscham quam Willelmus de Batheley' dedit Thome, patri meo, in concordiam, scilicet unam bovatam terre cum pertinenciis quam Radulfus Smethe tenuit, et dimidiam bovatam terre cum pertinenciis quam Robertus Tuppe tenet, cum tota sequela sua cum omnibus catallis suis. Tenendum et habendum sibi et heredibus suis vel assignatis suis libere, quiete et pacifice cum omnibus libertatibus et aisimentis ad predictam terram intra villam et ex pertinentibus. Reddendo inde annuatim Willelmo de Batheley capitali domino vel heredibus suis tres solidos ad tres terminos, scilicet ad festum sancti Thome apostoli xii denarios, ad clausum Pasce xii denarios, ad nativitatem beate Marie xii denarios, pro omni servicio consuetudine et exaccione salvo forinseco servicio quantum pertinet ad predictam terra.

Et ego predictus Johannes et heredes mei warantizabimus prenominata[1] Henrico et heredibus vel assignatis suis totam predictam terram cum pertinenciis et Robertum Tope cum sequela sua et catallis suis contra omnes homines in perpetuum. Et ut hec mea donacio concesso et confirmato[2] rata sit et stabilis presentem cartam sigilli mei apposicione roboravi. Hiis testibus: Roberto de Burstall', Willelmo de Batheley, Radulfo de Muscham, Hugone Gernon, Rogero de Anigton', Willelmo filio Odonis de Muscham, clerico, Henrico filio Henrici de Carleton, Ricardo de Muscham, clerico, et aliis.

[1] MS *sic*   [2] MS *sic*

Date   After **44** and while Robert III de Burstall was active (*Thurgarton*, cxxiii–cxxiv).

Note   William of Bathley, elder brother of Thomas, and uncle of John of Ingham, active *c*. 1252 × 1275. Hugh Gernon witnessed **551–4**, **556–8**. Ralph of Muskham, William son of Odo of Muskham and Hugo Gernon witnessed *c*. 1240–8 (*Rufford*, 199).

44   *Grant by Thomas de Innocents, son of Henry de Bale, to Henry, son of Hugh de Pascy, his brother, of one bovate of land sometime of Henry, his father, in South Muskham for 1d rent per annum*   [1219 × 1245]

Alia carta de Suthmushcam

Sciant presentes et futuri quod ego Thomas de Innocentibus, filius Henrici de Bale, dedi, concessi et hac mea presenti carta confirmavi Henrico filio Hugonis de Pascy, fratri meo, pro homagio et servicio suo unam bovatam terre cum pratis et pasturis et cum pertinenciis libertatibus et asiamentis predicte terre adiacentibus in territorio de Suthmuscham que fuit quondam Henrici, patris mei, iacentem inter terram quam Ricardus Tupe tenet et terram[1] [quam] Radulfus filius Pagani Smethe tenet de eodem feodo. Tenendam et habendam sibi et heredibus suis vel assignatis suis de me et heredibus meis libere, quiete et pacifice, reddendo inde annuatim mihi et heredibus meis unum denarium ad Pasca pro omni servicio consuetudine et exaccione salvo forinseco servicio quantum pertinet ad tantam terram. Et ego prenominatus Thomas et heredes mei warantizabimus predicto Henrico, fratri meo, et heredibus suis vel assignatis suis, predictam bovatam terre cum pratis et pasturis et cum omnibus pertinenciis libertatibus et assiementis predicte adiacentibus contra omnes homines in perpetuum. Et in huius autem securitatem et testimonium huic scripto sigillum meum apposui. Hiis testibus: domino Hugone filio Ade, domino Willelmo de Crely, domino Henrico de Notingham, canonico Suthwell', Willelmo de Bale, Henrico de Muscham, Gilberto le Harpur et aliis.

[1] Followed by *et*

Date   While Henry of Nottingham was a canon; see **37n**.

Note   The names Hugh and Adam were fairly common in the extensive Muskham family. William de Bale may be identified with William of Bathley (**43**), who also frequently occurs as a witness to Rufford charters in the mid-thirteenth century.

45   *Notification by the Chapter of the appointment of John of Hoton, chaplain, as vicar of South Muskham by order of John [Le Romeyn], archbishop of York, at his last visitation and by the presentation of John of Penistone, canon*   Southwell, 6 May 1295

Southmuscham vicaria

Universis Christi fidelibus hoc presens scriptum visuris vel audituris capitulum collegiate ecclesie sancte Marie Suwelliensis salutem in domino sempiternam. Noverit universitas vestra nos dilectum nobis in Christo dominum Johannem de Hoton, capellanum, ad vicariam de Suthmusham de novo per nos creatam secundum decretum et preceptum reverendi patris domini Johannis, Dei gracia Ebor' archiepiscopi, Anglie primatis, in ultime visitacione sua Suwell' facta per dilectum concanonicum et confratrem nostrum Johannes de Penigeston eiusdem loci prebendarium nobis legitime presentatum admisisse, ipsumque vicarium instituisse canonice in eadem. Que quidem vicaria consistit in porcionibus infrascriptis, videlicet, in uno tofto et mesuagio cum pertinenciis in villa de Suthmuscham sitis inter toftum Roberti dicti Petit et toftum domini Willelmi le Ros, quod Willelmus Trewlove tenet de eo in eadem. Item in lana et agnis totius parochie citra sortem remanentibus quod interpretamur a numero quinario descendendo, et decima croftorum que modo sunt clausa vel esse solebent. Item in primo legato quod comuniter dicitur mortuarium, et in omnibus minutis decimis, oblacionibus et proventibus universis. In cuius rei testimonium eidem Johanni fieri fecimus has literas nostras patentes. Valete. Datum in capitulo nostro pridie nonas Maii anno domini m° cc° nonagesimo quinto.

Margin   The centred heading *Southmuscham vicaria* is written in large formal Fere textualis in the same hand as the charter which has been transcribed by the registrar, John Martiall, around 1600.

Note   John of Hoton may be the man who later became prebendary of Oxton I (*c.* 1331–before 1337), *Reg. Melton*, iii, no. 192; iv, no. 541 and v, nos 473 and 491. For the arrangements leading to this appointment see **40**.

Halloughton Prebend, 46–56

46   *Bull of Alexander III confirming to Roger, brother of Martin de Capella, clerk of Henry II, prebendary of Halloughton, the grant of lands made to him by Roger [de Pont-l'Évêque], archbishop of York in the presence of the papal legate, Cardinal Henry, and the bishops of Lincoln, Durham, Lisieux, Évreux and Sées*   Anagni, 6 April [1173 × 1176]

Bulla Urbani[1] de prebenda de Haltona   p. 26

Alexander[2] episcopus servus servorum Dei, dilecto filio Rogero, fratri Martini de Capella, clerico Henrici illustris Anglorum regis salutem et apostolicam benedictionem. Justis petentium desideriis facilem nos convenit impartiri consensum et vota que a rationis tramite[3] non discordant effectu sunt prosequente complenda. Eapropter, dilecte in domino fili, tuis iustis postulationibus grato concurrentes assensu tam terram de Halton' cum pertinentiis suis et beneficium a Willelmo bone memorie Turstini quondam Eboracensis archiepiscopi dapifero detentum, quam terram et beneficium venerabilis frater noster Rogerus Eboracensis archiepiscopus in presentia dilecti filii nostri Henrici sancte Romane ecclesie presbiteri cardinalis, apostolice sedis legati, et fratrum nostrorum Roberti Lincolniensis, Hugonis Dunelmensis, Arnulfi Lexoviensis, Rotroci Ebroicensis, Frogeri Sagiensis episcoporum in prebendam tibi noscitur canonice contulisse, sicut ea in presentiarum rationabiliter possidere dinosceris, devotioni tue auctoritate apostolica confirmamus et presentis scripti patrocinio communimus. Nulli ergo omnino homini liceat hanc paginam nostre confirmationis ausu temeritatis infringere vel ei aliquatenus contraire.[4] Si quis autem hoc attemptare presumpserit indignationi omnipotentis Dei et beatorum Petri et Pauli apostolorum eius se noverit incursurum. Datum Anagn' viii idus Aprilis.

[1] Followed by *pape* which has been erased [2] Decorated initial *U* corrected to *A*; rest of the original name erased and replaced with *–lex*' [3] MS *tremate* (cf. the comparable arenga in **9**, '... *consensum et vota que a rationis tramite non discordant...*' [4] MS *contramire*

Note NA, M 494, f. 107[r–v] for a copy made for Thoroton. Text edited by Holtzmann, *PUE*, ii, 340–1, no. 150, which has been compared with MS; also pd. in *Mon. Ang.* vi, pt iii, 1314–15 (ix). See **50–3** and **55** and *Thurgarton*, xxxiv, ccii, 94–5; no. 153.

47 *Writ by Henry II to the bailiffs of the archbishop of York at Southwell to deliver to Mr Roger de Capella, the king's clerk, all liberties and customs that William Das' his ancestor had*

Feckenham, [1163 × May 1172]

Carta regis Henrici de consuetudinibus et libertatibus de Haltona

Henricus, rex Anglie et dux Normannie et Aquitanie et comes Andegavie ballivis archiepiscopi Ebor' [de] Suthwella salutem. Precipio vobis quod plenarie et iuste faciatis habere magistro Rogero de Capella, clerico meo, omnes libertates [et] consuetudines suas in bosco et plano et pratis et pasturis et in omnibus aliis rebus sicut racionabiliter monstrare poterit quas Willelmus Das', antecessor suus, eas habuit anno et die quo rex Henricus, avus meus, fuit vivus et mortuus. Et nisi feceritis, Rogerus archiepiscopus Ebor' faciat. Teste Ricardo, archiepiscopo[1] Pictav'. Apud Fecheham.

[1] MS *sic* for *Archidiacono*

Date After Henry II's return to England and the promotion of Richard of Ilchester as archdeacon of Poitou, but before introduction of *Dei gratia* clause (*Acta Henry II*, no. 507).

Note *Acta Henry II*, no. 507, rejected the identification of *Fecheham* with Fécamp (Eyton, *Itinerary*, p. 55), but identified William the steward of Archbishop Thurstan, before 1140, with *Willelmus Da[cu]s* (**49**). Mr Roger was brother of another royal clerk, Martin de Capella. He was confirmed in his prebend by Alexander III, 6 April 1173–6 (*PUE*, ii, 106, 150; **46**), and was dead by 1211. He was a benefactor of Thurgarton priory (*Thurgarton*, 153; *EEA York 1070–1154*, no. 70).

48 *Writ of Henry II to the archbishop of York and his bailiffs at Southwell not to permit any infringement of the rights of Mr Roger, the king's clerk, in the pasture of Halloughton as William the steward, his predecessor held* Westminster, [1163 × May 1172, ?1163 × March 1166]

Carta regis Henrici de libertatibus de pastura de Haltona

Henricus, rex Anglie et dux Normannie et Aquitanie et comes Andegavie archiepiscopo Ebor' et ballivis suis de Suthwell' salutem. Precipio vobis quod non patiamini quod aliquis iniuriam vel contumelliam faciat magistro Rogero, clerico meo, de libertate quam debet habere in pastura de Halton' de sicut Willelmus, dapifer, antecessor suus, eam habuit tempore regis Henrici, avi mei. Teste Simone filio Petri, apud Westmonasterium.

Date After the promotion of Roger de Capella (**47**) and return of Henry II to England in 1163, but probably before he crossed to Normandy in March 1166 (*Acta Henry II*, no. 2232).

Note For Archbishop Thurstan's grant to William, his steward, see **49**. Thoroton, iii, 72 briefly notes this charter.

49 *Grant in hereditary fee by Thurstan, archbishop of York to William the steward of a thorn-brake at Halloughton in augmentation of his land in return for the service he owed on other land for one third of a knight's fee* [1125 × 1135]

Litera Turstini archiepiscopi de prebenda de Haltona

Turstinus Dei gratia Ebor' archiepiscopus omnibus successoribus suis et omnibus hominibus suis de Notinghamsira, clericis et laicis, Francis et Anglis salutem. Sciatis me dedisse et presentis cartule testimonio confirmasse Willelmo dapifero et heredibus[1] suis et[2] feudo et hereditate frutectum quoddam apud Halton' in crementum terre sue pro eodem servitio pro quo aliam terram suam tenet, videlicet pro servitio tertie partis militis. Hiis testibus, Hugone decano Ebor', Hugone Sotta Sac', Willelmo filio Tole archidiacono, Willelmo preposito, Rogero de Suthwella canonico, Willelmo elemosinario et aliis.

[1] MS *heredis*   [2] Thus in MS: ? should be *in*

Date Hugh was appointed dean of York before December 1093 and retired to become a monk at Fountains in 1135 (*Fasti 1066–1300*, vi, 8). Archdeacon William, son of Tole, occurs as archdeacon without territorial title *c*. 1125–33 and *c*. 1125–35 (ibid., 31 cf. *EEA York 1070–1154*, no. 70).

Note Pd. in Hodgson, *Thomas II*, 52n; Nicholl, *Thurstan*, 248–9; cal. in *EEA York 1070–1154*, no. 70, where the grant is said to be of an orchard. Hugh Sottovagina was a canon of York by *c*. 1109, perhaps before 21 May 1108, but he may appear as cantor, which dignity he held from before August 1133 until his death (or resignation) in July 1139 (*Fasti 1066–1300*, vi, 14, 112–13). Burton identifies William the provost as provost of the archbishop (*EEA York 1070–1154*, xxxv). Roger was probably canon of Southwell rather than of York. William the almoner witnessed two other charters of Thurstan between *c*. 1121 and 1140 (ibid., nos 79 and 82).

50 *Notification by Rotrou, bishop of Évreux that in his presence Archbishop Roger [de Pont-l'Évêque], in the court of the papal legate, Cardinal Henry of Pisa, had granted to Master Roger, king's clerk, the land at Halloughton previously held by William the steward by grant of Archbishop Thurstan, over which the archbishop had been in dispute with Martin de Capella, Roger's brother* [*c.* April 1162]

Litera R. episcopi de Haltona

Rogerus[1] Dei gratia Ebr' episcopus[2] omnibus sancte matris ecclesie filiis salutem. Noverit universitas vestra Rogerum archiepiscopum me presente concessisse et dedisse coram Henrico de Pisa sancte Romane ecclesie cardinali et apostolice sedis legato magistro Rogero clerico domini regis totam terram de Halton, quam Willelmus dapifer Turstini archiepiscopi de eo tenuit, cum omnibus pertinentiis suis in perpetuam prebendam Suthwell', et quicquid archiepiscopus contra Martinum de Capella fratrem predicti Rogeri in dominio suo tenend' calumpniatus est, et me super hoc veritatis testimonium perhibere et idem archiepiscopus predictam terram eidem Rogero defendere et sicut dominicum suum warantizare pepigit.

[1] MS *sic* (see Note)   [2] *Ebr' episcopus* over erasure

Date   See **55n**.

Note   NA, SC7/1/5, f. 6ᵛ for a 15ᵗʰ-c. copy. The bishop concerned is Rotrou of Warwick, bishop of Évreux (1139–late May 1165), then archbishop of Rouen until 26 November 1183.

51 *Notification by Robert, bishop of Lincoln that in his presence Roger, archbishop of York, assigned to Mr Roger, brother of Martin de Capella, the land in Halloughton and whatever William the steward of Archbishop Thurstan held in chief* [*c.* April 1162]

Litera Roberti episcopi Lincoln' de Haltona

Robertus Dei gratia Linc' episcopus omnibus sancte matris[1] filiis ad quos carta ista pervenerit salutem. Notum sit universitati[2] vestre quod Rogerus Ebor' archiepiscopus in presentia mea assignavit et concessit in prebendam in ecclesia de Suthwell' magistro Rogero fratri Martini de Capella totam terram de Haltona cum omnibus pertinentiis suis, et quicquid Willelmus dapifer Turstini archiepiscopi de ipso et predecessoribus suis | tenebat in capite, predictam quoque terram adversus omnes sicut dominium suum defendet. Factum est hoc[3] presentia nostra. Hiis testibus, Henrico sancte Romane ecclesie presbitero cardin[ali], Hugone Dunelm[ensi] episcopo.

[1] MS omits *ecclesie* which normally formed part of Robert Chesney's usual style though it was occasionally omitted   [2] MS *universitate*   [3] MS omits *in*

Date   See **55n**.

Note   This charter of Robert Chesney, bishop of Lincoln (19 December 1148–27 (probably) December 1166), is not in *EEA Lincoln 1067–1185* or in the addenda in *EEA Lincoln, 1186–1206*. Hugh de Puiset, bishop of Durham (20 December 1153–3 March 1195).

52 *Notification by Froger, bishop of Sées that in his presence Roger, archbishop of York assigned to Mr Roger, brother of Martin de Capella, all the land in Halloughton and whatever William the steward of Archbishop Thurstan held in chief* [*c*. April 1162]

Litera Rogeri episcopi Sag' de Haltona

Rogerus[1] Dei gratia Sag' episcopus omnibus sancte matris ecclesie filiis ad quos carta ista pervenerit salutem. Notum sit universitati vestre quod Rogerus Ebor' archiepiscopus in presentia nostra assignavit et concessit in prebendam in ecclesia de Suthwell' magistro Rogero fratri Martini de Capella totam terram de Haltona cum omnibus pertinentiis suis et quicquid Willelmus dapifer Thurstini archiepiscopi de ipso et predecessoribus suis tenuit in capite, predictam quoque terram adversus omnes sicut dominicum suum defendet. Factum est in presentia nostra hiis assidentibus episcopis, Roberto Lincoln', Hugone Dunnelm'[2] et Rotrodo Eboracensi.[3]

[1] MS *sic* for *Frogerus* (see Note)   [2] MS *sic* for *Dunelm'*   [3] MS *sic* for *Ebroicensi*

Date   See **55n**.

Note   Froger, bishop of Sées (20 December 1159–85): 'Perhaps from Lisieux, he had previously been a *domesticus* of Arnulf of Lisieux, as well as archdeacon of Derby and almoner of the king. He was intruded by Henry II upon the electors of Sées, who had chosen Achard, abbot of Saint-Victor as the next bishop in 1157. He was active in the royal court throughout his career, playing a significant role in the Becket controversy. A generous benefactor of the abbey of Mortemer both before and after his election, he was buried in the choir of the abbey'. (Details kindly provided by Dr Richard Allen, who is preparing an edition of *Les actes des évêques de Sées (XIe siècle–1220)*.

53   *Notification by Cardinal Henry, papal legate, that in his presence Archbishop Roger of York assigned to Mr Roger, brother of Martin de Capella, all the land at Halloughton and whatever William the steward of Archbishop Thurstan held in chief* [*c*. April 1162]

Litera Henrici cardinalis de Haltona

Henricus Dei gratia sancte Romane ecclesie presbiter cardinalis et apostolice [sedis] legatus omnibus sancte matris ecclesie filiis ad quos carta ista pervenerit salutem. Notum sit universitati vestre quod Rogerus Ebor' archiepiscopus in presentia nostra assignavit et concessit in prebendam in ecclesia de Suthwell magistro Rogero fratri Martini de Capella totam terram de Halton' cum omnibus pertinentiis suis et quicquid Willelmus dapifer Turstini archiepiscopi de ipso et predecessoribus eius tenebat in capite. Predictam vero terram adversus omnes sicut dominicum suum defendet. Factum est in presentia nostra hiis assidentibus episcopis Roberto Lincoln', Hugone Dunelm', Frogero[1] Sag'.

[1] Holtzmann prefers *Frog[erio]*

Note   Pd. *PUE*, ii, 292, no. 106. Henry of Pisa was legate to the English and French bishops from 1160 (Tillmann, *Die päpstlichen*, 53; *EEA* 20, no. 95n). This notification was perhaps issued at the same time as Archbishop Roger's (**55**), *c*. April 1162 (*EEA York 1154–1181*, no. 95n).

54 *Grant by William the steward of Halloughton and his wife, ?Avicia, in free alms to Southwell, of forty acres of land and one messuage in Halloughton and tithes of orchards, gardens and flying ducks, the right of the priest's cattle to share pasture with the lord's cattle, and his other flock to use the common pasture. Also in time of pannage, the priest's swine may be sent to the wood with the lord's, with the right to take wood whenever necessary by agreement with the lord's officers* [1139 × 1153]

Carta Willelmi senescalli de ordinatione vicarie de Haltona

Omnibus sancte matris ecclesie filiis Willelmus senescallus de Haltona et Anina[1] uxor eius in Cristo salutem. Notum sit omnibus nos dedisse et concessisse in perpetuam elemosinam ecclesie sancte Marie in Suthwella et canonicis ibidem Deo servientibus quadraginta acras terre et unam mansuram in Haltona libere et quiete absque omni servitio pro salute anime nostre, videlicet xiii acras apud Wineleswellam et xi apud Odecroft, et xvi in Westriding et totam decimam de pomerio et horto et de volatilibus, et ut boves sacerdotis pascantur cum bobus domini [in] eodem pascuo et alia pecora eius in communi pascuo. Item in tempore glandis proprii porci predicti sacerdotis cum porcis domini ad silvam mittantur et ut de nemore habeat quicquid ad necessarium ei fuerit sine wasto consensu et assensu ministri domini et domine. Valete. Hiis testibus Radulpho Debarum, Galfrido Turcople archidiacono, Rogero Maito, Ricardo, Nicholao, Rogero Cras, Herberto, Hugone, Thoma canonicis,[2] Willelmo capellano et multis tam clericis quam laicis.

[1] MS *sic* for ?*Avicia*   [2] MS *canonici*

Date William became Archbishop Thurstan's steward at Halloughton before Thurstan's resignation 20/21 January 1140, and he died on 5 or 6 February 1140 (**49**; *Fasti 1066–1300*, vi, 2). Geoffrey Turcople, archdeacon of Nottingham, occurs 1137 × 1140 and last 1151 × 14 October 1153 and his successor first occurs 13 December 1157. Ralph de Baro was archdeacon of Cleveland, 1139 × 1140–57 × 1158.

Note The list of at least seven canons of Southwell as witnesses is the fullest evidence for membership of the Chapter at such an early date. Hugh, Nicholas, Roger Cras (also Grasso), Roger Maito (also Macro) and Thomas all occur as witnesses in Rufford abbey charters around 1150.

55 *Notification by Roger, archbishop of York, to Robert, dean of York, and the chapters of York and Southwell that he has confirmed to Mr Roger, brother of Martin de Capella, all the land in Halloughton which William the steward of Archbishop Thurstan held of him as a perpetual prebend of Southwell* [c. April 1162]

Carta Rogeri archiepiscopi Ebor' de prebenda de Halton'[1]

R[ogerus] Dei gratia Ebor' archiepiscopus R[oberto] decano Ebor' et capitulo Ebor' et capitulo Suthwell', salutem. Sciatis me donasse et concessisse m[agistro] R[ogero] fratri Martini de Capella totam terram de Haltona quam Willelmus dapifer Turstini archiepiscopi tenebat de me, et quicquid ad eandem villam pertinet, in perpetuam prebendam ecclesie sancte Marie de Suthwell'. Quare volumus et precipimus ut teneat illam bene et in pace et libere et honorifice cum omnibus pertinentiis suis, et sicut ullus canonicorum in eadem ecclesia melius et liberius tenuit. Testibus hiis: Henrico de Pisa Romane ecclesie presbitero cardinali et apostolice sedis legato, Hugone episcopo Dunelm', Roberto[2] Lincoln' episcopo, Arnulfo Lexoviens' episcopo, et aliis multis etc.

[1] Title and transcription by Scribe 4 as is **56**   [2] MS *Ric[ardo]*

Margin   *Rogerus archiepiscopus t. 1154, Halton preb.* (16th–17th c.)

Date   Marie Lovatt (*EEA York 1154–1181*, no. 95n) dates this 1160–4, and thinks the most likely date of issue was in Normandy *c*. April 1162. Henry of Pisa became legate to English and French bishops in 1160 and Roger himself legate in 1164. All the witnesses were in Normandy with Henry II in the spring of 1162, and since the charter makes no mention of Thomas Becket it was probably issued before he was elected archbishop.

Note   NA, SC7/1/5, f. 6v for another 15th-c. copy. Pd. in *EEA York 1154–1181*, no. 95. For Robert, dean of York, see **56**.

56   *Confirmation by Robert II, dean of York and the Chapter of York of the grant by Roger, archbishop of York to Roger, brother of Martin de Capella of the land which William the steward of Archbishop Thurstan held in Halloughton for a prebend*   [Probably April × 23 September 1162]

Confirmationis carta Roberti decani secundi de terra in Halton[1]

Robertus secundus decanus et capitulum ecclesie sancti Petri Ebor' omnibus sancte matris ecclesie filiis ad quos iste litere pervenerint salutem et fraternam dilectionem. Sciatis nos concessisse et presentium harum attestatione confirmasse donationem Rogeri venerabilis archiepiscopi Ebor' quam Rogerus fratri Martini de Capella fecit. Dedit vero illi predictus Rogerus archiepiscopus ut carta sua testatur totam terram de Haltuna quam W[illelmus] dapifer Turstini archiepiscopi tenebat et quicquid ad eandem villam predictam in perpetuam prebendam ecclesie sancte Marie de Suwella. Hanc igitur donationem ratam et firmam volumus permanere. Hii sunt testes Robertus decanus, Johannes thesaurarius, Robertus magister, Geroldus canonicus et aliis multis etc'.

[1] Title, marginalia and text in the same hand (Scribe 4) as **55**

Margin   *Halton preb.*

Date   After **55** and before John of Canterbury (or Bellesmains) became archbishop of Poitiers in 1162 and was consecrated at Déols on 23 September 1162 (*Fasti 1066–1300*, vi, 22). He was treasurer of York from just after 20 December 1153 until he was made bishop.

Note   Mr Robert Butevilain occurs as dean of York 6 May 1158 and died in office July 1186. Robert occurs as *magister scholarum* of York 1157 × *c*. 1158 and he died 27 September 1177. Gerold is probably Gerold, son of Serlo, who occurs from before 1143 to after 1165 (*Fasti 1066–1300*, vi, 9, 18, 120–1).

57 *Letters of John [Le Romeyn], archbishop of York, establishing the church of Eaton, of which he is the patron, as a prebend of St Mary's, Southwell, with the consent of the Chapters of York and Southwell, reserving to himself the presentation of a vicar for whom an appropriate portion will be assigned in consultation with the Chapter at Southwell; also reserving the rights of himself and his successors to name prebendaries of Eaton, who are to have stalls in the choir and Chapter House and the right to name vicars choral to carry out their duties as other prebendaries do, with the usual rates of remuneration*   Southwell, 30 January 1290

p. 28   **Litera Johannis Ebor' archiepiscopi de ordinatione prebende de Eton'**

Universis sancte matris ecclesie filiis ad quorum notitiam pervenerit hec scriptura Johannes permissione divina Ebor archiepiscopus Anglie primas salutem in sanctissimis amplexibus salvatoris. Inter alias solicitudines quibus ex debito officii occupamur illam mentalius amplectimur qua divini cultus augmentum promovere cupimus ad laudem altissimi et decorem ecclesie in ministris. Cum itaque ecclesiarum prelatis pontificali prefulgentibus dignitate prebendas et numerum prebendarum ecclesiarum suarum, necessitate vel utilitate ingruente, augendi potestas a iure canonico sit concessa, nos hanc utilitatem ut premisimus precordialiter intuentes et pro nostre fragilitatis humane modulo affectantes ut decus sancte matris ecclesie succrescat cumuletur[1] et amplificetur per maiorem numerum canonicorum qui gratos Deo se facient et ydoneos servitores cultus per divini exercitum in latitudine caritatis quod ecclesia de Eton', nostre dioc', cuius ad nos pertinet patronatus ecclesie nostre Suthwell' cum vacaverit in perpetuum sit annexa, et in eadem ecclesia Suthwell' habeatur et de cetero sit prebenda de consensu[2] et assensu unanimi dilectorum in Cristo filiorum capitulorum nostrorum Ebor' et Suthwell' ecclesiarum duximus ordinandum et tenore presentium ordinamus, reservata nobis in prefata ecclesia de Eton' collatione vicarii tantomodo ista vice persone ydonee per nos[3] conferende que in dicta ecclesia de Eton' personaliter resideat et per quam ipsius ecclesie debeat cura regi; collatione autem dicte vicar[ie] ista unica pars per nos facta ordinamus de consensu capituli Suthwell' predicti quod postmodum[4] proximo et perpetuo cum vicariam memorate ecclesie de Eton' vacare contigerit vicarius qui in eadem ecclesia de Eton' debeat ordinari et in eadem ut premittitur personaliter residere ac curam regere ecclesie antedicte nobis et successoribus nostris a canonico prebende huiusmodi qui pro tempore fuerit presentetur et per nos et successores nostros instituatur ibidem. Reservata etiam vicario qui pro tempore fuerit iuxta taxationem ipsam de consensu eiusdem capituli Suthwell' congrua portione. Prefata etiam prebenda per nos et successores nostros cum eam vacare contigerit conferenda a prestatione cuiuslibet[5] oneris ordinarii sit libera et immunis, et ipsius prebende canonico stallus in choro et locus in capitulo per capitulum Suthwell' debite assignetur, qui canonicus vicario suo in dicta ecclesia Suthwell' suo nomini ministranti ac dicto capitulo Suthwell' per prebendarium presentato et per idem capitulum de choro inibi instituendo sicut de aliis vicariis chori fieri consuevit iuxta morem capituli supradicti solvat stipendia annua sicut alii dicte ecclesie solvunt canonici consueta. Omnia autem onera ordinaria dictus vicarius de Eton' subeat et subportat. Onera vero extraordinaria[6] quecumque contigerint subeunda tam ad dicte prebende canonicum quam ipsius de Eton vicarium pro rata pertineant portionis. In cuius rei testimonium sigillum nostrum presentibus[7] est appensum. Datum apud Suthwell' iii kalend' Februarii anno gratie m° cc° octogesimo nono et pontificatus nostri quarto.

[1] MS *cunuletur*   [2] MS *concensu*   [3] MS *mos*   [4] MS corr. from *postomodum*   [5] MS *cuislibet*   [6] MS as two words   [7] MS *presitibus*

Margin   Heading at top of page: *Prebend' de Eton* (Scribe 4); alongside text: *John Roman 1289* (16th–17th c.); rubricated title and text in usual hand for this section (Scribe 1).

Note   NA, SC7/1/5, f. 7r for another 15th-c. copy. Pd. in *Mon. Ang.*, vi, pt iii, 1315 (x) and *Reg. Romeyn*, i, no. 1088.

VICARS CHORAL, 58

58   *Confirmation by the Vicars Choral of Southwell, to Richard of Sutton, canon, that on days that masses for the dead are celebrated in the church for brothers and benefactors, a special prayer will be said for Richard and another for Robert of Sutton, his father, and Alice, his mother, and that a candle will be lit for him in perpetuity at the daily mass of the Virgin*   Southwell, 13 January 1261

Litera de communi vicariorum de Suthwell' pertinens ad Ricardum de Sutton canonicum eiusdem ecclesie

Omnibus presens scriptum visuris vel audituris vicarii ecclesie beate Marie Suthwell' salutem in domino. Noveritis nos pro nobis et successoribus nostris concessisse domino Ricardo de Suttona canonico Suthwell' quod singulis diebus in perpetuum quando missa de defunctis[1] celebrabitur in ecclesia nostra pro fratribus et benefactoribus ecclesie nostre dicetur ad missam illam una oratio specialis pro dicto Ricardo et alia oratio specialis pro animabus Roberti de Suttona patris sui et Alicie matris sue. Concessimus etiam eidem quod inveniemus in perpetuum pro anima predicti Ricardi unum cereum ardentem ad missam beate Marie que singulis diebus celebratur sollempniter in ecclesia nostra. Et ut hec nostra concessio robur perpetue firmitatis optineat presenti scripto sigillum nostrum communie una cum sigillo capituli Suthwell' ecclesie apponi fecimus. Datum apud Suthwell' idibus Januarii anno domini m° cc° sexagesimo. Hiis testibus magistro Petro de Radonora,[2] magistro Henrico de Skypton', Henrico de Mora, Reginaldo de Stouwe, Roberto Malore, canonicis et aliis.

[1] MS *defuctis*   [2] MS *sic* for *Radenor*

Margin   *Nota de I cereo providetur ad Luminare sancte Marie Virginis missas celebratas in perpetuo* (15th–16th-c. hand). *Anno domini 1260* (16th–17th c.)

Note   Mr Richard of Sutton had been a canon since at least 1241 (*Reg. Greenfield*, 84); further details on him and his family can be found in the **Introduction**, pp. xciii–xcv, and in the notes to the entries concerning the chantry founded in his name (**61**–**71**), especially **61** and **62**. Mr Peter of Radnor, canon by 23 July 1257 (**192**) until his death in an affray in Oxford, probably in June 1276 (cf. *BRUO*, iii, 1548). Mr Henry of Skipton, canon since 1255, prebendary of Normanton, d. before 29 December 1286. Henry de Mora, canon before 1249–after 1261. Reginald of Stowe, canon from *c.* 1241, later prebendary of Rampton, d. by 17 June 1267. Robert Malore, already a clerk of the archbishop of York in 1238, canon by 1251 and still on 23 July 1257 (**192**); this appears to be his last appearance as witness.

Eaton Prebend, 59–60

p. 28a   Piece of parchment inserted into volume in hand of Scribe 4 (mid-15th c.)

59   *Ordination by John [Le Romeyn], archbishop of York, concerning the vicar of the prebendal church of Eaton, to receive various tithes and other payments, including four marks per annum while he resides from the prebendary, who is to remain in possession of the ecclesiastical manse and the great tithes, providing suitable books and ornaments for the church*   [Bishop] Wilton, 27 June 1290

Ordinacio vicarie de Eton per archiepiscopum

Omnibus sancte matris ecclesie filiis ad quorum noticiam pervenerit hec scriptura Johannes permissione divina Ebor' archiepiscopus Anglie primas salutem in sinceris amplexibus salvatoris. Assumpti officii vigilans sollicitudo ac canonica instituta nos multipliciter exhortantur ut vicariis ecclesiarum qui tenentur continue residentiam facere personalem portio conveniens[1] assignetur. De vicaria itaque in ecclesia prebendali de Eton' inperpetuum optinenda et portionibus in quibus debeat vicaria consistere supradicta de consensu et assensu unanimi dilectorum in Cristo filiorum capitulorum nostrorum Ebor' et Suwelln' ecclesiarum ordinamus et disponimus in hunc modum: videlicet quod vicarius qui pro tempore fuerit in ecclesia prebendali predicta habeat agnos, lanam, mortuaria, oblationes et ceteras minutas decimas totius parochie de Eton' quocumque nomine censeantur, una cum turbaria ad dictam ecclesiam pertinente. Prebendarius insuper dicte ecclesie de Eton', qui pro tempore fuerit, vicario, qui in dicta ecclesia personaliter, ut premittitur, residebit, solvat singulis annis quatuor marcas sterlingorum bone et usualis monete in pecunia numerata in festo beati Martini in yeme et Pentecosten per portiones equales. Habeat vero prebendarius memoratus totum mansum ecclesie cum edificiis constructis ibidem et omnes decimas maiores quocumque nomine censeantur, cum tota terra et prato ad dictam ecclesiam de Eton' spectantibus, cum feno etiam nomine decime seu quovis alio modo ad ipsam ecclesiam pertinente. Et prefatus vicarius dicte ecclesie de Eton' per se et ministros sufficientes in debito et consueto numero ydonee deserviat et honeste qui omnia onera ordinaria subeat et supportet. Onera quippe extraordinaria quecumque et quandocumque contigerint subeunda tam ad prebendarium quam ad ipsum vicarium pro rata pertineant portionis. In libris etiam et ornamentis sufficientibus idem prebendarius dicte ecclesie de Eton' provideat competenter. In cuius rei testimonium hoc scriptum bipartitum, cuius una pars penes prebendarium vel ipsius procuratorem et altera penes ipsum vicarium resideat, sigilli nostri munimine duximus roborand'. Datum apud Wylton' v kalendas Julii anno gratie millesimo ducentesimo nonagesimo et pontificatus nostri quinto.

¹ MS conve^s

Margin   Heading and text by Scribe 4. *Johannes Roman[...] archiepiscopus 1290* (16th–17th c.)

Note   Copy in *Reg. Romeyn*, i, 293. Bishop Wilton, East Riding, Yorks., held by the archbishop at Domesday, established as a prebend by Archbishop Gray and usually held by the treasurer (*York Fasti*, i, 86).

60   *Letters of the official of the court of York about a dispute between Mr Gerard de Ceyzériat, former canon and prebendary of Eaton, and Thomas of Burton, then rector of Ordsall, continued before the court by Mr John of Barnby, now prebendary of Eaton, and Laurence de Hercy, now rector of Ordsall, reciting the reasons for the original dispute, which arose from competing claims to tithes raised on various lands (of which full details are given), and for the resumption of the case between Barnby and Hercy, now issuing a definitive sentence condemning Hercy to restore to Barnby half the tithes which had been unjustly raised*   1 March 1333

Universis sancte matris ecclesie filiis ad quos presentes littere pervenerint   p. 28b
officialis curie Ebor' salutem in omnium salvatore. Noverit universitas vestra nos in causa decimarum que primo in dicta curia vertebatur inter magistrum Gerardum de Sesiriaco dudum canonicum ecclesie collegiate Suwellen' et prebendarium prebende de Eton' in eadem actorem ex parte una et dominum Thomam de Burton' tunc rectorem ecclesie de Ordesale reum ex altera et postmodum¹ coram nobis inter magistrum Johannem de Barneby nunc prebendarium dicte prebende dictam causam resumentem ex parte una et dominum Laurentium de Hercy nunc rectorem dicte ecclesie de Ordesale eandem causam defendentem ex altera legitime procedentes sententiam diffinitivam tulisse sub hac forma. In Dei nomine amen. Cum dudum magister Gerardus de Se\si/riaco canonicus in ecclesia collegiate Suwell' Ebor' diocesis ac prebendarius prebende de Eton' in eadem dominum Thomam de Burton' tunc rectorem ecclesie de Ordesale dicte diocesis occasione spoliationis medietatis decimarum garbarum et feni provenientium de terris cultis et pratis videlicet de una platea que vocatur Kildecroft sita inter terram Stephani preposito ex una parte et unam hayam iuxta viam regiam ex altera et de decem selionibus iacentibus a tribus selionibus del hegge in loco qui vocatur Brecland' de una acra iacente in le Longerodes versus Retford sita inter terram Johannis Pratt ex una parte et terram quondam Stephani prepositi ex altera et de viginti una acris in le Succihlay de quibus octo site sunt inter terram Johannis Pratt ex una parte et Stephani prepositi ex altera et alie octo acre inter

terram dicti Johannis Pratt ex una parte et terram Stephani prepositi ex altera et de octodecim acris in le Southelay de quibus octo acre site sunt iuxta locum qui vocatur Wellecroft et alie octo acre et[2] ... et de duabus acris buttantibus ad domum carpentarii sitis inter terram Johannis de Ripariis ex parte una et terram dicti Stephani prepositi ex parte altera et una acra buttante super Kildecroft sita inter terram Johannis Pratt ex una parte et terram Stephani prepositi ex altera et de tribus acris tendentibus se ultra viam que ducit a la Redecancy sitis inter terram Johannis Pratt ex parte una et terram Stephani prepositi ex altera et de tota terra que iacet in le Northcroft et le Halletoft cum prato adiacente sita inter terram Johannis Pratt ex parte una et quendam locum qui vocatur Gildeslane ex parte altera et de octo acris in le Mydelclay de quibus sex buttant super unum locum qui vocatur Aldemore et alie due acre site sunt in loco qui vocatur Conlewong et de toto prato iacente in tofto Johannis de Ripariis in loco qui vocatur Sewyng' et de una acra prati iacente in Dalcroft buttante super aqua que vocatur Idel et de duabus acris prati in le Mikelmore sitis inter pratum Johannis Pratt ex parte una et pratum Stephani prepositi ex altera et de duabus acris prati in Northmore sitis inter pratum Johannis Pratt ex parte una et pratum Stephani prepositi ex altera et de tribus acris prati in Aldemore sitis inter pratum Johannis Pratt ex parte una et pratum Stephani prepositi ex altera et de duabus acris prati in le Southcroft sitis inter pratum Johannis Pratt ex parte una et pratum ecclesie de Ordesale ex altera et de una acra et dimidia prati iacente in loco qui dicitur le Redyng siti inter pratum Johannis Pratt ex parte una et pratum Stephani prepositi ex altera infra parochiam ecclesie de Eton et loca decimationum eiusdem existentibus ut dicebatur coram officiale curie Ebor' traxisset in causam partibus ipsis per procuratores suos in iudicio comparentibus oblato libello liteque legitime contestata ad eundem libellum per procuratorem dicti domini Thome partis ree sub hac forma: duo narrata prout narrantur vera non esse et ideo petria prout petuntur fieri non debere proposito quia[3] pro partem ream quodam facto contrario et sub certa forma admisso iuramento a partibus ipsis huic et inde prestito de calumpnia et de veritate dicenda iuxta ipsius cause qualitatem et naturam traditis positionibus et securis responsionibus ad easdem productis ac scilicet iuratis examinatis et eorum dictis publicatis datis terminis ad dicendum attestes [et][4] eorum dicta \et/ proponendum omnia in facto consistentia propositisque quibusdam exceptionibus contra testes ex parte dicti prebendarii productos et eorum dicta et sub certa forma admissis et testibusque productis super eisdem et eorum dictis publicatis ac postmodum[1] magistro Johanni de Barneby prebendario dicte prebende huiusmodi causam litem et processum resumente necnon domino Laurentio de Hercy rectore ecclesie de Ordesale antedicte defensionem ipsius litis et negotii ad hoc legitime vocato in se assumente ipsisque in statu in quo huiusmodi lis et causa fuit tunc admissis in forma iuris et agentibus causam antedictam iurisque ordine qui in hoc casu requiritur in omnibus observato. Nos officialis curie Ebor' antedicte ad sententiam diffinitivam in causa antedicta invocata spiritus sancti gratia procedimus in hunc modum auditis et intellectis[5] meritis huiusmodi[6] cause, quia invenimus partem prebendarii predicti in medietate decimarum in terris et pratis in articulis

suis deductis et contentis provenientium sufficienter fundasse medietatem
huiusmodi⁷ decimarum ad prebendam predictam et magistrum Johannem
prebendarium ipsius nomine pertinere et pertinere debere sententialiter et
diffinitive pronuntiamus et declaramus ipsumque dominum Laurentium
ad restitutionem medietatis huiusmodi decimarum iniuste subiectarum
cum omni sua causa condempnamus ipsumque magistrum Johannem ad
statum in quo fuit prebendarius dicte prebende tempore spoliationis facte
dicte prebende nomine restituimus predictumque dominum Laurentium
quo ad alia in dicto libello comprehensa ab impetitione ipsius prebendarii
penitus absolventes eundem dominum Laurentium in expensis in prefata
causa per prefatum magistrum Johannem factis quarum taxationem nobis
reservamus condempnantes. In quorum omnium testimonium sigillum
officii nostri presentibus est appensum. Datum et actum in kalend' Marcii
anno domini millesimo⁸ cccᵐᵒ tricesimo secundo.

¹ MS *posmodum* ² Rest of line illegible because of fold and wear to surface of parchment ³ Or *quod?* ⁴ MS difficult to read at this point ⁵ MS *intelectis* ⁶ Fold in MS at this point ⁷ Reading uncertain ⁸ MS *milesimo*

Note Original pasted in; Anglicana hand contemporary with date 1333. Mr Gerard de Ceyzériat, the first prebendary of Eaton, 1290–after 1320, dead by 30 June 1330. Mr John of Barnby, rector of Barnby on Don, was a notary and clerk of Archbishop Melton (*Reg. Melton*, iv, no. 202; v, no. 515). This document provides the first evidence for his succession as prebendary of Eaton. Laurence de Hercy became rector of Ordsall in 1322, finally resigning in 1364 (Train, *Clergy of North Notts.*, 147).

SUTTON CHANTRY AT ST PETER'S ALTAR, 61–72

Cantaria de Northmuscham in ecclesia Suthwell' p. 29
fundata pro anima Ricardi de Sutton'

61 *Letters patent by Edward I to Oliver [Sutton], bishop of Lincoln, of a licence in mortmain of one messuage, twelve acres of meadow, five marks and 10d rent per annum, and a moiety of one bovate in North Muskham and Holme to assign to a chaplain celebrating at Southwell*
Acton Burnell, 1 October 1283

Carta Edwardi regis Anglie de terris et redditibus pertinentibus ad prebendam de Northmuscham ad sustentacionem unius capellani divina celebranti in ecclesia beate Marie Suthwell'

Edwardus rex Anglie, dominus Hibernie et dux Aquitanie, omnibus ad quos presentes litere pervenerint, salutem. Licet de communi consilio regni providerimus quod non liceat viris religiosis seu aliis ingredi feodum alicuius ita quod non ad mortuam manum deveniat sine licencia nostra et capitalis domini de quo res illa in medietate tenetur. Volentes tamen venerabili patri Olivero Lincoln' episcopo graciam facere specialem dedimus ei licenciam quantum in nobis est quod unum mesuagium et duodecim acras prati et quinque marcas et decem denaratas redditus et medietatem unius bovate terre sue cum pertinenciis in Northmuscham et Holme iuxta Northmuscham dare possit et assignare viris religiosis vel cuidam capellano divina celebranti apud Suthwell'. Tenendum et habendum eisdem viris religiosis vel ipsi capellano et successoribus suis in perpetuum et eisdem religiosis seu huiusmodi capellano¹ quod predicta mesuagium, terram, pratum et redditum ab eodem episcopo possint recipere tenore presencium, scilicet licenciam concedimus specialem. Volentes quod idem episcopus aut predicti religiosi seu capellanus racione statuti predicti per nos vel heredes nostros inde occasionateur in aliquo vel graventur, salvis tamen capitalibus dominis feodi illius serviciis inde debitis et consuetis. In cuius rei testimonium has literas nostras fieri fecimus patentes. Teste me ipso apud Acton' Burnel, primo die Octobris anno regni nostri undecimo.

¹ The scribe alternates between *capelanus* (and endings) and *capellanus* (and endings) in this document; spellings have been rationalised as elsewhere

Margin   Section heading centred and in bold, *in ecclesia … Sutton'* added later by Scribe 4. Rubricated title in same hand as text (Scribe 1) beginning in left margin but concluding in right margin; *Oliver Sutton 1282* added just below in later (?16th-c.) hand.

Note   Eighteenth-century notes and extracts on this section concerning Richard of Sutton's chantry in NA, DDM 53/1. Oliver of Sutton (b. *c.* 1219), bishop of Lincoln, 1280–99, was in all probability the son of Roland of Sutton on Trent, and Elizabeth his wife (sometimes called Helysoud or Alice) of Laxton, sister to Robert of Laxton/Lexington, canon of Southwell, and his other brothers, Henry, Stephen and John, hence his concern to found a chantry locally for his nephew, Richard of Sutton, at Southwell. This foundation, unknown to Rosalind Hill, who has otherwise provided the fullest modern account of Oliver's career, confirms a number of her suppositions about his family relationships but necessitates some corrections (*Reg. Sutton*, iii, xiiiff; *ODNB online*: Rosalind Hill, 'Sutton [Lexinton], Oliver (*c.* 1219–99), bishop of Lincoln': http://www. oxforddnb.com/view/article/26801?docPos=32, accessed 14 December 2016).

62   *Grant in hereditary fee by Philip of Ponton to Arnold of Caunton, sometime executor of the late Sir Richard of Sutton, of 5 marks 5s 10d rent per annum in Holme for 1d rent per annum for which Arnold gave him £100*   [1270 × 1274]

Carta feoffamenti Arnaldi de Calneton' per quam infeodavit eum Philippus de Pawnton' de terra de Northmuscham et de Holme

Sciant presentes et futuri quod ego Philippus de Pawnton' dedi et concessi et hac presenti carta mea confirmavi Arnaldo de Calneton', quondam executori bone memorie domini Ricardi de Sutton' quinque marcas, quinque solidos et decem denarios sterlingorum annui redditus percipiendum in villa de Holme in locis sudistinctis, videlicet viginti et octo solidos et quatuor denarios de una bovata terre cum crofto quam Galfridus de Holme, capellanus, quondam libere per cartam de me tenuit una cum homagio et servicio eiusdem Galfridi et heredum suorum seu assignatorum suorum. Et quatuordecim [solidos] annui redditus de dimidia bovata terre cum crofto et tofto quam Gilbertus filius Radulfi filii Gamilli quondam libere per cartam de me tenuit cum homagio et servicio eiusdem Gilberti et heredum suorum seu assignatorum. Et tresdecim solidos annui redditus de dimidia bovata terre cum tofto et crofto quam Hugo de Winbetorp' quondam libere per cartam de me tenuit cum homagio et servicio eiusdem Hugonis et heredum suorum seu assignatorum. Et duos solidos annui redditus de terra quam Willelmus Le Sergant' quondam libere de me tenuit cum homagio et servicio suo et heredum suorum seu assignatorum. Et quatuordecim denarios annui redditus de terra quam Hugo le Sergant de me tenuit per cartam et homagio et servicio suo et heredum suorum seu assignatorum. Dedi[1] eciam eidem Arnaldo unam dimidiam bovatam terre et prati cum tofto et crofto quam Robertus Bene, nativus meus, quondam pro quatuordecim[2] solidis annui redditus de me tenuit in eadem villa et eundem Robertum Bene cum tota sequela et omnibus catallis suis ante confeccionem huius carte procreatis et post procreandis.[3] Et duodecim acras prati in pratis de Holme iacentes in locis subscriptis, quorum tres acre prati iacent in le Wroughegenge inter pratum Willelmi le Sergant' ex una parte et pratum Thome de Batheley ex altera parte. Et una acra et dimidia iacet in prato que vocatur Estmilne inter pratum Willelmi le Sergant et pratum fratris de Goswong'. Et una acra prati iacet super Crosiswad inter pratum Willelmi le Sergant' et pratum Arnaldi de Calenton'. Et una acra et dimidia iacet super Steniland dendis inter pratum Ade de Sutton' et prati mei ex altera. Et tres \acre/ et dimidia in australi parte de Wethow inter pratum quod fuit Willelmi Lestant'. Et dimidia acra prati iacet in australi parte iuxta pratum Ade de Sutton', cum omnibus libertatibus, aysiamentis, wardis, reliviis et eschaetis et serviciis aliis que aliquo modo de predictis tenementis racione dicti annui redditus accidere poterunt vel de iure pertinere debent et cum omnibus aliis pertinenciis ut in pratis, pascuis et pasturis et aliis communiis ad predictam terram cum prato infra villam et extra pertinentibus. Tenendum et habendum eidem Arnaldo et heredibus suis vel assignatis quibuscunque et quandocunque et ubicunque dare, vendere seu assignare voluerit libere, quiete, pacifice et integre, in feodo et hereditate de me et heredibus meis | in perpetuum p. 30 pro centum libris sterlingorum quas idem Arnaldus dedit mihi graciam suam pre manibus. Reddendo inde annuatim mihi et heredibus meis unum denarium argenti ad natale domini apud Holme pro omnibus serviciis forinsecis, sectis curie communis, wapentagiis et pro wardis, reliviis, homagiis, maritagiis, exchaetis et pro omnibus serviciis aliis et demandis que aliquo modo mihi et heredibus meis aliquo tempore de predictis terris cum prato et tenementis racione predicti annui redditus accidere poterunt. Ego vero Philippus et heredes mei totum predictum annuum redditum cum predictis terra et prato cum homagiis, wardis, releviis, exchaetis, aliis et cum omnibus aliis pertinenciis, de predictis terris cum prato et redditibus provenientibus pro predicto servicio sicut predictum est, predicto Arnaldo et heredibus suis vel suis assignatis quibuscunque contra omnes homines warantizabimus et defendemus. In cuius rei testimonium huic presento scripto sigillum meum apposui. Hiis testibus: domino Nicholao de Eyvil, Roberto de Sutton', Johanne Burdon', Waltero Gow'. Thoma de Muscham, Petro de Venella et aliis.

---

[1] *Dei*   [2] *quardecim*   [3] MS *procreendas* corrected in original hand to *proceandas*

Date After the death of Richard of Sutton and before **67**. Sir Nicholas d'Eyville of Caunton died *c.* 1270.

Note The Pawntons/Pontons, from Great Ponton, Lincs., held half a knight's fee in North Muskham of the abbot of Peterborough. Philip, succeeded his father Baldwin, in 1252 and became a knight, *c.* 1256–7 (TNA, Chancery Misc., C 47/1/1/ m. 8; *Thurgarton*, 580). He was sheriff of Nottinghamshire and Derbyshire in 1292–3 (Thoroton, iii, 153–4). Richard of Sutton was son of Robert of Sutton and his wife, Alice (**58**), whose position in the genealogy of the Sutton family is uncertain. Thoroton, iii, 110 makes Richard the son of a Robert who died in 1286 (as does Holdsworth, *Rufford*, i, cxi following him), but since he had been a canon of Southwell since at least 1241 (*Reg. Greenfield*, p. 84), the likelihood is that he was born before 1220, around the time of the birth of the man who died in 1286, who was a younger brother of William of Sutton known to have been born *c.* 1218. For the execution of his will see LA, Cragg MS 3/25. Nicholas II d'Eyville, lord of Caunton (De Ville, 'John Deyville', 28 and 38), who also witnesses **63** and **64**. *Walter Gow* is probably a misreading for Sir Walter *Towk/Touk* of Kelham, who succeeded Walter his father *c.* 1270, and witnessed other charters connected with this chantry (**63**, **65** and **70**). For Thomas IV of Muskham see *Dale*, 229–30. Peter de Venella occurs with his father, William, in **62**, **63** (*Rufford*, 333, 441), where he is sometimes styled 'Peter de Venell of Muskham' (**424**, **448**, **449**). He was probably the same as Peter in le Lane (**133**, **134**) and occurs as 'Petro in Venella' in an accord between the abbot of Peterborough and the prior of Thurgarton and their houses 'in crastino sancti Vincencii anno domini m° cc° lxx° nono' (Raban, *White Book of Peterborough*, no. 57, dated 22 January 1280, and *Thurgarton*, 317, with the date 23 January 1279, but for which the correct date is 23 January 1280 since 22 January is the feast of St Vincent and Easter style is being followed). He also occurs in several undated charters relating to Newark, where other witnesses include Richard of Sutton, canon of Southwell and Thomas of Muskham; (see NA, Newark Corporation/Borough Muniments, T1 (A1); T11 (A11); T17 (A-15–3); T21).

63 *Grant by Arnold of Caunton, executor of the will of Sir Richard of Sutton, canon of Lincoln, to Mr Oliver of Sutton of all rents and lands which he had bought from Sir Philip of Ponton, knight, in Holme for a chantry in memory of Richard of Sutton* [*c.* 1268 × 1274]

Carta Oliveri de Sutton' per quam feofetavit eum Arnaldus de terra in Northmuscham et Holme

Sciant presentes et futuri quod ego Ernaldus de Callenton', executor testamenti bone memorie quondam domini Ricardi de Sutton', canonici Linc' ecclesie, dedi, concessi et hac presenti carta mea confirmavi magistro Olivero de Sutton', predicti testamenti meo executori, totum illum redditum cum toftis, croftis, pratis et aliis pertinenciis suis quem nuper de bonis dicti defuncti de domino Philippo de Paunton', milite, emi in villa et territorio de Holm' in locis subdistinctis ad perpetuam cantariam pro anima memorati testatoris sustendandam, videlicet, viginti et octo solidos et quatuor denarios annui redditus de dimidia bovata terre cum tofto et crofto quam *Galfridus*[1] [...]²*us quondam libere de me tenuit una cum homagio et servicio eiusdem Galfridi et heredum suorum et assignatorum, et quatuordecim solidos annui redditus de dimidia bovata terre cum tofto et crofto quas* Gilbertus filius Radulfi filii Gamil quondam libere de me tenuit cum homagio et servicio eiusdem Gilberti et heredum suorum et assignatorum suorum, *et tresdecim solidos annui redditus de dimidia bovata terre cum tofto et crofto quam Hugo de Wymbethorp' quondam*

libere de me tenuit cum homagio et servicio eiusdem Hugonis et heredum
suorum et assignatorum, et duos solidos annui redditus de terra quam
Willelmus le Seriaunt libere de me tenuit cum homagio et servicio eiusdem
Willelmi et heredum suorum et assignatorum, et quatuordecim denarios
annui redditus de terra quam Hugo le Seriaunt libere de me tenuit cum
homagio et servicio suo[3] et heredum suorum et assignatorum. Dedi eciam
et concessi eidem magistro Olivero unam dimidiam bovatam terre et prati
cum tofto et crofto quam Robertus Bene, nativus pro quatuordecim solidis
annuis de me tenuit in eadem villa et eundem Robertum Bene cum tota
sequela sua et omnibus catallis qualitercumque et quocumque[4] tempore
de ipso et per ipsum provenientibus. Pratum autem superius nominatum
scilicet, duodecim acre in pratis de Holme iacent in locis subscriptis,
videlicet tres acre in le Wrongeng' inter pratum Willelmi le Seriaunt ex
una parte et pratum Thome de Batheley ex altera, et una acra et dimidia
iacet in prato que vocatur Estmilne inter pratum Willelmi le Seriaunt ex
una parte et pratum Ade de Sutton' ex altera parte[5] et una acra super le
Milne Holme buttans super le Horsgres inter pratum Galfridi Grobbe
ex una parte et pratum fratris de Goswong' et altera, et una acra super
le Crotiswad inter pratum Willelmi le Seriaunt ex una parte et[6] pratum
meum ex altera, et una acra et dimidia in Stanilandendes inter pratum
Ade de Sutton' *ex una parte et pratum domini Philippi de Paunton' ex*
altera, et tres acras et dimidia ex australi parte de Wethou inter pratum
quod fuit Willelmi Lefthand ex una parte et pratum domini Philippi de
Paunton' ex altera, et dimidia acra in prato australi iuxta pratum Ade
de Sutton' cum omnibus libertatibus, aysiamentis, wardis, releviis,
maritagiis, homagiis, eskaetis et serviciis aliis que aliquo modo de
predictis tenementis racione dicti annui redditus accidere poterunt vel de
iure pertinere debent cum omnibus aliis pertinenciis ut in pratis, pascuis,[7]
pasturis et aliis comuniis ad predictam terram cum prato infra villam et
extra pertinentibus. Tenendum et habendum eidem magistro Olivero ad
dictam sustenacionem ex inde faciendam et heredibus suis vel assignatis
quibuscunque et quandocunque et ubicunque dare, vendere vel assignare
voluerit libere, quiete, integre, bene et in pace absque aliquo servicio
seculari exaccione forinseca consuetudine et demanda[8] sectis curiarum
comitatus et wapentachi, wardiis, releviis, homagiis, maritagiis, eskaetis
et omnibus aliis serviciis que aliquo modo exigi[9] possunt in perpetuum
de premissis sub warantizacione, adquietacione et defensione domini
Philippi predicti michi in hac parte factis prout in carta sua expressius
continetur. In cuius rei testimonium sigillum meum huic scripto apposui
et cartam domini Philippi predictam | prefato magistro Olivero assignato　p. 31
meo tradidi et coexecutori.[10] Hiis testibus: dominis Nicholao de Evill',
Roberto de Sutton', Johanne Burdun', Waltero Tuk', militibus, Thoma
de Muschaump, Petro de Venella, Willelmo de Batheley, Roberto de
Muschaump, clerico.

[1] Passages in italics omitted in WB　[2] Two words obscured by former damp patch　[3] *suo*
added in WB　[4] WB omits *et quocumque*　[5] *parte* added in WB　[6] *et* repeated in
WB　[7] WB adds *et*　[8] WB adds *et*　[9] WB *eigi*　[10] WB *executori*

Date　Probably at the same time as **62**.

Note LA, Cragg MS 3/34 (formerly 3/25) for the original, on ruled parchment, formerly sealed on double tag through turn-up, with some damp stains obscuring a few words, used as base text here since the clerk of WB omits three passages through homeoteleuton. William of Bathley witnessed c. 1252–75 (*Rufford*, 257, 334), and may be William, son of Geoffrey of Bathley, who witnessed a grant of William, son of William son of Henry of Muskham, of half a toft to his brother, Thomas, before 1268 (NA, Newark Corporation/Borough Muniments, T1(A1)). For Peter de Venella, see **62n.** Robert of Muskham, clerk, may have been the son of Richard, younger brother of Thomas III of Muskham.

64 *Grant in free alms by Oliver [Sutton], bishop of Lincoln, to Mr Henry of Newark, archdeacon of Richmond, and prebendary of North Muskham of lands and tenements in North Muskham of Philip of Ponton which he has of the feoffment of Arnold of Caunton for 1d rent per annum*

[1287 × 1288]

Carta Oliveri episcopi Lincoln' de terra de Muscham et de Holme

Sciant presentes et futuri quod nos Oliverus, permissione divina Lincoln' episcopus, dedimus, concessimus et hac presenti carta nostra confirmavimus magistro Henrico de Newerk, archidiacono Richemund' et prebendario de Northmuscham in ecclesia Suthwell omnes terras et tenementa cum homagiis et serviciis liberorum hominum, catallis et sequelis villanorum in Northmuscham de predicto Philippo et heredibus suis una cum wardis, reliv[i]is, maritagiis que habuimus de feofamento[1] Ernaldi de Calneton' de quibus dominus Philippus de Paunton' feofavit predictum Ernaldum. Habendum \et/ tenendum eidem Henrico et successoribus suis prebendariis de Northmuscham de predicto Philippo et heredibus suis una cum wardis, reliviis, maritagiis, excaetis et omnibus libertatibus suis in liberam et perpetuam elimosinam. Reddendo inde annuatim predicto Philippo et heredibus suis unum denarium apud Holme in festo natalis domini pro omni servicio seculari exaccione demanda. Ita quod nec nobis vel heredibus nostra nichil inde remaneat in perpetuum. In cuius rei testimonium huic carte sigillum meum duximus apponendum. Hiis testibus: domino Waltero de Ludham', Johanne Burdun, Jacobo de Sutton', militibus, et aliis.

[1] MS *feoafamento*

Date Henry of Newark was collated to the prebend of North Muskham on 2 June 1287 (*Reg. Romeyn*, i, no. 1042) and acknowledged this grant in November 1288 (**72**).

Note This charter was inspected and confirmed by the king on 17 August 1290: *CPR 1281–92*, 383. It is interesting to note that the clerk who drafted the bishop's charter uses the phrase *sigillum meum* when the rest of the charter is written in the first person plural, an unusual mistake for this period.

65 *Confirmation by Philip of Ponton of 64 which Oliver of Sutton, bishop of Lincoln, made to Mr Henry of Newark, archdeacon of Richmond and prebendary of North Muskham, for 1d rent per annum*

[1287 × 1288]

Confirmacio Philippi de Paunton' illius carte quam fecit Oliverus de Sutton' magistro Henrico de Newerk de terra in Northmuscham et Holme

Omnibus Christi fidelibus ad quos carta presens pervenerit Philippus de Paunton', miles, salutem in domino. Sciatis me inspexisse cartam quam venerabilis pater dominus Oliverus Lincoln' episcopus fecit magistro Henrico de Newerk, archidiacono Rechemund' et prebendario de Northmuscham in ecclesia Suthwell' in hec verba: Sciant presentes … [*as 64, with no significant variants*] Ego vero predictus Philippus predictas donacionem, concessionem et carte confirmacionem et omnes et gratos eos pro me et heredibus meis prefato Henrico et successoribus suis prebendariis de Northmuscham tenore presencium testifico, ratifico et confirmo. Reddendo inde mihi et heredibus meis predictum annuum redditum unius denarii tantum ad terminum supradictum pro sectis curiarum comitatus, wapentakyorum et pro omnibus aliis serviciis secularibus et consuetudinibus tam forinsecis serviciis quam aliis quibuscunque et pro wardis et reliviis, homagiis et maritagiis, excaetis et omnibus aliis serviciis et demandis quas pro me vel heredes meos vel alios quoscunque de predictis terris et tenementis exigi vel vendicari poterunt in aliquo tempore in perpetuum. Et \ego/ predictus Philippus et heredes mei omnes terras et tenementa predicta cum homagiis, reliviis, excaetis et cum omnibus aliis pertinenciis suis de predicto servicio unius denarius redditus sicut predictum est predicto Henrico et successoribus suis prebendariis de Northmuscham contra omnes homines tam Christianos | quam Judeos warantizabimus, acquietabimus et p. 32 defendemus inperpetuum. In cuius rei testimonium presenti carte sigillum meum apposui. Hiis testibus: dominis Waltero de Ludham, Ricardo de Bekingham, Johanne Burdun, Waltero Tuk, Jacobo de Sutton', militibus, et aliis.

Date　Shortly after **64**.

Note　Sir James of Sutton succeeded his father, Robert, in 1286 and died in 1304 (Thoroton, iii, 110). He and Sir Walter Tuke were accused in 1295, along with Sir Richard of Bingham, by Beatrice, widow of Richard, son of Walter of Kelham, of instigating an ambush by John Cutte and thirteen others on her husband, which led to his death at Staythorpe, probably the result of a local feud. Although the case proceeded for several years no verdict was reached against the alleged instigators though some of the assailants were eventually outlawed (Crook, 'The Anatomy of a Knightly Homicide').

66　*Confirmation by Edward I of 64 for Oliver of Sutton, bishop of Lincoln*　　　　　　　　　　　　　Northampton, 17 August 1290

Carta Edwardi regis Anglie que confirmat cartam Oliveri episcopi Lincoln' de terra Northmuscham et Holme

Edwardus Dei gracia rex Anglie, dominus Hibernie et dux Aquitanie, omnibus ad quos presentes litere pervenerint, salutem. Inspeximus cartam quam venerabilis pater Oliverus, Lincoln' episcopus, fecit dilecto et fideli nostro magistro Henrico de Newerk, archidiacono de Richemund et prebendario de Northmuscham in ecclesia Suthwell' in hec verba: Sciant presentes [*as 64 with no significant variants*] Nos autem donacionem, concessionem et confirmacionem predictas ratas habentes et gratas eas pro nobis et heredibus quantum in nobis est concedimus et confirmavimus sicut carta predicta racionabiliter testatur. In cuius rei testimonium has literas nostras fieri fecimus patentes. Teste me ipso apud Norhamton' decimo septimo die Augusti anno regni nostri decimo octavo.

67 *Letters of attorney of Mr Oliver of Sutton, canon of Lincoln, executor of the will of Sir Richard of Sutton, canon of Lincoln, to William of Stockton, clerk, to accept delivery of lands and other rights which his own executor, Arnold of Caunton, had received by enfeoffment of Philip of Ponton* Lincoln, 21 October 1274

Omnibus ad quos presens scriptum pervenerit magister Oliverus de Sutton', canonicus Lincoln', executor testamenti bone memorie domini Ricardi de Sutton, eiusdem ecclesie canonici, salutem in domino sempiternam. Ad agnoscendum et recipiendum pro me et nomine meo assignacionem et corporalis possessionis, seysinam, redditum et terrarum cum toftis et croftis et pratis et aliis pertinenciis suis unde Ernaldus de Calneton', executor meus, per dominum Philippum de Paunton' feofatus existit pro ut in carta eiusdem Philippi plenius continetur mihi et heredibus meis et assignatis facienda Willelmum de Stoketon', clericum latorem presencium attornatum meum facio, constituo volens et concedens quod idem Willelmus tam fidelitatem de libere tenentibus in hac parte recipiendo quam de aliis rebus disponendo et alium loco sui de seysina continuanda sibi substituendo faciat et ordinet quo ego si presencia essem facere possem. Ratum habiturus quicquid per ipsum vel per ipsum substitutum factum fuerit in premissis. Et quia sigillum meum non est bene notum sigillum capituli Lincoln' presentibus apponi procuram. Datum Lincoln' xi kalendas Octobris anno domini m° cc° lxx° quarto.

Note Oliver of Sutton had probably been a canon of Lincoln since at least 1259. After spending most of the 1260s in Oxford, he returned to Lincoln where he became prebendary of Milton Manor, and was elected dean in 1275 (*ODNB online*).

68 *Letters of attorney by Oliver of Sutton, bishop of Lincoln, to Hugh of Normanton and Philip of Swayfield, clerks, to deliver seisin to Henry of Newark of lands and rights in North Muskham and Holme which Oliver had granted to him* [1287 × 1288]

Litera Oliveri de Sutton per quam tradidit seysinam magistro Henrico de Newerk de terra de Northmuscham et Holme

Oliverus permissione divina Lincoln' episcopus in Christo filiis Hugoni de Normanton' et Philippo de Swafeld, clericis, salutem, graciam et benedictionem. Ad inducendum nomine nostro magistrum Henricum de Newerk, archidiaconum de Richemund et prebendarium de Northmuscam in ecclesia Suthwell' in plenam seysinam et possessionem omnium

terrarum et tenementorum cum pertinenciis | in Northmuscham et   p. 33
Holme iuxta Northmuscham que habuimus ex feofamento Ernaldi de
Calneton'. Habendum et tenendum eidem Henrico et successoribus suis
prebendariis de Northmuscham secundum formam carte feofamenti
nostri et confirmacionis domini Philippi de Paunton' inde prefato Henrico
factarum vobis coniunctim et divisim committimus vices nostros. In cuius
rei testimonium has literas nostras patentes signari fecimus signo nostro.

Date   After **65**.

Note   Hugh of Normanton, successively prebendary of Thorngate (1295), Crackpole St
Mary (1295) and Norton (1305) (*Fasti 1066–1300*, iii, 63, 104). Philip de Swafeld probably
takes his name from Swayfield, Lincs., rather than Swafield, Norfolk (cf. ibid., 40 n. 2).

69   *Letters of attorney by Arnold of Caunton to Robert, his son, to deliver
seisin of rent of 5 marks 5s 8d per annum and twelve acres of meadow
in Holme that he bought from the executors of Richard of Sutton*
                                                    22 September 1274

**Litera Ernaldi de Calneton' de tradendo seysina magistro Olivero
de Sutton in Northmuscham et Holme**

Per presens scriptum pateat universis quod ego Ernaldus de Calneton' facio
et constituo Robertum, filium meum et heredem, procuratorum meum et
attornatum ad adsignandum et tradendum corporalem possessionem et
seysinam cuiusdam annualis redditus quinque marcis v. solidis et octo
denariis cum toftis et croftis et aliis pertinenciis suis in villa et territoria
de Holme ac duodecim acras prati ibidem una cum seysina Roberti
Bene, nativi, et terre et prati quas tenet quo omnia nuper emi de bonis
testamentoriis domini Ricardi de Sutton ad quandam cantariam pro
anima ipsius faciendam in perpetuum Willelmo de Stoketon', clerico
attornato magistri Oliveri de Sutton' executoris dicti testamenti mandans
et firmiter iugens[1] dictis libere tenentibus ut plenius de cetero eidem
Willelmo obediant in omnibus nomine domini sui respondeant et intendant
ratum habens quicquid idem Robertus fecerit in premissis. In cuius rei
testimonium presentibus sigillum meum apposui, x kalendas Octobris
anno domini mᵒ ccᵒ lxxᵒ iiii.

[1] MS is either *ingens* or *iugens* for *iniugens*

70   *Release and quitclaim by Robert, son and heir of Arnold of Caunton,
to Mr Henry of Newark of one messuage, a moiety of one bovate of land
and services in Holme that Oliver [of Sutton], bishop of Lincoln granted
to him*   [after 2 June 1287 × November 1288]

**Quieta clamacio Roberti de Calneton' de terra et redditu de Holme
liberanda magistro Henrico de Newerk vel capitulo Suthwell**

Noverint universi quod ego Robertus, filius et heres Ernaldi de Calneton',
pro me et heredibus meis remisi et omnino quietum clamavi magistro
Henrico de Newerk, prebendario de Northmuscham in ecclesia Suthwell',

totum ius et clameum quod unquam habui vel habere potui in uno mesuagio, medietate unius bovate terre, pratis, redditibus, serviciis liberorum hominum una cum serviciis, bonis, catallis et sequelis bondorum ac homagiis liberorum et omnibus aliis terris et tenementis cum pertinenciis de quibus venerabilis pater dominus Oliverus, Lincolniensis episcopus, feofavit predictum Henricum, habendum sibi et successoribus suis prebendariis ibidem in perpetuum pro ut in carta feofamenti predicti Oliveri eidem Henrico confecta plenius continetur. Ita quod nec ego predictus Robertus nec heredes mei aliquod ius vel clamium in predictis mesuagio, terra, redditibus, homagiis, serviciis, bonis, catallis aut sequelis possimus in perpetuum vendicare. In cuius rei testimonium huic scripto sigillum meum apposui. Hiis testibus: dominis Johanne Burdun, Waltero Tuk, Jacobo de Sutton', militibus, et aliis.

71 *Grant by Philip, son of Baldwin of Ponton to Hugh, son of Robert of Winthorpe, called knight, of one croft and a half a bovate of land in Holme for 13s 4d rent per annum* [*c.* 1270]

Carta Philippi de Pantona de terra et redditu de Holme et tradidit eam Hugoni de Wyntorp

Sciant presentes et futuri quod ego Philippus de Panton, filius Baldewini, dedi, concessi et hac presenti carta mea confirmavi Hugoni de Wintorp, filio Roberti eiusdem, dicti militis, unum croftum integrum cum crofto in villa de Holme et dimidiam bovatam terre arrabilis in territorio de Holme cum prato pertinente ad dictam terram quam Begine quondam tenuit. Tenendum et habendum dicto Hugoni et heredibus suis a corpore suo legitime procreatis ita quod non possunt alienare de me et heredibus meis vel assignatis libere, quiete, bene et \in/ pace et hereditate. Reddendo inde annuatim mihi et heredibus meis vel assignatis tresdecim solidos [iiii denarios] argenti a\d/ quatuor terminos anni. Ad annunciacionem beate Marie iii solidos iiii denarios, ad festum beati Johannis baptiste iii solidos iiii denarios, ad festum beati Michaelis iii solidos iiii denarios, ad festum beati Thome apostoli iii solidos iiii denarios, pro omnibus exaccionibus secularibus, consuetudinibus et demandis et sectis curiarum, salvo forinseco domini regis. Et ego vero Philippus et heredes vel assignati dicto Hugoni et heredibus dictum toftum cum crofto et dimidia bovata terre cum prato et cum omnibus pertinenciis, asyamentis in pascua et pasturis contra omnes homines warantizabimus. Et ad maiorem securitatem hanc cartam sigillo meo roboravi. Hiis testibus: Thoma de Muscham, Willelmo de Batheley, Hugone de Holme, Rogero filio Capelli, Radulfo Palmer et aliis.

Date Philip of Ponton became a knight *c.* 1256–7 (**62n**), but did not always mention his title in his charters.

Note Neither Thoroton nor Moor list any Winthorpes as knights. A succession of Thomases of Muskham and Williams of Bathley from the late twelfth century to the early fourteenth century makes identification problematic, but this Thomas and William are probably the witnesses to a grant in 1254 (*Rufford*, 504), while William witnessed a grant of Thomas, described as Thomas of (North) Muskham, son of Thomas of Muskham, *c.* 1250 (ibid., 524) and was still active 1271–3 (**428**).

72 *Notification by Henry of Newark, archdeacon of Richmond, preb-*
endary of North Muskham, of the endowment of his prebend with rents
to the value of 5 marks 5s 10d for the maintenance of a priest serving the
chantry of Richard of Sutton at Southwell

[North] Muskham, November 1288

Carta cantarie Ricardi de Suthon' in ecclesia de Suthwella

p. 34

Omnibus Christi fidelibus ad quos presentes litere pervenerint Henricus
de Newerk, archidiaconus Richemund',[1] idem prebendarius de
Northmuscham in ecclesia Suthwell', salutem in domino sempiternam.
Cum per venerabilem patrem dominum Oliverum, Dei gratia episcopum
Lincoln', sim ego predicta prebenda de Northmuscham et successores
mei in eadem prebenda infeodati de quinque marcis quinque solidis
decem denariis sterlingorum anni redditus percipiendum in villa de
Holm' in locis subdistinctis, videlicet viginti \et/ octo solidos et quatuor
denarios de una bovata terre cum tofto et crofto quam Galfridus[2] de Holm'
libere per cartam tenuit de Philippo de Pawentone, una cum homagio et
servicio eiusdem Galfridi et heredum suorum seu assignatorum suorum.
Et de quatuordecim solidis anni redditus et de dimidia bovata terre cum
tofto et crofto quam Gilbertus filius Radulfi Gamel quondam libere per
cartam tenuit de eodem Philippo de Pawentone cum homagio et servicio
eiusdem Gilberti et heredum suorum seu assignatorum suorum. Et de
tresdecim solidis anni redditus de dimidia bovata terre cum tofto et
crofto quam Hugo de Wynbethorp quondam libere per cartam tenuit de
eodem Philippo de Pawenton' cum homagio et servicio eiusdem Hugonis
et heredum suorum seu assignatorum suorum. Et duobus solidis anni
redditus de terra quam Willelmus le Seriaunt quondam libere per cartam
tenuit de predicto Philippo cum homagio et servicio eiusdem Willelmi
et heredum seu assignatorum suorum. Et de quatuordecim denariis anni
redditus de terra quam Hugo le Seriant quondam libere tenuit de predicto
Philippo per cartam cum homagio et servicio suo et heredum suorum seu
assignatorum. Et de una dimidia bovata terre et prati cum tofto et crofto
quam Robertus Bene, nativus predicti Philippi quondam pro quatuordecim
solidis annui redditus tenuit in villa de Holm' de eodem Philippo. Et
de eodem Roberto Bene cum tota sequela sua et omnibus catallis suis
procreatis in posterum procreandum. Et de duodecim acris prati in pratis
de Holme iacentibus in locis subscriptis in cartis antedictis cum omnibus
libertatibus aysimentis, wardis et reliviis, eschaetis et serviciis aliis que
aliquo modo de predictis tenementis racione dicti anni redditus accidere
poterunt vel de iure pertinere debent. Et cum omnibus aliis pertinenciis
ut in pratis, pascuis et pasturis et aliis communiis ad predictam terram
cum prato infra villam et extra pertinentibus in perpetuam et liberam
elimosinam ad sustentationem unius sacerdotis in ecclesia Suthwell'
perpetuo celebrantis pro anima felicis recordacionis quondam domini
Ricardi de Sutton' ipsius prebende prebendarii et animabus omnium
fidelium defunctorum accedente ad hoc excelentissimi principis domini
Edwardi, Dei gracia regis Anglie illustris, consensu[3] et licencia speciali
sic que[4] per venerabilem capitulum nostrum Suthwell' ac predictum
patrem nostrum statutum et immobiliter ordinatum ut predictus sacerdos

sic ut premittitur celebrans pro defunctis pro stipendiis suis annuis de me predicta prebenda et successoribus meis sex marcas sterlingorum duntaxat ad quatuor anni terminos pro equalibus porcionibus videlicet, ad festum sancti Thome apostoli viginti solidos, ad festum annunciacionis dominice viginti solidos et in festo nativitatis sancti Johannis baptiste viginti solidos et in festo sancti Michaelis viginti solidos in ecclesia Suthwell' annis singulis percipiat. Ne futuris temporibus solucio predictarum marcarum aliqualiter perire valeat aut differri me prebendam meam predictam successores que meos presencium tenore obligo et concedo ut si aliquo tempore contigerit quod absit solucionem ipsam pro toto aut pro parte per me aut successores meos impediri aut retineri quin suis loco temporibus persolvatur liceat predicto venerabili capitulo predictam prebendam et ipsius fructus quoscunque sequestrare et sub arto sequestro tenere ac eciam si necesse fuerit fructus ipsos omnimodos distrahere et vendere usque ad predictam summam sex marcarum absque contradictione mea aut successores meorum et nichilominus me et successores meos per suspensionis et excommunicationis sentencias ad predictam solutionem suis loco et temporibus faciendam compellere. Si legitime⁵ moniti infra octo dies immediate subsequentes, de pecunia non satisfecerimus antedicta. In cuius rei testimonium sigillum meum presentibus apposui. Datum apud Muscam mense Novembris anno domini m° cc° octogesimo octavo.

¹ MS *Richemud'*   ² *Galfridus* over erasure   ³ MS *concensu*   ⁴ *Sic* but might be *quod*?   ⁵ MS *ligitimi*

Margin   In left margin in late hand *Cantaria Ricardi Sutton* and, below, *6 marcarum annum clameum e prebendario de North Muskham* at the point where Richard of Sutton is mentioned.

Note   NA, SC7/1/5, f. 14ʳ⁻ᵛ for another 15ᵗʰ-c. copy.

BECKINGHAM PREBEND, 73

73   *Presentation by the Chapter, with the agreement of Peter de Dene, prebendary of Beckingham, of Robert of Saundby, priest, to the vicarage of Beckingham, setting out in detail the terms of his appointment, including payment of a pension of 40s per annum from the prebendary, with assignment of the priest's house (next door to that of Hugh de Wyburne) for which a rent of 6d per annum is to be paid, and various tithes, all to be worth ten marks a year, with the vicar promising to be resident*

Southwell, 1 May 1318

p. 35   ### Ordinacio vicarie de Bekyingham

Litera¹ de ordinatione vicarie de Bekingham per capitulum de Suthwelle

Capitulum ecclesie Suthwell' Ebor' dioc' discreto viro domino Roberto de Sandeby presbitero salutem in auctore salutis. Cum ecclesia parochialis de Bekingham dicte dioc' prebende venerabilis viri magistri² Petri de Dene³ canonici nostri quam optinet in ecclesia nostra Suthwell' predicta fuerit ab antiquo et a tempore cuius memoria non existit anexa canonice seu unita.[4] Idem canonicus instetit et instat debita diligentia et perpetuus vicarius instituatur canonice in parochiali ecclesia supradicta. De fructibus itaque provenientibus atque bonis eiusdem ecclesie ad sustentationem perpetui vicarii instituendi in ea portionem sufficientem et congruam assignavit, videlicet oblationes omnimodas in ecclesia annuatim obvenientes, ceragium et decimam de parochinarum[5] servientibus provenientem ad pasca, decimas de parochiariis vitulis, lacte, butiro, caseo, pullanis, porcis, aucis, gallinis, columbis, apibus, molendinis, pomis, piris, oleribus, lino et canape provenientes nec non mortuaria universaque superius assignata valent annis octo marcas et ultra. Preterea ad sustentationem vicarii assignavit idem canonicus quadraginta solidos sterlingorum in festis Pentecostes et sancti Martini in \h/yeme[6] per portiones equales annuatim et per ipsum canonicum et successores suos prefato vicario et suis successoribus erogandis. Insuper ut vicarius commodius,[7] honestius et diligentius valeat ecclesie deservire et animarum curam in parochia exercere[8] mansionem ecclesie ipsi vicinam que domus presbiteri appellatur, que situatur iuxta domos Hugonis de Wyburne, idem canonicus assignavit ipsi vicario et suis successoribus possidendum, reddendo eidem canonico et suis successoribus annuatim in festo omnium sanctorum sex denarios sterlingorum, premissa siquidem universa ad sustentationem perpetue vicarie et successorum suorum cum infrascriptis omnibus assignavit canonicus supradictus, videlicet quod vicarius qui pro tempore fuerit predicte parochiali ecclesie per se et ministros ydoneos deservire animarum curam exercere[9] ministrorum, librorum, ornamentorum et luminarium omnium necnon reparationes cancelli seu thori onera universa subire prout solebat et tenebat canonicus. Ac etiam in ecclesia quam extra eam omnia onera ordinaria et pro portione decem marcarum extraordinaria agnoscere teneatur. Porro fructus, decimas, obventiones, redditus et proventus necnon alia quelibet emolumenta ad ecclesiam supradictam spectantia quocumque nomine nuncupentur[10] que nominatim expresse non sunt superius assignata predictus canonicus sibi et successoribus suis retinet et reservat.[11] Ad vicariam autem huiusmodi te dictum Robertum presbiterum supradictum nobis prefatus canonicus presentavit, petens humiliter et instanter quatinus curaremus premissa prout ad nos pertinet approbare vicariam perpetuam ordinare et te ad eam presentatum admittere vicariumque[12] perpetuum instituere ac ulterius in hac parte facere quod continemur. Nos igitur, habitis super hiis examinatione diligenti et deliberatione, premissa omnia et singula per dictum canonicum assignata et facta acceptamus ac etiam approbamus ut in rebus cum omnibus \ ut/ premuntur assignatis vicariam perpetuam ordinamus te presbiterum supradictum per dominum canonicum canonice presentatum ad huiusmodi vicariam perpetuam ordinamus te presbiterum supradictum in eadem tibi curam animarum parochie committentes[13] ac mandantes in corporalem possessionem[14] vicarie huiusmodi inducendum recepto per nos a te corporali iuramento ad canonica obedientia et residentia[15] personali in predicta parochiali ecclesia iuxta iuris exigentiam facienda. In quorum omnium testimonium ac fidem sigillum nostrum commune presentibus est appensum. Actum et datum in capitulo nostro Suthwell' die apostolorum[16]

Philippi et Jacobi anno domini m° triscentesimo decimo octavo.

¹ MS *Litara*   ² MS adds *viri* and then expunges and crosses out   ³ MS *Bene*   ⁴ MS *unica*   ⁵ *Sic* for ?*parochianorum*   ⁶ MS corr. by same scribe   ⁷ MS *commodus*   ⁸ MS *excersere*   ⁹ MS *excercere*   ¹⁰ MS *nuncepentur*   ¹¹ MS *reservet*   ¹² MS *vicarium que*   ¹³ MS *comittentes*   ¹⁴ MS *posessionem*   ¹⁵ MS *residensia*   ¹⁶ MS *appostolorum*

Margin   Page heading, Scribe 4. Hand with pointing forefinger drawn in margin near *Porro fructus.*

Note   Mr Peter de Dene, prebendary of Beckingham, failed to appear at a visitation in October 1313 (*Reg. Greenfield*, i, no. 196). *Ceragium*, wax-scot (or wax-shot), a customary payment for maintaining lights in church.

RAMPTON PREBEND, 74–83

74   *Grant by Robert (II) Malluvel, with the consent of Pavia his mother, to Southwell of the church of Rampton for a prebend*   [*c.* 1191 × 1197]

p. 36   **Carta pertinens ad capitulum de Ramton'**

Omnibus sancte matris ecclesie filiis presentibus et futuris Robertus Malluvel in Cristo salutem. Noverit universitas vestra me de consensu¹ Pavie matris mee ecclesiam de Ramton' cum omnibus pertinentiis suis pro amore dei et animabus antecessorum meorum ecclesie beate Marie de Suthwella in puram et perpetuam elemosinam dedisse et hac presenti carta mea confirmasse ad prebendam in eadem ecclesia de Suthwell' ordinandam. Hiis testibus, Ada² abbate de Wellebek, Alano canonico de Ripon, Willelmo capellano, magistro Lisiardo,³ Willelmo de Eornell',⁴ Henrico de Gorham et aliis.

¹ MS *concensu*   ² MS *Adam*   ³ MS ? *Ligiardo*   ⁴ ? for *Gornell'*

Date   After Mr Lisiard de Musters became a canon of York (*c.* 1191–4, *Fasti 1066–1300*, vi, 124). Adam, abbot of Welbeck, from *c.* 1180 was succeeded by Richard of Southwell by 1197 (*HRH*, i, 198), but see **77n.**

Note   Another 15ᵗʰ-c. copy NA, SC7/1/5, f. 7ᵛ. Pd. in *Mon. Ang.*, vi, pt iii, 1315 (xi). On Archbishop Geoffrey's initiative, two other prebends were established (Norwell Tertia Pars, **29**, South Muskham, **525n**) in order to enhance the Chapter. In 1086 Rampton with the church was a substantial manor of Roger de Busli (honour of Tickhill) valued at 50s. With the consent of his unnamed wife and son, Robert Malunell (*sic*) confirmed to Blyth priory the land that Nigel of Rampton, father of Robert's wife, and the wife of Nigel of Rampton had granted, namely the land that Robert, uncle of Nigel, held in Rampton (*Blyth*, 149). Robert de Meinil (*Mainil*), with the consent of his son Robert, confirmed to Blyth priory the assarted land of the monks of Blyth in *Tirebec* in the land Harwin Specus held (*Blyth*, 151). In turn *Tirebec* was confirmed by Matthew I of Hathersage as the charter of Robert del Meinil (*sic*), his ancestor, testified, by Oliver de Albenia (Aubeney) and Joan, daughter of Robert del Mainil, his wife, Joan, daughter of Robert de Meynil in her widowhood, and Richard Musard and Isabel, his wife, daughter of Robert del Maynel (*Blyth*, 152–5). *Tirebec* is never located in the Blyth cartulary but it was assumed that *Tirebec* as confirmed by Robert de Mainill (*Blyth*, 151) and his descendants was included in the land confirmed by Robert Mallunel son-in-law of Nigel of Rampton (*Blyth*, 149), so that Robert Mallunel and Robert de Mainil were thus identified as the same person. But they are not: Robert de Meinill of Whitwell and Langley Meynell (Derbys.) died in 1194 when Sewall, son of Henry of Edensor gave fifty marks to have his daughters who were, from later evidence, Emma, married to Matthew I of Hathersage, Joan and Isabel (*PR 6 Richard I*, 84). William Meinil who was fined for default in 1177 (*PR 23 Henry II*, 62) may have been Robert's son but Robert's ultimate heirs were his daughters. Since the husbands of these daughters held of Frechville and Stuteville in the thirteenth century, but not of Tickhill, then Robert Meinill can be identified as having held five fees in 1166 of Hubert Fitz Ralph (barony of Crich). Meinill and Maluvell were thus not the same family (**77n**).

75 *Quitclaim by Hugh de Lisures, son of Matilda de Lisures, to Southwell, and Reginald, canon-prebendary of Rampton, of one toft which his mother Matilda had in the close of Rampton prebend in Southwell* [1256]

Alia carta pertinens ad prebendam de Ramton'

Universis Cristi fidelibus ad quos presens scriptum pervenerit Hugo de Lissoures filius Matildis de Lisoures salutem in domino. Noverit universitas vestra me concedisse et presenti carta mea confirmasse et quietum clamasse pro me et heredibus meis Deo et ecclesie beate Marie Suthwell' in puram et perpetuam elemosinam domino Reginaldo canonico prebendario de Ramton' unum toftum quod fuit Matildis matris mee quod quidem iacet infra clausum prebende de Rampton' in Suthwell' versus mansum canonici de Dunham. Tenendum et habendum eidem Reginaldo et successoribus suis libere, quiete, pacifice in perpetuum tamquam pertinens ad prebendam eandem. Ita quod nec ego Hugo nec heredes mei nec aliquis pro nobis vel per nos quicquam iuris vel calumpnie in dicto tofto aliqua ratione de cetero poterimus vendicare. In cuius rei testimonium sigillum meum apposuimus. Testibus dominis Hugone filio Radulfi, Thoma de Balla Aqua, Johanne Picot et Reginaldo de Anesbay militibus et aliis, presente domino Simone clerico Ebor' et suis, anno domini m° cc° quinquagesimo sexto.

Note Reginald of Stowe, prebendary of Rampton (1256–67). For Sir Hugh FitzRalph, see **37**; for Sir Thomas de Bella Aqua, **84**. John Picot is probably the man who made a grant at Kirklington (**88**). Sir Reginald (II) de *Anesbay*, recte *Anneslay*, active between c. 1223–c. 1265, issued a confirmation to his brother Ralph for land at Morton in 1241 (cf. *Thurgarton*, 513n, 1615 and passim). This is one of the earliest charters relating to the prebendal houses lying to the north and west of the Minster, and the plot in question presumably lay between the modern Rampton and Dunham prebendal houses on the west side of Westgate.

76 *Sale and quitclaim by William of Shirland, with the assent of his wife, Matilda, to Sir William, chaplain of the archdeacon of York, canon of Southwell, for the augmentation of his prebend, of one toft for which he gave two marks* [1220 × 1241]

Carta Willelmi de Shireland de tertia[1] pertinens prebendam[2] de Ramton'

Sciant presentes et futuri quod ego Willelmus de Schireland consensu[3] et assensu et bona voluntate Matildis uxoris mee concessi, vendidi et quietum clamavi domino Willelmo capellano domini archidiaconi Ebor' canonico de Suthwell' et successoribus suis ad emendationem prebende sue totum ius et clamium quod habui vel habere potui in illo tofto quod iacet inter mesuagium domini Roberti de Hayton et mesuagium[4] dicti domini Willelmi capellani pro duabus marcis argenti quas michi dedit. Ita tamen quod idem dictus dominus Willelmus et successores sui faciant servitium capitali domino sicut dicta carta facere consuevit. Et ut hec concessio, venditio et quieta clamatio rata sit et stabilis, hoc presens scriptum sigilli mei munimine roboravi. Hiis testibus, magistro Willelmo de Taney, magistro Willelmo de Marcam, domino Henrico de Notingham, domino Roberto de Laxton' et aliis multis.

[1] MS *sic* for *tofto*   [2] MS *sic* for *prebende*   [3] MS *concensu*   [4] MS *mesug'*

Date   After Robert of Laxton became a canon and before Mr William de Taney was appointed archdeacon of Nottingham.

Note   This appears to be the only occurrence of William the chaplain as prebendary of Rampton. Mr William de Taney, canon, witnessed a charter of Mr Walter de Taney, perhaps his brother (**524**).

77   *Grant by Pavia, daughter of Nigel of Rampton, with the consent of Robert (II) Malluvel her son, to Southwell of the church of Rampton for a prebend*   [*c.* 1191 × 1197]

Alia carta pertinens ad eandem prebendam

Omnibus sancte matris ecclesie filiis presentibus et futuris Pavia filia Nigelli de Ramton' in Cristo salutem. Noverit universitas vestra me de consensu[1] Roberti Malluvel filii mei ecclesiam de Ramton' cum omnibus pertinentiis suis pro amore dei et animabus antecessorum meorum ecclesie beate Marie de Suthwell' in puram et perpetuam elemosinam dedisse et hac presenti carta mea confirmasse ad prebendam in eadem ecclesia de Suthwell' ordinandam. Hiis testibus, Ada[2] abbate de Wellebek, Alano canonico de Ripon' et Willelmo capellano, Henrico de Gorham, magistro Radulfo de Hamton' et aliis.

[1] MS *concensu*   [2] MS *Adam*

Date   At a similar time to **74**. Mr Ralph de Hamton witnessed a charter of Geoffrey, archbishop of York, 1191–4 (*York Fasti*, i, 81–2).

Note   Exceptionally, in this note we have preserved the several different forms of the benefactors' family name as they appear in contemporary records or in modern calendars in order to show the wide variations. In 1130 Nigel of Rampton paid ten marks in order not to reply to Morcard's claim for his father's lands (*PR 31 Henry I*, 9). In 1165–6 Robert I Mallovel paid 100s relief for his unspecified fee held of Tickhill (*PR 12 Henry II*, 50). He probably witnessed with Robert II de Ferrers (dead by 1160–2) and Henry, his brother, the grant by Richard of Harthill to Adam Malet (Jeayes, *Derbys. Charters*, 216). In 1194–5 Adam of Bedingfield (**78**) and Gundreda de Musters, his wife (**79**), sought against Robert II Maluvel and Pavia, his mother, seven bovates of land in Rampton which Gundreda had in dower, awarded to her in Henry II's court, from Robert I Maluvel, Robert's father, which Stephen Maluvel, brother of Robert II, had given in dower and the cirograph was shown. Robert II Maluvel disseised Adam and Gundreda in the war against Count John when he was with John against King Richard I at Kingshaugh and the land was taken into the king's hand. Hugh Bardolf testified that Robert II fined with the king to have his peace and his lands and Gundreda received seisin. Pavia, by writ of right, sought the same land against Gundreda as her hereditament which her husband (Robert I) never had unless in custody. Gundreda sought full seisin of £27 and offered her champion Robert le Flamenc (*Rot. Cur. Reg.* i, 47–8). In 1194 Robert II Malluvel owed twenty marks to have his lands and the king's peace; he was quit of this debt in 1198 (*PR 6 Richard I*, 84; *10 Richard I*, 14). In the Easter term of 1198 Adam of Bedingfield claimed against Pavia of Rampton two messuages and two crofts and the church of Rampton. The jurors stated that Rampton church was situated on (*infra*) seven bovates of land which Geoffrey de Musters proved (*dirationavit*) against Pavia, and the church was then vacant. Gundreda de Musters proved concerning the seven bovates that she was seised of the crofts by Besmer, bailiff of the hundred, but the jurors did not know if the crofts pertained to the bovates. It was judged that Adam and Gundreda should have seisin of the advowson of Rampton church and the land and Robert II and Pavia were in mercy (*CRR* i, 32–3). In 1203 the case re-surfaced when an assize was summoned to determine if Stephen, father of Robert Malluvel, was seised in his demesne as of fee of seven bovates in Rampton on the day he died which land Adam of Bedingfield then held. Adam said it was true that Stephen was so seised but only as the marriage portion (*set sicut de maritagio*) of Gundreda, his wife, whereas Robert claimed that the land was of the hereditament of Stephen, his father (*CRR* iii, 66, 75). What was at issue was seisin by hereditary portion or seisin by marriage portion, on which the law was not yet fixed in the late twelfth century (Catherine McCauliff, 'The Medieval English Marriage Portion from Cases of Mort d'Ancestor and Formedon', 38 *Villanova Law Review* (1993) 933–1002 at 938–9). In the years 1223–5 Robert III Maulluvel made claims against Roger Maulluvel, Ralph Maulluvel, Robert Maulluvel of Rosliston (Derbys.) and Matilda Maulluvel, probably his uncles and aunt, and called Richard Maulluvel, Stephen's brother, to warrant, claiming that Pavia his grandmother was seised as of right in the time of Henry II and her right descended to Stephen her son, and to him as his father's heir. Stephen was the first-born son (*primogenitus*) of Robert I and he married without his father's permission. Robert was born posthumously and Roger became his guardian 'who took care of him in his infirmity when all his other friends had left him' (*CRR* xi, 975, 2192; xii, 481, 1214 1836; xiii, 1208; Thoroton, iii, 242). In 1242–3 all of Rosliston was held by Clemencia, countess of Chester (*Book of Fees*, 1001). William Rufus, perhaps the same who with Malveisin de Hercy held one and a half fees of Tickhill in Grove, the two being married to Isabel and Theophania, daughters of Gilbert de Arches (Yeatman, *Feudal History of the County of Derby*, 175, 436), gave twenty marks and a palfrey to have custody of seven bovates of land in Rampton that were in the king's hands by reason of Gundreda de Musters's children which Pavia, William's grandmother, claimed against Gundreda (*PR 3 John*, 86; *PR 5 John*, 169, 173; Thoroton, iii, 242). Robert III Maulluvel thus had a troubled inheritance. Pavia, daughter of Nigel of Rampton, married Robert I Maluvel who succeeded in 1165–6 and was dead before 1194–5, and they had two sons Stephen and Robert II. Stephen predeceased his father Robert I and his brother Robert II, but he had married Gundreda de Musters and with her held the seven bovates of land in Rampton. After Stephen's death Gundreda married Adam of Bedingfield, perhaps before or between 1189 and 1194 to be disseised by Robert II Maluvel, and he claimed the seven bovates in the right of his wife as the tenant. It is not certain if Robert II Mauluvel usurped his nephew or was his legal guardian after Robert I's death and if so probably in 1189–94 when Count John held Nottinghamshire and the honours of Tickhill, Peveril and Lancaster (Foulds, 'Siege of Nottingham', 20). In 1200 Robert II Maulovel owed 40s not to reply to Adam and Gundreda over the seven bovates (*PR 1 John*, 20). He owed for one fee of Tickhill in 1200 but Pavia owed 20s scutage for one fee in 1201 but only for a half-fee of Tickhill in 1202 until 1204 which would suggest that Robert II had died in 1200 when Robert III was still a minor. Robert III paid twelve marks for his relief in 1203–4 (*PR 2 John*, 19; *4 John*, 170, 173, 194, 197–8). In the Michaelmas term of 1223 Robert III offered himself against Walter Gray, archbishop of York, concerning the advowson of Rampton church but the archbishop failed to appear (*CRR* xi, 974). On 19 May 1224 Robert III and Archbishop Gray, by his attorney Richard of Southwell, made a final concord whereby Robert quitclaimed the advowson of Rampton to the archbishop and he was received into all the benefits and prayers of the church of Southwell (TNA, CP 25/1/182/1 no. 29). Robert III made final concords with Ralph Maulovel on 6 October 1226, Isabella widow of Robert Maulovel of Rosliston on 7 June 1232, and Matilda Maulovel on 25 June 1232 (TNA, CP 25/1/182/4 no. 73; CP 25/1/182/5 no. 166; CP 25/1/182/6 nos 146, 154). In 1230 Mr Alexander of Dorset claimed that Robert III should hold to him an agreement concerning one bovate and two tofts in Rampton which Robert acknowledged in 1231 (*CRR* xiv, 588, 1420). Alexander of Dorset was in royal service by 1205, presented to Knaresborough church by Nostell priory, prebendary of Ulleskelf, York Minster 1216–26, and justice of the Jews *c*. 1218–31 (*Fasti 1066–1300*, vi, 102–3; C. A. F. Meekings, *Studies in Thirteenth-Century Justice and Administration*, ed. R. F. Hunnisett and D. Crook (London, 1981), 178–9; N. Vincent, *Peter des Roches: An Alien in English Politics, 1205–1238* (Cambridge, 1996), 275, 288). In the Michaelmas term 17–18 Henry III (1233 or 1234) Robert III's plea against Matilda de Maulluvel rested as Robert was dead (*CRR* xv, 569). He was succeeded by Stephen his son (**80**). Joan, widow of Robert Maluvel, is mentioned under 'new oblations' in the Pipe Roll for 1237/8 (Yeatman, *Feudal History of the County of Derby*, 209).

78   *Quitclaim by Adam of Bedingfield to Southwell of the church of Rampton for a prebend*   [*c*. 1197–1208]

Alia carta pertinens ad prebendam de Ramton'

Sciant presentes et futuri quod ego Adam de Bedingefeld' dedi, concessi et quietam clamavi de me et heredibus meis in perpetuum ecclesie de Suthwell' ecclesiam de Ramton' cum omnibus pertinentiis suis in puram et perpetuam elemosinam ad prebendam ecclesie de Suthwell' faciendam. Et ut hec nostra[1] donatio rata et firma permaneat, sigilli mei appositione eam roboravi. Hiis testibus magistro Ricardo de Turri, magistro Rogero, Gaufrido de Dorkest', Willelmo de Bruug' et aliis.

[1] MS *sic*; should be *mea*

Date   The witnesses, all clerks of Archbishop Geoffrey Plantagenet, frequently acted together (cf. *EEA York 1189–1212*, xcix). Mr Richard de Turri was the second most frequent master to witness the archbishop's charters (ibid., cix). Mr Roger is probably the royal justice, Mr Roger of Arundel, canon of Southwell, active 1176–1208 (ibid., Index sub Arundel). Geoffrey of Dorchester was a canon by 1197 (**119**) and prebendary of Woodborough by *c*. 1200 (**521**). Mr William *de Bruug'* may have come from Bruges though a Gascon origin has also been proposed (ibid., xcix).

Note   On 3 February 1203 Robert III Malluvel and Adam of Bedingfield were to make their cirograph (*CRR* iii, 75). Adam I of Bedingfield (four miles south-east of Eye, Suffolk), son of Ernald, son of Peter, first witnessed charters to Eye priory 1189–91. He died between 1226 and 1230, probably in 1227, and was succeeded by his son, Adam II (Brown, *Eye Priory Cartulary* 2, 60–1). Adam I married Gundreda de Musters, widow of Stephen Malluvel (**77n**). His first appearance in a Nottinghamshire context was in 1193 when he owed five marks for replevin (*proplevina sua*) and he owed a half mark for false presentment in 1195 (*PR 5 Richard I*, 28; *7 Richard I*, 76). In 1198 he owed 20s scutage for a half-fee held of Tickhill, probably the result of the case of 1198 (**77n**; *PR 10 Richard I*, 118). In 1200 he owed fifty marks to have seisin of a half-fee in Rampton and a half-fee in Bedingfield of which he had been unjustly disseised (*PR 2 John*, 19). With Robert III Malluvel he owed three marks for a half-fee of Tickhill in 1202 (*PR 4 John*, 195).

79   *Grant by Gundreda de Musters to Southwell of the church of Rampton for a prebend*   [*c.* 1197 × 1208]

Alia carta pertinens ad prebendam de Ramton'   p. 37

Sciant presentes et futuri quod ego Gundere de Monasteriis \dedi et concessi/ ecclesie sancte Marie de Suthwell' ecclesiam de Ramtona cum omnibus pertinentiis suis in puram et perpetuam elemosinam ad faciendam prebendam ecclesie Suthwell'. Et ut hec donatio rata et concessa permaneat sigilli mei appositione eam roboramus. Hiis testibus magistro Coln', magistro Ricardo de Turri, magistro Rogero, Gaufrido de Dorkest', Willelmo de Schireburn', Philippo venatore et aliis.

Date   Probably at a similar time as **78** but on a different occasion. A William of Sherburn witnessed with Aimeric, archdeacon of Durham, *c.* 1197–1217 (Durham University Library, Durham almoner's small cartulary, pp. 102–3).

Note   See **77–78n**. It is not clear if Geoffrey de Musters (**77n**) was the father or brother of Gundreda de Musters, or lord of Kirklington (Yorks.). Geoffrey witnessed with Andrew canon of Southwell *c.* 1176–84 a grant to Rufford and confirmed to Rufford (*c.* 1170–99) the grant of his daughter Matilda (*Rufford*, 157, 970). His probable second wife, Avice, was a daughter of William Fitz Ralph, the founder of Dale abbey, and he was related to Hubert Fitz Ralph who held the barony of Crich (*Dale*, p. 12; *Darley*, pp. xxv, 548–9). Mr Richard de Thurre/Turri/Turry frequently witnessed charters of Archbishop Geoffrey Plantagenet along with Geoffrey of Dorchester and Mr Roger of Arundel (*EEA York 1189–1212*, xcix and passim). Mr Colin has not been identified.

80   *Settlement of the dispute between Mr Reginald of Stowe, canon and prebendary of Rampton, and Sir Stephen Malluvel concerning the breaking of Reginald's fishpond at Rampton. Stephen agreed that Reginald and his successors may build the fishpond towards the western pasture up to stakes fixed in the pasture in the presence of the parties. If flooding occurs in future beyond the stakes, Reginald and his successors may not benefit from this agreement*   1 November 1263

Litera dissensionis inter dominum Reginaldum canonicum Suthwell' et prebendarium de prebenda de Ramtona et dominum Stephanum Mallovell' et quosdam alios

Notum sit omnibus presentibus et futuris quod contentio mota esset inter dominum Reginaldum de Stowa canonicum Suthwell' de prebenda de Ramton' et dominum Stephanum Maulouell' et quosdam alios de villa de Ramton supra fractura piscarie eiusdem Reginaldi coram viris fide dignis, videlicet dominis Simone de Hedon' et Johanne de Raigate senescallo domini Ebor' militibus, pluribus etiam dictam villam inhabitantibus tunc presentibus. Pax inter eosdem fuit reformata, lis quorum quievit in hunc modum, videlicet quod dictus Stephanus de consilio et assensu sibi astantium concessit eidem Reginaldo et successoribus suis quod piscariam suam firmare possit et edificare sine contradictione versus pasturam occidentalem usque ad palos ibidem in pastura fixos in presentia predictorum ibidem astantium. Ita tamen quod si per undationem aquarum terra predicte pasture frangatur ultra palos versus occidentem dictus

Reginaldus vel successores suis dictam piscariam edificare non possint nisi de concessione et licentia Stephani memorati et heredum suorum succedentium. Quod quia ita ut ratum sit et stabile permaneat partes predicte presenti scripto alternatim apposuerunt sigilla sua. Et ad confirmationem compositionis predicte sigillum capituli Suthwell' utrique scripto in modum cyrographi confecto est appensum. Datum in festo omnium sanctorum anno domini m° cc° lx° tertio. Testibus magistro Henrico de Skipton' canonico Suthwell', dominis Simone de Hedun, Johanne de Raigate militibus, Ricardo de Conton', Willelmus de la Venelle, Ricardo de Stowa et aliis.

Note Stephen Malluvel held one in fee of Tickhill in Rampton in 1235–6 and 1242–3 (*Book of Fees*, 534, 979). On 14 April 1252 he made a final concord with Robert Ingemay concerning Robert's free tenement in Rampton and on 9 December 1257 with William Mauluvel concerning William's messuage and land in Rampton (TNA, CP 25/1/182/10, no. 203; 25/1/183/12 no. 28). He was still alive in 1272–3 and his son or grandson Stephen held one fee in 1302–3 (Yeatman, *Derby*, 237; *Feudal Aids* iv, 97). For his descendants see Thoroton, iii, 243–4. Sir Simon of Headon was assessor for the subsidy in Lincolnshire, Nottinghamshire, Derbyshire, Leicestershire. and Warwickshire, 4 June 1260, ceded the sheriffdom of Nottinghamshire, 15 April 1264, and was dead by 16 October 1272 (Moor, ii, 214). John de Reygate was escheator north of the Trent 1268–9 (*CFR 1267–8*, no. 250; *CFR 1268–9*, no. 348) and frequently served as a justice of assize, almost always in Yorkshire, in 1269–70 (*CFR 1268–69* and *CFR 1269–70*, various entries). He was appointed to inquire into the franchises of Southwell on 2 July 1271 and witnessed on 17 August 1272 (*Reg. Giffard*, 198; *Reg. Gray*, 50n).

81 *Memorandum by the Chapter concerning various disputes over tithes and other payments owing since the time that Henry of Bolsover was vicar of Rampton, as a result of agreements with successive prebendaries of Rampton, Mr Geoffrey de St-Médard, Mr Cynthius de Pinea and Mr Bonetus de St-Quentin, by Robert de Well'n [?Wells], who had been deprived of various lands after his appointment as vicar, now restoring his full rights by agreement with Mr Peter de St-Quentin, proctor of Mr Bonetus* 11 June 1287

Memorandum quod cum terra ecclesie de Rampton' in augmentum vicarie loci eiusdem sicut veritas negotii plenius exquisita testatur ab antiquo collata a domino Henrico de Bollesoure loci vicario culta nullo se opponere[1] ipsiusve posset omni perturbante ad firmam magistri G. de Sancto Medardo de Rampton' prebendarium ex ipsius vicar' traditione pro xxx solidis annui redditus fuisset[2] dimissam. Item prebendarius ipsas terras ex traditione huius diutius tenuit soluta vicario annuatim pecunia conventa. Post multum vero temporis, decedente[3] magistro G., collatus fuit in prebenda de Rampton dominus Cyncius[4] de Pyna, qui, facta denuo cum dicto vicario conventione pro xxx solidis annuis dictarum terrarum, per multa tempora tenuit; deinceps, decedente[3] dicto domino Cyncio de Pyna, collatus fuit a domino r[ege], vacante sede Ebor', ipsa prebenda magistro Boneto de Sancto Quintino. Et quia conpertum est dominum Robertum de Well'n presbiterum ad presentationem dicti devoti fratris nostri domini Cyncii de Pyna tunc prebendarium de R' ad vicariam[5] in ecclesia de R. vacantem et ad presentationem suam spectantem intuitum caritative admissum, ipsumque per capitulum in eadem cum pertinentiis corporaliter institutum, quod prout per certam inquisitionem ex mandato capituli super hoc factam acceptum est in portionibus consistit subscriptis, videlicet in quodam manso terre ecclesie decimis agnorum et lane et omnibus aliis decimis maioribus et minoribus, obventionibus omnimodis, decimis garbarum et secundum prebendar' dumtaxat salvis; eodem vero Roberto, vicario de R. ut premittitur, dictam terram alienatam et illicite distractam reperiente, et ipsam ad statum pristinum prout moris est revocare intendente, post aliquod tempus Magister Petrus de Sancto Quintino, dicti magistri Boneti procurator sufficienter constitutus, ad suasionem capituli receptus una marca argenti a dicto vicario ipsum gratum dicta terra persolvitur reinvestivit[6] et dicte vicarie readiunxit imperpetuum. Cum vero de premissis in pleno capitulo tertio id' Junii anno gratie millesimo cc octavo septimo ad plenum constaret capitulum huius facti nomine subiuxum nolens infirmari decrevit dictam terram eidem vicario integraliter facere restituendam et per ipsum capitulum dictus Robertus vicarius in plenam ipsius possessionem iudicialiter reintroductus.

¹ MS *opp're*   ² *fuisse?*   ³ MS *desce'te*   ⁴ MS *domino Cyncio*   ⁵ MS *vacar'*   ⁶ The reading *gratum dicta terra persolvitur reinvestivit* remains problematic

Margin   Text in hand of Scribe 4. *Rampton vicarii porciones* (16th–17th c.)

Note   Mr Geoffrey de St-Médard, prebendary of Rampton at time of his death at Viterbo, before 12 May 1281 (*Reg. Wickwane*, 11, 276, 318). Mr Cynthius de Pinea, provided by Martin IV to Rampton following the death of Geoffrey de St-Médard, resigned during the archiepiscopal vacancy 26/27 August 1285–16 April 1286 (*Reg. Wickwane*, 11, 198–9, 236, 318–19), and was subsequently elected archbishop of Capua (*Reg. Honorius IV*, 356, 25 May 1286), dead by 10 February 1291. He was succeeded at Rampton as this memorandum shows by Mr Bonetus de St-Quentin, appointed by Edward I during the vacancy at York, though he was subsequently challenged for possession by Roland de Ferentino, provided by Honorius IV, before 27 August 1288 (*CPL*, i, 493, 495–6).

82   *Notification by the Chapter concerning the portion of the vicar of Rampton*   Southwell, 27 June 1301

Litera capituli beate Marie Suthwell'¹ de ordinatione vicarie de Ramton   p. 38

Universis sancte matris ecclesie filiis presentes literas inspecturis capitulum ecclesie beate Marie Suthwell' Ebor' diocesis salutem in omnium salvatore. Universitati vestre innotescat quod cum nos in plena convocatione nostra super quibusdam ecclesie nostre statum tangentibus rite facta registrum nostrum super ordinatione vicarie prebendalis ecclesie de Rampton inspeximus² ac coram nobis legi fecerimus exquesite comperimus quod dicta vicaria in portionibus constat infrascriptis, videlicet in quodam manso iuxta ecclesiam cum terra et prato ecclesie antedicte et in decimis³ lane et aliis quibuscumque decimis, oblationibus seu proventibus dicte ecclesie pertinentibus, decimis garbarum et feni prebendario eiusdem dumtaxat salvis, quas quidem portiones cum manso terra decimis oblationibus et proventibus, ut est dictum, eidem vicarie per antecessores nostros antiquitus ordinatas decernimus et promittamus sententialiter ac diffinitive ad eandem vicariam pertinere. In cuius rei testimonium presentes literas fieri fecimus patentes sigillo nostro communi roboratas. Datum in capitulo nostro Suthwell' quinto kalend' Julii anno domini m° ccc° primo.

¹ *Suthwell'* over erasure? ² *inspeximus* underlined by the 16ᵗʰ–17ᵗʰ-c. marginal annotator ³ MS *indecimis*

Margin Page heading, *Ordinacio vicarie de Rampton* (Scribe 4); rubric and text (Scribe 1); *Inspeximus* (16ᵗʰ–17ᵗʰ c.)

83 *Confirmation by Pope Innocent III to the Chapter of the right to present to the church of Rampton granted as a prebend by [Geoffrey], archbishop of York, at the presentation of the patrons, and to the church of St Helen's, [South] Wheatley*   St Peter's, Rome, 5 April 1205

Confirmatio¹ pro ecclesia de Rampton'² et Wheateley³

Innocentius episcopus servus servorum Dei dilectis filiis canonicis Suthwell' salutem et apostolicam benedictionem. Solet annuere sedes apostolica piis votis et honestis petentium precibus favorem benevolum impartiri. Eapropter dilecti in domino filiis vestris iustis postulationibus grato concurrentes assensu ecclesiam de Rampton' quam venerabilis frater noster Ebor' archiepiscopus ad presentationem patronorum vobis in prebendam liberaliter⁴ contulit et ecclesiam sancte Elene de Whetley cum pertinentiis suis, sicut eas iuste ac pacifice possidetis, vobis et per vos ecclesie vestre auctoritate apostolica confirmamus et presentis scripti patrocinio communivimus.⁵ Nulli igitur omnino homini liceat hanc paginam nostre confirmationis infringere vel ei ausu temerario contraire. Siquis autem hoc attemptare presumpserit indignationi omnipotentis Dei et beatorum Petri et Pauli apostolorum eius se noverit incursuros. Datum Rome apud Sanctum Petrum nonas Aprilis pontificatus nostri anno octavo.

¹ Short word erased here ² Scribe 4, as is the main text ³ *et Wheateley* (16ᵗʰ–17ᵗʰ c.) ⁴ Omitted in *A* ⁵ Cheneys read *communimus*

Margin *Rampton* and *Wheteley* (16ᵗʰ–17ᵗʰ c.)

Note Another copy at **522**, listed by Cheney and Cheney, no. 612, and pd. in appendix p. 245, with this copy as A and the later one as B. Note that they abbreviate various formulae.

HEXGRAVE PARK, 84–7

84 *Quitclaim by Thomas de Bella Aqua releasing to Archbishop Walter [Gray] all his rights in the wood of Hexgrave and in a fief between the wood and a ditch which abuts Kirklington field*   [1236 × 1253]

p. 39 **Carta Thome de Bella \Aqua/¹feofamenti de Hekkesgrave**

Omnibus Cristi fidelibus ad quos presens scriptum pervenerit Thomas de Bella Aqua salutem in domino. Noveritis me concessisse et quietumclamasse pro me et heredibus meis imperpetuum venerabili patri domino Waltero Ebor' archiepiscopo Anglie primati et successoribus suis totum ius et clamium quod habui vel habere potui in bosco de Hekkesgrave sine aliquo retenemento in viis,[2] semitis, pascuis et pasturis et in omnibus locis infra clausum dicti bosci de Hekkesgrave. Concessi etiam et quietumclamavi pro me et heredibus meis in perpetuum dicto domino archiepiscopo et successoribus suis totum[3] feofamentum[4] cum bosco superexistente quod est de toto feudo meo et tenemento inter dictum boscum et campum de Kirthilington super quod fossatum dictum campum abbuttat, tenend' et habend' eidem domino archiepiscopo et successoribus suis libere, quiete,[5] integre et pacifice, ita quod nec ego nec heredes mei nec aliquis pro nobis vel per nos quodcumque[6] iuris vel calumpnie in predicto bosco de Hekkesgrave vel fossato memorato aut bosco superexistente vendicare poterimus vel exigere in perpetuum. Ego vero et heredes mei warantizabimus predicto domino archiepiscopo et successoribus suis predictam concessionem et quietam clamationem contra omnes homines et feminas. Et ut hec mea concessio quieta et clamatio et warantizatio[7] perpetuum robur optineat presenti scripto sigillum meum duxi apponendum. Testibus: magistro Willelmo de Suthwell' canonico et Roberto de Haget canonico Suthwell', Willelmo de Vescy, Jordano de Bingel, Odone de Richmund', Martino de Marisco clericis, Roberto de Gray et Willelmo Martil militibus et aliis.

[1] Insertion in same hand as rubric and text (Scribe 1)   [2] MS *vii*, i.e. 7   [3] MS *totam*   [4] MS *feofatum*   [5] MS *quite*   [6] MS *quicumque*   [7] MS *warantazatio*

Date   While Thomas de Bella Aqua was active (**412n**) and probably at a similar time to **85**. William II de Vesci died in 1253 (Sanders, *English Baronies*, 103).

Note   Calendared in *Reg. Gray*, Addenda, 329. William de Vescy also witnesses **85** and **430** (*c.* 1222), which Odo of Richmond also witnessed. The Bella Aqua family were generous benefactors of Rufford abbey and occur very frequently as charter witnesses (see also **85n**). Hexgreave wood lies to the west of the original Kirklington open field which rises up to a site still named 'Camp hill' as it was in Thoroton's day (Thoroton, iii, 100), before sloping down towards a flat low-lying piece of ground bordering the modern wood. No clear signs of older ditching, either on Camp hill, or in the adjacent low land are now evident.

85   *Quitclaim by Robert de Bella Aqua to Archbishop Walter [Gray] of all his rights in the hay (wood) of Hexgrave and the ditch and fief he has between the wood and Kirklington field*   [1236 × 1243]

Carta Roberti de Bella Aqua de[1] feofamento de Hekkesgrave

Omnibus Cristi fidelibus ad quos presens scriptum pervenerit Robertus de Bella Aqua salutem in domino. Noverit universitas vestra me concessisse et imperpetuum clamasse pro me et heredibus meis in perpetuum venerabili patri domino Waltero Ebor' archiepiscopo Anglie primati et successoribus suis totum ius et clamium si quod habui vel habere potui in haya de Hekkesgrave in viis et semitis, in planis et in pasturis, in herbagiis infra clausum dicte haye sine aliquo retinemento. Preterea concessi et quietum clamavi prenominato dicto archiepiscopo et successoribus suis pro me et heredibus meis totum fossatum meum cum bosco superexistente[2] infra fossatum predictum et extra quantum ad me pertinet ad totum tenementum meum et feodum meum inter hayam de Hekkesgrave et campum de Kyrthilington' tenendum et habendum eidem domino archiepiscopo

et successoribus suis libere, quiete, solute, pacifice, ita quod nec ego
Robertus nec heredes mei nec aliquis pro nobis vel per nos aliquod ius
vel clamium in predicta haya vel in fossato vel in bosco \super/[3] existente
aliquo modo vendicare vel exigere poterimus in perpetuum. Ego vero
predictus Robertus et heredes mei predicto domino archiepiscopo et
successoribus suis illam quietam clamationem et concessionem contra
omnes homines warantizabimus in perpetuum. Et ut hec mea concessio et
quieta[4] clamatio perpetuum robur optineat presenti[5] scripto sigillum meum
duxi apponendum. Testibus: magistris Willelmo de Suthwell' canonico
Ebor', et Roberto Haget et Ricardo de Hereford', canonicis Suthwell',
Galfrido de Hokeland' canonico Beverl', Willelmo de Vescy et aliis.

[1] Two letters erased   2 MS *superexiste*   [3] Same hand   [4] MS *quieata*   [5] *scri* erased here

Date   At a similar time to **84** and before the death of Robert de Bella Aqua which
occurred after 1236 but before 1243 (**565n**).

Note   Cal. in *Reg. Gray*, Addenda, 329. Robert (II) de Bella Aqua, brother of Adam
de Bella Aqua, and uncle of Thomas (**84**), witnessed *c.* 1200–43, and with his wife,
Dionisia, made two grants to Rufford (cf. *Rufford*, 807–8). He also occurs as a witness
to an agreement of 9 October 1236 as does Thomas de Bella Aqua, son of William (ibid.,
858). For Mr William of Southwell, canon of York and rector of Blaby, see **283**. Whether
he was also the William of Southwell, chaplain of Kirklington, who occurs in **88** is more
problematic. He is to be distinguished from William, son of Nicholas de Grauntcurt, also
known as William of Southwell, very active in the latter part of Henry III's reign (**398n**).
Richard de Hereford (his name very distinctly begins with an H in this quitclaim) is
probably identical with Richard de Bereford (**87**), although he also occurs as Hereford
in *Reg. Wickwane*, 339 no. 930, and ibid., 252 no. 615; see also **87n**. For Geoffrey de
Bocland (*Hokeland*), canon of Beverley, see **414n**. *Haya* in a post-Conquest context
is now usually interpreted as indicating a deer-park rather than just a wood (cf. John
Fletcher, 'The Rise of British Deer Parks: Their raison d'être in a Global and Historical
Perspective', *The History, Ecology and Archaeology of Medieval Parks and Parklands*,
ed. Ian D. Rotherham (= *Landscape Archaeology and Ecology* 6 (2007), 37–8).

86   *Quitclaim by Thomas of Kirklington, clerk, to Archbishop Walter
[Gray] of all his right in the ditch below Hexgrave wood in the field of
Kirklington for which the archbishop gave him 10s*   [1226 × 1249]

Carta Thome de Kyrtlingtone et de Hekkesgrave

Sciant presentes et futuri quod ego Thomas[1] de Kyrtlingtona clericus
dedi concessi et hac presenti carta mea confirmavi venerabili patri nostro
Waltero archiepiscopo et successoribus suis totum ius et clamium quod
habui seu aliquo modo habere potui sine aliquo retenemento in fossato
sub bosco de Hekkesgrave in campo de Kyrlinton' ubicumque tam in
ea[2] abbuttat[3] super predictum fossatum quod modo inclusum est infra
pratum de Hekkesgrave, tenendum et habendum eidem domino Waltero
archiepiscopo et successoribus suis, ita quod ego Thomas clericus nec
heredes mei nec aliquis pro nobis vel per nos clamium vel calumpniam

p. 40 | erga predictum fosatum de cetero movere poterimus. Pro hac autem
donatione, concessione et quietaclamatione dedit dominus Walterus
archiepiscopus Ebor' michi decem solidos argenti pre manibus. In
huius rei robur et testimonium presenti scripto sigillum meum apponere

dignum duxi. Hiis testibus, domino Willelmo de Windendune, Galfrido de Bocland, Hugone Picot et aliis.

[1] MS *Thoma* [2] MS *mea* for *in ea* [3] MS *abbuctat*

Date After William of Widdington was granted land in Southwell and before his death. Geoffrey de Bocland had become a canon of Beverley probably in 1227–8 and certainly by 1233 (**414n**). As he is not named a canon here perhaps a date 1226–8 may be preferred.

Note Cal. in *Reg. Gray*, Addenda, 329.

87 *Quitclaim by Hugh Picot to Archbishop Walter [Gray] of his rights in Hexgrave hay and his ditch in the wood pertaining to his tenement and fee between Hexgrave hay and Kirklington field for which the archbishop gave him ten marks and a rouncey worth three marks* [1231 × 1245]

Quieta clamatio Hugonis Picot de Hekkesgrave

Omnibus Cristi fidelibus ad quos presens scriptum pervenerit Hugo Picot salutem in domino. Noverit universitas vestra me concessisse et quietum clamasse pro me et heredibus meis in perpetuum venerabili patri domino Waltero Eboracensi archiepiscopo Angli[e] primati et successoribus totum ius et clamium si quod habui vel habere \potui/[1] in Haya de Hekkesgrave, in viis et semitis, in planis et pasturis, in boscis et pascuis et herbagiis infra clausum dicte haye sine aliquo retenemento. Preterea concessi et quietum clamavi prenominato domino archiepiscopo et successoribus suis pro me et heredibus meis totum fossatum meum in bosco superexistente infra fossatum predictum et extra quantum pertinet ad totum tenementum meum et feodum meum inter hayam de Hekkesgrave et campum de Kyrhelinton', tenendum et habendum eidem domino archiepiscopo et successoribus suis libere, quiete, solute, pacifice, ita quod nec ego nec heredes mei nec aliquis pro nobis vel per nos aliquid ius vel clamium in predicta haya vel in fossato vel in bosco superexistente aliquo modo vendicare vel exigere poterimus in perpetuum. Pro hac vero concessione et quieta clamatione et carte mee confirmatione dedit michi predictus dominus archiepiscopus decem marcas argenti et unum runcinum de pretio trium marcarum. Et ego Hugo Picot et heredes me warantizabimus predicto domino archiepiscopo et successoribus suis illam concessionem et quietam clamationem contra omnes homines et feminas in perpetuum. Et ut hec mea concessio et quieta clamatio rata et stabilis in posterum permaneat presenti scripto sigillum meum duxi apponendum. Testibus Willelmo archidiacono, Henrico de Notingham, Ricardo de Bereford', Roberto de Oxn' canonicis Suthwell' et aliis.

[1] Interlineation in 15th-c. hand

Date Richard de Bereford occurs as a canon of Southwell from at least 20 June 1231 (*Reg. Gray*, 238) and before the death of Henry of Nottingham (see **37n**).

Note The identity of William the archdeacon is ambivalent. Mr William of Bodham was archdeacon of Nottingham in 1221, possibly as early as 1218, being replaced by Mr Walter de Taney *c.* 1234, in turn replaced by another Archdeacon William, sometime between 1245 and no later than 21 September 1249 (*York Fasti*, ii, 43–4). Robert of

Oxford was active *c.* 1220–50 (*Thurgarton*, cxxii, 134). Hugh Pigot witnessed 1218 (*Rufford*, cxiii–cxiv, 846).

LIGHTS, 88–92

88 *Grant in free alms by John Picot to the chapel of St Swithun, Kirklington, and to Mr William of Southwell of one toft in Kirklington for Mr William and his successors to maintain a lamp burning on the high altar each day at mass, vespers, matins and compline. If not reversion of the toft to John's heirs as Lady Margaret, his mother, held*

[1236 × 1272]

Carta de lampade[1] in \capella de/ Kyrtlyngton[2]

Sciant presentes et futuri presens scriptum visuri quod ego Johannes Picot pro salute anime mee et animarum patris mei et matris mee et omnium successorum meorum et heredum meorum dedi, concessi et hac presenti carta mea confirmavi in liberam, puram et perpetuam elemosinam Deo et capelle beati Swythuni de Kyrtlington' et magistro Willelmo de Suthwell' et successoribus suis dictam capellam possidentibus toftum[3] unum in villa de Kirtlington', illud scilicet quod iacet inter toftum dicte capelle et toftum Ade Karlot cum omnibus pertinentiis, aisiamentis et libertatibus suis, ita scilicet[4] quod dictus magister Willelmus et successores sui invenient in perpetuum unam lampadem ardentem in dicta capella coram maiori altare eiusdem sumptibus suis singulis diebus anni ad missam, vesperas, matutinas et ad omnes alias horas et ad completorium. Quod si dictus magister Willelmus vel successores sui dictam lampadem ut predictum est minime invenire voluerint,[5] post ternam admonitionem[6] competenter a me vel heredibus meis eis factum, dictum toftum cum pertinentiis suis ad me vel heredes meos sine contradictione aliqua tenend' sicut domina Margareta mater mea illud tenuit revertetur. Quod ut firmum et stabile perseveret, presenti scripto in modum cyrographi[7] confecto sigillum meum apposui. Dictus vero magister Willelmus alteri parti huius scripti penes me et heredes meos remanenti signum suum apposuit. Hiis testibus domino Thoma de Bella Aqua, Johanne de Uffleth, Willelmo de Sutton', Roberto de Sutton' militibus et aliis multis.

[1] Scribe 1, as is text   [2] Addition (Scribe 4), with interlineation in a later 16th–17th-c. hand   [3] MS *tofptum*   [4] MS *silicet*   [5] MS *voluerunt*   [6] MS *amonitionem*   [7] MS *cyrografi*

Margin *Notum veterum apellacionem capellam de Kyrtlington dici et non ecclesiam parochialem* (16th–17th c.)

Date While Thomas de Bella Aqua was active (**412n**). William of Sutton died 1273 and Robert, son and heir of William, son of Roland of Sutton (died 18 August 1268), aged 27, dead by 8 March 1273 (Moor, iv, 317).

Note For the problem of identifying Mr William of Sutton, see **85n**.

There is an inserted leaf between p. 40 and p. 41. The recto of the insert is blank; the verso is p. 40a.

89 *Grant in hereditary fee by Robert son of Richard of Kersall to Hugh*
the Fleming of one bovate of land in Normanton with croft and toft for
one pound of incense rent per annum for which Hugh gave 3½ marks
                                                    [*c*. 1220 × 1230]

Carta de i libra incensi[1]   p. 40a

Sciant omnes tam presentes quam futuri quod ego Robertus filius Ricardi
de Kynesall' dedi, concessi et hac presenti carta mea confirmavi Hugoni
Flandr' et heredibus suis vel cui assignare voluerit, pro homagio et
servitio suo unam bovatam terre in Normantun' cum tofto[2] et crofto
et cum omnibus pertinentiis infra villa et extra, scilicet illam bovatam
quam Wlmarus tenuit, tenend' de me et heredibus meis illi et heredibus
suis vel suis assignatis in feodo et hereditate libere, quiete et pacifice,
reddendo unde annuatim michi et heredibus meis unam libram incensi
ad nativitatem beati Johannis baptiste pro omni servitio et exactione ad
me et heredes meos pertinente[3] salvo forinseco servitio. Et ego et heredes
mei warantizabimus prefatam bovatam terre cum pertinenciis prefato
Hugoni et heredibus suis vel suis assignatis contra omnes homines. Pro
hac autem donatione, concessione et confirmatione dedit michi predictus
Hugo tres marcas argenti et dimidiam nomine de gersuma. Hiis testibus:
domino Hugone decano de Suwell', Hugone[4] de Notingham, Roberto de
Laxinton', Rogero de Soweresby canonicis Suwell', Ricardo, Hugone,
Ricardo, Luca et aliis multis etc'.

[1] Scribe 4, as is text   [2] MS corr. from *crofto*   [3] MS *sic*   [4] *Sic* for ? *Henrico*; see note

Date After Robert of Laxton (1214) and Henry of Nottingham (*c*. 1219) became canons
and before the death of Hugh the dean.

Note This is the only occasion on which a Hugh of Nottingham is listed as a canon,
and it is clearly a scribal error for Henry of Nottingham (**92**).

90 *Grant by William Ribald to Andrew of Southwell for his homage*
and service of two bovates of land in Farnsfield for 15s 10d and a leather
surcoat and 12d rent per annum   [early 13th century]

Carta de lampade in ecclesia Suthwell' coram crucifixo in coro ecclesie.[1] p. 41
Carta de lampade in ecclesia beate Marie de Suthwelle[2]

Sciant presentes et futuri quod ego Willelmus Riba\l/d'[3] concessi et dedi
et hac presenti carta mea confirmavi Andreo[4] de Suthwell' pro homagio
et servitio suo et pro xv solidis et decem denariis[5] et pro una supertunica
pro unus[6] stivalis de cordewan'[7] duas bovatas terre in villa de Farnesfeld',
illas scilicet[8] quas Baldwinus de eadem villa tenuit cum tofto et crofto et
omnibus pertinentiis predicte terre in pratis et pascuis et in omnibus locis
infra villam et extra, illi et heredibus suis vel cui eam assignare voluerit
tenendam et habendam de me et heredibus meis libere quiete pacifice et
honorifice, reddendo michi vel heredibus meis annuatim pro omni servitio
et exactione ad me vel heredes meos pertinenti duodecim denarios ad
duos terminos, scilicet[8] sex denarios ad Pentecosten et sex denarios ad
festum sancti Martini salvo tamen forinseco servitio. Et ego et heredes

mei warantizabimus predicto Andree et heredibus suis et suis assignatis predictas duas bovatas terre cum omnibus pertinentiis contra omnes gentes. Et ut hec mea donatio et confirmatio firma et stabilis permaneat in perpetuum, eam sigilli mei appositione roboravi. Hiis testibus, domino H. decano, magistro W. de Marcam canonicis Suthwell' et aliis.

¹ Heading by Scribe 4, replacing the original rubric by Scribe 1   ² Deleted rubric by Scribe 1, who also writes text   ³ Insertion in same hand   ⁴ MS *sic*, post corr. ? from *Andree*   ⁵ MS *denarios*   ⁶ MS *unis*   ⁷ space of about three letters here   ⁸ MS *silicet*

Margin   Opposite bottom of **90**: *Vacat quod scribuntur iste carte in cantaria Andree Baylly* (late 14ᵗʰ c. or later)

Date   If Andrew is identified as Andrew the bailiff of Southwell, he was dead by 1228 and Hugh the dean was dead by 1230.

Note   William Ribald may be the same man as William Ribaud of Halam who witnessed 1237–43 (**235**).

91   *Grant by William Ribald to Richard son of Walter, for his homage and service of two bovates of land in Farnsfield for 3s rent per annum*
[early 13ᵗʰ century]

Carta Willelmi Ribald' de eadem terra¹

Sciant presentes et futuri quod ego Willelmus Ribald' dedi et concessi et hac presenti carta mea confirmavi Ricardo filio Walteri pro homagio et servitio suo duas bovatas terre in villa de Farnesfeld', illas scilicet² quas Baldewinus de eadem villa tenuit cum tofto et crofto et omnibus pertinentiis predicte \terre/ pratis³ in pascuis et pasturis et in omnibus locis infra villam et extra, illi et heredibus suis vel cui eam assignare voluerit, tenendam et habendam de me et heredibus meis libere et quiete et pacifice reddendo michi et heredibus meis annuatim pro omni servitio et omni exactione ad me sive ad heredes meos pertinenti tres solidos argenti scilicet² xviii denarios ad festum sancti Martini et xviii denarios ad inventionem sancte crucis salvo tamen forinseco servitio. Et ego et heredes mei warantizabimus predicto Ricardo et heredibus suis vel cui eam assignare voluerit predictam terram contra omnes homines. Et ut hec mea donatio stabilis sit et firma eam sigilli mei appositione roboravi. Hiis \testibus/⁴ Johanne filio Mathei de Halum, Waltero filio Petri, Rogero palmario, Henrico fratre suo et aliis.

¹ Scribe 1   ² MS *silicet*   ³ MS *prate*   ⁴ Added in red by Scribe 1

Date   After **90**.

92   *Grant by Robert, son of Richard of Kneesall, to Southwell of the homage of Hugh the Fleming for one bovate of land in Normanton for one pound of incense rent per annum*   [c. 1220 × 1230]

Carta de incenso in ecclesia beate Marie Suthwell'

Omnibus sancte matris ecclesie filiis hoc scriptum visuris vel audituris Robertus filius Ricardi de Kirneshale eternam in domino salutem. Noverit universitas vestra me intuitu Dei et beate Marie pro salute anime mee et pro animabus tam heredum meorum quam antecessorum meorum concessisse et dedisse et hac presenti carta mea confirmasse Deo et ecclesie beate Marie de Suthwell' in puram et perpetuam elemosinam homagium quod Hugo Flandrensis michi fecerat et homagium totum et servitium quod idem Hugo et heredes sui vel assignati eorum michi et heredibus meis facere debuerant de illa bovata terre in Normanton' cum pertinentiis quam Wulmarus tenuit quietum de me et heredibus meis in perpetuum ab omni servitio et exactione seculari salvo forinseco quantum ad predictam bovatam terre pertinet percipiendo inde memorate ecclesie de predicto Hugone et heredibus suis vel assignatis eorum unam libram incensi albi annuatim ad nativitatem beate virginis et omnibus diebus sabati per annum pro omni servitio. Ego vero Robertus et heredes mei warantizabimus hanc meam donationem Deo et predicte ecclesie sancte Marie contra omnes homines in perpetuum. Et ut mea donatio firma et stabilis in perpetuum perseveret, presenti carta mee sigillum meum apposui. Hiis testibus: Hugone decano, Henrico de Notingham, Roberto de Lexinton', canonicis Suthwell' et multis aliis.

Date   After **89**.

ROLLESTON, 93–103

93   *Grant by Henry, son of Thomas of Rolleston, to Thurgarton priory, for the souls of Thomas and Aviva, his father and mother, of the patronal right and advowson of Rolleston church*   [*c.* 1200 × 1208]

Carta Henrici filii Thome de Rorldeston' pertinens ad commune[1]   p. 42
capituli de Suthwell'

Omnibus filiis sancte [matris] ecclesie ad quos presentes litere pervenerint Henricus filius Thome[2] de Roldeston salutem. Noverit universitas[3] vestra me divine pietatis intuitu dedisse et presenti carta confirmasse Deo et beato Petro de Thurgarton' et canonicis ibidem Deo servientibus ius patronatus et advocationem quam habui in ecclesia de Roldeston' cum omnibus eidem pertinentibus in puram et perpetuam elemosinam[4] pro salute anime mee et uxoris mee Letitie et pro animabus patris mei Thome et matris mee Avive et pro animabus antecessorum meorum ita pure et quiete sicut aliqua elemosina[5] purius et liberius dari posset. Hiis testibus capitulo de Suthwell', Jolino de Nova Villa, Ingelramo et Willelmo Grantcurt, capellanis Suthwell', Reginaldo capellano,[6] Roberto de Somervil', Willelmo filio Radulfi et Henrico clericis et aliis.

[1] MS *commune?* *Thurgarton*, *115 reads *tociem*   [2] Followed in MS by a red line presumably to show scribe could not decipher the surname   [3] MS *universita*   [4] MS *elimosinam*   [5] MS *elimosina*   [6] MS *cappellano*

Date   'After Henry son of Thomas had succeeded his father and before the death of Jollan de Neville' (*Thurgarton*, *115, p. 75).

Note   Pd. as *Thurgarton*, *115.

94 *Grant by Jollan de Neville to Thurgarton priory, for the souls of himself and Amphelissa, his wife, of the advowson of Rolleston church*
[1176 × 1208]

Carta Jolini de eadem

Omnibus filiis sancte ecclesie ad quos presentes pervenerint Jollinus de Nova Villa salutem. Noverit universitas vestra me divine pietatis intuitu dedisse et presenti carta mea confirmasse Deo et beato Petro de Thurgarton' et canonicis ibidem deo servientibus advocationem quam habui in ecclesia de Roldeston' cum omnibus eidem ecclesie pertinentibus in puram et perpetuam elemosinam[1] pro salute anime mee et uxoris mee Amphelisse et pro animabus patris mei et matris mee ita pure et quiete sicut aliqua elemosina[2] purius et liberius dari potest. Hiis testibus: magistro Rogero de Arundel, Ingelramo et Willelmo capellanis[3] de Suthwell', Reginaldo capellano[4] Roberto de Sumervilla, Roberto de Forneus, Willelmo filio Radulfi et aliis.

[1] MS *elimosinam*   [2] MS *elimosina*   [3] MS *cappellanis*   [4] MS *cappellano*

Date While Jollan de Neville was active (*Thurgarton*, 111n). Probably to be dated shortly before **93** with which it shares several witnesses in common. Most charters witnessed by Mr Roger of Arundel seem to date to the 1190s, but he may have been active as a canon 1176–1208.

Note Another version of this charter is pd. in *CCR*, x, 21, which provides the name of Jollan's father (Roscelin), his mother (Alice) and a brother (Richard). His widow, Amphelissa, was still alive in 1219 (see *Thurgarton*, 111 for a comparative edition of the two versions).

95 *Grant by Henry, son of Thomas of Rolleston, to Robert the Grammarian of Rolleston church* [*c.* 1205 × 1221]

Carta alia de Roldeston'

Universis sancte matris ecclesie filiis Henricus filius Thome de Roldeston salutem. Noverit universitas vestra me karitatis intuitu donasse et concessisse Roberto Grammatico[1] ecclesiam de Roldeston' cum omnibus pertinentiis et libertatibus suis in puram et perpetuam elemosinam[2] pro salute anime mee et omnium predecessorum meorum et successorum meorum. Hanc autem donationem ut rata et firma in posterum permaneat sigilli mei appositione confirmavi. Hiis testibus, domino Philippo de Tymblund', Godefredo Andegavensi, Thoma filio Henrici, Andrea de Roldeston' et aliis.

[1] MS *gramatico*   [2] MS *elimosinam*

Date While Philip I of Timberland was active and before the death of Godfrey the Angevin (*Thurgarton*, 233n, 745n) and **96**.

Note Did Robert the Grammarian act as the local school teacher? Godfrey the Angevin's career from *c.* 1190 to his death *c.* Hilary Term 1229 is sketched in *Thurgarton*, 233, notes; see also **306, 565–6**. Philip (I) of Timberland is also cited frequently in the notes to the edition of that cartulary.

96 *Notification by Elias, prior of Thurgarton and the convent that they have granted to Walter [Gray], archbishop of York, the advowson of Rolleston church and surrendered to him the charters of Sir Henry of Rolleston and Jollan de Neville* Hilary term 1221

Carta Elye et conventus de Thurgarton' de ecclesia de Roldeston'

Omnibus sancte matris ecclesie filiis ad quos presens scriptum pervenerit Elyas dictus prior de Thurgarton et humilis eiusdem loci conventus eternam in domino salutem. Ad notitiam vestram volumus pervenire nos unanimi assensu et spontanee voluntate concessisse et dedisse reverendo patri nostro Waltero Dei gratia Ebor' archiepiscopo advocationem ecclesie de Roldeston' cum toto iure quod in ea habuimus vel habere potuimus conferendam cuicumque vel quibuscumque voluerit. Et ad maiorem huius donationis nostre firmitatem cartas Henrici de Roldeston' militis et Jollani de Nevill' super predicta advocatione collatas eidem reddidimus. Ne igitur supradicta alicui in posterum devenire possint[1] in dubium prenominato archiepiscopo hanc cartam nostram confecimus et eam sigilli capituli nostri corroboravimus.[2] Hiis testibus magistro Willelmo de Boham, archidiacono de Notingham, Henrico decano Suthwell', W. Mauclerc et Radulpho de Lexinton' et aliis.

[1] MS *possunt* [2] MS *coroboravimus*

Note Pd. in *Thurgarton*, *117 after this copy, with emendations from the enrolled copy (*CRR*, x, 21). William of Bodham first occurs as archdeacon of Nottingham in 1218 and last occurs probably in 1234 as his predecessor became dean of York on 20 September 1214 and his successor was in post by 9 October 1241 (*Fasti 1066–1300*, vi, 45). In *Visitations*, xxxvi, it is plausibly argued that 'Henry the dean of Southwell' is a copyist's misreading for Hugh, just as 'Ralph' should be Robert of Laxton. Walter Mauclerc became bishop of Carlisle in 1223, though he continued to appear in Chapter at later dates. See **93–5** for the charters handed back by Elias.

97 *Notification by Archbishop Walter [Gray] that Rolleston church has been returned to him by Thurgarton priory as patron at the wish of Henry of Rolleston and that he has granted it for the use of the canons of Southwell to augment their common fund, saving to Thurgarton priory the portion which pertains to them, for two stones of wax per annum for the lights of Southwell* [7 April 1221]

Litera Walteri archiepiscopi de ecclesia de Roldeston'

Omnibus Cristi fidelibus ad quos presens scriptum pervenerit Walterus Dei gratia Ebor' archiepiscopus Anglie primas salutem in domino. Noverit universitas vestra nos ob reverentiam Dei et beate virginis Marie ecclesiam de Roldeston' nobis a veris eiusdem patronis scilicet[1] prior et conventus[2] de Thurgarton' de assensu insuper et voluntate Henrici de Roldeston' militis qui aliquando ius advocationis sibi in eadem vendicavit concessam in usus Suthwell' ecclesie convertendam canonicis[3] in eadem ecclesie Suthwell residentibus in augmentum communie sue[4] cum omnibus ad eandem ecclesiam pertinentibus caritative[5] contulisse et salva dictis priori et conventui de Thurgarton' portione sua quam eis de pertinentiis memorate ecclesie concessimus sicut in carta capituli Suthwell' eis super hoc confecta continetur, solvende annuatim dicte ecclesie Suthwell' duas petras cere in augmentum luminariorum ad duos terminos sicut tam in dicta carta capituli quam in carta dictorum prioris et conventus inde confecta

p. 43   continetur.[6] | Quod ut ratum et stabile inconcussum duret in posterum presenti scripto sigilli nostri munimine consignato confirmandum duximus et corroborandum.[7] Hiis testibus: Willelmo thesaurario et magistro Ricardo Cornub', Serlone, Roberto de Wynton' canonicis Ebor' et aliis.

[1] MS *silicet*   [2] In nominative in MS   [3] MS *canonicus* with later correction to *canonicis*   [4] In MS the passage *ecclesie conventendam . . . communie sue*, has been underlined by a later hand   [5] MS *caritive*   [6] End of p. 42 here with catchwords *Quod ut*; start of p. 43   [7] MS *coroborandum*

Date After **96** and before **101** (21 April 1221). NA, SC7/1/5, f. 2, another 15th-c. version of this charter, is dated 7 April in the seventh year of Archbishop Gray's pontificate.

Note Pd. in Dickinson, *Southwell* (1819), 362 (with omissions) and *Visitations*, 201–2 where this version has been collated with a late sixteenth-century copy of the church's statutes (probably NA, SC1/2/2 or 3). William of Rotherfield first occurred as treasurer of York on 3 September 1220 and his predecessor, Hamo, last occurred as treasurer in 1216 and was dead by 1 March 1218. William, probably a relative of Walter Gray, was dead by 7 January 1242. Mr Richard of Cornwall, the archbishop's clerk, occurs 17 September 1216, canon 1217 and chancellor of York Minster by 1 July 1225. Serlo is probably Mr Serlo, canon of Beverley and of York, who was a canon of York by 17 June 1218 and is probably identifiable with Mr Serlo de Sunninges. Mr Robert of Winchester had become canon of York by 27 January 1217 and precentor by 4 December 1235. For Elias's acknowledgement to pay the two stones of wax per annum, and Southwell's grant to Thurgarton concerning the wax *c.* 1225, see *Thurgarton*, *121, 996–7.

98   *Quitclaim by Henry, son of Thomas of Rolleston, knight, to Southwell of the advowson of Rolleston church*   3 April 1221

Quieta clamatio Henrici filii Thome de ecclesia de Roldeston

Omnibus ad quos presens scriptum pervenerit Henricus filius Thome de Roldeston' militis eternam in domino salutem. Ad notitiam vestram volo pervenire me divine pietatis intuitu concessisse et quietumclamasse et hac presenti carta mea confirmasse ecclesie beate Marie Suthwell' et canonicis ibidem deo servientibus advocationem ecclesie de Roldeston' et totum ius quod in ea habui vel habere potui in eadem quietam eisdem ecclesie canonicis de me et heredibus meis in perpetuum. Et ne ego vel heredes mei aliquid iuris in eadem de cetero vendicare possimus hanc cartam sigillo meo signatam in testimonio[1] huius mee quiete clamationis predictis ecclesie et canonicis confeci. Hiis testibus: Willelmo de Roldeston clerico, Andrea filio Hugonis de Roldeston', Roberto Laycest', Andrea capellano[2] et aliis.[3] Actum in ecclesia Suwell' in vigilia dominice palmarum anno primo post translationem sancte Thome martiris.

[1] MS *testio'm*   [2] MS *cappellano*   [3] Following added in a 15th-c. hand

Date Thomas Becket was translated on 7 July 1220 by Archbishop Stephen Langton so this charter can be dated to Saturday, 3 April 1221.

99 *Quitclaim by Benedict, son of Thomas of Rolleston, knight, to Southwell of the advowson of Rolleston church. Also confirmation of the quitclaim of Sir Henry of Rolleston, his predecessor, for which Southwell gave him twenty marks* [1242 × 1272]

Quieta clamatio Benedicti filii Thome de Roldeston' de eadem ecclesia

Omnibus Cristi fidelibus ad quos presens scriptum pervenerit Benedictus filius Thome de Roldeston' miles salutem in domino. Noverit universitas vestra me caritatis intuitu concessisse, dimisisse et hac presenti carta mea confirmasse ecclesie beate Marie Suthwell' et canonicis ibidem Deo servientibus advocationem ecclesie de Roldeston' et omnia ab eadem ecclesia possessa cum omnibus suis pertinentiis in puram et liberam et perpetuam elemosinam[1] et totum ius et clamium quod in eis habui vel habere potui quietum eisdem ecclesie \et/ canonicis clamasse de me et heredibus meis in perpetuum. Concessionem et confirmationem et quietam clamationem quam predecessor meus dominus Henricus de Roldeston' fecit dictis ecclesie et canonicis de prenominatis cum suis pertinentiis ratas habeo et presentis scripti testimonio confirmo et in perpetuum permanere concedo. Pro hiis autem concessione, dimissione, confirmatione et quieta clamatione dederunt michi prenominati canonici xx[ti] marcas sterlingorum. Unde volo et concedo quod si aliquod scriptum penes me vel heredes meos fuerit aliquo umquam tempore repertum vel ostensum quod dictos canonicos super predictis aliquant' gravare possit, quod illud viribus penitus careat et michi seu heredibus meis nullatenus valeat. Et ut ego Benedictus vel heredes mei futuris temporibus aliquod iure in premissis vendicare possimus hanc cartam nostram in testimonium premissorum predictis ecclesie et canonicis fieri feci et signo meo sigillavi. Hiis testibus, dominis Thoma de Bella Aqua et Simone de Gringelthorp militibus, Willelmo de Blythewurd, Simone de Farnesfeld', Roberto de Gypesmer', Roberto filio Johannis et aliis.

[1] MS *elimosinam*

Date Benedict, son of Thomas of Rolleston, had succeeded Henry of Rolleston by 1242 (*Book of Fees*, 981, 989; *Thurgarton*, 112n) and before the death of Thomas de Bella Aqua (**412n**).

Note For Simon of Grimblethorpe see **415n**.

100 *Notification by Walter [Gray], archbishop of York, to the king's justices of the Bench that the prior and convent of Thurgarton has granted him the advowson of Rolleston church, which he has conferred on the canons of Southwell to augment their common fund* [*c.* April 1221]

Litera domini archiepiscopi Ebor' iust[iciis] domini regis de banco de advocatione ecclesie de Roldeston'

Viris venerabilibus et amicis in Cristo dilectissimis iusticiis domini regis de banco Willelmus[1] Dei gratia Ebor' archiepiscopus Anglie primas salutem et sinceram in domino dilectionem. Noveritis quod, cum dilecti filii prior et conventus de Thurgarton' suum ius quod habebant in advocatione ecclesie de Roldeston' nobis concesserit, nos pietatis intuitu eandem ecclesiam dilectis filiis canonicis ecclesie Suthwell' ad augmentationem ecclesie sue contulimus. Ideoque sciatis quod quicquid inter ipsos canonicos et Henricum de Roldeston' militem qui ius in advocationem eiusdem ecclesie vendicabat coram nobis actum fuerit ratum habemus et gratum. Valete.

¹ Thus in MS for *Walterus*

Date As **97** and before **101**.

101 *Final concord between Henry of Rolleston and Elias, prior of Thurgarton, concerning the advowson of Rolleston church whereby Henry has granted the advowson to Southwell. Prior Elias has surrendered the charters to Southwell* Westminster, 25 April 1221

Finalis concordia in curia domini regis de advocatione ecclesie de Roldeston'

Hec [est]¹ finalis concordia facta in curia regis domini apud Westem' a die pasche in quindecim dies anno regni regis Henrici filii regis Johannis quinto, coram Roberto de Ver, comite Oxon', Martino de Pat'hull', Ricardo Hareng', Stephano de Segrave, Thoma de Haydon, Roberto de Lexinton iusticiis et aliis domini regis fidelibus tunc ibidem presentibus inter Henricum de Roldeston' petentem et Eliam priorem de Thurgarton' deforciantem per Walterum de Ludham canonicum suum positum loco suo ad iurandum vel petendum² de advocatione ecclesia de Roldeston', unde assisa ultime presentationis summonita fuit inter eos in prefata curia scilicet³ quod predictus Henricus recognovit advocationem predicte ecclesie esse ius ipsius prioris ut illam quam habet ex dono ipsius

p. 44 Henrici et predictus prior ad petitionem ipsius Henrici dedit | et concessit advocationem eiusdem ecclesie Deo et sancte Marie de Suthwell' et canonicis eiusdem ecclesie habendam et tenendam eidem ecclesie et ipsis canonicis in puram et perpetuam elemosinam.⁴ Et sciendum quod idem prior reddidit canonicis predictis de Suthwell' cartas et munimenta que habuit de eodem Henrico de predicta ecclesia.

¹ *est* omitted ² MS appears to have *perdendum* ³ MS *silicet* ⁴ MS *elimosinam*

Note Robert de Vere had succeeded his brother as earl of Oxford in 1214 and died between 19 and 25 October 1221. Among the justices sitting with him on this occasion were two who held prebends at Southwell: Martin of Patishall (d. 1229), perhaps the most eminent of Henry III's early judges, held Rampton (*CRR*, x, 219); and Robert of Laxton (d. 1250) held Norwell Palishall.

102 *Ordinances of Walter [Gray], archbishop of York, for Southwell with the assent of the Chapter concerning conditions governing payments to canons and terms of residence; the old commons and Rolleston church to form one fund managed by wardens named annually by the canons; every canon resident, or passing through, present at matins, to receive 3d on ordinary feasts, and 6d on double feasts; the rest to be divided at Whitsuntide among resident canons equally; residence means three*

months at one time, or in two halves, in Southwell church or being a
student in theology; absence for urgent business with licence if made up
within the year Cawood, 20 April 1225

Litera domini \Walteri/[1] archiepiscopi de communia canonicorum residentium

Universis sancte matris ecclesie filiis ad quos presens scriptum pervenerit Walterus Dei gratia Ebor' archiepiscopus salutem in domino. Noverit universitas vestra nos de assensu capituli ecclesie nostre Suthwell' de communia taliter ordinasse videlicet quod antiqua communia dicte ecclesie et ecclesia de Roldeston' quam eis in aumentum[2] communie sue contulimus[3] quicquid in posterum accreverit communie memorate in unam summam coniungantur per manus custodum ad hoc annuatim de communi consilio provisorum hoc modo inter canonicos dividenda. ¶ Statuimus sane quod si quis canonicorum residentium vel etiam transitum faciendum matutinis novem lectionem interfuerit, tres denarios percipiet de communia. ¶ Qui vero duplici festo interfuerint sex denarios[4] percipiet de communia. ¶ In fine autem anni scilicet[5] in octabis Pentecostes totum residuum communie inter canonicos residentes equaliter dividuntur. Illos autem anno illo residentes interpretamur qui per tres menses continuos vel in duas partes divisos in ecclesia Suthwell' moram fecerunt. ¶ Similiter illos qui in theologia studuerint. ¶ Si quis autem fratrum infra tempus residentie necesse habuerit exire pro negotio urgenti de licentia fratrum tunc residentium ad certum tempus exire poterit et pro residenti nichilominus habeatur. Ita tamen quod quanto tempore residentie deputato absens fuerit, tanti temporis defectum eodem \anno/[6] suppleat per tot dies ibidem residendo. ¶ Ut autem hec nostra ordinatio perpetue firmitatis robur optineat presenti scripto sigillum nostrum pariter cum sigillo capituli sepe dicti dignum duximus apponendum. Datum apud Cawod' duodecimo kal' Maii pontificatus nostri decimo.

[1] Interlineation in black by Scribe 1   [2] MS *sic*   [3] Scribe writes *in* and crosses it out   [4] MS repeats *sex denarios*   [5] MS *silicet*   [6] Interlineation in 15th-c. hand

Margin marginal note (17th/18th c.): *Ordinatio de Devisione communii. de Residenciariis pro simplici festo et duplici in Choro quovislibet [?] tempore divinarum. De absentia residenc[iariorum]*

Note Pd. in Dickinson, *Southwell* (1819), 362 (where incorrectly dated to 1274; cf. *Visitations*, 201 n. c for explanation); *Reg. Gray*, 3–4 (from the Register of Walter Giffard, fo. 3b, and the White Book), and in *Visitations*, 202–3. Other later manuscript copies in the Chapter's possession include NA, SC1/2/3 and 8, 17th-c. and 19th-c. printed editions in nos 10–13, most probably derived from the White Book copy. It was confirmed by the Chapter in 1260 (**104**). As Edwards, *Secular Cathedrals*, convincingly showed, the thirteenth century was a very important period for early cathedral and collegiate church statute-making; for comment see Barrow, 'Statutes', 317–29.

103 *Letters of the Chapter following a dispute between Hugh, vicar of Rolleston, and Geoffrey, vicar of Morton, over tithes from houses in Rolleston and Morton which Hugh claimed were owing to his church, announcing that agreement had been reached by which five houses in*

Morton would pay all their tithes to Morton while other parishioners
would pay tithes on their properties in Rolleston to Rolleston and on
those in Morton to Morton Southwell, 14 October 1259

**Litera capituli Suthwell de mota facta in vicaria de Roldeston' et
vicaria de Morton'**

Noverit universi[1] per presentes quod cum contentio mota fuisset coram
nobis magistro Petro de Radenov'[2] et Henrico de Mora canonicis ecclesie
Suthwell' auctoritate capituli Suthwell cognoscentibus inter dominos
Hugonem et Galfridum vicarios ecclesiarum de Roldeston et de Morton'
super decimis stipendiorum de mercenariis quicumque domorum in
parochia de Roldeston et Morton' existentium quas decimas dixit dominus
Hugo ad ecclesiam suam de iure parochiali pertinere eandemque ecclesiam
in possessione earundem decimarum per magnum tempus extitisse. Et sic
utroque petente sibi iustitiam exhiberi et diutius super hiis contendente
tandem inter eos amicabiliter convenit sub hac forma, videlicet soluti
de quinque dictis domibus in villa de Morton' parochianis ecclesie
eiusdem ville servientes integrum decimas de suis stipendiis solvant
ecclesie de Morton licet de nocte iaceant in territorio[3] parochie de
Roldeston' et parochiani ecclesie de Morton' deservientes in parochia
de Roldeston ecclesie de Roldeston' decimas stipendiorum solvant,
omnibus aliis ecclesiis eisdem ab eisdem mercenariis[4] salvis. Nos autem
conventionem ipsam approbantes eam quantum in nobis fuit in nomine
domini confirmavimus. In huius rei testimonium presenti scripto sigillum
capituli nostri fecimus apponi. Actum apud Suthwell' pridie idus Octobris
anno domini m° cc° l° nono.

[1] MS *universis*   [2] i.e. *Radenoveria*   [3] MS *territorie*   [4] MS *mercinariis*

Note   Mr Peter of Radnor was a canon of Southwell by late 1257 (**192**) and was presented to the living of Bunny on 23 May 1270 (*Reg. Giffard*, 63). Mr Henry de Mora had
first witnessed before becoming a canon prior to May 1230 (**399, 412**), holding the living
of Eakring before receiving a canonry *c.* 1249, dying after 13 January 1261 (**58, 394–6**).

104   *Confirmation by the Chapter of the statutes issued by Archbishop*
Walter [Gray] (102), with interpretation of its terms; students in theology
to count as canons resident only if actually studying at the universities of
Paris, Oxford and Cambridge for at least two terms a year; absence from
urgent cause to break three-monthly residence, unless it be only twice
or thrice for preaching or other clerical duties within their prebendal
churches for not more than three nights away from Southwell at a time and
with leave from other canons; Warden of the Fabric to have a colleague
and not to begin any new work without leave of the Chapter; Wardens
of the Commons to render yearly accounts and then resign; two or three
days' deliberation to precede appointment of successors who may be the
same persons or not; deceased residentiaries to have apportioned part
of common fund Thursday, 23 September 1260

This page is an insert in hand of Scribe 4

Confirmatio statuti Walteri archiepiscopi Ebor' per capitulum Suthwell' facta

Anno domini m° cc^{mo} sexagesimo die Jovis proxima post festum sancti Mathei apostoli vocati convenerunt fratres et canonici ecclesie beate Marie Suthwell' in capitulo eiusdem ecclesie ut statui suo et profectui ecclesie providerentur. Et in principio consenserunt omnes tunc presentes et procuratores eorum qui erant absentes ut ordinatio et scriptura felicis memorie domini Walteri archiepiscopi sigillis eius et dicti capituli signata de communia sua percipienda servetur. Intelligentes illud in scripto illo insertum quod studentes in theologia percipienda communa dicuntur residentes de illis tamen qui student Parisiis, Oxon' vel Cantebrig' et qui theologiam audiunt vel legunt ordinare et ad minus per duos terminos illius anni quo pro residentibus habebuntur. Alioquin communiam non percipient. Intelligentes etiam illud quod ibidem inseritur de exeuntibus propter causam urgentem quod canonici, si infra suos tres menses tantum bis vel ter causa predicandi vel confessiones audiendi in suis ecclesiis ad prebendas suas pertinentibus, vel exercendi¹ in prebendis suis ea que ad curam et sollicitudinem earundem prebendarum requiruntur, exierint, et non ultra tres noctes extra villam Suthwell' moram fecerint, pro residentibus debent haberi. Ita tamen quod a canonicis tunc residentibus licentiam petierint aliquam dicta causarum assignantes sui² processus et super quo sue veraci assertioni credetur. Canonici vero qui ad aliquam ecclesiam suam ad prebendam suam non pertinentem eadem de causa consimilibus³ vicibus petita licentia et assignata causa sui recessus exierint perficient illos dies sue absentie infra annum vel communiam in fine anni non percipient. Item custos fabrice ecclesie socium habebit aliquem capellanum de ecclesia sibi a residentibus datum qui in compoto suo de receptis suis et expensis suis poterit ei testimonium perhibere. Nec novam fabricam incipiet in ecclesia vel extra nisi de consensu fratrum in generali congregatione compotum suum in fine anni reddent' modo debito ut alias est ordinatum. Et post compotum committent officium suum cum clavibus et omnibus sibi commissis in manus canonicorum tunc residentium qui per biduum vel triduum deliberabunt quibus scilicet illis vel aliis voluerint illud officium assignare et istud fiet singulis annis statim post compotum eorundem. Preterea supradicti canonici omnes tunc presentes et procuratores eorum qui erant absentes consenserunt quod illi canonici residentiarii qui infra tempus residentie sue inchoatum per mortem decedunt naturalem pro residentibus intelligantur, ita quod communam ceterasque distributiones dicte ecclesie saltim pro rato temporis percipiant effectu.

¹ MS *excercendi*   ² Or *sive*?   ³ MS *consilibus*

Margin   Note next to relevant part of text: *custos fabrice* in 15th-c. hand.

Note   Pd. in *Visitations*, 203–5.

105   *Confirmation by Henry III of free warren to Archbishop Sewall [de Bovill] in all his demesnes*   Westminster, 26 March 1257

p. 46   **Carta domini Henrici regis concessa Sewallo archiepiscopo de libera warenna in omnibus dominicis terris suis. In xviii peixide.**

Henricus, Dei gracia rex Anglie, dominus Hibernie, dux Aquitanie et comes Andegavie, episcopis, abbatibus, comitibus, baronibus, iusticiariis, vicecomitibus, prepositis, ministris et omnibus ballivis et fidelibus suis, salutem. Sciatis nos concessisse et hac carta nostra confirmasse pro nobis et heredibus nostris venerabili patri Sewallo, Ebor' archiepiscopo, Anglie primati, quod ipse et successores sui archiepiscopi Ebor' in perpetuum habeant liberam warennam in omnibus dominicis terris suis quas idem archiepiscopus in presenti habet in comitatibus Ebor', Notingham, Lincoln', Northumb', Gloucestr' ad dictum archiepiscopatum pertinentibus dum tamen terre ille non sint infra metas foreste nostre. Ita quod nullus intret terras illas ad fugandum in eis vel ad aliquid capiendum quod ad warennam pertineat sine licencia et volunte ipsius archiepiscopi vel successores suorum archiepiscoporum Ebor' super foresfacturam nostram decem librarum. Quare volumus et firmiter precipimus pro nobis et heredibus nostris quod predictus archiepiscopus et successores sui archiepiscopi Ebor' in perpetuum habeant liberam warennam in omnibus dominicis terris suis predictis sub pena predicta. Hiis [testibus]: Simone de Montoforti, comite Leyc', Ricardo de Clar', comite Glouc' et Herteford, Petro de Sabaud', Johanne Maunsell' et aliis. Datum per manum nostram apud Westmonasterium vicesimo sexto die Marcii anno regni nostri quadragesimo primo.

Margin   Heading and text of this and **106–8** in hand of Scribe 1.

Note   This grant to Sewald de Bovill, archbishop of York (1255–8), is enrolled on the Charter roll for 41 Henry III (TNA C 53/47), m. 7 (pd. in *CChR 1226–57*, 465). For another grant of free warren, to Mr John Clarell, see **361**. The additional rubricated note in the heading *In xviii peixide* appears to be one of the few indications surviving about how the medieval Chapter kept its records in caskets or chests (cf. **Introduction**, p. xlii). The witnesses form a very powerful team: Simon de Montfort, earl of Leicester (d. 1265), Richard de Clare, earl of Gloucester (d. 1262), Peter of Savoy, count of Savoy (1263–8), holder of the earldom of Richmond from 1241–68, and John Mansel, a leading royal councillor (d. 1265).

106   *Confirmation by Henry III of the forest bounds in Nottinghamshire following a perambulation of the forest by Hugh de Neville, Brian de Lisle and other justices [made in 1227]*   Lambeth, 16 July 1232

Carta domini Henrici ultimi de perambulacione foreste et de libera warenna concessa venerabili archiepiscopo Ebor' in omnibus dominicis terris suis in Notingham sira

Henricus, Dei gracia rex Anglie, dominus Hibernie, dux Normannie [et] Aquitanie et comes Andegavie, archiepiscopis, episcopis, abbatibus, prioribus, comitibus, baronibus, iusticiariis, vicecomitibus, forestariis, prepositis, ministris et omnibus ballivis et fidelibus suis, salutem. Sciatis nos concessisse et hac carta nostra confirmasse pro nobis et heredibus nostris in perpetuum quod perambulacio facta per dilectos et fideles nostros Hugonem de Nevill', Brianum de Insula et alios sibi associatos per preceptum nostrum predicto Hugoni de Nevill', tunc existente iusticiario foreste nostre. Inter partes illas que deforestande erant et partes illas que foresta remanere in perpetuum et quod partes ille de comitatu predicto deforestate per\re/maneant per metas et loca inperambulacione inde facta plenius expressa et inferius subscripta:

Incipit autem predicta perambulacio ad vadam de Cuningeswath per chiminum quod se extendit usque ad villam de Welhage versus Notingham. Ita quod clausum ville de Welhage est extra forestam, et sic deinde per idem chiminum quod se extendit inter Welhage et Notingham usque ad Baxtonhou, et sic deinde ad locum ubi rivulus[1] de Doverbec pertransit predictum cheminum, sic deinde sicut predictus rivulus de Doverbec descendit usque in aquam que vocatur Trenthe. Ita quod illa pars de Notinghamsyra que vocatur Cley, et quedam particula que vocatur Hatfeld' ab aquilonari parte magni chimini de Notingham, quod se extendit a predicto vado de Cuningeswath et extendens se ad predictum rivulum de Doverbec, sunt deforestate per predictas metas versus aquilonem et orientem. Que quidem pars predicta que vocatur le Cley et particula predicta que vocatur Hatfeld' sunt inter rivulum de Doverbec et Bikeresdich et Syrwoud et Trenthe.

Incipit autem predicta perambulacio in eodem comitatu Notingham ad predictum vadum de Coningeswath ascendendo versus occidentem per aquam[2] que vocatur Medine usque ad villam que vocatur Warsope, et ab eadem villa ascendendo usque ad Mammesheved' et Selegh',[3] et de inde ascendendo per ipsam aquam usque ad Heyeredebrigg' et deinde[4] divertendo per magnum chiminum de Notingham usque ad pontem de Mulneford, et deinde ascendendo usque ad Mammesheved, et deinde inter campos de Herdewik et de Kirkeby et moram de Kyrkeby usque ad angulum que vocatur Nunnekere, et deinde per assartum Ywain Briton' usque ad Tharlesty, et deinde usque ad Stolegate, et deinde per magnum chiminum usque subtus vetus castellarium de Aneslay, et ab ipso ca[s]tellario per magnum chiminum usque ad villam de Lindeby, et deinde per mediam villam de Lyndeby usque ad molendinum de eadem villa, quod est super aquam de Lene, et deinde ascendendo per ipsam aquam[5] usque ad villam de Lenton', | et deinde sicut ipsa aqua antiquitus currere solebat usque in aquam que vocatur Trenthe. Ita quod illa pars in Notinghamsyra que est inter aquam de Coningeswath et villam de Blye, scilicet[6] que vocatur Hatfeld est deforestata extraqua parte magni chimini inter predictam aquam de Coningeswath et predictam[7] villam de Blye et similiter tota illa pars de Notinghamsyra, que est ex occidentali parte aque de Medine ascendendo versus austrum usque in aquam de Trenthe inter predictas divisas in comitatu de Derby, est deforestata. Ita quod quicquid est extra predictas metas est deforestatum et quicquid est infra metas remanet foresta, salvis eciam nobis et heredibus nostris haya de Welleye et omnibus dominicis

p. 47

nostris in predicto comitatu Notingham ex parte occidentali aquilonari et orientali ville de Notingham et ex parte australi eiusdem ville usque in aquam de Trente que sunt et remanent foresta. Concessimus eciam et carta nostra confirmavimus pro nobis et heredibus nostris omnibus de comitatu predicto Notingham manentibus in partibus predictis deafforestatis que partes predicte secundum metas et loca predicta deafforestate sint quiete in perpetuum de vasto reguardo visu forestariorum et de omnibus que ad forestam, forestarios, viridarios, regardatores vel eorum ministros pertinent, et quod nullus predictorum hominum qui manet in predictis partibus deafforestatis vel alibi in eodem comitatu extra forestam nec eorum heredes aliquo tempore per nos vel heredes nostros fiant agistatores sive viridarii sive regar\da/tores in foresta predicta in comitatu Notingham. Concessimus eciam eisdem hominibus et hac carta nostra confirmavimus pro nobis et heredibus nostris quod nullus qui sit de partibus predictis deafforestatis veniat per communem summonicionem coram iusticiariis itinerantibus ad placita foreste, nisi attachiatus sit pro aliqua transgressione foreste vel sit plegius alicuius qui coram predictis iusticiariis venire debeat ad respondendum pro aliqua transgressione foreste. Quare volumus et firmiter precipimus pro nobis et heredibus nostris quod perambulacio predicta facta per metas et loca superius expressa in comitatu Notingham firma sit et in perpetuum stabilis permaneat quod partes predicte sicut in eadem perambulacione superius notata sint deafforestate imperpetuum. Ita quod quiete sint de vasto regardo visu forestariorum et de omnibus que ad forestam pertinent. Hiis testibus: venerabili P[etro] Wynton', J[oscelino] Bacthon' et W[altero] Karleol' episcopis, H[uberto] de Burg' comite Kant', iusticiario Anglie et Hibernie et aliis. Datum per manus venerabilis patris R[adulpho] Cycestr' episcopi cancellarii nostri apud Lambt' sextodecimo die Julii anno regni nostri sextodecimo.

¹ MS *Ruvulus* ² *per aquam* repeated ³ The description of the boundary is garbled here: *ad Mammesheved' et Selegh'* should read *per eandem aquam usque ad parcum de Pleselly* ⁴ MS *deinden* ⁵ MS *equam* ⁶ MS *silicet* ⁷ Followed by *aquam* struck out

Note Dickinson, *Southwell* (1819), 353 for an abbreviated translation; cal. in *CChR 1226–57*, 165–6, and see also **348** for an abbreviated version. For another version see *Sherwood Book*, 33–8, where on p. 37 the reference to Mansfield is an error for Mamshead. For the identification of the places on the boundaries see Crook, 'Spigurnels', 50–70, and 'Struggle', 35–45. The witnesses listed here are Peter des Roches, bishop of Winchester (1205–38), Jocelin of Wells, bishop of Bath (1206–42), Walter Mauclerc, bishop of Carlisle (1223–48), Hubert de Burgh, earl of Kent (1227–32, 1234–43), justiciar of England since 1215, appointed justiciar of Ireland on 16 June 1232 but dismissed shortly after the issue of this charter on 29 July 1232, and deprived of the justiciarship of England, probably on 21 September 1232, a post he finally resigned in late May 1234. The charter was given under the hand of Ralph Neville, bishop of Chichester (1222–44), chancellor of England from 1226, deprived of seal 1238, but retaining the title. The copy in the *Sherwood Book*, 38 lists a further eight lay witnesses omitted here.

107 *Confirmation by Edward I to Archbishop Thomas [of Corbridge] of free warren in his demesnes of Cawood, Beverley and Southwell*
Westminster, 8 March 1303

Carta domini Edwardi regis Anglie concessa Thome archiepiscopo Ebor' de libera warenna de omnibus dominicis terris suis de Cawode et Beverlaco et Suthwell'

Edwardus, Dei gracia rex Anglie, dominus Hibernie et dux Aquitanie, episcopis, abbatibus, prioribus, vicecomitibus, prepositis, ministris et omnibus ballivis et fidelibus suis, salutem. Sciatis me concessisse et hac carta nostra confirmasse venerabili patri Thome archiepiscopo Ebor', Anglie primati, quod ipse et successores sui imperpetuum habeant liberam warennam in omnibus dominicis terris suis de Cawode [et] Beverlaco in comitatu Ebor' et Suthwell' in comitatu Notingham, dum tamen terre ille non sint infra metas foreste nostre. Ita quod nullus intret terras illas ad fugandum in illis vel ad aliquid capiendum quod ad warennam pertineat sine licencia et voluntate ipsius archiepiscopi vel successorum suorum super foresfacturam nostram decem librarum. Quare volumus et firmiter precipimus pro nobis et heredibus nostris quod predictus archiepiscopus et successores sui in perpetuum habeant liberam warennam in omnibus dominicis suis predictis super foresfacturam decem librarum sicut predictum est. Hiis testibus: Johanne de Warenna comite Surr', Johanne de Brictannia, Hugone le Despenser, Roberto de Tatessale et aliis. Datum per manum nostram apud Westmonasterium octavo die Marcii anno regni nostri tricesimo primo.

Note   Mentioned in *CChR 1300–26*, 34. The witnesses are John de Warenne, earl of Surrey (1240–1304), John of Brittany, earl of Richmond (1268–1305), Hugh Despenser the elder (1261–1326) and Robert, 2nd Lord Tattershall, who was dead by late July 1303.

ECCLESIASTICAL LITIGATION, 108–12

108 *Letters dimissory of William [la Zouche], archbishop of York, reporting that after various charges had been alleged against the Chapter, it had produced letters, instruments and muniments both from the pope and from his predecessors, which had been displayed to the Chapter of York and others, and that it was agreed that the charges made at the recent visitation were without foundation*
Southwell, 17 September 1344

Dimissio domini archiepiscopi   p. 48

Universis sancte matris ecclesie filiis ad quorum notitiam presentes litere pervenerint Willelmus permissione divina Ebor' archiepiscopus Anglie primas, sedis apostolice legatus salutem in sinceris amplexibus salvatoris. Noverit universitas vestra quod cum nuper dilecti filii capitulum nostre ecclesie collegiate beate Marie Suthwell' coram nobis super nonnullis articulis contra ipsos in ultima visitatione nostra quam nuper exercuimus[1] in capitulo antedicto compartis fuissent iudicialiter petiti. Idem capitulum ad certos diem et locum eis per nos assignatos \per/ procuratorem suum legitimum sufficientem in hac parte potestatem habentem coram nobis comparentes diversa literas et instrumenta ac munimenta tam Romanorum pontificum quam quorundam predecessorum nostrorum. Ac etiam capituli ecclesie nostre beati Petri Ebor' et aliorum exhibuerunt. Quibus quidem literis instrumentis ac munimentis penes nos diligenter[2] examinatis et de iuris peritorum consilio nobis assistentium ad plenum discussis habitaque consideratione pleniori ad illa legitima documenta evidentias et rationes per partem dicti capituli coram nobis ostensis allegatis et probatis ipsos quoad[3] omnes et singulos articulos contra eos in dicta visitatione nostra ut premittitur compertos videlicet capitulum dicte ecclesie nostre collegiate ut capitulum cocernentes[4] statutis irrationabilibus per idem capitulum absque nostra seu alia auctoritate[5] sufficientius in preiudicium nostrum aut aliorum editis dumtaxat[6] exceptis ab ulteriori impetitione officii nostri quietos dimittimus per presentes quibus sigillum nostrum apponi fecimus in fidem et testimonium premissorum. Datum apud Suthwell' xvii[mo] die mensis Septembris anno domini millesimo ccc[mo] quadragesimo quarto et pontificatus nostri tertio.

[1] MS *excercuimus*   [2] MS *dilegenter*   [3] MS *quo ad*   [4] MS *sic*   [5] MS *autoritate*   [6] MS *dum taxat*

Note   This was one of the first occasions when some quires of the White Book may have been available to the Chapter for the defence of its privileges, though the tone of the archbishop's letter suggests that originals were displayed at York (cf. **Introduction**, p. xlii).

109   *Letters of Henry [of Newark], archbishop of York, about a dispute which had arisen over the presentation made by Mr Nicholas of Wells, canon of Southwell, of Richard of Halloughton to the vicarage of Dunham, citing the Chapter to appear in his court on Thursday after the feast of St Augustine next wherever he might be, together with Nicholas and Richard, to hear his judgment*   Monkton, 28 April 1299

Citatio archiepiscopi Ebor' facta capitulo Suthwell'

Henricus permissione divina Ebor' archiepiscopus Anglie primas dilectis in Cristo filiis capitulo nostro Suwell' salutem gratiam et benedictionem. Cum curam parochie ecclesie de Dunham et parochianorum eiusdem ac spiritualem iurisdictionem plenarum in omnibus ad forum ecclesiasticum pertinentibus notor' habeamus quod in nostra diocesi non notorium nullatenus poterit reputari et vos ad presentationem magistri Nicholai de Welles canonici ecclesie nostre Suwell' Ricardum de Halughton ad vicariam predicte ecclesie de Dunham ut refertur admittere presumpsistis curam animarumque non ad vos sed ad nos dinoscitur pertinere committentes eidem ipsumque Ricardum in corporalem possessionem eiusdem vicarie induci facientes quam idem Ricardus sic detinet occupatam in nostri et nostre Ebor' ecclesie preiudicium ipsorumque parochianorum periculum animarum. Quo circa tenor presentium peremptorum vos citamus quantumque compareat' sufficienter et libere coram nobis die Jovis proximo ante festum sancti Augustini ubicumque tunc fuerimus in nostra diocesi super premissis responsuros facturos ulterius et recepturos quod iustitia suadebit. Ad hoc citet' seu citari faciat peremptor' prefatos magistrum Nicholaum et Ricardum quod dictis die et loco sufficienter compareant coram nobis. Magister Nicholaus videlicet super presentatione huiusmodi et consensu admissioni predicti Ricardi prestito; Ricardus vero super iniusta occupatione vicarie huius et aliis se obiciend' ex officio responsuros facturos et recepturos ulterius quod consonum fuerit rationi. Nos super huius executione mandati citra diem certificantes predictum per vestras patentes literas harum seriem continentes. Valete. Datum apud Monketon iiii kalendas Maii pontificatus nostri anno primo.

Margin Heading and text, Scribe 4, as is **110**.

Date The 'feast of St Augustine' poses problems since it is not clear whether it refers to St Augustine of Hippo or St Augustine of Canterbury. Since the main feast day of the former was celebrated on 28 August, and his translation on 11 October, and the latter's main feast day was 26 May (translation 13 September), given the date of the archbishop's letter (28 April 1299), it is likely that Thursday following 26 May 1299, that is 28 May, was intended, but it was also Ascension day that year.

Note Henry of Newark, archbishop of York (15 June 1298–15 August 1299). Nicholas of Wells, canon by 1279 (*Reg. Wickwane*, no. 181A), prebendary of Dunham, d. by 1 March 1312 (*Reg. Greenfield*, i, no. 158 and p. 296), was chancellor to Archbishops Wickwane and Le Romeyn and archdeacon of Northumberland by 1291.

110 *Letters dimissory of Archbishop William [la Zouche] about the sequestration of the revenues of the prebends of Dunham, Rampton and Beckingham, and citing Thomas de Hewell, John de Sandale, canons, and Richard of Normanton, perpetual vicar of Southwell, to appear as proctors of the Chapter to discuss the matter*

Cawood, 14 December 1349

Dimissio archiepiscopi Ebor' facta capitulo Suthwell'

Universis sancte matris ecclesie filiis pateat per presentes quod cum dilecti filii capitulum ecclesie nostre collegiate beate Marie Suthwell' nostre diocesi fuissent coram nobis Willelmo permissione divina Ebor' archiepiscopo Anglia primati apostolice sedis legato super eo quod sequestratur[1] nuper auctoritate nostra ordinaria in fructibus reddi et proventibus prebendarum de Donham, Rampton et Bekyngham \in/ hunc interpositum debuissent temeritate propria violasse ac etiam alia per se et suos ministros attemptasse quod in preiudicium et usurpationem iurisdictionis nostre archiepiscopalis tendere videbatur iudicialiter impetiti. Idem capitulum certis die et loco sibi in hac parte assignatis per discretos viros dominos Thomam de Hewell' et Johannem de Sandale dicte Suthwellen' ecclesie canonicos et Ricardum de Normanton' perpetuum vicarium parochie de Suthwell' procuratores suos sufficientem in hac parte potestatem habentes coram nobis comparuerunt et auditis ac ad plenum discussis rationibus et excusationibus per eosdem procuratores nomine dicti capituli duorum suorum quoad[2] premissa obiecta coram nobis proposit' et allegat' nos idem capitulum ac omnes et singulas personas eiusdem immunes reputavimus in premissis ipsosque ab ulteriori impetitione officii nostri quoad[2] premissa quietos et absolutos dimittimus per presentes quibus sigillum nostrum apponi fecimus in testimonium premissorum. Datum apud Cawode xiiii die mensis Decembris anno domini millesimo ccc quadragesimo nono et pontificatus nostri octavo.

¹ Or *sequestrabatur?* MS reads *sequesten'* ² MS *quo ad*

Note Thomas de Helwell/Holwell, provided to a prebend on 10 August 1342 (*CPL*, iii, 93), prebendary of Beverley (1347–55), *BMF*, 25. John de Sandale, holding prebend of Normanton by 30 July 1318 (*CPL*, ii, 148; *CPR 1317–21*, 194), was a nephew of John de Sandale, bishop of Winchester (1316–19). This is the latest evidence for him at Southwell (cf. also **112**). Richard of Normanton was still perpetual vicar in 1369 (**221**). Three vacant prebends may suggest the impact of the Black Death locally. William of Barnby held Beckingham from at least 1329 to 1361 and William of Retford occupied that of Rampton from 1347 to 1373. The only possible vacancy in 1348–9 was at Dunham, where John of Winwick, prebendary of South Muskham (1347–8), was eventually promoted although firm evidence for him holding the prebend has not been found before 1354 (*CPL*, iii, 241; *CPR 1350–4*, 179, 182, 324; *CPR 1354–8*, 26).

III   *Notarial instrument, drawn up by Edward of York, recording proceedings before the court of the Official of York of a case in which Hugh le Milner, chaplain of Southwell, was accused by Henry of Normanton, chaplain, of defamation; and citing the letters of the Chapter, dated at Southwell, 4 January 1304, appointing Mr William of Thornhaugh as their proctor in the case*   York, 9 January 1304

p. 49   **Instrumentum dimissionis \in causa diffamacionis/ factum per dominum officialem Ebor' domino Hugoni Le Milner capellano ecclesie Suthwell'**

In nomine domini amen. Per presens scriptum publicum instrumentum universis Christi fidelibus pateat evidenter quod cum nono die mensis Januarii sub anno ab incarnatione domini secundum cursum ecclesie Anglicane millesimo ccc^{mo} iii° indictione secunda dominus Hugo le Milner capellanus minister ecclesie Suthwell' Ebor' diocesis et cuidam altari ut asseritur in eadem ecclesia deserviens in divinis coram reverendo domino officio curie Ebor' ad instantiam domini Henrici de Normanton capellani personaliter tunc temporis in iudicio comparentis super petitione eiusdem domini Henrici cuius petitionis tenor dinoscitur esse talis. Coram vobis domine iudex dicit et de iure proponit Henricus de Normanton capellanus contra dominum Hugonem le Milner capellanum et contra quemlibet legitime intervenientem in iudicio pro eodem quod idem Hugo dominum Henricum apud bonos et graves penes quos prius diffamatus non fuerat nequiter diffamavit crimen falsi falso et maliciose inponendo ac etiam dicendo publice et asserendo Dominum Henricum fidem suam violasse per virum excommunicatum irregularem incorrigibilem capitulum Suthwell et canonica mandata eiusdem existere extitisse contemptorem dicti Henrici preiudicium non modicum gravamen unde dicit ipsum in sententiam maioris excommunicationis contra tales in sancta synodo Ebor' provide promulgatam disponabiliter incidisse in qua prestitit animo indurato, que sunt publica et notoria et manifesta in partibus Suthwell' locis et convicinis, ac super hiis in dictis locis laborat publica vox et fama. Quare petit probatis vel in iure confessatis hiis vel eorum aliquo que vel quod sibi debeant seu debeat sufficere in premissis dictum Hugonem sic in sententiam excommunicationis incidisse per vos pronuntiari petit etiam sibi in omnibus iustitie complementum exhiberi. Premissa proponit divisim seu coniunctim actans se tantum ad ea probanda que sibi sufficere poterunt in premissis iuris beneficio in omnibus sibi salvo. Acta. Ex prefixcione dicti domini officii diem ad deliberandum in eadem curia habuisset pro ut nichil notario publico infrascripto[1] per inspectionem actorum iudicialium in eadem curia super huiusmodi negotio habitorum evidentius apparebat. Quidam vero magister Willelmus de Thorhawe clericus procurator venerabilis capituli sancte ecclesie Suthwell' litteratorie constitutus, cuius procuratorium vero, sigillo communis eiusdem venerabilis capituli consignatum, non cancellatum, non abolitum, non abrasum, non vitiatum in aliqua parte sui, vidi palpavi et diligenter examinavi, tenorem continens infrascriptum:

Tenore presentium pateat universis quod nos capitulum ecclesie beate Marie Suthwell' in omnibus causis, negotiis et querelis nos qualitercumque contingentibus coram quibuscumque iudiciis ordinariis delegatis vel quicumque iuris notionem habentibus. Dilectum nobis magistrum Willelmum de Thornhawe clericum procuratorem nostrum facimus ordinamus et constituimus dantes eidem potestatem et mandatum speciale nomine nostro agendi, defendendi, ponendi, propositionibus respondendi, appellandi, appellationem causas prosequendi, transigendi, alium procuratorem substituendi, substitutum revocandi et officium procuratoris reassumendi, in loca et iudices consentiendi, iuramentum de calumpnia et omne illud licitum nomine nostro prestandi ac omnia alia faciendi que mandatum requirunt speciale. Pro eodem vero procuratore et eius substituto rem ratam haberi et iudicatum solvi rerum nostrarum ypoteca exponimus cautiones. Hoc omnibus et singulis quorum interest per presentes significamus. In cuius rei testimonium sigillum nostrum communie presentibus est appensum. Datum apud Suthwell' pridie nonas Januarii, anno domini m° ccc^mo tertio.

Acta. Nomine dictorum dominorum suorum sine scriptis eadem die et loco declinatorie proposuit, allegando quod ecclesia beate Marie Suthwell' et eiusdem ecclesie canonici iure consuetudinario de omnibus eiusdem ministris ecclesie cognitiones primatias sine calumpnia ordinar' cuiuscumque habuerant a tempore cuius memoria non existit et quod ecclesia huiusmodi et canonici eadem usi fuerant hactenus libertate et quod se optulit[2] idem procurator nomine dominorum suorum predictorum eisdem die et loco coram domino offic' memorato in forma iuris legitime probaturum. Demum exceptione huiusmodi declinatoria fori nomine memorate ecclesie Suthwell' et eiusdem venerabilis capituli ut premittitur allegata per eundem dominum officialem audita diligentius et etiam intellecta[3] ac deliberatione[4] cum iurisperitis secum assedentibus habita super ea et hiis que venerabilis in Christo patet dominus [p. 50] Thomas[5] Dei gratia Ebor' archiepiscopus Anglie primas et iurisperiti quam plures alii huiusmodi consuetudine non ignorari[6] ipsi domino . . . offic' exposuerat in hoc facto cum quibus super dicto negotio prius cum effecti tractaverat, ut dicebat, habitoque rescriptu ad dispositionem magistri Thome de

Uffynton clerici ad sancta Dei ewangelia ab eodem super hoc tunc temporis prestito corporaliter iuramento, qui iuratus iudicialiter et super huiusmodi consuetudine diligenter requisitus in premissa omnia deposuit esse vera. Idem dominus offic' dictum dominum Hugonem \le/ Milner capellanum tunc personaliter in iudicio existentem omnesque et singulos dicti venerabilis capituli ministros quoscumque ab eius examine pretextu ecclesie Suthwell' huiusmodi prehibite libertatis. Ex tunc dimisit totaliter per decretum quia tunc temporis sibi facta fuerat ut premittitur plena fides quod dictus dominus Hugo le Milner capellanus minister extitit venerabilis capituli dicte ecclesie Suthwell' et quod primarie cognitiones de ministris suis dicto venerabili capitulo spectabant notorie ut est dictum. Acta fuerunt hec in pleno consistorio dicte ecclesie Ebor', sub anno, die, mense et indictione prenotatis, presentibus domino Willelmo de Jaford,[7] rectore ecclesie de Croft', magistro Johanne de Wodhouse, rectore ecclesie de Burghthorpe Ebor' diocesi, domino Willelmo de Wintringham capellano et Johanne de Sutton clerico testibus ad premissa vocatis specialiter et rogatis.[8]

[*Several lines of space are then left before the final part of the document follows*]

Et ego Edwardus de Ebor' clericus publicus sacrosancte Romane ecclesie autoritate notarius premissis omnibus una cum testibus suprascriptis presens interfui et ea scribere rogatus scripsi et in hanc publicam formam redegi signoque meo solito roboravi, et illud verbum habuerant in vicesima octava linea ante appositionem signi mei inter lineam propria manu mea.

[1] MS as two words   [2] MS *opptulit*   [3] MS *intelecta*   [4] MS *diliberatione*   [5] Rubricator has wrongly assumed this is start of new document and put a big T in blue in the margin, but has then spotted error and tried to erase it   [6] MS *ignari*   [7] MS adds *et*   [8] Followed by what looks like an attempt to imitate a notarial mark

Margin   Heading and text of this item is by Scribe 1, including interpolations; although he continues to supply the text from p. 50, he ceases to supply the rubrics and no *litterae notabiliores* are stroked in red. p. 49, alongside the passage beginning *Acta*, in a ?15th-c. hand, *Nota de cognicionibus primariam causarum*. p. 50 at top of page, probably in same hand, *primarie cogniciones de ministris capituli Suthwell procuratore ad dictam causam*

Note   If Mr John of Woodhouse, rector of Burghthorpe, is the man who was prebendary of Botevant (1339–55), he will have enjoyed a very long career (*Fasti 1300–1541*, vi, 37). He and William of Yafford, rector of Croft on Tees, North Riding Yorks., were already acting together in the service of Archbishop Corbridge in 1302 (*Reg. Corbridge*, i, 13). The latter had been inducted into Croft in November 1300 and was the archbishop's receiver at York by January 1303 (ibid., 247, 286), going on to serve Archbishop Greenfield in the same capacity until 1314 (cf. *Reg. Greenfield*, iii, nos 1222, 1251, 1269, 1334, and iv, passim). Mr Edward of York had been created notary by Archbishop Corbridge on 23 July 1300 (*Reg. Corbridge*, i, 28, no. LXXVI; for his title of Master, see ibid., i, 141–2 no. CCCLXXVIII, 28 November 1303). As 'clerk of the Chapter of York' he received two sums of 40s for providing confirmations of documents to Bolton priory in 1302–3 and 1303–4 (*The Bolton Priory Compotus 1286–1325, together with a priory account roll for 1377–1378*, ed. Ian Kershaw and David Smith, with the assistance of T. N. Cooper (YAS, RS, CLIV, 2000), 152, 169). In 1306, as 'Edward of York, clerk' he had to purge himself of an accusation of theft allegedly committed two years earlier at 'Appeleyheued' in the deanery of Retford along with John de Laughton, clerk, of Morthing (*Reg. Greenfield*, i, nos 379, 382, 388 and 401).

112   *Another copy of* **110** *with the titles written by two separate late*   p. 50
medieval hands different from the main text which is by Scribe 1, **Litera
archiepiscopi de dimissione facta capitulo Suthwell'** (in hand of Scribe
4) *and* **pro Dunham, Rampton et Bekyngham** (in an unidentified medieval hand) *but otherwise few orthographical differences.*

STATUTES OF ARCHBISHOP CORBRIDGE, 113

113   *Statutes issued by Archbishop Thomas Corbridge for the Chapter,
recalling a visitation in February 1301; canons to provide statutes against
neglect of services; two or three canons always to be resident; no order
made by a canon in residence to be revoked by a successor, unless it is
plainly wrong, and then only by a general chapter; in absence of all canons, the church to be entrusted to some discreet person under oath; two
deputies of canons to inspect buildings of canons every other year and
compel repairs; books to be examined by the Precentor, and discordances
corrected; two sides of choir to be balanced evenly; only fit and sufficient
ministers to be admitted; stipends to vicars to be paid more punctually
to prevent them wandering about the country creating disturbances as
previously; no prebend to be leased to canons except by special licence;
perpetual vicars to be instituted in all prebendal churches within a year;
no one is to be presented by letters of the Chapter for ordination or beneficed except after examination before the Chapter; these statutes to be
read after Martyrology in the Chapter House once a month*
                                           Scrooby, 4 June 1302

Statuti domini Thome de Corbryg', Ebor archiepiscopi, capitulo   p. 51
Suthwell'

Thomas, Dei gracia Ebor' archiepiscopus, Anglie primas, dilectis in Christo
filiis capitulo nostre Suthwell' ecclesie salutem, graciam et benedictionem.
Dudum apud vos, videlicet octavo idus Februarii anno gracie m° ccc°
visitacionis officium, pro ut ex pastorali nobis incubuit debito, paternis
affectibus exercentes, quedam comparata personalia, que presentibus non
inserimus pro ut expedire vidimus, coreximus[1] tunc ibidem, et aliqua alia
corectione digna, ut subsequitur, duximus reformanda.
    Statuentes in primis et firmiter inju[n]gentes quod vos canonici, in
quorum absencia nec cultus divinus nec missa gloriose virginis Marie, in
cuius honore prefata fundatur ecclesia, sustentatur congrue, nec corectiones
fiunt in choro seu capitulo debite, de excessibus ministrorum, ad faciendum
residenciam secundum statuta ecclesie, que in admissione vestra observare
iurastis, vos de cetero coaptetis, per statuta vestra specialia, providentes,
quod ne cultus negligatur divinus, aut excessus remaneant incorecti. Sic
de facienda residencia disponatur, quod [de] omni tempore anni, tres, vel
ad minus, duo canonici sint in ecclesia residentes, qui capitulum celebrent,
ipsius que negocia consulte dirigant et pertractent.
    Et si contingat ipsos, dum sic presint capitulo, aliquid diffinire, illud
succedentibus sibi futuris residentibus canonicis non liceat revocare, nisi id

errorem contineat manifestum, et tunc ob hoc facta speciali convocacione confratrum per commune consilium decidatur, et postmodum pro ut iustum fuerit, racionabiliter emendetur.

Quod si forsan, ex causa inevitabili et legitima, licencia a nobis optenta, ad tempus, nullum contingat canonicum residere, committatur alicui discreto iurato regimen ecclesie, quouscunque canonici ad faciendum residenciam revertantur.

Item, volumus et districte precipiendo mandamus, quod alternis annis ad minus, per duos discresciores de capitulo, per vos communiter eligendos, canonicorum omnium, tam presencium quam absencium, edificia subic[i]antur oculis[2] diligenter, et defectus comperti, quam cicius per predictos duos electos vobis constare poterit, de eisdem, infra annum ex tunc iuxta qualitatem et quantitatem ipsorum, congrue reparentur. Ad quos omnes, quos principaliter huius[modi] defectus contingunt, sine accepcione qualibet personarum, per sequestrum in prebendis suis arcius interponendum, et in reparacionem defectum huiusmodi, si opus fuerit, convertendum premissa monicione canonica compellatis.

Omnes libri saltem notati bene examinentur per precentorem, vel eius vicem gerentem, ne sibi invicem contrarientur, vel discordent in nota. Et de choro eciam et cantoribus talia disponantur, quod non claudicet in psallendo, una parte eiusdem[3] altera[4] in numerum prevalente, et iuxta discrecionem vestram equaliter pocius dividatur.

Item, cum non umquam confusionum pareat multitudo, statuimus quod nisi apti, necessarii, et qui sufficiant, in ecclesiam recipiantur ministri, quibus solito promcius de suis stipendiis satisfaciatur, ne pro defectu huius[modi], obsequio divino, ad quod tenentur cotidie, et in quo vigiles et assidui esse debent, neglecto in vestrum et ecclesie scandalum, ad suscitandum iurgia, ut solebant, in patria vagari cogantur. Si quis vero de canonicis, statutis terminis, eisdem ministris sua stipendia solvere tardaverit, omni die quo a solucione cessaverit, ad duplum salarii communis et soliti, quo usque satisfacerit, teneatur.

Preterea inhibemus, ne alicui quam canonico prebenda de cetero dimittatur ad firmam, sine[5] capituli licencia speciali.

Statuentes, quod in singulis ecclesiis vestris parochialibus, sive sint prebendate sive prebendis anexe, habeatis infra hunc annum, a data presencium computandum, perpetuos vicarios institutos qui curam habeant animarum. Alioquin in vestri defectu ex ordinare proponimus de eisdem, sicut viderimus expedire. Et providentur in huius[modi] ecclesiis de libris sufficientibus, et aliis necessariis ornamentis, ne manus, ad hoc vobis negligentibus, apponere compellamur.

Omnes[6] autem presbiteri, pro defunctis in Suwellensi ecclesia celebrantes, ante horam celebrent magne misse, ne postquam incepta fuerit existentes in choro impediant sicut solent.

Nulli omnino ad ordines per literam capituli amodo presententur, aut ad vicarias vacantes in chori vel extra aliqualiter admittantur, nisi qui, examinacione coram capitulo prehabita diligenti, digni inventi fuerint, et diucius in ecclesia laudabiliter conversati.

Nullus[7] vicarius aut minister ecclesie de negociacionibus aut contractibus, de quibus scandalum umoriri poterit, de cetero intromittere se presumat; ceterum provideatis vobis de sufficienti et ydoneo cicius quo poteritis auditore, sicut vos habere nolumus aliqualiter sicut nec decet aut expedit conjugatum.

Hec nostra statuta salubria, correctiones et injuncta, plene et distincte, singulis mensibus semel ad minus, in capitulo post lectum martilogium, ut dum singulorum inprimitur cordibus, fructus perveniat placidus, in virtute obediencie perlegi, et observare per omnia faciatis, quousque ad vos nos contingat alias declinare, et tunc cognito plenius statu ecclesie possimus, si opus fuerit, aliqua addere vel mutare, *scituri*[8] *quod transgressores, si qui fuerint in premissis, reliquere nolumus secundum sua demerita canonice impunitos.* Valete. Datum apud Scroby, pridie nona Junii anno gracie m° ccc° secundo, pontificatus nostri tercio.

[1] The scribe here spells *corrigere, correctio* and variants as *corigere, corectio*; thus *coreximus* does not mean 'we ruled jointly' but 'we corrected'   [2] *occlis*   [3] Followed by *quam* struck out   [4] *m* struck out   [5] Followed by the erasure of an illegible word   [6.]
[7 & 8] Clauses in italics added from the copy in Corbridge's Register (see Note below)

Margin   There are at least eight notes in the left margin, most in late medieval or early modern hands alongside relevant clauses: *de residencia canonicorum*; *reservatum de duobus residentibus canonicis ... non est ...*; *pro reparacione domorum*; *nota de ... precentore*; *ministri non apti non sunt recipiendi*; illegible; *nota vicariorum examinaciones ... ad capitulum*; *statuta debent legi.*

Note   Pd. in *Visitations*, 212–15 after this copy; the version in *Reg. Corbridge*, ii, 14, no. DCCCXLVI is dated at Scrooby, 2 June 1302, with the note that they were delivered during a visitation. This had taken place on 6 February 1301. Besides minor orthographical differences, this enrolled version has three further clauses added at 6, 7 and 8 above. There are several later copies including NA, SC 1/2/1, a single sheet of parchment in an otherwise unidentified fifteenth-century hand, with a partial copy of 1, Alexander III's bull of 28 July 1171 in a different hand on the other side, while SC 1/2/2, 3 and 8 provide late sixteenth- and seventeenth-century copies, and SC 1/2/10–13, copies of a printed nineteenth-century edition, probably all after the White Book copy. The archbishop issued almost identical statutes for Beverley at Scrooby on 5 June (*Reg. Corbridge*, ii, no. DCCCXLVII). He had also issued a short set of statutes around 1300 which are not found in the White Book (*Visitations*, 212, probably after the copies in NA, SC 1/2/2 or SC 1/2/3).

Statutes of Archbishop Le Romeyn, 114

114   *Statutes of Archbishop John Le Romeyn for the Chapter following a visitation: vicars and clerks not to laugh or talk in choir, on pain of expulsion for repeated offences; Sacrist to sleep in church and ring bells at proper times; door-keepers to be under him; women, unsuspect relations excepted, to be removed from vicars' houses; benefices within the Minster should be conferred by at least three canons; benefices outside the Minster to be given by the whole chapter; the great seal to be under seals of three canons, and seal for citations under the seal of one canon; muniments not to be shown, except in Chapter; music books to be made concordant; prebends not to be let to laymen; canons to pay their vicars £3 a year regularly, as they are burdened by having to share oblations* *and obits with the vicars of two newly created prebends; every canon to have a proxy; perpetual vicars to be established in all prebendal churches before the next visitation; houses of alien canons to be repaired within a year, on pain of heavy fine for fabric of the new Chapter House; successive residentiaries not to give contradictory orders*

Southwell, 12–13 January 1294

p. 52

Statuta Johannis archiepiscopi

Johannes, permissione divina Ebor' archiepiscopus, Anglie primas, dilectis[1] in Christo filiis, capitulo nostro Suthwell', salutem, graciam et benedictionem. Hesterna die martis proxima post festum epiphanie domini, anno gracie m° cc° nonagesimo tercio apud vos, ad recreacionem animarum vestrarum, visitacionis officium paternis affectibus exercentes, ea que tunc corectione digna reperimus, reformavimus in hunc modum:

In primis, itaque firmiter vobis iniungendo, mandamus et precipimus quod vicarii et clerici se a confabulacionibus et risu in choro, maxime ubi divino iugiter intendere tenentur obsequio, de cetero abstineant, et si, per capitulum moniti et corepti, id facere neglexerint, a choro protinus expellantur.

Item, sacrista iaceat infra ecclesiam et secundum orlogium debitis pulset horis.

Item, clerici, ad servanda ostia ecclesie deputati, coripiantur per ipsum, et, nisi ei obedierint, alias que se honeste habuerint, ipsos amoveri volumus per eundem.

Amoveantur mulieres a domibus vicariorum, personis conjunctis que omni careant suspicione exceptis, sub pena substractionis stipendiorum et privacionis officiorum et beneficiorum suorum, si eorum pertinacia id exposcat.

Item, de consensu omnium vestrum tunc presencium statuimus et decernimus statuendo, quo[d] de cetero beneficia interiora ecclesie per tres ad minus canonicos, qui comodius haberi poterunt, conferantur. Pro exterioribus autem conferendis beneficiis[2] qui in ecclesia plus laboraverunt preferantur, et si secus actum fuerit, viribus careat huiusmodi collacio et effectu.

Item, sigillum magnum sub sigillis trium canonicorum, et parvum ad citaciones, sub sigillo unius canonici habeantur.

Munimenta qui contingunt ecclesiam non exhibeantur alicubi de cetero, nisi coram fratribus in capitulo, vel eciam instrumenta.

Fiant grad[u]alia, processionaria et troporia concordancia citra visitacionem nostram proximam, sub pena centum solidorum, quos a nobis levari mandabimus, si fuerit secus actum.

Quo ad dimittendum prebendas ad firmam, uti poteritis sicut hactenus fieri consuevit, proviso quod laicis de cetero nullatenus dimittantur, sub pena contravenientibus graviter infligenda.

Statuimus eciam ordinando quod singuli canonici suis, absque contradictione, solvant vicariis, ad re\le/velacionem[3] vicariorum ipsorum, qui per duos vicarios iam pro duabus prebendis de novo creatos dum in percepcione oblacionum et obituum concurrunt, cum aliis nimis gravantur, sexaginta solidos annuatim, et ad hoc per vos capitulum districtius compellantur, vobis firmiter iniungentes quod si qui apparuerint forsan[4] canonici, vel procuratores ipsorum, qui huiusmodi solvere stipendia statutis terminis neglexerint, ipsos, scilicet tam presentes quam absentes, ad id per omnes vias, quibus de iuris rigore poteritis compellatis.

Item, quilibet absens canonicus procuratorem sufficientem habeat qui capitulo terminis, ad quod per vos absens quilibet compellantur.

Statuimus eciam et decernimus statuendo, quod in omnibus ecclesiis parochialibus prebendis anexis, citra primam visitacionem nostram, ordinetur et fiant vicarii perpetui, qui curam habeant animarum in eisdem. Alioquin ex tunc ordinabimus in causa vestre negligencie de eisdem.

Domus alienigenarum canonicorum minantes ruinam, infra annum reparentur debite, ad quarum reparacionem ipsos per vos compelli volumus, et mandamus sub gravi pena per vos capitulum iuxta defectus taxanda, que ad fabricam novi capituli deputetur.

De cetero, caveant residentes canonici, quod nullus eorum succedens alii residendo, mandatum scribat, illi contrarium quod ad precedentem suum residentem canonicum, nomine capituli, emanavit, sed antequam scribat, circumspecte deliberet, ne super scriptura sua redargui valeat, sicut contigit aliquando.

Hoc supradicta omnia apud vos in virtute obediencie precipimus observari. Datum Suthwell', die mercurii in octavo epiphanie anno gracie supradicto et pontificatus nostri octavo.

[1] Followed by *Capitulo* struck out   [2] A small passage omitted here according to the copy in *Reg. Romeyn*, ii, no. 1186, probably through homeoteleuton by the Southwell clerk: ... *fiat fratrum convocacio consueta, collacionibus quibuslibet factis hactenus in suo robore duraturis; volentes quod secundum statutum vestri capituli in conferendis beneficiis* (then as text above)   [3] The scribe clearly intended to correct *revelacionem* to *relevationem* but has not made a very good job of it   [4] MS *forsay*

Margin   Title in different hand (Scribe 4) from main text. As with **113** at least nine notes appear in right margin alongside appropriate clauses all, apart from one, in a mixture of medieval hands: *nota de confabulacione in choro*; *nota de Sacrista*; *nota de mulieribus suspectis*; *nota de beneficiis interioribus et exterioribus*; *nota pro collacione beneficiorum*; *nota de sigillis*; *Munimenta non exhibeantur* (early modern hand); *nota de lx solidis pro vicariis etc.*; *nota quod quilibet canonicus absens tenetur constituere procuratorem ad respondendum capitulo.*

Note   Pd. in *Visitations*, 210–12 after **114** and cf. *Reg. Romeyn*, ii, no. 1186 for the copy in the archbishop's register. Dickinson, *Southwell* (1819), 360–1 for an earlier edition. As with Corbridge's statutes of 1302 (**113**), several later copies survive in NA, SC 1/2/2, 3 and 8, and the printed edition in nos 10–13, which we have not attempted to collate since they all appear to derive from the White Book copy. The provision whereby fines levied for failure to repair canons' houses should be used for the fabric of the new Chapter House, alongside a similar order of 25 January 1288 (*Reg. Romeyn*, i, no. 1058) and the fines levied for arrears from the prebendaries of North Muskham, South Muskham, Beckingham, Oxton I and Oxton II and Rampton on 11 September 1290 (ibid., no. 1110), is the most significant surviving documentary evidence for dating the work that produced 'a building which contains the most brilliant achievements of late 13th century sculpture' (ibid., 1058n).

115   *Letters of John [Le Romeyn], archbishop of York, determining that*
revenues coming from the tithes of sheaves and hay at Upton, which had
previously been enjoyed by three prebendaries, should be used to augment
the common fund of residentiaries   Southwell, 20 October 1291

p. 53   **Ordinatio firme de Uptun commune residentium**

Universis sancte matris ecclesie filiis ad quorum notitiam pervenerit
hec scriptura Johannes permissione divina Ebor' archiepiscopus Anglie
primas subscripta ad perpetuam memoriam eorundem. Considerationis
nostre intuitus qui est et erit erga subditos deo propitio semper pius in
eos presertim oculos[1] dirigit benevolos[2] quos bene meritos conspicimus
et divinis obsequiis laudabiliter intendentes, inter quos capitulum nostre
ecclesie Suthwell' affectione sincerrima[3] intuemur quod in canonicis
collegii eiusdem collegiate ecclesie habet ab antiquo in ipsa ecclesia
residentiam ordinatam qui quidem canonici in eadem ecclesia libenter et
devote resident quamquam communes[4] redditus seu proventus residentium
usibus deputatis pauci fuerint et exiles. Cupientes itaque statum dictorum
capituli et canonicorum oportuna subventione favorabiliter relevare ut
iidem canonici et eorum successores ad divini cultus augmentum et
honorem sanctissime virginis matris sue que prefate ecclesie patrona
specialis existit eo pronius excitentur quo ipsis residentibus proventus
accreverint pinguiores[5] ad meram et spontaneam submissionem dilectorum
filiorum magistri Johannis Clarell per magistrum Benedictum de Halum
canonicum Suthwell procuratorem suum legitimum eius nomine dominorum
Willelmi de Retherfeud' et Ricardi de Bamfeud' dicte ecclesie Suthwell'
canonicorum congrua deliberatione habita cum partibus[6] accedente Ebor'
et Suthwell capitulorum nostrorum assensu et voluntate expressa dictorum
nominatorum canonicorum sic[7] in dei nomine duximus ordinandum.
Ordinamus siquidem et decernimus ordinando quod portiones garbarum
et feni in parochia de Upton iuxta Suthwell' ad prebendas prefatorum
magistri Johannis Clarell et Willelmi de Retherfeud[8] et Ricardi de Bamfeud[9]
in dicta ecclesia Suthwell' pertinentes que hactenus consueverint ad
ipsas pertinente prebendas quas portiones a dictis prebendis per hanc
nostram ordinationem separavimus auctoritate pontificali et dividimus
ad communam seu communes[4] usus prefatorum capituli et canonicorum
residentium perpetuis ex tunc temporibus pertineant atque spectent
quas ad eorum communam et communes usus perpetuo assignamus
ipsorum capituli et canonicorum residentium sicut de bonis eorum
communibus per predecessores nostros antiquitus ordinatum extitit ac
secundum eiusdem ecclesie consuetudinem communibus usibus de cetero
profuturas. In quarum portionum corporalem possessionem capitulum et
canonicos predictos huius auctoritate ordinationis plenarie inducimus et
decreti. In cuius rei testimonium sigillum nostrum una cum predictorum
capitulorum nostrorum sigillis presentibus est appensum. Actum et datum
in capitulo Suthwell' ecclesie xiii kalendas Novembris, anno gratie m^mo
cc^mo nonagesimo primo et pontificatus nostri sexto.

¹ MS *occlo's*   ² MS *benivolos*   ³ MS *sincerima*   ⁴ MS *communies*   ⁵ corr. from *pinnguiores*   ⁶ MS *par'tis*   ⁷ MS *sicut* with final two letters expunged   ⁸ MS *Retherfuend'*   ⁹ MS *Bamfend'*

Margin   Title in different 15ᵗʰ-c. hand (Scribe 4) from text which is by Scribe 1.

Note   NA, SC 7/1/5, f. 3ʳ⁻ᵛ for another fifteenth-century copy. Pd. in *Mon. Ang.*, vi, pt iii, 1315 (xii) after an inspeximus of Edward III, Pat. 9 E III, part 2 m. 8, 14 Dec. 1335 = TNA C 66/186; Pd. in *CPR 1334–8*, 187 and **116**. Mr John Clarell, prebendary of Norwell Overhall (1256–95). Mr Benedict of Halam, canon since at least 1286 (**574**) and named the first prebendary of North Leverton on 24 Oct. 1291 (**41**). Mr William of Rotherfield, canon since at least 1257 (**192**) and prebendary of Beckingham when it was divided from the new prebend of North Leverton. Richard de Bamfield, prebendary of Norwell Tertia Pars (*c.* 1287–*c.* 1302/4). This new arrangement was clearly part of the archbishop's re-ordering of life at Southwell following the creation of the two new prebends which brought the strength of the Chapter up to sixteen prebendaries at which it would remain until its abolition in 1841.

116   *Ratification by Edward III of letters of Archbishop John Le Romeyn, Southwell, 20 October 1291 (115), relating to the provisions made for support of the canons*   Auckland (Co. Durham), 14 December 1335

Ratificatio regis Edwardi super ordinacione et confirmacione proximis prescriptis   p. 54

Edwardus, Dei [gratia] rex Anglie, dominus Hybernie et dux Aquitannie, omnibus ad quos presentes litere pervenerint, salutem. Inspeximus literas patentes Johannis nuper archiepiscopi Ebor' in hec verba: *text as* **115**

Nos autem ordinacionem, separacionem, divisionem et decretum predicta rata habentes et grata ea pro [nobis]¹ et heredibus nostris quantum in nobis est concedimus et confirmamus sicut litere predicte racionabiliter testantur. In cuius rei testimonium has literas nostras fieri fecimus patentes. Teste me ipso apud Aukesland quartodecimo die mensis Decembris anno regni nostri nono.   per ipsum regem ad instanciam Henrici Edenstowe.²

¹ Supplied by different hand in margin   ² *per . . . Edenstowe* added in later medieval hand

Note   Pd. in *Mon. Ang.*, vi, pt iii, 1315 after an enrollment in Patent Roll, 9 Ed. III, part 2, m. 8 (TNA C 66/186; Pd. in *CPR 1334–8*, 187). Edward III was returning from a major, but largely unsuccessful, expedition to Scotland, which he had invaded in July 1335; on 26 November he was at Newcastle (Ranald Nicholson, *Edward III and the Scots. The Formative Years of a Military Career 1327 to 1335* (Oxford 1965), 203–36, 244). Henry of Edwinstowe, king's clerk, keeper of the Great Seal in 1332 (*CPR 1327–30*, 201; Tout, *Chapters*, vi, 12), prebendary of Oxton II since 13 May 1327 (*Reg. Melton*, iv, no. 440 and v, no. 228).

KIRKLINGTON, 117–19

p. 55
Kirtlington capella

117 *Quitclaim by John, son of Thomas de Bella Aqua, to the Chapter of all his rights in the advowson of the chapel of Kirklington*

[1286 × 1301]

Omnibus sancte matris ecclesie filiis hoc scriptum visuris vel audituris Johannes filius Thome de Bella Aqua salutem in domino sempiternam. Noverit universitas vestra me pro salute anime mee et animarum tam antecessorum quam successorum meorum me concessisse[1] confirmasse pro me et heredibus meis in perpetuum totum ius et clamium quod habui vel aliqua ratione habere potui Deo beate Marie et capitulo Suthwell' in advocatione capelle de Kirtlington'. Ita quod nec ego nec heredes mei poterimus de cetero aliquem ad ipsam capellam presentare aut aliquid iuris vel clamii in ipsa vendicare. Et si contingat quod ego Iohannes vel heredes mei aliquem ad dictam capellam presenteremus vel litem contra dictum capitulum super advocatione dicte capelle de cetero moveamus vel in terris tenementis et libertatibus ad ipsam capellam pertinentibus eidem capitulo omnes expensas quas circa ipsius litem et defensionem imposuerint[2] secundum arbitrium dicti capituli refundemus. Et ego Iohannes et heredes mei predicta ius clamium et confirmationem dicto capitulo contra omnes gentes inperpetuum warantizabimus. In cuius rei testimonium presens scriptum sigillo meo roboravi. Hiis testibus: Ricardo de Sutton, Roberto de Weston', Ricardo de Marnam et aliis.

[1] MS omits *et*   [2] MS *inposuerint*

Margin   Page heading in 17th-c. hand; main text Scribe 1, but without rubric as are **118–28a**.

Date   After Richard of Sutton had come of age (*Rufford*, 868) and before the death of John de Bella Aqua, unless Richard of Marnham is to be identified as the man instituted to Lambley on 24 September 1295 (*Reg. Romeyn*, i, 330).

Note   The perfect infinitive *quietum clamasse* would appear to have been omitted. John de Bella Aqua had succeeded his father Thomas by 1272 (**412n**). On 18 January 1298 he made homage for Kirklington, Normanton and Burn (Yorks.) and for one fee in Kirklington and Normanton and a half fee in Burn to Archbishop Corbridge, 18 July 1300 (*Reg. Romeyn*, ii, 254; *Kirkby's Inquest*, 399, 403). He died shortly before 18 August 1301 (*CIPM*, iv, no. 45). He married Laderana or Laderina, fourth and youngest sister and co-heiress of Peter III de Brus died 1272 (Sanders, *English Baronies*, 78; *Kirkby's Inquest*, 219n; *Yorkshire Inquisitions*, ed. Brown, 139, 147–9). She died (*c.* 1276) giving birth to her youngest daughter Joan. Her heirs were her two daughters: Isabel, wife of Miles of Stapleton and, she having died before 1301, her heir was her son Nicholas aged fifteen years in 1301, and Joan aged twenty-four years in 1301 and wife of Aucher son of Henry (*CIPM*, iv, no. 45). John de Bella Aqua married secondly Isabel and they had a son William. On 30 December 1301 Archbishop Corbridge granted the lands of John de Bella Aqua's heir and his marriage to William le Vavasour and on 17 November 1302 Corbridge granted seisin of Kirklington to Isabel to hold as her dower (*Kirkby's Inquest*, 424–5). Isabel acquired her son's marriage for 200 marks which she granted to William her son. On 2 November 1309 William quitclaimed to her for her life all his father's lands in Kirklington, Hockerton, Roe Wood (Hockerton), Middlethorpe and Earlshaw (both Caunton, Notts.) and Swinton, Rawmarsh and Wildthorpe (Yorks. W.R.). In return Isabel granted William his reasonable estovers, two robes per annum, fodder for two horses and two boys, and 40s per annum for the boys' robes. On 17 July 1309 Isabel made homage to Archbishop Greenfield, witnessed by Mr William of Pickering, archdeacon of Nottingham, and Richard of Whatton, bailiff of Southwell (*Kirkby's Inquest*, 424–7). On 7 September 1309 William de Bella Aqua, son and heir of John, made homage for his father's lands but he was uncertain as to what these were and Archbishop Greenfield ordered an inquiry to be made (*Kirkby's Inquest*, 409). This is the only occurrence of Sir Robert of Weston and Sir Richard of Marnham as witnesses in the White Book. Richard of Marnham witnessed a late thirteenth-century charter to Blyth Priory (*Blyth*, 520).

118   *Quitclaim by Adam de Bella Aqua to the Chapter of all his rights in the advowson of the chapel of Kirklington*   [1215 × 1221]

Omnibus sancte matris ecclesie filiis hoc scriptum visuris vel audituris Adam de Bella Aqua eternam in domino salutem. Noverit universitas vestra me intuitu Dei et pro salute anime mee et pro animabus antecessorum meorum concessisse et quietum clamasse de me et heredibus meis inperpetuum Deo et beate Marie et capitulo Suthwell' totum ius quod habui in advocatione capelle de Kirtlington', ita quod nec ego nec heredes mei de cetero aliquem ad ipsam capellam presentare aut aliquid iuris in ea vendicare. Et ut hec mea concessio rata sit in posterum et inconcussa presenti carte mee sigillum meum apposui. Hiis testibus: magistro Stephano de Lexinton, Willelmo de Marcam, Thoma de Anneslay et aliis.

Date   After Mr Stephen of Laxton, the future abbot of Clairvaux, was appointed prebendary of Oxton I by King John on 23 May 1215, and before he entered Quarr abbey after his flight from the schools in Oxford *c*. 1221 (cf. *ODNB*).

Note   For Adam de Bella Aqua see **309n**. William of Markham is probably the future canon and prebendary of South Muskham by 31 May 1228 (*Reg. Gray*, 24). Thomas of Annesley witnessed a charter of Reginald II of Annesley in 1241 (*Thurgarton*, 1165, and see 1160n for an important discussion of the various branches of the family).

119   *Agreement between the Chapter and William de Bella Aqua concerning the chapel of Kirklington following a dispute over the nomination of the parson who is to serve it, and stipulating an annual payment of 30s by the Chapter*   [*c*. 1191 × 1196]

Hec conventio est inter capitulum de Suthwella et Willelmum de Bella Aqua de capella de Kyrtlington' de qua ipse Willelmus ei litem movebat quod post decessum vel recessum eius qui inito[1] huius conventionis[2] eam possidebat unam tantum personam quam ipse vel aliquis ex heredibus suis eis[3] optulerit proximo loco post decessum et recessum predictum recipiet, et prefatam capellam eidem ab eodem capitulo et tota iura sua tenendam pro triginta solidis annuatim nomine pensionis reddendis assignabit. Post decessum autem eius qui ad presentationem predicti Willelmi vel alicuius ex heredibus suis in predicta capella admissus fuerit liberum erit eidem capitulo de cetero de predicta capella pro arbitrio suo disponere. Nec deinceps sepedictus[4] Willelmus vel heredes sui aliquam querelam sepedicto[4] capitulo poterunt movere. Pensio autem supradicta triginta solidorum debet duobus terminis persolvi, medietas infra octabas sancti Martini et medietas infra octabas Pentecosten. Hiis testibus: A. abbate de Welbek, Galfrido et Matheo canonicis eiusdem, R. de Karlent', magistro Lisiardo, Alexandro capellano et multis aliis.

¹ MS *sic* ² After correction, MS ³ MS *eit* ⁴ As two words, MS

Margin *Kirtlington capella*, 17ᵗʰ c.

Date After Mr Lisiard de Musters became a canon of York (*Fasti 1066–1330*, vi, 6) and before the death of William de Bella Aqua.

Note Mr Lisiard de Musters also witnessed **74**. Adam, abbot of Welbeck *c.* 1180–97 (*HRH*, i, 198). William de Bella Aqua was probably the son of Robert de Bella Aqua who, with Pain de Bella Aqua (*Belewe*), witnessed (1146–54) a notification to Rufford abbey (*Rufford*, 319). Robert de Bella Aqua witnessed five other charters to Rufford in the period 1146–53 (*Rufford*, 180, 198, 201, 203, 668). He may have been the son or grandson of Robert de Bella Aqua who, in the time of Archbishop Thomas I (1070–1100), granted (1078–87) to Selby abbey lands in Monk Fryston, Hillam and Little Selby (Yorks.). In a confirmation of Archbishop Thomas II (1109–14) to Selby, Robert had granted a half-carucate in Hillam (*EYC*, i, 49–50; *Selby Coucher*, i, 292; *EEA York 1070–1154*, no. 20). William de Bella Aqua held one and a quarter fees of the archbishop of York in 1166 which probably comprised the vill of Kirklington, parts of the soke of Southwell and Burn (Yorks). He married an unnamed daughter of John, 4th baron Deyncourt, perhaps Beatrix (**307, 309n**), with whom he received land in Creswell (Derbys.), Sutton in Granby and Hockerton, although he already held a half-fee of old feoffment of Walter, 3rd baron Deyncourt in 1166 prior to his marriage (*Thurgarton*, xlv, lxxix). Although William witnessed a number of grants to Rufford he was not a prolific monastic patron, making only one grant to Rufford (*Rufford*, 189) and none to the Deyncourt foundation of Thurgarton priory. He died in 1196 (*PR 8 Richard I*, 189) and his heir was Adam, probably his grandson (**309n**). He seems to have had two other sons: Ralph (**308**) and Thomas de Bella Aqua of Stallingborough (**416n**).

PARISH ALTAR, 120–6

p. 56 **Depositiones et processus super oblationibus**

120 *Testimony of Sir Robert Brun about oblations collected on various altars at Southwell* [*c.* 1259]

Dominus Robertus Brun iuratus requisitus an parochiani ecclesie Suthwell' communiter solebant diebus natalis domini, Pasce, Pentecosten et omnium sanctorum accedere et offerre ad altare maius Suthwell' dicit se nil scire. Quod an altare \de/ parochia solebant communiter offerre dicit quod suo tempore recepit uno anno die natalis domini xxii denarios et anno sequenti xxvi denarios et tertio anno triginta et sub illo anno quando primo archiepiscopus Walterus statuit ne darentur decima de stipendiis mercenariis sed colecent¹ ecclesie oblationibus eorundem. Requisitus autem ut \m/² idem decime offerent³ ibi vel aliter ex devotione dicit quod se nescire de die Pasce. Requisitus dicit quod inhibitum fuit ad altare de parochia suis temporibus ne alicui coniugati sive terram tenentes ibidem offerent vel in posterum⁴ fecit prohibitionem ad mandatum ecclesie et missus fuit clericus quod propter illos qui non poterant expectare altam missam qui stetit iuxta ipsum altare et quando venerint tales coniugati scilicet[5] vel[6] tenentes recepit eorum oblationem et reportavit ad maius altare et ipse recepit residuum nec unquam fuerat ab eo petitum.

[1] MS *sic* for *colligent* or some form of *collect-*? The first of several odd readings in the Latin of this entry   [2] MS *sic*, though it might be better as *si* since a question is being asked   [3] Should this read *offerentur*?   [4] The reading *vel in posterum* is uncertain   [5] MS *silicet*   [6] MS adds *non* but expunges

Margin   Page heading in 17th/18th-c. hand. In right margin alongside the head of the text: *Nota de questione an parochiani Ecclesie Suthwell pocius tenentur ad maius altare vel ad altare parochiale* (15th-c. hand).

Date   This and further testimony in **121–3** was presumably collected after the appointment of Sir Robert, *c*. 27 January 1259 (**125**), to gather evidence in the case of the custodians of the Commons against Henry de Mora over the collection and distribution of oblations.

Note   A Robert Brun, chaplain, occurs as a witness *c*. 1275 (**421, 423**). Archbishop Gray's first surviving regulations for the common fund and other financial matters were issued in 1225 (**102**).

121   *Testimony of Sir William the parson about oblations collected at various altars at Southwell*   [*c*. 1259]

Dominus Willelmus dictus persona iuratus et diligenter examinatus dicit quod parochiani ecclesie Suthwell' solebant communiter venire diebus natalis domini, Pasce et Pentecosten et omnium sanctorum ad maius altare ecclesie Suthwell' et ibi facere oblationes suas diebus tamen Pasce mercatores et mercenarii et alii minores ad altare de parochia decimas et oblationes dederunt et omnes alios et etiam aliquando mercatores vidit ea die ad maius altare offerre; dicit etiam quod hoc vidit sex annos et amplius triginta annis elapsis et amplius et sit semper postmodum fuit. Dicit etiam quod ad altare de parochia nullus offerebat nisi in die pasce nisi forte aliquando ex gratia fieret vel quia altam missam expectare nollet aliquis nec aliter fieri deberet nec fieri aliter consuevit. Dicit etiam vehementer quod credit quod illi qui ibi offerrunt et obtulerunt. Hoc faciunt et fecerunt quia molestum est eis altam missam expectare et tunc offerre. Dicit etiam quod ad altare \de/ parochia consueverunt presbiteri de eodem altari propter oblationes[1] laborantes et transeuntes summo mane dominicis diebus et aliis novem lectionum matutinas ibidem solempniter cantare et missam ita quod extranei et alii omnibus diebus quanti in aurora missam ibidem poterunt audire et postmodum dietam suam facere libere quod modo omnino dimittitur post adventum domini Henrici.

[1] MS expunges

Date   As **120** and **125**.

Note   William is identified as William of Averham in **123**. As **125** shows 'Sir Henry' is Henry de Mora, who first witnessed charters before May 1230 (**399, 412**), parson of Eakring (*Rufford*, 11, 36–7, 40, 596, 773 and 798), canon by 1249 (**349**) and still in office after January 1261 (**58**).

122 *Testimony of Sir Thomas the Sacristan about the collection of oblations at Southwell* [*c.* 1259]

Dominus Thomas dictus sacrista iuratus et diligenter examinatus dicit quod parochiani ecclesie Suthwell' omnes diebus natalis domini, Pasce et Pentecosten et omnium sanctorum consueverunt communiter venire ad maius altare et ibi offerre et nullus suis temporibus venit ad altare de parochia ad offerend' nisi iuvenes non coniugati et non tenentes terram qui diebus Pasce ibidem offerebant[1] et non alii. Queritur si viderit umquam diebus natalis domini, Pentecosten et omnium sanctorum aliquis ibidem offerre dicit quod sic sed paucos et credit quod propter paucitatem eorum et parvitatem oblationis tunc temporis mentio de eo non fiebat. Dicit etiam de pauperibus coniugatis et mendiciis non fiebat vis ubi offerrent diebus Pasce. Sed postmodum audivit solempniter in pulpito prohiberi ne alibi quam ad maius altare accederent aliqui parochiani ad offerendum[2] diebus predictis nec alibi admittentur et credit quod tempore pascali facta fuit inhibitio et quod vehementer credit quod illi qui ibi offerrunt hoc faciunt propter tedium expectandi altam missam et ibidem offerre. Dicit etiam quod miratur unde provenit quod tot modo offerrunt ad altare de parochia quia non consuevit sic fieri. Dubitat quin sinistra exhortatio hoc operetur. Queritur si viderit umquam aliquem vel aliquos ad altare de parochia missos ad oblationem nomine maioris altaris ibidem recipiend' qui oblationem ibi a parochianis factam reciperet et ministris ecclesie defferrent dicit se non recolere. De officiis vero altaris de parochia idem dicit quod dominus W. persona.

[1] MS *offerrebant*   [2] MS *offerrendum*

Date As 120 and 125.

123 *Testimony of Sir Richard Bateman, chaplain, over the collection of oblations at Southwell* [*c.* 1259]

p. 57   Dominus Ricardus Bateman capellanus iuratus et dicit erat concordiam cum domino Willelmo de Egru'. Dicit tamen se vidisse clericos missos ad altare de parochia ad oblationem ibi factam a parochianis ecclesie de Suthwell' recipiendam reportare ipsam oblationem set satis notorium est quod reportaverunt sed quantum nescit.

Date As 120 and 125.

124 *Memorandum recording the appearance in St Mary's, Southwell, on 27 January 1258/9, of Simon and Thomas, proctors or custodians for the Commons, testifying that all parochial oblations were brought to the main altar where they were ceded to the common fund, namely on the four feasts of Christmas, Easter, Pentecost and All Saints, except that at Easter the priest of the parish received income from single people not holding land not owing oblations, and that Henry the parish priest had, despite prohibition, often received oblations at that altar, resulting in a loss of one mark to the common fund; they petition for Henry to make restitution*   Southwell, 27 January 1259

Memorandum quod vi kalendas Februarii anno domini m° cc^mo l viii°
comparuerunt in ecclesia beate Marie Suthwell' domini Symon et Thomas
procuratores sive custodes communie ecclesie predicte proponentes
sub hac forma. Nos procuratores sive custodes communie sancte Marie
Suthwell' proponimus et dicimus quod omnes oblationes parochianorum
illam ecclesiam communiter frequentantium a longo retro temporibus ad
maius altare illius ecclesie deferri et fieri solent et commune concedere
debent scilicet natalis domini, Pasce et Pentecosten et omnium sanctorum
eo excepto quod in festo Pasce recepit presbiter de parochia de solutis
terram non tenentibus oblationes et quod dictus Henricus presbiter de
parochia post adventum suum ad altare de parochia contra prohibitionem
auctoritate ecclesie sepius factam de eisdem oblationibus ad illud altare
recepit et retinet ad estimationem unius marce communiam predictam
spoliando unde petimus ipsum Henricum ad restitutionem detentorum
prout probate poterimus nobis nomine communie illius ecclesie faciendam
compelli ipsumque ab huiusmodi receptione illicita et rectitudine arceri.

Note   For Henry (de Mora) see 121n.

125   *Sir Henry [the parish priest] denies the claims of the custodians
or proctors of the Commons and states that he and his predecessors
have been accustomed to take oblations peaceably at Easter, and that
no injury or spoliation had occurred for which he owed restitution; Sir
Robert is appointed to hear witnesses for the Commons and for Sir Henry
de Mora*   [c. 1259]

Dominus Henricus presens in iudicio respondit non esse vera ut credit
que proponunt domini custodes sive procuratores quia ipse suo tempore
semper recepit dictas oblationes pacifice et tenuit preter quam in die
Pasce de terram tenentibus tantum et sic[1] fecerunt sui predecessores ut
credit unde nullam fecit iniuriam vel spoliationem nec aliquam tenetur
restitutionem et si teneatur reverenter faciet et iuraverunt partes huic
inde de veritate dicenda et dominum Robertum induxerunt testem pro
se communiter et dominum Henricum de Mora.

[1] MS corrected from *sint*

Date   Shortly after 124.

126   *Sentence issued in the case over the collection and distribution
of oblations, confirming the ancient custom of parishes bringing their
offerings to Southwell at Christmas, Easter, Pentecost and All Saints,
and condemning Sir Henry (the parish priest) to pay 12d*
[after 27 January 1259]

Auditis et intellectis[1] omnibus hinc inde propositis et probatis cum
nobis constet evidenter per testium dispositiones et etiam notorium est
et publicum quod diebus natalis domini, Pasce, Pentecosten et omnium
sanctorum venerunt et venire solebant a longis retro temporibus communiter
omnes terram tenentes et etiam coniugati de parochia ecclesie Suthwell'

ad maius altare illius ecclesie et ibidem oblationes suas reverenter offerre sepius quod[2] inhibitum esse solempniter auctoritate eiusdem ecclesie ne alibi offerrent dicti parochiani nec ad offerend' reciperentur dictis diebus et quod ab aliquibus ad altare de parochia oblatum fuit ibidem receptum fuisse ad maius altare deleant.[3] Constet per confessionem domini Henrici ipsum oblationes a quibusdam prenominatis recipisse et non solvisse ad estimationem xii denarii ipsum ad rectitudinem et restitutionem eorundem maiori altari sive communi faciendam condempnantes. Inhibuimus eidem in virtute sacramenti diebus predictis mandat oblata ibidem a predictis recipiend' ne de quantitate oblatarum contentio inter eos oriatur.

[1] MS *intelectis*   [2] Or *quia?*   [3] Possibly corr. to *deleat?*

RENTS, WAX AND MONEY, 127–9

127 *Notification by Thomas, prior of Shelford, that half the church of North Muskham, of which he held the advowson, had become vacant by the resignation of Robert of Muskham, clerk, and that he placed this at the disposition of W[alter], archbishop of York, to whom the right of patronage belonged, who conferred that half on Shelford because of its poverty, for three stones of wax per annum to Southwell* [1220 × 1225]

p. 58

Appropriatio medietatis ecclesie de Northmuskham

Universis sancte matris ecclesie filiis ad quos presens pagina pervenerit frater Thomas prior de Schelford' et humilis eiusdem loci conventus salutem in domino. Noverit universitas vestra quod cum medietas ecclesie de Northmusc\h/am per resignationem Roberti de Musc\h/am clerici qui eam de nostra tenuit advocatione vacaret, nos ordinationem dicti beneficii dispositioni domini W. dei gratia Ebor' archiepiscopi quantum ius patronatus pertinebat sponte et absolute commisimus, qui paupertati nostre paterna compatiens pietate dictam medietatem cum omnibus ad eam pertinentibus in proprios usus domus nostre convertendam et possidendam ad hospitalitatis augmentationem karitative concessit. Ita tamen quod nos inde annuatim persolvemus ecclesie beate Marie Suthwell' tres petras cere contra tres sollempnes dies ad luminariorum augmentationem s[cilicet] unam contra Pascam aliam contra Pentecosten tertiam contra nativitatem beate Marie salvo sibi et successoribus suis iure pontificali et parochiali et salva in omnibus Ebor' ecclesie dignitate. In huius autem annue solutionis testimonium huic scripto sigillum capituli nostri apponere dignum duximus. Hiis testibus magistro Willelmo archidiacono Notingham', Galfrido archidiacono Norwic', magistro Ricardo Cornub' canonico Ebor' et multis aliis.

Margin   Title, 17th/18th c. as in most of items to **137**. In right margin at head of document *Schelford* (late medieval) and then *3 petr' cera* (17th c.).

Date   Thomas of Laxton first occurs as prior of Shelford 1219–23 (his predecessor last occurred 7 June 1220), and last occurs December 1228–December 1229 (*HRH*, ii, 458). Geoffrey de Burgh, archdeacon of Norwich, was in post 1200–25, and elected bishop of Ely before 2 June and consecrated on 29 June 1225 (*Fasti 1066–1300*, ii, 64).

Note   Mr Richard of Cornwall, canon of York since 1216, was chancellor of York by 1 July 1225 (*York Fasti*, i, 18–19). Mr William of Bodham first occurs as archdeacon of Nottingham in 1218 to probably 1234, although his predecessor, also a Mr William, had become dean of York in 1214 (*Fasti 1066–1300*, vi, 45).

128   *Notification by Elias, prior of Thurgarton. and the convent that they are obliged to pay two stones of wax annually to St Mary's, Southwell to maintain lights at Christmas and at the Assumption in return for all the tithes ceded to them by the Chapter*   [7 June 1220 × 27 January 1223]

Concessio 2 petrarum cere capitulo per priorem de Thurgarton

Omnibus Cristi fidelibus ad quos presens carta pervenerit Elyas prior de Thurgarton totusque eiusdem loci conventus salutem in domino. Universitati vestre notum fieri volumus quod nos tenemur solvere annuatim ecclesie beate Marie Suthwell' in perpetuum duas petras cere ad augmentationem[1] luminariarum scilicet[2] unam petram ad natale et unam petram ad assumptionem[3] beate Marie pro omnibus decimis nobis a capitulo predicte ecclesie concessis et carta sua ecclesie beati Petri de Thurgarton et canonicis ibidem deo servientibus sicut predicta carta testatur confirmatis. In huius rei testimonium hanc cartam sigillo capituli nostri roboravimus. Hiis testibus domino Roberto abbate de Rucford, domino Ric[ardo] abbate de Wellebek, Rogero priore de Lenton, Thoma priore de Schelford' et multis aliis.

[1] MS *aumentationem*   [2] MS *silicet*   [3] MS *asumptionem*

Margin   Title in 17th-c. hand. *Thurgarton 2 petras cere* in right margin.

Date   The date of this notification is probably 7 June 1220 × 27 January 1223. Elias' predecessor as prior, Henry, last occurred on 6 October 1218. Elias first occurs on 25 June 1219, last occurred 25 April 1221 and his successor, John, first occurs in Trinity term 1227 (*Thurgarton*, ccii–cciii). For Thomas of Laxton see **127**. R. prior of Lenton occurs 1214, and Roger, prior of Lenton, occurs 17 November 1225 and thereafter until 16 August 1240 (see also Foulds, 'Lenton Priory', no. 33). Robert, abbot of Rufford first occurs on 13 January 1219 (his predecessor last occurs 25 July 1215 and possibly died 1217), and last occurred 20 January 1228 (his successor was elected 25 January 1231). Richard of Southwell was probably elected abbot of Welbeck in 1197 and last occurred in 1217–24 and on 20 January 1222. He was dead by 24 October and his successor first occurs on 27 January 1223 (*HRH*, i, 198).

Note   Pd. in *Thurgarton*, *121, and with reference to Southwell's grant of tithes at Fiskerton to Thurgarton to sustain this payment (*Thurgarton*, 996).

128A   *Notification by Henry, prior of Worksop and the convent that they are obliged to pay 3s 8d per annum for the land they hold of the Chapter in Brampton*   [1200 × 1214]

Concessio 3 s' annuorum capitulo per priorem de Wirksop'

Universis sancte matris ecclesie filiis ad quos presens scriptum pervenerit H. prior et conventus de Wirkesop salutem. Noveritis quod tenemur solvere annuatim tres solidos scilicet[1] octodecim denarios ad festum sancti

Martini capitulo beate Marie et octodecim denarios ad Pentecosten pro terra quam tenemus de eodem capitulo in Bramtuna.

¹ MS *silicet*

Margin   Title in usual 17ᵗʰ-c. hand to **137**. *Worksop* in right margin.

Date   While Henry was prior of Worksop (*HRH*, i, 191; *Thurgarton*, p. 198).

Note   It is not clear why this item was omitted from the main modern numeric sequence since it is quite clearly a separate item after **128**. Is the land in question linked to that later granted to the Chapter by William of Brampton (**35**) on which a rent of 3s 4d was owing? The rent may come from some of the land mentioned in **35**.

129   *Agreement between the Chapter and the Chapter of Launde (Leics.) by which Southwell has granted its lands in Tilton, of eight bovates and one manse, for 20s per annum*   [late 12ᵗʰ century]

p. 59

Tilton

Hec est conventio facta inter capitulum Suthwell' et capitulum de Landa. Capitulum Suthwell' concessit capitulo de Landa in perpetuum terram quam habent in Tiltona, videlicet viii bovatas et unum mansum pro viginti solidis per singulos annos ad vincula sancti Petri et de tali moneta que currit in Suthwella, teste presente cyrographo.

Margin   *De Landa* (at top right in hand of Scribe 1). *Landa* (left margin, late medieval).

Date   Before Innocent III's bull of 11 May 1200 concerning this payment (**5**).

Note   Tilton is nine miles east of Leicester. It is not clear how Southwell obtained land here. The advowson of Tilton had been granted to the Austin canons of Launde before 1162 and the church appropriated by 1220 (*VCH Leics.*, ii, 10–13).

WOODBOROUGH, 130

130   *Grant by Agatha, daughter of Geoffrey, sometime canon of Southwell, to Southwell of half an acre of land in Woodborough*

[1224 × 1245]

D. acre terre in Woodburgh

Omnibus Cristi fidelibus ad quos presens scriptum pervenerit Agatha filia Galfridi quondam canonici de Suthwell' salutem in domino. Noveritis me dedisse concessisse et hac presenti carta mea confirmasse Deo et ecclesie beate Marie Suthwell' et canonicis ibidem Deo servientibus dimidiam acram terre in territorio de Woudeburgh', scilicet¹ unam rodam que iacet iuxta terram Willelmi de Karleton' versus orientem, et unam rodam super Lidegath que iacet inter terram Nicolai et terram predicte Agathe, tenendam et habendam in puram et perpetuam elemosinam libere quiete et pacifice pro omni servitio salvo forinseco domini regis. Et ut hec mea donatio rata et inconcussa permaneat, huic scripto sigillum meum dignum duxi apponere. Hiis testibus magistro Waltero Thaneth, Henrico de Notingh', magistro Willelmo de Marcam, Willelmo capellano et aliis.

[1] MS *silicet*

Margin Title in 17th-c. hand as for others in this section. *Woudburgh'* (left margin, late medieval).

Date While Walter de Taney was a canon of Southwell and before his appointment as archdeacon of Nottingham and the death of Henry of Nottingham.

Note Agatha appears to be the daughter of Geoffrey of Dorchester, prebendary of Woodborough *c*. 1200, who witnessed **521**.

CAUNTON, 131–5

131 *Grant in free alms by Robert of Daiville to Southwell of seven acres of land and one house in Caunton* [*c*. 1150 × 1168]

12 acr' et unum mansum in Calneton'

Robertus de Dayvilla omnibus sancte matris ecclesie filiis necnon heredibus et successoribus suis salutem. Notum sit benignitati[1] vestre me dedisse et concessisse[2] in elemosinam perpetuam Deo et ecclesie sancte Marie de Suthwella et canonicis ibidem Deo servientibus vii acras terre et unum mansum in Calneton et hanc elemosinam dedi liberam et quietam ab omni servitio et consuetudine et seculari exactione pro redemptione anime mee et pro animabus patris mei et matris mee et pro salute omnium amicorum meorum. Et hoc feci concessione domini Robert de Chalz et Radulfi de Herovilla. Ipse est inde testis et Galfridus de Calx et Ricardus Ursel.

[1] MS *benignitate* [2] MS *concecisse*

Margin Title in usual 17th-c. hand for this section. *De Calneton* (Scribe 1, heading top right). *Calneton* (left margin, late medieval).

Date While Robert of Daiville was active and before the death of Robert de Caux (see Note).

Note Robert II of Daiville held a moiety of Langford and Kilburn (Yorks.) of Roger de Mowbray and Robert de Stuteville, to whom he was related by marriage, in 1154–70, and died in 1186. He was married to Juliana (living 1202), daughter of Thurston de Montford, and was succeeded by his son John (*EYC*, ix, 17, 222; *Mowbray Charters*, xxxivn, and *passim*; *Complete Peerage*, iv, 130–1n; De Ville, 'John Deyville', 17–40). Robert of Daiville held one fee, Geoffrey de Caux and Richard Ursel a half-fee each of Robert de Caux in 1166 (*Red Book*, 343; *Rufford*, 490n). Robert de Caux held half the barony of Shelford before 1161 and is last mentioned in 1168 (Sanders, *English Baronies*, 76). He witnessed a grant to Rufford 1146–56 and Richard Ursel witnessed *c*. 11 November 1171 (*Rufford*, 431, 719; *Thurgarton*, 172n). In 1242–3 Reginald Ursel and Hugh of Tithby held a half-fee of Everingham (barony of Shelford) in Gedling, Carlton and Stoke (*Book of Fees*, 982, 990). Ralph de Heroville witnessed the grant by Robert of Daiville to St Peter's hospital, York, of 13d from his mill in Baxby, Husthwaite parish, Yorks. (Clay, *Early Yorkshire Families*, 110). Perhaps he may be an ancestor of William de Heroville (Heronville) who, in 1182, obtained the manor of Wednesbury (Staffs.) in the right of his wife, a daughter of Ralph Boteler, held of the earls of Warwick (*Book of Fees*, 142, 544, 595). Doun Bardolf (1171–1205) had connections with Heroville near Caen. He was the son of Thomas Bardolf and his wife, Rose, daughter of Ralph II Hanselin, the other holder of half the barony of Shelford.

132 *Confirmation in hereditary fee by Hugh of Caunton to Richard, his brother, of all the land with toft that he holds of the Chapter in Caunton for 2s rent per annum. Also grant in hereditary fee of six acres of land in Caunton for 14d rent per annum* [early 13th century]

Carta Henrici[1] Calneton de terra et tofto

Sciant etc' quod ego H[ugo] de Calneton' etc' et confirmavi Ricardo fratri meo filio H. pro homagio et servitio suo totam terram cum tofto et omnibus pertinentiis quam teneo de Deo et beate Marie de Suthwell' et capitulo Suthwell' in Calneton' sicut carta quam habeo de capitulo protestatur tenendum et habendum sibi et heredibus suis de me et heredibus meis in feudo et hereditate libere quiete et pacifice, reddendo inde michi annuatim et heredibus meis duos solidos pro omni servitio dicte terre pertinente, scilicet[2] ad festum sancti Martini duodecim denarios et xii denarios ad Pentecosten. Ego etiam Hugo dedi predicto Ricardo ad incrementum sex acras terre arabilis in campis de Calneton' etc' tenendum et habendum sibi et heredibus suis de me et heredibus meis in feudo et hereditate libere quiete et pacifice, reddendo michi inde michi annuatim et heredibus meis quatuordecim denarios ad predictos festos, scilicet[2] ad festum sancti Martini vii denarios et ad Pentecosten, vii denarios pro omni servitio et exactione tam pro forinseco quam pro alio servitio dicte terre pertinente et dimidiam acram prati. Et ego et heredes mei warantizabimus predicto Ricardo et heredibus suis predictum tenementum contra omnes homines. Testibus capitulo de Suthwell', Nicolao de Daivilla et Nicolao filio suo et aliis.

[1] MS *sic*   [2] MS *silicet*

Margin   Title, 17th c.

Date   Nicholas I of Daiville was the brother of John (**131n**). He held the manor of Caunton before 1194 and was a juror in 1212 (*Book of Fees*, 148); his son Nicholas was deputy sheriff of Nottinghamshire in 1264 (see also **428** and **579**). Hugh of Caunton (more than one) witnessed many charters to Rufford.

p. 60   This is an inserted leaf, smaller than the rest, and has two items by Scribe 4 (mid-15th c.).

133 *Grant by the Chapter to Richard, clerk of Caunton, for his life of twelve acres of land, half an acre of meadow and one house in Caunton for a rent of 2s per annum* [mid-13th century]

Terra in Calneton

Humile capitulum beate Marie Suellensis omnibus hanc presentem cartam intuentibus vel audientibus salutem in omnium salvatore. Vestre equitatis fraternitati manifestum fieri volumus quod omnium nostrum communi assensu et consensu dedimus concessimus et presentis carte testimonio corroboravimus[1] Ricardo clerico de Calnatona tam heredibus quam ipsi xii acras de terra arabili in eiusdem ville territorio et dimidiam acram in prato et unam mansuram in eadem villa ita quod nec predictus Ricardus nec heredes sui nec aliquis heredum eorum ultra terminum vite sue aliquo modo poterit alienare pro duobus solidis per singulos annos ad horum prescriptionem terminorum reddend', videlicet quod reddet nobis xii nummos ad Pentecosten et residuos xii ad festum sancti Martini. Et hii sunt testes Willelmus de Upton' presbiter, Rogerus Westhorp' presbiter, Godfridus de Wodhous, Nicholaus de Eyvile miles, Petrus in le Lane et alii plures.

¹ In MS preceded by *confirmavimus*, expunged

Margin　Title in 17ᵗʰ-c. hand. *2s per annum* in right margin (17ᵗʰ c.).

Date　After **132**. Sir Nicholas of Daiville probably died *c.* 1270, and Peter in the Lane is probably the same as Peter de Venella (**62–3**).

Note　This and **134** probably provide the names of the two earliest known vicars of Caunton.

134　*Grant by Hugh, clerk of Caunton, to Richard, clerk of Caunton, for life of twelve acres of land, half an acre of meadow and one house in Caunton for 2s rent per annum paid to the Chapter*　[mid-13ᵗʰ century]

Carta H. clerici de eadem

Omnibus Christi fidelibus filiis ad quos presens carta pervenerit Hugo clericus de Calnatona salutem in domino sempiternam. Noveritis me dedisse, concessisse et presentis carte testimonio corroborasse Ricardo clerico de Calnatona tam heredibus quam ipsi xii acras de terra arabili in eiusdem ville territorio et dimidiam acram in prato et unam mansuram in eadem villa, ita videlicet quod nec ipse Ricardus nec heredes sui nec aliquis heredum eorum ultra terminum vite sue predictas xii acras terre, pratum vel mansuram aliquo modo poterit alienare, pro duobus solidis per singulos annos ad horum prescriptionem terminorum annuatim reddendis capitulo sancte Marie Suwelensis, videlicet quod reddet eidem capitulo xii nummos ad Pentecosten residuos xii ad festum sancti Martini. Hii sunt testes, Nicholaus de Eyvile, Petrus in le Lane, Godewinus Kent, Ricardus Kent, Petrus in le Est et alii plures.

Margin　Title in 17ᵗʰ-c. hand. *2s per annum* in right margin (17ᵗʰ c.).

Date　Similar to that of **133** with which it shares some witnesses.

Note　Richard Kent of Caunton witnessed charters to Rufford in 1250, 1254 and 1260 (*Rufford*, 496, 503, 515) as well as many dated 'mid-13ᵗʰ c.' (ibid., 490–2, 494, 501, 509, 513, 514). Other members of the Kent family were still living in Caunton at the begining of the fifteenth century (**379**).

135　*Memorandum in the top right margin in late medieval hand:* Per　p. 61
inquisicionem pro vicaria de Northwell' de iiii marcis et ii solidis debitis vicariis choralibus sic concordat[am] [...]. An early foliation, now illegible, has also been erased.

WESTHORPE, 136–7

136 *Grant by Mr William of Rolleston, son of Richard, to Southwell,* *of four strips of land and meadow* [1201 × 1236]

Carta Willelmi de Roldeston de 4 selionibus terrae

Omnibus sancte matris ecclesie filiis ad quos presens scriptum pervenerit magister Willelmus de Roldeston filius Ricardi salutem. Noverit universitas vestra me divine pietatis intuitu pro salute anime mee et antecessorum meorum dedisse et hac presenti carta mea confirmasse a me et heredibus meis in perpetuum in puram liberavi et perpetuam elemosinam Deo et ecclesie beate Marie de Suthwell duas seliones terre arabilis in Amerlandes iacentes inter terram Alicie de Mora vidue et terram Willelmi Kyndud' et pratum quod iacet inter pratum eiusdem Alicie et toftum Rogeri Chapman et duas seliones in Fulwudeclive iacentes prope viam que extendit se de Westorp' usque ad Halthon' et que iacent inter terram Symonis filii Hugonis Snelling et terram Willelmi filii Hugonis Albloth' et que se abbuttant[1] super Fulwudebec'. Et ego et heredes mei vel successores mei predictas terras cum prato prenominato warantizabimus deo et predicte ecclesie sancte Marie de Suthwell' et defendemus in omnibus et contra omnes homines nec ego et heredes mei vel successores mei a prefata ecclesia obtentu istius donationis, concessionis et confirmationis mee de predictis terris vel prato prescripto aliquod exigemus servitium vel demandam. Et ut hec mea donatio concessio et confirmatio firma et stabilis in perpetuum permaneat hoc scriptum[2] munimine roboramus.[3] Hiis testibus Ricardo de Marcam, Hugone de Westorp, Gilberto, Willelmo de Egrum capellano, Adam[4] de Bella Aqua, Ricardo de Eddynglay et aliis.

[1] MS *abbuctant* [2] MS *scriptim* [3] *Sic:* should be *huius scripti munimine robora-mus* [4] MS *sic*

Margin Title, 17th c. *Hic* ... [two or three erased words] just above title in medieval hand. Text of this and **137**, Scribe 1.

Date While Adam de Bella Aqua was active (**309n**) and Richard of Edingley witnessed 1220–4 (**505**).

137 *Grant and quitclaim by Mr William of Rolleston to Southwell of* *one furlong of his land between Southwell and Halloughton and one strip* *of two he has below Westhorpe* [1230 × 1249]

Carta Willelmi de Roldeston' de una cultura & 1 selione terrae

Sciant presentes et futuri quod ego magister Willelmus de Roldeston dedi, concessi et quietam clamavi Deo et beate [Marie] de Suthwell' et canonicis ibidem deo servientibus unam culturam terre mee que iacet inter Suthwell' et Halthon' que vocatur Redynwang' et unam selionem de duabus quas habeo sub Westorp' tenendam et habendam in puram et perpetuam elemosinam quiete et pacifice sine omni servitio ad me vel heredes meos pertinente et seculari exactione. Et ego magister Willelmus et heredes mei warantizabimus prefatam terram dictis canonicis ut dictum est contra omnes homines. Et ut hec mea donatio, concessio quieta clamatio et confirmatio firma et stabilis permaneat huic carte sigillum meum apposui. Hiis testibus, Willelmo persona de Bildestorp', Henrico de Mora capellano, Thoma filio Willelmi clerico, Rogero filio Walteri Malet et aliis.

Margin Title 17ᵗʰ c. *notetur bene hec carta* (late medieval) and *Redingwonge* (17ᵗʰ c.) in right margin with line bracketing this item.

Date William of Southwell, clerk, was instituted to the vicarage of Bilsthorpe on 28 May 1230 (*Reg. Gray*, 35) and before Henry de Mora became a canon.

Note For Roger and Walter Malet see **235** and **236n**.

NORWELL VICARAGE, 138–9

138 *Mr Richard de Bamfield, papal chaplain and canon, Richard of Upton, warden of the Commons, and Richard of Halloughton, vicar at Southwell, report to the Chapter the testimony of a jury (members named) concerning the vacant vicarage of the prebendal church of Norwell, rights of presentation and its value*   Norwell, 6 August 1284

Ordinacio vicarie de Northwell'

Viris¹ venerabilibus et discretis dominis capitulo ecclesie collegiate beate Marie Suthwell' devoti sui Ricardus de Baumfelld', domini pape capellanus eiusdem ecclesie frater et concanonicus, Ricardus de Upton', custos commune canonicorum ecclesie supradicte et Ricardus de Haluthton', vicarius in ecclesia memorata, salutem obedienciam et reverenciam omni subieccionem plenam, ad mandatum vestrum vocatis coram nobis fideidignioribus de parochia ecclesie prebendalis de Northwell' tam clericis quam laycis diligentem fecimus inquisicionem super vacacione vicarie eiusdem, scilicet per dominos Henricum et Robertum, capellanos parochiales loci eiusdem, Walterum Freeman, Hugonem de Ybernia, Robertum dictum Sympyle, Robertum clericum, Robertum de Esthorpe, Hugonem filium Ricardi, Robertum filium Rogeri, Henricum Donne, Henricum Chymung', Rogerum Page, Willelmum filium Reginaldi, Radulfum Kolfe, iuratos, qui dicunt quod predicta vacat vicaria per mortem Henrici Legat', quondam vicarii in eadem et vacavit a quadraginta et octo annis iam elapsis. Magister Paulus Dentaynty est verus patronus presentandi ad eandem vicariam pro rata porcionis sue quam habet in eadem ecclesia prebendali de Northwell'. | Non recolunt quis ultimo presentavit ad eandem propter lapsum termini temporis. Non est litigiosa. Est pensionaria ecclesie Suthwellensis in quatuor marcis duobus solidis annuis solvendis vicario qui pro tempore \de/ servierit stalo in choro pertinenti ad prebendam quam dictus magister Paulus modo tenet. Consistat autem prefata vicaria in uno mesuagio, in xxx acris terre arabilis, quinque acris prati, quinque solidis vii denariis annuis redditibus percipiendis de duobus tenentibus in Northwell' et Carleton' et in omnibus decimis maioribus et minoribus, oblacionibus et obvencionibus quibuscumque

p. 62

ad porcionem dicti magistri Pauli pertinentibus, decimis garbarum et feni duntaxat exceptis que ad prefatum canonicum spectant integraliter. Dicunt eciam quod ipsa vicaria non est integra set divisa. Quod nichil omnino percipiat de porcione prebende que pertinet ad prebendam magistri Johannis Clarell' nisi pro rata porcionis dicti magistri Pauli. Valet autem ipse dicta vicaria annuatim vii librarum xiii solidorum ii denariorum. De persona presentata ad eandem, dicunt quod est bone conversacionis et honeste et habilis ad illud et ad maius beneficium obtinendum nec obstat presentanti seu presentato aliquod canonicum quod sciamus. In cuius rei testimonium sigilla nostra bona cum sigillis aliquorum contestancium presenti inquisicionem sunt appensa. Datum apud Northwell' die dominica proxima post festum beati Petri apostoli quod dicitur ad cathedram, anno domini millesimo cc° octogesimo quarto.

¹ A space has been left for a larger decorated initial V here and in the copy in **139**

Margin   Title underlined in same hand as text (a mid-15ᵗʰ-c. hand, also used in **139**, very similar to that of Scribe 4), but lacking the rubrication used to this point, omitting his own opening initials. An earlier title, which has been erased but may also have read *Ordinacio vicarie de Northwell*, occurs two lines below **137** and five lines above **138**.

Note   Richard de Bamfield, steward of the household of Archbishop Wickwane in 1280, canon by 1291, later prebendary of Norwell Tertia Pars, resigning in 1304. Mr Paul de Dentaynty/Dentayicty, sometimes called Paul de Casaviti, an Italian from Rome, held the prebend of Norwell Tertia Pars, dying before 9 August 1298. Probably since the creation of the prebend around 1190–4 (cf. **29**), its holder had shared with the prebendary of Norwell Overhall, the right each to present a vicar, a system which prevailed until the early eighteenth century. This document provides the name of the earliest known vicar of the Tertia Pars moiety, Henry Legat (d. *c.* 1236) and confirms the prebendary's right of patronage. The phrasing of the document, with short disconnected sentences, might be the result of those giving the ruling working their way through a list of questions to which they have been asked to provide answers, cf. **40**, where, for example, the phrase *Non est litigiosa* also occurs.

139   *A verbatim copy of 138, with only very minor differences, but with the heading:* Inquisicio facta de Vicaria de Northwell' prebende Pauli

Margin   Title in same hand as text (cf. **138**).

p. 63   **De cantaria de Calneton'**

140   *Grant in the form of an indenture by Robert of Collingham, Walter of Caunton, William of Bathley and William of Folksworth, executors of the will of Robert of Caunton, reciting his indenture establishing a chantry in Caunton church, 29 June 1349, and the mortmain licence of Edward III, 2 November 1351*   [after 2 November 1351]

Omnibus Christi fidelibus ad quos presentes litere pervenerint Robertus de Colyngham, Walterus de Caunton', Willelmus de Batheley et Willelmus de Folkesworth', executores testamenti Roberti de Calneton', salutem in domino sempiternam. Noverit universitas vestra quod predictus Robertus de Calneton' per quoddam scriptum suum indentatum nuper domino Willelmo Porter de Calneton', perpetuo capellano, et successoribus suis, ad altare beate Marie in ecclesia parochiali de Calneton' divina singulis diebus iuxta ordinacionem in hac parte faciendam celebraturo dedisset ac concessisset quendam annuum redditum quinque marcarum argenti percipiendum singulis annis imperpetuum de manerio et de duabus carucatis terre cum suis pertinenciis ipsius Roberti de Calneton' in Calneton' que sunt de feodo prebendarii de Northmuskam ad quatuor anni redditus, videlicet ad assumpcionis beate Marie, sancti Martini in yeme, prime dominice quadragesime et Pentecostes per equales porciones. Ac illustrissimus dominus Edwardus, rex Anglie et Francie et dominus Hibernie, ad requisicionem nostram predictum scriptum annui redditus quinque marcarum per cartam suam confirmasset, ratificasset et approvasset prout in eadem carta regia et dicto scripto indentato plenius continetur. Quorum tenores inseriem subscribuntur:

Noverint universi per hanc indenturam me Robertum de Calneton' dedisse ac concessisse domino Willelmo Porter de Calneton', perpetuo capellano altaris beate Marie in ecclesia parochiali de Calneton', et successoribus suis ad altare predictum celebraturo pro me dum vixero, filiis, filiabus, fratribus et sororibus meis vivi, et pro Roberto Wyte de Colyngham dum vixerit, et pro animabus Alicie, uxoris mee, patris mei et matris mee, fratrum et sororum mearum et antecessorum meorum et omnium fidelium defunctorum et post mortem meam et mortem predictorum filiorum, filiarum, fratrum, sororum vivorum et Roberti, pro anima mea et animabus eorundem filiorum, filiarum, fratrum, sororum et Roberti ac omnium prenominatorum quendam annuum redditum quinque marcarum argenti[1] ad valorem sterlyngorum percipiendum singulis annis imperpetuum de manerio meo de Calneton' et de duabus carucatis terre cum pertinenciis in eadem[2] villa que sunt de feodo prebendarii de Northmuskham ad quatuor anni terminos, videlicet ad festa sancti Martini in yeme, prime dominice quadragesime, Pentecostes et assumpcionis beate Marie per equales porciones. Ad quem quidem annuum redditum quinque marcarum terminis predictis fideliter persolvendum obligo me, heredes meos et omnia bona et specialiter manerium et terram predictam districcioni cuiuscunque Iudiciis ecclesiastici vel secularis. Et si contingat dictum redditum annuum quinque marcarum terminis predictis vel eorum aliquo in parte vel in toto aretro esse volo et concedo pro me et heredibus meis quod bene liceat dicto domino Willelmo, capellano, et eius successoribus imperpetuum, in predicto manerio et duabus carucatis terre libere distringere et districciones huiusmodi fugare, abducere et retinere quousque de dicto annuo redditu sic aretro existent et arreragiis quibuscumque una cum dampnis et expensis si que ea occasione incurrerit vel fecerit; eidem capellano et successoribus suis, qui pro tempore erunt, fuerit plenarie satisfactum. In cuius rei testimonium parti huius indenture penes dictum dominum Willelmum, capellanum, et eius successores remanentes sigillum meum apposuit, et alteri parti huius indenture penes me et heredes meos remanenti sigillum dicti domini Willelmi, capellani, est appensum. Hiis testibus: Thoma de Nevill', milite, Johanne de Sutton' de Averham, Johanne Bray de Upton', Roberto Wyte de Colyngham, Henrico de Northwell', Ricardo de Hertehyll', Roberto Waren, Johanne filio Thoma de Besthorpe et aliis. Datum apud Calneton' die lune in festo apostolorum Petri et Pauli anno regni regis Edwardi tercii a conquestu Anglie vicesimo tercio.

Edwardus Dei gracia rex Anglie et Francie et dominus Hibernie, omnibus ad quos presentes litere pervenerint, salutem. Supplicarunt nobis executores testamenti Roberti de Calneton' ut cum idem Robertus dum vixerit dedisset et assignasset cuidam capellano divina ad altare[3] beate Marie in ecclesia parochiali de Calneton' iuxta ordinacionem ipsius Roberti, vel executorum suorum predictorum, in hac parte faciendam celebraturo quinque marcas annuas exeuntes de manerio sue de Calneton' et duabus carucatis terre cum pertinencis in eadem villa que de nobis non tenentur in capite ut dicitur, habendum | et percipiendum dicto capellano et successoribus suis capellanis divina ad altare predictum iuxta ordinacionem predictam celebraturis imperpetuum dictus que capellanus de eodem annuo redditu virtute donacionis et assignacionis predictarum seisitus existat licencia nostra super hoc non obtenta volumus transgressionis in hac parte factam generose pardonare. Nos de gratia nostra speciali et pro quinque marcis nobis solutis dicte supplicatione annuentes perdonavimus transgressionem predictam et concessimus pro nobis et heredibus nostris dicto capellano quod ipse annuum redditum predictum cum pertinenciis percipeat et habeat sibi et successoribus suis predictis divina iuxta ordinacionem supradictam ut premittitur celebraturis imperpetuum sine occasione vel impedimento nostri vel heredum nostrorum iusticiariorum escaetorum vicecomitum aut aliorum baillivorum seu ministrorum nostrorum quorumcumque ita quod liceat dictis capellanis et successoribus suis quociens dictus redditus sibi retro fuerit in parte vel in toto in predictis manerio et terra distringere et districtiones retinere quousque sibi de arreragiis redditus illius fuerit satisfactum statuto de terris et tenementis ad manum mortuam non ponendis edito non obstante. In cuius rei testimonium has literas nostras fieri fecimus patentes. Teste me ipso apud Westmonasterium secundo die Novembris anno regni regis Anglie vicesimo quinto regni vero[4] nostri Francie duodecimo.[5] Nos vero Robertus de Colyngham, Walterus [de Calneton'], Willelmus de Batheleye et Willelmus [de] Foulkesworth audeam[6] et fea... et augmentum cultura termini de unanimi consensu volumus et ordinamus quod prefatus Willelmus capellanus et successores sui capellani qui pro tempore fuerint divina singulis diebus ad altare beate Marie in ecclesia parochiali de Calneton' celebranda parentibus Roberti[7] de Colyngham, A[licie] uxori[8] eius, filiabus [et] fratribus.

p. 64

---

[1] Followed by half a line blank   [2] After *edem* struck out   [3] Followed by *predictum iuxta ordinacionem predictam* struck out   [4] Written once, cancelled and then written again   [5] The material following the dating clause of the writ in the White Book does not appear in the patent roll, where at the end the note *Et predicte quinque marce solute sunt in hanaperio* added on the same line in a smaller hand   [6] The MS is badly faded at this point and the reading of the next few words uncertain   [7] MS *Roberto*   [8] *Sic*; *recte* Calneton'?   [8] MS *uxore*

Margin Page heading (Scribe 4). Main text, an unidentified mid-15th-c. hand.

Note The writ only is calendared in *CPR 1350–4*, 180, from TNA, C 66/235, m. 12; there are no significant textual differences between the two versions. The possible relationship between Robert of Caunton and a person of the same name active in the 1270s and 1280s (**69, 70, 449**) is not clear. This Robert held a third of a knight's fee in Caunton and North Muskham, together with Richard Herthill and Thomas Barry, according to a jury in 1348 (Thoroton, iii, 139). Among those who witnessed his will, Sir Thomas de Neville (of Rolleston) would in 1362 give land at Barnby, near Newark, as well as the advowson of its church to endow the choristers at Southwell (a grant witnessed *inter alia* by John Sutton of Averham, and pd. below in Appendix **A2**). John Bray is probably the man who, also in 1349, founded a chantry at Upton (**213**). Henry of Northwell witnessed **480**, while Robert Waren is probably identical with Robert Waryn of Sutton (cf. **465–72**). The chantry of Our Lady to which William Porter was appointed first chaplain survived to the Dissolution when a copy of this document was shown to the commissioners ('Chantry Certificate Rolls', *TTS* 17 (1913), 91–2). It is not clear whether Walter of Caunton, an executor, was a son, brother, uncle or cousin of Robert. William of Bathley is probably the son of the man already described as William of Bathley senior, in 1323 (**465, 466, 470**). The close links between Caunton and the priory of Newstead are well illustrated in *Cart. Newstead*, 189–97.

BECKINGHAM, 141

141 *Grant by Thomas Haxey of two messuages in Beckingham to the Chapter*   Southwell, 24 November 1415

Sciant presentes et futuri quod ego Thomas Haxey, canonicus ecclesie collegiate beate Marie Southwell, per licenciam metuendissimi domini regis pro salute anime mei, dedi, concessi et hac presenti carta mea confirmavi capitulo ecclesie collegiate beate Marie Southwell duo messuagia, sex tofta, centum et sexaginta acras terre, triginti acras prati, sex bosci et tresdecem solidatos et quatuor denarios redditus cum pertinenciis in Beckingham in the Clay, \et/ Normanton iuxta Southwell. Habendum et tenendum omnia predicta messuagia, tofta, terram, pratum, boscum et redditum predicta cum omnibus suis pertinenciis in villis predictis, prefato capitulo et successoribus suis ad quedam onera et pietatis opera in ecclesia Southwell predicta iuxta ordinacionem meam in hac parte faciendam de capitalibus dominis feodi per servicia inde debita et de iure consueta, in puram et perpetuam elemosinam \in perpetuum/. Et ego predictus Thomas et heredes mei omnia predicta messuagia, tofta, terram, pratum, boscum et redditum predictum cum omnibus suis pertinenciis in villis predictis, prefato capitulo et successoribus suis in forma predicta contra omnes gentes warantizabimus et imperpetuum defendemus. In cuius rei testimonium sigillum meum presentibus apposui. Hiis testibus: dominis Nicholao Stanley et Willelmo Neville, militibus, Johanne Briggesforde, Thoma Newton, Willelmo Rothwell, armigeris, Edmundo Archer, Willelmo Shyre et aliis. Datum apud Southwell in vigilia sancte Katherine[1] virginis anno regni regis Henrici quinti post conquestum Anglie tertio.

---

[1] After *Katherine* struck out

Margin   In left margin *Carta Thome Haxey de terris et tenementis in Beckingham Capitulo donates* in post-1583 hand, text also in late 16th-c. hand of John Martiall, Registrar.

Note   Thomas Haxey, prebendary of Rampton (1388–1425); for his interest in the land in Normanton see **596–604**. He is most remembered for his petition attacking the expenses of Richard II's household, presented to the Parliament of January 1397. This led to his arrest and a short period of imprisonment: see McHardy, 'Haxey's Case', 93–114. For his patronage of the Chantry priests, see **Introduction**, p. lxxxv.

LIBERTIES, 142–51

p. 65   **Libertates ecclesie collegie beate Marie Suthwellie et prebendarum in eadem ecclesia a tempore cuius contrarii memoria non existit usitate ac etiam per diversos reges Anglie concesse et confirmate etc.**

142   *Another copy of* **19** *with no significant variations, see also* **25**, **144** *and* **148**.

Margin   Heading in bold, in hand of Scribe 4, who was also responsible for text of this and items to **148**.

143   *Another copy of* **21**, *see also* **26** *and* **148**.

Margin   *Consuetudines de archiepiscopi*, 17th c.

Note   The text breaks off after ... *Et si quis super hoc ali* ..., and the final two lines have been erased. Sharpe, *Acta Henry I*, York 18 (forthcoming) discusses the different versions of this charter in detail.

p. 66   This page is blank.

p. 67   **Libertates ecclesie collegie beate Marie Suthwellie et prebendarum in eadem ecclesia a tempore cuius contrarii memoria non existit usitate ac etiam per diversos reges Anglie concesse et confirmate hic incipiunt**

144   *Another copy of* **19** *with no significant variations, see also* **25**, **142** *and* **148**.

145   *Record of the Quo warranto case brought against the Chapter of Southwell in the Nottinghamshire eyre which began at Nottingham on 13 November 1329 by the king, after a presentment by the jury of the wapentake of Thurgarton and Lythe of the Chapter's claim to view of frankpledge of their tenants in Southwell, Norwell, South and North Muskham, Caunton, Oxton, Calverton, Woodborough, Cropwell, Blidworth, Halloughton,*

Beckingham, Dunham, Edingley and Normanton from time out of mind. They also presented the Chapter's claim that the king's justices in eyre were accustomed to sit at the south door of the church of Southwell to hear and determine the pleas relating to the Chapter's tenants, and to answer the justices through twelve jurors and not otherwise. The Chapter is represented by its attorney, Thomas of Ashbourne[After 13 November 1329]

William of Deanham, who sues for the king, pleads that the claim by prescription is not valid, because in the previous eyre, before justices led by John de Vaux [which began on 3 November 1280], the Chapter had been summoned to answer to the king [Edward I] concerning by what warrant it claimed the right to correct breaches of the assize of bread and ale in Southwell, Norwell, South and North Muskham, Caunton, Oxton, Calverton, Woodborough and Blidworth. It had then claimed the right to correct breaches of the assize of bread and ale in all those places except South Muskham, where it claimed only for breaches of the assize of ale. In this present eyre the Chapter has also been summoned to show by what warrant it claims correction of the assize of bread and ale in Southwell, Norwell, North and South Muskham, Caunton, Oxton, Calverton, Woodborough, Cropwell, Blidworth and Halloughton, to which it answers that, as regards South Muskham, it claims only the assize of ale. As regards the assize of bread and ale in Cropwell and Halloughton it claims nothing at present because before Vaux and again now it claims nothing except those things which are parcels of the view, so now it seeks judgment that it may claim view of frankpledge in these vills.

The Chapter also claims that in Vaux's eyre it was not summoned to show by what warrant it claimed view of frankpledge or anything else in Beckingham and Dunham, and nothing had been presented concerning any other liberties in those places, so the Chapter should not have to answer for them now. It has held view of frankpledge of its tenants in those two places from time immemorial. Deanham asks for a jury to inquire into this, and it confirms that the liberty has been held from time immemorial. The jury also says that it has always been the custom of the Chapter to punish those who broke the assize of bread and ale with a monetary penalty, never subjecting them to corporal judgment. When asked how much the view was worth each year in all the vills except Beckingham and Dunham, the jurors said that the view of the tenants in Edingley, Halum, Halloughton, Normanton and Southwell, held at Southwell, was worth 2s a year; the view of the tenants of Cropwell, Calverton, Blidworth and Oxton, held at Oxton, also yielded 2s a year; that of Caunton and North Muskham, held at North Muskham, 12d a year; the view of the tenants at North Muskham 12d a year; and that in Woodborough 12d a year. All the views in all those vills are to be taken into the king's hand.

Afterwards John of Wainfleet and Peter del Wych made a fine of 40s with the king on behalf of the Chapter nevertheless to regain the views in Beckingham and Dunham, and it was to be able to use them as it wished, and it was to go without day in respect of those views, saving the king's right. The sheriff is to answer to the king for the issues of the other views.

Afterwards the king orders, by a writ to his justices here, that the record and process of the claim of the Chapter concerning these liberties should be sent to the King's Bench at the octaves of Michaelmas, through Adam of Newton, chaplain.

Placita de quo waranto coram Willelmo de Herle et sociis[1] iusticariis domini regis itinerantibus apud Not' die lune proxima post festum sancti Martini anno regni regis Edwardi tercii a conquest tercio

Herle

Presentatum est per xii[2] iuratores wapentacii de Thurgarton' et de Lyth quod capitulum de Suthwell'[3] habet visum franci plegii de omnibus tenentibus suis in Suthwell' Northwell'[4] Southmuscham[5] Northmuscham[6] Calneton' Oxton' Calverton' Wodeburgh Crophill' Blythworth[7] Halghton'[8] Bekyngham Dunham Halum Edyngley[9] et Normanton' quo waranto vel a quo tempore ignorant. Et eciam presentant quod in quolibet itinere iusticariorum etc. iusticiarii itinerantes solebant sedere in ostio[10] australi ecclesie de Suthwell' predicte et ibidem terminare placita de itinere de omnibus tenentibus dicti capituli et respondere coram iusticiariis per xii et non alibi. Ideo predicte libertates capiantur in manu domini regis. Postea venit predictum capitulum per Thomam[11] de Ashburn' attornatum suum in omnibus placitis et querelis et similiter ad libertates suas calumpniandas etc. et petit predictum visum[12] per plevinam. Et habet. Et dicit quod ipsum capitulum a tempore quo non extat memoria habuit predictum[13] visum in predictis villis ut de iure ecclesie sue beate Marie Suthwellie.[14]

Et Willelmus de Denum qui sequitur pro[15] rege dicit quod capitulum predictum ad huiusmodi clamat titulo prescriptionis admitti non debet. Dicit enim quod idem capitulum alias coram Johanne de Vallibus et sociis suis iusticiariis ultimo[16] itinerantibus hic tempore regis Edwardi avi domini regis nunc summonitus fuit ad clamium suum proprium ad respondendum predicto Edwardo regi etc. quo waranto clamat emendas assise panis et cervisie etc. in predictis villis de Suthwell' Northwell' Suthmuscham Northmuscham[17] Calneton' Oxton' Calverton' Wodeburgh et Blythworth.[18] Et idem capitulum tunc tamen clamat ad[19] emendas assise panis et cervisie in predictis villis de Suthwell' Northwell' Northmuscham[20] Calneton' Oxton' Calverton' Wodeburgh et Blythworth.[21] Et emendas assise \cervisie/[22] fracte tam in Suthmuscham.[23] Et similiter[24] idem capitulum nunc[25] in itinere isto summonitus est ad respondendum etc. quo waranto[26] clamat emendas assise panis et cervisie etc. in predictis villis de Suthwell' Northwell' Northmuscham Suthmuscham[27] Calneton' Oxton' Calverton'

---

[1] A adds *suis.*   [2] B omits.   [3] B *Suthwelle*   [4] B *Northwelle*   [5] A *Suthmuskham*; B *Suthmuscham*   [6] A *Northmuskham*   [7] A, B *Blitheworth*   [8] B *Halgthon'*   [9] A *Eddyngleye*; B *Edyngle*   [10] A, B *hostio*   [11] B *Johannem*   [12] B *predictas libertates*   [13] B *illum*   [14] B *Suthwell'*   [15] B adds *domino.*   [16] B omits.   [17] A *Southmuskham Northmuskham*   [18] A *Blitheworth*; B *Blytheworth*   [19] A, B omit.   [20] A *Northmuskham*   [21] A *Blitheworth*   [22] As well as being interlined, *cervisie* is also written in the right-hand margin, preceded by a caret.   [23] A *Suthmuskham.* B omits this sentence.   [24] B omits.   [25] B *tunc*   [26] B omits the preceding ten words.   [27] A *Northmuskam Suthmuskham*;

Wodeburgh Crophill' Blythworth[28] et Halghton' ad quod clamat idem capitulum respondere[29] quo ad Suthmuscham[30] quod ipsum non clamat nisi emendas assise panis et[31] cervisie fracte tam ibidem. Et quo ad emendam assise panis et cervisie in Crophill' et Halghton'[32] nichil clamat ad presens unde dicit quod cum idem capitulum coram Johanne de Vallibus etc. ad breve ad quod tunc summonitus fuit et similiter ad breve ad quod nunc[33] summonitus est etc. non clamat nisi illa que sunt parcelle visus etc. et hoc in quibusdam villis etc. et in quibusdam non unde petit iudicium si predictum capitulum titulo supradicto visum franci plegii etc. in eisdem villis clamare possit vel debeat in hac parte etc.

Et capitulum dicit quod ipsum alias in predicto itinere Johannis de Vallibus etc. non fuit summonitus ad respondendum predicto regi avo etc. quo waranto clamat visum franci plegii vel aliquid aliud in predictis villis de Bekyngham et Dunham[34] etc. nec aliquid tunc presentatum fuit super ipsum capitulum de aliquibus libertatibus in eisdem villis unde dicit quod de illo ad quod tunc non fuit positum ad respondendum admitti debet ad presens ad clamandum etc. Et dicit quod ipsum capitulum a tempore quo non extat memoria habuit visum franciplegii apud Bekyngham de tenentibus suis ibidem. Et eciam visum franciplegii apud Dunham de tenentibus suis ibidem ut de iure ecclesie[35] predicte.

Et Willelmus de Denum qui sequitur pro rege petit quod inquiratur pro rege si predictum capitulum habuit predictum visum in predictis villis de Bekyngham et Dunham etc.[36] Et si sic tunc qualiter[37] illis usum est etc. Ideo inquiratur etc. Juratores dicunt super sacramentum suum quod predictum capitulum | a tempore quo non extat memoria habuit in Bekyngham visum per se de omnibus tenentibus suis ibidem et[38] in Dunham visum per se de omnibus tenentibus suis residentibus ibidem. Et dicunt[39] idem capitulum semper usum est punire illos qui deliquerunt contra assisam panis et cervisie etc. per penam pecuniariam et nunquam ponere eos ad iudicium corporale. Et iuratores quesitum quantum[40] predicti visus in omnibus illis[41] villis exceptis Bekyngham[42] et Dunham valent per annum dicunt quod visus de tenentibus suis in Edyngley[43] Halum Halghton' et[44] Normanton' et Suthwell' tenta apud Suthwell' valet per annum duos solidos. Et visus de tenentibus[45] in Crophill'[46] Calverton' Blythworth[47] et Oxton' tenta apud Oxton' valet duos solidos per annum. Et visus de tenentibus[48] in Calneton' et Northmuscham[49] tenta apud Northmuscham[50] valet[51] duodecim denarios per annum. Et visus de tenentibus suis in Suthmuscham[52] duodecim denarios per annum. Et visus in Wodburgh[53] tenta ibidem per se duodecim denarios per annum. Ideo predicti[54] visus in omnibus predictis villis capiantur in manum domini regis etc.

p. 68

B *Suthmuscham Northmuscham* [28] A *Blitheworth*; B *Blytheworth* [29] B *respondend'* [30] A *Suthmuskham* [31] A, B omit *panis et.* [32] A *Haghton'* [33] B *tunc* [34] B *Dounham* [35] B adds *sue.* [36] B omits. [37] B adds *et quo modo.* [38] A omits. [39] A adds *quod.* [40] A omits. [41] A, B omit. [42] A *Beckyngham* [43] A, B *Eddyngley* [44] A omits. [45] B adds *suis.* [46] A *Crophull'* [47] A, B *Blitheworth* [48] B adds *suis.* [49] A *Northmuskam* [50] A *Northmuskam* [51] A, B omit. [52] A *Suthmuskham* [53] A, B *Wodeburgh* [54] B *predictus*

Postea Johannes de Waynflete[55] et Petrus del Wych'[56] de[57] eodem comitatu[58] fecerunt finem cum domino rege de quadraginta solidis pro predictis visibus in Bekyngham et Dunham tamen eidem capitulo rehabendis. Ideo predictum capitulum rehabeat visus illos utendi illis modo quo[59] decet etc. Et quo ad visus illos inde sine die[60] salvo iure regis etc.[61] Et vicecomes respondeat domino regi de exitibus aliorum visum.[62] Postea dominus rex mandat breve suum iusticiariis suis[63] hic quod recordum et processum super clamorem capituli predicti super libertatibus predictis coram domino rege mitteret in octabis sancti Michaelis ubicumque etc. Ideo recordum mittatur per Adam de Newton capellanum.[64]

Note Pd. in *Placita de Quo Warranto*, 615–16, from TNA, JUST 1/687, rot. 5, A in this entry. In the Rex roll, JUST 1/684, the entry is found on rot 5, B in this entry. The footnotes refer to differences in the texts of the two enrolments, A and B, from the version in the White Book. The plea roll versions are superior, crucially for the meaning in note 31. The text of the record forms part of the enrolment of the continuing proceedings in King's Bench, in **147** below; cf. also **14**. For Archbishop Wickwane's defence of his rights at Southwell in 1280 see *Reg. Melton*, v, no. 333; ibid., no. 334 provides a summary of further proceedings in the Quo warranto inquiry on 13 November 1329, when Archbishop Melton was summoned to answer for his rights at Southwell and Laneham, of which the original is TNA, JUST 1/687, rot. 19.

146 *Record of a Quo warranto case brought against the Chapter of Southwell by the king in the Nottinghamshire eyre which began at Nottingham on 13 November 1329. The Chapter has been summoned to answer the king by what warrant it claims to have the right to correct breaches of the assize of bread and ale by their tenants in Southwell, Norwell, North and South Muskham, Caunton, Oxton, Calverton, Woodborough, Cropwell, Blidworth and Halloughton, and appears through its attorney, Thomas of Ashbourne. The Chapter claims the liberty as by right of the church of Southwell from time immemorial in Southwell, Norwell, North Muskham, Caunton, Oxton, Calverton, Woodborough and Blidworth. In South Muskham it claims correction of breaches of the assize of ale as by right of the church of Southwell from time immemorial, but does not claim the assize of bread at present; and in Cropwell and Halloughton it does not claim the assize of bread and ale at present. William of Deanham, who sues for the king, says that the Chapter cannot have these liberties, and nor can it have pillory or tumbrel or any other judicial privileges that pertain to those liberties, and is prepared to prove this. The Chapter says it is unable to gainsay this, but that its liberties should not be prejudiced thereby, because from time immemorial its practice has been to punish trespassers against the assize of bread and ale among its tenants by monetary penalties. Deanham says that since the Chapter claims those liberties and sufficiently acknowledges that it does not have*

[55] A, B *Waynflet* [56] A *Wich* [57] B omits. [58] A omits *de eodem comitatu*. [59] B omits. [60] The version in TNA, JUST 1/684, rot. 5 ends here, omitting the *postea*. [61] B ceases at this point. [62] A adds *etc.* [63] A omits. [64] The remainder of this entry is a separate enrolment on JUST 1/687, rot. 15d, printed in *Placita de Quo Warranto*, 636. The version in JUST 1/684 is on rot. 16d.

pillory, tumbrel or any other judicial liberties but says, to maintain its liberties, that it always used monetary penalties in the place of corporal judgment, it is rather an abuse and corruption of the liberty because it is against the liberty, and asks for the liberties to be taken into the king's hand. [After 13 November 1329]

Deanham says that it is presented here in court by the jurors of the wapentake of Thurgarton and Lythe that the Chapter has view of frankpledge in these vills, which it claims. He said that in Vaux's previous eyre under Edward I it claimed nothing in those vills except the right to correct breaches of the assize of bread and ale nevertheless, and in certain of those vills correction of the assize of ale which are nothing but parts of the view, and in as much as the Chapter claims view of frankpledge by prescription, alleging in this to have had a view before that last eyre which it does not now claim, he asks for judgment as to whether the Chapter can claim that liberty through the excessive claim of that view, and that they ought to forfeit it. They are given a day to hear judgment on this at Derby on 23 July 1330. At that date Deanham and the Chapter's attorney appear and are given a new day to hear judgment at Derby on 15 October 1330. In the meantime the sheriff is to answer for the issues of the other views. Afterwards the king ordered by his writ to the justices that the record and process on the Chapter's claim to those liberties are to be sent to the King's Bench on 6 October, through Adam of Newton, chaplain.

Capitulum Suthwellie[1] summonitus fuit ad respondendum domino regi de placito quo waranto clamat habere emendas assise panis et cervisie fracte de tenentibus suis in villis de Suthwell'[2] Northwell et Northmuscam[3] Suthmuscham[4] Calneton' Oxton' Calverton' Wodeburgh Crophill'[5] Blythworth[6] et Halgton'[7] etc. Et capitulum per Thomam Asshborne[8] attornatum suum venit.[9] Et quo ad hoc quod ipsum summonitus[10] etc. quo waranto clamat habere emendas assise panis et cervisie fracte de tenentibus suis in villis de Suthwell'[11] Northwell'[12] Northmuscham[13] Calneton' Oxton' Calverton' Wodeburgh et Blythworth[14] dicit quod ipsum capitulum ut de iure ecclesie beate Marie Suthwellie[15] a tempore quo non extat memoria habuit emendas assise panis et cervisie fracte de tenentibus suis in eisdem[16] villis etc. Et eo waranto clamat habere emendas assise panis et cervisie fracte de tenentibus suis in predictis villis etc. Et quo ad hoc quod ipsum summonitus est quo waranto clamat habere emendas assise panis et cervisie etc. in Suthmuscham[17] Crophill' et Halghton' quo ad emendas assise cervisie etc. de tenentibus suis in Suthmuscham[18] dicit quod idem capitulum ut de iure ecclesie sue predicte a tempore quo non extat memoria habuit emendas assise cervisie etc. de tenentibus suis in

---

[1] A *de Suwell'*; B *de Suthwell'*   [2] B *Suthwelle*   [3] B *Northmuscham*   [4] A *Southmuscam*; B *Suthmuscham*   [5] B *Crophille*   [6] A *Blitheworth*; B *Blythe-worth*   [7] A *Halghton'*   [8] A *Assheburn*; B *de Assheburn'*   [9] Repeated in error.   [10] B adds *est*.   [11] B *Suthwelle*   [12] B *Northwelle*   [13] A *North-muscam*   [14] A, B *Blitheworth*   [15] A *Suwell*; B *de Suthwelle*   [16] B *predictis*   [17] A *Southmuscam*   [18] A *Southmuscam*

Suthmuscham.[19] Et eo waranto clamat habere [emendas] assise cervisie fracte tam de tenentibus suis in eadem villa de Suthmuscham etc. Et quo ad emendas assise panis etc. in Suthmuscam nichil clamat ad presens. Et quo ad emendas assise panis et cervisie fracte etc. de tenentibus suis in Crophill' et Halghton' nichil clamat ad presens etc. Et Willelmus de Denum qui sequitur pro rege etc. dicit quod idem capitulum non habet[20] huiusmodi libertates habere non potest etc. Dicit enim quod idem capitulum non habet pillore neque tumbrell' neque aliqua iudicialia que ad huius[21] libertates pertinent. Et hoc paratus est verificare etc. Et capitulum dicit quod non potest hoc deducare[22] set dicit quod per hoc non debet ipsum capitulum a libertatibus suis predictis preiudicari. Quia dicit quod a tempore quo non extat memoria ipsum usum est punire transgressores assise panis et cervisie de tenentibus predictis per penam pecuniariam et ita facere et habere emendam[23] etc. Et Willelmus qui sequitur etc. dicit quod ex quo idem capitulum clamat predictas libertates et satis expresse cognovit quod ipsum non habet pillore tumbrell' neque alia iudicialia que ad huius[24] libertates pertinent set pro libertatibus suis manutenendis dicit quod ipsum semper usum est capere penam pecuniariam loco punicionis corporalis etc. que potius est abusio libertatis et corruptela[25] quia[26] versus libertatis etc. petit quod predicte libertates capiant[27] in manum domini regis etc.

p. 69   Et idem Willelmus qui sequitur etc. dicit quod presentatus est in curia hic per iuratores wapentachii de Thurgarton' et Lyth[28] quod idem capitulum habet visum franciplegii in eisdem villis ad quod idem capitulum placitando clam' visum predictum etc. Et idem Willelmus qui sequitur etc. dixit quod capitulum predictum in itinere Johannis de Vallibus et sociorum suorum iusticiariis ultimo itinerantibus hic tempore regis Edwardi avi etc. nichil clamat in quibusdam villarum predictarum nisi emendas assise panis et cervisie tamen et in quibusdam earumdem[29] villarum[30] emendas assise cervisie tamen que non sunt nisi parcelle visus etc. et exquo idem capitulum clamat visum franciplegii titulo prescriptionis etc. in hoc allegando ipsum habere visum ante predictum iter etc. quem quidem visum tunc non clamat etc. petit iudicium etc. si idem capitulum[31] emendas predictas clamere possit etc. que[32] superfluitatem clamei predicti visus etc. forisfieri debent de iure etc. datus est eis[33] dies de audiendo inde iudicio suo apud Derby[34] die lune in crastino sancte Marie magdal'[35] etc. ad quem diem venit tam predictus Willelmus qui sequitur etc. quam predictum capitulum per dictum[36] attornatum suum. Et datus est ei dies de audiendo inde iudicium suum[37] ibidem die lune proxima post quindenam sancti Michaelis etc. Et vicecomes respondet domino rege de exitibus aliorum visuum etc. Postea dominus rex mandavit breve suum iusticiariis hic quod recordum et processum super clamium capituli predicti super libertatibus predictis

---

[19] A *Southmuscam*; B adds *etc.*   [20] B omits *non habet.*   [21] B *huiusmodi*
[22] *Sic*; A, B *dedicere*   [23] A, B *emendas*   [24] B *huiusmodi*   [25] B *coruptela*
[26] A, B *quam*   [27] B *capiantur*   [28] A *Lith*   [29] B omits.   [30] B adds
predictarum.   [31] B adds *etc.*   [32] B adds *per.*   [33] B *ei*   [34] A *Derb'*
[35] B *Magdalene.* The version in JUST 1/684, rot. 16d ends here; the *postea* is omitted.
[36] A *predictum*   [37] A *iudicio suo*

coram domino rege mitteret in octabis sancti Michaelis ubicumque etc.
Ideo recordum mittitur etc. per Adam de Neuton' capellanum.

Note Pd. in *Placita de Quo Warranto*, 636 from TNA, JUST 1/687, rot. 15d. In the
Rex roll, JUST 1/684, the entry is found on rot. 16d.

147 *Record of the case between the king and the Chapter and canons
of Southwell in a plea of Quo warranto in the court of King's Bench at
Westminster in Easter term, 5 Edward III (1331), enrolled on rotulus 115
of the plea roll. The king has sent to the justices, by writ close, a petition
by Henry of Edwinstowe, Robert of Woodhouse and other canons of
Southwell, exhibited before the king and his council, together with the
process previously held before William of Harle and his associates, justices in eyre at Nottingham in 1329, concerning the liberties claimed by
the Chapter and challenged there by the king [see 14–16, 145 and 146].
The justices are instructed to inspect the petition and its endorsement,
and also the process concerning the fine made by the canons to recover
the liberties mentioned in it, and then to proceed to the final determina-
tion of these matters, notwithstanding that the liberties claimed in other
earlier eyres did not stand, and in the meantime not to levy charges or
impose any burdens on the canons or the Chapter.*

*The petition from Edwinstowe, Woodhouse and other canons, is recited
in the original French: they show the king and council that in the lands
and tenements of their prebends they have and use view of frankpledge
and what pertains to it; and have been accustomed to be able to correct
breaches of the assize of bread and ale from time immemorial; and also
that the king's justices in eyre in Nottinghamshire are accustomed to hear
and determine, at the door of the church, the pleas touching the church
and its tenants. The franchises claimed by the Chapter have not been
allowed by the justices of the recent eyre because they are not so wide as
those claimed at the previous eyre forty-five years before [in fact held in
1280]. The canons pray for restitution of the view, which is worth no more
than 7s each year, as appears in the transcript of the process in the same
eyre, under the seal of William of Harle, the chief justice, in Chancery,
attached to the petition, together with the other franchises; having regard
to the fact that their letters and muniments, which would have assisted
their claim, have been carried away, when the church was robbed, as is
known to the whole country; the church should not be disinherited of all
the franchises previously mentioned. The endorsement on the petition
provides that the whole process is to be placed before the king's justices
assigned to hold these pleas, and examined there, and the fine made by
them for having back their liberties is to be recovered, notwithstanding
that the franchises were not fully claimed in earlier eyres; and that, while
the matter is still undetermined, no charges should be levied or any injury
done to them for that reason.*

*The process before Harle and his associates at Nottingham in November
1329 concerning the claim to view of frankpledge is then recited in full
down to the end of the postea in which it is recorded that Waynflete
paid the fine for the restoration of the view of Beckingham and Dunham*

[see 145]. Current proceedings in King's Bench then continue with the appearance of Robert de Totel' as attorney for the Chapter. Inspection of the petition and process established that the claim to view of frankpledge in Beckingham and Dunham had been upheld, but that it was not clearly established that the Chapter had claimed any other liberty in the eyre. The canons are asked on what account they caused the process to be brought, and if the Chapter and the canons held those liberties in common or not, and further that they should show the court by what right and in what way they used the liberties; the canons then ask the court for licence to imparl, to consult among themselves. Having deliberated, they say that the canons are prebendaries of the church and constitute a Chapter, and that they hold their prebends separately; and that the Chapter holds other liberties and lands, tenements and fees pertaining to itself, and each of the canons in the lands, tenements and fees of their own prebends, the Chapter holding view frankpledge of all their men and tenants and residents in its fee of Southwell, Halam and Edingley, twice a year. They claim that the justices in eyre come to Southwell to hear and determine, at the door of the church, all pleas touching the Chapter, the canons, their tenants and ministers, except pleas of the crown, which the justices hear and determine at the house of a canon outside the sanctuary. Of the canons, Robert of Woodhouse, prebendary of Norwell, holds view of frankpledge for all the men, tenants and residents in his fee of Norwell, at Norwell twice a year; Robert of Nottingham, prebendary of Oxton and Cropwell, for his in Oxton, Blidworth, Calverton, Woodborough and Cropwell; Lambert of Threckingham, prebendary of Halloughton, twice a year at his prebend; Henry of Edwinstowe, prebendary of Oxton and Cropwell, in his fee of Oxton, Blidworth, Calverton, Southwell, Woodborough and Cropwell; Robert of Bridlington, prebendary of Woodborough, in his fee of Woodborough and Edingley; William of Barnby, prebendary of Beckingham, in his fee of Southwell, Edingley and Beckingham; William of Newark, prebendary of North Muskham, in his fee of North Muskham, Caunton, South Muskham and Normanton by Southwell; Thomas of St Albans, prebendary of Dunham, in his fee of Dunham; and John de Sandale, prebendary of Normanton, in his fee in Southwell and Normanton. These uses had been accustomed, and they ask that they may be accepted as the liberties claimed.

Adam of Fincham, who sues for the king, contends that the liberties claimed in the eyre, and the view of frankpledge in Beckingham and Dunham, had been judged, as recorded in the process, and that they do not exist and should not be allowed; and the canons now acknowledge that they form a Chapter and hold the claimed liberties separately, but they had used them contrary to their claim through the Chapter, so he asks for all the liberties to be taken into the king's hand.

Afterwards the king sent a letter close to Geoffrey le Scrope and his fellow justices of King's Bench, dated at Windsor on 18 February 1331, referring to the petition from Woodhouse, Edwinstowe and the other canons stating that the Chapter and the individual prebendaries had exercised the right to view of frankpledge and the correction of breaches of the assize of bread and ale by their tenants, and other liberties, which the eyre justices deferred allowing although it was before them, as well as the process they were sent from Chancery under the foot of the king's seal, ordering them to examine the process and the petition, having a fine from them for recovering those liberties by plevin, and proceed to a final decision on the matter; now, on behalf of the clerks, the king accepts that the prebendaries and Chapter, questioned before him whether these liberties were in common of the Chapter itself and used by the prebendaries themselves, they answered before the king that they had always exercised the liberties in the lands, tenants and fees of their prebends, not in common, and claimed them on that basis, so that the basis on which the liberties were claimed in the eyre could not be valid, so they asked the king to provide a remedy. The king therefore orders that, from each of the prebendaries, a fine shall be taken for recovery of the liberties which they wish to claim in their lands, tenements and fees, from themselves and from the Chapter, and then proceed to the final decision, notwithstanding that they had not been claimed in the eyres of earlier justices, or that the Chapter claimed them to be separate but pertaining to it, and, the final decision pending, no charges should be levied or any injury done to them for that reason. On the basis of the writ, the Chapter and canons through their attorney asked for their liberties to be restored, and the court agrees. For this, for the recovery by plevin, the Chapter gives the king a fine of half a mark by plea of Robert Vissell. Through him also Robert of Woodhouse, prebendary of Norwell, pays 40d; [Robert of Nottingham, prebendary of Oxton and Cropwell, 40d]; Lambert of Threckingham, prebendary of Halloughton, 40d.; Henry of Edwinstowe, prebendary of Oxton and Cropwell, 40d; Robert of Bridlington, prebendary of Woodborough, half a mark; William of Barnby, prebendary of Beckingham, half a mark; William of Newark, prebendary of North Muskham, half a mark; Thomas of St Albans, prebendary of Dunham, half a mark; John of Sandale, prebendary of Normanton, half a mark.

Under a heading, the claim of the Chapter and prebends is recited in full. The Chapter claims view of frankpledge of all men, tenants and residents in its soke in Southwell, Halam and Normanton, held twice a year at Southwell. It also claims view of frankpledge of all men, tenants and residents in its fee of Edingley, held twice a year. It also claims that in each eyre by the justices itinerant in Nottinghamshire the justices shall come to Southwell to hear and determine, at the door of the church, all pleas touching the Chapter, the canons, their tenants of the church and their ministers, except pleas of the crown, which the justices shall hear and determine at the house of a certain canon outside the sanctuary. Robert of Woodhouse, prebendary of Norwell, claims view of frankpledge in Norwell, Woodhouse, Willoughby and Middlethorpe, at Norwell twice a year, and waif in the same places. Robert of Nottingham, prebendary of Oxton and Cropwell, claims view of frankpledge in Oxton, Blidworth, Calverton and Woodborough, and waif in the same places. He also claims view of frankpledge in Cropwell and Hickling, held twice a year, and waif. Lambert of Threckingham, prebendary of Halloughton, claims in his manor of Halloughton view of frankpledge twice a year, and waif and stray. Henry of Edwinstowe, prebendary of Oxton and Cropwell, claims view of frankpledge in Oxton, Blidworth, Calverton, Southwell and Woodborough, held twice a year at Oxton, and waif in the same places. He also claims view of frankpledge in Cropwell and Hickling, held twice a year, and waif in the same places. Robert of Bridlington, prebendary of Woodborough, claims view of frankpledge in Woodborough and Edingley, held twice a year. He also claims waif in his lands and fees. William of Barnby, prebendary of Beckingham, claims view of frankpledge in Southwell and Edingley, held twice a year at Southwell. He also claims view of frankpledge in Beckingham, held at Beckingham twice a year. William of Newark, prebendary of North Muskham, claims view of frankpledge in North Muskham, Caunton, South Muskham, North Carlton and Normanton by Southwell, held at North Muskham twice a year. He also claims waif in the same places. Thomas of St Albans, prebendary of Dunham, claims view of frankpledge in Dunham, Darlton, Whimpton and Ragnall, held at Dunham twice a year. John of Sandale, prebendary of Normanton, claims view of frankpledge in Southwell and Normanton, held twice a year at Southwell.

Then, on the morrow of Ascension [9 May 1331] the Chapter, through their attorney Robert de Totel', and Woodhouse and the other prebendaries, through their attorney, claim singularly view of frankpledge in those places, and the prebendaries also claim waif and stray, from time immemorial, used in right of their prebends. They ask for enquiry to be made by a jury, and Adam of Fincham similarly. The sheriff is ordered to cause a jury of twenty-four to come to King's Bench on the morrow of St John the Baptist [25 June 1331] from the visne of Southwell, Edingley, Norwell, Oxton, Crophill, Woodborough, Halloughton, Beckingham, North Muskham and Dunham, with no affinity with the Chapter or the canons, to acknowledge whether the claims are true or not. The Chapter claims that the justices in eyre sat at the church door for Southwell pleas, with crown pleas in the house of a canon, in the most recent eyre and the ones before that, and vouch the rolls of the justices for that; so an order is sent to the treasurer and chamberlains of the Exchequer to search the rolls and certify this to the court by 25 June. On that day Fincham, the Chapter and all the prebendaries come, and also the chosen jurors: namely Hugh of Normanton, Richard Ingram, Thomas de Whatton of Stoke, William de la Basage, Henry Cotel, John in le Wilewes, Ranulph of Kilvington, Robert de Whiten', Hugh of Colston, Ralph of Bulwell, Ralph the clerk of Langar and Alan of Raby. The jurors relate all the claims in detail and swear that they are valid, and so the Chapter and canons are allowed to go without day, saving the king's right.

Placita coram domino rege apud Westmonasterium de termino Pasche anno regni regis Edwardi tercii post conquestum quinto Rotulo CXV[1]

Dominus rex misit iusticiariis suis hic per breve suum clausum quandam peticionem dilectorum clericorum suorum Henrici de Edenstow[2] et

---

[1] A has the heading *Adhuc de crastino Ascensionis* at the top of the rotulus.

Roberti de Wodehous[3] et aliorum canonicorum ecclesie beate Marie
Suthwellie[4] coram ipso domino[5] rege et consilio suo exhibitam ac quemdam
processum de quibusdam libertatibus coram Willelmo de Herle et sociis
suis iusticiariis nuper in comitatu Notingh' itinerantibus per capitulum
ecclesie de Suthwell' et canonicos predictos clamatis ac eciam coram
eisdem iusticiariis presentatam. Et per breve predictum iusticiariis suis
hic mandans quod inspectis petitione illa et indorsamento facto ad eandem
necnon processu predicto finem ab eisdem canonicis pro libertatibus in
predicto processu contentis habendis per plevinam recipiant et ulterius ad
finalem discussionem eiusdem negocii procedant eo non obstante quod
libertates ille in aliis itinerantibus iusticiariorum itinerancium in comitatu
predicto clamate non extiterunt ac dicto negotio coram eisdem iusticiariis
indiscusso pendente de quicquam ab eisdem canonicis seu de capitulo
predicto levandis sine ipsos premissa occasione onerandis seu gravandis
supersederi faciatis qui quidem peticio et processus sequuntur in hec verba.

Peticio.[6] A nostre seignur le roi et son conseil monstront[7] ses clers
Robert de Wodehous Henri de Edenstow[8] et les autres chanoignes de
leglise de Suthwell'[9] en le countee[10] de Notingh' que come le chapitre de
mesmes[11] leglise en les terrez[12] et tenementz appurtenanz a ycel[13] et les
ditz provendres[14] en lour provendes en mesme leglise ont eu et use daver
vewe de franciplegg' et quant qe a veue appertient et auxint amendes
dassise de payne[15] et de cerveise enfreinte de lour tenantz puis temps
de memorie et auxint qe en chescun eyre en mesme[16] le countee[17] qe les
justices soleient seer en le eus del eglise et illeoqes terminer lez pleez
touchant[18] la dite eglise et les tenantz dycell'[19] et tout soit il qe present[20]
fuit en leir[21] de Notingham qe le dit chapitre avoit lez ditz[22] fraunchises
si ne voleient[23] lez[24] justices de mesme leiyre a lower[25] au dit chapitre
mesmes[26] les fraunchises[27] | ne a les chanoignes susditz priee[28] qe il ne   p. 70
clameront pas si largement en le darrein eyre devant[29] qe estoit a qaurant[30]
et cynk[31] aunz passez dont les ditz chanoignes prient qils purrent[32] aver
restitucion de la dit vewe qe ne vaut par an forsque vii s. come poet apparer
per le transcript'[33] du processe en fait en mesme leyre qe vyent desus[34]
le seal monser William[35] Herle en chauncellerie et qe ore est attache a
ceste peticion ensemblement ad toutez[36] les autres franchises avantditz
eyant[37] regard qe toutez[38] lour letres et autres munimentz depar quelx ils
se poent[39] aver eyde furent enportez[40] qant leglise estoit de robbe come
conu chose est a toute le paiis[41] issint qe la dit[42] eglise ne soit disherite.[43]

[2] A *Ednestowe*   [3] A *Wodehouses*   [4] A *Suwelle*   [5] A omits.   [6] Written in the right margin; see also **14**, where the prebendaries concerned are identified in the Note.   [7] A *monstrent*   [8] A *Edenestowe*   [9] A *Suwell'*   [10] A *counte*   [11] A *meisme*   [12] A *terres*   [13] A *icel*   [14] A *provenders*   [15] A *pain*   [16] A *meisme*   [17] A *counte*   [18] A *tochanz*   [19] A *dicele*   [20] A *presente*   [21] A *leyre*   [22] A *les dites*   [23] A *voileient*   [24] A *les*   [25] A *meisme leyr allower*   [26] A *meismes*   [27] Superscript erasure above this word.   [28] A inserts *ceo.*   [29] A *devaunt*   [30] A *quaraunt*   [31] A *cink*   [32] A *puissent*   [33] A *transescrit*   [34] A *vint desouz*   [35] A inserts *de.*   [36] A *od totes*   [37] A *avantdites eant*   [38] A *tentz*   [39] A *poienit*   [40] A *eide feuret emporter*   [41] A *tote le pais*   [42] A *dite*   [43] A *desherite*

INDORSAMENTUM PETICIONIS PREDICTE TALE EST: Soit toute ceste[44] processe mande[45] devant les justices le roi a ces pleez tenir assignez od la peticioun[46] et veues et examinez illeoqes mesme[47] le processe[48] preignent mesmes[49] justices pur les fraunchises clamez reaver per plevine fin et outre aillent a finale discussioun de la bosoigne nient contrsteant[50] qe les fraunchises nont mye este clames[51] en autres eyres et pendant la bosoigne nient termine soit mande[52] a surseer de rien lever charger ou grever par cele[53] enchesoun.

PROCESSUS CORAM WILLELMO HERLE SEQUITUR IN HEC VERBA: Placita de quo waranto coram Willelmo Herle et sociis suis iusticiariis domini regis itinerantibus apud Not' die lune proxima post festum sancti Martini anno regni regis Edwardi tercii a conquestu tercio rotulo quinto. Presentatum est per xii iuratores wapentachii de Thurgarton et de Lyth quod capitulum de Suthwell habet visum franciplegii de omnibus tenentibus suis in Suthwell' Northwell' Suthmuscham[54] Northmuscham[55] Calneton' Oxton' Calverton' Wodeburgh Crophill' Blythworth[56] Halghton' Bekyngham Dunham Halum Edyngley et Normanton' quo waranto vel a quo tempore ignorant. Et eciam presentant quod in quolibet itinere iusticiariorum etc. iusticiarii itinerantes solebant sedere in ostio australi ecclesie Suthwell' predicte et ibidem terminare placita de itinere de omnibus tenentibus dicti capituli et respondere coram iusticiariis per xii et non alibi. Ideo predicte libertates capiantur in manum domini regis.

Postea venit predictum capitulum per Thomam de Asshborne[57] attornatum suum in omnibus placitis et querelis et similiter ad libertates suas calumpniandas etc. Et petit predictum visum per plevinam. Et habet et dicit quod ipsum capitulum a tempore quo non extat memoria habuit predictum visum in predictis villis ut de iure ecclesie beate Marie Suthwellie[58] etc. Et Willelmus de Denum qui sequitur pro rege dicit quod capitulum predictum ad huiusmodi clamium admitti non debet titulo prescripcionis.[59] Dicit enim quod idem capitulum alias coram Johanne de Vallibus[60] et sociis suis iusticiariis ultimo itinerantibus hic tempore regis Edwardi avi domini regis nunc summonitus fuit ad clamium suum proprium ad respondendum predicto Edwardi regis etc. quo waranto clamat emendas assise panis et cervisie etc.[61] in eisdem villis de Suthwell' Northwell' Northmuscham Suthmuscham[62] Calneton' Oxton' Calverton' Wodeburgh et Blythworth.[63] Et idem capitulum tamen clamat emendas assise panis et cervisie in predictis villis de Suthwell' Northwell'[64] Northmuscham Calneton' Oxton' Calverton' Wodeburgh et Blythworth.[65] Et emendam assise cervisie fracte tamen in Suthmuscham.[66] Et similiter idem capitulum nunc in itinere isto summonitus est ad respondendum[67]

[44] A *cest*　[45] A *maunde*　[46] A *peticion*　[47] A *meisme*　[48] A *proces*　[49] A *meismes*; and inserts *les* here.　[50] A *contrstant*　[51] A *clamez*　[52] A *maunde*　[53] A *cel*　[54] A *Suthmuscam*　[55] A *Northmuscam*　[56] A *Blitheworth'*　[57] A *Assheburn'*　[58] A *Suthwell'*　[59] A *titulo prescriptionis admitti non debet*　[60] A *Wall'*　[61] A omits.　[62] A *Suthmuscam Northmuscam*　[63] A *Blitheworth'*　[64] In A followed by another name, possibly South Muskham, struck through and then erased.　[65] A *Blitheworth'*　[66] A *Suthmuscam*　[67] A inserts *etc.*

quo waranto clamat emendas assise panis et cervisie etc. in predictis villis de Suthwell' Northwell' Northmuscham Suthmuscham[68] Calneton' Oxton' Calverton' Wodeburgh Crophill' Blythworth[69] et Halghton' ad quod clamium idem capitulum respondet quo ad Suthmuscham[70] ad ipsum non clamat nisi emendas assise panis et[71] cervisie fracte tamen ibidem. Et quo ad emendas assise panis et cervisie in Crophill' et Halghton' nichil clamat ad presens. Unde dicit quod cum idem capitulum coram Johanne de Vallibus etc. ad breve etc. ad quod tunc summonitum fuit et similiter ad breve ad quod nunc summonitus est etc. non clamat nisi illa que sunt parcelle visus[72] et hoc in quibusdam villis etc. et in quibusdam non. Unde petit iudicium si predictum capitulum titulo supradicto visum franciplegii etc. in eisdem villis clamare possit vel debeat in hac parte etc. Et capitulum dicit quod ipsum alias in predicto itinere Johannis de Vallibus etc. non fuit summonitus ad respondendum predicto regi avo etc. quo waranto clamat visum franciplegii vel aliquid aliud in predictis villis de Bekyngham et Dunham etc. nec aliquid tunc presentatus fuit super ipsum capitulum de aliquibus libertatibus in eisdem villis unde dicit quod de illo ad quod tunc non fuit positum ad respondendum admitti debet ad presens ad clamandum etc. | Et dicit quod ipsum capitulum a tempore quo non extat memoria p. 71
habuit visum franciplegii apud Bekyngham de tenentibus suis ibidem et eciam visum franciplegii apud Dunham de tenentibus suis ibidem ut de iure ecclesie predicte etc. Et Willelmus de Denum qui sequitur pro rege[73] etc. petit quod inquiratur pro rege si predictum capitulum habuit predictum visum in predictis villis de Bekyngham et Dunham etc. Et si sit tunc qualiter illis usum est etc. Ideo inquiratur etc. Juratores dicunt super sacramentum suum quod predictum capitulum a tempore quo non extat memoria habuit in Bekyngham visum per se de omnibus tenentibus suis ibidem. Et in Dunham visum per se de omnibus tenentibus suis residentibus ibidem. Et dicunt quod idem capitulum semper usum est punire illos qui deliquerunt contra assisam panis et cervisie etc. per penam pecuniariam et nunquam ponere ipsos[74] ad iudicium corporale. Et iuratores quesitus quantum predicti visus valent per annum in omnibus villis exceptis Bekyngham et Dunham[75] dicunt quod visus de tenentibus suis in Edyngley[76] Halum Halghton' Normanton' et Suthwell' tentus apud Suthwell' valet per annum duos solidos. Et visus de tenentibus in Crophill' Calverton' Blythworth[77] et Oxton' tentus apud Oxton' valet duos solidos per annum. Et visus de tenentibus in Calneton' et Northmuscham[78] tentus apud Northmuscham[79] xii denarios per annum. Et visus de tenentibus[80] in Suthmuscham[81] duodecim denarios per annum. Et visus in Wodeburgh tentus ibidem per se duodecim denarios per annum. Ideo predicti visus in omnibus predictis villis capiantur in manu domini regis etc. Postea Johannes de Waynflete[82] Petrus del Wych'[83] de eodem comitatu fecerunt finem cum domino rege de quadraginta solidis pro predictis visibus in

---

68 A *Northmuscam Suthmuscam*   69 A *Blithworth*   70 A *Suthmuscam*   71 A omits *panis et*.   72 A inserts *etc.*   73 A omits *pro Rege*.   74 A *eos*   75 In A *valent per annum* comes here; different word order.   76 A *Edyngleye*   77 A *Blitheworth'*   78 A *Northmuscam*   79 A *Northmuscam*   80 A inserts *suis*.   81 A *Southmuscam*   82 A *Weyflet*; and inserts *et.*   83 A *Wyche*

Bekyngham et Dunham tamen eidem capitulum rehabendis. Ideo predictum capitulum rehabeat visus illos utendi illis modo quo decet etc. Et quoad visus illos inde sine die salvo iure regis nostri[84] etc.

Et modo venit hic coram rege tam capitulum predictum quam canonici predicti per Robertum de Totel' attornatum suum et inspectis petitione et processu predictis pro eo quod compertum est quod libertates predicte per predictum capitulum in itinere predicto clamate fuerunt et libertas \visus/ franciplegii in villis de Bekyngham et Dunham eidem capitulo adiudicata fuit et per predictum processum non est compertum[85] quod predicti canonici aliquam libertatem predictarum in itinere illo clamarunt. Quesitus est ab[86] eisdem canonicis ob quam causam venire fecerunt hic processum predictum et si dictum capitulum libertates predictas superdictas simul cum canonicis predictis in communi teneant vel non et dictum est eis quod ulterius ostendant curie qualiter et quo modo illis libertatibus utuntur etc. Qui quidem canonici petunt inde licenciam loquendi etc. Et habita inde deliberacione dicunt quod ipsi canonici sunt prebendarii ecclesie predicte et faciunt capitulum et quod tenent prebendas suas separatim. Et quod idem capitulum tenet aliquas libertates libertatum predictorum in terris tenementis et feodis ad illud spectantibus per se et quilibet canonicorum predictorum per se aliquas libertates earumdem libertatum in terris tenementis et feodis prebendarum suarum ecclesie predicte videlicet predictum capitulum visum franciplegii de omnibus hominibus tenentibus suis et residentibus in feodo suo de Suthwell' Halum et Edyngley[87] tenendum bis per annum. Et quod in quolibet itinere iusticiariorum itinerancium in comitatu Not' iusticiarii ibidem itinerantes veniant apud Suthwell' audiant et terminent ad ostium[88] ecclesie predicte omnia placita tangencia capitulum canonicos tenentes suos de ecclesia predicta et ministros suos preter placita corone que predicti iusticiarii audient et terminabunt ad domum alicuius canonici extra sanctuarium. Et Robertus de Wodehous unus canonicorum predictorum et prebendarius prebende de Northwell' in ecclesia predicta tenet visum franciplegii et ea que ad visum pertinent de omnibus hominibus tenentibus et residentibus in feodo suo de Northwell' ut de iure ecclesie[89] sue predicte apud Northwell' bis per annum etc. Et Robertus de Notyngham[90] prebendarius prebende de Oxton' et Crophill' in ecclesia predicta visum franciplegii in ea que ad visum pertinent de omnibus hominibus tenentibus et residentibus suis in Oxton' Blythworth[91] Calverton' Wodeburgh et Crophill' ut de iure prebende sue predicte. Et Lambertus de Trikyngham prebendarius prebende de Halghton' in ecclesia predicta visum franciplegii et ea que ad visum pertinet tenendum ibidem bis per annum ad prebendam suam predictam. Henricus | de Edenstow[92] prebendarius prebende de Oxton' et Crophill' in ecclesia predicta visum franciplegii et ea que ad visum pertinent de omnibus hominibus tenentibus et residentibus in feodo suo in Oxton' et

p. 72

---

[84] A omits.   [85] *Canonici non ?clamatus in predicto itinere* is written in the margin at this point, in the same hand as the pointing finger in the next note and both may be of fifteenth-century date.   [86] A pointing finger is drawn in the margin at this point. [87] A *Edyngleye*   [88] A *hostium*   [89] A *prebende*   [90] A *Notingham*   [91] A *Blitheworth'*   [92] A *Edenestowe*

Blythworth[93] Calverton Suthwell' Wodeburgh[94] et Crophill'[95] ut de iure prebende sue predicte. Robertus de Bridlyngton'[96] prebendarius prebende de Wodeburgh[97] in ecclesia predicta visum franciplegii et ea que ad visum pertinent de omnibus hominibus tenentibus et residentibus in feodo suo in Wodeburgh[98] et Edyngley ut de iure prebende sue predicte. Willelmus de Barneby prebendarius prebende de Bekyngham in ecclesia predicta visum franciplegii et ea que ad visum pertinent de omnibus tenentibus residentibus in feodo suo in Suthwell' Edyngley Bekyngham ut de iure prebende sue predicte. Willelmus de Newerk prebendarius prebende de Northmuscham[99] in ecclesia predicta visum franciplegii et ea que ad visum pertinent de omnibus hominibus tenentibus et residentibus in feodo suo in Northmuscham[100] Calneton' Suthmuscham[101] Normanton' iuxta Suthwell' ut de iure prebende sue predicte. Thomas de Sancto Albano prebendarius prebende de Dunham[102] in ecclesia predicta visum franciplegii et ea que ad visum pertinent de omnibus hominibus tenentibus et residentibus in feodo suo in Dunham[103] ut de iure prebende sue predicte. Johannes de Sandehale[104] prebendarius prebende de Normanton' in ecclesia predicta visum franciplegii et ea que ad visum pertinent de omnibus hominibus tenentibus et residentibus in feodo suo in Suthwell'[105] Normanton' ut de iure prebende sue predicte. Et sic hactenus illis uti consueverunt et petunt admitti ad libertates illas clamandas et placitandas in forma predicta.

Et Adam de Fyncham qui sequitur pro domino rege petit quod exquo omnis libertates predicte in itinere predicto per predictum capitulum clamate fuerunt et visus franciplegii in predictis villis de Bekyngham et Dunham ibidem dicto capitulo adiudicata fuit prout per predictum processum manifeste liquet et quod libertas aliqua in predicto itinere per canonicos predictos clamata non extitit nec eisdem adiudicatus fuit. Et modo iidem canonici cognoscunt quod ipsi faciant capitulum et quod dictum capitulum aliquas libertates libertatum predictarum scilicet de omnibus tenentibus et residentibus in feodo eiusdem capituli separatim tenet et quilibet canonicorum predictorum per se aliquas libertates libertatum predictarum de omnibus tenentibus et residentibus in feodis illis prebendarum suarum predictarum ut supradictum est separatim tenet et quod sic illis utantur in contrarium clamii supradicti per predictum capitulum in itinere predicto facti petit quod omnes libertates predicte capiantur in manum domini regis. Ideo omnes libertates supradicte capiantur in manu domini regis etc.

Postea dominus rex mandavit breve suum clausum iusticiariis suis hic in hec verba: Edwardus Dei gratia rex Anglie et dominus Hibernie et dux Aquitanie dilectis et fidelibus suis Galfrido le Scropp'[106] et sociis suis iusticiariis ad placitum coram tenend' assignatis salutem. Cum nos nuper ad prosecutionem dilectorum clericorum nostrorum Roberti de Wodehous et[107] Henrici de Edenestow[108] et aliorum canonicorum ecclesie beate Marie

---

[93] A *Blitheworth'*   [94] A *Wodburgh'*   [95] A *Crophull'*   [96] A *Brydelyngton'* [97] A *Wodburgh'*   [98] A *Wodburgh'*   [99] A *Northmuscam*   [100] A *Northmus-cam*   [101] A *Suthmuscam*   [102] A *Donham*   [103] A *Donham*   [104] A *Sandale* [105] A inserts *et.*   [106] A *Scrop'*   [107] A omits.   [108] A *Edenestowe*

Suthwell' in comitatu Not'[109] per peticionem suam coram nobis et concilio nostro exhibitam nobis suggencium quod capitulum ecclesie illius in terris et tenementis ad idem capitulum spectantibus et eciam prebendarii prebendarum eiusdem ecclesie in prebendis suis usi fuerunt habere visum franciplegii et quicquid ad huiusmodi visum pertinet et emendas assise panis et cervisie de tenentibus suis fracte necnon quasdam alias libertates in eadem petitione contentas et quod iusticiarii nostri nuper itinerantes in eodem comitatu libertates illas ei allocare distulerunt quamquam coram eis quod idem capitulum libertatibus illis usum fuerit presentatum extiterit peticionem predictam simul cum tenore tocius processus inde coram prefatis miserimus nostris in itinere illo habitis quem coram nobis in cancellaria nostra venire fecimus nobis inferius sub pede sigilli nostri mandantes quod visis et examinatis processu et peticione predictis finem ab eis pro eisdem libertatibus per plevinam rehabendis recuperetis et

p. 73 ulterius ad finalem discussionem negocii illius procederetis et iam ex | parte ipsorum clericorum nostrorum accepimus quod predicti prebendarii et capitulum coram nobis allocuti utrum libertatibus illis in communi an idem capitulum per se et predicti prebendarii per se usi fuerunt coram nobis responderunt quod capitulum predictum in terris tenementis et feodis ad illud spectantibus aliquibus earumdem libertatum per se et quilibet eorum prebendariorum in terris tenementis et feodis prebendarum suarum aliquibus predictarum libertatum per se semper hactenus usi fuerint et sic eis uti et habere clamium et non in communi per quod exitus finalis inde modo quo predicte libertates in itinere illo fuerunt clamate coram nobis fieri non potest super quo nobis supplicarunt eis per nos de remedio provideri. Nos volentes supplicationi ipsorum clericorum nostrorum pretextu laudabilis obsequium progenitoribus nostris regibus Anglie et nobis per ipsos hactenus impensi quatinus[110] bono remedio[111] potuerimus in hac parte subvenire vobis mandamus quod a quolibet prebendariorum predictorum pro libertatibus quas iidem prebendarii coram nobis clamare voluerint in terris tenementis sive feodis suis prebendarum illarum per plevinam rehabendam sive per se et a predicto capitulo pro libertatibus quas coram vobis clamare voluerit in terris tenementis sive feodis ad idem capitulum spectantibus per plevinam rehabendis finem per se recipiatis et ulterius ad finalem discussionem inde procedatis non obstante quod libertates ille in aliis itineribus iusticiariorum in eodem comitatu clamate non extiterint[112] seu quod idem capitulum libertates predictas tam in terris tenementis et feodis ipsorum prebendariorum a possessionibus ipsius capituli seperatis quam in terris tenementis sive feodis ad predictum capitulum spectantibus clamat ut predictum est et dicto negotio indiscusso pendente de quicquam ab eisdem prebendariis sive aliquo eorum sive de predicto capitulo levandi seu ipsos ea occasione onerandis seu gravandis supersederi faciatis. Teste me ipso apud Wyndesore xviii die Februarii anno regni nostri quinto. Et super hoc venit tam predictum capitulum quam canonici predicti per attornatum suum predictum et petunt libertates predictas per plevinam rehabendas et quod possint admitti ad libertates

---

[109] A *Notingh'*   [110] A *quatenus*   [111] A *modo*   [112] A *extiterunt*

suas clamandas et placitandas iuxta formam brevis predicti et eis concedit videlicet capitulum predictum beate Marie Suthwell' dat domino regi de fine pro libertatibus suis rehabendis per plevinam per placitum Roberti Vissell' dimidiam marcam. Robertus de Wodehous[113] prebendarius prebende de Northwell pro eodem per idem placitum xl d.[114] Lambertus de Trikyngham[115] prebendarius prebende de Halghton' pro eodem per idem placitum xl d. Henricus de Edenstow[116] prebendarius prebende de Oxton' et Crophill' pro eodem per idem placitum xl d. Robertus de Bridlyngton'[117] prebendarius prebende de Wodeburgh[118] pro eodem per idem placitum dimidiam marcam. Willelmus de Barneby prebendarius prebende de Bekyngham pro eodem per idem placitum[119] dimidiam marcam. Willelmus de Newerk prebendarius prebende de Northmuscham pro eodem[120] per idem placitum dimidiam marcam. Thomas de Sancto Albano prebendarius prebende de Dunham pro eodem per idem placitum dimidiam marcam. Johannes de Sandale[121] prebendarius prebende de Normanton' pro eodem per idem placitum dimidiam marcam.

CLAMIUM CAPITULI et prebendariorum ecclesie de Suthwell' ut[122] patet super hac forma.[123] Capitulum ecclesie beate Marie Suthwellie[124] in comitatu Not'[125] clamat habere visum franciplegii et ea que ad visum pertinet de omnibus hominibus tenentibus et residentibus in soca suo in Suthwell' Halum et Nouton tenendum per annum bis apud Suthwell'. Item clamat habere visum franciplegii et ea que ad visum pertinet de omnibus[126] tenentibus[127] et residentibus in feodo suo in Edyngley[128] tenendum bis per annum. Idem capitulum clamat quod in quolibet itinere iusticiariorum itinerancium in comitatu Notynghime[129] quod iusticiarii ibidem itinerantes veniant apud Suthwell' audiant et terminent ad hostium ecclesie predicte omnia placita tangencia capitulum canonicos tenentes suos de ecclesia predicta et ministros suos preter placita corone que predicti iusticiarii audient et terminabunt ad domum alicuius canonici extra sanctuarium. Robertus de Wodhous[130] prebendarius prebende[131] de Northwell' in ecclesia beate Marie de Suthwell' clamat habere visum franciplegii et ea que ad visum pertinent de omnibus hominibus tenentibus et residentibus in feodo suo in Northwell' Wodhous Wyleghby et Mydelthorp'[132] apud Northwell' | bis per annum et wayff[133] in eisdem villis ut de iure prebende sue predicte. Robertus de Notingh'[134] prebendarius prebende de Oxton' et Crophill' in ecclesia beate Marie de Suthwell' clamat[135] visum franciplegii et ea que ad visum pertinent de omnibus hominibus tenentibus et residentibus in

p. 74

---

[113] A *Wodhous*   [114] A inserts *Robertus de Notingham prebendarius prebende de Oxton' et Crophull' pro eodem per idem placitum xl d.*   [115] A *Trychyngham*   [116] A *Edenestowe*   [117] A *Bridelyngton'*   [118] A *Wodburgh'*   [119] A *per placitum predictum*   [120] A omits *pro eodem*.   [121] A *Sandhale*   [122] A omits.   [123] *nota bene* is written in the margin at this point.   [124] A *Suthwell'*   [125] A *Notingh'*   [126] A inserts *hominibus et*.   [127] *De libertatibus Eddyngly et Suthwell'* is written in the margin in a seventeenth-century hand.   [128] A *Edyngleye*   [129] Reading uncertain; A has *Notingham*.   [130] A *Wodehous*   [131] *Norwell'* is written in the margin in a late-fifteenth or sixteenth-century hand.   [132] A *Middelthorp'*   [133] A *wayf*   [134] A *Notingham*   [135] A inserts *habere*.

Oxton' Blythworth[136] Calverton Wodeburgh'.[137] Clamat eciam habere wayff[138] in terris et feodis suis in eisdem villis ut de iure prebende sue. Idem clamat habere visum franciplegii et ea quod ad visum pertinent de omnibus hominibus tenentibus et residentibus in feodo suo in Crophill' et Hykelyng'[139] tenendum bis per annum et wayff[140] in eisdem villis ut de iure prebende sue predicte. Lambertus de Trikyngham[141] prebendarius prebende de Halghton' in ecclesie beate Marie Suthwell' clamat habere[142] in manerio suo de Halghton' visum franciplegii et quicquid ad visum pertinet tenendum ibidem bis per annum et[143] wayff[144] et stray pertinenci ad prebendam suam predictam. Henricus de Edenstow[145] prebendarius prebende de Oxton' et Crophill'[146] in ecclesie beate Marie Suthwell' clamat habere visum franciplegii et ea quod ad visum pertinent de omnibus tenentibus et residentibus in feodo suo in Oxton' Blithworth[147] Calverton' Suthwell' et Wodeburgh tenendum bis per annum apud Oxton' et wayff[148] in eisdem villis ut de iure prebende sue predicte. Idem clamat habere visum franciplegii et ea quod ad visum pertinent de omnibus hominibus tenentibus suis et residentibus in feodo suo de Crophill' et Hiklyng'[149] tenendum bis per annum et wayff[150] in eisdem villis ut de iure prebende sue predicte. Robertus de Bridlygton'[151] prebendarius prebende de Wodburgh in ecclesia beate Marie de Suthwell' clamat habere visum franciplegii et ea que ad visum pertinent de omnibus hominibus tenentibus suis et residentibus in feodo suo in Wodeburgh et Edyngley tenendum bis per annum. Clamat eciam habere wayff[152] in terris et feodis suis ut de iure prebende sue predicte. Willelmus de Barneby prebendarius prebende de Bekyngham in ecclesia beate Marie de Suthwell' clamat habere visum franciplegii et ea que ad visum pertinent de omnibus hominibus tenentibus et residentibus in feodo suo de Suthwell' et Edyngley ut de iure prebende sue predicte apud Suthwell' bis per annum. Idem clamat habere visum franciplegii et ea que ad visum pertinent de omnibus hominibus tenentibus et residentibus in feodo suo de Bekyngham[153] ut de iure prebende sue predicte tenendum apud Bekyngham bis per annum. Willelmus de Newerk prebendarius prebende de Northmuscam in ecclesia beate Marie de Suthwell' clamat habere visum franciplegii et ea que ad visum pertinent de omnibus hominibus tenentibus suis et residentibus in feodo suo in Northmuscham[154] Calneton' Suthmuscham[155] North Carlton' Normanton' iuxta Suthwell' tenendum apud Northmuscham[156] bis per annum. Clamat eciam habere wayff in terris et feodis suis in eisdem villis ut de iure prebende sue predicte. Thomas de Sancto Albano prebendarius prebende de Dunham in ecclesia beate Marie de Suthwell' clamat habere visum franciplegii et ea que ad visum pertinent de omnibus hominibus tenentibus et residentibus in feodo suo in Dunham[157] Derlton' Wymton' et

---

[136] A *Blitheworth*   [137] A *Wodeburgh'*   [138] A *wayf*   [139] A *Hickelyng*
[140] A *wayf*   [141] A *Trikingham*   [142] Followed by *clamat habere* expunged.
[143] A omits.   [144] A *wayf*   [145] A *Edenstowe*   [146] A *Crophull'*   [147] A *Blitheworth'*   [148] A *wayf*   [149] A *Hickelyng'*   [150] A *wayf*   [151] A *Bridelyngton*   [152] A *wayf*   [153] *Northmuscham* is written in the margin in a late-fifteenth or early-sixteenth century hand.   [154] A *Northmuscam*   [155] A *Southmuscam*
[156] A *Northmuscam*   [157] A *Donham*

Ragenhull' ut de iure prebende sue predicte tenendum apud Dunham[158] bis per annum. Johannes de Sandehale[159] prebendarius prebende de Normanton' in ecclesia beate Marie de Suthwell' clamat habere visum franciplegii et ea que a visum pertinent de omnibus hominibus tenentibus et residentibus in feodo suo in Suthwell' et Normanton ut de iure prebende sue predicte bis per annum apud Suthwell'.

Et modo scilicet in crastino ascensionis domini venit predictum capitulum per Robertum de Totel attornatum suum et similiter predicti Robertus de Wodehous et alii prebendarii per attornatum suum et dicunt quod ad hoc quod ipsi singillatim clamant habere visum franciplegii de omnibus hominibus tenentibus suis[160] et residentibus in feodis suis in villis predictis. Et similiter quo ad libertates quas dicti[161] prebendarii clamant habere wayff[162] et stray in predictis villis dicunt quod ipsi et predecessores sui a tempore quo non extat memoria semper hactenus usi fuerint libertatibus illis in predictis villis ut de iure | prebendarum suarum predictarum. Et hoc petunt quod inquiratur per patriam etc. Et Adam de Fyncham qui sequitur pro domino rege similiter. Ideo preceptum est vicecomiti quod venire faciat coram domino rege in crastino sancti Johannis baptiste ubicumque etc. xxiiii[or] tam milites etc. de visum de Suthwell' Edyngley Northwell' Oxton' Crophill'[163] Wodeburgh[164] Halghton' Bekyngham Northmuscham[165] et Dunham[166] per quos etc. Et qui capitulum et prebendarios predictos nulla affinitate etc. ad recognoscendum si predicti capitulum et prebendarii separatim usi fuerint libertatibus predictis in forma predicta necne. Quia etc. Et quo ad hoc quod predictum capitulum[167] in quolibet itinere iusticiariorum itinerancium in comitatu Notingh' iusticiarii itinerantes veniant apud Suthwell' et sedeant in ostio[168] ecclesie predicte et ibidem terminent placita etc. ut predictum est. Idem capitulum dicit quod semper hactenus a tempore quo non extat memoria seisitum fuit quod iusticiarii itinerantes venerunt ibidem et sederunt in ostio[169] ecclesie de Suthwell'[170] et ibidem audiverunt et terminaverunt omnia placita tangencia capitulum canonicos et tenentes suos de ecclesia predicta et ministros suos preter placita corone que prefati iusticiarii audierunt[171] et terminaverunt ad domum cuiusdam canonici extra sanctuarium. Et dicunt[172] quod in ultimo itinere iusticiariorum in comitatu predicto ante istud iter iusticiarii itinerantes venerunt ibidem ad predicta placita tenenda et similiter in aliis itineribus precedentibus a tempore predicto. Et de hoc vocant recordum rotulorum eorumdem iusticiariorum itinerancium etc. Ideo mandatum est thesaurario et camerariis suis[173] quod scrutatis rotulis suis de itineribus suis[174] regem inde certificent ad prefatum terminum etc. ad quem crastinum sancti Johannis baptiste, scilicet anno[175] domini regis nunc quinto, venit predictus Adam qui sequitur pro domino Rege et similiter predictum

p. 75

---

[158] A *Donham* [159] A *Sandale* [160] Repeated in error. [161] A *predicti* [162] A *wayf* [163] A *Crophull'* [164] A *Wodburgh'* [165] A *Northmuscam* [166] A *Donham* [167] A inserts *clamat quod.* [168] A *hostio* [169] A *hostio* [170] The four lines from *Et quo ad hoc…ecclesie de Suthwell'* are bracketed by an orange line in the margin, next to which *Nota* is written three times in a late 16th- or early 17th-century hand. [171] A *audierunt* [172] A *dicit* [173] A omits. [174] A *predictis* [175] A inserts *Regni*.

capitulum Robertus de Wodehous Robertus de Notingh'[176] et omnis et[177] alii prebendarii[178] in ecclesia predicta de Suthwell'. Et eciam iuratores scilicet Hugo de Normanton' Ricardus Ingram Thomas de Whatton' de Stoke. Willelmus de la Basage. Henricus Cotel. John in le Wilewes[179] Ranulphus de Kylvyngton' Robertus de Whiten'. Hugo de Colston', Radulphus de Bulwell' Radulphus clericus de Langar et Alanus de Raby ad hoc electi et triati. Qui dicunt super sacramentum suum quod capitulum predictum et similiter predictus Robertus de Wodehous[180] et omnes prebendarii predicti et eorum predecessores a tempore quo non extat memoria singillatim usi sunt habere visum franciplegii et ea que ad visum pertinent de omnibus hominibus[181] tenentibus suis et residentibus in feodis ipsorum in villis predictis tenendum bis per annum apud Suthwell' et alibi prout superius clamant etc. Et similiter quod predicti[182] Robertus de Wodehous Robertus de Notingh'[183] Lambertus de Trikyngham[184] Henricus de Edenstow[185] et Robertus de Bridlyngton'[186] et predecessores sui prebendarii in ecclesia predicta a tempore quo non extat memoria singillatim usi sunt habere libertatem que dicitur wayff[187] in terris et feodis suis prout superius clamant ut de iure prebendarum suarum predictarum. Et quod predictus Lambertus de Trikyngham et eciam[188] predecessores sui a tempore quo non extat memoria semper usi sunt habere libertatem que dicitur stray in manerio suo de Halghton' ut de iure prebende sue predicte. Ideo idem capitulum Robertus de Wodehous et omnis alii prebendarii predicti quo ad libertatem visus franciplegii habendum separatim et similiter predicti Robertus de Wodehous Robertus de Notingh'[189] Lambertus de Trikyngham Henricus de Edenstow[190] et Robertus de Brydlyngton'[191] prebendarii quo ad libertatem habendum wayff[192] in terris tenementis et feodis suis separatim et predictus Lambertus de Trikyngham quo ad libertatem habendum stray prout superius separatim clamant et prout per predictam iuratam compertum est inde sine die salvo iure domini regis.

Margin Heading in bold in same medieval hand as text (Scribe 4); other marginalia in this item are signified in the notes at the appropriate place.

Note This entry is enrolled on the King's Bench plea roll for Easter term 5 Edward III (1331), TNA, KB 27/284, rot. 115 (consisting of two membranes). The whole entry was exemplified in letters patent enrolled on the patent roll for 7 Edward III (TNA, C 66/182, mm. 8–7), and this exemplification appears in **14**. The original petition of Henry of Edwinstowe and others, quoted in full in this entry, has not survived.

---

[176] A *Notingham* [177] A omits. [178] A inserts *predicti*. [179] A *Wylewes*
[180] A *Wodhous* [181] A inserts *et*. [182] A *predictus* [183] A *Notingham*
[184] A *Trykyngham* [185] A *Edenstowe* [186] A *Bridelyngton'* [187] A *wayf*
[188] Followed by *et eciam* repeated in error. [189] A *Notingham* [190] A *Edenestowe*
[191] A *Bridelyngton'* [192] A *wayf*

148 *Inspeximus by Richard II of (1) a charter of Henry I, ?17 October 1109 (21); (2) of a writ-charter of Henry I, 1100–7, to William Peveril, Richard the sheriff and the shire court of Nottinghamshire, informing them that Archbishop Gerard is to have the same services, rents and customs as his predecessor Archbishop Thomas had in the time of William I and William II; (3) a charter of Henry II (19)*

Westminster, 4 December 1381

Carta regis Ricardi que est ratificatio, et cetera de terris archiepiscopi   p.76
Ebor'

Ricardus etc. Omnibus ad quos presentes litere pervenerint salutem. Inspeximus quandam cartam domini Henrici, quondam regis Anglie, progenitoris nostri, in hec verba: (1) *copy of Henry I's charter (21) with no major differences.*

Inspeximus eciam quandam aliam cartam eiusdem progenitoris nostri in hec verba (2): Henricus etc. Willelmo Pevrello et Ricardo vicecomiti etc. salutem. Mando et precipio ut Girardus archiepiscopus habeat omnes consuetudines quas antecessor suus Thomas habuit de equitibus et de sochemannis et de villanis tam in serviciis quam in redditibus, et ita bene omnes consuetudines suas habeat sicut melius antecessor suus habuit tempore patris mei et fratris. Teste Ricardo de Redveirs apud Wincestram.

Inspeximus insuper quandam cartam domini Henrici secundi, quondam regis Anglie, progenitoris etc.: (3) *copy as 19 with no major differences.*

Nos autem cartas predictas et omnia contenta in eisdem rata habentes et grata ea pro nobis et heredibus nostris quantum in nobis est acceptamus, approbamus et ratificamus et nunc canonicis ecclesie Suthwellensis et successoribus suis tenore presencium concedimus et confirmamus prout carte predicte racionabiliter testantur et prout iidem canonici et eorum predecessores a tempore confectionis cartarum predictarum hucusque libertatibus et consuetudinibus predictis racionabiliter uti et gaudere consueverunt. In cuius rei etc. Teste me ipso apud Westmonasterium quarto die Decembris anno regni nostri quinto.

Pro quinque marcis solutis in hanaperio. Horbury.[1]

---
[1] Added in different late medieval hand

Margin Heading part in bold and same hand as text (Scribe 4), the last phrase in cursive late medieval hand. *Southwell possessiones et libertates* halfway down left margin (17th c.).

Date Sharpe, *Acta Henry I*, York 7 (forthcoming) will provide the fullest edition of (2) the writ-charter and other details; Richard fitz Gotse had ceased to be sheriff and his successor was probably in post by Michaelmas 1107.

Note *CPR 1381–5*, 57 for Richard II's inspeximus. This confirmation was also confirmed by Henry V in 1415 (*CChR 1341–1417*, 479) and by many subsequent monarchs (cf. Sharpe).

148A   *Writ of Richard II to the sheriff of Nottingham ordering him to respect the privileges and liberties of the canons granted by charters of the king's predecessors, which he has confirmed*   Westminster, 8 December 1381

Breve allocacionis eiusdem patens

Ricardus, Dei gracia rex Anglie et Francie et dominus Hibernie, vicecomiti de Notyngham salutem. Quia dilecti nobis canonici ecclesie collegiate beate Marie Suthwell' per cartas progenitorum nostrorum quondam regum Anglie, quas confirmavimus, clamant habere diversas libertates et consuetudines, quibus ipsi et predecessores sui canonici ecclesie predicte a tempore confectionis cartarum predictarum semper hactenus usi sunt et gavisi, sicut dicuntur, tibi precipimus quod ipsos canonicos libertatibus et consuetudinibus predictis in comitatu predicto uti et gaudere permittas, iuxta tenorem cartarum et confirmacionis predictarum, et prout eis uti debent ipsi que et predecessores sui canonici ecclesie predicte libertatibus illis a tempore predicto semper hactenus racionabiliter uti et gaudere consueverunt. Teste me ipso apud Westmonasterium octavo die Decembris anno regni nostri quinto.

Margin   Title centred in late medieval hand (Scribe 4a or 4b), also for this item and those to **157**.

Note   W. A. James transcribed this as part of **148**, but since it constitutes a separate item added in a different late medieval hand, it has been listed here as **148A**. This item is not enrolled in *CCR 1381–5*.

149   *Writ of Richard II, following a request of the canons, to Adam of Everingham and his fellow justices of weights and measures to allow the canons their rights in Southwell and fifteen other townships*
Westminster, 6 December 1381

p. 77   **Aliud breve allocacionis**

Ricardus [etc.] Ade de Everyngham et sociis suis iusticiariis nostris ad statutum de mensuris et ponderibus editum conservandum et ad quedam alia in literis patentibus inde confectis contenta faciendum in comitatu Notingham salutem. Ex parte canonicorum ecclesie collegiate beate Marie Suthwell' nobis est ostensum quod cum ipsi habeant ipsique et omnes alii canonici ecclesie predicte a tempore quo non extat memoria semper hactenus habere consueverunt emendas assise panis, vini et cervisie, fracte de omnibus hominibus et tenentibus suis ac residentibus infra [villas] de Suthwell', Northwell', Suthmuscham, Northmuscham, Calneton', Oxton', Calverton', Wodeburgh, Crophill', Blyworth, Halghton', Bekyngham, Dunham, Halum, Edyngley et Normanton'. Et licet iidem canonici, pistores, tabernarios et brasiatores infra villas predictas residentes pro huiusmodi assisa fracta ac abusu mensurarum et ponderum ibidem per amerciamenta et alios modos per ministros suos punire et amerciamenta illa ad opus suum levari fecerint, vos cum dictos pistores, tabernarios, brasiatores, tenentes suos et alios residentes predictos, pro huiusmodi assisa fracta et abusu mensurarum et ponderum ac si prius ea de causa puniti non fuissent, per amerciamenta gravia iterato punire intenditis, quod si fieret in ipsorum canonicorum prejudicium et tenencium ac residencium predictorum opposicionem cederet manifeste. Et quia in magno consilio domini Edwardi, nuper regis Anglie, avi nostri, apud Westmonasterium tento extitit concordatum quod in inquisicionibus et punicionibus pro huiusmodi transgressionibus factis libertates dominorum et aliorum semper salventur. Nolentes prefatis canonicis in hac parte iniuriari vobis mandamus, quod si vobis constare poterit ipsos canonicos et omnes alios canonicos ecclesie predicte assisas mensurarum et ponderum ac emendas assise panis, vini et cervisie, fracte de hominibus et tenentibus suis ac residentibus infra villas predictas semper hactenus habuisse et habere, debere tunc huiusmodi punicionibus pistorum, tabernariorum et brasiatorum infra villas predictas residencium pro huiusmodi assisa fracta et abusu mensurarum et ponderum pro quibus per ministros ipsorum canonicorum puniti fuerint coram vobis iterato faciendo supersedatis omnino districtiones si quas eis ea occasione feceritis sine dilacione relevari facientes. Proviso semper quod mensure et pondera tenencium et residencium predictorum standardo fuit concordancia iuxta formam statuti inde editi, et quod omnia falsa mensure et pondera ibidem conburantur et adnullentur, et quod omnes illi de huiusmodi delictis culpabiles, qui prius inde per ministros ipsorum canonicorum puniti non fuerint, per vos puniantur prout decet. Teste me ipso apud Westmonasterium vi die Decembris anno regni nostri quinto.

Note Not enrolled in *CCR 1381–5*.

150 *Writ of Richard II, at the request of Richard of Chesterfield, William of Gunthorpe and Mr James de Staunton, canons and prebendaries, upholding their privilege to take views of frankpledge of their own men, and ordering the sheriff of Nottingham to cease citing them before his court of Thurgarton and Lythe* Westminster, 8 December 1381

Aliud breve allocacionis

R[icardus etc.] vicecomiti Not' salutem. Ex parte dilectorum nobis Ricardi de Chestrefeld', Willelmi de Gunthorpp' et magistri Jacobi de Staunton', canonicorum ecclesie collegiate beate Marie Suthwell' nobis est ostensum quod cum ipsi prebendarii prebendarum de Northwell' et Halghton existant et ibidem habere debeant ipsi que et predecessores sui prebendarii prebendarum predictarum a tempore quo non extat memoria semper hactenus habere consueverunt visum franciplegii cum omnibus ad huiusmodi visum spectantibus de hominibus et tenentibus suis prebendarum predictarum cum nichilominus homines et tenentes ipsorum Ricardi, Willelmi et Jacobi de prebendis predictis ad veniendum ad visum franciplegii coram te in curiis nostris de Thurgarton' et Lythe, singulis annis prius festa sancti Michaelis et Pasche ad presentandum ea ibidem que in curiis nostris predictis ibidem presentari deberent graviter distringis iam de novo, et ipsos ea occasione multipliciter inquietas nimius iuste in ipsorum hominum et tenencium grave dampnum et prebendarum ipsorum Ricardi, Willelmi et Jacobi exheredacionis periculum manifestum, et aliter quam retroactis temporibus fieri consueverunt. Et quia eisdem

prebendariis aut hominibus seu tenentibus suis predictis iniuriari nolumus in
hac parte et precipimus quod si ita est tunc ipsos prebendarios visum suum
predictum cum omnibus ad huiusmodi visum spectantibus de hominibus et
tenentibus suis predictis absque impedimento habere permittas prout ipsi
visum huiusmodi habere debent et ipsi et predecessores sui prebendarii
prebendarum predictarum visum illum a tempore predicto huiusque
racionabiliter habere consueverunt prefati homines et tenentes ad vivendum
ad visum franciplegii curie predictarum ibidem ad presentacionem
ibidem faciendum ea que in curiis nostris predictis presentandis existunt
nullatenus distringens aliter quam retroactis temporibus fieri consuevit.
Et districciones si quas eis ea occasione feceris sine dilacione relaxari
facis eisdem. Teste me ipso apud Westmonasterium viii die Decembris
anno regni nostri quinto.

Note　Not enrolled in *CCR 1381–5*. Richard of Chesterfield, prebendary of Norwell
Overhall (1370–1405). William of Gunthorpe, former treasurer of Calais (1368–73), prebendary of Norwell Palishall (by 1380–1400). Mr James de Stanton/Staunton, prebendary
of Halloughton (by 1380–after 1395).

151　*The customs applied by the Chapter since ancient times with respect
to their tenants*　　　　　　　　　　　　　　　　　　　[s.d.]

p. 78　**Consuetudines laudabiles capituli predicti antiquitus usitate et
approbate sequuntur in hunc modum**

Prima consuetudo est quod quilibet residens infra dominium capituli hoc
est quod de qualibet domo occupata principalis persona illius domus sive
sit vir sive mulier sive sit principalis tenens tenementorum de capitulo
tentorum, sive tenens tenentis, talis tenementi faciet ad minus duas
apparencias ad curiam capituli per annum, videlicet ad proximum visum
post festum sancti Michaelis et ad proximum visum post festum Pasche,
et si non faciat debet amerciari quia essoniari non potest.

Item quod quilibet alius tenens dicti capituli libere secundum formam
carte sue faciet sectam vel non sectam.

Item quod quilibet nativus[1] tenens de dicto capitulo faciet communem
sectam si curia teneatur de tribus septimanis in tres septimanas.

Item quod quilibet nativus de sanguine succedens in hereditatem suam
post mortem antecessoris sui dabit capitulo pro herieto suo ad suum
ingressum tantum v solidos iiii denarios.

Item quod quilibet nativus capituli qui habet filias vel filiam maritatam
dabit pro mercheto tantum v solidos iiii denarios. Et si \illa/ filia fuerit
deflorata ante matrimonium dabit pro letherwyte tantum v solidos iiii
denarios.

Et post mortem dicti tenentis si habeat uxorem superstitem et filium
vel filios, vel filiam vel filias, dicat uxor post mortem viri sui tenebit
tenementa sua integra ad terminum vite sue dum tamen tam diu vivere
contingat sine marito et sic dicta uxor sustenabit exitum inter ipsam et
maritum suum exeuntem et precipue heredem mariti sui sive sit masculus
sive femella quam diu tenuerit tenementa predicta.

Et dicta uxor dabit ad ingressum post mortem viri sui v solidos iiii denarios.

Et si contingat quod ipsa capiat alium maritum liberum hominem sive nativum capituli sive alicuius alterius tenementa sua \predicta/ debent rese\si/ri in manus capituli et reddi heredi qui dabit ad ingressum suum pro herieto suo v solidos iiii denarios, non obstante quod mater sua antea tantum solvit.

Et si contingat quod vivente marito prima uxor decedat et habeat exitum cum prima uxore sua filiam et cum secunda uxore habeat filium, filius succedet patri suo post eius mortem solvendo pro herieto suo v solidos iiii denarios, non obstante quod sit de secunda uxore, set secunda uxor post mortem viri sui habebit nomine dotis sue unam domum in qua possit honeste morari et in quolibet campo dimidiam acram terre arabilis quas domum et terram heres tenentur erga dominum exonerare quam diu dictam uxorem secundam vivere contingat sine marito, quia si alium virum capiat domus et terra debent reseisiri et reddi heredi etc.

Et si contingat quod nativus de sanguine teneat aliqua tenementa de capitulo et procreaverit de uxore sua plures filias nullum habens masculum post mortem dicti nativi ultima filia succedet in hereditate post mortem patris sui tantum et dabit pro herieto suo v solidos iiii denarios.

Et si illa filia capiat virum sive liberum hominem sive nativum capituli vel alicuius alterius sine licencia tenementa sua debent reseisiri et dicta heres dabit pro mercheto v solidos iiii denarios, non obstante reseisina predicta.

Et si vir talis heredis faciat finem cum capitulo tenendi tenementa predicta ad terminum vite uxoris sue licet habeant exitum inter se ille exitus sive sit vir sive mulier nunquam hereditabit illam terram post mortem matris nisi ad voluntatem capituli eo quod talis exitus semper est liber de sanguine.

Et regula generalis | talis est quod liber homo numquam potest hereditare terram que tenetur de domino de bondagio nisi ad voluntatem domini. p. 79
Set post mortem predicte ultime filie hereditas predicta descendere debet sorori sue juniori si sola sit, sin autem non potest calumpniare.

Item nullus nativus nec aliquis alius tenens per copiam curie ad terminum annorum vel ad terminum vite sine licencia capituli debet alienare tenementa sua que de capitulo tenentur neque parcellam eorundem per scriptum neque sine scripto alicui alteri extra curiam capituli sine licencia.

Et si faciat tenementa sua debent seisiri et teneri quousque fecerit finem ad voluntatem capituli pro tenementis rehabendis, nec faciet vastum vel vendicionem seu destruccionem in tenementis que de capitulo tenet.

Et si faciat tenementa sua debent seisiri quousque fecerit finem etc. vel debet amerciari ad voluntatem capituli.

Et si sit liber homo qui tenet de capitulo aliqua tenementa ad terminum vite vel annorum per copiam curie et faciat vastum, vendicionem vel destruccionem in tenementis illis durante termino suo prosequatur contra ipsum per breve de vasto etc.

Item si error aliquis sive difficultas aliqua inveniatur sive assignetur in aliquo placito infra curiam alicuius prebende capituli predicti per favorem senescalli[2] ignoranciam vel aliquam aliam causam in favorem alterius partis, ad sectam partis que prosequi voluerit ad capitulum predictum placitum illud debet removeri a curia predicta, in curiam capituli, et terminari per inquisicionem capiendam de magis discrecioribus tocius iurisdiccionis capituli, secundum formam iuris, ut patebit inferius pluribus modis, que quidem consuetudines semper hucusque \similiter/ utuntur sive uti deberent in qualibet prebenda eiusdem capituli.

¹ MS *native* ² MS *senascalli*

Margin Heading in bold, in a late medieval hand probably the same as text, in which clauses have been set out individually here for ease of reference.

Date Dickinson, *Southwell*, 132 states that these 'Laudable Customs' date from the fifth year of Richard II (1381–2), presumably on the basis of proximity of **151** to **149** and **150**, but we have found no further evidence to support this suggestion.

Note Pd. in Dickinson, *Southwell*, 351–2.

p. 80 This page is blank.

PLEAS IN THE MANOR COURTS, 152–84

152

p. 81 **Placita in diversis curiis prebendarum infra iurisdiccionem capituli ecclesie beate Marie Suthwell' placitata propter errores iudiciorum in eisdem assignata ad instanciam partium remota ad curiam capituli predicti. Ut ibi terminentur prout ius expostulat et consuetudo eiusdem capituli. Ut exempla patebit inferius per diversa.**

Pleas in different Prebendal Courts within the jurisdiction of Southwell Chapter, removed to the court of the Chapter at the instance of the parties because of errors of judgment, there to be concluded according to right and the customs of the Chapter

Curia capituli ecclesie beate Marie Suthwellie tenta ibidem die sabbati proximo ante festum nativitatis sancti Johannis baptiste, anno regni regis Edwardi tercii post conquestum Anglie primo.

Case in the court of Southwell Chapter, 20 June 1327, John, son of Stephen Claryce complaining against Henry, son of Richard Helwys, concerning a false judgment made at view of frankpledge of the prebend of Robert of Nottingham at Oxton, concerning property in Calverton, prebendal inheritance customs and right of dower on 20 May 1327
Southwell, 20 June 1327

Johannes filius Stephani Claryce queritur de Henrico filio Ricardi Helwys de iniusta vexacione per ipsum sibi illata per iudicium erroneum in curia domini sui apud Oxton' adiudicatum in forma que sequitur etc.

Ad visum franciplegii domini Roberti de Notingham prebendarii alterius prebendarum de Oxton' et Crophill' in ecclesia collegiata beate Marie Suthwell' tentum apud Oxton' die mercurii in crastino sancti Dunstani episcopi, anno regni regis Edwardi tercii post conquestum primo. Venit Henricus filius Ricardi Helwys sicut alias et optulit se

versus Johannem filium Stephani Claryce de Calverton' et petit unum
mesuagium et duas bovatas terre cum pertinenciis in Calverton' ut ius
suum secundum consuetudinem prebende, eo quod Stephanus Claryce
quondam tenens dictorum tenementorum desponsavit quandam mulierem
nomine Margeriam de qua genuit quandam filiam nomine Agnetis et
ipsam filiam maritavit Ricardo Helwys tenenti alterius prebendarum
in villa predicta de qua iste Henricus est exitus legitimus. Et dicit quod
consuetudo istius prebende est quod exitus prime uxoris sive sit masculus
sive femella debet habere hereditatem patris sui non obstante quod pater
habuerit plures uxores de quibus procreavit masculos. Et quod tale sit
ius suum ponit se super curiam. Et predictus Johannes venit et cognovit
quod dictus Stephanus Claryce duxit in uxorem predictam Margeriam et
de ea progenuit dictam Agnetem cuius exitus predictus Henricus est. Set
dicit quod dictus Stephanus post mortem predicte Margerie uxoris sue
desponsavit quandam mulierem nomine Beatricem de qua genuit ipsum
Johannem. Et petit iudicium si dictus Henricus qui est liber quantum ad
dominum et liberi status et de alio domino habeat melius ius in dictis
tenementis quam ipse qui est nativus domini tenens dicta tenementa in recta
linea descendente de patre suo. Unde tota curia per communem assensum
dicit quod idem Henricus habet melius ius ad dicta tenementa habenda
secundum consuetudines prebende quam dictus Johannes tenenda. Et quia
videtur senescallo dictum iudicium essere erroneum et dissonum legi, eo
quod Henricus, qui petens est, est liberi status quantum ad dominum et
dictus Johannes est navitatis condicionis. Ideo execucio predicti iudicii
ponitur in respectum usque consultum fuerit cum domino vel quod dominus
inde mandaverit voluntatem suam. Postea dominus mandavit literam
suam Thome de Radeclyve senescallo suo predicto quod inquireret de
tenentibus prebendarum habencium curiam infra iurisdiccionem capituli
predicti de consuetudinibus earumdem et quod faceret execucionem iudicii
predicti secundum consuetudines earumdem prebendarum interpretatas
predictas. Unde convocatis tenentibus prebendarum Oxton', Wodeburgh',
Crophill', Halghton', Northwell' et Muscham apud Suthwell' in pleno
capitulo die sabbati \proximo/ ante festum nativitatis sancti Johannis
baptiste, anno predicto. Facta fuit inquisicio de xxiiii[or] tenentibus dictarum
prebendarum, quorum xvii iurati de Oxton', Crophill et Wodeburgh'
et Halghton', dicunt quod predictum iudicium bonum est et usitabile
secundum consuetudines prebendarum predictarum. Et vii iuratores de
Northwell' et Muscham dicunt quod credunt predictos xvii jurati bene
dixisse secundum suam consuetudinem, tamen dicunt quod ea consuetudo
non est inter eos in prebendis predictis. Et quia quatuor prebende hinc
prebende viciniores concordant | in consuetudinibus isti prebende. Ideo p. 82
consideratum est quod dictus Henricus recipiat predicta tenementa petita
videlicet unum mesuagium et duas bovatas terre cum pertinenciis in
Calverton' versus dictum Johannem. Et predictus Johannes pro iniusta
detencione in misericordia.

Et super hoc venit supradicta Beatrix secunda uxor predicti Stephani
et petit dotem suam de dictis tenementis, versus dictum Henricum. Et
dictus Henricus dicit quod ipsam dotem habere non debet, eo quod
secunda uxor tenencium predictarum prebendarum post mortem mariti

sui dotari debet de uno cotagio cum uno curtilagio et dimidia acra terre in quolibet campo, dum tamen se solam tenet et si iterum maritaverit illam dotem amittet. Dicit eciam quod illa Beatrix maritata est cuidam Willelmo de Marnham. Unde petit iudicium etc. Et tota curia dicit quod dicta Beatrix non debet inde dotari eo quod se iterum maritavit et secundum consuetudines prebendarum predictarum, uxor que se iterum maritaverit dotem suam amittet. Ideo consideratum est quod dicta Beatrix nichil respondet ad presens set sit in misericordia pro falso clamore et condonatur quia pauper etc.

Margin 2ⁿᵈ paragraph, right-hand margin, *Southwell'* and 3ʳᵈ paragraph, right-hand margin, *Oxton cur'* (17ᵗʰ c.).

Note Robert of Nottingham, prebendary of Oxton I (1323–c. 1333).

153 *Chapter proceedings overturning judgment in the case John, son of Stephen Claryce v Henry, son of Richard Helwys* 2 June 1328

Postea in convocacione residenciariorum et aliorum existencium in eadem convocacione facta in capitulo predicto die iovis proximo post festum sancte Trinitatis, anno regni regis predicti secundo. Declarata fuit tota materia in isto recordo contenta coram eisdem et eorum consilio, coram quibus iudicium inter predictos Johannem querentem et Henricum defendentem in curia capituli predicti fuit inventum erroneum et iniuste iudicatum eo quod dictus Henricus fuit liber homo et libere condicionis quo ad dominum prebende predicte et sit extraneus ad habendum tenementa predicta. Ideo pro defectu placitacionis declaratum fuit placitum predictum irritum et inane sicut probari potest per articulos antique consuetudinis ante istud tempus prius recitatos. Item in eadem.

   Item in eadem convocacione ordinatum fuit quod senescallus curie capituli qui nunc est vel futuris temporibus pro tempore erit examinari faciat rotulos curie confratrum capituli in thesaurario existentes et consuetudines probabiles in eisdem rotulis inventas et usitatas inscribi faciat in registro capituli predicti pro evitacione malignorum consuetudines predictas probabiles et usitatas adnichilare volencium virtute cuius ordinacionis sequitur processus in hunc modum.

154 *Action in the court of Southwell Chapter between Richard Dyoth, plaintiff, and Geoffrey Augeny and his wife, Beatrice, tenants of holdings in Edingley, involving a false oath sworn by jurors* 11 September 1344

Curia capituli beate Marie Suthwell' tenta ibidem die sabbati proximo post festum nativitatis beate Marie virginis, anno regni regis Edwardi tercii post conquestum decimo octavo.

Attincta inter Ricardum Dyoth petentem et Galfridum Augeny et Beatricem, uxorem eius, et Henricum Aubrey et Ceciliam, uxorem eius, tenentes de quibusdam tenementis in Edyngley unde dictus Ricardus dicit quod iuratores inquisicionis de tenementis predictis capte falsum fecerunt iuramentum eo quod dixerunt quod consuetudo manerii fuit talis quod quilibet nativus tenementa sua dare et vendere potest per voluntatem domini de se et heredibus suis inperpetuum et quo ad hoc fecerunt falsum iuramentum et dicta attincta ponitur in respectum usque ad proximam curiam. Postea partes comcidunt[1] ut patet in proxima curia sequenti. Ideo etc. Set verum est quod falsum fecerunt sacrosanctum ut querentes dicunt. Et ut probabitur in sequentibus pluribus modis.

Judicium veridicti cuiusdam inquisicionis capte inter Julianam, que fuit uxor Willelmi Knyght, petentem et Ricardum Tauntelyn' et Aliciam Tauntelyn' tenentes de placito terre ponitur in respectum usque ad proximam curiam.

p. 83

[1] MS *sic*

Margin *Southwell'* in left margin (17th c.).

155 *View of frankpledge of the court of Southwell Chapter, essoins and non-appearances; respite of verdict in case of Juliana, widow of William Knyght, against Richard and Alice Tauntelyn* 2 October 1344

Visus franciplegii cum curia predicti capituli tentus ibidem die sabbati proximo post festum sancti Michaelis archangeli, anno regni regis E[dwardi][1] post conquestum decimo octavo.

Essonia Johannes de Waynflete de adventu per Johannem filium suum
erronea Sibilla Bakster de eodem per Willelmum servientem suum
Willelmus Brounynge de eodem per Robertum servientem suum
Johannes atte Esshe de eodem per Hugonem de Holbek'
Elias Cressy de eodem per Willemum de Batheley
Dominus Willelmus de Hundon' de eodem per Robertum Maundevile

Pro quibus essoniatis sciendum est quod omnes residentes infra dominium capituli sive sit[2] tenentes capituli sive tenentes tenentium capituli debent venire bis per annum ad duos visus franciplegii et si non faciat apparentem suam debet amerciari. Quia non iacet ibi essonium. Quare talis processus essonie erroneus est.

Juratores presentant quod Henricus Marchell' de Northwell', Johannes Wallesby, Johannes de Roldeston', dominus Johannes Wellys et Johannes Ferrour' de Laxton' non veniunt. Ideo in misericordia. Set quia morantur extra villam queratur causa pro capitulo pro quibus tenementis facerent adventum sive sectam et in quibus villis. Quia ut supponitur dictus Henricus Marchell' tenuit certa tenementa in Northwell' de capitulo etc.

Ad huc veredictum cuiusdam inquisicionis capte inter Ricardum Tauntelyn' et Aliciam Tauntelyn' tenentes et Julianam, que fuit uxor Willelmi Knyght, petentem de placito terre ponitur in respectum usque ad proximam curiam.

[1] *tercii* probably missing [2] MS *sit* for *sint*

Margin *Southwell'* in right margin (17th c.), and lower down opposite clause *Pro quibus* ... in same late hand *Sic est rotulus consuetudinum Capituli.* Opposite clause *Juratores presentant* is *quere* in same medieval hand as text.

Note John of Wainfleet first occurs as a witness to Southwell charters early in the century (cf. **527, 529, 531–4, 536, 539**), often being the first named. He last occurs in April 1349 (**540**) and may have been a victim of the Black Death since his son begins to witness regularly from 1350 (**590**), though since the latter continues to distinguish himself as John of Wainfleet, junior, as late as 1353 (**331**), his father may not have died until after this date. The younger John also usually witnessed first (**323, 331, 334**), a reflection of the family's high standing in the town, and was still active in 1373 (**577**). For William of Hundon, see **535n.**

156–156A   *Court of Southwell Chapter, two respites of verdict in the case of Juliana, widow of William Knyght, against Richard and Alice Tauntelyn*   23 October 1344 and 13 November 1344

Curia capituli beate Marie Suthwell' tenta ibidem die sabbati proximo post festum sancti Luce evangeliste, anno regni regis E[dwardi] tercii post conquestum xviii°.

Ad huc iudicium veredicti cuiusdam inquisicionis capte inter Julianam, que fuit uxor Willelmi Knyght, petentem, et Ricardum Tauntelyn' et Aliciam Tauntelyn, querentes de placito terre ponitur in respectum usque ad proximam curiam.

p. 84   **Curia capituli beate Marie Suthwell' tenta ibidem die sabbati proximo post festum sancti Martini, anno regni regis Edwardi tertii post conquestum xviii°.**

Iudicium veredicti cuiusdam inquisiticionis capte inter Julianam que fuit uxor Willelmi Knyght petentem et Ricardum Tauntelyn' et Aliciam Tauntelyn' tenentes de placito terre ponitur in respectum usque ad proximam curiam.

Margin   *Southwell'* in right margin (17th c.).

Note   W. A. James treated **156** and **156A** as one entry although it is clear from the heading on p. 84 that they ought to have formed two separate items.

157   *Court of Southwell Chapter, proceedings in case of Juliana, widow of William Knyght, against Richard and Alice Tauntelyn, relating to dower in land at Woodborough*   1 January 1345

Curia capituli ecclesie beate Marie Suthwell' tenta ibidem die sabbati proximo post festum sancti Thome martiris, anno regni regis E[dwardi] tercii post conquestum xviii°.

Juliana que fuit uxor Willelmi Knyght de Wodeburgh' petit versus Ricardum Tauntelyn' et Aliciam Tauntelyn' unam bovatam terre cum pertinenciis in Wodeburgh, quam clamat habere ad vitam suam post mortem predicti Willelmi quondam viri sui secundum consuetudinem prebende etc. Et in quam iidem Ricardus et Alicia non habent ingressum nisi post dimissionem quam Willelmus quondam vir ipsius Juliane inde fecit Radulpho Knyght fratri ipsius Willelmi ad terminum qui preteriit. Et que ad ipsam Julianam post mortem dicti Willelmi viri sui remanere debet ad terminum vite sue secundum consuetudinem prebende etc.

Et Alicia Tauntelyn' venit et dicit quod ipsa non tenet de predicta bovata terre nisi unam acram et dimidiam terre ex assignacione dicti Ricardi Tauntelyn' post mortem viri sui, tenendum ad terminum vite secundum consuetudinem prebende. Et vocat inde ad warantizandum dictum Ricardum Tauntelyn' qui presens in curia ei warantizavit. Et tam de dicta acra terre et dimidia quam de toto residuo predicte bovate terre dicit quod dicta Juliana nichil iuris clamare potest, que dicit quod dictus Willelmus Knyght quondam vir ipsius Juliane alias in curia magistri Symonis de Curia maiori tunc temporis prebendarii de Wodeburgh' petiit illam bovatam terre versus Willelmum Tauntelyn' avum ipsius Willelmi cuius heres ipse est ut suum ius et illam bovatam terre per inquisicionem xii hominum iure recuperavit et totum ius et clameum quod habuit in dicta bovata terre dedit que concessit cuidam Radulpho fratri suo seniori in plena curia. Et postea Willelmus Tauntelyn' senciit se iniuste gravari per illam falsam inquisicionem. Adivit magistrum Henricum de Newerk' tunc temporis archiepiscopum Ebor' et conquerebatur coram eo de iniuria sibi illata per illam falsam inquisicionem. Et archiepiscopus literas suas capitulo beate Marie Suthwell' direxit precipiendo quod diligenter per predictum capitulum veritas inquireretur. Et quod predicto Willelmo de iniuria sibi illata emendaretur. Et capitulum beate Marie Suthwellie ad preceptum dicti archepiscopi fecit xxiiii homines bonos et legales de predicto capituli prebendar' citare ad convincendum predictos xii iuratores prime inquisicionis et diligenter inquirere super predictas. Et illi xxiiii iuratores dixerunt in pleno capitulo quod predicti xii iuratores falsum fecerunt sacramentum. Et quod predictus Willelmus Tauntelyn' habuit ius hereditarie in predicta bovata terre et predictus Radulphus Knyght nullum ius omnino. Et sic iuratores prime inquisicionis capte in curia magistri Symonis de Curia maiori tunc temporis prebendarii de Wodeburgh' convicti fuerunt. Et consideratum fuit quod dictus Willelmus Tauntelyn' recuperaret seisinam suam dicte bovate terre et positus fuit in seisina in eodem statu quo prius fuit. Et fecit iudicium si dicta Juliana aliquod ius vel clameum in dicta bovata terre racione alicuius possessionis viri sui que adnullata fuit in forma predicta decetero exigere vel vendicare potest. Et ad testificandum istud recordum et processum nullum recordum ostendit nisi duas literas sigillatas videlicet unam de capitulo Suthwell' et aliam de custodibus capituli in hiis verbis.

Capitulum ecclesie beate Marie Suthwell' Reginaldo de Westhorpp clerico salutem. Ad ponendum in seisinam unius bovate terre cum suis pertinenciis in Wodeburgh' et ad restituendum predictam terre Willelmo Tauntelyn' secundum quod ius habuit in eadem iuxta mandatum |¹ venerabilium virorum domini archiepiscopi et capituli Ebor' nobis in hac parte directis tibi mandamus et committimus potestatem per presentes. Et in huius rei testimonium sigillum nostrum presenti est appensum. Datum in capitulo nostro Suthwell' die veneris proximo ante festum sancte Margarete virginis, anno domini millesimo ccc^{mo} septimo decimo.²   p. 86

Thomas de Hokerton' unus de custodibus capituli ecclesie beate Marie Suthwell' et Adam de Kelsolt' ballivus dicti capituli Rogero de Hokerton' eiusdem subballivo salutem. Ex parte capituli predicti tibi mandamus firmiter iniungentes quatinus ponas Willelmum Tauntelyn' de Wodeburgh' in seisina de i bovata terre cum pertinenciis in eadem quam idem Willelmus coram nobis in curia predicti capituli die sabbati proximo post festum Ascensionis domini, anno domini millesimo ccc nonagesimo quinto[3] tanquam ius suum versus Radulphum Knyght de Wodeburgh per recognicionem cuiusdam attincte denicit, necnon ipsum Radulphum pro i marca argenti per nos secundum taxacionem predicte attincte predicto Willelmo Tauntelyn' adiudicato distringas. In cuius rei testimonium sigillum predicti Thome de Hokerton' est appensum. Datum apud Suthwell' die et anno supradictis.

Preterea dicit quod dictus Willelmus Knyght quondam vir ipsius Juliane numquam seisitus fuit de predicta bovata terre postquam ipsam Julianam desponsavit et hoc petit quod inquiratur.

Et ipsa Juliana respondet et dicit quod illa attincta ei nocere non debet quare dicit quod Radulphus Knyght tempore quo predicta attincta transivit nullum statum habuit in dicta bovata terre nisi ad terminum annorum ex dimissione Willelmi Knyght viri sui et ius feodi illius bovate terre tempore illius attincte et ante et post semper remansit in persona predicti Willelmi sui viri ut illud recordum illius attincte ostendit. Unde petit iudicium si per illam attinctam de iure suo illius bovate terre excludi debeat. Et quod dictus Willelmus quondam vir suus fuit seisitus de predicta bovata terre postquam ipsam desponsavit. Ita quod dictam bovatam terre habere debet ad totam vitam suam secundum consuetudinem prebende parata est verificare etc.

Et Ricardus dicit quod predictus Radulphus Knyght versus quem predictam attinctam transivit habuit feodum in predicta bovata terre ex concessione dicti Willelmi Knyght fratris sui prout superius dictum est, et quod dictus Willelmus quondam vir etc. postquam ipsam Julianam desponsavit numquam fuit seisitus de predicta bovata terre ut de feodo. Ita quod ipsa Juliana terram illam secundum consuetudines prebende ad terminum vite sue tenere non debet et de hoc ponit se in inquisicionem et Juliana similiter.

Ideo preceptum est ballivo quod venire faciat xii probos et legales homines de prebenda de Wodburgh et de aliis prebendis proximis per quos veritas melius sciri poterit in premissis quod sint ad proximam curiam.

Qui quidem iuratores postea venerunt et de assensu partium electi et jurati fuerunt, videlicet Johannes Pelle de Wodeburgh, Radulphus de eadem, Hugo Thurston' de eadem, Johannes atte Esshe de eadem, Johannes Wlsi de eadem, Willelmus Herbert' de Halum, Ricardus super montem de Blythworth, Johannes super montem de eadem, Ricardus le Rede de Oxton', Robertus Osbern de eadem, Ricardus Genyuer' de eadem, Johannes Helwys de Calverton'.

Qui quidem iuratores dicunt super sacramentum suum quod dictus

p. 87 Willelmus Knyght quondam vir | ipsius Juliane fuit seisitus de predicta bovata terre ut de feodo et iure postquam ipsam Julianam desponsavit. Et dicunt eciam quod dictus Radulphus Knyght tempore quo predicta attincta transivit nullum statum habuit in dicta bovata terre nisi ad terminum annorum ex dimissione dicti Willelmi Knyght quondam viri ipsius Juliane. Et dicunt quod uxor habebit totum tenementum quod fuit viri sui postquam sponsalia in feodo post mortem viri sui ad terminum vite sue ut nomine dotis secundum consuetudines prebende.

Ideo consideratum est quod predicta Juliana reciperet seisinam suam
versus predictam Aliciam de predicta acra terre et dimidia. Et versus
predictum Ricardum de toto residuo predicte bovate terre. Et quod
predicta Alicia quo ad tenenciam suam habeat de terra eiusdem Ricardi
ad valenciam. Et idem Ricardus in misericordia.

¹ *Sic*; for p. 85 which has been inserted later, see below, **158**.   ² 15 July 1317   ³ 20
May 1395, certainly a scribal error for 1295 (cf. **458**, 1286 × 1296, for Thomas de
Hokerton)

Margin   p. 84, *Southwell* (17ᵗʰ-c. hand) alongside title; *Woodburgh* in a different 17ᵗʰ-c.
hand, at the beginning of the paragraph starting *Juliana que fuit...*

Note   This case had been dragging on for a very long time since it refers to letters
given by Archbishop Henry of Newark (elected 7 May 1296, died on 15 Aug. 1299). Mr
Simon de Courtmayor, canon from April 1296 and probably enjoying the prebend of
Woodborough from shortly afterwards, though orders had to be given on 7 September
1329 to install him (**216**). He resigned a few years later to become rector of Clayworth
from which benefice he had also resigned by 29 May 1336 (*Reg. Melton*, iv, nos 758, 785,
815). Did he originally come from Courmayeur in the Bernese Alps, one of the latest
to gain a benefice in the English church thanks to the influence of the Savoyards Peter
of Aigueblanche, bishop of Hereford (1240–68), Boniface, archbishop of Canterbury
(1243–70), and others?

158   *Instrument of John de Tyverington, notary public, on the appeal to
the Chapter of St Peter's Cathedral, York, in the case between Richard
Tantelyn of Woodborough against Juliana Frigg, lately wife of William
Knyght of Woodborough*   5 July 1345

IN DEI NOMINE AMEN. Per presens publicum instrumentum   p. 85
cuntis appareat evidenter quod anno domini ab incarnacione eiusdem
secundum cursum et computacionem ecclesie Anglicane millesimo
trecentesimo quadregesimo quinto indiccione tertiadecima pontificati
sanctissimi in Christo patris et domini nostri domini Clementis divina
providencia pape sexti anno quarto mense Julii die quinto. IN MEI
NOTARII publici infrascripti et testium subscriptorum presencia
comparuit magister Gilbertus de Welton' canonicus ecclesie collegiate
de Suthwell' coram reverendis viris magistris Johanne de Warrenna
et Thoma Sampson ecclesie cathedralis beati Petri Ebor' canonicis
in domo sua capitulari presentibus et capitulum facientibus petens
cum instancia quatinus dicti reverendi viri capitulum ut premittitur
facientes sentenciam et processum coram dicto venerabili capitulo
Ebor' et eiusdem capituli senescallo alias habitas et gestas pro quodam
Ricardo Tantelyn de Wodeburg' petente unum mesuagium et unam
bovatam terre cum pertinenciis in villa de Wodeburgh' contra Julianam
Frigg' que fuit uxor quondam Willelmi Knyght de Wodeburgh'
partem defendentem tamquam minus rite habitas et gestas per dictum
venerabilem capitulum, totaliter subducerent et cum effectu facta
que aliquali deliberacione predicti reverendi viri videlicet magistri
Johannes et Thomas capitulum ut prefertur facientes predictos
sentenciam et processum inter prefatos Ricardum et Julianam habitas
ut est dictum revocarunt sub hac forma.

Quicquid in causa dicti Ricardi Tauntelyn de Wodeburgh' contra memoratam Julianam Frigg' nuper coram nobis et deinde coram nostro senescallo de nostro expresso mandato mota et agitata temere et non debite fuit et est attemptatum subducimus et revocamus penitus cum effectu dictoque senescallo nostro cum coram nobis in domo nostra capitulari comparueret precipiemus quod quicquid per eundem temere ut prefertur et non debite fuit et est attemptatum in causa Ricardi supradicti illud sine mora revocetur seu faciat revocari. Acta sunt hec Ebor' anno domini, indiccione, pontificati, mense, die ac loco predictis, presentibus dominis Henrico Ketell', rectore ecclesie de South Whetelay Ebor' diocesis, Johanne de Wistowe, capellano, et Henrico de Welton', clerico Lyncoln' diocesis, testibus ad premissa vocatis et specialiter rogatis.

Et ego Johannes de Tyverington', clericus Ebor' diocesis publicus auctoritate apostolica notarius, premissis omnibus et singulis dum sic ut premittitur per venerabilem capitulum ecclesie Cathedralis beati Petri Ebor' predictum agerentur dicerentur et fierent una cum prenominatis testibus anno domini, indiccione ac pontificati mense die et loco predictis presens interfui eaque sic fieri vidi et audivi scripsi publicavi et in hanc publicam formam redegi meisque signo et nomine consuetis signavi in fidem et testimonium premissorum rogatus.

On reverse
Instrumentum super revocacionem processus de Wodeburgh factam apud Ebor' (late medieval) and *Southwell, Woodburgh* in early modern hand.

Margin **158** is an original public instrument on a separate sheet bound in at right-angles to the main text. In left-hand margin of 1st paragraph, written vertically, *Revocacio processus* in later 17th-c. hand: on left hand side before indented 2nd paragraph, *signum* of public notary.

Note Mr Gilbert of Welton, prebendary of Eaton (3 Aug. 1343–53), when he became bishop of Carlisle (1353–62). For Tyverington's notarial *signum* see Purvis, *Notarial Signs*, pl. 29 (1371). Henry Ketill, rector of South Wheatley, priest and minister of Southwell as early as 17 November 1322 (*Reg. Melton*, v, no. 136), when he was also warden of the fabric (**258**).

159 *View of frankpledge of the Southwell Chapter, on non-appearance of John le Ferrour and others* 29 April 1346

Visus franciplegii capituli beate Marie Suthwell' tentus ibidem die sabbati proximo post festum sancti Marci evangeliste, anno regni regis E[dwardi] tercii a conquestu vicesimo.

Johannes le Ferrour' de Maunnesfeld, dominus Rogerus atte Vikers, Seuwall' de Edyngley, dominus Ricardus de Wylughby, Rogerus Gryme, dominus Robertus de Roderham, Galfridus de Esthorpp', dominus Robertus de Somerby, Elias Cressy, Ricardus filius Nicholai de Normanton', quia non veniunt ideo in misericordia.

Margin Title and text of **159–84**, Scribe 4a or 4b. Left-hand margin, 1st paragraph, *Southwell* (17th c.); 2nd paragraph, *misericordia* (late medieval).

160 *View of frankpledge of Southwell Chapter, on purchase of tenements in Edingley by Thomas de Meyeley and non-appearance of Robert of Halam and others*   18 December 1346

Visus franciplegii capituli beate Marie Suthwell' tentus ibidem die lune proximo post festum sancte Lucie virginis, anno regni regis E[dwardi] tercii a conquestu vicesimo.

Thomas de Meyeley perquisivit tenementa in villa de Edyngley que tenentur de capitulo et non fecit fidelitatem

Robertus de Halum non venit. Ricardus Wode, Ricardus Dryng', Johannes Kydyher', Johannes de Hundon', Johannes de Roldeston', Emma de Crumwell', quia non veniunt ideo in misericordia.

Margin   Left-hand margin, first paragraph, *Southwell* (17ᵗʰ c.); 3ʳᵈ paragraph, *misericordia* (late medieval).

161 *Proceedings of the court of Henry of Edwinstowe, prebendary of Oxton and Cropwell, for the presentment against Matilda Northeron, tenant in bondage, for leasing tenements to Roger Galoway and William Alcok without licence*   16 October 1346

Curia domini Henrici de Edenstowe prebendarii alterius prebendarum de Oxton' et Crophill' in ecclesia collegiata beate Marie Suthwell' tenta ibidem die lune proximo ante festum sancti Luce evangeliste, anno regni regis E[dwardi] tercii xx°.

Presentatum est quod Matillda Northeron' tenens domini in bondagio dimisit tenementa illa Rogero Galoway et Willelmo Alcok' sine licencia domini. Ideo in misericordia \xl denarii/. Postea in proxima curia sequenti predicti Rogerus et Willelmus fecerunt finem cum domino de v solidis pro termino habendo etc.

Margin   Opposite title *Oxton'* (late medieval).

Note   Henry of Edwinstowe, prebendary of Oxton II (1327–d. by 1 February 1350).

162 *Proceedings of the court of the Prebendary of Oxton, payments by Geoffrey of Arnold and William Clerk of Blidworth for licence to let tenements at Blidworth to Sarah Bonde and Nicholas de Hoghton*   29 November 1346

Curia predicti prebendarii tenta ibidem die mercurii proximo post festum sancti Clementis pape, anno supradicto.

Galfridus de Arnall' dat domino pro licencia habenda tenendi Sarre Bonde in Blithworth prout convenire possit cum eadem Sarra hic in curia domini sui. Dando per annum domino pro licencia habenda quam domini tenere debet dicta tenementa   xii d.

Willelmus Clerk' de Blithworth nativus domini dat domino pro licencia   p. 88
habenda dimittendi ii acras terre sue Nicholao de Hoghton' ad terminum quinque vesturarum   xii d.

Margin   Opposite title *Oxton'* (late medieval).

163 *Proceedings of the court of the Prebendary of Oxton, ruling on merchet to be given by Isabella, daughter of John Pelle of Woodborough, for her marriage to John Alcok* 8 February 1346

Curia predicti prebendarii tenta ibidem die mercurii proximo post festum purificacionis beate Marie, anno supradicto.

Presentatum est quod Isabella filia Johannis Pelle nativi domini in Wodeburgh maritatur cuidam Johanni Alcok' nativo domini tamen dicit quod non debet dare merchet eo quod maritata est nativo domini et non alicui alteri. Set quia videtur senescallo domini quod merchet datur pro maritagio solummodo non habendo respectum ad quam personam. Ideo adiudicatur quod det pro mercheto suo prout moris est de consuetudine antiquitus usitata et approbata. v s. iiii d.

Margin Opposite title *Oxton'* (late medieval).

164 *View of frankpledge of Southwell Chapter, for the essoin of suit of court* 15 May 1349

Visus franciplegii capituli beate Marie Suthwell' tentus ibidem die veneris proximo ante festum sancti Dunstani archiepiscopi, anno regis predicti xxiii°.

Essonia Hugo de Osmanthorpp de adventu per Hugonem filium suum Robertus de Halum de eodem per Hugonem apparitorem

Margin Opposite title *Suthwell'* (late medieval).

165 *View of frankpledge of Southwell Chapter, claims of Robert Fraunseys to a messuage and land at Edingley, Thomas, son of Robert of Halum, to his father's holdings at Halam, and Hugh, son of William of Epperstone, to his father's holdings at Halam* 13 December 1351

Visus franciplegii predicti capituli tentus ibidem die martis in festo sancte Lucie virginis, anno domini millesimo ccc^mo li°.

Robertus Fraunseys de Edyngley venit in curiam et fecit fidelitatem et clamat tenere de capitulo unum mesuagium et unam bovatam terre cum pertinenciis in Edyngley in bondagio per servicium octo solidorum per annum et faciendo ulterius communem sectam et quo ad alia servicia inquiratur.

Thomas filius Roberti de Halum infra etatem existens seisitus est racione iunioris etatis quia eius maritagium pertinet ad dominum de iure prout patet per cartam versus capitulum de dono domini Willelmi de Wedynton' remanentem cuius tenementa quondam patris sui in Halum postea devenerunt ad manus Willelmi Golde et [blank] uxoris sue.

Presentatum est quod Willelmus de Epurston' nativus qui tenuit de capitulo unum mesuagium et i bovatam terre et dimidiam cum pertinenciis in Halum in bondagio diem clausit extremum. Ideo capiantur tenementa sua predicta in manus capituli salvo iure etc. Et super hoc venit Hugo filius et heres dicti Willelmi infra etatem existens et clamat dicta tenementa tenenda in bondagio per servicium xii solidorum per annum et communem sectam curie. Et quia dictus Hugo est infra etatem concessa sunt dicta tenementa Johanni de Haywode habenda usque ad legitimam etatem dicti Hugonis una cum maritagio suo faciendo pro dictis tenementis servicia debita capitulo durante minori etate eiusdem Hugonis. Et dictus Johannes dat pro dicta concessione xl d. Et pro herieto dicti Hugonis v s. iiii d. \per/ plegium Ricardi de Walesby.

Margin Opposite title *Suthwell'* (late medieval).

Note For William of Widdington/Wyddington, seneschal of the archbishop of York in Southwell, in the mid-thirteenth century and his chantry, see **Introduction**, pp. lxxxix–xciii and **390–420**. His charter about this land in Halam does not appear to survive.

166 *Court of Southwell Chapter, seizure by the Chapter of messuages and lands in Halam and Edingley held by Thomas atte Crosse*
22 November 1350

Curia predicti capituli tenta ibidem die lune in festo sancte Cecilie virginis, anno regni regis E[dwardi] tercii xxiiii°.

Ad istam curiam seisiti sunt in manus capituli ii mesuagia et ii bovate terre cum pertinenciis in Halum et Edyngley que Thomas atte Crosse tenuit de dicto capitulo per servicium ii s. et sectam curie per annum ut de cantaria beati Nicholai fundata pro anima Willelmi de Wydynton' pro defectu heredum ex parte matris sue salvo iure etc.

Margin Opposite title *Suthwell'* (late medieval).

Note This document is connected with a long-running case most fully set out in **171**.

167 *View of frankpledge of Southwell Chapter, William of Lincoln's claim to hold a messuage and land at Caunton, seizure by the Chapter of the holdings of Elias Cressy in South Carlton and seizure by the Chapter of the holdings of Henry Catte (location not given)*
3 July 1352

Visus franciplegii tentus ibidem die martis proximo post festum sancti Swithuni, anno millesimo ccc lii°. p. 89

Willelmus de Lincoln' venit in curiam et fecit fidelitatem capitulo et cognovit se tenere de eodem capitulo per legem Anglie ad terminum vite sue post decessum Matilde Dragun de Calneton uxoris sue i mesuagium et dimidiam acram terre in Calneton' per servicium ii s. per annum, quondam Ricardi Dragun'. Et queratur de aliis serviciis que et qualia sunt.

Presentatum est quod Elias Cressy qui tenuit de capitulo certa tenementa in Suthcarlton' libere per cartam diem suum clausit extremum. Ideo capiantur predicta tenementa in manus capituli quousque etc., racione minoris etatis filii et heredis ipsius Elie.

Item presentatum est quod Henricus Catte qui tenuit de capitulo certa tenementa in [*blank*] diem suum clausit extremum et quod heres eius infra etatem. Ideo capiantur tenementa predicta in manus capituli salvo iure etc.

Margin Opposite title *Suthwell'* (late medieval).

168   *View of frankpledge of Southwell Chapter, claims of Robert de Tame of a toft at Southwell, John of Farndon of a messuage at Southwell, and Richard O the More of Southwell of a messuage*   26 November 1352

Visus franciplegii capituli predicti tentus ibidem die martis proximo post festum sancte Katerine virginis, anno regni regis E[dwardi] tercii xxvi°.

Robertus de Tame venit in curiam et fecit fidelitatem capitulo et cognovit se tenere de capitulo i toftum in Suthwell' per servicium xviii d. per annum.

    Johannes de Farnedon' venit in curiam et fecit fidelitatem capitulo et cognovit se tenere de capitulo unum mesuagium in Suthwell' per servicium viii s. per annum.

    Ricardus O the More de Suthwell' venit in curiam et fecit fidelitatem capitulo et cognovit se tenere de capitulo unum mesuagium cum pertinenciis de iure Isabelle uxoris sue per servicium ii s. per annum.

Margin   Opposite title *Suthwell'* (late medieval).

169   *Proceedings of the court of Southwell Chapter, Richard Dryng of Halam claims to hold a moiety of two bovates of land in Halam and Edingley*   13 December 1352

Curia capituli predicti tenta ibidem die lune in festo sancte Lucie virginis, anno regni regis E[dwardi] tercii xxiiii°.

Ricardus Dryng' de Halum qui tenet medietatem unius bovate terre cum pertinenciis in Halum post decessum patris sui venit in curiam et clamat tenere de capitulo illam medietatem ut parcellam duarum bovatarum terre quondam Roberti Donne cum pertinenciis in Halum et Edyngley ex concessione Roberti filii Ricardi Kyng' de Edyngley per servicium quantum pertinet ad illam parcellam.

Margin   Opposite title *Suthwell'* (late medieval).

Note   This document is connected with the long-running case most fully set out in **171**. Extracts entered in the White Book from proceedings in the court at Southwell break off at this point in 1352, before resuming in 1388 (**170**). However an original roll covering the years 1355–1419 has survived (NA, DD SP 4/0/1), though there is very little overlap in content between material in the White Book (to **184**) and the roll.

170   *View of frankpledge of Southwell Chapter, claim of John Dryng to two messuages and two bovates of land at Halam, and counter-claim of John Broun of Edingley*   3 February 1388

Visus franciplegii capituli Suthwell' tentus ibidem die lune proximo post festum purificacionis beate Marie virginis, anno regni regis Ricardi secundi xi°.

Johannes Dryng' qui tenet de capitulo ut de altera cantariarum beati Nicholai duo mesuagia duas bovatas terre cum pertinenciis in Halum post mortem Agnetis Dryng' matris sue venit in curiam in propria persona sua et dicit quod quedem Matill' Douwe fuit seisita de predictis mesuagiis et ii bovatis terre in feodo simplici et obiit seisita post cuius mortem predicta tenementa descenderunt | cuidam Ricardo Dryng' patri suo ut proximo heredi. Et sic idem Johannes verus tenens ut dicit paratus est facere fidelitatem suam. Set quia quidam Johannes Broun' de Edyngley dicit se esse rectum heredem tenementorum predictorum differtur fideliter usque ad proximum diem. Et dicitur per quosdam quod dictus Ricardus Dryng' non fuit consanguineus predicte Matilde Douwe ut de eius sanguine.

p. 90

Margin Opposite title *Suthwell'* (late medieval).

Note This document is connected with the long-running case most fully set out in **171**.

171 *View of frankpledge of Southwell Chapter, proceedings in the case of John Broun and John Dryng as above* **170**, *reciting a number of deeds and charters, and a writ of novel disseisin*

[unspecified day before 20 July 1388]

Visus franciplegii capituli predicti tentus ibidem proximo ante festum sancte Margarete, anno regni regis Ricardi secundi xii⁰.

Johannes Dryng de Halum liber homo clamat tenere de capitulo ecclesie beate Marie Suthwell' \sicut alias/ duo mesuagia et duas bovatas terre cum pertinenciis in Halum ex dono et feoffamento cuiusdam domini Henrici quondam vicarii de Halum ad terminum vite sue reddendo certum redditum suum \scilicet duos solidos/ alteri cantarie sancti Nicholai in eadem ecclesia Suthwell' facit sectam curie et profert se facere fidelitatem. Set eam accipere senescallus curie predicti capituli refutavit, eo quod alias invenitur, videlicet quod capitulum Suthwell' predictum seisivit tenementa predicta ut escaeta sua pro defectu heredum in prima pestilencia \[*in margin*] anno regni regis Edwardi tercii xxiiii⁰/ eo quod quidam Willelmus Donne de Halum tenuit duo mesuagia et ii bovatas terre cum pertinenciis in Halum libere per cartam de Rogero de Lanum clerico per redditum ii s. per annum per fidem et sectam curie etc., qui quidam Rogerus redditum illum cum servicio sibi pertinentem alienavit cuidam Willelmo de Wydington' qui quidem Willelmus de Wydyngton' postea dedit eundem redditum cum servicio una cum aliis terris et tenementis capitulo de Suthwell' ad sustentacionem unius capellani divina celebrantis ad altare sancti Nicholai in eadem ecclesia. Virtute cuius doni dictum capitulum fuit seisitum tam de redditu quam aliis serviciis per manus Thome Donne filii predicti Willelmi Donne ut patet per cartam etc. a tempore cuius contrarii memoria non existit. De quo quidem Thoma Donne venit Ricardus Donne filius suus et heres qui solvit redditum predictum. De Ricardo Donne venit Matill' Donne que desponsata fuit cuidam Ricardo atte Cross qui fuerunt seisiti de tenementis predictis et solverunt redditum predictum etc. De quibus venit Thomas atte Crosse filius et heres tenementorum predictorum et solvit redditum predictum et obiit seisitus sine herede de \sanguine suo/ ex parte matris sue, ex cuius parte tenementa predicta descenderunt Ricardo atte Crosse patri suo et Matilde uxori sue matri eiusdem Thome cuius heres ipse fuit exceptis xvii selionibus de ii bovatis terre predicte continentibus per estimacionem dimidie bovate terre ut dicebatur per Robertum Donne proavum ipsius Thome atte Crosse alienatis Roberto filio Ricardi Kyng' de Edyngley ut patet per cartam eiusdem Roberti in hec verba.

Notum sit omnibus tam presentibus quam futuris, quod nos Robertus Donne de Halum et Hauwisia uxor mea dedimus concessimus et hac presenti carta nostra confirmavimus Roberto filio Ricardi Kyng' de Edyngley et heredibus suis in feodo et hereditate septemdecim seliones in territoria de Halum et Edyngley arabiles, quorum unus selio iacet etc. et unam placeam prati etc. Tenendum et habendum dicto Roberto et heredibus suis in feodo et hereditate cum omnibus pertinenciis libertatibus et aisiamentis in boscis planis pratis pascuis pasturis viis et in semitis infra villam et extra quantum ad tantam terram pertinet imperpetuum. Reddendo inde annuatim nobis et heredibus nostris vel assignatis nostris unum denarium tamen die Pasche pro omnibus serviciis secularibus exaccionibus sectis curie et omnimodis demandis. Et nos vero dicti Robertus et Hauwisia dictos seliones cum prato predicto dicto Roberto et heredibus suis in feodo et hereditate cum omnibus pertinenciis ut predictum est pro predicto servicio contra omnes homines et feminas warantizabimus, | acquietabimus et imperpetuum defendemus. Et ut hec nostra donacio concessio et presentis carte nostre confirmacio rata et stabilis imposterum perseveret hoc presens scriptum sigilli nostri munimine duximus roborando. Hiis testibus Hugone de Osmonthorpp', Roberto filio Roberti, Willelmo Paumer, Johanne de Thorpp', Willelmo de Seggisbrok', Hugone filio Hugonis, Haudewyno de Osmunthorpp', Johanne de Osmunthorpp', Roberto de Osmunthorpp', Rogero de Alneto, Roberto filio Gerardi de Edyngley, Henrico Franceys de Halum et multis aliis.

p. 91 [in margin]

Postea iidem Robertus et Hauwisia uxor eius fecerunt confirmacionem de selionibus predictis in forma que sequitur.

Omnibus hoc scriptum visuris vel audituris Robertus dominus de Halum et Hauwisia uxor eius salutem in domino sempiternam. Noverit universitas vestra nos unanimi consensu et voluntate nostra concessisse et confirmasse Ricardo Kyng de Edyngley totam terram quam habet penes se de dono Johannis Kyng' advunculi sui de hereditate nostra sicut carta feoffatoris testatur. Tenendum et habendum de nobis et heredibus nostris dicto Ricardo et heredibus suis vel suis assignatis vel heredibus assignatorum vel cuicumque dare legare vendere vel assignare voluerint tam in egritudine quam in sanitate. Reddendo inde annuatim nobis et heredibus nostris unum denarium argenti ad festum Pentecosten pro omnibus serviciis secularibus exaccionibus sectis curie et demandis. Et ego Robertus et Hauwisia et heredes nostri predictam terram cum omnibus pertinenciis dicto Ricardo et heredibus suis vel suis assignatis vel heredibus assignatorum sicut predictum est contra omnes homines et feminas warantizabimus acquietabimus et defendemus imperpetuum. Et ut hec nostra donacio concessio et carte nostre confirmacio rata et stabilis permaneant imperpetuum presentem cartam sigilli nostri munimine roboravimus. Hiis testibus magistro Hugone de Upton', Roberto filio Roberti de Halum, Thoma filio Alexandri de eadem, Hugone de Osmunthorpp', Willelmo le Paumer, Roberto de Osmunthorpp', Roberto eius filio, Roberto filio Gerardi de Edyngley, Rogero filio Radulphi de Alneto et aliis etc.

Et sic dictus Ricardus Kyng' virtute primi doni et confirmacionis sequentis tamen fuit seisitus de septemdecim selionibus et prato in dictis scriptis contentis, tenendis de capitulo etc., qui fuerunt nisi \parcella/ duarum bovatarum terre predictarum pro quibus Ricardus Dryng' fecit fidelitatem ut patet in curia capituli Suthwell' tenta ibidem die lune in festo sancte Lucie virginis, anno regni regis Edwardi tercii a conquestu xxiiii°.[1]

Et quia dictus Thomas atte Crosse obiit seisitus de mesuagio et duabus bovatis terre predictis exceptis xvii selionibus alienatis Ricardo Kyng' de Edyngley ut supra que continent ut supponitur dimidia bovata terre sine herede de sanguine suo ex parte matris sue ex cuius parte tenementa predicta sibi descenderunt. Capitulum Suthwellie seisivit tenementa illa ut escaeta sua pro defectu heredis in prima pestilencia scilicet anno xxiiii° regis Edwardi tercii ut superius. Et post illam seisinam sic factam per capitulum Ricardus Kyng' pater predicti Johannis Dryng' alias vocatus Johannes Kyng' ut filius Ricardi Kyng' prenominati et ista fuit causa quare Ricardus Kyng' fuit nativus domini sui; et \ad/ evitandum illam navitatem Johannis Kyng' filius suus serviebat cuidam N. Dryng' de Halum de quo ipse Johannes filius Ricardi Kyng' nativi supradicti cepit nomen magistri sui et vocabatur Johannes Dryng' et cepit tenementa predicta de capellano cantarie, tenendum sibi ad voluntatem capituli ut dicebatur reddendo per annum ii s., et faciendo sectam etc., qui quidem Ricardus Kyng' tenementa predicta postea per cartam suam alienavit cuidam N. vicario de Halum, quo precepto capitulum seisivit, eo quod sine licencia capituli predicti tenementa predicta alienavit etc. Et sic capitulum seisitum fuit c'[2] quousque disseisitum per dictum Johannem alio nomine et recto vocandus Johannes Kyng'. Et quia Johannes Broun' de Edyngley clamat ius in eisdem tenementis | ut proximus heres prefati Thome atte Crosse   p. 92
qui ultimo obiit seisitus de tenementis predictis exceptis preexceptis sine herede de sanguine suo ex parte matris sue ex qua parte dicta tenementa sibi descenderunt iure hereditario. Ideo capta fuit assissa nove disseisine versus eosdem Johannem Dryng' et Johannem Broun' in hec verba.

Ricardus Dei gracia rex Anglie et Francie et dominus Hibernie vicecomiti Notingh' salutem. Questum est nobis capitulum ecclesie collegiate beate Marie Suthwell' quod Johannes Broun' de Edyngley et Johannes Dryng' de Halum iniuste et sine iudicio disseisiverunt predictum capitulum de libero tenemento suo in Edyngley post primam transfretacionem domini Henrici regis filii regis Johannis \in/ Vascon'. Et ideo tibi precipimus quod si predictum capitulum fecerit te securem de clamio suo prosequendo tunc facies tenementum illud reseisiri de catallis que in ipso fuerint et ipsum tenementum cum catallis esse in pace usque ad certum diem quem dilecti et fideles nostri Willelmus Thirnyng' et Johannes Woderoue tibi scire facient. Et interim facies xii liberos et legales homines de visneto illo videre tenementum illud et nomina eorum imbreviari. Et summonebis eos per bonos summonitores quod tunc sint coram prefatis Willelmo et Johanne et hiis quos sibi associabunt ad certum locum quem iidem Willelmus et Johannes tibi scire facient parati inde facere recognicionem. Et pone per vadia et salvos plegios predictos Johannem et Johannem vel ballivos suos si ipsi inventi non fuerint, quod tunc sint ibi audire illam recognitionem. Et habeas ibi summonitores nomina plegii et hoc breve.

Teste me ipso apud Westm' xviii die Junii anno regni nostri vicesimo.[3]
Roderh[am]

In quo brevi capitulum querelabatur se disseisiri de duobus mesuagiis et duabus bovatis terre cum pertinenciis in brevi nominatis etc.

Nomina panellatorum dicto brevi consuta
Summonitores Johannes Skathlok' manucaptus per Hugonem Poge
Johannes Walker manucaptus per Hugonem Poge

Ricardus Walhyll'	Willelmus Golde de Halum
Willelmus de Gelston'	Willelmus Clerk' de Gedlyng'
Willelmus atte Vykers de Sutton'	Johannes Bryce de Stokbardolf iunior
Thomas de Crumwell' de Carleton'	Johannes Edward de Loudeham
Johannes Johnnson' de Weston'	Johannes Cryche de Hokerton'
Johannes Julyane de Holme	Radulphus Bykerstafe de Bulcote
Johannes de Evyngton de Suthwell'	Johannes Fyssher' de Suthwell' senior
Johannes de Ledenham de eadem	Johannes Lysurs de Wylughby
Radulphus de Hokerton'	Johannes de Crumwell' de Starthorpp'
Robertus Whitberd de Bathley	Willelmus Clerk' de Roldeston'
Robertus Mabe de Areham	Robertus Hawys de Holme
Ranulphus Morey de Starthorpp	Johannes Fyssher' iunior de Suthwell'

Que quidem assisa postea discontianta fuit ad instanciam predictorum amicorum predictorum Johannis Broun' et Johannis Dryng'. Et ad huc remanet indiscussa, et dicti Johannes Broun' et Johannes Dryng' mortui sunt et Johannes filius Johannis Dryng' post mortem parentum suorum eadem tenementa usque ad presens occupavit.

[1] 13 December 1350   [2] MS seems to be clear that the reading is 'c'', but it is possible that it ought to be 't'', i.e. it is the tenement that has been seized. It may also, however, be 'c[apella]', though given what is said above is it more likely to be 'cantaria'?   [3] 18 June 1397

Margin   p. 90, left margin, opposite title *Suthwell'* (late medieval); right margin 1st paragraph line 2 *Halum'*; line 6 *anno regni Regis Edwardii tercii xxiiii°*; right-hand margin, 2nd paragraph *Carta* (all late medieval but different hands); p. 91, left margin at the beginning of the Robert Donne deed *Cart'*; twenty-five lines further down *Kyng' alias Dryng'* in later medieval hands; p. 92, right margin *Dies visus die Sabbati proximo post festum Sancti Jacobi apostoli* (late medieval).

Note   The land in Halam at the centre of this long-running case appears to be that held by William Donne of Roger of Laneham, clerk, who sold it to William of Widdington, before 1250 (**400**). Its descent from William Donne to his great-great-grandson Thomas atte Cross appears to be clearly set out at the start: William Donne, Thomas Donne, Richard Donne, Matilda (née Donne, wife of Richard atte Cross), and their son Thomas. But then mention of Robert Donne, great-grandfather (*proavus*) of Thomas atte Cross, together with his wife, Hawisia, granting seventeen strips of the parcel in Halam and Edingley to Robert, son of Richard Kyng of Edingley, together with the donors' later confirmation of this deed, both cited in full and to be dated *c.* 1300, introduce elements of confusion into the Donne genealogy. Has the clerk muddled the names Robert and Richard Donne as well as their generations? Later, the death of Thomas atte Cross without direct heirs allowed for other competing claims. He was almost certainly a victim of the Black Death as is suggested by mention here of seizure by the Chapter of his tenement *pro defectu heredum in prima pestilencia*, with an added marginal date of 24 Edward III, i.e. 1350–1. For this seizure, see **166**, 22 Nov. 1352. Among those now putting forward claims was Richard Dryng of Halam who asked for a moiety by 13 December 1352 (**169**).

A generation later, by 3 February 1388, another claimant had also emerged, John Broun of Edingley, who said he was Thomas's closest heir, though this was disputed by John Dryng (**170**). Curiously in fact, Dryng was the son of the man to whom Robert Donne had granted the seventeen selions and for which his father, Richard Kyng, performed fealty to the Chapter on 13 December 1350 as **171** relates, But, apparently taking advantage of new opportunities following the Black Death which enabled social mobility, he had changed his name from Kyng to Dryng in an effort to escape the stigma of serfdom, by attaching himself to the service of a certain N. (almost certainly Richard) Dryng of Halam, whose name he took (*cepit nomen magistri sui et vocabatur Johannes Dryng'*). Later still, as the brief mention of the inquest following Richard II's order of 18 June 1397 shows, by then both John Broun and John Dryng were dead, and John Dryng, junior, currently held the tenement. But the ramifications of the dispute were by no means concluded as further proceedings between 1402 and 1409 reveal (**172**–8, **180**). In Richard II's letters to the sheriff of Nottingham, 18 June 1397, which are cited in full, there is mention of the Chapter having first held the tenement in dispute since the time of Henry III's first expedition to Gascony, i.e. 1242.

172   *View of frankpledge of Southwell Chapter, claim of John, son of John of Osmanthorpe, to a toft of land at Osmanthorpe, and of John Broun of a messuage and land in Edingley and two messuages and land at Edingley and Halam*   22 June 1402

Visus franciplegii predicti capituli tentus ibidem die iovis in festo sancti Albani martiris, anno regni regis Henrici quarti tertio.   p. 93

Ad istam venit Johannes filius Johannis de Osmonthorpp. Et fecit fidelitatem capitulo et clamat tenere de eo unum toftum cum crofto nuper mesuagium edificatum et ii seliones super Goldhille cum pertinenciis in Osmonthorpp' que quondam fuerunt Willelmi Helwys de Suthwell' per fidelitatem et servicium duorum solidorum per annum, faciendo ulterius duos adventus et duos visus franciplegii, videlicet ad proximum post festum Michaelis et ad proximum post festum Pasche tenendos.

Presentatum est quod Johannes Broun' qui tenuit de capitulo i mesuagium et i bovatam terre cum pertinenciis in Edyngley ad voluntatem dimisit de bovata terre predicte Johanni Asselyn' dimidiam acram terre iacentem super Rawensty, Johanni Smyth de Edyngley iii acras terre in diversis locis campi, Ricardo Parker de Farnesfeld ii acras prati sub gardino quod Johannes de Roldeston' tenet de capitulo extra curiam sine licencia capituli. Ideo capiantur tenementa predicta in manus dicti capituli.

Item dictus Johannes Broune vendidit in feodo cuidam Johanni Hudson' de bovata predicta dimidiam acram iacentem super Holgatebuskes. Ideo capiantur etc. ut plures. Postea dictus Johannes Hudson' fecit finem pro terra habenda ad terminum vite sue qui modo mortuus est. Et sic in manu capituli cum predicta terra quondam Johannis Broun' que tenementa Johannes filius et heres predicti Johannis Broun' pro manutenencia habenda feoffavit ut dicitur Willelmum de Westhorpp et Emmam uxorem eius, ut ipsi manutenerent illa tenementa contra capitulum non obstante seisina capituli predicta, unde oportet remedium fieri etc.

Ad huc remanent seisita duo mesuagia et ii bovate terre cum pertinenciis in Halum et Edyngley que Johannes Drynge de Halum iniuste occupat de iurisdiccione capituli in Halum et Edyngley clamando tenementa illa sibi perquisita per cartam que tenementa sunt de lescaeta[1] capituli et illa de causa seisita etc. Et de quibus nullam habet cartam etc.

Item ad huc remanent seisita tenementa Johannis Broun' in Edyngley prius seisita, causa prius assignata.

[1] MS *sic*

Margin   Opposite title *Suthwell'* (late medieval); 2nd paragraph at top *Nota bene*, 2nd paragraph at bottom *Remedium* (both late medieval).

Note   For John Dryng, see **171n.**

173   *View of frankpledge of Southwell Chapter, relating to the claims of John Asselyn and John Hudson to lands in Edingley, of Robert Couper and Henry, son of John the park-keeper, of a messuage and land at South Carlton, and of John Dryng to a messuage and lands at Edingley*
28 October 1402

Visus franciplegii predicti capituli tentus ibidem die sabbati in festo apostolorum Symonis et Jude, anno regni regis Henrici quarti quarto.

Ad huc sicut in proxima curia precedente dimidia acra terre iacens super Rawensty cum pertinenciis in Edyngley quam Johannes Asselyn' clamat habere et tenere ex concessione Johannis Broun' qui terram illam tenuit ad voluntatem capituli remanet seisita causa quousque etc.

Ad istam curiam venit Johannes Hudson' liber homo et cepit de capitulo dimidiam acram terre cum pertinenciis iacentem super Holgatebusk' in campis de Halum et Edyngley parcellam cuiusdam bovate terre quam Johannes Broun' nuper tenuit de capitulo predicto ad voluntatem seisitam

p. 94 | in manus capituli ad proximam curiam precedentem pro eo quod ipse Johannes Broun' dimidiam acram terre predictarum[1] alienavit in feodo dicto Johanni Hudson' sine licencia capituli, habendum et tenendum predictarum[1] dimidiam acram terre cum pertinenciis in villis predictis prefato Johanni Hudson' ad terminum vite sue de dicto capitulo. Reddendo inde annuatim domino Willelmo Ketill' capellano cantarie beati Nicholai in ecclesia Suthwell' et successoribus suis ii d, per annum ad duos anni terminos usuales in partem solucionis quatuor solidorum annui redditus exeuntis de i bovata terre integra predicta et dicto capellano[2] debitorum prout in curia precedente plenius continetur. Ulterius veniendo bis per annum ad duos visus franciplegii apud Suthwell' cum ceteris tenentibus euisdem capituli et fecit fidelitatem domino etc.

Robertus Couper de Starthorpp' et Johannes filius Henrici parcenarius suus fecerunt fidelitatem capitulo separatim et clamant tenere de eo libere per cartam i mesuagium et ii bovatas terre cum pertinenciis in Southcarleton' quondam Elie Cressy ut de iure Johanne et Isabelle uxorum \suarum/ ~~suarum~~ filiarum et heredum Johannis Smyth de Northwell' qui tenementa predicta perquisivit de Johanne filio Willelmi de Batheley per servicium xvi s. per annum solvendum domino Willelmo Ketull' capellano alterius cantariarum beati Nicholai episcopi in ecclesia Suthwell' et successoribus suis capellanis cantarie predicte. Ulterius veniendo bis per annum ad duos visus franciplegii dicti capituli apud Suthwell'¹ pro omni alio servicio.

Ad huc sicut in curia precedente remanent seisiti unum mesuagium et una bovata terre cum pertinenciis in Edyngley que Johannes Dryng de Halum iniuste occupat de iurisdiccione capituli in Halum clamando tenementa illa tenere hereditarie per cartam que sunt de escaeta capituli. Et pertinent cantarie beati Nicholai episcopi quam dominus Willelmus Kydyer modo occupat, qui quidem Johannes nunquam fuit de sanguine Thome atte Crosse post cuius mortem clamat hereditatem predictam etc.

¹ MS *sic* for *predictam*   ² MS *sic* for *Capitulo*

Margin   Opposite title *Suthwell'* (late medieval); 2ⁿᵈ paragraph *Super holegatebusk'* in a later hand, with *?Nota* written above it; 3ʳᵈ paragraph *Messuagium et 2 bovatas terre in South Carlton*, and *16s per annum*, both in the same hand.

Note   For John Dryng and Thomas atte Cross, see **171n**.

174   *View of frankpledge of Southwell Chapter, at which fealty was rendered to the Chapter in customary form by William Scotte, formerly a bondman of Thomas atte Lude, acquired by the late William of Gunthorpe, canon, when endowing his chantry of the Blessed Virgin, of the claims of John Best to a messuage and land in Sutton, Margery Mauger of a messuage at Carlton, John Asselyn of land at Edingley. Also recital of an indenture dated 11 September 1392, demising two acres of meadow in Edingley by John Broun of Edingley to Richard Robynson of Farnsfield for 18 years, with extension after that term by Robynson to Richard Parker. Also, remedy as to the right of John, son of John Dryng to a messuage and land at Halam and Edingley*   8 June 1403

Visus franciplegii eiusdem capituli tentus ibidem die veneris in festo sancti Willelmi Ebor' archiepiscopi, anno regni regis Henrici quarti quarto.

Willelmus Scotte nativus de sanguine quondam cuidam Thome atte Lute cuius statum dominus Willelmus de Gunthorpp nuper canonicus capituli perquisivit ad quandam cantariam misse beate Marie ordinatam fecit fidelitatem capituli ut nativus facere tenetur. Et postea petit de quodam Johanne Beste de Sutton' unum mesuagium et unam bovatam terre cum pertinenciis in Sutton' que Hugo Scotte nativus dicti Thome atte Lutte nuper tenuit ut ius et hereditatem suam etc. Et dictus Johannes Beste presens in curia dicit quod ipse cepit tenementa predicta de domino Willelmo de Gunthorpp tunc domino tenementorum predictorum. Reddendo sibi annuatim xiii s. iiii d. Et capitali domino feodi illius per annum ii s. v d. faciendo ulterius pro dictis tenementis officium franciplegii quolibet anno sub tali condicione quod si aliquis heres de sanguine bondagii venerit ad calumpniandum tenementa predicta quod quemcumque fore contigerit prius concordet cum tenente tenementorum predictorum de misis expensis et | custagiis necessariis pro melioracione tenementorum predictorum in suo tempore factis quare ipse tenens dicit quod si placeat dicto petenti satisfacere sibi in forma predicta quod ipse paratus est ad liberandum

p. 95

sibi ad proximam curiam sequentem etc. Ad quod petens consentit. Ideo datus est partibus predictis dies usque ad festum sancti Michaelis infra quod tempus possunt concordare etc.

Item presentatum est quod Margeria Mauger nativa quondam uxor Thome Souter' de Sutton' perquisivit unum mesuagium cum parcella terre in Carleton' predicta que tenementa post perquisicionem factam seisita fuerunt. Et non obstante seisina dicta Margeria tenementa predicta alienavit cuidam Johanni filio Johannis de Barneby de Carleton' sine licencia. Ideo prosequatur etc.

Ad huc remanet seisita in manibus capituli ut patet in curia precedente dimidia acra terre iacens super Rawensty in campo de Eddyngley quam Johannes Asselyn' iniuste occupat ex dimissione Johannis Broun' qui terram illam et aliam terram tenuit de capitulo ad voluntatem et sine licencia extra curiam fecit dimissionem dicto occupatori per indenturam sigillatam. Et iii acre terre iacentes cum pertinenciis diversis locis eiusdem ville quas Johannes Smyth iniuste occupat ex dimissione eiusdem Johannis Broune causa predicta. Et due acre prati cum pertinenciis in eadem villa iacentes sub gardino Johannis de Roldeston' quas Ricardus Parcarius de Farnesfeld iniuste occupat causa predicta ut patet per indenturam sigillatam huic rotulo consuta in hec verba.

Hec indentura facta die mercurii proximo ante festum sancte Lucie virginis anno regni regis Ricardi secundi sextodecimo¹ inter Johannem Broun' de Edyngley ex una parte et Ricardum Robynson' de Farnesfeld ex altera parte testatur quod dictus Johannes tradidit et ad firmam dimisit prefato Ricardo Robynson' ii acras prati simul iacentes in pratis de Edyngley² inter pratum Ricardi Parker' ex parte occidentali et pratum Willelmi Sewalson' ex parte orientali et abbutat ad unum caput super Prestestubbyng', habendum et tenendum predictas duas acras prati predicto Ricardo Robynson' heredibus et assignatis suis usque ad terminum xviii annorum proximo sequentem post datum presencium plenarie completorum. Et dictus Johannes Broune et heredes sui predictas duas acras prati prout iacent in pratis predictis prefato Ricardo Robynson' heredibus et assignatis suis durante termino predicto contra omnes gentes warantizabunt et defendent. In cuius rei testimonium partes predicte sigilla sua alternatim apposuerunt. Hiis testibus Ricardo Parker' de Farnesfeld, Willelmo Sewallson' de Edyngley, Ricardo Brokestow, Johanne Smyth, Willelmo Couper', et aliis. Datum apud Edyngley die et anno supradictis.

Quem terminum xviii annorum predictorum Ricardus Parker' continuavit [expunged] continuavit in eodem prato per assignacionem ipsius Ricardi Robynson' etc.

Item remanent seisita unum mesuagium et una bovata terre cum pertinenciis in Halum et Edyngley que Johannes Dryng' senior iniuste occupat clamando tenementa illa teneri per cartam hereditarie que sunt de escaeta capituli et illa de causa seisita in manus capituli ut pluries patet in curia precedente. Fiat igitur remedium erga tenentem, scilicet Johannem filium et heredem predicti Johannis Dryng' pro quibus tenementis capta fuit assisa pro capitulo que discontinata fuit ut prius dicitur.

¹ 11 December 1392   ² Followed by *in pratis de Edyngley* repeated

Margin   Opposite title *Suthwell'* (late medieval); 3rd paragraph left margin (p. 95),
Carlton; 4th paragraph, at top, left-hand margin, *Rawensty, Pyngley, no'8* (early modern?); half-way down, *Indentura* (late medieval); 5th paragraph, left margin, *Remedium* (late medieval).

Note   For Margaret Mauger and her family, villeins of Sutton and Carlton on Trent, see **175, 178** and also various documents connected with William of Gunthorpe's foundation (**491–503**); for Thomas Lude and his acquisition of lands in Norwell, see **373, 487, 488, 491** and **495**; for John Dryng, see **171n**.

175   *View of frankpledge of Southwell Chapter, claim of John Asselyn to land at Edingley and seizure by Chapter of the holding of William Scotte and Robert Mauger in North Carlton*   29 March 1404

Visus franciplegii eiusdem capituli die sabbati in septimana Pasche, anno regni regis Henrici quarti post conquestum Anglie quinto.   p. 96

Ad huc remanet seisita ut pluries patet in curia precedente in manus capituli dimidia acra terre iacens super Rawensty in campo de Edyngley quam Johannes Asselyn' de Halum iniuste occupat eo quod Johannes Broun' qui illam tenuit ut parcellam cuiusdam bovate terre quam ipse tenuit de capitulo in bondagio, illam dicto tenenti dimisit extra curiam sine licencia et nullo modo vult dimittere clamando eam tenere per cartam dicti Johannis sibi factam ad grave scandalum dominorum capituli. Ideo fiat inde remedium etc.

Item presentatum est ad istam curiam quod Willelmus Scotte de Sutton' super Trent' nativus capitulo et Robertus Mauger nativus capitulo ut de tenemento in North Carleton' morantur extra dominium capituli sine licencia. Ideo capiantur per eorum corpora etc., quousque finem pro eorum mora fecerint.

Margin   Opposite title *Suthwell'* (late medieval); 2nd paragraph, right margin, *Remedium* (late medieval).

176   *View of frankpledge of Southwell Chapter, claims of Elisota, daughter of John of Barley, and Richard Cryche to a messuage and land at Halam*   11 October 1404

Visus franciplegii eiusdem capituli tentus ibidem die lune proximo ante festum sancti Luce evangeliste, anno regni regis Henrici quarti post conquestum Anglie vi^{to}.

Presentatum est quod Elisota que fuit uxor Johannis de Barley qui tenuit de capitulo unum mesuagium et i bovatam terre cum pertinenciis in Halum ad voluntatem capituli prout in quadam curia precedente plenius apparet per redditum octo solidorum per annum debitum cantarie sancti Nicholai in ecclesia Suthwell' quam dominus Willelmus Ketull' capellanus modo occupat concordat[1] cum quodam Ricardo Kyng' de Halum pro certa summa pecunie sibi soluta quod ipsa Elisota tenementa predicta relinqueret et moraretur in alio loco que se removebat causa predicta extra feodum capituli cum omnibus bonis et catallis suis ante festum sancti Michaelis proximum preteritum et permisit tenementa illa stare vacua, non occupata.

Ideo capiantur tenementa illa in manus capituli quousque etc. Et super hoc venit quidam Ricardus Cryche de Halum liber homo ex consensu Ricardi Kyng' superius nominati et cepit de capitulo mesuagium et bovatam terre predicte cum omnibus eorum pertinenciis in Halum predictis, habendum et tenendum sibi et heredibus suis sub tali condicione tamen quod nec ipse Ricardus Cryche nec aliquis heredum suorum faciet vastum vel destruccionem in tenementis predictis set quod quilibet eorum quem pro tempore fore contigerit domos infra mesuagium predictum edificatas vel edificandum sumptibus suis propriis competenter reparabit sustentabit sub pena amissionis status sui quem clamat habere in tenementis predictis. Et quod nec dictus Ricardus Cryche nec aliquis eius heres post eius mortem mesuagium et terram predictam neque aliquam parcellam eorumdem alicui alteri dimittat relinquat nec vendat extra curiam predicti capituli sine licencia speciali petita et optenta sub pena predicta. Et quod quilibet heres hereditarie succedens post mortem predicti Ricardi Cryche nunc tenentis dabit capitulo ad ingressum suum post mortem antecessoris sui tamen v s. faciendo ulterius omnia alia servicia et redditus sicut supradictum est. Reddendo annuatim pro tenementis predictis tam dictus Ricardus Cryche quam heredes sui capellano cantarie predicte qui pro tempore erit in ecclesia predicta – viii s. ad duos anni terminos usuales per equales porciones. Ulterius faciendo communem sectam ad curiam predicti capituli apud Suthwell' de tribus septimanis in tres septimanas cum ceteris tenementibus eiusdem capituli. Et quod dictus Ricardus Cryche

p. 97 et heredes sui erunt | bedelli dicti capituli videlicet ad summoniendum curiam eiusdem capituli et extractus curie illarum colligendum quociens et quum[2] per senescallum eiusdem capituli onerati vel per curiam electi sub pena supradicta. Et si contingat dictum mesuagium stare vacuum ita quod sufficiens districcio in eodem pro aliquo eius redditu debito et non soluto aliquo tempore futuro a retro inveniri non poterit quod extunc bene licebit dicto capitulo et successoribus suis ut supra dictum est mesuagium et terram predictam in manus suas reseisire et ea sit seisita retinere imperpetuum ista concessione superius facta non obstante. Et dictus Ricardus Cryche dabit capitulo ad ingressum suum pro fine suo – xx s. plegium de solucione summe predicte Ricardus Kyng' de Halum de cuius consensu et voluntate ipse tenens venit ad tenementa predicta. Et fecit fidelitatem capitulo.

[1] MS *concordant*   [2] MS *sic* for *cum*

Margin Opposite title *Suthwell'* (late medieval).

Note For Richard Kyng of Halam, see **171n**.

177 *View of frankpledge of Southwell Chapter, claims of William Golde to a messuage and land at Halam, Thomas of Averham to land of the Chantry of St John of Southwell, William of Overton and Thomas Cade to lands of the Chantry of St Nicholas of Southwell in Westhorpe and Morton, respectively and of John, son of John Broun to lands in Edingley*
9 November 1407

Visus franciplegii predicti capituli tentus ibidem ix die Novembris, anno regni regis Henrici iiii[ti] ix°.

Willelmus Golde presens in curia cognovit se tenere de capitulo ut de iure cantarie sancti Nicholai fundate per Willelmum de Wydyngton' i mesuagium et certam parcellam terre eidem pertinentem quondam Roberti Halum in Halum ut de iure Alicie uxoris sue per homagium et fidelitatem et redditum – v s. vi d. per annum, veniendo ulterius bis per annum ad duos visus franciplegii capituli.

Thomas de Averham presens in curia clamat tenere de capitulo certam parcellam terre de cantaria sancti Johannis in Suthwell' et reddere per annum ii d. et duos adventus per annum.

Willelmus de Overton' tenet i toftum et i croftum cum pertinenciis in Westhorpp' quondam Roberti Mathew ut patet per unam cartam inde confectam presentatem in curia, reddendo inde per annum iiii s. ad cantariam sancti Nicholai per Willelmum Wydyngton' fundatam pro omnibus serviciis preter forinsecum servicium domini regis ut dicta carta testatur.

Thomas Cade de Morton' venit in curiam et cognovit se tenere de capitulo de iure cantarie sancti Nicholai per Willelmum Wydyngton' fundate i tenementum in Morton' ut de iure Isabelle uxoris sue et reddere per annum xiiii d. et duos adventus per annum pro omnibus etc.

Presentatum est quod Johannes Broune de Edyngley qui tenuit de capitulo unum mesuagium et i bovatam terre cum pertinenciis in Edyngley in bondagio ut de iure cuiusdam cantarie sancti Nicholai fundate quam dominus Willelmus Ketull' occupat per certa servicia etc., diem suum clausit extremum. Ideo capiantur tenementa illa in manus capituli. Et super hoc venit Johannes filius et heres predicti Johannis Broun'et clamat tenementa predicta ut proximus heres tenementorum predictorum et quia predictus Johannes Broune in vita sua vastavit omnes domos nuper edificatos super mesuagium predictum et terram eidem pertinentem diversis personis alienavit et dimisit extra curiam capituli. Et dictus Johannes filius suus modo petens, impotens ad satisfaciendum capitulo pro vasto[1] ac eciam dicta tenementa sunt de bondagio capituli et ipse petens liber homo est sicut pater suus fuit, quare iure hereditarie nullo modo ad tenementa predicta habenda venire potest. Et ideo remanent seisita in manu[2] capituli quousque etc. Et non obstante seisina pro capitulo facta dictus Johannes filius et heres occupavit tenementa predicta et postea illa alienavit Willelmo de Westhorpp' per cartam suam in manutenanciam contra capitulum ut prius dictum est et recitatum in registro capituli etc.

[1] *vasto* repeated   [2] MS *sic*

Margin   Opposite title *Suthwell'* (late medieval); 5th paragraph left margin *Remedium* (late medieval); at bottom of page as catch words: *Visus franciplegii* (late medieval).

Note   For John, son of John Broun of Edingley, see **171n**.

178   *View of frankpledge of Southwell Chapter, seizure by the Chapter of land of Thomas de Leke of Holme by Muskham, arrest of Robert Keruer for seizing land at Halam, claim of John of Rolleston to a messuage and* *land at Edingley, alienation by Margery Mauger to John of Beverley of land at Carlton, and distraint of John, son of John Osmonthorpp, a minor, concerning land at Osmanthorpe* 6 May 1408

p. 98 **Visus franciplegii capituli predicti tentus ibidem sexto die Maii, anno regni regis Henrici quarti ix°.**

Juratores presentant quod Thomas de Leke de Holme iuxta Muscham tenet parcellam terre continentem i mesuagium pro acre terre ad voluntatem capituli antea in possessione Johannis Julian' et non venit. Ideo etc. Et ideo capiantur in manus domini.

Item presentant quod ubi Willelmus Ketull' unus capellanus alterius cantariarum in ecclesia Southwell' beati Nicholai fundate pro anima Andree Baylly in ecclesia predicta precepto capituli distrixit super terram cuiusdam Johannis Frankys in quodam loco iuxta Kynalbryg' in campo de Halum que tenetur de capitulo ut de capitali domino feodi illius per servicium viii s. per annum et pro redditu a retro sic districta, quidam Robertus Keruer de Suthwell' post arestacionem predictam sic factam vi et armis vesturam terre predicte sic arestate cepit et abduxit etc. Quare presentatum est ut dictus Robertus capiatur ad respondendum etc. capitulo de transgressione predicta.

Ad istam curiam venit Johannes de Roldeston' senior liber homo et cepit de capitulo unum mesuagium et medietatem unius bovate terre cum pertinenciis in Edyngley nuper seisita in manus capituli eo quod Johannes Broune qui dicta mesuagium et terram tenuit de capitulo predicto in bondagio et mesuagium et terram predicta alienavit per scriptum suum eidem Johanni de Roldeston' sine licencia capituli, qua de tenementa illa seisita fuerunt ut predicitur ut patet in quadam curia precedente. Et quia idem Johannes de Roldeston' pauper sic deceptus credens feoffamentum fore sufficiens supplicavit capitulo de gracia ut patet etc., ad quod tempus concessum fuit quod ipse idem Johannes de Roldeston' teneret tenementa predicta de capitulo per servicium etc. ad terminum vite predicti Johannis Broune ut patet in quadam curia precedente pro quadam fine capitulo facto sine aliquo inde dicto Johanni Broune reddendo. Et quia dictus Johannes Broune mortuus est ut patet in curia precedente ipse idem Johannes ad huc petit gratiam ut supra. Et ad presens conceditur quod teneat tenementa predicta sibi Johanne uxori sue et Johanni filio eorumdem ad terminum vite eorum diutius viventis reddendo et faciendo inde annuatim dicto capitulo omnia servicia inde debita et consueta, videlicet faciendo communem sectam et portando onus bedelli quum¹ eligi contigerit. Et dabunt capitulo ad ingressum pro fine tenementorum habendo vi s. viii d. Set quia invenitur de recordo in quadam curia precedente occupat ii acras prati pertinentes dictis tenementis de favore capituli pro eo quod dictus Johannes solvet de cetero redditum dicte cantarie pro tenementis integris debitum. Ideo respectuatur finis in gracia capituli. Et dictus Johannes fecit fidelitatem.

Item presentatum est quod quedem Margeria Mauger' nativa capituli quondam uxor Thome Souter' de Sutton' perquisivit unum mesuagium cum certa parcella terre in Carlton' que seisita fuerunt in manus capituli. Et non obstante seisina dicta Margeria dicta tenementa alienavit cuidam

Johanni filio Johannis de Beverley de Carlton' sine licencia que tenementa pertinent capitulo ut de iure cantarie beate Marie. Ideo fiat inde remedium.

| Item preceptum est distringere Johannem filium et heredem Johannis p. 99
Osmonthorrp qui infra etatem est et in custodia domini Johannis Zouch militis domini de Kyrtlyngton' ut de iure uxoris sue tenens unius tofti cum crofto quondam edificato et ii selionibus iacentibus super Goldhill' cum pertinenciis in Osmunthorpp' pro redditu ii s. exeuntium de dictis tenementis et capitulo debita ut de iure alterius cantariarum beati Nicholai etc.

¹ MS *sic* for *cum*

Margin   Opposite title *Suthwell'* (late medieval); 2ⁿᵈ and 3ʳᵈ paragraphs, *Nota bene* (probably early modern); 5ᵗʰ paragraph right margin *Remedium* (late medieval).

179   *Proceedings in the court of Southwell Chapter, claim of Peter Chaumburleyn to a messuage at Easthorpe belonging to the Chantry of St Nicholas*   12 August 1408

Curia capituli predicti tenta ibidem xii° die Augusti, anno regni regis Henrici iiiiᵗⁱ ix°.

Petrus Chaumburleyn' de Barneby venit in curiam et fecit fidelitatem et clamat tenere de capitulo unum mesuagium in Esthorpp' ut de cantaria sancti Nicholai quam Willelmus Kydyer occupat libere reddendo per annum cantarie predicte v s. et veniendo ulterius bis ad duos visus franciplegii etc. pro omni alio servicio quod quidem mesuagium Willelmus Sutton' antea tenuit etc.

Margin   Opposite title *Suthwell'* (late medieval).

180   *View of frankpledge of Southwell Chapter, seizure by the Chapter of a messuage and land at Halam leased by Richard Crych to Isabella Dryng and her son Richard without permission, and of lands at Halam and Edingley unjustly occupied by John Asselyn*   22 November 1408

Visus franciplegii capituli predicti tentus ibidem die iovis in festo sancte Cecilie virginis, anno regni regis Henrici quarti post conquestum Anglie x°.

Juratores presentant quod Ricardus Crych tenens unius mesuagii et unius bovate terre cum pertinenciis in Halum per copiam curie dimisit tenementa illa Isabelle Dryng' et Ricardo filio suo extra curiam capituli contra formam dimissionis sibi factam. Ideo capiantur illa in manus capituli etc.

Item presentatum quod Johannes Asselyn' de Halum iniuste occupat ii acras terre et prati cum pertinenciis in Halum et Edyngley que sunt de bondagio capituli. Ideo capiantur in manus capituli etc.

Margin   Opposite title *Suthwell'* (late medieval); between 2ⁿᵈ and 3ʳᵈ paragraphs, with lines indicating both, *Remedium* (late medieval).

Note   The relationship of Isabelle Dryng and her son Richard to the Richard Dryng of **171** is uncertain, though Isabelle may have been a daughter or grand-daughter.

181 *Proceedings in the court of Southwell Chapter, fraudulent holding by John of Langford, barker, of a messuage at Westgate, date as 180*

~~Curia capituli predicti tenta ibidem in vigilia exaltacionis sancte crucis, anno regni regis Henrici iiii~~^{to} ~~x°.~~[1]

Item presentant quod Johannes de Landforth barker' ingrediebatur quedam mesuagium de Westgate in Suthwell' quod tenetur de capitulo ut de iure cantarie Willelmi de Wydyngton' etc. et illud occupavit per sex annos elapsos et dimidium in partem maioris termini xii annorum ex certis convencionibus inter ipsum Johannem et Robertum Barker' ex sua parte et Willelmum Kydyar' capellanum cantarie predicte loco capituli ex altera parte factis et fractis per prefatum Johannem de Landesforth minus iuste et in fraudem capituli quare senescallus capituli fecit sigillare ostium mesuagii predicti et seisiri fecit mesuagium illud in manus capituli una cum bonis et catallis in eodem mesuagio adtunc inventis quousque etc., eo quod dictus Johannes [de] Landforth mesuagium illud reparare debuisset et manutenere durante termino xii annorum ut predictum est que non fecit ut terminum complevit set infra terminum se cum bonis et catallis removebat pro quibus causis sigillacio et arestacio infra mesuagium predictum facte fuerunt, quas quidem sigillacionem et arestacionem
p. 100 dictus Johannes de Landforth | fregit in regis contemptum ipsius capituli preiudicium dampnum non modicum et gravamen et aliorum exemplum perniciosum. Ideo etc. quod attachietur per corpus contra proximum ad quod tempus venit. Ut patet in proxima curia sequenti. Et fecit finem pro transgressione predicta facta in gracia capituli pro – xiii s. iiii d. per plegium Willelmi de Overton' et Johannis Ketyll'.

[1] Crossing out for Chapter court on 13 September 1409; see **182** below

Margin   Opposite title *Suthwell'* (late medieval).

182 *Court of Southwell Chapter, taking by Roger Hanson of a messuage and land at Morton, and claim of William Henryson Dykonson to land at Edingley* 13 September 1409

Curia capituli beate Marie Suthwell' tenta ibidem in vigilia exaltacionis sancte crucis, anno regni regis Henrici iiii^{ti} x°.

Ad istam curiam Rogerus Hanson' de Morton' venit et cepit de capitulo ut de iure fabrice ecclesie i mesuagium iiii acras terre et ii rodas prati cum pertinenciis in Morton' iacentia inter priorem de Thurgarton' ex parte orientali et vicarios chori Suthwell' ex altera parte que tenementa Walterus filius Ricardi quondam tenuit. Tenendum et habendum sibi ad terminum vite sue de dicto capitulo ut de fabrica ecclesie predicte et Isabelle uxori sue et Johanni filio eorumdem sub tali condicione quod dictus Rogerus, Isabella et Johannes sustentabunt reparabunt et manutenebunt domos in dicto tofto existentes sumptibus suis propriis durante termino predicto. Et in fine termini sui in adeo bono statu quo eas receperunt dimittent vel meliori et quilibet eorum qui diutius vixerit dimittet sub pena amissionis status predicti. Et faciet duas apparencias ad curiam capituli bis per annum. Et dabit ad ingressum pro fine suo predicte fabrice ii libras cere.

Et fecit fidelitatem, reddendo inde annuatim eidem capitulo x s. ad duos anni terminos usuales.

Ad istam curiam venit Willelmus Henryson' Dykonson' de Edyngley et clamat tenere de capitulo i rodam et dimidiam terre in Edyngley inter terram Margarete Qwhenyld' ex parte australi et terram Johannis Falk ex parte orientali et reddendo per annum cantarie sancti Nicholai fundate per Andream Baylly i d. et faciendo duas apparencias ad curiam capituli per annum et fecit fidelitatem.

Margin   Opposite title *Suthwell'* (late medieval); 2nd paragraph, right margin, at top, *Messuagium et alia in Morton*: at bottom, *10s per annum* (both 17th c.).

183   *View of frankpledge of Southwell Chapter, claims of Henry Scheperd to a messuage and land in Westhorpe and Alice, wife of John Wryght, of a moiety of a bovate of land in Westhorpe*   8 May 1410

Visus franciplegii capituli predicti tentus ibidem die iovis proximo post festum ascensionis domini, anno regni regis Henrici iiii[ti] post conquestum xi°.

Ad istam curiam venit Henricus Scheperd et clamat tenere de capitulo unum mesuagium cum pertinenciis in Westhorpp' et parcellam alterius mesuagii proximi iacentis ex parte orientali quondam Henrici Wryght, reddendo per annum ad altarem beate Marie xi d. et faciendo duas apparencias ad curiam pro omni alio servicio et fecit fidelitatem.

Alicia que fuit uxor Johannis Wryght' fecit fidelitatem et clamat tenere de capitulo parcellam medietatis unius bovate terre cum pertinenciis in Westhorpp' quam dictus Henricus Wryght ante tenuit reddendo per annum servicium quantitatem tenure sue.

Margin   Opposite title *Suth'* (late medieval).

184   *View of frankpledge of Southwell Chapter, wardship of N. the son and heir of Robert of Newton relating to holdings in Newton near Bingham*   8 August 1411

Visus franciplegii capituli Suthwell' tentus ibidem die sabbati proximo ante festum sancti Laurencii, anno regni regis Henrici iiii[ti] xii°.

Presentatum est quod Robertus de Newton' qui tenuit de capitulo certa tenementa in Newton' iuxta Byngham per forinsecum servicium ut de iure cantarie beati Johannis evangeliste diem suum clausit extremum. Et quia N filius et heres dicti Roberti infra etatem existens cuius custodia ad dictum capitulum pertinet durante minori etate eo quod tenementa predicta tenentur de capitulo per homagium et fidelitatem elongatus est extra patriam per amicos suos in preiudicium capituli unde fiat remedium.

Margin   Opposite title *Suthwell'* (late medieval); 2nd paragraph, *Newton* (17th c.).

These pages are blank, apart from some preliminary marking out, and the traces of former foliation in top right corner of right hand folio (e.g. p. 104, *fo. lii°*, p. 114, *fo. xxxiii*). A folio seems to have been torn or cut out between pp. 115 and 116 (cf. **Introduction**, p. xxxiv).   pp. 102–15

ROYAL AND OTHER LETTERS, 185–212

185 *Letters patent of Edward II revoking the nomination of his clerk, William Aylmer, to the prebend [Normanton] held by another royal clerk, Ingelard de Warle, because the king had been incorrectly informed that Ingelard was dead* Westminster, 28 October 1317

p. 116 **Carta regis de revocacione cuiusdam prebende in Suthwell' per ipsum collate**

Edwardus, Dei gracia rex Anglie, dominus Hibernie et dux Aquitanie, omnibus ad quos presentes litere pervenerint, salutem. Licet nuper credentes prebendam quam dilectus clericus noster, Ingelardus de Warle, habet in ecclesia de Suthwell' per mortem eiusdem Ingelardi vacasse, eandem prebendam dederimus et concesserimus dilecto clerico nostro, Willelmo Aylmer', habendum cum suis iuribus et pertinenciis quibuscunque, quia tamen constat nobis quod idem Ingelardus gaudet corpore sospitate, collacionem nostram prefato Willelmo de dicta prebenda sic factam tenore presencium duximus revocandam. In cuius rei testimonium has literas nostras fieri fecimus patentes. Teste me ipso apud Westmonasterium xxviii die Octobris anno regni nostri undecimo.

Margin Title and text in late medieval hand (Scribe 4a).

Note On 18 August 1314 Ingelard de Warle was collated to the prebend of Normanton (*Reg. Greenfield*, i, no. 211). Aylmer had been named to succeed him on 24 October 1317 (*CPR 1317–21*, 37), and this revocation was also enrolled (ibid., 41).

186 *Letters of the Chapter of York confirming the union of the churches of Kneesall and Boughton following letters of Archbishop Richard Le Scrope appointing John of Southwell and John of Stanton as his commissioners to discuss with the Chapter over this matter* York, 7 January 1404

Knesall et Bughton ecclesiarum unionis confirmacio

UNIVERSIS sancte matris ecclesie \filiis/ ad quos presentes litere pervenerint, capitulum ecclesie cathedralis Ebor', decano eiusdem in remotis agente, salutem in omnium salvatore. Noverit universitas vestra quod nos capitulum antedictum visis et perlectis quibusdam literis reverendi in Christo patris et domini domini Richardi, permissione divina Eboracensis archiepiscopi, Anglie primatis et apostolice sedis legati, discretis viris magistris Johanni de Southwell et Johanni de Stanton, clericis, ipsius venerabilis patris commissariis ad tractandum nobiscum de et super negocio ac causis unionis et annectionis ecclesie de Bughton ecclesie parochiali de Kneesall, Ebor' diocesis, per ipsum reverendum patrem faciendum, sub certa forma verborum confecta, convocacionem confratrum et concanonicorum nostro per absentium in ea parte debita requisitam, ex causis in eisdem verbis expressis ad septimum diem mensis Januarii decrevimus fere faciendam. Quo quidem die septimo advenient (vocatis et ad hunc diem citatis legitime dictis confratribus et concanonicis nostris secundum morem ecclesie Ebor' antedicte) ad comparendum in domo nostra capitulari in huiusmodi negocio, ac ad ostium domus nostre capitularis publice preconizatis, diutius expectatis et nullo modo comparentibus, contumacias per nos quo ad acta huiusmodi pronunciatis, decrevimus, ipsorum absentia non obstante, cum dictis commissariis in negocio huiusmodi de iustitia fore procedendum. Unde nos capitulum supradictum in domo nostra capitulari predicta termino huiusmodi ad hoc ut prefertur assignato de et super contentis in dictis literis prefati venerabilis patris, huiusmodi negocium unionis concernentibus, ac etiam literis certificatoriis cuiusdam inquisicionis inde captis, et coram nobis ac dictis commissariis exhibitis, ac causis huiusmodi solemniter diligenter et communem tractatum habuimus cum commissariis supradictis, necnon causis huiusmodi in dictis literis expressatis per nos et dictos commissarios examinatis et ad plenum discussis, veris et legitimis inventis, eadem una cum eisdem commissariis approbamus, necnon unioni et annexioni dictarum ecclesiarum parochialium prefati venerabilis patris pontificali auctoritate pure simpliciter et libere faciendi absque aliqua annua pensione nobis aut nostris successoribus ratione huiusmodi unionis per eundem venerabilem patrem taxanda seu imponenda certis et legitimis ex causis nos ad id moventibus, nostrum prebuimus consensum ac prebemus tenore presentium periter et assensum. Que omnia et singula universitati vestre predicta innotescimus per presentes. In quorum omnium testimonium sigillum nostrum presentibus est appensum. Data in domo nostra capitulari Ebor' septimo die mensis predicti anno domini millesimo cccc° tertio.

Margin   Title in right margin and text in hand of Scribe A (John Martiall).

Note   The church at Boughton had been given to the priory of Blyth shortly after its foundation and much material on the medieval parish and its inhabitants survives in its cartulary (cf. *Blyth*) though the decision to release the advowson in 1403–4 is not recorded there. The union with Kneesall continued until 1866, when Boughton became an independent perpetual curacy. In 1987 it was united in one benefice with Ollerton.

Diverse littere capituli et concanonicorum Suthwell'   p. 117

187   *Letters of the Chapter to all prebendaries and their proctors recalling the decision taken unanimously by those present at the last Chapter meeting on 30 September [1294] that to pay certain pressing expenses the prebendaries were to contribute one seventh of the income of their prebends (to be paid in two instalments on 3 November [1294] and 2 February [1295]) but that since some were in default they were to do so by 12 March, summoning the prebendaries of Dunham, Beckingham, Oxton (I), Halloughton, Sacrista, Rampton and Eaton to be present (or to send proctors to answer for them) on that day on pain of excommunication for their failure to pay the required sum*
                                 Southwell, 18 February 1295 n.s.

Capitulum ecclesie collegiate beate Marie Suwell' in Christo sibi dilectis fratribus et concanonicis omnibus et singulis per prebendas nostre communitatis constitutis vel eorum procuratoribus seu locum tenentibus salutem in auctore salutis. Cum in ultima convocatione nostra in crastino beati Michaelis anno instanti facta de unanimi fratrum et procuratorum tunc presentium[1] deliberatione provida sit provisum quod pro arduis ecclesie nostre negotiis necessariis expediendis fratres septimam partem prebendarum suarum contribuant secundum ultimam taxationem cuius medietatem in crastino commemorationis animarum et aliam medietatem in festo purificationis beate Marie iam lapsis pro anno dumtaxat instanti persolverent et huiusmodi pecunia levanda communie nostre custodibus sit facta commissio prout vobis satis constare credimus multi tum vestrum eisdem custodibus nostris in nullo huc usque in parte satisfacere curarunt. Intendentes siquidem quod validissima presumptio contra vos operatur quod auctoritatem nostram contempnitis pro eo quod mandatum nostrum per custodes nostros iamdictos vobis directum multi vestrum minus reverenter quam deceret hactenus executi estis de quo admiramur. Quocirca vobis in virtute sancte obedientie qua nobis tenemini firmiter iniungendo mandamus quatinus singuli vestrum citra festum sancti Gregorii pape de portione prebendam suam contingente dictis custodibus nostris plenarie in ecclesia nostra Suthwell' satisfaciant ut tenentur. Et quia vos de Doneham, de Bekyngham, de Oxton et Crophill', Halugton', Sacristarie, Rampton' et de Eton prebendarii de predicta septima in parte vel in toto nobis huc usque minime satisfacere voluistis, vobis auctoritate presentium mandamus ymo verius citamus quod compareatis personaliter seu per procuratores sufficienter instructos coram nobis vel vices nostras gerentibus in capitulo nostro Suthwell' die sancti Gregorii pape iam dicti ad satisfaciendum nobis totaliter et integraliter de septima iamdicta sub pena excommunicationis quam ex nunc in ipsos inferimus ac promulgamus qui tunc de predicta septima nobis minime satisfecerint. Bene valete. Datum apud nos xii kalendas Marcii anno domini m⁰ cc nonagesimo quarto.

[1] MS *pervertium*

Margin Page heading in bold, in same hand as text (Scribe 4), as are subsequent headings and titles to p. 130 unless otherwise mentioned. Left margin p. 117 near head of document, *Septima pars prebende pro arduis negociis collegii allocatur consensu prebendariorum omnium sive eorum procuratorum* (?16th-c. hand).

Note This document reveals the problems of administering the collegiate church efficiently when many prebendaries were absentees. Those in arrears were: Dunham: probably Mr Nicholas of Wells, canon by 1281 until his death in 1312, a civil and canon lawyer who certainly held this prebend 1298–1312; Beckingham: Mr Reginald of St Albans (1292–1311), king's clerk, often absent at the papal curia; Oxton I, John Landulfi de Colonna (1289–1318), papal chaplain (see **188n**); Halloughton, probably Nicholas de Cnovile/Knoville, canon by 1265–after 1306; Rampton, probably Roland de Ferentino (1290–8), papal chaplain; Eaton, Mr Gérard de Ceyzériat (1290–c 1330), king's clerk. The holder of Sacrista in 1295 is unknown.

188   *Letters of excommunication issued by the Chapter against Giles de Olye, proctor of Mr John Landulfi de Colonna, prebendary of Oxton and Crophill*   Southwell, 8 October 1297

Litera excommunicationis aggravate

Capitulum ecclesie beate Marie Suthwell' in Christo sibi dilectis eiusdem ecclesie custodibus salutem in auctore salutis. Cum Egidius de Olye, qui se gerit pro procuratore magistri Johannis Landulfi de Columpna, prebendarii parciarii de Oxton' et Crophill' maioris excommunicationis sentenciam in ipsum propter offensam suam manifestam per nos promulgatam diutius animo sustinuerit indurato claves ecclesie dampnabiliter contempnendo nec ab ipsa se absolvi procuret licet per nos ad hoc multipliciter excitatus ne oneris morbida sui contagione gregem dominicum inficiat, vobis mandamus quatinus prefatum Egidium diebus dominicis et festivitis inter missarum solempnia in ecclesiis de Oxton' et Crophill' cum omnibus eidem qualitercunque comitantibus preter quam in casibus a iure premissis | sic excommunicatum denuncietis seu denunciari faciatis. Ceteris   p. 118 Christi fidelibus sub pena consimilis sententie arcuis inhibentes, ne sibi quoquo modo communicent quousque satisfacione premissa beneficium absolutionis optinere meruit in forma iuris. Et quid super hiis feceritis nobis ad plenum constare faciatis cum super hoc fuerit congrue requisiti, ut contra ipsum in obstinacia sua perseverantem ad invocationem auxilii brachii secularis si opus fuerit precedamus. Valete. Datum in capitulo nostro viii idus Octobris anno domini millesimo cc nonagesimo septimo.

Margin   *aggravate* in the title added in 17th c. hand. p. 118, in top right corner, *fo. xxxvij*

Note   John, son of Landulph Colonna, citizen of Rome, was inducted to the prebend of Oxton I by a mandate of 19 April 1289 (*Reg. Romeyn*, i, no. 1072) and was provided to another at Lincoln on 17 March 1298, to hold alongside those he already had at Oxton, Troyes and St Martin's of Tours (*CPL*, i, 569). This excommunication probably arose from his failure to obey **187** or **190**; see also *Reg. Romeyn*, i, xxvi–xxviii for further details on his family and connections.

189   *Letters of the Chapter ordering the vicar of Bleasby to cite Robert de la Cressoner to appear in court before the Chapter on Monday before the feast of St Peter ad vincula (1 August) to answer the charges of John de Monte Claro, canon*   27 July 1318

Litera citationis

Capitulum ecclesie collegiate beate Marie Suthwell' in Christo sibi dilecto vicario de Bleseby salutem in auctore salutis. Citetis peremptorie Robertum de la Cressoner' de Bleseby quod compareat coram nobis vel locum nostrum tenenti in ecclesia nostra Suthwell' die lune proximo ante festum sancti Petri apostoli quod dicitur ad vincula domino Johanni de Monte Claro, concanonico nostro, super sibi canonice proponendum ad eodem ut dicit responsurus ulterius facturus et recepturus quod iuris ordo dictaverit et rationis. Et ad probam huius citationis facte, remittatis nobis citra diem per presentes sigillo vestro pendente signatas. Datum in capitulo nostro Suthwell' \vi/ kalendas Augusti anno domini millesimo ccc decimo octavo.

Note   Cressoner was ordered to appear on 31 July. Mr John Humbert de Monte Claro, prebendary of Sacrista (1309–c. 1347 or later).

190   *Letters of monition issued by the Chapter to John d'Évreux, Mr John Landulfi de Colonna, prebendary of Oxton [I], Mr Gerard [de Ceyzériat], prebendary of Eaton, and the prebendary of Sacrista ordering them, by virtue of a mandate of the prior of Worksop, collector of a fifth levied on the clergy of the Archdeaconry of Nottingham, to deliver the money owing from their canonries*   Southwell, 28 August 1297

Litera monitionis

Capitulum ecclesie beate Marie Suthwell' in Christo sibi dilectis fratribus et concanonicis Johanni de Everoys, magistro Johanni Landulfi de Columpna, prebendario de Oxton', magistro Gerardo, prebendario de Eton' et prebendario Sacristarie ecclesie memorate, salutem et fraterne dilectionis in domino semper augmentum. Mandatum venerabilis viri domini prioris de Wyrkesopp' collectoris quinte cleri archidiaconatus Not' recepimus, quod vobis inspiciendum nobis que transmittimus remittendum, cuius autoritate mandati vos omnes et singulos peremptorie monemus per presentes quatinus iuxta formam peritus et tenorem mandati memorati de quinta parte prebendarum et bonorum vestrorum satisfaciatis ut tenemini[1] sicut penam in dicto mandato comminatam vitare volueritis. Datum apud nos v kalendas Septembris anno domini m° cc nonagesimo septimo.

[1] For *teneamini?*

Note   John d'Évreux, canon from *c.* 1282, prebendary of Oxton II by *c.* 1290, still active 13 August 1309 but dead by 22 October 1310 (*Reg. Greenfield*, i, no. 96). For John Landulfi de Colonna, prebendary of Oxton I, see **188n**. Mr Gérard de Ceyzériat was the first prebendary of Eaton, installed on 2 March 1290 (*Reg. Romeyn*, i, nos 811 and 1008n), still active in 1320 but dead by 30 June 1330 (*Reg. Melton*, iv, no. 202 and v, no. 338). For John de Monte Claro, prebendary of Sacrista (1309–c. 1347) see **189n**; the name of the prebendary of Sacrista in 1297 is not known, but he, as well as those of Oxton I and Eaton, were already in arrears in 1295 (**187**). John of Tickhill, prior of Worksop (1303–14).

191   *The Chapter orders an inquiry into clerical misdemeanours*
10 January 1265

Inquisicio de delictis ministrorum ecclesie S[uwell'] facta per capitulum

Pateat quod anno domini m° cc lxiiii[to] die[1] sabbati proximo post diem Epiphanie in aliquibus diebus interpollatim sequentibus facta fuit diligens inquisitio in capitulo Suwell' super quibusdam rebus dictis et factis que possent honorem et honestatem illius ecclesie et ministrantium in ea impedire coram dominis Riginaldo de Stowe, Henrico le Vavasur' et magistro Henrico de Skypton', canonicis et custodibus commune canonicorum, et multis aliis de eadem ecclesia. Et cum constabat quod dominus J. de Hokerton', vicarius, unam mulierem solutam cognoverat, que pregnans fuit, et de ipso non constabat, exclusus fuit a choro per viii dies. Et si alias de consimili delicto diffimatus se purgare non poterit vel noluerit, erit in voluntate canonicorum tunc presencium quod excludatur ab omni officio et beneficio ecclesie Suwell' per unum annum, vel quod tunc conficiat scriptum et signatum sigillo suo tradat canonicis vel canonici presenti.

¹ MS *de*

Note   Reginald of Stowe, canon since *c.* 1241, prebendary of Rampton, d. by 17 June 1267 (*Reg. Giffard*, 23). Henry Le Vavassour, prebendary of Norwell Palishall by 23 July 1257 (**192**), d. by 13 September 1280 (*Reg. Wickwane*, no. 36). Henry of Skipton, canon by 1255, prebendary of Normanton, d. by 29 Dec. 1286 (*Reg. Romeyn*, i, no. 1032). John of Hockerton may be identical with 'John of Hockerton, chaplain, called Walur' who held land of the Chapter (**285**, before 1268) and 'Sir John of Hockerton, vicar' who acted as a witness *c.* 1284 (**443–5**).

192   *Memorandum recording that a full meeting of the Chapter had been summoned for 23 July 1257 to discuss certain matters, especially a response to letters sent by the Chapter of York; the names of those present were recorded, but since certain canons failed to appear or to send their excuses another meeting was convened for 17 September 1257, an answer was prepared (as appeared from a schedule then attached but now lost); other matters discussed included a subsidy to meet the archbishop's debts, and various decrees were also passed for the punishment of William de Gray, canon, who was still contumacious; Robert Le Pettit, vicar of the Minster, was warned to pay 23s 4d which he owed, and a general visitation of prebends was to be held by those canons who were in residence or lived close by*   Southwell [17 September 1257 or shortly afterwards]

Decreta capituli super negociis et contumacia cuiusdam confratris   p. 119

Memorandum quod cum per capitulum ecclesie Suwell' vocati fuissent omnes canonici eiusdem ecclesie quod in virtute obedientie comparerent in ecclesia predicta in crastino festi beate Marie Magdalene anno domini mᵒ cc l septimo super quodam urgenti negotio ecclesiam ipsam contingente tractaturi eodem crastino comparuerunt in ecclesia predicta personaliter domini Henricus de Mora, Robertus Mallore, Ricardus de Sutton', Henricus le Vavassour et magistri Willelmus phisicus et Petrus de Radenouere, canonici eiusdem ecclesie. Magistri vero Henricus de Skypton' et Willelmus de Rotherefeld, canonici eiusdem¹ [ecclesie] se literatorie excusaverunt, promittentes et se ratum et gratum habituros quicquid per presentes de eodem negotio fieret. Dominus vero Ricardus de Gimpton' vices suas domino Henrico de Mora commisit promittens² etiam se ratum habiturum quod per ipsum fieret nomine suo. Ceteri vero canonici diutius expectati nullatenus comparuerunt. Unde predicti presentes post diutinum tractatum inter eos habitum super literis capituli Ebor' sibi directis tandem eidem capitulo Ebor' responderunt sicut in cedula presentibus appensa continetur, decernentes loco eodem generaliter conveniendum die lune proxime post [festum] exaltationis sancte crucis proximo sequens cum contumatione die ad providendum de subsidio patri eorundem spirituali domino archiepiscopo Ebor' faciendo ad sui exonerationem debitis variis in sua confirmatione requirenda contractis et de aliis negociis eiusdem ecclesie tractaturi et quod expediens fuerit cum effectu facturi et predictos absentes peremptorie vocandos quod in virtute obedientie sub pena sacramenti ecclesie Suthwell' prestiti compareant dictis die et loco premissa facturi et etiam inobedientiam eorundem in modo et alias non veniendo canonice si poterunt purgaturi. Alioquin penam condignam pro eadem contumacia recepturi. Et quia constat dominum Walterum de Gray monitum fuisse et eidem sub pena suspensionis iniunctum esse quod duas marcas et dimidiam de decima prebende sue ad expensas in communibus negotiis ecclesie expediendis factas, secundum capituli decretum certo termino solveret, nec solvit ut dicebatur, decreverunt iidem presentes in litera sua vocationis fore addenda quod dictas duas marcas et dimidiam citra diem lune predictum plenare solvat. Alioquin sit auctoritate predicte ecclesie Suwell' tunc excommunicatus, et talis publice denunciandus, donec tam de eisdem expensis quam de suo contemptu plene satisfecerit. Eundem etiam monendum in eadem litera decreverunt quod dicto[3] domino Roberto le Petitt, vicario eiusdem ecclesie, de xx tribus solidis et quatuor denariis in quibus, ut dicit, tenetur eidem citra terminum eundem eidem Roberto competenter satisfaciat. Alioquin eodem termino sibi respondeat peremptorie super eisdem[4] et quod ius dictaverit recipiat. Dicto vero crastino predictus dominus Ricardus de Sutton', vices suas prefato domino Henrico de Mora commisit ad ordinandum et expediendum negotia dicte ecclesie ipsius nomine in omni convocatione quando ipsum abesse contingeret se ratum habere et perpetuo habiturum promittens, quicquid per ipsum nomine suo fieret. Eodem eciam crastino decretum fuit et provisum quod canonici tunc presentes ratum habere et perpetuo habiturum promittens quicquid per ipsum nomine fieret. Eodem eciam crastino decretum fuit et provisum quod canonici tunc presentes qui morari vellent et possent propinquas visitarent prebendas et reformarent reformanda et corrigenda in forma iuris corrigerent. In premissorum attestacionem commune sigillum ecclesie Suwell' presentibus est appensum.

[1] MS reads *eorundem* and omits *ecclesie*   [2] MS *promittentes*   [3] *dicto* marked for deletion by three subscript points   [4] *super eisdem* repeated

Margin   Title at top of page in bold and text by Scribe 4. Left margin at head *ecclesie* (late medieval).

Note   The July meeting was attended by six canons in person (Henry de Mora, Robert Malure, Richard of Sutton, prebendary of North Muskham, Henry Le Vavassour, prebendary of Norwell Palishall, Mr William de Fécamp and Mr Peter of Radnor), two (Mr Henry of Skipton, Mr William of Rotherfield) sent letters of excuse, and another (Mr Richard de Gimpton) had given a proxy, leaving five canons unaccounted for since the Chapter numbered fourteen at this point. One of them, Mr Walter de Gray, was still absent in September and was excommunicated as the memorandum shows. Fécamp later held the prebend of Norwell Tertia Pars, Skipton that of Normanton, and Rotherfield that of Beckingham. It is not clear which stalls Mora, Malure, Radnor and Gray held; this is the only mention so far found of Gimpton.

193 *Inquiry into various rights enjoyed by prebendaries and their tenants held in the court of the Sheriff of Nottingham by order of letters of 2 April 1287*

Inquisicio capta super quibusdam consuetudinibus tangentibus tenentes capituli Suthwell' coram vicecomite Notingham virtute cuiusdam \literis/ inde sibi directis die mercurii in septimana Pasche anno regni regis Edwardi xv per sacramentum Johannis de Kyrnesale, Johannis le Boteler' de Hokerton', Willelmi de Normanton', Henrici Gernon' de Carleton', Walteri filii Radulphi de Suthmuscham, Willelmi filii Ode de eadem, Ade de Batheley, Henrici, clerk de Suthmuscham, Henrici le Clerk de Holm', Willelmi de Etona in Suthwell', Roberti le Petytt de Suthmuscham, Willelmi le Palmer' de Halum, Roberti filii Odonis de eadem, Hugonis de Osmundthorpp' in Halum. Qui dicunt super sacramentum suum quod omnes prebende beate Marie Suwelliensis ecclesie et tenentes eorum de pontagio liberi sunt omnino et quieti, nec inter gildabiles in scotto seu lotto esse debent aliqualiter etc. In cuius rei testimonium hinc inquisicioni iuratores predicti sigilla sua apposuerunt.

Margin The initial word, *Inquisicio*, is written in left margin alongside which has been added *Libertates prebendariorum et tenementum suorum* in 17th-c. hand, and below towards the end in a late medieval hand *Tenentes prebendarum de pontagio et cetera sunt liberi*. Main text Scribe 4b.

Note Several of the witnesses occur in other charters (cf. William le Palmer and Hugh of Osmanthorpe of Halam). John of Kersall had given testimony in 1272 when an inquisition was held to determine whether the canons of Southwell enjoyed the same liberties and customs as the Dean and Chapter of York (*IPM Notts. 1279–1329*, 130–1).

Litere concanonicorum capituli Suthwell' diverse p. 120

194 *Letters of Elias of Cowton, canon, announcing to the Chapter that he has been appointed attorney of Henry, archbishop-elect of York*
Cambridge, 22 November 1297

Litera attornata

Venerabilibus viris capitulo ecclesie Suwellen' eorum concanonicus Elyas de Couton' salutem reverenciam peritam et honorem. Ad audiendum que ex parte reverendi patris domini Henrici, Dei gratia Ebor' electi, fuerint proponenda, nec non et tractanda[1] nomine meo vobiscum et consentiendum omnibus que canonice duxeritis facienda dilectum mihi in Christo dominum de Couton', presbiterum, procuratorem meum constituo per presentes, promittens me ratum habiturum quicquid per eundem factum fuerit in premissis. In cuius rei testimonium sigillum meum presentibus est appensum. Datum Cantebrig' in festo sancte Cecilie virginis anno gratie millesimo ducentesimo nonagesimo septimo.

[1] Part of this letter is missing at this point where Cowton announces that he is citing Archbishop-elect Henry's letters which resume at *nomine meo* ...

Margin Main title at top of page in bold; title for charter centred in bold, and text, as are **195–9** (Scribe 4).

Note   Henry of Newark, prebendary of North Muskham 1287, archbishop of York 1296–9. Mr Elias of Cowton, apostolic notary, prebendary of Norwell Overhall (1295–1329). More than twenty-five instruments alone written by him relating to the dispute between Antony Bek, bishop of Durham, and the monks of Durham survive, as well as an early fourteenth-century manuscript, now Winchester Cathedral, MS 9, which he owned as an inscription on f. 2^v shows: *Liber \quondam/helie de Coutona Canonici Ecclesie Southwellen' \et prebende de ouerhalle apud Northwell./* It is described in Ker and Piper, IV, 586–7. The principal original contents are Martinus Polonus, *Chronicon pontificum et imperatorum*; Dares Phrygius, *De excidio Troiae*; Geoffrey of Monmouth, *Historia regum Britanniae*; and brief annals of England AD 185–24 Feb. 1307 (coronation of Edward II). Among later additions is a narrative of the vision of St Wilfrid at Meaux that led to his foundation of Southwell Minster, added during the early fifteenth century.

195   *Letters of William Bomere, prebendary of North Muskham, presenting William Yole, priest, to the Chapter for admission as vicar of a mediety of North Muskham*   Ghent, 11 July 1346

Litera presentacionis

Venerabilibus viris et discretis capitulo ecclesie collegiate beate Marie Suthwell', Ebor' diocesis, suus concanonicus et confrater Willelmus Bomere, prebendarius prebende de Northmuscham in ecclesia antedicta, obedienciam cum reverencia et honore debitis tantis viris. Ad vicariam medietatis ecclesie prebendalis de Northmuscham iam vacantem et ad presentacionem meam spectantem dilectum mihi in Christo dominum Willelmum Yole de Northmuscham, presbiterum, vobis presento in tuitu caritatis, attencius exorans quatinus ipsum benigne velitis admittere et iuxta consuetudinem ecclesie vestre feliciter expedire ad Dei laudem et regimen ecclesie sue altissimus vos conservet. Datum apud Gandavum in Flandria, xi die mensis Julii anno domini millesimo ccc xlvi^{to}.

Margin   Right margin *Presentacio vicarii de Northmuscham per prebendarium ibidem* (late medieval).

Note   Mr William Bomere was given the prebend of North Muskham by Edward III on 1 May 1340, which he held till his death in 1351. He was a Flemish clerk from Dixmuide coopted to the king's council (cf. *CPR 1338–40*, 468), who served as a go-between with the king's ally, Jacob van Artevelde, at Ghent, performing many diplomatic missions (H. S. Lucas, *The Low Countries and the Hundred Years' War, 1326–1347* (Ann Arbor, 1929), passim).

196   *Letters of B., a humble brother, asking the Chapter to excuse him from a meeting because of sickness and promising to support whatever decisions are taken in his absence*   [early–mid-14th century]

Litera excusatoria

Venerabili collegio capituli Suwellen' devotus ipsorum B., frater humilis, salutem et reverenciam cum honore. Reumate contactus algoribus hiis diebus absque maris¹ mali periculo exponere me non possem. Et id circo si placet in convocacione vestra ad diem jovis proximum post festum commemoracionis animarum facta absenciam meam habere velitis excusatam. Quicquid autem pro statu ecclesie per vos ad tunc fuerit ordinatum, me ratum et gratum habiturus promitto per presentes. Valeat devota fraternitas vestra in dulci Jhesu per tempora longa.

[1] Reading uncertain

Date Since most of this small collection of form letters seem to date to the late 13th or early 14th c., it is tempting to ascribe the model of this letter to a canon like Benedict of Halam, very active in the Chapter's affairs before being named the first prebendary of North Leverton in 1291, dead by 31 July 1307.

197 *Nomination by John Clarell, prebendary of Norwell [Overhall], of Richard and Thomas, custodians of the Chapter of Southwell, to proceed as quickly as possible in the matrimonial dispute between Alice of Staythorpe and Roger of Norwell, clerk, which had been delayed by the death of Richard of Upton previously appointed to settle the matter*
Norwell, 2 April 1293

Litera Johannis Clarell' committendo causam matrimonialem aliis

Johannes Clarell', prebendarius de Northwell', dilectis suis dominis Ricardo et Thome, custodibus communie capituli Suwellen', salutem in auctore salutis. Causam matrimonialem inter Aliciam de Starthorpp', actricem ex parte una, et Rogerum de Northwell', clericum, reum ex parte altera motam alteri vestrum una cum collega suo domino Ricardo de Upton', iam defuncto alias commissam, et per ipsius mortem diutius suspensam vobis coniunctim et divisim cum canonice cohercionis potestatem iuxta processum habitum committimus audiendam et sine delicto terminandam. Datum apud Northwell' iiii nonas Aprilis, anno domini m⁰ cc nonagesimo tercio.

Note For Clarell's career see **30, 115, 138, 360, 361, 371, 407, 444** and notes.

198 *Letters of the Chapter ordering prebendaries and their proctors to make certain payments of 1d for every pound of their income, as instructed by the Chapter of York, at a meeting of the Chapter to be held on Saturday in Mid-Lent*
Southwell, 11 March 1297

Litera monitoria custodum ecclesie directa prebendariis p. 121

Venerabilibus viris dominis ac magistris prebendariis omnibus et singulis capituli ecclesie Suthwell' constitutis et eorum procuratoribus seu locum tenentibus devoti sui ecclesie memorate custodes salutem in omnium salvatore. Cum per dominum officialem curie Ebor' capitulo nostro memorato nobis que per idem capitulum firmius sit iniunctum de singulis libris prebendarum vestrarum singulos obolos[1] secundum taxacionem Northwyc' levare qualiter excusacione cessante vos auctoritate curie Ebor' et capituli nostri cuius vices gerimus in hac parte peremptorie requirimus et monemus quatinus quilibet vestrum de memoratis obolis prebendam suam contigentibus latori presencium in alleviand' laboris nostri satisfaciat. Alioquin vos omnes et singulos peremptorie citamus per presentes quod compareatis in ecclesia Suwell' coram capitulo nostro antedicto die sabbati in media quadregesima de eisdem obolis satisfacturi ad plenum. Scientes quod qualiter de predictis obolis¹ fuerit satisfactum vel satisfacere neclectum dicto domino officiali prout iniunctum est fideliter intimabitur per capitulum nostrum. Datum Suwell' v idus Marcii anno domini m° cc nonagesimo sexto.

¹ MS *obalos*

Date We have assumed that although the Roman calendar is being used here, the normal practice of Lady Day as the beginning of the New Year in England is also being followed.

Note The valuation of Norwich for the collection of a tax imposed on all English clergy by Innocent IV, at the request of Henry III, takes its name from one of the commissioners, Walter Suffield, bishop of Norwich, and was carried out between 1250 and 1254, but the returns for York have not survived (*The Valuation of Norwich*, ed. W. E. Lunt (Oxford 1926), 52–3). It is thus impossible to compare the amounts due from Southwell under this assessment with those due from the later *Taxatio* of 1291. May the use of the former assessment on this occasion have been preferred because it was lighter?

199 *Letters of William of Newark, having been named prebendary of North Muskham by Archbishop Henry, appointing Robert, called Roger William of Westhorpe, and John, called Sewale of Southwell, priests, as his attorneys to receive possession of his prebend*

[Bishop]Thorpe by York, 19 July 1298

Litera attornata sive procuratorium

Pateat universis quod ego Willelmus de Newerk', canonicus ecclesie Suwellen', ad recipiendum nomine meo possessionem prebende de Northmuscham eiusdem ecclesie quam michi venerabilis pater dominus Henricus, Dei gratia Ebor' archiepiscopus, Anglie primas, caritative contulit in eadem, et ad omnia alia facienda que ad hoc iure et consuetudine pertinent infra ecclesiam Suwell' et extra, dilectos michi in Christo dominos Robertum, dictum Rogerum Willelmum de Westhorpp' et Johannem, dictum Sewale de Suwell', presbiteros, coniunctim et divisim procuratores meos ordino, facio et constituo per presentes, dans eisdem et eorum cuilibet specialem potestatem prestandi in manum meam quodlibet genus liciti sacramenti ratum habiturus et gratum quicquid iidem procuratores mei vel eorum aliquis nomine meo fecerint vel fecerit in premissis aut in aliquo premissorum. In cuius rei testimonium venerabilis patris predicti apponi presentibus procuravi. Datum apud Thorpp' iuxta Ebor' xiii kalendas Julii anno gracie millesimo cc° nonagesimo octavo.

Margin In title *sive procuratorium* added in 17ᵗʰ-c. hand.

Note Whether William of Newark, alias William of Hemingbrough, was related to Archbishop Henry of Newark has not been clearly established though it is very likely. He had been collated to the prebend on the previous day (*Reg. Newark*, no. 26) and held it until 1340. In 1305, as 'parson of the church of North Muskham' he was attacked and taken prisoner by Walter Touk of Kelham and his son, Henry, following an amorous liaison with Walter's daughter, Beatrice, that led to a lawsuit which provides much colourful detail on the affair (Brown, *Newark*, i, 88).

200   *Letters of Mr Peter of Radnor, Mr Thomas de Ludham, Henry de Mora and Robert Malure, canons, about estimating the value of the goods of the late Mr William de Shendon, canon*   20 September 1259

Commisio fructus estimandi

Universis sancte matris ecclesie filiis presentes literas inspecturis magister Petrus de Radenour', magister Thomas de Ludham, dominus Henricus de Mora, dominus Robertus Malure, canonici Suwell', salutem. Noverit universitas vestra nos in vigilia beati Mathei apostoli, anno domini m° cc l° nono, in capitulo nostro Suwell' ad ordinandum de bonis quondam fratris nostri et concanonici magistri Willelmi de Senedon' scilicet quod eiusdem anime saluti et ecclesie nostre tranquillitati magis congruere[1] credebamus personaliter, et sub forma subscripta cuiuslibet contencionis seu contradiccionis amputata materia ordinasse. Videlicet quod aliqui iuris prudentes et fidedigni ex | parte capituli ad prebendam de Muscham   p. 122 destinabuntur ad estimandum fructus ibidem existentes et secundum estimacionem ab eisdem factam auctoritate capituli magistro Thome dicti magistri Willelmi in dicta prebenda successori tradentur recepta tamen ab eodem securitate sufficienti de dicte estimacionis solucione tribus annuis terminis, videlicet ad festum beati Andree apostoli proximum sequentis tercie partis, et ad festum purificacionis beate Marie tercie partis, et ad festum invencionis Sancte Crucis tercie partis, nostro capitulo et dictis executoribus fideliter facienda si ad dictum fratrem nostrum secundum nostrorum tenorem privilegiorum et consuetudines generales et approbatas et a tempore ex quo non extat memoria sine cuiusdam contradictione optentam debeant fructus instantis anni pertinere. Ut ista nostra ordinacio stabilis inconcussa permaneat, dum tamen fratres nostri absentes huic ordinacioni suum prebere duxerunt consensum eam sigilli nostri impressione duximus roborandum etc.

[1] MS *congrue*

Margin   Title, centred, in 17th-c. hand; main text, Scribe 4b.

Note   William de Shendon, canon by 1241, prebendary of South Muskham at his death. This appears to be the first mention of Thomas de Ludham (?Lowdham) as a canon.

201   *Walter de Gray, William de Shendon and Reginald of Stowe, canons, inform fellow canons in the Chapter that they have agreed the lease by Walter de Taney, archdeacon of Nottingham, to Robert, his brother, of lands at Norwell*   York, 1 April 1244

Peticio confirmacionis

Viris venerabilibus confratribus et amicis suis karissimis capitulo Suwell' sui Walterus de Gray, Willelmus de Senedon' et Riginaldus de Stowa salutem in domino. Attendentes quod in collacione tofti quam venerabilis vir dominus Willelmus archidiaconus Nottingham fecit Roberto fratri suo in Northwell' ex magna firma pro eo annuatim solvenda, indempnatti ecclesie nostre satis ut credimus est provisum, si confirmacionem capituli nostro ei concedere decreveritis, nos id gratum habebimus et acceptum. In cuius rei testimonium has literas nostra vobis mittimus patentes. Actum apud Ebor' kalendas Aprilis, anno domini m° cc^{mo} xliiii^{to}.

Margin   Title in right margin in early modern hand. Main text, Scribe 4b, though added on later occasion than **200** if darker shade of ink is an indication.

Note   The Chapter also confirmed this grant, noting that the messuage was that *in quo idem Walterus et predecessores sui solebant manere* (**433**). Walter de Gray, the younger, nephew of Archbishop Gray, a canon of York and prebendary of Masham and Beverley (d. 11 Nov. 1271, *Reg. Giffard*, 34) was later excommunicated for failing to attend Chapter (**192**). Mr William de Shendon, canon by 1241, prebendary of South Muskham (1242–59). Reginald of Stowe, later prebendary of Rampton (1263–7). Mr Walter de Taney, canon by 1224, archdeacon by 9 October 1241, prebendary of Norwell Palishall by 1244, dead by 1249. The toft was part of the prebendal manor of Palishall in Norwell which Walter had otherwise specifically retained when he made the grant to his brother (**425–9**).

p. 123   **Litere archiepiscoporum Ebor' directe capitulo Suthwell**

202   *Letters to the Chapter from [Thomas of Corbridge], archbishop of York enclosing a copy of a mandate of Edward I, York, 8 July 1302, informing him that Mr Nicholas of Wells had appeared in the Court of the Exchequer at York at the quindene of St John the Baptist's day (8 July) to respond to Jacopo Brabazon, merchant of Siena (*Cene*), in a plea of debt and ordering him to relax any sequestration of Nicholas's benefices, which he instructs the Chapter to implement*   Laneham, 13 July 1302

Litera relaxationis sequestri

Dilectis in Christo filiis capitulo nostro Suthwell' salutem gratiam et benedictionem. Mandatum domini regis nuper recepimus in hec verba: Edwardus Dei gratia rex Anglie, dominus Hibernie, dux Aquitanie venerabili in Christo patri Thome eadem gratia archiepiscopo Ebor', Anglie primati salutem. Sciatis quod magister Nicholaus de Well' fuit coram baronibus de scaccario nostro apud Ebor' a die sancti Johannis baptiste prox' futur' in xv dies ad respondend' Jacobo Brabazonn' mercatori de Cene de placito debiti. Et ideo vobis mandamus quod sequestrum, si quod in beneficiis ipsius magistri Nicholai ecclesiasticis ea actione apponi feceritis, id sine dilatione relaxari faciatis eidem. T[este]: P. de Lexc' apud Ebor' viii die Julii anno regni xxx. Quocirca vobis mandamus quatinus sequestrum in bonis prefati Nicholai ecclesiasticis actione premissa per vos auctoritate nostra interpositum relaxetis. Valete. Datum apud Lanum' iii idus Julii pontificatus nostri anno tertio.

Margin   Page heading, charter title and text in hand of Scribe 4, as are **203** and **204**.

Note   Mr Nicholas of Wells had been a canon of Southwell since at least 1279 and by 1298 was prebendary of Dunham. An expert canon and civil lawyer, he was dead by 1 March 1312; for earlier proceedings against him over these debts see **209**. Peter of Leicester, baron of the Exchequer, as deacon had once briefly held the church of Lowdham, Notts. (*Reg. Romeyn*, i, 327, cf. also 322). He may be the prebendary of Bishopshull, Lichfield, who died before 28 March 1304, and whose will was proved on 8 March 1305 (*Fasti 1066–1300*, xi, 43).

203   *Letters of Thomas [of Corbridge], archbishop of York to the Chapter, reminding them that he had ordered them to do justice to the claim of Osbert Geven' of Oxton and his wife, Ivetta, which they should now do without further delay so that he would not be compelled to take the case into his own hands*   Sibthorpe, 28 September 1303

Litera pro iustitia facienda

Thomas Dei gratia Ebor' archiepiscopus Anglie primas dilectis in Christo filiis capitulo nostro Suwell' salutem, gratiam et benedictionem. Alias vobis meminimus nos scripsisse quod audita querela Osberti Geven' de Oxton' et Ivette uxoris sue eisdem celerem impendi iustitiam faceretis. Ad quod vos ut eam in hac connotatione[1] tenore presentium vos iterum excitamus ita quod in vestri destin' ad nos sub iteratis laboribus recurrere non cogantur et in casu vestre negligentie manus ad hoc exundere[2] suadente iustitia compellamur. Valete. Datum apud Sibthorpp' iiii kalendas Octobris pontificatus nostri anno quarto.

[1] *Ad quod ... connotatione* is expunged by scribe   [2] Reading uncertain; James reads *exercendere?*

204   *Letters of Thomas [of Corbridge], archbishop of York, to the Chapter, warning Mr John d'Évreux, canon of Southwell, to pay to the Canons of Ripon arrears of 3½ marks for tithes owing to the Fabric on account of the prebend which he had recently obtained there and 100s for various vestments which he had taken from that church as well as a cope, within a month of this warning being delivered to him, ordering the Chapter to send letters confirming the action they had taken*   Monkton, 5 October 1301

Litera monitoria

Thomas Dei gratia Ebor' archiepiscopus Anglie primas dilectis in Christo filiis capitulo nostro Suwell' vel suum locum tenenti salutem, gratiam et benedictionem. Moneatis et officialiter inducatis magistrum Johannem de Ebroicis canonicum vestrum quod dilectis filiis canonicis nostris Ripon' de tribus marcis et dimidia in quibus pro arreragio decime ad fabricam ecclesie Ripon' occasione[1] prebende quam nuper in eadem optinuit assignate tenetur et de centum solidis etiam eidem capitulo ratione cuiusdam vestimenti a dicta ecclesia asportati per eum debit', sicut dicunt, et de una capa in qua eidem ecclesie iuxta consuetudinem eiusdem tenetur infra mensem a die monitionis huius sibi facte satisfaciat competenter. Ad quod cum ratione previa per censuram ecclesiasticam canonice compellatis nisi aliquid canonicum seu rationabile pro se proposuit coram vobis quarum non debeat ad premissa. Super quo et de die etiam receptionis presentium et quicquid feceritis in hac parte extunc per vestras literas harum continentes tenorem distincte et apte studeatis reddere certiores. Ut nos quod iusticie convenire viderimus ulterius si opus fuerit in prefato negotio faciamus. Valete. Datum apud Munketon' iii nonas Octobris pontificatus nostri anno secundo.

[1] MS appears to read *actione*

Note   Pd. in *Mems. Ripon*, i, 297. Mr John d'Évreux had received permission as a canon of Southwell and Ripon to study for three years on 24 July 1286 (*Reg. Romeyn*, i, no. 1018); by *c.* 1290 he was prebendary of Oxton II until replaced by William Melton on 2 January 1305, returning again on 13 August 1309 when Melton acquired Norwell Palishall, but was dead by 22 October 1310 (*Reg. Greenfield*, i, nos 96, 126–7 and p. 297). See **219** and **220** for more peaceable relations between the two chapters of Southwell and Ripon.

205 *Letters of William [Melton], archbishop of York to the Chapter, enclosing an order to him of Edward II, Westminster, 9 June 1318, for the sequestration of the goods of the late Ingelard de Warle because of debts owing to the king from when he was keeper of the Wardrobe and elsewhere, and instructing him to report to the Exchequer by 24 June what ecclesiastical goods had been sequestered; the archbishop now instructs the Chapter to report on what Ingelard had held in the church of Southwell when he was a canon and to send a certificate of what they had seized* Humbleton, 29 June 1318

p. 124   **Litera ad faciendum sequestrum**

Willelmus permissione divina Ebor' archiepiscopus Anglie primas dilectis filiis capituli ecclesie nostre Suwell' salutem gratiam et benedictionem. Mandatum regium die confectionis presentium recepimus in hec verba: Quia Ingelardus de Warle qui diem suum clausit extremum[1] ut accepimus tenebatur in diversis debitis nobis die quo obiit tam de tempore quo fuit custos garderobe nostre quam aliunde, vobis mandamus quod omnia bona ecclesiastica que dictus defunctus habuit in diocesi vestra die quo obiit supradicto sine dilatione aliqua sequestrari et ea omnia sub salvo sequestro custodiri faciatis donec aliud inde habueritis in mandatis. Et constare faciatis thesaurario et baronibus de scaccario nostro apud Westm' a die[2] nativitatis sancti Johannis baptiste in quindecim dies que et cuiusmodi bona ecclesiastica que fuerunt predicti defuncti sequestrari feceritis occasione predictarum ubi. Et remittatis ibi hoc breve. Teste I. Abel apud Westm' ix die Junii anno regni nostri undecimo. Quocirca vobis mandamus firmiter iniungentes quatinus omnia et singula bona predicti Ingelardi in eadem ecclesia Suwell' dum vixit canonici infra iurisdictionem vestram die quo obiit existentia et inventa sequestretis arctius[3] vice nostra et sub sequestro huiusmodi faciatis fideliter custodiri sicut de hiis rendere volueritis cum super hoc fueritis requisiti certificantes nos super hiis que feceritis in hac parte ac que et qualia bona sequestraveritis et valore bonorum eorundem quam cito commode poteritis per vestras patentes literas harum seriem continentes. Valete. Datum apud Humbelton' iii kalendas Julii anno gratie m ccc decimo octavo et pontificatus nostri anno primo.

[1] MS adds *extremum* and crosses it out   [2] MS *adie*   [3] MS *arcius*

Margin   Heading and text, Scribe 4.

Note   Ingelard de Warle was a king's clerk before 28 October 1283, keeper of the Wardrobe (8 July 1309–December 1311 and 25 February 1312–1 December 1314) and chief baron of the Exchequer (1316–17). He was collated to the prebend of Normanton on 18 August 1314 (*Reg. Greenfield*, i, no. 211 and p. 296); for his political role in 1313–15, see Phillips, *Edward II*, 205, 239, 265.

206 *Letters of Thomas [II], archbishop of York, ordering all the parish-*
ioners of Nottinghamshire to make their Pentecostal procession to South-
well instead of York, in order to enable them more easily to aid the building
of the church there [27 June 1109 × 24 February 1114]

Litera archiepiscopi pro sustentatione ecclesie Suthwell'

Thomas Dei gratia omnibus parochianis suis de Notinghamscira salutem et
Dei benedictionem. Precamur vos sicut filios karissimos ut in remissionem
peccatorum vestrorum adiuvetis de beneficio elemosine vestre ad faciendam
ecclesiam sancte Marie de Suwella. Et quicunque ibi vel de minimo
auxilium fecerit, erit usque in finem[1] huius seculi particeps omnium
orationum et beneficiorum que fient in ea et in omnibus ecclesiis nostris.
Et \ut/ hoc libentius debetis facere quo vobis relaxamus ne vos oporteat
per singulos annos visitare Eboracensem ecclesiam, sicut omnes alii
parochiani nostri faciunt, sed ecclesiam sancte Marie de Suwella cum
ibi habetis idem perdonum quod habetis Ebor'.[2] Valete etc.

[1] MS adds *us*, then crosses out   [2] *Ebor(aco)* in *EEA* – but should be locative, which
is *Eboraci*

Margin Heading and text, Scribe 4. In lower right margin *Relaxati sunt subditi in*
hoc com(itatu) ab annua visitatione ecclesie Ebor ea lege, ut ecclesiam Southwell
visitent, 17th-c. hand.

Note Pd. in Dimock, 'Architectural History', 53 n. 9; Hodgson, *Thomas II*, 80–1;
EEA, York 1070–1154, no. 22; translated in Beaumont, *Chapter*, 10, with facsimile,
Plate I (and cf. 4th edn, 3 and 10). Pentecostal processions to cathedral churches in the
earlier twelfth century are commented on by Brett, *English Church*, 162–4, with mention
of this document (p. 163). In 1171 Alexander III confirmed that the clergy and laity of
Nottinghamshire should process to Southwell as ancient custom dictated (**1**), and (in
the translation of Dickinson, *Southwell*, 120) 'that every year, according to the old and
rational usage of that church, a synod should there be celebrated, and that thither the
chrisma should be brought by the deans of the county from the church of York, to be
thence distributed through the other churches'. Also according to Dickinson (121), the
practice of holding the synod ordered by the papal bull was only finally abolished by
Archbishop Drummond (1761–76), though 'How far he was empowered thus to alter
the constitution of the church may be a matter of great doubt; but, as the institution
abolished was become, since the reformation, an useless ceremony, and attended with
some trouble to the officers of the church, the mandate of the archbishop received a very
ready obedience'. Dickinson (121–6) further provides an undated, probably late, list of
the Pentecostal offerings which each parish in the four Nottinghamshire deaneries and
the Peculiar of Southwell were expected to pay, totalling £15 18s 7¼d. Of this sum, a
tenth was allotted to Sacrista prebend, and the remainder was to be divided into two equal
portions, one belonging to the prebend of Normanton, 'and the other is to be applied to
the commons of the resident canon'. The town of Nottingham's share was 13s 4d, a sum
certainly being paid in the early seventeenth century, and we can probably assume that
payments were still being collected down to the moment the Chapter was abolished in
1841. In Thoroton's notes, evidence survives from a case in 27 Elizabeth I (1584–5) in
which Laurence Broadbent, receiver for Nottinghamshire and Derbyshire, tried to recoup
arrears which had occurred in Edward VI's and Mary's reigns when the Chapter estates
were in royal hands and thus were still owing to the crown (NA, M 494 ff. 22^r–27^v).

Attached at the bottom of p. 124 is a paper slip with a transcription of **206** in the hand
of Richard Beaumont, Minster librarian (fountain pen, black ink), with a few errors.

**Nota bene pro vicariis et capellanis cantariarum ecclesie de
                           Suthwell**

207   *Lease by Cardinal John Kempe, archbishop of York, leasing to the
Chapter for 100 years at an annual rent of 8s 11½d various plots, cottages,
waste ground and other land in Southwell to be used for maintenance of
the chantry chaplains*   Manor of Rest, Cawood, 10 November 1446

**Carta domini archiepiscopi Ebor' de placeis, cotagiis, terris et vastis
concessis capitulo Suthwellie ad terminum centum annorum ad opus
et utilitatem capellanorum Deo ibidem serviencium pro annuali
summa octo solidorum undecim denariorum cum obolo**

Omnibus Christi fidelibus ad quos presentes litere pervenerint, Johannes,
miseracione divina sacrosancte Romane ecclesie titulo sancte Balbine
presbiter cardinalis, Ebor' archiepiscopus, Anglie primas et apostolice
sedis legatus, salutem in domino et fidem indubiam presentibus adhibere.
Noveritis nos concessisse ac presenti carta nostra confirmasse capitulo
ecclesie nostre collegiate beate Marie Suthwellie unam placeam edificatam
super vastum nostrum inter portas cimiterii Suthwellie predicte, ex
parte una, et placeam Roberti Sampson' ex parte altera, reddentem
nobis annuatim sex denarios sterlingorum, ac unam placeam captam de
vasto nostro in vico vocato vulgariter Westgate, ville nostre Suthwellie
predicte, iacentem inter mesuagium Roberti Fissher, ex parte boriali, et
unam venellam ducentem usque ad stansile vulgariter nuncupatum Will
Robert stihil, reddentem nobis annuatim novem denarios sterlingorum, in
qua placea Willelmus Hude quondam habitavit. Nec non unam parcellam
soli vasti cum uno gardino iacentem in Westgate predicta inter toftum
Roberti Farnedon' ibidem et altam viam vocatam Seynt Thomas Street, que
reddit nobis per annum decem denarios sterlingorum, ac unum cotagium
in Westgate antedicta super corneram, quondam captum de vasto nostro,
nuper in tenura Nicholai Wolces, reddens nobis per annum tres denarios
sterlingorum, et unum toftum vastum iacens in Esthorp inter mesuagium
nuper Thome Averham, ex parte orientali, et toftum nuper Willelmi
Kydyer, ex parte occidentali, quod reddit nobis annuatim septemdecim
denarios et unum obolum, ac unum cotagium in Westgate predicta de
vasto nostro edificatum ex parte boriali portarum manerii nostri Suthwellie
cum uno parvo gardino, que quidem gardinum et cotagium reddunt nobis
annuatim quatuordecim denarios sterlingorum, ac unum toftum in vico
predicto ex parte orientali tenementi Roberti Sewall' quod reddit nobis
anuatim octodecim denarios sterlingorum, necnon duo cotagia edificata
de vasto nostro in Farthingate, infra villam nostram predictam, cum
fundo vasto adjacente et tribus acris terre in campis de Westgate, que
nuper erant Roberti Barbor, senioris, que reddunt nobis annuatim duos
solidos et sex denarios sterlingorum. Habendum et tenendum placeas,
parcellam vasti cum gardino, cotagia, tofta, fundum vastum et tres acras
terre predicta omnia et singula cum suis pertinenciis prefato capitulo de
nobis et successoribus nostris ad opus et utilitatem capellanorum Deo
serviencium in ecclesiam nostram collegiatam predictam usque ad finem
centum annorum a datis presencium continue numerandorum et plenarie

complendorum. Reddendo nobis et successoribus nostris annuatim de dictis placeis, parcella vasti cum gardino, cotagiis, toftis, fundo vasto et tribus acris terre omnibus et singulis cum pertinenciis octo solidos undecim denarios et unum obolum sterlingorum durante termino predicto ad duos anni terminos, videlicet ad festa sancti Martini et Pentecostes per equales porciones. In cuius rei testimonium sigillum nostrum presentibus apposuimus. Datum in manerio nostro de Rest iuxta Cawod decimo die mensis Novembris anno domini millesimo quadringentesimo quadragesimo sexto, et nostre translacionis anno vicesimo secundo.

Margin   Page heading, title of charter midway down left margin and main text in late 15ᵗʰ-c. hand of Scribe 7.

Note   This charter reveals the considerable extent of urban decay that seems to have occurred at Southwell both widely in the town and its surrounding fields by the mid-fifteenth century, almost certainly local evidence for the impact of successive waves of the Black Death over the previous hundred years. Some revival of local economic fortunes is also suggested as new cottages were being erected on former waste ground.

Diverse litere officialium curie archiepiscopi Ebor' et commissariorum   p. 126

208   *Letters of the Official of York sending letters of Archbishop William [Melton] containing letters of Edward II proroguing the parliament summoned at Lincoln on 27 January, first to 12 March and then to 26 June at Lincoln, Westminster, 3 March 1318, and ordering all archdeacons and clergy of his diocese to appoint two suitable proctors, Thorpe next York, 25 April 1318, with instructions of the Official to the Chapter to send a proctor by 25 May 1318 for this purpose*   York, 15 May 1318

Dominus officialis curie Ebor' [et] commissarius generalis, venerabili capitulo Suwell' salutem in auctore salutis. Mandatum infrascriptum recipimus in hec verba:

Willelmus, permissione divina Ebor' archiepiscopus, Anglie primas, dilecto filio officiali Ebor', vel eius commissario generali, salutem, graciam et benedictionem, mandatum regium recepimus in hec verba:

Edwardus, Dei gracia rex Anglie, dominus Hibernie et dux Aquitanie, venerabili in Christo patri, eadem gracia, archiepiscopo Ebor', Anglie primati, salutem. Licet \nuper/ super diversis et arduis negociis nos et statum regium nostri specialiter tangentibus parliamentum nostrum apud Lincoln' in quindena sancti Hillarii proxima preterito temere vobiscum ac cum ceteris prelatis, magnatibus et proceribus dicti regni habere proposuissemus colloquium et tractatum, mandassemus quod dictis die et loco omnibus aliis pretermissis personaliter interessetis ibidem nobiscum, et cum ceteris prelatis, magnatibus et proceribus predictis super dictis negociis tractaturi vestrum que consilium impensuri, et postmodum parliamentum predictum apud locum predictum tenendum usque ad primam dominicam quadragesime proxime future ad requisicionem prelatorum dicti regni duxissimus prorogandum, vobis mandantes quod ad dictum locum in dicta dominica ex causa premissa interessetis. Ad requisicionem tamen dictorum prelatorum ac cleri regni nostri predicti parliamentum predictum ad huc usque in crastinum sancte Trinitatis proximi futuri apud locum predictum tenendum duximus prorogandum. Et ideo vobis mandamus in fide et dilecione quibus nobis tenemini, firmiter injungentes quod loco et crastino predicti omnibus aliis pretermissis personaliter intersitis ibidem nobiscum, et cum ceteris prelatis, magnatibus et proceribus predictis super dictis negociis tractaturi vestrum que consilium impensuri, premunientes decanum et capitulum ecclesie vestre Ebor', archidiaconos totum que clerum vestre diocesis, quod idem decanus et archidiaconi in propriis personis suis et dictum capitulum per unum. Idemque clerus per duos procuratores ydoneos plenam et sufficientem potestatem ad ipsis capitulo et clero habentes una vobiscum intersint modo omnibus tunc ibidem, ad faciendum et consenciendum hiis que tunc ibidem de communi consilio favente, domino ordinari contigerit super negociis antedictis. Et hoc nullatenus omittatis. Teste me ipso apud Westmonasterium tercio die Marcii anno regni nostri undecimo.

Quo circa vobis mandamus quatinus omnes archidiaconos ac totum clerum nostre diocesi super hiis premuniatis celeriter vice nostra, quod dicti archidiaconi personaliter clerus vero, per duos procuratores ydoneos plenam et sufficientem potestatem[1] ab eodem clero habentes, dictis die et loco prefato parliamento intersint super hiis que feceritis in hac parte et qualiter hoc ipsum mandatum fueritis executi citra dictum crastinum per viii dies per literas vestras patentes harum seriem et predicti cleri procuratorem nomina continentes. Valete. Datum apud Thorpp prope Ebor' vii kalendas Aprilis anno gracie m ccc decimo octavo, et pontificatus nostri primo.

Vos igitur capitulum memoratum tenore presencium peremptorie citamus et per vos clerum jurisdictionis vestre citari volumus et mandamus quod compareatis et compareat coram dicto domino officiali, vel nobis, per unum procuratorem sufficientem potestatem ad hac habentem, in majori ecclesie Ebor' die jovis proximo post festum sancti Dunstani, ad consenciendum et ordinandum duos procuratores sufficientem potestatem p. 127 habentes ad instans parliamentum domini regis | nomine tocius cleri Ebor' destinandum, necnon ad tractandum faciendum ulterius et recipiendum quod ipsius literis regii natura exigit et requirit. Certificantes dictum dominum officialem vel nos ad eundem diem iovis super hiis quod feceritis in premissis, per vestras patentes literas harum seriem continentes. Datum Ebor' idus Maii anno gracie m° ccc decimo octavo.

[1] Followed by *habentes* struck out

Margin Page heading in same hand as text (Scribe 4, who also writes **209–12**); *premonicio parliamenti* in 17th-c. hand in right margin.

Note The parliament summoned to Lincoln in January 1318, and prorogued as evidenced here, was eventually cancelled on 8 June because of the alleged need to repel the Scots, though more obviously because of the king's negotiations with Thomas of Lancaster preceding the treaty of Leake, 9 August 1318. It next met at York on 20 October 1318, when the clerical proctors for the archdiocese of York were Mr John of Skerne, rector of Marton (N. Yorks) and Mr John of Lutton, rector of a moiety of Rillington (N. Yorks) (J. R. L. Maddicott, *Thomas of Lancaster 1307–1322* (Oxford, 1970), 213ff.;

Denton and Dooley, 93, 110; PROME, Introductions to Parliaments of January 1318 and October 1318).

Litera citacionis et sequestri

209 *Letters of the Official of York sending to the Chapter letters of Archbishop Thomas [of Corbridge] to the Official, enclosing a copy of a writ of Edward I ordering the archbishop to summon Nicholas of Wells, clerk, to appear before the barons of the Exchequer at York to answer charges of Jacopo Brabazon and his associates of Siena for a debt of twenty marks, York, 27 November 1301, instructing the Official to execute these, Cawood, 19 December 1301, which he now does by ordering the Chapter to sequestrate Nicholas's goods and order him to appear at York by 13 January 1302*   York, 21 December 1301

Officialis curie Ebor' venerabili capitulo Suthwell' salutem in auctore salutis. Mandatum domini nostri domini Thome, Dei gracia Ebor' archiepiscopi, Anglie primatis, recepimus continencie infrascripta:

Suo officiali Ebor', vel eius commissario generali, salutem, graciam et benedictionem. Mandatum domini regis recepimus in hec verba:

Edwardus, Dei gracia rex Anglie, dominus Hibernie et dux Aquitanie, venerabili in Christo patri, Thome, eadem gracia, archiepiscopo Ebor', Anglie primati, salutem. Quia Nicholaus de Wellis clericus est et non habet laicum feodum, unde aliquod debitum levari possit, prout vicecomes nostri Notingham nobis signavit, baronibus de scaccario nostro apud Ebor' in octavo sancti Michaelis proximo preterito vobis mandamus quod ipsum Nicholaum distringatis per beneficium suum ecclesiasticum quod habet in archiepiscopatu vestro predicto. Ita quod sit coram prefatis baronibus nostris apud Ebor' in octavo sancti Hillari ad respondendum Jacobo Brabazon' et sociis suis, mercatoribus de Sene, de xx marcis quas eis debet, ut dicunt, sicut racionabiliter monstrare poterunt, quod inde respondere debet in partem solucionis debitorum que iidem mercatores nobis debent. Remittentes ibi tunc hoc breve. Teste Willelmo de Carleton' apud Ebor' xxvii die Novembris anno regni nostri xxx°.

Quo circa vobis mandamus quatinus predictum mandatum secundum ipsius formam et effectam diligencius exequamini[1] vice nostra, nos super execucione eiusdem citra diem tempestive predictum certificantes per vestras patentes literas harum seriem continentes. Datum apud Cawode xiiii kalendas Januarii pontificatus nostri anno secundo.

Huius que auctoritate mandati vobis firmiter injungendo mandamus quatinus prefatum Nicholaum peremptorie citetis et per bonorum suorum ecclesiasticorum sequestracionem distringatis, quod sit coram prefatis baronibus in scaccario domini regis, ad diem et locum in dicto brevi contentos, prefato Jacobo et sociis suis predictis, secundum formam eiusdem literis regii, responsurii. Ad hoc iiii solidos sterlingorum de bonis suis ecclesiasticis predictis pro expensis circa execucionem presencium per nos factis levari celeriter faciatis. Ita quod dictam pecuniam citra instans festum sancti Hillarii apud Ebor' modis omnibus habeatis per vos vel per alium nobis plenare munerandam. Et certificetis nos vel commissarium nostrum super presentis execucione mandati citra festum sancti Hillarii predictum per vestras patentes literas harum seriem continentes. Datum Ebor' xii kalendas Januarii anno gracie millesimo ccc primo.

¹ MS *exequumini*

Margin Title, centred, in bold; *pro debito regio* in 17ᵗʰ-c. hand in left margin.

Note Wells had risen to prominence in the personal service of successive archbishops, serving Walter Giffard as treasurer (by 1275), and as chancellor to William Wickwane and John Le Romeyn (*York Fasti*, i, vii, 20n, 26n). Already a canon of Southwell by 1279 (*Reg. Wickwane*, no. 181A), he was dispensed both for illegitimacy and, as learned in both laws, to hold additional benefices on condition of taking suitable orders and residing (*CPL*, i, 500, 1 Aug. 1289). Among other posts he was archdeacon of Northumberland by 24 February 1291 (*Fasti 1066–1300*, ii, 42). After his death (by 1 March 1312) his goods, including books, which were to be displayed for potential buyers to view, were sold; and his prebendal manor of Dunham was left in poor repair (*Reg. Greenfield*, i, nos 158, 160, 162). See **202** for a continuation of this case.

p. 128   **Litera monicionis et citacionis, pro procurationibus debitis sedi apostolice**

210 *Letters of the Official of York to the Chapter sending them an order of Rigaud d'Assier, canon of Orléans, papal chaplain and nuncio in England, to the Official, informing him that since his mission was a long one it was necessary, as was customary in such instances, to levy a tax of 7s on the clergy for his first and second years to defray his expenses, London, 1 October 1318, and ordering them to carry out the mandate*

York, 26 October 1318

Officialis curie Ebor' venerabili capitulo Suwelliensis, salutem in auctore salutis. Mandatum infrascriptum recepimus in hec verba:

Rigaudus de Asserio, canonicus Aurelianensis, domini pape capellanus et eiusdem in Anglia nuncius, discreto viro domini Ebor' archiepiscopi officiali, vel eius locum tenenti, salutem in domino. Cum pro negociis ab apostolica sede commissis iam per annum et ultimus per non modicam tempus in Anglia moram traxerimus in civitate London' et ad huc nos oporteat immorari. Idcirco pro secundo anno more nostre in Anglia procuraciones nostras quas tam nos, quam predecessores nostri, percipere consuevimus exnunc imponendum decrevimus ac eciam exigendum. Quo circa vobis in virtute obediencie quam sedi apostolice teneri, firmiter iniungendo precepimus et mandamus ac tenore presentis una canonica monicione pro omnibus vos monemus, sub pena excommunicacionis quam in vos exnunc et extunc fecimus in hiis scriptis. Si mandatis nostris ymo verius apostolicis plene parendis non duxeritis in hac parte, quatinus infra quindecim dies a recepcione presencium canonice ac peremptorie moneatis seu moneri faciatis singulariter et nominatim omnes personas ecclesiasticas, religiosos et seculares exemptas et non exemptas, dignitates vel parsonatus habentes vel non habentes. Necnon capitula et collegia, conventus civitatis et diocesis Ebor' que procuraciones nunciorum sedis apostolice hactenus solvere consueverunt, ut procuracionem septem solidorum per dictam sedem nobis concessam per ipsos debitos prout predecessoribus nostris solvere consueverunt infra instans festum sancti Andree apostoli, tam illas procuraciones quas nobis debent pro primo anno, quam eciam secundo anno more nostre in Anglia nobis apud London' in hospicio decanatus London' quod inhabitamus, sine dilacione solvant. Alioquin omnes personas ecclesiasticas predictas quas auctoritate apostolica nobis in hac parte commissa in hiis scriptis excommunicamus capitula, collegia et conventus que in hiis scriptis interdicimus excommunicatas et interdictas publice denunciatas seu denunciari faciatis, diebus dominicis et festivis in ecclesiis et locis vero, videlicet a dicto festo sancti Andree,[1] in antea nullo a nobis alio expectato mandato, de die vero confectionis presencium et aliis que feceritis in premissis nos per vestras literas patentes harum seriem continentes infra terminum clare et distincte certificare curetis. Datum London' primo die mensis Octobris anno domini millesimo ccc decimo octavo.

Quo circa tenore presencium vos monemus quatinus de dictis procuracionibus septem solidorum prefato magistro Rigaudo debitis tam pro primo anno quam secundo anno more suo in Anglia infra instans festum sancti Andree apostoli dicto hospicio decanatus London', quod idem magister Rigaudus, ut pretenditur, inhabitat solvatis, et eidem de procuracione huiusmodi satisfacere non tardetis. Alioquin singulares personas capituli vestri et ipsum capitulum per dictum magistrum Rigaudum excommunicatas et interdictas faciemus publice et solempniter nunciari et eciam puplicari nullo alio expectato mandato. Et quid feceritis in premissis nobis citra octabas sancti Martini distincte et aperte constare faciatis per vestras literas harum seriem continentes. Datum Ebor' vii kalendas Novembris anno domini m° ccc xviii°.

[1] From this point the colour of the ink changes but without change of hand which is that of Scribe 4.

Margin Centred heading and main text by Scribe 4 but *pro procurationibus debitis sedi apostolice* added in later medieval hand.

Note Rigaud d'Assier, papal chaplain, was appointed nuncio to England on 1 May 1317, and acted as general papal collector 1316–23. He was provided to the bishopric of Winchester on 26 November 1319, dying on 12 April 1323; his accounts for the period 1317–19 survive (Wright, *Church and Crown*, 313 with further references).

Litera absolucionis de perjurio

p. 129

211 *Letters of Cardinal Gaucelme, vice-chancellor of the Roman Church and universal nuncio, absolving William, son of John of Hemingbrough of Newark, priest, York diocese, from perjury or other sins committed in acquiring and selling lands which the late Archbishop Henry of Newark had promised to give to the church* London, 15 April 1318

Gaucelmus, permissione divina titulo sanctorum Marcellini et Petri presbiter cardinalis, sancte Romane ecclesie vicecancellarius, apostolice sedis nuncius, universis presentes literas inspecturis, salutem in domino. Noverit universitas vestra quod nos Willelmum filium Johannis de

Hemyngburgh' de Newerk', presbiterum Ebor' diocesis, latorem presencium qui olim, sicut asseruit, a bone memorie Henrico de Newerk', quondam Ebor' archiepiscopo, certos redditus et terras predictos ex causa pure donacionis optinuit, cui domino archiepiscopo sub proprio iuramento propter hoc per eum ad sancta Dei evangelia prestito firmiter promisit, quod redditus et terras predictos nullo tempore absque voluntate executorum ipsius archiepiscopi venderet vel alienaret, quos quidem redditus et terras idem Willelmus post ipsius domini archiepiscopi obitum, et absque suorum executorum voluntate, propria auctoritate pro certa pecunie summa vendidit et alienavit, a reatu perjurii huiusmodi quod premissorum occasione perpetravit, et ab aliis peccatis suis que penetenciario nostro, sua confessione detexit, auctoritate apostolica nobis in hac parte commissa, quatenus nobis eadem auctoritate, conceditur per eundem penitenciarium, absolvi fecimus et injungi sibi pro modo culpe penitenciam salutarem. In quorum testimonium presentes literas nostro sigillo munitas sibi duximus concedendas. Datum London' die xv mensis Aprilis anno domini millesimo ccc xviii, pontificatus sanctissimi patris domini Johannis, providencia divina, pape xxii, anno secundo.

Margin Title centred in bold at top of page in same hand as main text (Scribe 4).

Note Gaucelme de Jean was created Cardinal of SS Marcellinus et Petrus by his uncle, Pope John XXII, in December 1316, who named him nuncio to England with Cardinal Luca Fieschi on 17 March 1317. His mission terminated on August 1318 and he was back in Avignon by 5 November 1318; he died in 1348 (Wright, *Church and Crown*, 293–6, 333–41). William, son of John of Hemingbrough (or Hemingford), alias William of Newark, was almost certainly related to Archbishop Henry of Newark. He held the prebend of North Muskham 1298–1340. See also **199n**.

Instrumentum tangens executores domini Roberti[i] de Barneby

212   *Public instrument of John of Cropwell, dean of Nottingham, clerk of York diocese and apostolic notary, for Robert of Barnby, perpetual vicar of Southwell, and John of Wainfleet, executors of William of Barnby, late prebendary of Beckingham, agreeing terms for the administration of his goods with the Chapter*   [Southwell], 26 May 1361

In Dei nomine Amen. Per presens publicum instrumentum cuilibet appareat evidentum quod anno ab incarnacione domini secundum cursum et computacionem ecclesie Anglicane m° ccc lx primo, indicione quartadecima, pontificatus sanctissimi in Christo patris ac domini, domini Innocencii, divina providencia pape sexti, mensis Maii die vicesimo sexto, in mei notarii presenti et testium subscriptorum presencia constituti personaliter discreti viri, dominus Robertus de Barneby, perpetuus vicarius ecclesie collegiate beate Marie Suthwell', et Johannes de Waynflet, executores testamenti domini Willelmi de Barneby, nuper canonici dicte ecclesie ac prebendarii prebende de Bekyngham, defuncti, se precendentes coram reverendo viro, domino Roberto de Edenstow, canonico et residenciario antedicte ecclesie, faciente ac celebrante capitulum tunc ibidem nomine suo et executorum suorum, dixerunt, asseruerunt et affirmarunt bona fide quod ad huc non fluxissent decem dies a die quo idem dominus Willelmus de Barneby diem suum clausit extremum, infra quos taxe vel residui dicte prebende ac firmarum suarum optio eis de jure datur. Volentes tanquam filii obediencie canonicis in hac parte obedire mandatis taxam tam prebende predicte quam firmarum suarum optio[2] pro dicto defuncto sibi optarunt et eligerunt et dicto capitulo ipsam opcionem notificarunt, tunc ibidem presentibus | discretis viris dominis Waltero de Ulseby et   p. 130 Willelmo de Gryngley, prefate ecclesie collegiate vicariis, testibus ad premissa vocatis diligenter que rogatis.

Et ego Johannes de Crophill', decanus de Notyngham, clericus Ebor' diocesis, publicus auctoritate apostolica notarius, premissis omnibus et singulis dum sic ut premittur fierent et agerentur presens interfui eas sic fieri, vidi et audivi variis negociis prepeditus scribi feci meo que signo consueto signavi rogatus in fidem premissorum et testimonium veritatis. Constat mihi notario de rasura in tercia linea a capite computando Waynflett, et rasura in quarte linea similiter a capite computando Roberto.

[1] MS *sic* for *Willelmus*   [2] Followed by *ex* struck out

Margin   Title centred in bold and main text, Scribe 4.

Note   William of Barnby, canon by 1318, prebendary of Beckingham by 1329. Robert of Edwinstowe, prebendary of Woodborough since 1338 (*Reg. Melton*, v, nos 501, 502). John of Wainfleet is probably to be identified with John, son of John of Wainfleet (**155, 331, 541, 590**), who may first have intended to lead a clerical life, since John, son of John of Wainfleet, jr of Southwell, was presented to the living of Barnburgh by the Chapter on 7 December 1349 (*Fasti Parochiales*, i, 27). But since he does not appear with a clerical title here or in other later charters, we may assume that he renounced his clerical status on resignation from Barnburgh in 1351. Walter of Ulceby remained active in the service of the Minster as chaplain, clerk, warden, vicar choral and vicar until at least 1395. John of Cropwell was the rural dean (or dean of Christianity) of Nottingham.

UPTON CHANTRY, 213

Composicio Cantarie de Upton' iuxta Southwell' etc.   p. 131

213A–F *John Bray, Usher of the Receipt of the Exchequer, founds a chantry with an annual revenue of six marks in the parish church of Upton to be served by Hugh atte Welle, perpetual chaplain of Upton and his successors, to pray for Bray, William, his son, William Edington, bishop of Winchester, and Robert of Caldwell, and for the souls of the late Ysolde, John's wife, and their parents, brothers and sisters as well as friends and benefactors, on terms agreed by the abbot and monastery of Rufford, reciting Edward III's licence to Rufford to burden lands not held in chief with twelve marks a year for two chaplaincies worth six marks each in the parish churches of Upton and Newark, Westminster, 18 November 1349 (B), and letters of Thomas, abbot of Rufford, enfeoffing Hugh atte Welle with six marks a year from the manors of Northlathe, Southlathe and Wilkynsefeld, Rufford, 10 May 1350 (C), with Bray's reservation to name to vacancies of the chaplaincy during his lifetime* *for presentation by the Chapter, Upton, 10 April 1352 (A, **D**). Letters of the Chapter accepting these arrangements, Southwell, 17 October 1352, follow, with the approval of John, abbot of Cîteaux, in a general chapter of the Order, noting Bray's donation to Rufford, Cîteaux, 1358 (E–F)*

1349–58

[**A**]   Omnibus Christi fidelibus ad quos presentes litere pervenerint Johannes Bray, ostiarius recepte scaccarii domini regis salutem in domino sempiternam. Noverit universitas vestra quod cum illustrissimus dominus Edwardus, rex Anglie et Francie et dominus Hibernie, ad requisicionem meam per cartam suam nuper religiosis viris abbati et conventui de Rufford' concessisset et licenciam dedisset quod ipsi terras et tenementa sua cum pertinenciis in comitatu Notyngham sub certa forma obligare possint et onerare in sex marcis annuis uni capellano et successoribus suis in ecclesia parochiali de Upton' iuxta Suthwell' divina singulis diebus iuxta ordinacionem in hac parte faciendam celebraturis, ac iidem abbas et conventus pro se et successoribus suis ac domo eorundem dedissent et concessissent et scripto eorum indentato confirmassent domino Hugoni atte Welles de Upton', perpetuo capellano, et successoribus suis divina singulis diebus ad altare beate Marie virginis in ecclesia de Upton' predicta celebraturis pro salubri statu dicti Johannis Bray et Willelmi, filii eius, domini Willelmi de Edyndon', episcopi Wynton', et Roberti de Caldewell', quo advixerint, necnon animabus suis cum ab hac luce migraverint, ac animabus Ysolde, que fuit uxor predicti Johannis, patrum, matrum, fratrum, sororum, parentum, amicorum et benefactorum ipsorum Johannis et Ysolde et omnium fidelium defunctorum quendam annuum redditum sex marcarum argenti percipiendum prout in carta regia et eodem scripto indentato plenius continetur, quorum tenores in serie subscribuntur:

[**B**]   Edwardus, Dei gracia rex Anglie et Francie et dominus Hibernie, omnibus ad quos presentes litere pervenerint salutem. Sciatis quod de gracia nostra speciali et ad requisicionem dilecti valetti nostri, Johannis Bray, ostiarii scaccarii nostri, concessimus et licenciam dedimus pro nobis et heredibus nostris quantum in nobis est dilectis nobis in Christo abbati et conventui de Rufford' quod ipsi terras et tenementa sua cum pertinenciis in comitatu Notyngham que de nobis in capite non tenentur obligare possint et onerare in duodecim marcis annuis duobus capellanis, videlicet in sex marcis annuis uni capellanorum eorundem in ecclesia parochiali de Upton' iuxta Suthwell' et in sex marcis alteri capellanorum eorundem in ecclesia parochiali de Newerke divina singulis diebus iuxta ordinacionem in hac parte faciendam celebraturis percipiendis et habendis ipsis capellanis et successoribus suis divina singulis diebus in ecclesiis predictis in forma predicta celebraturis imperpetuum. Ita quod uterque capellanorum eorundem et ipsorum utriusque successores quociens aliquid de porcione sua dictorum sex marcarum annuarum aretro fuerit, possint licite in terris et tenementis predictis distringere et districciones retinere quousque sibi de arreragiis illis plenare fuerit satisfactum. Et eisdem capellanis quod ipsi et successores sui predicti predictas duodecim marcas annuas de terris et tenementis predictis percipere possint et habere imperpetuum sicut predictum est tenore presencium. Similiter licencias dedimus specialem statuto de terris et tenementis ad manum mortuam non ponendis edito non obstante. Nolentes quod ipsi dicti abbas et conventus seu successores sui aut prefati capellani vel successores sui racione premissorum seu statuti predicti per nos vel heredes nostros inde occasionentur in aliquo seu graventur, salvis tamen capitalibus dominis feodi illius serviciis de terris et tenementis predictis debitis et consuetis. In cuius rei testimonium has litteras nostras fieri fecimus patentes. Teste me ipso apud Westmonasterium decimo octavo die Novembris anno regni nostri Anglie vicesimo tercio, regni vero nostri Francie decimo.[1]

[C] Omnibus Christi fidelibus ad quos presens scriptum indentatum [pervenerit][2] Thomas, abbas de Rufford', et eiusdem loci conventus, salutem in domino sempiternam. Noverit universitas vestra quod nos abbas et conventus predicti pro nobis et successoribus nostris ac domo nostra de Rufford' predicta dedimus, concessimus et hoc presenti scripto indentato confirmavimus domino Hugoni atte Welle de Upton', perpetuo capellano, et successoribus suis divina singulis diebus in ecclesia sancti Petri de Upton' iuxta Suthwell', ad altare beate Marie virginis in eadem ecclesia pro salubri statu Johannis Bray et Willelmi, filii eius, domini Willelmi de Edyndon', episcopi Wynton' et Roberti de Caldewell', quo advixerint, necnon pro animabus suis cum ab hac luce migraverint, ac animabus Ysolde,[3] que fuit uxor predicti Johannis, patrum, matrum, fratrum, sororum, parentum, amicorum et benefactorum ipsorum Johannis et Ysolde et omnium fidelium defunctorum celebraturis quendam annuum redditum sex marcarum argenti ad valorem sterlingorum percipiendum annuatim de maneriis nostris de Northlathe, Southlathe et Wilkynesfeld in comitatu Notyngham ad duos anni terminos, videlicet ad festa Pentecosten et sancti Martini in yeme per equales porciones. Et si, quod absit, in solucionem dicti annui redditus aretro fuerimus in toto vel in parte terminis predictis vel eorum aliquo voluimus et concedimus pro nobis et successoribus nostris ac domo nostra predicta quod bene liceat dicto domino Hugoni, perpetuo capellano, et eius successoribus imperpetuum in maneriis nostris predictis et eorum singulis libere distringere et districciones huiusmodi fugare, abducere et retinere quousque de dicto annuo redditu sic aretro existente et arreragiis quibuscunque una cum dampnis et expensis si que ea occasione incurrerint seu fecerit eidem capellano et successoribus suis qui pro tempore erint plenarie fuerint satisfactum. In cuius rei testimonium huic presenti | scripto indentato sigillum nostrum commune una cum   p. 132 sigillo dicti abbatis apposuimus. Datum apud Rufford' in capitulo nostro decimo die mensis Maii anno regni regis Edwardi tercii a conquestum Anglie vicesimo quarto, et regni eiusdem regis Francie undecimo.

[D] Ego Johannes Bray antedictus affectans augmentum cultus domini volo et ordino quod prefatus dominus Hugo atte Welle, capellanus, et successores sui capellani qui pro tempore fuerint divina singulis diebus ad altare beate Marie virginis in ecclesia de Upton' supradicta celebrent pro salubri statu meo et Willelmi, filii mei, domini Willelmi de Edyndon', episcopi Wynton' et Roberti de Caldewell' dum vixerimus, necnon pro animabus nostris cum ab hac luce migraverimus, ac animabus Ysolde, quondam uxoris mee, patrum, matrum, fratrum, sororum, parentum,

amicorum et benefactorum meorum et dicte Ysolde et omnium fidelium
defunctorum, quod que percipient et habeant quendam annuum redditum
sex marcarum argenti ad valorem sterlingorum de abbate et conventu
predictis et successoribus suis ad duos anni terminos, videlicet ad
festa Pentecosten et sancti Martini in yeme per equales porciones. Ita
quod solucio cuiuslibet termini esse referat ad tempus sequens, sic
videlicet quod si contingat capellanum qui pro tempore fuerit in aliquo
predictorum terminorum plenarie satisfieri ac ipsum ante terminum
proximum sequentem solucionis faciendum ut premittitur decedere,
successori suo capellano qui pro tempore fuerit de bonis eiusdem defuncti
pro rata temporis satisfaciat competenter. Et ego Johannes Bray dum
vixero quociens dicta cantaria vacaverit, capellanum idoneum capitulo
ecclesie beate Marie Suthwell'; infra mensem a tempore cuiuslibet note
vacacionis dicte cantarie presentabo. Et per ipsum capitulum instituendum
canonice in eadem. Et si ego dictus Johannes vel heredes mei infra
mensem antedictum a tempore vacacionis dicte cantarie ut premittitur
computandum capellanum ydoneum non presentabo seu presentabunt
ut superius est expressum extunc potestas providendi eidem cantarie
et ipsam conferendi illa vice ad prefatum capitulum absque prejudicio
futuri temporis devolvatur. Et predictus Hugo, perpetuus capellanus,
et successores sui qui pro tempore erunt et instituti canonice in eadem
pro animabus superius nominatis celebraturi dicent singulis diebus pro
mortuis, videlicet commendacionem, placebo et dirige ac missam de
sancta Maria, matre Dei gloriosa, singulis diebus celebrabunt, diebus
dominicis ac solempnibus festis duntaxat exceptis quibus de die celebrare
teneantur, memoriamque singulis diebus pro defunctis faciant specialem,
quilibet eciam capellanus qui pro tempore fuerit in cantaria predicta statim
in admissione sua coram capitulo ad sancta Dei evangelie iuramentum
prestet corporale, personalem residenciam se factuendum et omnia onera
premissa sibi et cantarie predicte incumbencia sine aliquo fraude seu
collusione pro suis viribus adimplere. Et si forte huiusmodi capellanus qui
pro tempore fuerit per vi dies dictam cantariam absque causa racionabili et
impedimento legitimo deserverit et in premissis faciendis vel exequendis
negligens repertus fuerit vel remissus et super hiis et aliis excessibus
notabilibus legitime convincatur ipso pro suis excessibus notoriis rite
amoto, confestim alius capellanus ydoneus ad dictam cantariam in forma
predicta admittatur et instituatur canonice in eadem. In quorum omnium
testimonium presenti scripto quod ad perpetuam rei memoriam necnon
pro maiori securitate feci triplicari, quorum unum penes dictum Hugonem,
capellanum, et successores suos, et aliud penes predictum capitulum, et
tercium penes me et heredes meos, volo perpetuis temporibus remanere,
sigillum meum apposui. Datum apud Upton' iuxta Suthwell' decimo die
mensis Aprilis anno domini millesimo ccc^{mo} quinquagesimo secundo.

[E] Nos vero capitulum ecclesie collegiate beate Marie Suthwell'
premissa omnia et singula suprascripta que ad divini cultus augmentum
tendere conspicimus manifeste diligencium recensentes ac volentes ea
piis affectibus consonere. Ipsa omnia et singula prout in serie superius
conscribuntur de consensu omnium et singulorum interest in hac parte

quatinus ad nos attinet, acceptamus, ordinamus, approbamus et ratificamus et ea in suo robore perpetuo durature et in omnium sui parte ac singulis suis articulis fideliter observandis confirmamus per presentes. In cuius rei testimonium sigillum nostrum presentibus est appensum. Datum in domo nostra capitulari Suthwell' sexto decimo kalendas Novembris anno supradicto.

[F] Nos frater Johannes, abbas Cistercii, notum facimus universis quod   p. 133 nos dilecti nobis in Christo Johannis Bray donacionem et elemosinas largas monasterio de Rufford' factas relacione fidedigna attendentes cantariam sue missam perpetuam quam predicti monasterium, abbas et conventus in capella de Upton' concesserint imperpetuum celebrandam secundum formam et tenorem scriptorum inde confectorum approbamus, ratificamus, hac auctoritate nostra et capituli generalis confirmamus. Et si defectus fuerit in predicta continuacione misse celebrande, volumus quod per abbatem Rieuvalt ad satisfaccionem per censuram ecclesiasticam compellantur. In cuius rei testimonium sigillum nostrum presentibus duximus apponi. Datum in Cistercio, anno domini millesimo ccc^mo lviii^vo tempore capituli generalis, etc.

¹ *Per breve de privato sigillo. eodem. pro duodecim marcis Regi solvendi* added in original (see below Note)   ² *pervenerit* added from original   ³ Holdsworth reads as *Joulde* in original

Margin Title in box at top of page and main text in hand of a mid-15th-c. scribe who only contributes this one document; *nota // – // – // nota* in left margin, p. 131, where **C** begins; p. 132, *d* half way down right margin.

Note **213A–D** are written as a continuous paragraph, and **E** and **F** as separate items but all have been separately distinguished here for clarity. *Rufford*, 992 and 993 for editions of **B** and **C** from the originals, NA, Saville Charters, DDSR 102/183. **B** is calendared in *CPR 1348–50*, 429; cf. also *Rot. Orig.*, ii, 205. **C**, the original of which is endorsed *Irrotulatur in memorandis scaccarii videlicet inter commissiones litteras patentes et scripta recognita de termino sancte Trinitatis anno xxxvii ex parte rememoratoris regis* can indeed be found on the King's Remembrancer's Memoranda Roll, 37 Edward III (TNA, E 159/139, *Commissions, letters patent and recognisances*, rot. 5), where, as Holdsworth noted, 'it is preceded by the statement that Hugh of Upton appeared before the Barons of the Exchequer on 7 June [1363] to ask that the enrolment be made'. Although the office of Usher of the Exchequer is briefly mentioned in Tout, *Chapters* (i, 94 n.2; v, 240, 252, 342 n.3) no named holders are cited.

It appears Bray made two chantry foundations, both endowed with an income of six marks, that of Upton, for which **213** provides the main evidence, and another dedicated to Corpus Christi at Newark. For this latter Edward III granted a similar licence to Rufford as in **B** on 7 November 1351, with rents assigned on Rufford's manor of Parkelathe (Park Leys Grange, Kelham; cf. *Rufford*, 382 for an extent drawn up in 1390, with modern map of boundaries) and other properties in Calverton and Kelham. With the consent of Robert of Caldwell and other members of the guild of Corpus Christi, William of Coddington was instituted chaplain (Brown, *Newark*, i, 221). Caldwell, who left over £300 at his death, *c.* 1381, also established another chantry in honour of the Holy Trinity at St Mary's, Newark, under the patronage of the premonstratensian house of Newbo, Lincs. (Brown, *Newark*, i, 220). Both Bray and Caldwell occur frequently as witnesses in deeds relating to Newark and they were also occasionally employed collecting taxes on wool (Brown, *Newark*, i, passim).

William Edington, bishop of Winchester (1345–66), treasurer of England (1344–56), had probably appointed Bray as usher and acted as his patron. C seems to be a unique charter of Thomas, abbot of Rufford, who had been replaced by 1352 (*HRH*, ii, 306). *Northlathe* (now Crateley), *Southlathe* and *Wilkynesfeld* (now Winkerfield) are all in Rufford.

RAVENDALE PRIORY, 214

214 *Letters patent by Henry VI, following the petition of Archbishop John Kempe relating the declining value of its present endowments and difficulties in maintaining a chapter of some sixty persons at Southwell, agreeing to the appropriation of the alien priory of [West] Ravendale, Lincolnshire, up to the value of £14 per annum, to relieve their poverty and increase support for forty lesser clergy serving in the Minster*
St James's next to Westminster, 18 March 1439

Magna gracia regis Henrici sexti de Ravendale

Henricus Dei gracia rex Anglie et Francie et dominus Hibernie omnibus ad quos presentes littere pervenerint salutem. Monstravit nobis venerabilis pater Johannes archiepiscopus Ebor' qualiter possessiones et proventus ecclesie collegiate beate Marie de Southwell ad ecclesiam cathedralem sancti Petri Ebor' que de fundacione inclitorum progenitorum nostrorum et nostro patronatu existit pertinentis in qua quidem ecclesia de Southwell persone canonicorum, vicariorum, capellanorum cantariarum, diaconorum, subdiaconorum, choristarum et aliorum ministrorum ad numerum sexaginta personarum vel circiter se extendunt ad tantam exilitatem devenerunt ac intantum decreverunt et sunt diminute quod nec vicarii, diaconi, subdiaconi aut capellani supradicti paucis saltem eorundem capellanorum exceptis nec alii inferioris gradus ministri supradicti qui videlicet vicarii, diaconi, subdiaconi, capellani cantariarum et alii inferioris gradus ministri numerum quadraginta personarum aut circiter attingunt de porcionibus et proventibus eis assignatis possunt sustentari quin ymmo ob congrue sustentacionis defectum sunt ab ipsa ecclesia de Southwell verisimiliter recessuri et eadem ecclesia desolacionis subitura dispendium et divinis officiis destituenda nisi per nos in hac parte celerius succurratur eidem. Nos premissa considerantes de gracia nostra speciali et in relevamen paupertatis et inopie dicte ecclesie de Southwell ac ministrorum eiusdem ac ad continuacionem divinorum serviciorum in eadem necnon pro summa trescentarum marcarum nobis per prefatum archiepiscopum soluta concessimus capitulo eiusdem ecclesie de Southwell, prioratum de Ravendale in comitatu Lincoln' alienigenam cum suis pertinentiis qui valorem quatuordecim librarum per annum ultra onera et reprisas non excedit. Habendum et occupandum prioratum predictum unacum advocacionibus ecclesiarum, pensionibus et aliis commoditatibus, proficuis, emolumentis et pertinentiis suis quibuscumque predicto capitulo et successoribus suis imperpetuum absque aliquo nobis heredibus seu successoribus nostris inde solvendo disponendam in relevamen et sustentacionem omnium sue aliquorum ministrorum predicte ecclesie de Southwell iuxta discrecionem et ordinacionem archiepiscopi supradicti. Concessimus eciam pro nobis et heredibus nostris quantum

in nobis est quod si contingat predictum prioratum versus predictum capitulum seu successores suos per debitum iuris processum in futurum evinci vel recuperari eo casu nos seu heredes nostri faciemus eidem capitulo in et de aliis terris et tenementis, redditibus aut possessionibus annui valoris quatuordecim librarum recompensari. Et ulterius de uberiori gracia nostra concessimus et licencia dedimus predicto capitulo quod ipsi et eorum successores terras, tenementa, redditus et alias possessiones ad valorem viginti librarum per annum que de nobis non tenentur in capite perquirere possint et recipere absque impedimento nostri heredum seu successorum nostrorum iusticiariorum, escaetorum aut aliquorum aliorum ministrorum nostrorum quorumcumque absque fine vel feodo nobis heredibus vel successoribus nostris per prefatum archiepiscopum vel capitulum aut successores suos aliquo modo in hac parte solvendo. Statuto de terris et tenementis ad manum mortuam non ponendis edito non obstante. Dumtamen per inquisiciones inde in forma debita capiendas et in cancellaria nostra vel heredum nostrorum predictorum rite retornandas compertum sit quod id fieri possit absque dampno seu prejudicio nostri vel heredum nostrorum seu aliorum quorumcumque. In cuius rei testimonium has literas nostras fieri fecimus patentes. Teste me ipso apud sanctum Jacobum iuxta Westmonasterium decimo octavo die Marcii anno regni nostro decimo septimo.   Per ipsum Regem
                                                                    KYRKEHAM

Margin   Heading (apart from *de Ravendale* which has been added later), main text and marginalia in late 15th-c. hand (Scribe 7). Two notes in left margin have been abridged when the folio was cut during a rebinding, ends of lines being indicated here by slashes (/): *Donum/ Henrici/ de conces[sione]/ capitulo/ de Suth[well]/ prioratus/ [alien]igenam de/ [Rave]ndale in/ Lincoln'/ et pertinencium* and *Gracia eiusdem/ concessum/ eodem capitulo/ [re]dditus et pos/[...] ad viginti/[...] per annum/ [...]adquiri/[... ma]num mortuam/ ut patet infra.*

Note: Pd. in *Mon. Ang.*, vi, pt iii, 1316 (xv), after copy in Patent Roll, 17 H. VI, pt 1 m. 2 (*CPR 1436–41*, 261). LA, Cragg MS 4/22 (formerly 4/7), for the original, sealed with the Great Seal (damaged) in green wax on a cord of alternate green and blue silk laces, endorsed: *Irrotulatum in memorandis Scacarii de anno xxxi° regis Henrici sexti, videlicet inter recorda de termino sancte Trinitatis rotulo (blank) ex parte remembratoris Thesaurii,* of which W. A. James made a transcript (NA, SC11/4/82 pp. 9–12). The initial H includes a drawing of the Annunciation and other letters of the first line are much ornamented. For an early 16th-c. copy see NA, SC7/1/5, f. 2[r]. Accounts for West Ravendale in 1454–7, presented to the Chapter by John Hateclif, prior, and Richard Bielby, receiver, survive in NA, SC/5/3/1. The document is 'signed' at the bottom by the Chancery clerk Robert Kirkham, who was active from about 1432 to 1482 but at the time of this instrument was still quite junior (information from the card index of Chancery clerks at TNA, kindly supplied by Dr Paul Dryburgh).

ROYAL AND OTHER LETTERS, 215–20

Litere archiepiscopales directe capitulo Suthwell'

215 *Letters of Archbishop Henry [of Newark] to the Chapter renewing an earlier order to sequestrate the income of the prebend of Mr John d'Évreux* Shelton [April 1297 × 15 August 1299]

Litera ad faciendum sequestrum

Henricus, permissione divina Ebor' archiepiscopus, Anglie primas, dilectis in Christo filiis capitulo nostro Suwell' salutem, graciam et benediccionem. Licet nuper vobis mandaverimus quod ex certis causis fructus et proventus prebende magistri Johannis de Ebroyc', canonici vestri in ecclesia Suwell', sequestraretis, et sub arco donec aliud super hoc vobis mandavemus, teneretis sequestro. Intelleximus tamen postmodo quod non nulli sequestrum huiusmodi violentes fructus et proventus predictos dissipant et consumunt in non modicum suarum periculum animarum. Quo circa vobis districte iniungendo mandamus, quatinus omnes fructus et proventus memorate prebende iterum sequestretis et sub arciori teneatis sequestro donec a nobis aliud in mandatis recepitis sicut nobis respondere volueritis de eodem, de huiusmodi presumptorum nominibus diligencius inquirentes et nos certificantes per vestras literas harum continentes tenorem, cum vobis lumen constiterit de eisdem. Valete. Datum apud Schelton'.

Margin Sectional title at head of page (centred and bold), charter title (underlined) and main text by Scribe 4 as is **216**.

Date Mr John d'Évreux, prebendary of Oxton II since *c.* 1286, had received a protection as canon of Southwell and Ripon from Archbishop Le Romeyn on 20 April 1292 (*Reg. Romeyn*, ii, no. 1144). He resigned his Ripon prebend before 3 July 1297 (*Reg. Newark*, no. 53), so this letter probably dates between then and the death of the archbishop on 15 August 1299; Newark's itinerary shows him at Shelton, Notts., across the Trent a few miles south-east of Southwell, on at least eight occasions between April 1297 and August 1299 (*Reg. Newark*, 333–5).

Note See also **204** for later proceedings in the case against Mr John d'Évreux.

216 *Letters of Archbishop William [Melton] to the Chapter to install Simon de Courtmayor as prebendary of Woodborough through his proctor, John of Newent* Cawood, 7 September 1329

Litera pro installacione canonici per procuratorem

Willelmus, permissione divina Ebor' archiepiscopus, Anglie primas, dilectis in Christo filiis salutem, graciam et benediccionem. Quia prebendam de Wodeburgh in ecclesia Suthwell' vacantem Symoni de Curtemaiori, clerico, duximus conferendam vobis mandamus firmiter iniungentes, quatinus eundem Symonem[1] in fratrem et canonicum admittentes, Johanni de Newent, clerico, presencium portitori predicti Symonis, nomine stallum in choro et locum in capitulo assignetis, quod vestrum est ulterius in hac parte celeriter exequendo. Valete. Datum apud Cawod' vii idus Septembris pontificatus nostri anno duodecimo.

¹ Followed by *et* struck out

Margin   Title centred in bold and main text in smaller version of hand of Scribe 4 as 217-22; a pointing finger in right margin.

Date   These letters are dated in the twelfth year of Melton's pontificate. Although elected on 16 January 1316, he was not consecrated until 25 September 1317 and did not receive his temporalities until 8 October 1317 (*HBC*, ed. Fryde, 282), so the twelfth year of his pontificate was late Sept./Oct. 1328-9; if counted from his election the date would be 7 September 1328.

Note   Simon de Courtmayor was already a canon by April 1296 (**457**) and on 8 April 1324 had been commissioned by Archbishop Melton along with the prior of Thurgarton and Mr Elias of Cowton, prebendary of Norwell Overhall, to inquire into the ownership of tithes on assarted land at Norwood (*Reg. Melton*, v, no. 169). He was certainly still acting as a canon in 1328, though he later became rector of Clayworth (ibid., iv, nos 550, 758, 785, 815). There is considerable confusion over the sequence of prebendaries of Woodborough at this point.

217   *Monition of Archbishop William [Melton] to the Chapter of Southwell and the rural dean of Retford to threaten Robert de* Wolryngton' *of Eaton with excommunication if he fails to pay the arrears of an annual rent of 33s 4d he owes to the Fabric*   Lowdham, 10 August 1322

Monicio de iudicato, sub pena excommunicacionis, solvendo, quam exnunc etc.

Willelmus, permissione divina Ebor' archiepiscopus, Anglie primas, dilectis filiis capitulo ecclesie nostre Suwell' et decano de Retford' salutem, graciam et benediccionem. Cum Robertus de Wolryngton' in Eton, nostre diocesis, in triginta tribus solidis et quatuor denariis annui redditus ad fabricam ecclesie Suwell' ab eodem Roberto et suis progenitoribus ab antiquo debitis, quos idem Robertus per duosdecim annos subtraxerat minus iuste, coram magistris Alano de Neusum, rectore ecclesie de Byngham, Thoma de Sancto Leonardo, rectore de Egmanton' et Willelmo de Hundon', rectore ecclesie de Barnburgh, commissariis nostris sub certa forma in hac parte legitime deputatis, presentibus hiis quorum intererat seu interest, concurrentibus omnibus et singulis que de iure requiruntur, ordine iuris in omnibus observato, rite ac legitime cum arreragiis dicti annui redditus pro xii annis memoratis et ad solucionem eiusdem redditus in futurum iuxta conformam suam fideliter faciendam extiterat condempnatus sub pena excommunicacionis quam extunc si prefate condempnacione non pereret tulerunt in eundem nostri commissarii antedicti prout super omnibus premissis et singulis nobis extitit \facta/¹ fides. Vobis mandamus quatinus dictum Robertum de Wolryngton', peremptore moneatis et efficaciter inducatis, quod de dicto annuo redditu et eiusdem arreragiis prout de eisdem superius plenior sit mencio supradicte ecclesie et custodibus fabrice eiusdem infra triduum a tempore huiusmodi monicionis sibi facte plenare satisfaciat ut est iustum. Alioquin sepefactum Robertum in dicte excommunicacionis sentenciam

diebus et locis quibus² videritis expedire, dampnatum incidisse palam et
p. 135 puplice nuncietis | et per alios faciatis nunciari quousque dicte ecclesie in
premissis omnibus et singulis satisfacerit competenter. Ad que omnia et
singula facienda, vobis et utrique vestrum per se et insolidum committimus
vices nostras. Et de omni eo quod in premissis duxeritis faciendis non
curetis aut alter vestrum curet reddere certiores tempore opportuno per
literas vestras patentes harum seriem continentes. Valete. Datum apud
Loudham iiii idus Augusti anno gracie m° ccc vicesimo secundo. Et
pontificatus nostri quinto.

¹ After *firma* struck out   ² Followed by *poneritis* struck out

Margin Title in post-1583 hand; *Nota de xxxiii solidis et iiii denariis ad fabricam
ecclesie S[. . .]* in right margin in late medieval hand probably different from main text;
the word beginning S.., presumably Southwell, has been cut off when the MS was later
trimmed.

Note For the grants of Robert de Wolryngton [Wilfrunton]'s ancestors and this
long-standing dispute over the rents due, see **226**, **227**, **229-34**. When he died (before
8 June 1326), this Robert held two parts of the manor of Eaton with his wife, Margery, of
which their four daughters, Elizabeth, Eleanor, Isabel and Alice were heiresses, though
Robert's son, also Robert, probably by a previous marriage, was heir to his other lands
(*IPM Notts. 1321–50*, 10–12). Mr Adam of Newsham, rector of Bingham by 1311, the
archbishop's official in Durham during a vacancy in that year, was frequently employed
on commissions, including one with Thomas de St Leonard in January 1314 (*Reg.
Greenfield*, i, nos 199n, 213n, 227, 307). He was dead by 14 April 1329 (*Reg. Melton*, iv,
no. 542). Between 1311 and 1315 St Leonard served as vicar of Laneham, sequestrator in
the archdeaconry of Nottingham and as rural dean of Southwell, Laneham and Retford
(*Reg. Greenfield*, i, nos 139, 196, 199, 227, 646 and 653; iv, 194). By 1318 he was rector
of Egmanton and acting on commissions with William of Hundon (for whom see **535n**).
They were joined by Neusum between 1320 and 1322 (*Reg. Melton*, iv, nos 67, 166, 192,
277). St Leonard received a new commission as sequestrator in the archdeaconry and
dean (with judicial powers) of Southwell in 1323 but was replaced by Gregory Fairfax,
rector of Headon, by 16 November 1324 (ibid., nos 297, 372).

218   *Notification by the Chapter that by authority of the pope the case
pending between Stephen, cardinal priest of Santa Maria in Trastevere,
canon of Southwell, and the prior and convent of St Katherine's [without
Lincoln], over the collation to the schools of Newark had been amicably
settled by the abbot of Roche, proctor of the cardinal in England, with the
assent of the Chapter, in the year of Our Lord 1238, allowing the prior
and convent to present to the Chapter and to the canon or warden of the
prebend (if the canon were absent or the prebend vacant) a fit clerk to
instruct boys in grammar, who was to swear obedience to the canon of
the prebend and to the Chapter, with provision for correcting him if he
infringed the rights of the church of Southwell and the prior and convent
failed to discipline him*   1238

p. 136 **Litera de iure presentationis scolarum de Newerk**

Noverint universi sancte matris ecclesie filii ad quorum notitiam presentes
litere pervenerint quod cum lis esset mota auctoritate domini pape inter
Stephanum tituli sancte Marie Transtiberim presbiterum cardinalem,

canonicum Suwell' ex una parte et priorem et conventum canonicorum sancte Katherine ex altera super collatione scolarum de Newerk' tandem dicta lis inter dominum abbatem de Rupe procuratorem ipsius cardinalis in Anglia de consensu capituli Suwell' amicabili compositione conquievit in hunc modum anno scilicet incarnationis dominice millesimo ducentesimo tricesimo octavo videlicet quod dicti prior et conventus clericum ad regimen scolarum predictarum ad instruendum pueros in arte grammatica ydoneum canonico, sive custodi dicte prebende quicumque pro tempore fuerit, si canonicus presens non fuerit, quotienscumque eas vacare contigerit in capitulo Suwell' presentabunt qui quidem clericus a canonico vel custode dicte prebende sine difficultate qualibet admittetur, idemque clericus canonico dicte prebende et capitulo obedientiam canonicam iurabit. Si vero dictus clericus in aliquo contra libertates ecclesie Suwell' vel dicte prebende deliquerit si incorrigibilis existat et dicti prior et conventus in corripiendo eum fuerint negligentes[1] super excessibus ipsius corrigend' recepto prius mandato super hiis a canonico ipsius prebende sive a capitulo predicto per eosdem priorem et conventum amovebitur et alius per eosdem loco ipsius presentare recipietur. Ut vero hec concessio perpetue firmitatis robur optineat capitulum Suwell' et predicti prior et conventus sigilla sua autentica huic scripto hinc inde apposuerunt.

[1] MS *necligentes*

Margin   In top right corner of page *Litera de Ripon facta ecclesia de Suthwell pro mutuo celebracione exequiarum* (a reference to **219** below). Main heading (bold and centred) and text in same hand (Scribe 4). In right margin in another late 15th-c. hand: *Quia collationes scolarum grammaticalium per totum archidiaconatum Notyngham solum et insolidum pertinent ad prebendarium de Normanton in colleg[iata] ecclesia de Sutht' ut cancellarium eiusdem ecclesie et quamvis aliqua pretensa compositio super collationes scolarium grammaticalium ville de Newerk fuerit facta illa tamen nullius potest existere auctoritatis ut liquet ex tenore eiusdem quia peccat in pluribus.*

Note   Brown, *Newark*, ii, 177 provides a facsimile of this important document, which is the first evidence for the existence of a grammar school at Newark, and also a complete translation, including the testy marginal note. Because the prebendary of Normanton usually exercised the right to appoint or approve nominations of school masters throughout the archdeaconry of Nottingham on behalf of the Chapter in the later Middle Ages, as the unknown annotator asserts and other evidence proves, it is argued by modern authorities that Cardinal Stephen occupied that prebend and was both *magister scolarum* and chancellor of the collegiate church, an arrangement that certainly pertained at York (cf. *Visitations*, xli–xlii, clearly followed by Brown, *Newark*, ii, 175). Leach even comments that 'the *Magister Scolarum* was the earliest dignitary' of the collegiate church of Southwell on the basis of the note. There remain problems with these suggestions, however, since there are no other known references to medieval chancellors of Southwell apart from this late one (cf. **Introduction**, p. lxxvi). Cardinal Stephen is Stefano Normandis dei Conti (d. 1254), elected cardinal-deacon of San Adriano in 1216 and cardinal-priest of Santa Maria in Trastevere in 1228. Among his English benefices he was also a prebendary of Lincoln, York and Norwich where he was also for a time archdeacon of Norwich (see *Fasti 1066–1300*, vi, 86 and Salvador Miranda, 'The Cardinals of the Holy Roman Church' (2015) at http://www2.fiu/~miranda/bios1216.htm#Normandis (accessed 22 July 2017)). The small Gilbertine house of St Katherine's, Lincoln, had been founded *c.* 1148 and among early endowments it received the advowson of St Mary's, Newark, from Bishop Robert de Chesney, a grant confirmed by Henry II. The abbot of Roche (West Riding, Yorks) was Richard who occurs *c.* 1229–41.

219 *Letters of the Chapter of St Wilfrid, Ripon, to the Chapter of South-well, proposing that they should mutually celebrate obits on behalf of canons who had died and also, once annually, for the souls of late vicars and other clerks who had served the two churches* 29 September 1239

Litera capituli de Rypon' fact' capitulo Suthwell' pro mutua celebratione exequiarum

Viris venerabilibus et amicis in Cristo dilectissimis capitulo Suwell' humile capitulum beati Wilfridi de Rypon salutem eternam in domino. Cum misero data sit lux[1] ut sibi possit providere ne corruat, ad hoc etiam valet si labatur ut resurgat, ideo dominus misericorditer dispensando quem predestinavit lumine sue claritatis illustrat ut statum suum si ceciderit consideret et non solum ad iustitiam quam amisit hanc let'[2] verum eciam ut in ea perseveret omni circumspectione meritis intendat. Cum igitur ad hoc facilius consequenda specialiter valeant mutuarum orationum devota suffragia et alterna beneficia sepe contingit ut quod possibilitas propria non optinet aliorum intercessione donetur. Huic est quod vestram caritatem attendentes et quod pie postulatis vobis benigne credimus et ut idem nobis faciatis devote postulamus. Scilicet ut alterna sint ecclesiarum nostrarum imposterum beneficia et maxime ut scita alicuius canonicorum morte quam cito si ingesserit oportunitas, plene fiat pro eo servitium in choro dies obitus eius scribatur in martilegio[3] et singulis annis anno revoluto cum placebo et dirige et commendatione anime et missa in choro celebretur. Simili modo etiam fiat semel in anno die ad hoc specialiter assignato pro animabus vicariorum et aliorum clericorum Deo et beate Marie de Suwell' et beato Wilfrido de Rypona ministrantium. Quod quidem necesse est ut tanto arcius custodiamus quanto magis cuius res prius in iudicium deduci debeat ignoratur. Ne igitur hoc tantum beneficium tanta caritate concessimus communi assensu provisum posteritate temporum negligentia[4] vel ignorantia frustrari vel tradi possit oblivioni quod ore et mente vobis concedimus presenti scripto sigilli nostri appositione roborato quantum in nobis est confirmamus. Actum in anno gratie m° cc° xxxix in festo [sancti] Michaelis. Valete semper in domino.

[1] cf. Job 3, 20, *data est misero lux*   [2] The MS reads *hanclet*, perhaps a mis-transcription for *habundet*? However, Raine (see Note) reads *anhelet*, literally 'he may pant' but also 'he may strive'   [3] Thus for *martirologio*   [4] MS *necligentia*

Note Pd. in *Historians of York*, iii, 150–1 and *Mems. Ripon*, i, 294. This carefully composed letter reveals a clerk well schooled in the formalities of ecclesiastical correspondence, perhaps adapting phrases from formularies to suit the occasion.

220 *Letters of the Chapter of St Wilfrid, Ripon, setting out some of the privileges they have enjoyed from the days of King Athelstan, and sending a recommendation for their liege man, I. clerk* [early 13th century]

p. 137 **Litera testimoniales tanquam ecclesie beati Wilfridi de Ripon**

Omnibus sancte matris ecclesie filiis ad quos presentes litere pervenerint capitulum sancti Wilfridi de Rypon salutem in domino. Noveritis ab Adestano rege et successoribus suis regibus Anglie imposterum concessum fuisse et confirmatum a pontificibus Romane ecclesie corroboratum Deo et sancto Wilfrido de Rypon et omnibus legiis hominibus suis liberas consuetudines et regales infra leucam circa villam de Rypon et quod nominatim ire debent per totam Angliam in qualibet negotiatione sua sive per aquam sive per terram libere et quiete tam ab omni paagio[1] quod vocatur thur tol, ut autem homines beati Wilfridi benignius et cum maiori veneratione et sine omni vexatione sui vel catallorum suorum a nobis suscipiantur scire vos volumus statutum esse in ecclesia nostra imperpetuum singulis diebus tres missas celebrari, scilicet unam missam pro salute vivorum et duas missas pro refrigerio defunctorum omnium qui liberas ecclesie consuetudines et homines beati Wilfridi manutenuerint et aliqua beneficia ecclesie nostre largiti fuerint. Hinc est quod fraternitatem vestram obsecramus et in Cristo rogamus quatinus I. clericum ligium hominem beati Wilfridi et nutritum ecclesie nostre ob reverentiam beati Wilfridi in remissionem omnium peccatorum nostrorum benigne suscipiatur in negotiis suis expediendis et in nullo vexari permittatis. Si quis autem contra ecclesie nostre statuta eundem clericum iniuste vexare presumpserit vel aliquem ligiorum hominum beati Wilfridi sciat se involvi sententia Romanorum pontificum a tempore regis Aldestani data et ter in anno in ecclesia nostra renovata. Valete in domino.

[1] MS *sic* for *pedagio*

Date The earliest reference to the charter of King Æthelstan mentioned here is in a record of a trial held in the Chapter House at Ripon in 1228, for which TNA, DL 41/270 provides the first manuscript copy in the early 15th c. (Woodman, *Charters*, 260, 264–5).

Note Pd. in *Mems. Ripon*, i, 292. For Æthelstan's two known but spurious charters for St Wilfrid's, Ripon, see Woodman, *Charters*, nos 15 and 16, of which the latter is the one referred to above, but he does not bring this copy into his discussion of when the spurious charter was confected. The description of I. as a *nutritus* (literally 'foster-ling') suggests that he had been committed to Ripon Minster in boyhood and that he had perhaps been educated there.

PARISH ALTAR AND VICARAGE, 221

221 *Indenture between the Chapter and Richard of Normanton, paro-chial vicar of the altar of St Vincent, over the ornaments and other furniture belonging to the vicar's manse* Southwell, 6 August 1369

Indentura capituli Suthwell' tangens vicarium parochialem eiusdem pro ornamentis altaris et mansi p. 138

Hec indentura inter nos capitulum ecclesie collegiate beate Marie Suthwell', ex una parte, et dominum Ricardum de Normanton', vicarium nostrum parochialem, altaris sancti Vincencii in eadem, ex altera, de ipsius domini Ricardi consensu expresso confecta, testatur quod infrascripta sunt ornamenta sive bona dicti altaris, que omnia et singula prefatus dominus Ricardus se fatetur teneri dimittere, sive restituere, successori suo cuicunque, in eadem vicaria vicario canonice instituendo.

In primis, videlicet, habentur in altari predicto duo calices argentei et deaurati quorum, minor ponderat xxx solidos vel amplius, et maior xxxv solidos, usualis monete, et deservitur minor communiter pro celebracione divinorum in eodem altari, et maior, diebus Pasche, pro communicacione parochianorum.

Habentur insuper ibidem duo frontalia, quorum unum de serico, precii iii solidorum iiii denariorum, et aliud de armis domini regis, precii ii solidorum. Quatuor insuper tobalia,[1] precii cuiuslibet ii solidorum, et duo ferialia, precii xvi denariorum, quorum unum inveteratum est.

Habentur eciam ibidem quatuor vestimenta integre, videlicet, casualia, stola, fanula, alba, amictus, zona et corporale. De quibus vestimentis quo sunt principalia, et unum eorum cum tunicis, precii xl solidorum, et aliud sine tunicis, precii l solidorum, tercium vero dominicale, precii xx solidorum. Et quartum feriale, precii x solidorum.

Habetur eciam ibidem quintum vestimentum preter casulam, videlicet, alba et duo amictus cum stola et fanula, precii xiii solidorum. Et duo cervicalia cooperta syndone rubeo, cum uno lectrino pro altari, cum xi manutergiis, precii xv solidorum, quorum duo longiora sunt pro mensa domini diebus Pasche. Et uno tapeto struendo coram altari duplicibus festis, sub pedibus sacerdotis.

Et habetur ibidem unus habitus choralis competens, precii xx solidorum, videlicet, capa, almicium, rochetum et superpellicium, et secundum superpellicium pro visitacione infirmorum, cum lucerna.

Inveniuntur ibidem nichilominus unum missale competens, precii xl solidorum, unum epistolare, precii xiii solidorum iiii denariorum. Et duo gradalia nova cum tropariis inclusis pro diebus saltem dominicis et festivis, precii utriusque xxvi solidorum, unum portiforium notatum et bene apparatum, precii c solidorum, unum antifonarium, quod non est de usu Eboraci, precii x solidorum. Et una legenda vetus, precii .vi. solidorum viii denariorum. Et duo manualia, quorum unum vetus est, precii ii solidorum, et aliud competens, precii v solidorum.

Item unus liber qui vocatur *Summa summarum*, precii iiii librarum. Et unus liber qui vocatur *Manuele peche*, lingua gallica conscriptus, precii iii solidorum iiii denariorum.

Item unus liber sermonum tam de epistolis quam de evangeliis dominicalibus per annum, precii iiii solidorum. Et unus liber expositorum evangeliorum dominicalium per annum, precii iii solidorum. Et unus libellus qui vocatur *Pars oculi sacerdotis*, precii vi solidorum viii denariorum.

Item unum candelabrum ferreum breve pro altari et duo lignea cum una absconso de latonne, precii predictorum quatuor ii solidorum.

Item habetur una crux portatilis, argentea et deaurata, cum baculo ad eam congruo, et honeste deagentato, precii vii librarum.

Item una cuppa de cupro deaurato, pendens supra altare pro corpore Christi inibi reponendo et adorando, precii iii solidorum. Et una capsula brevis et lata pro eukaristia similiter conservanda, precii ii solidorum.

Item duo ciste maiores pro vestimentis et libris inibi repondendis, quarum precium unius vii solidorum et precium alterius iiii solidorum vi denariorum.

Item tercia cista minor pro cera conservanda, precii ii solidorum vi denariorum.

Item due capsule, quarum una minor pro cereis ymaginis beate Marie conservandis, precii xviii denariorum. Et alia maior pro[2] cereis gilde sancti Vincencii, precii xii denariorum.

Item in manso ipsius vicarie, videlicet, in aula una tabula mensalis duplicata de fraxino, cum tribus tristellis ad eam congruis, precii xviii denariorum. Et una alia tabula mensalis de quercu, cum duobus tristellis ad eam consuetis, precii xiii denariorum. Et una mappa cum manutergio meliori, precii ii solidorum vi denariorum, una pelvis cum lavatorio meliori, precii iiii solidorum.

Item in camera ibidem una[3] studualis cathedra, cum uno desco versatili, precii ii solidorum. Et uno panno depicto et supra lectum confixo, | precii xvi denariorum.

p. 139

Item in coquina due fornaces, precii xiii solidorum iiii denariorum, cum i olla enea[4] et patella enea meliori, precii viii solidorum, et quatuor plumba in fornilibus positis, precii x solidorum.

Item unum par molarum pro brasio molendo, cum toto apparatu, precii iii solidorum iiii denariorum. Et unum dolium pro farina conservanda, precii xvi denariorum, cum uno alviolo pro pasta conficienda, precii xiiii denariorum, et tabula ad item consueta cum tristellis, precii x denariorum.

Item citula, cum corda et cathena ad hauriendum aquam de fonte, precii xviii denariorum, cum uno alvo lapideo ibidem reposito, precii xii denariorum.

Et nos capitulum antedictum prefatum dominum Ricardum de ipsius consensu expresso ad dimittendum sive restituendum omnia et singula ornamenta sive bona premissa vel equivalencia successori suo vicario in eadem quiscunque fuerit condempnamus, et non solum ipsum dominum Ricardum set eciam quemlibet vicarium in eadem vicaria futurum ad similiter dimittendum sive restituendum omnia et singula ornamenta sive bona premissa vel equivalencia suo successori vicario in eadem canonice compellendum esse decernimus modo et forma que[5] sequitur, quod videlicet futuri vicarii successive in admissione sua ad predictam vicariam iuramentum prestent corporale de conservando predicta bona fideliter vel eorum estimacionem ad usum futuri successoris sui, quod que submittant se pure, sponte et absolute heredes et executores suos iurisdiccioni laudo et decreto capituli in hac parte. Et ipsum capitulum sine strepitu et figura iudicii simpliciter et de plano procedendo licite possint compellere per omnes censuras ecclesiasticas, dictos vicarios et executores suos ad observandum omnia et singula premissa et restituendum, ablata si que fuerint quod absit, vel eorum estimacionem omni appellacione, supplicacione et querela et alii iuris remedio quocunque remotis, quibus omnibus renunciet expresse dicendo renuncio. In cuius rei testimonium sigillum nostrum commune ac eciam sigillum dicti domini Ricardi partibus huius indenture alternatim sunt apposita. Datum apud Suthwell' vi die mensis Augusti, anno domini m⁰ ccc lx⁰ nono.

---

[1] *tobalia* is a variant of *tuallia* (*tuallia* or *tuallium*, here neuter plural) = an altar cloth or towel   [2] *pro* repeated   [3] Followed by *ecclesia* struck out   [4] MS *erea*   [5] Followed by *vid* struck out

Margin   In the title, *et mansi* added in later medieval hand; p. 139 *Juramentum vicarii*

Southwell de bonis ecclesie in left margin, added in post-1583 hand. The text is continuous in the MS but has been split up here for ease of reference.

Note *Visitations*, 197–200 for an earlier edition. The *Summa summarum* may be identical with BL, Harley MS 106 m (or certainly one very similar to it) containing 'extracts from Summulae on the Decretals, the *Summa Raymundi* on penitentials, the *Summa Predicantium* of [Walter] Bromyard' and so on. The *Manuel peche* was probably the mid-thirteenth-century work of William of Widdington (translated in 1303 by Robert of Bourne as *Handlyng Synne*). Leach's comment that it 'is an odd book for a vicar, as, under the guise of a religious work, it is really a collection of Boccaccian stories' seems to be very wide of the mark; see Sullivan, 'Textual History' and **Introduction**, p. xci for further discussion of content and possible identification of this manuscript. The *Pars oculi sacerdotis* may be part of the *Pupilli Oculi* attributed to John de Burgh, chancellor of Cambridge in 1384, whose second book begins *Libri secundus vel dextera pars oculi sacerdotis* and provides instructions on the Seven Sacraments, the Decalogue etc. Leach comments 'if this is the same book an earlier date must be assigned to it than has hitherto been supposed', noting that since it is said to be *compilata* the book mentioned here 'may be one from which it was compiled'. Cf. *BRUC*, 107 for Burgh.

EDINGLEY, 222

222 *Confirmation in hereditary fee by the Chapter to Robert, nephew of Turkill, and his heirs of a house below* Colihaa *for a rent of 6d per annum to the altar of St Giles of Edingley* [late 12th century]

Carta vi denariorum redditus in Coliha pertinentis ecclesie de Eddyngley

Prona sunt presentis etatis in malum studia adeo ut in verbis fides in pactis stabilitas vix inveniatur, hac racionis intuitu sub presentis scripti testimonio tam presentibus quam futuris volumus notum fieri quod nos capitulum sancte Marie de Suewella concessimus Roberto, nepoti Turkilli, mansuram sub Colihaa in feodum et hereditatem tenendam libere, quiete et ab omni servicio pro vi denariis annuatim percipiendis altari sancti Egidii de Eddyngley in festo sancti Egidii, eo tamen tenore si Robertus vitam suam mutaverit vel decesserit, ille quem sibi lege testamenti heredem constituerit iure hereditario imperpetuum pretaxatum teneat mansum. Hiis testibus: magistro Willelmo, clerico archiepiscopi, Willelmo, Rodberto, Rogero, Aldredo, Alexandro et aliis multis etc.

Date Alexander, Roger, Robert and William all witnessed as chaplains of Southwell to a number of grants made to Rufford abbey in the last quarter of the twelfth century. Alexander and Roger witnessed together 1175–1200 (*Rufford*, 246) and Alexander and Robert 1180–1200 (*Rufford*, 963). Alexander and Roger both witnessed with Mr Vacarius (*Rufford*, 172, 338). Mr William, the archbishop's clerk, is more difficult to identify, since none of the Williams listed as clerks of Archbishop Geoffrey in *EEA York 1189–1212* appear with the title *magister*, whilst the only Mr William to witness a charter of Archbishop Roger did so in 1157–63 (*EEA York 1154–1181*, no. 26).

NORTH MUSKHAM PREBEND, 223–4

223 *Inspeximus by the Chapter of the grant by John Pakenham, prebendary of North Muskham, to William Rows, bailiff of his prebend, and his heirs, for his long service, with various tofts (many vacant or wasted) in North Muskham, Holme and Bathley for 46s rent per annum. Also letters of attorney to Richard Bielby, chaplain, Thomas Thorpe, John Hawkyn and William Fulwode to deliver seisin, 27 December 1443*

Southwell, 23 April 1445

Universis sancte matris ecclesie filiis presentes literas inspecturis capitulum   p. 140 ecclesie collegiate beate Marie Suthwell' salutem in eo qui est omnium vera salvus. Noverit universitas vestra nos cartam quam dilectus frater noster et canonicus magister Johannes Pakenham, prebendarius prebende de Northmuskham in ecclesia collegiata nostra predicta fecit et tradidit Willelmo Rows, ballivo prebende sue predicte, heredibus et assignatis suis cum diligencia inspexisse cuius tenor sequitur in hec verba: Sciant presentes et futuri me Johannem Pakenham, prebendarium prebende de Northmuskham in ecclesia collegiata beate Marie Suthwell' attendentem grata et laudabilia obsequia que Willelmus Rows, serviens \ et/ ballivus prebende mee predicte tam michi quam eidem prebende mee multipliciter hactenus impendit et presertim[1] inter cetera graves labores et diligencias quas circa operaciones manerii prebendalis prebende predicte idem, ac circa supervisionem eorundem, nec non et super diligencia et laboribus per ipsum impensis circa disquisicionem scrutinium et introduccionem iurium eiusdem prebende per nonnullos dies et annos elapsos subtractio non absque sui corporis et mentis fatigacione et expensas effucione diu sustinuit, dedisse, concessisse et hac presenti carta mea confirmasse prefato Willelmo, heredibus et assignatis suis diversa tofta, terras et tenementa cum suis pertinenciis iacentia infra territoria villatarum de Northmuskham, Batheley et Holm' iuxta Newerk' in comitatu Notingham subscripta, que quondam de dicta prebenda tam libere quam per rotulos curiarum ad voluntatem et secundum consuetudinem manerii eiusdem tenebantur et que in manibus meis et predecessorum meorum prebendariorum prebende predicte per escaetam perquisicionem et sursum reddicionem tenentum devenerunt. Videlicet, quoddam toftum vastatum in Northmuskham predicta una cum omnibus illis terris, pratis, pascuis et pasturis cum suis pertinenciis, vocatum Beregething' que Willelmus Grayve et postea Johannes Bate dudum tenuerunt. Unum cotagium ibidem edificatum una cum omnibus illis terris, pratis, pascuis et pasturis cum suis pertinenciis, vocatum Daunserthing' que Robertus Baxster nuper tenuit. Unum toftum ibidem vastatum una cum omnibus illis terris, pratis, pascuis et pasturis cum suis pertinenciis, vocatum Skynnerthing' que Johannes Skynner et postea Johannes Bek' nuper tenuerunt. Unum toftum ibidem similiter vastatum una cum crofto ex parte boriali mansi Stephani Marschall', quondam Johannis Lysers, cum suis pertinenciis vocatum Danyelthing'. Unum eciam toftum eidem contiguum cum crofto vocatum Wallerthing' prout iacet ex parte orientali dicti capitalis mesiagii quondam Johannis Lysers versus aquam de Trent et abbuttat ad finem borialem super predictum toftum quondam Johannis Skynner et ad finem australem super venellam ducentem ultra predictam aquam de Trent, quedam tofta et tenementa ibidem vocata Symkynsonthing' una cum omnibus illis terris, pratis, pascuis et pasturis cum suis pertinenciis que Robertus Symkynson' et postea Robertus Wennesley de prebendariis prebende predicte infra territoria villatarum predictarum quovismodo tenuerunt. Unum cotagium iuxta ecclesiam parochialem de Northmuskham predicta in quo Johannes Samon' inhabitat cum suis pertinenciis ac cum duobus croftis iuxta eandem ecclesiam quorum unum in tenura dicti Johannis Samon' simul cum predicto cotagio et aliud affirmatum per priorem de Shelford'. Unum mesuagium in Batheley predicta una cum omnibus illis terris, pratis, pascuis et pasturis cum suis pertinenciis infra territoria villatarum predictarum vocatum Sowterthyng' que Ricardus Sowter et postea Thomas Smyth tenuerunt iam in tenura Willelmi Tille. Unum toftum ibidem quondam edificatum ex parte australi eiusdem mesuagii una cum omnibus illis terris, pratis, pascuis et pasturis cum suis pertinenciis vocatum Hansonthing' que Robert Hanson' et postea

p. 141 Henricus Taylour quondam tenuerunt | iam in tenura dicti Willelmi Tille. Unum toftum in Holm' predicta vastatum una cum omnibus illis terris, pratis, pascuis et pasturis cum suis pertinenciis vocatum Gybsonthyng' que Johannes Julyan' et postea Thomas Leke tenuerunt, et unum toftum vastatum ibidem una cum omnibus illis terris, pratis, pascuis et pasturis cum suis pertinenciis vocatum Grayvethyng' que Johannes Grayve et postea Willelmus Denton' quondam tenuerunt. Habendum et tenendum omnia et singula tofta, terras et tenementa prescripta cum suis pertinenciis prefato Willelmo Rows, heredibus et assignatis suis imperpetuum. Reddendo inde annuatim michi prefato Johanni Pakenham et successoribus meis prebendariis prebende predicta pro illis toftis, terris et tenementis vocatis Beregethyng' sex solidos et octo denarios, Daunserthyng' tres solidos et quatuor denarios, Skynnerthyng' duos solidos, Danyelthing' quatuor denarios, Wallerthyng' decem denarios, Symkynsonthyng' quatuor solidos et sex denarios, illo cotagio cum crofto in tenura Johannis Samon, tres solidos, illos crofto affirmato per priorem de Shelford', tres solidos et quatuor denarios, illis mesuagiis et toftis vocatis Sowterthyng' quatuor solidos, Hansonthyng' quatuor solidos, Gybsonthyng' decem solidos et Grayvethyng' quatuor solidos. Et ego prefatus Johannes Pakenham et successores mei prebendarii prebende predicte omnia predicta terras et tenementa cum omnibus pertinenciis suis prefato Willelmo Rows, heredibus et assignatis suis contra omnes gentes warantizabimus et per presentes imperpetuum defendemus.

Atturnatorium pro seisina liberande

Noveritis insuper me prefatum Johannem Pakenham assignasse et loco meo posuisse dilectos michi in Christo Ricardum Bielby, capellanum, Thomam Thorpp', Johannem Hawkyn' et Willelmum Fulwode, coniunctim et divisim, ad deliberandum vice et nomine meo predicto Willelmo Rows, heredibus et assignatis suis plenam et pacificam seisinam de et in omnibus toftis, terris et tenementis predictis cum eorum pertinenciis iuxta vim, formam et effectum huius presentis carte mee cui in testimonium premissorum sigillum meum apposui vicesimo septimo die mensis Decembris anno domini millesimo cccc^{mo} quadragesimo tercio et anno regni regis Henrici sexti post conquestum Anglie vicesimo secundo.

Nos autem capitulum supradictum attendentes predictam concessionem nobis et ecclesie nostre Suthwell' ac prebende predicte in nullo fore prejudicialem sicut per fidelem inquisicionem coram nobis presentatam et declaratam sumus plenius informati ipsam concessionem ratificamus et presenti scripto nostro confirmamus. In cuius rei testimonium presentibus sigillum nostrum commune fecimus apponi. Datum in domo nostra capitulari Suthwell' vicesimo tercio die mensis Aprilis anno domini millesimo cccc^mo quadragesimo quinto, et anno regni regis Henrici sexti post conquestum Anglie vicesimo tercio.

¹ *precipue* in **224**

Margin *carta vi. denariorum annui redditus pertinentis ecclesie de Edingley* written in cursive late medieval hand in top right hand corner of page, but irrelevant to the following entry. *Northmuskham* lower in right margin probably added in later medieval hand from main text (which has not been identified). p. 141 *Atturnatorium pro seisina liberande* in left margin in post-1583 hand. **223–4** are written in same unidentified late 15th-c. hand.

Note Mr John Pakenham had previously been prebendary of Oxton II (1442), and he appears to have held North Muskham until 1450. Hugh and/or Thomas Pakenham are also sometimes named by modern authorities as prebendaries 1445–50 but as **224** states Hugh, a layman, was John's brother.

224 *Grant by William Rows, bailiff of the prebend of North Muskham, to Hugh Pakenham, brother of John Pakenham, of all his tofts, lands and tenements in North Muskham, Bathley and Holme next Newark (223, recited in full)*   [after 27 December 1443, probably *c.* 23 April 1445]

Omnibus Christi fidelibus ad quos presens scriptum pervenerit Willelmus Rows, ballivus prebende de Northmuskham in ecclesia beate Marie Suthwell' salutem in domino. Cum venerabilis vir magister Johannes Pakenham, prebendarius prebende predicte per cartam suam dederit et concesserit michi prefato Willelmo Rows, heredibus et assignatis meis diversa tofta, terras et tenementa cum suis pertinenciis infra territoria villatarum de Northmuskham, Batheley et Holm' iuxta Newerk' in comitatu Notingham iacencia prout in eadem carta plenius continetur cuius tenor sequitur in hec verba:

Sciant | presentes … [*charter of John Pakenham, 27 December 1443, and his letters of attorney, as above* **223**]   pp. 142–3

Sciatis me prefatum Willelmum Rows omnia predicta tofta, terras et tenementa cum suis pertinenciis infra territoria villatarum de Northmuskham, Batheley et Holme iuxta Newerk' predicta adeo plene et integre sicut in eadem carta annotantur et specificantur dedisse, concessisse et hac presenti carta mea confirmasse Hugoni Pakenham, fratri prefati Johannis Pakenham, prebendarii prebende predicte, habendum et tenendum omnia illa tofta et terras et tenementa cum suis pertinenciis predicto Hugoni, heredibus et assignatis suis de capitalibus dominis feodorum illorum per redditum et servicia inde debita ac de iure consueta imperpetuum. In cuius rei testimonium etc.

Margin p. 141 *Carta Willelmi Rows* in left margin in post-1583 hand. p. 142.

225 *Confirmation in hereditary fee by the Chapter to Richard of Oxton of two bovates of land in Laxton, held by Robert, son of Geoffrey, reeve, which they had of Robert of Laxton, their fellow canon, paying annually two stones of wax for two candles used daily in the Mass of the Virgin celebrated at the hour of Prime* [1214 × 1230]

p. 144 **Munimenta fabrice ecclesie beate Marie Southwell', Laxton**

Capitulum ecclesie beate Marie salutem in salutis auctore. Noverit universitas vestra nos dedisse, concessisse et hac presenti carta nostra confirmasse Ricardo de Oxton duas bovatas terre cum pertinenciis quas habemus in Laxton' de dono Roberti de Laxton, concanonici nostri, et quas Robertus filius Galfridi prepositi tenuit in eadem villa. Tenendum et habendum ipsi Ricardo et heredibus suis de nobis in feodo et hereditate libere, quiete et pacifice. Reddendo inde annuatim ecclesie nostre Suthwellie duas petras cere ad nativitatis sancti Johannis baptiste pro omni servicio seculari et exaccione, ad inveniendum duos cerios singulis diebus per annum ad missam beate Marie que ad horam primam celebratur in eadem ecclesia. Et ut hac nostra confirmacio rata et inconcussa in futurum permaneat presenti carte nostre sigillum nostrum apposuimus. Hiis testibus: Hugone decano, magistro Rogero de Souresby, Henrico de Notingham, Roberto de Laxton' concanonico, etc.

Margin Heading at top of page, in bold, in same hand as text (Scribe 4, who is also responsible for all following entries to **343** as are the page headings and most marginal notes); after *Suthwell*, *pro ii petria cere* added later, and after *Laxton*, the same later hand has added *Stretton*. *2 petre cere annue* in right margin. Foliation *l* in top right corner.

Date After Robert of Laxton became a canon and before the death of Hugh the dean (*Reg. Gray*, 35).

Note Another fifteenth-century copy in NA, SC 7/1/5, f. 15ᵛ. Robert of Laxton, prebendary of Norwell Palishall, *c.* 1220–50, founder of a chantry at Southwell (**455, 456, 460, 505–7**) (cf. *ODNB*, 33, 683; Crook, 'Dynastic Conflict', 193–214, and 'Robert of Lexington', 149–75). Roger of Sowerby, prebendary of South Muskham (1210–after 1222). Henry of Nottingham, prebendary of Normanton (*c.* 1219–*c.*1244), also founded a chaplaincy later amalgamated with that of William of Gunthorpe (cf. **502**).

226 *Notification that Robert de Wlryngton' [Wilfrunton/Wolrington] held certain tenements in Stretton le Clay [now Sturton le Steeple] from Henry of Southwell, paying a rent of 40s, which Henry subsequently granted by his charter to the Chapter for use of the Fabric, as Robert recognised by a fine in the king's court. After Robert's death, these descended to Walter de Wlryngton, who sold them because of debt, having enfeoffed Gilbert of Welton, bishop of Carlisle, who in turn enfeoffed John of Sandale and others as his charter shows (227)* [mid-14ᵗʰ century]

Sciendum est quod Robertus de Wlryngton' quondam seisitus fuit de diversis tenementis in Stretton' in le Clay que tenuit de Henrico de Suthwell' per redditum quadraginta solidorum per annum quem redditum dictus Henricus per cartam suam dedit capitulo ecclesie beate Marie Suthwell' ad opus fabrice eiusdem ecclesie, quem statum dictus Robertus de Wlryngton' postea confirmavit per finem in curiam domini regis etc. Et obiit seisitus. Post eius mortem tenementa in villa predicta descenderunt Waltero de Wlryngton' qui quidem Walterus solvit capitulo sibi debitum etc. ut patet inferius in proximo folio sequenti. Et postea dictus Walterus feoffavit Gilbertum de Welton' episcopum Karliol' in tenementis predictis, reddendo dicto capitulo et faciendo servicia debita etc. ut patet in carta eiusdem Walteri et postea dictus Gilbertus feoffavit dominum Johannem de Sandale et alios ut patet inferius per cartam eiusdem Gilberti.

Margin *Stretton'* in same hand as text in right margin.

Date After **227**?

Note For the various forms of Sturton, see *EPNS Notts.*, 40. The succession after Robert, son of Thomas de Wolrington (**231**) is unclear. A Thomas de Wolrington witnessed charters to Rufford principally in the period 1250–68 (*Rufford*, 72, 109, 542, 544, 650, 728, 949, 968). A Robert de Wlryngton witnessed a document of 22 December 1290 (*Blyth*, A 74) and he may have witnessed a charter to Rufford (*Rufford*, 615). In 1286–7 Robert de Wolrington had defaulted against the prior of Worksop concerning the advowson of Eaton (Thoroton, iii, 259) and on 16 June 1314 he and his wife Margery made a final concord with Henry, son of Roger of Bradbourne, concerning the manor of Eaton which Henry had of the gift of Robert and Margery with reversion to the right heirs of Robert (TNA, CP 25/184/21 no. 78). When he died, before 8 June 1326, Robert held two parts of the manor of Eaton and he had four daughters: Elizabeth, Eleanor (*Elienora*), Isabel and Alice and his son Robert was his male heir. Agatha, mother of Robert was still living and she held in dower of Tickhill two parts of two fees. In Sturton Robert held one messuage, thirty acres of land and twelve acres of meadow of Southwell for 33s 4d per annum (*CIPM* vi (2), 413, no. 679; *IPM Notts. 1321–50*, 10–12). On 13 November 1329 Simon de Wolryngton and Agatha de Wolryngton made a final concord concerning one messuage, fifty-six acres of land, two and a half acres of meadow and 16s rent in Eaton, Ordsall and Sturton (TNA, CP 25/1/185/27 no. 67). Simon was granted a pardon on 28 May 1327 (*CPR 1327–30*, 48). Robert, son of Robert de Wolfryngton, and Amice his wife made a final concord (18 November 1336) with Richard of Willoughby, knight, who gave them twenty marks, for one messuage, fourteen acres of land and a moiety of one acre of meadow in Eaton (TNA, CP 25/1/185/29 no. 152). Walter de Wolrington may have been the son of Robert and Amice. Bishop Welton made a final concord (4 May 1354) with Roger de Bothale (Bothal, Northumberland) and Margaret, his wife for two messuages, land, meadow, pasture and 12s rent in Eaton and Milton (TNA, CP 25/1/185/32 no. 312).

Munimenta fabrice ecclesie de Southwell. Stretton   p. 145

227 *Confirmation by Gilbert of Welton, bishop of Carlisle, to John of Sandale, clerk, Walter of Ulceby and John Schyre, chaplains, of all the lands, meadow, rents and tenements he holds of the gift of Walter de Wlryngton in Sturton le Steeple, together with letters of attorney for William of Hackenthorpe and William of Bathley to deliver seisin*
Retford, 1 July 1339 (*sic* for 1359?)

Sciant presentes et futuri quod ego Gilbertus de Welton', permissione divina Karliolensis episcopus, dedimus, concessimus et hac presenti carta nostra confirmavimus Johanni de Sandale, clerico, Waltero de Ulseby et Johanni Schyre, capellanis, omnia terras, prata, redditus et tenementa cum omnibus suis pertinenciis que habemus et habuimus ex dono et feoffamento Walteri de Wlryngton' in villa, campis et pratis de Stretton', habendum et tenendum omnia predicta terras, prata, redditus et tenementa cum suis pertinenciis prefatis Johanni, Waltero et Johanni et eorum heredibus et assignatis de capitalibus dominis feodi illius per servicia inde debita et consueta imperpetuum. In cuius rei testimonium huic presenti carte sigillum nostrum apposuimus. Hiis testibus: domino Johanne de Loungvilers, Hugone de Hercy, Johanne de Leseus, Thoma de Saundeby, militibus, Johanne Power', Willelmo de Hoselbech' de Stretton et aliis. Datum apud Retford' die Iovis proximo post festum apostolorum Petri et Pauli, anno regni regis Edwardi tercii post conquestum Anglie xiii°.[1]

Attornatorium eius

Noverint universi nos Gilbertus de Welton', permissione divina Karliolensis episcopus, attornasse et loco nostro posuisse dilectos nostros in Christo Willelmum de Hacunthorpp et Willelmum de Batheley coniunctim et divisim ad liberandum nomine nostro Johanni de Sandale, clerico, Waltero de Ulseby et Johanni Schyre, capellanis, seisinam de omnibus terris, pratis, redditibus que habuimus de dono Walteri de Wlyrungton' in villa, campis et pratis de Stretton' secundum tenorem carte eisdem Johanni, Waltero et Johanni et heredibus et assignatis imperpetuum per nos inde facte. Rata et grata habiturus quicquid iidem Willelmus et Willelmus seu unus eorum nomine nostro fecerint seu fecerit in premissis per presentes sigillo nostro signatas. Datum apud Retford' die iovis proximo post festum apostolorum Petri et Pauli, anno regni regis Edwardi tercii post conquestum xiii°.[1]

[1] MS *sic*, probably for *XXXIII°*

Margin   Heading in later (?16th-c.) hand. *Carta Episcopi Carleolensis* in left margin in same hand.

Date   Gilbert of Welton, prebendary of Eaton (1343–53), was nominated bishop of Carlisle by Pope Innocent VI on 13 February 1353, on the grounds that his predecessor, Clement VI, had reserved the see for papal collation (*CPL*, iii, 482), and he died in late December 1362 (*Reg. Welton*, xxiv).

Note   Bishop Welton had appointed Mr John of Welton as his attorney to lease and farm all his lands and tenements in Eaton by Retford, Sturton le Steeple and Littleborough by letters patent dated at Rose Castle, 23 March 1354 (*Reg. Welton*, no. 529). John of Sandale, a nephew of John of Sandale, bishop of Winchester (1316–19), prebendary of Normanton (1318–after 1340). Bishop Sandale held the manor of Wheatley within Long Sandale by Doncaster (Yorks.). With Roger of Willoughby, William of Hackenthorpe (Derbys.) granted lands in Nottinghamshire and Lincolnshire to Nicholas le Monboucher and Margaret, his wife, on 24 and 30 April 1365 (NUM, Ne D 1885–6).

228   *Grant by Walter of Ulceby, chaplain, to William of Gunthorpe, clerk, Richard Andrew of Southwell, Hugh of Ulceby, Thomas of Rolleston, William of Cropwell, John Pikinam and Thomas of Linby, chaplains,* *of all lands, meadows, rents and tenements which he held by grant and enfeoffment of Mr Gilbert of Welton, late bishop of Carlisle, in Sturton le Steeple*   Sturton le Steeple, 24 July 1383

Sciant presentes et futuri quod ego Walterus de Ulseby, capellanus, dedi, concessi et hac presenti carta mea confirmavi domino Willelmo de Gunthorpp, clerico, Ricardo Andrew de Suthwell', capellano, et Hugoni de Ulseby, capellano, Thome de Roldeston', capellano, Willelmo de Crophill', capellano, Johanni Pikinam, capellano, et Thome de Lyndeby, capellano, omnia terras, prata, redditum et tenementa cum omnibus suis pertinenciis que habui ex dono et feoffamento magistro Gilberti de Welton' nuper episcopi Karliolensis in villa, campis et pratis de Stretton'. Habendum et tenendum omnia predicta terras, prata, redditus et tenementa cum suis pertinenciis prefatis Willelmo, Ricardo, Hugoni, Thome, Willelmo, Johanni et Thoma, heredibus et assignatis eorum, de capitalibus dominis feodi illius per servicia inde debita et de iure consueta imperpetuum. In cuius rei testimonium huic presenti carte mee sigillum meum apposui. Hiis testibus: Johanne Jankynson' de Stretton', Johanne de Doncastre de eadem, Francisco de Burton' de eadem, Ricardo in le Willowes, Hugone de Warrewyk' et aliis. Datum apud Stretton' die veneris in vigilia sancti Jacobi apostoli, anno regni regis Ricardi septimo etc.

Margin   *Carta Walteri Ulsbye* in late (?16ᵗʰ-c.) hand in left margin.

Note   William of Gunthorpe, former treasurer of Calais (1368–73), following its capture by Edward III in 1347, prebendary of Norwell Palishall (by 1380–1400). Richard Andrew was one of the wardens of the commons in 1395 (**500**) and vicar of Southwell in 1414 (**357**).

Munimenta fabrice ecclesie beate Marie Suthwellie   Stretton'   p. 146

229   *Grant in free alms by Henry of Southwell to the Fabric of 40s rent per annum which Robert de Wlryngton owes him in Sturton le Steeple*
[1235 × 1240]

Omnibus Christi fidelibus hoc presens scriptum visuris vel audituris Henricus de Suthwell' salutem in domino. Noveritis me ob veneracionem Dei et genitricis eius pro salute anime mee et uxoris mee et animarum patris et matris et omnium antecessorum et successorum meorum benefactorum et omnium fidelium defunctorum dedisse, concessisse et hac carta mea confirmasse in liberam, puram et perpetuam elemosinam Deo et fabrice ecclesie beate Marie Suthwellie quadraginta solidos annui redditus quos Robertus de Wlryngton' et heredes sui mihi debent pro tenementis et pratis que de me tenent in territorio de Stretton' secundum tenorem carte que idem Robertus et heredes sui de me habeant. Tenendum et habendum in liberam, puram et perpetuam elemosinam cum omnimodis eschaetis que aliquo iure vel casu imposterum poterint mihi vel heredibus meis de predictis tenementis accidere. Et ut hec mea donacio et concessio rata sit et stabilis imperpetuum presenti scripto sigillum meum apposui. Hiis testibus: domino Willelmo de Sutton' etc. et aliis.

Margin Page heading in bold, in same late medieval hand as text. *Carta Henrici Southwell* in later (?16th-c.) hand in right margin. *Strettone in le Clay* in right margin in same hand as text.

Date Henry of Southwell, clerk, granted (1241–9) to the Chapter three tofts in Southwell with no mention of his wife (*Rufford*, 36). Sir William Sutton was born *c.* 1218 and died on 18 August 1268 (Moor, iv, 317).

230 *Grant by Juliana, sister of Henry of Southwell, clerk, in her free widowhood of **229*** [1235 × 1250]

Sciant presentes et futuri quod ego Juliana soror Henrici de Suthwell', clerici, in libera viduitate et potestate mea concessi et presenti carta mea confirmavi Deo et fabrice ecclesie beate Marie de Suthwell' quadraginta solidos annui redditus quos Robertus de Wlryngton' et heredes eius debent Henrico de Suthwell', fratri meo, pro terris et pratis que de eo tenent in Stretton' et quos xl solidos predictus Henricus, frater meus, dedit et carta sua confirmavit fabrice dicte ecclesie. Tenendum et habendum in puram et perpetuam elemosinam secundum tenorem carte predicti Henrici, fratris mei, quam predictam ecclesiam inde habet. In cuius rei testimonium presenti scripto sigillum meum apposui. Hiis testibus: Thoma de B. etc. et aliis.

Margin *Carta Juliane Southwell* in later (?16th-c.) hand in right margin.

Date After **229**.

231 *Acknowledgement by Robert de Wlryngton' recognising that he and his heirs owe Henry of Southwell 40s rent per annum for lands in Sturton le Steeple* [1230 × 1250]

Sciant presentes et futuri quod ego Robertus de Wlyrngton' et heredes mei vel assignati mei et eorum heredes tenemur Henrico de Suthwell', clerico, et heredibus suis vel assignatis suis et eorum heredibus vel successoribus suis ad solucionem quadraginta solidorum annuatim redditorum, scilicet ad solucionem viginti solidorum ad Pascha et viginti solidorum ad festum sancti Michaelis, videlicet pro una bovata terre cum pertinenciis in territorio de Stretton' cum tofto et crofto que fuerunt Suuayn filii Gamell', quam bovatam terre cum pertinenciis et cum dictis tofto et crofto idem habuit de Hugone filio Ade de Stretton', et pro quatuor acris terre cum pertinenciis in territorio eiusdem ville, quas dictus Henricus tenuit de Olivero[1] de Stretton' filio de Staywath, et pro quatuor acris terre cum pertinenciis in eodem territorio, quas idem Henricus tenuit de Roberto filio Hugonis de Stretton'. Et pro una acra cum pertinenciis in territorio predicte ville de Stretton' quam idem Henricus tenuit de Hugone de Wiburg', et pro quodam essarto cum pertinenciis in territorio eiusdem ville. Scilicet quantum pertinet ad dimidiam bovate terre, quod quidem essartum dictus Henricus tenuit de Simone filio Hugonis de Lechburg', et pro duabus acris terre cum pertinenciis in lemens'[2] in territorio predicte ville, quas idem Henricus tenuit de Hugone filio Raynery, et pro iii rodis prati cum pertinenciis in prato de Stretton', quas sepe dictus Henricus tenuit de

Radulpho filio Thome de Burton', quas quidem terras cum pertinenciis et cum dictis tofto et crofto essarto et prato predictus Henricus mihi et heredibus meis vel assignatis dedit, concessit et carta sua confirmavit quam mihi inde fecit. Et in huius rei testimonium presens scriptum sigilli mei munimine roboravi. Hiis testibus: domino Waltero etc. et aliis.

[1] MS *Oliveto* but cf. **233**   [2] *Le Merche* in **233**

Margin   *Carta Roberti de Ulrington* in late (?16th-c.) hand in right margin.

Date   After **229** but before **232**.

Note   Robert de Wlryngton and his brother, Thomas (*Rufford*, 616), were the sons of Thomas de Wulvrington who held two fees of the honour of Tickhill in 1208–13 (*Book of Fees*, 32). In 1200 Thomas de Wlurinton owed three marks for one and a half fees and with his wife, Rametta, 23s 4d for one fee (*PR 2 John*, 14). In 1211–12 Thomas de Wolwrintone and Ralph of Misterton held two fees although Ralph only held a third of a fee, and Thomas de Wolurintone held by serjeantry a certain meadow for 5s. Thomas de Werfrintone, Ralph of Misterton and Robert of Ordsall held two fees in 1201–12 (*Red Book*, 182, 593–4). Thomas owed two marks for a false claim in Shropshire in 1190 which he still owed in 1196 (*PR 2 Richard I*, 125; *8 Richard I*, 131). In 1202 he owed one mark for an assize between himself and Rametta, his wife (*PR 4 John*, 193). Thomas de Wlrigtun and Rametta de Ripers, his wife, granted to Rufford (1194–1200) pasture and meadow in Eaton for which they were given three and a half marks and a horse worth three marks, and Thomas de Wlurinton witnessed (*c.* 1196–1206) a grant to Rufford (*Rufford*, 912, 969). In 1195 Rametta, wife of Thomas de Wurlinton, owed 40s to have 20s rent in Ordsall, Retford and Eaton of which she had been disseised when Thomas was with Count John (*PR 7 Richard I*, 22; Foulds, 'Siege of Nottingham', 27). Thomas and Rametta granted the church of Eaton to Worksop priory, which was confirmed by his son, Robert, and Robert, son of Herbert de Wolrington also confirmed the grant on 21 October 1286 (Thoroton, iii, 258 citing the lost cartulary of Worksop, f. 84). With Robert, abbot of Newbo, Henry, prior of Worksop (*c.* 1200–14), Henry of Rolleston, Godfrey the Angevin and Richard, his brother, Thomas de Wlrington witnessed the agreement between Welbeck abbey and Robert de Somerville of Oxton, Hugh de Capella and Walter of Strelley concerning rights in Oxton (Thoroton, iii, 44; *Thurgarton*, pp. 197–8, 112n). Robert de Wlryngton had succeeded Thomas by the Easter term of 1229 when Robert de Ripers, son of Robert of Ordsall, brought a case against him concerning a third of the manor of Eaton and in the Hilary term 1231 Robert de Ripers offered himself against Robert de Wulfrinton that he should hold to him (Ripers) an agreement made between Thomas de Wulfrington and Rametta, his wife, Robert's mother, and Robert de Ripers, father of Robert de Ripers, whose heir he is, concerning common of wood in *Wachinglegh* (*CRR*, xiii, 465; xiv, 250). John, prior of Torksey (occurs 1234), quitclaimed to Remeta de Ripers and Robert, her son, after the death of Thomas de Wilfrinton, two and a half bovates in Eaton and sixteen quarters of corn which Torksey had been granted during Thomas's lifetime (*Blyth*, 426; *HRH*, ii, 187)). In 1235–6 Robert de Wlfreton held two fees in Eaton and all of Eaton for two fees in 1242–3, but one of the fees was also held by John of Eaton in 1235–6 and 1242–3 (*Book of Fees*, 534, 536, 978, 986). Robert, Herbert and Thomas de Wlrington witnessed the exchange of lands between Richard, abbot of Roche (1238–54), and Robert de Ripers (J. R. Aveling, *History of Roche Abbey* (London and Worksop, 1870), 142–4).

232   *Agreement between the Chapter and Robert de Wlryngton concerning 40s annual rent given by Henry of Southwell for two and a half marks paid by Robert to the Fabric*   [1230 × 1257]

Sciant presentes et futuri quod ita convenit inter capitulum Suthwell' petens et Robertum de Wlryngton' impedientem de quadraginta solidis annui redditus quos idem Robertus reddere consuevit Henrico de Suthwell', clerico, pro tenementis que tenuit de eo in villa et territorio de Stretton' et quos dictus Henricus dicto capitulo contulit pro salute anime sue, scilicet quod predictum capitulum dedit, concessit et confirmavit dicto Roberto omnia predicta tenementa sine aliquo retenemento. Tenendum et habendum eidem Roberto et heredibus suis vel suis | assignatis et eorum heredibus libere, quiete et hereditarie cum omnibus pertinenciis et libertatibus in omnibus locis faciendo inde pro capitulo predicto dominis feodorum homagia, sectas curie, si debeantur, et relevia et omnia servicia que ad dicta tenementa pertinent sicut continetur in cartis per quas dictus Henricus feoffatus fuit de dictis tenementis quas sepe dictus Robertus penes se habuit. Et solvendo inde dicto capitulo ad opus fabrice ecclesie de Suthwell' duas marcas argenti et dimidiam singulis annis. Scilicet medietatem ad Pascha et aliam medietatem ad festum sancti Michaelis pro omnibus serviciis et demandis. Deinde vero dictum capitulum dicto Roberto et heredibus suis vel suis assignatis et eorum heredibus omnia predicta tenementa contra omnes gentes warantizare poterunt qui quidem dictum Henricum de dictis tenementis feoffaverunt. Et quum dicti feoffatores de warantia defecerint cessabit solucio dicti redditus dicto capitulo facienda. Et cessent similiter servicia que feoffatoribus fieri deberent. Si vero dictus Robertus et heredes sui vel sui assignati et eorum heredes defecerint licebit vicecomiti Notingham, qui pro tempore fuerit, distringere eos per omnia sua mobilia et immobilia donec dictus redditus plene persolvatur sine aliquo placito et sine contradiccione et impedimento dicti Roberti et heredum suorum vel assignatorum suorum et heredum. Ut autem omnia in hoc scripto continentur rata et stabilia permaneant partes hoc presens scriptum in modum cirograffi confectum sigillorum suorum impressionibus roborari fecerunt. Hiis testibus: domino Johanne de Lexinton' etc. et aliis.

Margin   *Conventio inter Capitulum et dictum Robertum de annuo reditu predicto* in later (?16ᵗʰ-c.) hand in right margin. p. 147 page heading *Stretton fabrica* (this last word added in 17ᵗʰ c.).

Date   After **231** and before the death of John of Laxton.

Note   Probably the youngest of the Laxton/Lexington brothers, John's career can be followed from 1235. A steward in the royal household, and briefly chancellor of England September 1247–August 1248 and 15 October 1249–May 1250, he inherited most of Robert's estates, but was dead by 18 January 1257 (*Rufford*, xcvii–xcviii; *ODNB*, 33, 682–3; and articles by Crook cited in **225n**).

p. 147

233 *Recognition by Robert de Wlryngton of Eaton to the Chapter of 33s 4d annual rent which he holds in Sturton le Steeple*

Southwell, 24 November 1308

Noverunt universi quod cum controversia exorta fuisset inter capitulum Suthwell' ex una parte et Robertum de Wlryngton' in Eton' ex altera super detencione arreragiorum cuiusdam redditum annualis triginta trium solidorum et quatuor denariorum in qui quidem redditu idem Robertus predicto capitulo tenetur pro pluribus tenementis que tenet de eodem capitulo in Stretton' vel in eius territorio, videlicet pro una bovata terre cum pertinenciis in territorio de Stretton' cum tofto et crofto que fuerunt Sauuen filii Gamell' quam bovatam terre cum pertinenciis et cum dictis tofto et crofto quidam Henricus de Suthwell', clericus, tenuit in Stretton'. Et pro quatuor acris terre cum pertinenciis quas dictus Henricus tenuit de Olivero de Stretton' filio Roberti de Staywarth', et pro iiii acris terre cum pertinenciis quas idem Henricus tenuit de Roberto filio Hugonis de Stretton', et pro i acra terre cum pertinenciis quam idem Henricus tenuit de Hugone filio Wyburg', et pro quodam essarto cum pertinenciis, scilicet quantum pertinent ad dimidiam bovate terre quo quidem assartum dictus Henricus[1] tenuit de Simone filio Hugonis de Letheburg'. Et pro ii acris terre cum pertinenciis in le Merche quas idem Henricus tenuit de Hugone filio Reynery, et pro iii rodis prati cum pertinenciis quas dictus Henricus tenuit de Radulpho filio Thome de Burton'. Amicis communibus intervenientibus, demum ita convenit quod predictus Robertus de Wlryngton' recognovit pro hoc scriptum se tenere omnia predicta tenementa cum suis pertinenciis de predicto capitulo imperpetuum et obligavit se et heredes suos et omnia predicta tenementa ad quorumcumque manus devenire contigerint de cetero ad solucionem predicti redditus annualis xxxiii solidorum et iiii denariorum predicto capitulo vel eius certo attornato ad duos anni terminos solvendum, videlicet ad terminos Pasche et sancti Michaelis pro equali porcione. Et si ad aliquem terminum predictus redditus in parte vel in toto aretro fuerit quod bene liceat predicto capitulo vel eius ballivo cum sua litera patente omnia predicta tenementa tanquam in proprio feodo eiusdem capituli pro sua voluntate intrare et districcionem facere et districcionem predictam prout sibi placuerit inde fugare et retinere contra vadium et plegium quousque de predicto redditu et suis arreragiis predicto capitulo plene fuerit satisfactum simul cum dampnis et interesse si qua incurrerit ex occasione. Et pro ista recognicione predictum capitulum omnia arreragia predicti redditus a primo mundi usque in diem confeccionis presencium existencia predicto Roberto penitus relaxavit. In cuius rei testimonium huic presenti scripto in modum cirographi confecto | utraque pars sigillum suum apposuit. Hiis testibus: dominis Willemo de Hokerton', Hugone Leverick', custodibus commune eiusdem ecclesie, domino Roberto de Wython', capellano, Thoma Pistore, Henrico Austyn et aliis. Datum in capitulo Suthwell' die dominica in crastino sancti Clementis martiris, anno regni regis Edwardi filii Edwardi secundo.

p. 148

[1] *dictus Henricus* repeated in MS

Margin   *Carta recognicionis de eodem eiusdem annui reditus* in later (?16th-c.) hand in left margin. cf. **217**

Note   This seems to be the only mention of William of Hockerton and Hugh Leverick as wardens of the commons. For Robert de Wlryngton see **226n**. In the surviving accounts of Robert Sampson and John Chetill, wardens of the Fabric in 1428–9 and 1429–30, John le Wode of Sturton paid 20s per annum for one bovate of land and meadow with the toft and croft, eleven acres of land with one assart, and three roods of meadow in Sturton sometime of Robert de Wolryngton (NA, SC5/2/1, 2).

WILLOUGHBY IN WALESBY, 234–6

Weloby

234   *Grant by Walter Malet of Willoughby, knight, to the Fabric for the souls of himself and Avicia, his wife, of seven acres of land in his wood of* Thirneclive   [early 13th century]

Omnibus sancte matris ecclesie filiis hoc scriptum visuris vel audituris Walterus Malett de Weloby, miles, eternam in domino salutem. Noverit universitas vestra me in tuitu Dei et pro salute anime mee et pro animabus antecessorum et heredum meorum et Avicie, uxoris mee, concessisse, dedisse et hac presenti carta mea confirmasse Deo et fabrice ecclesie beate Marie Suthwell' septem acras terre in bosco meo de Thirneclive ex parte occidentali eiusdem bosci mensuratas per perticam viginti quatuor pedum. Tenendum et habendum in puram et perpetuam elemosinam. Ita quod liceat assignatis eiusdem ecclesie pro voluntate sua assartare predictas vii acras aut permittere eas crescere in boscum. Ego eciam Walterus et heredes mei warantizabimus eidem fabrice ecclesie prenominate vel assignatis eiusdem ecclesie predictas septem acras in omnibus et contra omnes homines. Et ut hec mea donacio rata et inconcussa in futurum permaneat eam presenti carte mee attestacione et sigilli mei apposicione dignum duxi roborare. Hiis testibus: Hugone decano et aliis etc.

Margin   The heading at the top of p. 148 is *Weloby* (in same hand as text) *fabrica* (in later hand). Section heading in same hand as text, as is title in right margin *Carta Walteri Mallet'* with addition of *de 7 acris in Thirneclive* in later (?16th-c.) hand.

Date   Walter Malet was dead by 1229–30 (Thoroton, i, 165) and before the death of Hugh the dean who was dead by 28 May 1230.

Note   *Thirneclive/Thorncliffe* not recorded in *Pn Nt*, nor is the spelling *Weloby* but the latter is to be identified with Willoughby in Walesby rather than Willoughby by Norwell where a ridge, still wooded along its crest and lying to the east of the present two farmsteads which constitute the hamlet of Willoughby, rises up steeply from about 100 feet above sea level to over 250 feet in an imposing cliff-like formation. Henry, son of Robert de Burun, quitclaimed to Walter Malet his claim in half the land held of the barony of Burun in Cotgrave in 1219–20. Robert de Burun was said to be the heir of Roger de Buron but why he lost the barony is unknown. In 1200 Walter Malet offered twenty marks for an assize of mort d'ancestor for ten fees in Ossington, Horsley and Cotgrave (Sanders, *English Baronies*, 123n; Thoroton, i, 166–7; ii, 284–5). Curiously the Malet family also came to hold an interest in the manor of Willoughby by Norwell (Jones, *Willoughby by Norwell*, 17).

235 *Confirmation and quitclaim by Roger, son of Walter Malet of Willoughby, to William, his son, of seven acres of land in* Tirneclive *wood in Willoughby and two and a half acres of land in Halam which the Chapter has of the grant of William Ribaud of Halam* [1237 × 1243]

Sciant presentes et futuri quod ego Rogerus, filius Walteri Malett de Weloby, dedi, concessi et hac presenti carta mea confirmavi quietum clamavi Willelmo, filio meo, totum ius et clameum quod habui vel habere potui in vii acris terre in bosco de Weloby qui vocatur Tirneclive ex parte orientali eiusdem bosci mensuratis per perticam xxiiii pedum et in duabus acris et dimidia terre arabilis in campis de Halum. Tenendum et habendum illi et heredibus suis vel eorum assignatis libere, quiete et integre prout continetur in cartis meis de concessione et dono capituli beate Marie Suthwell' de predictis vii acris bosci et de concessione et dono Willelmi Ribaud' de Halum de ii acris et dimidia terre arabilis in campis de Halum. Et in huius rei testimonium sigillum meum apposui huic scripto. Hiis testibus: magistro V. de Lanum, archdiacono Dunelm', magistro Willemo de Berford' etc.

Margin *Carta Rogeri Mallet de iisdem et aliis* in later (?16th-c.) hand in right margin.

Date Mr William of Laneham, archdeacon of Durham (1224–43) and canon of York Minster (*Fasti 1066–1300*, ii, 38–9; vi, 57, 74). Perhaps related to Roger of Laneham (**396n**). A Mr William de Bereford was instituted to the church of Sockburn (County Durham) by Archbishop Gray on 17 October 1237 (*Reg. Gray*, 79). He may have been related to Richard de Bereford who occurs as canon of Southwell *c*. 1231–44 (*Reg. Gray*, 239; see **395**, **400** and **432**).

Note In **234** the wood was said to have been measured from the west (*occidentali*).

236 *Notification by Alan, son of Walter Malet of Willoughby, to the Fabric of 6d rent per annum for seven acres of wood in* Tirneclive *which Walter, his father, and Roger, his brother, gave* [1237 × 1243]

Omnibus hoc scriptum visuris vel audituris, Alanus filius Walteri Malett de Welheby salutem in domino. Noveritis me et heredes meos teneri ad solvendum annuatim fabrice ecclesie beate Marie Suthwellie infra octavum Pentecostem sex denarios pro vii acris terre iacentibus in Tirneclive quas Walterus, pater meus, Rogero, fratri meo, dedit. Tenendum et habendum de eadem ecclesia per idem servicium. In cuius rei testimonium huic scripto sigillum meum apposui. Hiis testibus: domino W. et aliis.

Margin *Carta Alani Malet* in later (?16th-c.) hand in right margin, and just below in the same hand is written *6d per annum*.

Date At about the same time as **235**.

Note Alan Malet had succeeded Walter (**234**) by 1229–30 (Thoroton, i, 166–7). He witnessed the grant (1223–34) by Robert, son of Thomas of Muskham, to Thomas of Cromwell (*Rufford*, 218). In 1235–6 and 1242–3 Alan Malet and the prior of Lenton held one and a half fees in Cotgrave of Burun (*Book of Fees*, 532, 537, 997; Sanders, *English Baronies*, 123n; Foulds, 'Lenton Priory', 34–42). He is probably to be identified with the man who asserted land in Norwell parish at this time (**425**, **427**) and ancestor of the later Malet lords of Willoughby by Norwell (Jones, *Willoughby by Norwell*, 17–19), since Robert, son of Alan Malet of Willoughby granted to Hugh Lisurs lands sometime of Henry and Alan Malet and the lands he had of the gift of Henry Malet, his brother (Thoroton, iii, 165).

ROLLESTON, 237–43

p. 149 **Roldeston'** **Fabrica**

237 *Grant by Thomas, son of Reginald, to the Fabric of one acre of meadow in* Seggisdale [*c.* 1200 × 1230]

Sciant omnes tam presentes quam futuri quod ego Thomas filius Riginaldi concessi, dedi et hac presenti carta mea confirmavi Deo et fabrice ecclesie sancte Marie de Suthwell' unam acram prati in Seggisdale que co[n]tinet duas perticatas et dimidia in latitudine pro salute anime mee et patris et matris mee et parentum meorum in puram et perpetuam elemosinam. Ego eciam et heredes mei warantizabimus predictam donacionem fabrice ecclesie in omnibus et contra omnes homines imperpetuum. Et ut hec mea donacio firma et stabilis permaneat presenti carte sigillum meum apposui. Hiis testibus etc.

Margin *Roldeston'* in medieval hand; *Fabrica* in post-1583 hand as is title *Carta Thome filii Reginaldi de una acra* in left margin.

Date While Henry, son of Thomas of Rolleston was active, before the death of Hugh the dean and **241**.

Note The majority of donors in this small group of charters concerning Rolleston (**237–43**) seem to be otherwise unattested so that their relationship (with the exception of Benedict, son of Thomas of Rolleston, **243**) to the two knightly families who seem to have dominated the village in the late twelfth and early thirteenth centuries is unclear (cf. *Rufford*, cvi–cvii; *Thurgarton*, pp. 69–78). These charters also supply several field and other minor names not included in *EPNS Nottinghamshire*.

238 *Grant by Agnes, daughter of Hugh Lumbard of Rolleston, in her widowhood to the Fabric of eight strips of land and one acre of meadow in Rolleston* [*c.* 1200 × 1230]

Universis sancte matris ecclesie filiis hoc scriptum visuris vel audituris Agnes filia Hugonis Lumbard de Roldeston' salutem in salutis autore. Noverit universitas vestra me in viduitate et propria potestate mea consistentem in tuitu Dei et beate Marie et pro salute anime mee et pro animabus antecessorum meorum et heredum meorum concessisse, dedisse et hac presenti carta mea confirmasse Deo et fabrice ecclesie beate Marie de Suthwell' in puram et perpetuam elemosinam octo seliones terre arabilis in campis de Roldeston', scilicet, duas seliones que se extendunt super Padoc Pit et continent quinque perticatas in latitudine et sunt de feodo Henrici militis, et duas seliones eiusdem latitudinis et de eodem feodo in Aldehill', et duas seliones eiusdem latitudinis et de eodem feodo in Hillis et duas seliones eiusdem latitudinis et de eodem feodo in Winehalnaker', et unam acram prati in Seggesdale continentem ii perticatas et dimidiam in latitudine. Tenendum et habendum memorate ecclesie Suthwell' et assignatis eiusdem libere et quiete ab omni servicio seculari et exaccione imperpetuum. Ego vero Agnes et heredes mei warantizabimus predictas octo seliones terre arabilis et unam acram prati prenominatam sepe dicte ecclesie beate Marie Suthwell' contra omnes homines. Et ut hac mea donacio firma et stabilis permaneat imperpetuum eam presenti carte mee munimine et sigilli meo apposicione roboravi. Hiis testibus: Henrico filio Thome de Roldeston' etc.

Margin *Carta A. filie H. Lumbarde de dicta acra et aliis* in post-1583 hand in left margin and *8 seliones* in same hand lower down.

Date After **237** but before **241**.

Note Hugh le Lumbart witnessed the grant by Henry, son of Thomas of Rolleston, to Rufford *c*. 1190–1209 (*Rufford*, 308).

239 *Confirmation by Robert, son of Philip of Rolleston, to the Fabric of the grant that his mother, Agnes, made of eight strips of land and one acre of meadow in Rolleston* [*c*. 1200 × 1230]

Omnibus sancte matris ecclesie filiis hoc scriptum visuris vel audituris Robertus filius Philippi de Roldeston' salutem. Noveritis me in tuitu Dei et pro salute anime mee et pro animabus matris et patris mee et antecessorum et heredum meorum concessisse et confirmasse Deo et fabrice ecclesie beate Marie Suthwell' donacionem quam Agnes, mater mea, fecit predicte ecclesie Suthwell', scilicet, octo seliones terre arabilis in campis de Roldeston' de feodo Henrici militis, videlicet, duas seliones que se extendunt super Paddokpro[1] et continent quinque perticatas in latitudine et duas seliones eiusdem latitudinis in Aldehill', et duas seliones eiusdem latitudinis in Hillis et duas seliones eiusdem latitudinis et de eodem feodo in Winehalnaker, et unam acram prati in Seggesdale continentem ii perticatas et dimidiam in latitudine. Tenendum et habendum memorate ecclesie Suthwell' in puram et perpetuam elemosinam libere et quiete ab omni servicio seculari, exaccione et demanda. Ego Robertus et heredes mei warantizabimus Deo et sepe dicte ecclesie prefatas octo seliones terre arabilis et prenominatam acram prati contra omnes homines. Et ut hac mea donacio et confirmacio rata stet et stabilis in futurum presenti carte mee sigillum apposui. Hiis testibus: Henrico filio Thome et aliis.

[1] MS *sic*

Margin *Carta Roberti filii Philippi de Roldeston* in post-1583 hand in left margin.

Date After **238**.

Note This is the only mention of Robert and his father currently known.

240 *Grant by Agnes, daughter of Hugh Lumbard of Rolleston, in her own power and widowhood, to the Fabric of four strips of land and one acre of meadow in Rolleston* [*c*. 1200 × 1230]

Omnibus Christi fidelibus hoc scriptum visuris vel audituris Agnes filia p. 150

Hugonis Lumbard' de Roldeston' salutem. Noverit universitas vestra quod ego in propria[1] potestate et viduitate et per concessionem heredum meorum concessi et dedi et hac presenti carta mea confirmavi Deo et fabrice ecclesie sancte Marie de Suthwell' duas seliones terre arabilis que continent quinque [. . .][2] in campis de Roldeston' que se extendunt super sicham que vocatur Padokpitt et duas seliones super Aldehill' et unam acram prati in Seggesdale que continet duas perticatas et dimidiam in latitudine pro salute anime mee et patris et matris mee et parentum meorum in puram et perpetuam elemosinam. Et ego Agnes et heredes mei warantizabimus predictam elemosinam fabrice[3] ecclesie de Suthwell' in omnibus et contra omnes homines. Et ut hec mea donacio firma et stabilis permaneat imposterum presenti carte sigillum meum apposui. Hiis testibus: domino Henrico filio Thome de Roldeston', Willelmo clerico, et aliis.

[1] Followed by *viduitate* struck out   [2] A phrase like *perticatas in latitudine* missing from text; cf. **238**   [3] MS followed by *terre* struck out

Margin   *Roldeston'. . . Fabrica* at head of page in same hands as on p. 149. *Carta Agnetis filie Hugonis Lumbard'* in same hand as text in right margin.

Date   As **238**.

Note   Henry, son of Thomas of Rolleston, appears here with the title *dominus* suggesting that he had been knighted since the issue of **238**.

241   *Acknowledgement by Andrew of Rolleston that he owes the Fabric 4d annual rent for four strips of land and two acres of meadow in Rolleston which Southwell has of the gifts of Agnes, daughter of Hugh Lumbard, and Thomas son of Reginald*   [*c.* 1200 × 1230]

Omnibus hoc scriptum visuris vel audituris Andreas de Roldeston' salutem in domino. Noveritis me et heredes meos teneri ad solvendum annuatim fabrice ecclesie beate Marie Suthwell' in assumpcione eiusdem virginis quatuor denarios pro quatuor seliones terre arabilis in campo de Roldeston' et duabus acris prati in Seggesdale in territorio eiusdem ville quas teneo de memorata ecclesia Suthwell' et quas eadem ecclesia habet ex dono et feoffamento Agnetis filie Hugonis Lumbard' et Thome filii Riginaldi. Ego vero Andreas tactis sacrosanctis iuravi quod predictos quatuor denarios solvam fideliter fabrice prenominate ecclesie ad prescriptum terminum et heredes mei vel assignati mei similiter facient cum predicte terre ad ipsos fuerint devolute. In cuius rei testimonium presenti scripto sigillum meum apposui. Hiis testibus: Hugone decano, magistro Rogero de Soureby et aliis etc.

Margin   *Carta Andree de Roldeston'* in same hand as text in right margin.

Date   After **238**.

Note   Andrew of Rolleston witnessed a grant to Rufford 1220–36 (*Rufford*, 311). Mr Roger of Sowerby, prebendary of South Muskham (1210–after 1222).

242 *Acknowledgement by William, son of Thomas of Staythorpe, that he owes 2d annual rent to the Fabric for two strips of land in Rolleston which Thomas, son of Reginald of Rolleston gave* [c. 1200 × 1230]

Omnibus Christi fidelibus hoc scriptum visuris vel audituris Willelmus filius Thome de Starthorpp' eternam in domino salutem. Noveritis me teneri ad solvendum annuatim fabrice ecclesie sancte Marie Suthwellie in assumpcione eiusdem virginis duos denarios pro duabus selionibus terre arabilis continentibus quinque rodas terre in campo de Roldeston' super Hillis quas teneo de dicta ecclesia et quas eadem ecclesia Suthwell' habet de dono Thome filio Riginaldi de Roldeston'. Hanc autem solucionem sepe dicte ecclesie fideliter faciendum annuatim ad terminum prescriptum. Ego Willelmus tactis sacrosanctis iuravi coram predicto capitulo ecclesie, et heredes vel assignati mei similiter facient cum predicte due seliones ad ipsos fuerint devolute. In cuius rei testimonium presenti scripto sigillum meum apposui. Hiis testibus: Hugone decano, magistro Rogero et aliis etc.

Margin *Carta Willelmi filii Thome de Starthorpp* in same hand as text in right margin.

Date After **237**.

Note Is William to be identified with the William of Staythorpe who exchanged two strips in Kelham with Rufford abbey in the mid-thirteenth century (*Rufford*, 276)?

243 *Grant and quitclaim by Benedict, son of Thomas of Rolleston, to the Chapter of Roger, son of William of Rolleston, his bondsman, for which the Chapter gave him four marks* [1242 × 1256]

Sciant presentes et futuri quo ego Benedictus filius Thome de Roldeston' dedi, concessi et quietum clamavi de me et heredibus meis imperpetuum Rogerum filium Willelmi de Roldeston', nativum meum, et totam sequelam suam et omnia catalla sua que habet vel adquirere poterit ubicunque fuerint[1] et eciam totum ius et clameum quod habui vel habere potui in corpore suo vel in sequela sua vel in catallis suis capitulo beate Marie Suthwell' in perpetuam libertatem. Ita quod nec ego nec heredes mei de cetero in dicto Rogero vel in eius sequela nec in catallis aliquod ius vel clameum nobis possimus vendicare. Pro hac autem donacione, concessione et quieto clameo dedit mihi predictum capitulum quatuor marcas argenti premanibus. Et ne ego vel heredes mei predictam donacionem, concessionem et quietam clamacionem imposterum venire possimus aliquo modo presenti scripto pro me et heredibus meis sigillum meum apposui. Hiis testibus: domino Galfrido de Stok', milite, [et] aliis.

[1] Followed by *invenienta* struck out

Margin *Carta \Benedicti filii/ Thome de Roldeston de nativo et eius sequela cum bonis* in post-1583 hand in right margin.

Date While Benedict, son of Thomas of Rolleston was active and before he became a knight after 1256 (*Thurgarton*, 112n).

Note There was also a Benedict the parson of Rolleston (**511**) when Andrew of Southwell was bailiff of Southwell. A Geoffrey of Stoke witnessed a grant of Hugh fitz Ralph to William Lupus 1224–32 (*Rufford*, 516).

SOUTHWELL, BURGAGE, 244–65

p. 151   **Burg'**   **Suthwell'**   **fabrica**

244   *Space left for a grant of John Augre of six tofts in the Burgage to the Fabric, as noted in the left margin:*

Istud spacium relinquitur pro carta Johannis Augre de vi toftis in burgagio per ipsum datis fabrice

Margin   Heading *Suthwell'* centred in bold, as on most following pages to p. 172, with *Burg'* in same late medieval hand (Scribe 4) to left, and *fabrica* in early modern hand to right.

Note   For John de Auger/Augre see **256n**, and for other missing charters of his, see **267, 270, 273**.

245   *Notification by Mr Gilbert of Eaton, clerk, that he holds six tofts of the Fabric from John de Auger for life for 7s rent per annum*

7 July 1274

Noverint universi presens scriptum inspecturi quod cum ego magister Gilbertus de Eton' clericus sex tofta tenerem in burgo Suthwell' fabrice ecclesie beate Marie eiusdem burgi a Johanne de Augre in liberam elemosinam collata tandem advertens ius ipsius ecclesie in eisdem totum ius et clameum quod in eisdem habui vel aliquo modo habere potui capitulo ecclesie predicte dimisi et quietum clamavi prout carta mea deinde confecta plenius continetur. Idem vero capitulum habita diucius seisina de eisdem pacificata ad instanciam amicorum ipsa tofta mihi concessit tenenda[1] ad vitam meam reddendo inde annuatim custodibus dicte fabrice vii s. sterlingorum medietatem scilicet ad festum sancti Martini in yeme et aliam medietatem ad Pentecosten ita videlicet quod si infra octavum alicuius terminorum eorumdem firmam ipsam non solvero custos dicte ecclesie qui pro tempore fuerit ipsa tofta ingrediatur libere et dicte fabrice commode inde faciat secure mea vel alterius cuiuslibet contradiccione vel impedimento nullatenus obstante. In cuius rei testimonium sigillum meum presenti apposui. Datum anno domini m° cc lxx° quarto vi kalendas Augusti.

[1] MS *sic*

Margin   *Carta Gilb. Eton de 6. toftis supradictis* in left margin in 17th-c. hand.

Notes   For Mr Gilbert of Eaton see **261n**.

246   *Grant and quitclaim by Mr Gilbert of Eaton to the Fabric of all the right he has, by the gift of his mother or by lease of Agnes de Auger, in six tofts in Southwell with which it was enfeoffed by John de Auger as attested in Gilbert's charters*   [1250 × 1274]

Omnibus Christi fidelibus ad quos presens scriptum pervenerit magister Gilbertus de Eton' salutem in domino sempiteram. Noveritis me dedisse concessisse et omnino quietum clamasse pro me et heredibus meis imperpetuum totum ius et clamium si quod habui de dono matris mee aut ex dimissione Agnetis de Aug' vel aliqua alia racione habere potui in sex toftis in burgo Suthwell' Deo beate Marie et fabrice ecclesie beate Marie de Suthwell' de quibus dicta fabrica fuit feoffata per Johannem Augre prout carte mee testantur ita quod nec ego Gilbertus nec aliquis nomine meo de cetero poterimus in dictis toftis aliquid exigere vel vendicare. In cuius rei testimonium presenti scripto sigillum meum apposui. Hiis testibus: magistro Petro de Radenowr' et aliis.

Margin   *Eiusdem Gilb. quieti clamatio* in left margin in 17th-c. hand.

Date   After **261** and before **245**.

Note   On 3 November 1271 Richard, son of Ralph of Nottingham, and Alice, his wife, by their attorney, Roger de Suthcote, and Sewall Brien, by his attorney, Gilbert of Eaton, made a final concord concerning one croft in Nottingham (TNA, CP 25/1/183/13).

Southwell'   **Burg'**   p. 152

247   *Lease and quitclaim by William of Eaton to the Fabric of six tofts in Southwell with which it was enfeoffed by John de Auger as attested in William's charters*   [1274 × 1286]

Omnibus Christi fidelibus ad quos presens scriptum pervenerit Willelmus de Eton' salutem in domino sempiternam. Noveritis me dimississe concessisse et quietum clamasse pro me et heredibus meis imperpetuum Deo et fabrice ecclesie beate Marie Suthwell' pro salute anime mee et antecessorum meorum totum ius et clameum si quod habui vel habere potui in sex toftis in burgo Suthwell' de quibus dicta fabrica fuit feoffata per Johannem de Augre prout carte mee testantur ita quod nec ego Willelmus nec aliquis nomine meo poterimus in dictis toftis aliquid iuris exigere vel vendicare. In cuius rei testimonium presenti scripto sigillum meum apposui. Hiis testibus: magistro Henrico de Skypton' archidiacono Notingh' etc.

Margin   *W. Eton de ii den' 6 cot. quieti clamo* in right margin in 17th-c. hand.

Date   After **245** and **246** and before the death of Henry of Skipton, archdeacon of Nottingham.

248   *Grant and quitclaim by Walter of Eaton, with the consent of Petronilla, his wife, to the Fabric of two tofts in Southwell sometime of Hugh the Fleming*   [mid-13th century]

Sciant presentes et futuri quod ego Walterus de Eton' assensu et consensu Petronille uxoris mee et heredum meorum dedi concessi et hac presenti carta mea confirmavi et quietum clamavi Deo et fabrice ecclesie beate Marie Suthwell' pro salute anime mee et antecessorum meorum totum ius et clameum quod habui vel habere potui in duobus toftis in burgagio Suthwellie in Fildingate que quondam fuerunt Hugonis Flandrens' ita quod nec ego nec heredes mei nec aliquis per nos in dictis toftis aliquid iuris vel clamei decetero habere poterimus vel nobis vendicare. Tenend' et habend' dicte fabrice libere quiete integre et pacifice imperpetuum faciend' servicium domino feodi quantum pertinet ad dicta tofta. Et ut hec mea donacio concessio et quieta clamacio et carte mee confirmacio rata et stabilis permaneat imperpetuum presenti scripto sigillum meum apposui. Hiis testibus: Johanne de Augustin', Galfrido scissore et aliis.

Margin *Carta Walt' de 2 cotagiis* in right margin in 17th-c. hand.

Date Hugh the Fleming was active in the 1220s and 1230s (**431, 434, 509, 566**) thus after his death, and Geoffrey the tailor (*scissore*) occurs 1235–49 (**414, 530**).

249 *Grant and quitclaim by Petronilla, wife of Walter of Eaton, of two tofts in Southwell sometime of Hugh the Fleming* [mid-13th century]

Sciant presentes et futuri quod ego Petronilla uxor Walteri de Eton' bona voluntate mea assensu et consensu heredum meorum dedi concessi et quietum clamavi Deo et fabrice ecclesie beate Marie Suthwell' pro salute anime mee et antecessorum meorum totum ius et clameum quod habui vel habere potui in duobus toftis in burgo Suthwell' in Fildingate que quondam fuerunt Hugonis Flandrens'[1] ita quod nec ego nec heredes mei nec aliquis per nos in dictis toftis aliquid iuris vel clamei de cetero habere poterimus vel nobis vendicare. Habend' et tenend' dicte fabrice libere quiete integre et pacifice imperpetuum faciend' inde servicium domino feodi quantum pertinet ad predicta tofta. Et ut hec mea donacio concessio et quieta clamacio firma et stabilis permaneat imperpetuum presenti scripto sigillum meum apposui. Hiis testibus: Johanne etc. et aliis.

[1] MS followed by *ita quod* in another hand crossed through

Margin *Carta Petronille eius relicte de iii d.* in right margin in 17th-c. hand.

Date After **248**.

250 *Grant in free alms by Botilda at the Gate End of Southwell to the Fabric of the third part of one toft in Southwell* [1249 × 1267]

Omnibus Christi fidelibus presens scriptum visuris vel audituris Botilda ad le Gatehende de Suthwell' salutem in domino. Noveritis me in libera viduitate mea pro salute anime mee patris et matris parentum amicorum antecessorum et successorum et omnium benefactorum meorum dedisse concessisse et hac presenti carta mea confirmasse Deo et fabrice ecclesie beate Marie Suthwell' terciam partem unius tofti in burgo Suthwell' iacentem propinquius iuxta toftum quod fuit quondam Mille cum omnibus suis pertinenciis et aisiamentis. Tenend' et habend' dicte fabrice quiete pacifice et honorifice in liberam puram et perpetuam elemosinam. Et ego Botilda et heredes mei dicte fabrice dictam partem tofti prout predictum est contra omnes gentes warantizabimus et defendemus imperpetuum. Ut hec autem donacio concessio et presenti carte confirmacio | rata et stabilis imperpetuum permaneat huic scripto sigillum meum apposui. Hiis testibus: dominis Ricardo de Sutton', Henrico de Mora, Riginaldo[1] de Stouwra et aliis.

p. 153

[1] MS *sic*

Margin   *Carta Botilde de 3º parte tofti* in right margin in 17th-c. hand.

Date   After Henry de Mora had become a canon and before the death of Reginald of Stowe (*Reg. Giffard*, 23).

Note   The name clearly written in the MS as *Mille* is unusual; is it a version of Matilda?

Burg'   **Suthwell'**   **fabrice**

251   *Grant in free alms by Robert of Laxton to the Fabric of 18d rent per annum owing from Robert le Verer*   [*c.* 1236 × before 29 May 1250]

Omnibus sancte matris ecclesie filiis ad quos hoc presens scriptum pervenerit. Robertus de Lesington' salutem eternam in domino. Noverit universitas vestra me in tuitu Dei et pro salute anime mee dedisse concessisse et hac presenti carta mea confirmasse Deo et beate Marie et fabrice ecclesie Suthwell' octodecim denariatas redditus quas Robertus le Verer mihi annuatim reddere consuevit in ville Suthwell'. Habend' et tenend' in liberam elemosinam imperpetuum. Et ut hec mea donacio concessio et carte mee confirmacio robur perpetue firmitatis habeat presenti scripto sigillum meum apposui. Hiis testibus: Thoma de Bella Aqua etc.

Margin   Page heading as p. 151. *Carta Rob. de Lesington de annuo red. 18ᵈ* in left margin in 17th-c. hand with *18d p. a* lower down.

Date   While Thomas de Bella Aqua was active (**412n**). Matthew Paris reports that Robert of Laxton died on 29 May 1250 (*Chron. Majora*, v, 138).

Note   The surname Le Verer (glazier or glass worker) is well attested in medieval England, and in the 1230s and 1240s glaziers were important at Southwell for the construction and, presumably, glazing of the new Early English choir.

252   *Grant by Hubert de Barra to the Fabric of part of his toft*
[*c.* 1210 × 1230]

Universis sancte matris ecclesie filiis hoc scriptum visuris vel audituris Hubertus de Barra salutem in domino. Noverit universitas vestra me pro salute anime mee et uxoris mee et parentum meorum concessisse et dedisse Deo et fabrice ecclesie beate Marie Suthwell' quandam partem tofti mei versus occidentem iuxta grangiam beate Marie in puram et perpetuam elemosinam scilicet in latitudine triginta pedum in longitudine quantum toftum meum extendit extransverso a tofto Roberti le Ferrum usque ad venellam. Quare volo quod predicta ecclesia habeat et teneat libere et pacifice predictam terram ab omni exaccione quietam. Et ne ista mea concessio imposterum possit in irritum revocari huius scripti testimonio et sigilli mei apposicione roboravi. Hiis testibus: Hugone decano Suthwell', Rogero de Souresby et aliis.

Margin   *Carta Huberti de Barra pro parte tofti* in left margin in 17th-c. hand.

Date   After Roger of Sowerby became a canon (certainly by 1219) and before the death of Hugh the dean.

253 *Quitclaim by Agnes, widow of John Pierrepont of Kirkby, to the Fabric of one toft in Southwell that she had of the gift of Thomas of Laneham for which the wardens of the Fabric gave 10s and received her and John, her husband, into fraternity* [1262 × 1286]

Omnibus sancte matris ecclesie filiis ad quos presens scriptum pervenerit Agnes relicta Johannis Perpount de Kyrkeby salutem. Noveritis me concessisse imperpetuum in pura viduitate mea quietum clamasse beate Marie et fabrice ecclesie de Suthwell' totum ius et clameum quod habui vel habere potui nomine hereditarie dotis vel alterius alicuius accionis in uno tofto cum pertinenciis suis in burgo Suthwell' quod habui de dono et feoffamento Thome de Lanum' \eius tenentes/ scilicet Willelmum Symmuoch' et Matild' uxorem suam de eodem tenemento[1] implacitavi per breve regis coram iusticiariis ita quod nec ego Agnes nec heredes mei nec aliquis per nos ius vel clameum in dicto tofto cum pertinenciis decetero exigere vel vendicare poterimus. Pro hac autem donacione et quieta clamacione dederunt mihi custodes ecclesie et fabrice predictarum decem solidos premanibus et me et Johannem maritum meum in fraternitate eiusdem receperunt. In cuius rei testimonium huic presenti scripto sigillum meum apposui. Hiis testibus: magistro Henrico de Schypton' et aliis.

[1] MS followed by *capitulum ecclesie predicte* crossed through and dotted for deletion

Margin *Agnetis Pierpont de tofto quiti clamo* in left margin in 17th-c. hand, with *Thoroton p 265* (modern, pencil) and then *queratur pro recordo placiti infrascripti* (medieval) below.

Date After John Pierrepont ceased being active (*Thurgarton*, 513–15) and before the death of Henry of Skipton.

Note Another quitclaim of land in Kirkby by Agnes as John's widow, and of roughly the same date, is in *Thurgarton*, 514.

Suthwell' **Burg'**

254 *Release and quitclaim by Richard, son of John le Skinner of South-well, to Richard Fulcher of Southwell and Felicia, his wife, of one mes-suage in Southwell that they have of the gift of William, son of Thomas called Baker of Southwell* Southwell, 28 July 1323

Omnibus Christi fidelibus hoc scriptum visuris vel audituris Ricardus filius Johannis le Skynner' de Suthwell' salutem in domino sempiternam. Noveritis me de me et heredibus meis relaxasse et imperpetuum quietum clamasse Ricardo Fulcher' de Suthwell' et Felicie uxori sue et assignatis eorum totum ius et clameum meum quod habui vel quoquo modo habere potui in uno mesuagio cum pertinenciis iacente in burgo Suthwell' iuxta mesuagium Willelmi de Walborue et quod quidem mesuagium dictus Ricardus et Felicia habent de dono et feoffamento Willelmi filii Thome dicti pistoris de Suthwell' ita quod nec ego Ricardus filius Johannis le Skynner' nec heredes mei nec aliquis nomine nostro etc. In cuius rei testimonium etc. Datum apud Southwell' die jovis proximo post festum sancti Jacobi apostoli anno regni regis Edwardi filii regis Edwardi septimo decimo.

Margin   Top of page as p. 152. In right margin: *Ricardus filius*/ *Jo.**le*/ *Skynner* *de Southwell*/ *de mess. in burgo quieti clam*^{o} in 17th-c. hand.

255   *Release and quitclaim by Thomas of Blyth to John son of Felicia and Thomas, his brother, of one messuage with buildings in Southwell*

Southwell, 30 July 1329

Pateat universis per presentem quod ego Thomas de Blythe relaxavi et omnino pro me et heredibus meis quietum clamavi Johanni filio Felice[1] et Thome fratri suo et eorum heredibus et eorum assignatis totum ius et clameum quod habeo habui vel aliquo modo habere potero in futurum in uno mesuagio cum edificiis suprapostitis iacente in burgo Suthwell' inter mesuagium Roberti le Wryght' ex una parte et mesuagium Willelmi de Walborue ex altera parte ita quod nec ego Thomas de Blyth' nec heredes mei nec aliquis pro me seu nomine meo etc. In cuius rei testimonium etc. Datum apud Suthwell' die dominica proximo post festum sancti Jacobi apostoli anno regni regis Edwardi tercii post conquestum tercio.

[1] MS *sic*

Margin   *Tho. de Blyth de eodem quieti clam*^{o} in right margin in 17th-c. hand.

256   *Grant and quitclaim by Matilda de Burbeck to John de Auger and Agnes, his wife, of one burgage plot in Southwell for 2s rent per annum paid to the archbishop of York*   [1226 × 1249]

Omnibus ad quos presens scriptum pervenerit[1] Matill' de Burbeck' salutem eternam in domino. Noverit universitas vestra me dedisse concessisse et de me et heredibus meis imperpetuum quietum clamasse Johanni de Augre et Agneti uxori sue et heredibus suis vel cuicumque dare vendere legare vel assignare voluerint sive in prosperitate sive in egritudine unum burgagium cum pertinenciis in villa de Suthwell' scilicet illud quod iacet inter burgagium Rogeri Haraz et burgagium Roberti Gaynok'. Tenend' et habend' predictis Johanni et Agneti et heredibus suis vel cuicumque assignare voluerint ut predictum est adeo libere et quiete sicut illud umquam liberius tenui cum omnibus pertinenciis libertatibus et aisiamentis ad predictum burgagium pertinentibus infra villam et extra ita scilicet quod nec ego Matill' nec heredes mei nec aliquis pro nobis vel per nos ius vel clameum de cetero erga predictum burgagium exigere poterimus reddendo inde annuatim domino archiepiscopo ii s. argenti tamen scilicet medietatem ad Pentecosten et medietatem ad festum sancti Martini in yeme pro omni servicio et exaccione seculari. In huius autem rei robur et testimonium presenti scripto sigillum meum apponere dignum duxi. Hiis testibus: domino Willelmo de Wedyndon' etc.

[1] MS followed by *salutem* crossed through and dotted for deletion

Margin   *Matilda de Burbeck de uno mess. quieti clam*^{o} in right margin in 17th-c. hand.

Date   After William of Widdington was granted land in Southwell and before his death.

Note   Matilda de Burbeck was named in the pipe roll of 34 Henry III (1249/50) (pd. in

Yeatman, *Feudal History of the County of Derby*, 217). Agnes de Burbeck was perhaps a daughter or sister of Matilda. The charters in which John de Auger (Augre) is either mentioned or appears as witness have extreme limits of 1219 to 1252 (**265, 569**), thus he would be a contemporary of William of Widdington. John witnessed one charter as serjeant of Southwell (**398**) and two as bailiff of Southwell (**395, 565**). When he held the office of bailiff is difficult to determine precisely; **565** cannot be dated to before 27 November 1235 and Thomas of Treswell was bailiff sometime in the period 1235–41 (**400**). On 29 October 1238 Richard was bailiff of Southwell when he was allowed ten marks which he delivered to John de Auger, and Roger of Osberton (**392n**) had ceased being bailiff by 10 January 1247 when he was described as Archbishop Gray's 'former bailiff' (*Reg. Gray*, 257–8). It would seem that John was bailiff after Richard but before Roger of Osberton and that he held the office of serjeant in the period 1241–9 (**398**) after being bailiff, unless he had more than one term of office. On balance the evidence would suggest that he was bailiff from after 1235 but before 1247, probably 1238–c. 1241 with, perhaps, a conjectural second term 1247–c. 1252, that is, after Roger of Osberton and before Sewal, bailiff from c. 1250 (**403, 412**). In an undated entry in Archbishop Gray's register, probably September 1235, John de Auger had been granted the dower lands of Alice of Sproxton (Yorks.) for he was allowed the seed sown on the land when Gray gave Alice the custody of her son, William, and the land in Beverley and South Burton (Yorks.) of his father William of Carthorpe (*Reg. Gray*, 246, 252–3). John de Auger (*de Augii*) witnessed (1241–9) the notification by Southwell of the grant made by Henry of Southwell (*Rufford*, 36).

257   *Confirmation by Matilda de Burbeck in her free widowhood to the Fabric of the gift of John de Auger of one bovate of land and two tofts in Southwell that she bought from Lecia, daughter of Ranulph of Bradley*
[mid-13th century]

Omnibus Christi fidelibus hoc scriptum visuris vel audituris Matill' de Burbek' salutem. Noverit universitas vestra me in libera viduitate et propria potestate mea concessisse de me et heredibus meis imperpetuum Deo et fabrice ecclesie beate Marie Suthwell' donacionem quam fecit Johannes de Auger' Deo et dicte fabrice ecclesie unius bovate terre quam quondam emi de Lecia filia Ranulphi de Bradleg' et duorum toftorum in burgo Suthwell'. Tenend' et habend' dicte fabrice imperpetuum sicut continetur in carta quam custodes dicte fabrice habent penes se de dono dicti Johannis de Augre ita quod nec ego Matill' nec heredes mei nec aliquis per nos vel pro nobis aliquid iuris vel clamii de cetero in dictis bovata terre et toftis poterimus exigere vel nobis vendicare. In cuius rei testimonium etc. Hiis testibus: Roberto de Barra etc.

Margin   *Relax° i bovat' terre et ii toft' quondam J. Augre* in right margin, with signum of a hand *nota bene*, all in 17th-c. hand.

Date   After **256** and see **271**.

258   *Release and quitclaim by Matilda, widow of William Mynnot of Southwell, in her lawful widowhood to Sir Robert of Morton and Sir Henry Ketell, wardens of the Fabric, of messuages and tenements in Southwell that William Mynnot sometime held*   Southwell, 3 August 1322

Pateat universis per presentem quod ego Matill' relicta Willelmi Mynnot de Suthwell' in legia viduitate concessi remisi relaxavi et omnino quietum

clamavi capitulo et fabrice ecclesie Suthwell' ac dominis Roberto de
Morton' [et] Henrico Ketell', custodibus fabrice ecclesie predicte, totum
ius et clameum quod habui vel habere potui in mesuagiis et tenementis
| aliis que et quod dictus Willelmus Mynnot quondam tenuit in burgo   p. 155
Suthwell' ita quod nec ego Matill' nec heredes mei nec aliquis nomine
meo aliquod ius vel clameum in dictis mesuagiis et tenementis vel aliqua
parte eorumdem de cetero exigere vel vendicare poterimus imperpetuum.
In cuius rei testimonium huic presenti quiete clamacione sigillum meum
apposui. Hiis testibus: domino Willelmo de Hokerton' et aliis. Datum
apud Suthwell' iii nonas Augusti anno domini m° ccc° vicesimo secundo.

Margin   *Matilda Minot de mess. et aliis in burg' quieti clamatio* in right margin in
17th-c. hand.

259   *Grant by the Chapter to William son of Mynnot and Matilda Kaue
of Hockerton of the third part of one toft in Southwell sometime held by
Nicholas Parker for 2s rent per annum paid to the Fabric*
[before 3 August 1322]

Universis Christi fidelibus hoc scriptum visuris vel audituris capitulum
ecclesie beate Marie Suthwell' salutem in domino sempiternam. Noverit
universitas vestra nos dedisse concessisse et hac presenti carta nostra
confirmasse Willelmo filio Mynnot et Matild' Kaue de Hokerton' terciam
partem eiusdem tofti in burgo Suthwell' quod quondam fuit Nicholai Parker
iacentem immediate iuxta illam partem quam quidem dicti Willelmus et
Matild' de nobis nomine fabrice ecclesie nostre Suthwell' et tenent ex parte
australi. Tenend' et habend' sibi et heredibus suis vel assignatis de nobis
libere quiete pacifice et honorifice in feodo et hereditate imperpetuum
reddendo fabrice ecclesie nostre Suthwell' annuatim duos solidos ad
duos anni terminos videlicet ad festum sancti Martini in yeme xii d. et
ad Pentecosten xii d. pro omni servicio seculari consuetudine exaccione
et demanda ad nos spectante salvo forinseco sicut alii vicini faciunt. In
huius rei testimonium etc. Hiis testibus: etc.

Margin   *Carta Capituli de 3. parte tofti in burg* in left margin in 17th-c. hand.

Date   Before **258**, probably by some years, possibly soon after **260**?

260   *Grant by the Chapter to Hugh, son of Robert at Cross, of the third
part of one toft in Southwell that Nicholas the parker sometime held for
3s rent per annum paid to the Fabric*   [1249 × 1261]

Omnibus Christi fidelibus hoc scriptum visuris vel audituris capitulum
beate Marie Suthwell' salutem in domino. Noveritis nos dedisse concessisse
et hac presenti carta nostra confirmasse Hugoni filio Roberti ad crucem
terciam partem cuiusdam tofti in burgo Suthwell' quod Nicholaus parcarius
quondam tenuit incipientem a tofto Gervasii fabri et tendentem usque
ad toftum Hugonis Baw. Tenend' et habend'¹ sibi [et] heredibus suis vel
assignatis suis et eorum heredibus libere quiete in feodo et hereditate
reddendo inde annuatim tres solidos et duos denarios fabrice ecclesie
videlicet ad festum sancti Martini in yeme xix d. et ad Pentecosten xix

d. pro omni servicio seculari exaccione et demanda salvo forinseco. In cuius rei testimonium sigillum capituli nostri fecimus apponi. Hiis testibus: domino Henrico de Mora etc.

¹ MS *et habend'* repeated

Margin *Carta Capituli de 3 parte tofti in burgo* in left margin in 17ᵗʰ-c. hand.

Date After Henry de Mora had become a canon and he was still active *c.* 1261.

261 *Grant and quitclaim by Hugh, son of Robert at Cross of Southwell, to Mr Gilbert of Eaton of one messuage in Southwell that Nicholas the parker sometime held for 3s rent per annum paid to the Fabric*
[1274 × 1282]

Omnibus sancte matris ecclesie filiis hoc scriptum visuris vel audituris Hugo filius Roberti ad crucem de Suthwell' salutem in domino sempiternam. Noveritis me dedisse concessisse quietum clamasse et hac presenti carta mea confirmasse magistro Gilberto de Eton' et heredibus suis vel assignatis suis quibuscumque totum ius et clameum quod habui vel habere potui in uno mesuagio in burgo Suthwell' illo¹ videlicet quod quidem Nicholaus parcarius quondam tenuit et quod quidem capitulum beate Marie Suthwell' mihi dedit concessit et sua carta confirmavit iacente inter toftum quondam Gervasii fabri et toftum Hugonis Bau fine viam regiam que dicitur Fildingate. Tenend' et habend' sibi et heredibus suis vel assignatis suis et eorum heredibus quibuscumque dare legare vendere vel assignare voluerit tam in egritudine quam in prosperitate libere quiete integre pacifice in feodo et hereditate imperpetuum reddendo inde annuatim fabrice ecclesie eiusdem tres solidos et duos denarios ad duos terminos anni videlicet ad festum sancti Martini in yeme novemdecim denarios et ad festum Pentecosten novemdecim denarios pro omni servicio seculari exaccione et demanda salvo forinseco si quod ad dictum mesuagium spectat. In cuius rei testimonium huic presenti carte sigillum meum apposui. Hiis testibus: domino Roberto de Burstall' et aliis.

¹ MS followed by *quidem* crossed through and dotted for deletion

Margin *H. ad cruc' de uno mess. in burgo quieti clam°* in left margin in 17ᵗʰ-c. hand.

Date While Mr Gilbert of Eaton was active from before 1274 (**245, 424, 515, 517**) and before the death of Robert III de Burstall (*Thurgarton*, cxxiv).

262 *Grant by the Chapter to Matilda of Hockerton, niece of the late John Edmund, chaplain, of the third part of one toft in Southwell sometime of Nicholas the parker for 2s rent per annum paid to the Fabric*
[early 14ᵗʰ century]

Universis etc. capitulum ecclesie beate Marie Suthwell' salutem in domino sempiternam. Noverit universitas vestra nos dedisse concessisse et hac presenti carta nostra confirmasse Matild' de Hokerton' quondam nepti¹ Johannis Edmundi capellani terciam partem cuiusdam tofti in burgo Suthwell' quod quondam fuit Nicholai parcarii que iacet inter toftum

Matild' quondam uxoris Gervasii ex parte australi et mesuagium Thome Barnfader ex parte boriali. Tenend' et habend' de nobis in feodo et hereditate libere quiete pacifice et honorifice imperpetuum sibi et heredibus suis vel cuicumque dare assignare vendere vel legare quali hora et quando voluerit sive in prosperitate sive in egritudine reddendo inde annuatim fabrice ecclesie nostre de Suthwell' duos solidos argenti ad duos terminos anni | videlicet duodecim denarios ad festum sancti Martini in yeme et   p. 156 xii d. ad Pentecosten pro omni servicio seculari consuetudine exaccione secta curie et demanda ad nos spectante salvo forinseco. Pro hac autem donacione concessione et carte nostre confirmacione dedit nobis ad opus fabrice dicte ecclesie predicta Matild' unam marcam argenti premanibus. In cuius rei testimonium huic scripto sigillum nostrum fecimus apponi. Hiis testibus: Thoma le Veriuse et aliis.

¹ MS *sic* for *nepti quondam*, i.e. 'to the niece of the late John Edmund, chaplain'

Margin   *Carti Capituli de 3⁰ parte tofti in burgo* in left margin, with *2ᵈ annum* below, in 17ᵗʰ-c. hand.

Date   Perhaps at the same time as **259** as Matilda of Hockerton is probably the same woman as Matilda Kaue of Hockerton.

Suthwell' **Burg'**

263   *Grant by the Chapter to Hugh of Scrooby of the third part of one toft in Southwell that Nicholas the parker sometime held for 2s rent per annum paid to the Fabric*   [mid-13ᵗʰ century]

Omnibus Christi fidelibus hoc scriptum visuris vel audituris capitulum beate Marie Suthwell' salutem in domino. Noveritis nos dedisse concessisse et hac presenti carta nostra confirmasse Hugoni de Scroby terciam partem cuiusdam tofti in burgo Suthwell' quod Nicholaus parcarius quondam tenuit incipientem a tofto Roberti filii Dande et tendentem a via regia usque ad toftum Gervasii fabri. Tenendum et habendum sibi et heredibus suis vel suis assignatis et eorum heredibus libere quiete et pacifice in feodo et hereditate reddendo inde annuatim duos solidos fabrice ecclesie nostre videlicet ad festum sancti Martini in yeme xii d. et ad Pentecosten xii d. pro omni servicio seculari exaccione et demanda salvo forinseco. In cuius rei testimonium huic presenti scripto sigillum capituli nostri fecimus apponi. Hiis testibus: dominis Henrico de Mora, Ricardo de Lincoln' canonicis Suthwell' et aliis.

Margin   *Carta Capituli de 3⁰ parte tofti pred.* in right margin with *2ˢ annum* below, both in 17ᵗʰ-c. hand.

Date   Richard of Lincoln occurs as a canon from *c.* 1248 to the mid-1250s and Henry de Mora, canon from *c.* 1249–*c.*1261.

264   *Agreement in the form of a bipartite indenture between the Chapter and Henry Augustine, clerk, that the Chapter has leased at farm to him one plot with one house on it at the bar of Southwell for 10s rent per annum paid to the Fabric*   1295

Anno domini millesimo cc^{mo} nonagesimo quinto facta fuit ista convencio inter capitulum ecclesie beate Marie Suthwell' ex parte una et Henricum Augustin' clericum ex parte altera videlicet quod dictum capitulum concessit dimisit et ad firmam tradidit dicto Henrico et assignatis suis unam placeam spectantem ad fabricam ecclesie Suthwell' memorate iacentem in barra ut se extendit versus Halum que vocatur le Kyrkecrofte cum una domo supersita. Tenend' et habend' dictam placeam cum dicta domo sibi et assignatis suis usque ad terminum decem annorum plenarie completorum reddendo inde annuatim custodibus fabrice ecclesie memorate qui pro tempore fuerint decem solidos argenti ad duos anni terminos videlicet ad Pentecosten et ad festum sancti Martini in yeme pro equalibus porcionibus ita videlicet quod dictus Henricus sustinabit sepes clausuras arbores crescentes una cum dicta domo in equo bono statu quo et ipse recepit easdem adiectum est eciam huic convencioni quod si dictus Henricus in dicta solucione dicte fabrice custodibus terminis supranotatis facienda ultra quindenam quod absit deficere contigerit eo ipso cadat ab omni iure firme supranotate dictum vero capitulum dictam placeam una cum domo superedificata dicto Henrico et assignatis suis pro firma iam dicta usque ad terminum supranotatum contra omnes et in omnibus warantizabit acquietabit et defendet. In quorum omnium testimonium huic scripto in duas partes diviso partes alternatim sua sigilla apposuerunt. Hiis testibus: Ricardo de Normanton' et aliis.

Margin *Locatio placee per capitulum* in right margin in 17th-c. hand.

265 *Quitclaim by John, son of Elias of Bellerby, and Amicia, his wife, to John de Auger of two tofts in Southwell sometime of Hugh the Fleming for 2s rent per annum paid to the archbishop of York for which he gave fifteen marks* [1246 × 1250]

Sciant presentes et futuri quod ego Johannes filius Elie de Bellerby et Amicia uxor mea concessimus et quietum clamavimus totum ius et clamium quod habuimus vel habere poterimus in duobus toftis in burgo Suthwell' que quondam fuerunt Hugonis Flandrens' et que iacent inter toftum Rogeri filii Galfridi et toftum Radulphi Gannok' cum omnibus edificatis in predictis toftis positis[1] Johanni Augre et heredibus suis vel suis assignatis et eorum heredibus reddendo inde annuatim domino archiepiscopo duos solidos ad terminos consuetos. Et ego Johannes et Amicia uxor mea warantizabimus predicta tofta contra omnes qui de nobis possint defendere. Pro hac vero concessione et quieta clamacione dedit mihi dictus Johannes de Augre quindecim marcas argenti premanibus. In huius rei testimonium quia non habui sigillum proprium sigillum domini mei Elie de Ellerby huic scripto apposui. Hiis testibus: domino Jollano de Nevilla et aliis.

[1] MS *ponitis*

Margin *Johannis Bellarby et uxor' de 2. toftis quieti clam°* in left margin with *2^s annum* below in 17th-c. hand.

Date Perhaps Jollan de Neville, the well-known royal justice, who had succeeded his brother, John, in possession of lands in Rolleston by 1219, died before 5 October 1246, but more likely his son and heir, Jollan, who died between 12 November 1249 and 12 March 1250 (*EYC* v, 156–7; *ODNB online*: Henry Summerson, 'Neville, Jollan de (*d.* 1246)': http://www.oxforddnb.com/view/article/19948, accessed 7 May 2012).

This page is blank.   p. 157

SOUTHWELL, EASTHORPE, 266–82

Suthwell'   Esthorpp'   p. 158

266   *Grant by William, son of Lecia Tirry, to John de Auger of one bovate of land with meadow except his toft for 3s rent per annum for which he gave five marks*   [*c.* 1241 × 1247]

Sciant presentes et futuri quod ego Willelmus filius Lecie Tyrry dedi concessi et hac presenti carta mea confirmavi Johanni de Augre et heredibus suis vel cuicumque assignare dare vendere vel legare voluerit sive in prosperitate sive in egritudine unam bovatam terre cum prato ad illam bovatam terre pertinente et cum omnibus aliis pertinenciis suis preter toftum meum illam scilicet bovatam unde quatuor seliones iacent in Mortunstegh' prope terram Roberti de Barra et i selio in Mortongate et i selio inter terram Willelmi Scott et Willelmi predicatoris et i selio in Spiteldale et i selio in Dockyland' et i selio in Waterfurris et i selio iuxta Caldewell' et iii seliones abuttantes super Mortonbek' et i selio in Ryland' et i selio in Sywardakyr' et una cultura continens quinque acras iacet in Frithsyk' et i selio in Mylneholm' et ii seliones et dimidius in Esfurlang' et i selio in Clerkfurlang' et i selio super Brekhyll' et unus selio super Duneakr' et i selio super Clayhill'. Tenend' et habend' eidem Johanni et heredibus suis vel cuicumque assignare voluerit ut predictum est in feodo et hereditate de me et heredibus meis libere quiete integre plenarie et pacifice imperpetuum reddendo inde annuatim mihi et heredibus meis tres solidos argenti ad duos anni terminos scilicet decem et octo denarios ad festum sancti Martini et decem et octo denarios ad invencionem sancte crucis pro omni servicio seculari exaccione et demanda. Pro hac autem concessione dedit mihi predictus Johannes quinque marcas argenti pre manibus ad negocia mea expedienda. Et ego Willelmus et heredes mei ut supradictum est contra omnes homines warantizabimus et pro predicto servicio acquietabimus et defendemus imperpetuum. Et ut hec mea donacio et carte mee confirmacio rata et stabilis imposterum remaneat presenti carte sigillum meum in testimonium apposui. Hiis testibus: Roberto de Osberton tunc ballivo etc.

Margin   Page heading, Scribe 4. *Carta W. Tirry de una bovata terre et prato* in right margin with *18ᵈ annum* below in 17ᵗʰ-c. hand.

Date   While Robert (*recte* Roger) of Osberton was bailiff of Southwell (**256n, 392n**).

267 *Missing charter of John Auger granting land mentioned in* **266** *to the Fabric*

Margin In right margin: *Deficit carta Johanni Augr' de bovata terre predicta facta fabrice ecclesie predicte* (medieval).

p. 159 **Esthorpp'** **Suthwell'** **fabrica**

268 *Lease by the Chapter to Sir Robert of Morton and Sir Henry Ketell, priests, for their lives of one bovate of land with meadow in Easthorpe that the Chapter has of the gift of John de Auger for 12s rent per annum paid to the Fabric* Southwell, 10 July 1324

Universis presentes litteras inspecturis vel audituris capitulum ecclesie beate Marie Suthwell' eternam in domino salutem. Noveritis nos de unanimi fratrum nostrorum consensu concessisse et dimisisse dominis Roberto de Morton' et Henrico Ketell' presbyteris in ecclesia nostra Suthwell' vel eorum alteri qui diucius vixerit unam bovatam terre cum prato et suis pertinenciis universis in campo de Esthorp quam habuimus de dono pie memorie Johannis Augr'. Tenend' et habend' predictis domino Roberto et Henrico vel eorum alteri qui diucius vixerit \vel/ quam diu vixerint libere quiete integre et pacifice cum omnibus iuribus libertatibus asiamentis in pratis pascuis pasturis et aliis communis ad tantam terram infra villam et extra pertinentibus reddendo inde annuatim custodibus fabrice ecclesie nostre Suthwellie pro omnibus serviciis secularibus duodecim solidos argenti ad duos anni terminos videlicet medietatem ad festum sancti Martini in yeme et aliam medietatem ad Pentecosten sine retenemento aliquali. In cuius rei testimonium huic presenti scripto sigillum nostrum commune est appensum. Hiis testibus: magistro Nicholao de Oxon', dominis Willelmo de Newerk et Johanne de Monte Claro canonicis, dominis Willelmo de Hokerton' et Hugone Leuerik' commune canonicorum custodibus, Roberto Gervays et Johanne Godwyne vicariis et aliis. Datum in capitulo nostro Suthwell' vi idus Julii anno gracie millesimo ccc vicesimo quarto.

Margin Page heading, *Esthorpp'* and *Suthwell'* (Scribe 4), *fabrica* (17th c.). *Locatio dimidie bovate per capitulum* in left margin, 17th c.

Note Mr Nicholas of Oxford, prebendary of Oxton II (1310–d. by 18 January 1327); William of Newark, prebendary of North Muskham (1298–1340); John de Monte Claro, prebendary of Sacrista (1309–c. 1347), prosecuted in 1311 for non-residence, but in dispute with Newark over the farm of Edingley in 1314 when he claimed residence (*Reg. Greenfield*, i, nos 149 and 199).

269 *Grant by William, son of Lecia Tirry, to John de Auger of two and a half acres of land in Easthorpe for 1d rent per annum for which he gave one mark* [1230 × 1245]

Omnibus hanc cartam visuris vel audituris Willelmus filius Lecie Tyrry salutem in domino. Noverit universitas vestra me dedisse et hac carta mea confirmasse Johanni de Augr' et heredibus suis vel suis assignatis duas acras et dimidiam terre in campo de Esthorpp' cum omnibus pertinenciis quarum una roda et dimidia iacet in Dockyland' et i roda iacet iuxta Mortonstygh' et dimidia roda iacet iuxta Caldewell' et i roda in Ryland' et dimidia acra in Waterfurris et i roda in Holmis et i roda et dimidia in Esfurlang' et i roda et dimidia in Duneacr'. Tenend' et habend' eidem Johanni de Augr' et heredibus vel assignatis suis de me et heredibus meis libere quiete bene et integre ita quod nullus per me vel heredes meos de cetero in dicta terra aliquod vel clameum poterit vendicare vel exigere reddendo inde annuatim mihi et heredibus meis unum denarium ad Pascha pro omnibus. Et pro hac donacione et concessione et carte mee confirmacione dedit mihi dictus Johannes unam marcam argenti. Et ego Willelmus et heredes mei predictas duas acras et dimidiam cum pertinenciis dicto Johanni et heredibus vel assignatis suis contra omnes homines warantizabimus acquietabimus et defendemus ut predictum est. In cuius rei testimonium presenti carte sigilli mei munimine apposui. Hiis testibus: domino Willelmo de Eton' etc.

Margin   *Carta Will. Tirrie de 2 acr' et d terre in Esthorpe* in left margin in 17th-c. hand.

Date   Probably at a similar time to **280**.

270   *Space left for another charter of John Auger*

In bottom left margin: *Relinquitur spacium pro <alia> carta Johannis Augr' de ii acris terre et dimidia data fabrice etc.*

Suthwell'   **Esthorpp'**   p. 160

271   *Grant in hereditary fee by Lecia, daughter of Ranulph Bradley, widow of William of Rolleston, in her free widowhood to Matilda de Burbeck of one bovate of land in Easthorpe that Godwin held of her father for 5s rent per annum*   [1221 × 1244]

Sciant presentes et futuri quod ego \Lecia/ filia Ranulfi Bradleg' quondam uxor Willelmi de Rolueston' in libera viduitate mea et propria potestate corporis mei assensu et voluntate heredum meorum dedi et hac presenti carta mea confirmavi Matild' de Burbek' et heredibus suis vel cuicumque vendere assignare vel legare voluerit sive in prosperitate sive in egritudine pro homagio et servicio suo unam bovatam terre in teritorio de Esthorpp' cum omnibus pertinenciis infra villam et extra scilicet illam bovatam quam Godewynus tenuit de patre meo. Tenend' et habend' ipsi Matild' et heredibus suis vel cuicumque assignare voluerit sicut predictum est in feodo et hereditate de me et heredibus meis vel successoribus meis libere quiete integre et pacifice reddendo inde annuatim mihi et heredibus meis vel successoribus meis quinque solidos per annum pro omni servicio seculari exaccione et demanda salvo forinseco servicio scilicet ad festum sancti Martini in yeme duos solidos et sex denarios et ad festum sancte crucis in estate duos solidos et vi d. Et ego Lecia et heredes mei vel successores mei warantizabimus predictam bovatam terre cum omnibus suis pertinenciis dicte Matild' et heredibus suis vel cuicumque voluerit assignare sicut predictum est in omnibus contra omnes homines et feminas imperpetuum. Et ut hec mea donacio concessio et confirmacio firmitatem optineat imperpetuum presentem cartam sigilli mei munimine roboravi. Hiis testibus: magistro Waltero de Tauney et aliis.

Margin   *Carta Lecie filie Ra. Bradleg de una bovata terre in Esthorpe* in right margin in 17th-c. hand.

Date   After Mr William de Taney became a canon and before his appointment as archdeacon of Nottingham.

272   *Grant and quitclaim by Matilda de Burbeck in her free widowhood to John de Auger of one bovate of land in Easthorpe that she bought from Lecia, daughter of Ranulph of Bradley, for 5s rent per annum for which he gave eighteen marks*   [1226 × 1249]

Sciant presentes et futuri quod ego Matild' de Burbek' in libera viduitate et potestate mea propria dedi concessi et presenti carta sigillo mea impressa quietum clamavi de me et heredibus meis imperpetuum Johanni de Augre et heredibus suis vel cuicumque dare assignare vendere voluerit sive in prosperitate sive in egritudine totum ius et clameum quod habui vel habere potui in una bovata terre cum pertinenciis in teritorio de Esthorp scilicet in una bovata terre cum pertinenciis quam ego emi quondam de Lecia filia Ranulphi de Bradlege. Tenend' et habend' eidem Johanni de Augr' et heredibus suis vel cuicumque assignare voluerit sicut predictum est in feodo et hereditate libere quiete et pacifice cum omnibus pertinenciis libertatibus et aisiamentis ad predictam pertinent infra villam et extra reddendo inde annuatim dominis feodi qui pro tempore fuerint quinque solidos argenti pro omni servicio et exaccione seculari salvo forinseco servicio quantum pertinet ad unam bovatam terre de eodem feodo scilicet medietatem ad Pentecosten et medietatem ad festum sancti Martini in yeme ita scilicet quod nec ego Matild' nec heredes mei nec aliquis pro nobis vel per nos ius vel clameum decetero erga predictam terram cum pertinenciis exigere poterimus. Pro hac autem donacione concessione et quieta clamacione dedit mihi prefatus Johannes de Augre decem et octo marcas premanibus in gersummam. Hiis testibus: domino Willelmo de Widendune et aliis.

Margin   *Carta Matilde de Burbeck de dicta bovata terre* in right margin in 17th-c. hand.

Date   After **271** and after William of Widdington had been granted land in Southwell and before his death.

Notes   cf. **256n** for possible relationship of John Auger and Matilda de Burbeck.

273   *Space left for a charter of John Auger*

In bottom right margin: *Spacium pro carta Johannis Augr' de bovata terre predicte data fabrice etc.*

Esthorpp'   **Suthwell'**   **fabrica**

274   *Confirmation by Mr William, son of Richard son of Albert, to the Fabric of his toft with an assart in Easthorpe that Ulf held and that Roger and Stennewar, his wife, gave to the Fabric, concerning which there was a dispute between the Chapter and Richard his father*
                                              [early 13th century]

Omnibus sancte matris ecclesie filiis tam presentibus quam futuris magister Willelmus filius Ricardi filii Alberti salutem in domino. Noverit universitas vestra me concessisse et hac mea presenti carta confirmasse Deo et fabrice ecclesie beate et gloriose virginis Marie de Suthwell' in puram et perpetuam elemosinam pro anima patris mei et matris mee et antecessorum meorum toftum quoddam in Esthorpp quod tenuit Ulf cum sarto in Prestgrave quod appellatur Wlfcrofte quod Rogerus et Stennewar' uxor sua et antecessores sui dederunt fabrice predicte ecclesie super que vertebatur contraversiam inter capitulum ecclesie Suthwell' et Ricardum patrem meum libere quiete in omnibus et sine aliquo retenemento tenend'. Ut autem hec mea concessio et confirmacio firma imposterum permaneat presentis scripti munimine et sigilli mei apposicione roboravi. Hiis testibus: Hugone de Pykeryng' et aliis.

Margin   *Carta W. filii Ricardi de tofto in Easthorp* in left margin in 17th-c. hand.

Date   Before the death of Hugh of Pickering (by May 1230), frequently called Hugh the dean towards the end of his life. Mr William, son of Richard son of Albert may be the same as Mr William, son of Richard (**431, 434–6**). *Stennewar* is an anglicisation of the Scandinavian feminine personal name *Steinvör*.

275   *Grant in hereditary fee by Alan of Westhorpe, deacon, at the instance of Sir Hugh called Scot, chaplain, to the Fabric of three roods of meadow in Easthorpe that he bought from Avicia, daughter of Hay of Southwell, for 2d rent per annum*   [mid–late 13th century]

Sciant presentes et futuri quod ego Alanus de Westhorpp' diaconus dedi concessi et hac presenti carta mea confirmavi ad instanciam domini Hugonis dicti Scott' capellani Deo et fabrice ecclesie beate Marie Suthwellie et custodibus dicte fabrice qui pro tempore fuerint tres rodas prati iacentes in prato de Esthorpp' iuxta pratum eiusdem fabrice quod quidem pratum emi de Avicia filia Hay de Suthwell'. Tenend' et habend' de domino feodi libere quiete et pacifice in feodo et hereditate dicte fabrice et custodibus imperpetuum reddendo inde annuatim domino feodi duos denarios scilicet unum denarium ad Pentecosten et unum denarium ad festum sancti Martini in yeme pro omni servicio seculari secta curie exaccione et demanda prout carta attestatur quam habui de dono predicte Avicie filie Hay. Et ut hec mea donacio concessio et carte mee confirmacio rata et stabilis imperpetuum permaneat presenti scripto sigillum meum apposui. Hiis testibus: etc.

Margin   *Carta Alani de W. de 3 rodis prati* in left margin, with *2d* lower down, in 17th-c. hand.

Date   Avicia, daughter of Hay of Southwell, is perhaps the same as Avicia called Schott of Southwell, wife of Roger Marshall of Norwell (**437**). Hugh called Scott witnessed **401** and Alan of Westhorpe is mentioned in **421**.

276 *Grant in free alms by William of Newton, called nephew of the dean, to the Fabric and for his fraternity of seven strips of land in Southwell*
[early–mid-13th century]

Sciant presentes et futuri quod ego Willelmus de Newton' dictus nepos decani pro salute anime mee et antecessorum meorum et omnium benefactorum meorum dedi concessi et hac presenti carta mea confirmavi in liberam puram et perpetuam elemosinam Deo et fabrice ecclesie beate Marie Suthwell' et pro fraternitate dicte ecclesie septem seliones terre arabilis in teritorio de Suthwell' cum omnibus suis pertinenciis continue iacentes in illa cultura que vocatur Redwonge ex parte aquilonari terre Henrici Gaynnoch' de eadem cultura. Tenend' et habend' dicte fabrice ecclesie Suthwell' in liberam puram et perpetuam elemosinam imperpetuum. Et ego Willelmus et heredes mei dicte fabrice prenominatos seliones cum omnibus suis pertinenciis et aisiamentis infra villam de Suthwell' et extra sicut predictum est warantizabimus acquietabimus et defendemus contra omnes gentes imperpetuum. Et ut hec mea donacio concessio et carte mee confirmacio rata et stabilis imperpetuum permaneat presenti scripto sigillum meum apposui. Hiis testibus: Johanne de Goverton' et aliis.

Margin *Carta W. Newton de 7 selionibus* in left margin in 17th-c. hand, with *Redwonge* (medieval) below.

Date William may have been the nephew of Hugh the dean (d. by May 1230).

277 *Missing charter of Geoffrey Wykes*

In bottom left margin in medieval hand, with space also left at the top of p. 162 *Deficit carta Galfridi Wyke' post per cartam immediate sequentem.*

278 *Quitclaim by Alice, widow of Geoffrey de Wykes, to the Fabric of the lands and tenements of which she was enfeoffed by Geoffrey, her husband, in divers places* [1260 × 1280]

p. 162 Omnibus sancte matris ecclesie filiis ad quos presens scriptum pervenerit Alicia relicta Galfridi de Wykys salutem in domino. Noveritis me concessisse ac quietum clamasse capitulo beate Marie Suthwellie et fabrice ecclesie eiusdem totum ius et clameum quod umquam habui vel habere potero nomine dotis vel alterius alicuius accionis in terris et tenementis in quibus feoffata fui per dictum Galfridum quondam maritum meum per diversa loca ita quod nec ego nec aliquis per me nomine meo ullum ius vel clameum in dictis terris et tenementis de cetero vendicare vel exigere poterimus. In cuius rei testimonium huic presenti scripto sigillum meum apposui. Hiis testibus: domino Henrico le Vavasour, Stephano de Wycheton' canonicis et aliis.

Margin No page heading; *Alicie Wykes quieti clam°* in right margin in 17th-c. hand.

Date While Henry le Vavassour was a canon.

Note This appears to be the only occurrence of Stephen of Wycheton (Weighton), prebendary of Rampton (d. 1283), as a witness in the *White Book.*

279 *Lease in the form of a chirograph by the Chapter to Sir Henry of Staythorpe, perpetual vicar of Halloughton, Isabella, his sister, and Richard the mason, their brother, for their lives of four acres of land in Southwell for 2s 6d rent per annum paid to the Fabric*

3 September 1296

Universis presentes inspecturis vel audituris capitulum ecclesie beate Marie Suthewell' eternam in domino salutem. Noveritis nos de unanimi fratrum consensu concessisse et dimisisse domino Henrico de Starthorp, perpetuo vicario de Haluton', Isabelle sorori suo, et Ricardo cementario, fratri ipsorum, quatuor acras terre arrabilis in campo de Suthewell' videlicet tres[1] acras et dimidiam super Prestegrave inter terram Roberti Brun[2] et terram Johannis person' et dimidiam acram super le Redewong' inter terram Roberti Brun[2] et terram Elye Packe. Tenend' et habend' dictis Henrico, Isabelle sorori sue vel eorum alteri quamdiu vixerint vel vixerit et post utriusque decessum dicto Ricardo cementario toto tempore vite sue libere, quiete et pacifice sine alicuius impedimento. Reddendo inde annuatim custodibus fabrice nostre pro omnimodo servicio duos solidos et sex denarios ad duos anni terminos videlicet medietatem in festo beati Michaelis et aliam medietatem in festo Pentecosten. Ita videlicet quod dicti Henricus, Isabella et Ricardus vel alterius ipsorum qui supervixerit dictam terram in cultura et compostura in eque bono statu quo [eam][3] invenerint seu meliori sustinebunt vel sustinebit, nec licebit ipsis vel eorum alteri dictam terram vel partem ipsius aliis locare vel quocumque alio titulo dimittere suo tempore quod si forte factum fuerit reservamus nobis potestatem illam terram sic dimissam in manus nostras reassumendi et plenam firmam nichilominus exigendi quod si dicti Henricus, Isabella et Ricardus vel eorum alteri qui pro tempore tenuerint in alicuius termini solucione defecerint vel defecerit, quod absit, licebit custodibus nostris in ipsos vel eorum alterum monicione premissa post lapsum decem dierum tamquam pro manifesta offensa maioris excommunicacionis sentenciam usque ad condignam satisfaccionem fulminare. Ipsis vero successive cedentibus vel decedentibus vel eorum altero qui superfuerit cedente vel decedente dictam terram sine alicuius reclamacione ad nos pleno iure redibit. In cuius rei testimonium presenti cyrograffatim[4] incisis sigillum nostrum commune parti penes dictos Henricum, Isabellam et Ricardum residenti est appensum dicti Henrici sigillo parti nostre similiter appenso. Actum et datum die lune proximo post festum sancti Augustini anno domini millessimo cc[mo] nonagesimo sexto. Testibus presentibus: domino Ricardo de Baumfeld', magistro Johanne Deuerus, magistro Benedicto de Halum, magistro Simone de Curtmaiurum, magistro Elye de Couton', canonicis eiusdem, dominis Thoma de Hokerton, Simone Breinde, Roberto de Witton, capellanis, et aliis.

[1] WB *iii*   [2] WB *Broun'*   [3] supplied by WB   [4] WB *cirographatim*

Margin   *Carta Capituli sive locacio 3 acr' d.* in right margin, with *Prestgrave* (medieval), *Redwonge* (medieval), and *2ˢ 6ᵈ per annum*, below in 17th-c. hand.

Note   For the original charter see LA, Cragg MS 3/19, formerly sealed on double tag through turn up, from which corrections and additions to **279** (which only names the first two witnesses), have been made. Mr Richard de Bamfield, prebendary of Norwell Tertia Pars (*c.* 1287–1302/4); Mr John d'Évreux, prebendary of Oxton II (*c.* 1290–1305), when replaced by William Melton, but returning in 1309 and d. by 22 Oct. 1310 (*Reg. Greenfield*, i. fo. 38ᵛ); Mr Benedict of Halam, prebendary of Rampton (*c.* 1286–91) then North Leverton (1291–1307); Mr Simon de Courmayeur, prebendary of Woodborough (though his title was long challenged); Mr Elias of Cowton, prebendary of Norwell Overhall (1295–1327/9). Thomas of Hockerton occurs as a churchwarden around this period (**458**), Simon Brainde was already a chaplain by 1281 (**457**) and Robert of Weighton/ Witton was chaplain by 1288 (**317**) and warden of the Fabric in 1295 (**40**). Was Richard *cementarius* one of the masons who had worked on the Chapter House?

p. 163　**Esthorpp'**　　　　　　　　**Suthwell'**

280　*Confirmation in hereditary fee by William, son of Lecia, daughter of Tirry, to Matilda de Burbeck of one acre of land in Easthorpe for 1d rent per annum for which she gave 16s*　　　　[1230 × 1245]

Sciant presentes et futuri quod ego Willelmus filius Lecie¹ que fuit filia Tyrry assensu et consensu heredum meorum et hac carta mea confirmavi Matild' de Burbek' et heredibus suis vel cuicumque assignare dare vendere vel legare voluerit sive in prosperitate sive in egritudine pro homagio et servicio suo unam acram \terre/ in teritorio de Esthorpp' in Clerkfurlang' scilicet illam acram que iacet inter terram Roberti de Barra et inter terram Walteri filii Thome. Habend' et tenend' ipsi Matild' et heredibus sui vel cuicumque assignare voluerit sicut predictum est in feodo et hereditate de me et heredibus meis vel successoribus meis libere quiete integre et pacifice reddendo inde annuatim mihi et heredibus meis vel successoribus meis unum denarium infra natalem domini in domo ipsius Matild' in Moregate per annum pro omni servicio seculari exaccione et demanda. Et pro hac donacione concessione et carte mee confirmacione predicta Matild' dedit mihi sexdecim solidos sterlingorum. Et ego Willelmus et heredes mei vel successores mei warantizabimus predictam acram terre dicte Matild' et heredibus suis vel cuicumque assignare voluerit sicut predictum est contra omnes homines et feminas imperpetuum. Et ut hec mea donacio concessio et confirmacio firmitatem optineat imperpetuum presentem cartam sigilli mei munimine roboravi. Hiis testibus: magistro Waltero de Thaney archidiacono Notingh', magistro Willelmo de Marcham, Henrico de Notingh' canonicis Suthwell' ecclesie, Henrico de Mora, Roberto de Lecestria, Willelmo sacrista capellanis eiusdem ecclesie, Rogero de Osbertona, Johanne de Burstall', Henrico de Suthwell' clerico, Roberto de Barra, Willelmo Cosyn' etc.

¹ MS followed by *Tyrry* crossed through

Margin　Page heading, Scribe 4; *Carta W. filii Lecie de una acra in Esthorpe Matildae Burbeck fecit* in left margin in 17ᵗʰ-c. hand.

Date　While John de Burstall was active (*Thurgarton*, cxxii–cxxiii) and before the death of Henry of Nottingham (see **37n**).

281 *Grant by Matilda de Burbeck in her free widowhood to the Fabric of all her meadow in Halam of the gift of Roger of Laneham, clerk, and one acre of land in Easthorpe that she bought from William, son of Lecia, daughter of Tirry* [mid-13th century]

Sciant presentes et futuri quod ego Matild' de Burbek' in libera viduitate mea dedi concessi et hac presenti carta mea confirmavi Deo et fabrice ecclesie beate Marie Suthwell' pro salute anime mee et antecessorum meorum totum pratum quod habui in teritorio de Halum' de dono Rogeri de Lanum' clerici illud videlicet pratum quod nominatur Halumholme iacens iuxta molendinum de Marthorn' et unam acram terre arabilis in teritorio de Esthorpp' quam quondam[1] emi de Willelmo filio Lecie filie Tyrry iacentem in Clerkfurlang' inter terram Roberti de Barra et terram Roberti filii Thome. Tenend' et habend' dicte fabrice libere quiete integre pacifice et honorifice imperpetuum faciendo inde servicium pro predictis terris sicut continetur in cartis quas habui de dictis Rogero et Willelmo quas custodes dicte fabrice habent penes se. Ut hec autem mea donacio concessio et carte mee confirmacio rata et stabilis imperpetuum permaneat presenti scripto sigillum meum apposui. Hiis testibus: Willelmo de Thorniton', Johanne de Guverton', Galfrido de Ledenham', Roberto de Gipismer', Roberto de Barra et aliis.

[1] MS followed by *emit* crossed through and dotted for deletion

Margin *Carte dicte Matildae de prato in Halome et dimidia acra terre in Esthorp* in left margin in 17th-c. hand.

Date After **280**.

Note For Roger of Laneham see **396n**.

282 *Grant and quitclaim by William, son of Richard of Edingley, with the consent of Matilda de Burbeck, his mother, to Southwell of one toft in Easthorpe* [1234 × 1249]

Sciant omnes tam presentes quam futuri quod ego Willelmus filius Ricardi de Eddyngley' consensu et voluntate matris mee Matild' de Burbek' dedi concessi et hac presenti carta mea confirmavi Deo et ecclesie beate Marie de Suwell' pro salute anime mee et anime patris mei unum toftum in Esthorpp' cum edificiis propinquiorem tofto Ricardi Pacg[1] versus aquilonem et totum ius meum quod in eo habui vel habere potui imperpetuum dicte ecclesie quietum clamavi cum omnibus pertinenciis et libertatibus ut in pasturis et aliis asiamentis ad predictum toftum pertinentibus. Et ut hec mea donacio et quieta clamacio firma et stabilis permaneat tactis sacrosanctis coram capitulo iuravi et presenti scripto sigillum meum apposui. Hiis testibus: m[agistro] Willelmo de Roldeston', domino Henrico de Mora, Ricardo [de] Marcham' et aliis multis.

[1] MS *sic*

Margin *Carta W. filii Ricardi de tofto in Esthorpe* in left margin in 17th-c. hand.

Date While Henry de Mora was active and before he became a canon, and see **413**.

Note For Richard of Markham see *Rufford*, xcix–c.

p. 164 **Suthwell'**

283 *Grant by Geoffrey of the parish of Southwell to Matilda, daughter of Geoffrey Fleming, of one toft with house that he bought from William Bullur for 4d rent per annum* [*c*. 1235 × 1250]

Sciant presentes et futuri quod ego Galfridus de parochia de Suthwell' dedi concessi et hac presenti carta mea confirmavi Matild' filie Galfridi Flamyng' unum toftum cum domo quod emi de Willelmo Bullur quod iacet iuxta prebendam de Wodeburgh' de me et heredibus meis Matild' et heredibus suis vel assignatis suis libere \et/ quiete reddendo inde annuatim iiii d. in die Pentecosten Willelmo Bullur' vel heredibus suis pro omnibus secularibus serviciis et demandis. Ut autem hec donacio et confirmacio rata maneat et stabile imperpetuum huic presenti scripto sigillum meum apposui. Hiis testibus: magistro Willelmo de Suthwellia rectore ecclesie de Blaby et aliis etc.

Margin *Carta Galfridi de tofto iuxta prebend. de Woodburgh* in right margin with *4^d per annum* below in 17th-c. hand.

Date After 1235 and before **284**.

Note William de Sywell', clerk, was instituted as rector of Blaby at the presentation of the abbot and convent of Leicester on 27 December 1235 (*Robert Grosseteste as Bishop of Lincoln. The Episcopal Rolls, 1235–1253*, ed. Philippa M. Hoskin (LRS, Kathleen Major Series of Medieval Records, 1, 2015), no. 1529). He is most probably the Mr William of Southwell, who witnessed 3 April 1229 with *W. de Makham, R. de Burton, Willelmo capellano, R. de Oxen canonicis Suwelensibus, Willelmo de Wisbech canonico Bever'*, *Odone de Richmund, Reginaldo de Stowa clericis* and as canon of York, 4 December 1235 (*Pontefract cartulary*, 74, 76; *Fasti 1066–1300*, vi, 132), **84** and **85**. As Hoskin notes, he later became a canon of Lincoln, *c*. 1250, prebendary of Asgarby from *c*. 1256, official for Bishop Gravesend in 1259–60, dying before 29 September 1276 (*Fasti 1066–1300*, iii, 50).

284 *Grant by Matilda, daughter of Geoffrey the Fleming, to William of Blidworth, chaplain, of one plot for 4d rent per annum for which William gave two marks* [1250 × 1268]

Sciant omnes presentes et futuri quod ego Matild' filia Galfridi le Flamyng' dedi concessi et hac presenti carta mea confirmavi Willelmo de Blideworth' capellano unam placeam que iacet iuxta prebendam de Wodeburgh' versus occidentem et placeam dicti Willelmi versus orientem. Tenend' et habend' dicto Willelmo et heredibus suis vel assignatis quibuscumque de me et heredibus meis libere quiete et pacifice reddendo inde annuatim mihi et heredibus meis vel domino capitali feodi prout elegerit quatuor denarios pro omni servicio seculari exaccione secta curie et demanda. Pro hac autem donacione et carte mee confirmacione dedit mihi dictus Willelmus duas marcas argenti premanibus. In cuius rei testimonium presenti scripto sigillum meum apposui. Hiis testibus: domino Ricardo de Sutton' et aliis.

Margin *Carta Matilde filiae Galfridi de placea versus preb. de Woodb.* in right margin in 17th-c. hand.

Date After **283** and before the death of Richard of Sutton.

285 *Grant by the Chapter to John of Hockerton, called Walur, chaplain, of one plot in Southwell for 4d rent per annum paid to the Fabric and 1d per annum for other service* [1250 × 1268]

Universis Christi fidelibus hoc scriptum visuris vel audituris capitulum ecclesie beate Marie Suthwell' salutem in domino. Noverit universitas vestra nos dedisse concessisse et hac presenti carta nostra confirmasse Johanni de Hokerton' capellano dicto Walur' unam placeam iacentem in villa Suthwell' inter toftum thesaurarii Ebor' et toftum Matild' Lefthand' et extendentem se in longitudine a via regia usque ad toftum quod quondam fuit Gilberti Dande capellani. Tenend' et habend' sibi et assignatis suis de nobis et successoribus nostris libere quiete et pacifice imperpetuum reddendo inde annuatim domino feodi quatuor denarios et fabrice ecclesie nostre Suthwell' unum denarium pro omnibus serviciis secularibus exaccionibus et demandis. Ut hec autem donacio concessio et presenti carte confirmacio rata et stabilis imposterum permaneat presens scriptum sigilli nostri munimine duximus roborand'. Hiis testibus: domino Ricardo de Sutton' etc.

Margin *Carta Capituli de placea* in right margin in 17th-c. hand.

Date After **284** and before the death of Richard of Sutton.

Note John of Hockerton, chaplain, is probably identical with John of Hockerton, vicar by 1284 (**442–4**). For Gilbert Dande, alias Gilbert of Laxton, chaplain, see **289n**. The tofts of Matilda Lefthand and Mr John of Penistone, canon of Southwell (1268–96), are mentioned in the grant in free alms by Thomas de Belew (Bella Aqua) to Thurgarton priory of 5s 6d annual rent in Southwell for a pittance (*Thurgarton*, 489).

286 *Grant by John le Walur, chaplain, to Sir William of Blidworth of one toft in Southwell for 4d rent per annum and 1d per annum to the Fabric* [late 13th century]

Sciant presentes et futuri quod ego Johannes le Walur' capellanus dedi concessi et hac presenti carta mea confirmavi domino Willelmo de Blideworth' unum toftum in villa de Suthwell' iacens inter toftum quondam Gilberti Dande versus orientem et toftum quondam Matild' Lefthande versus occidentem et abuttat versus aquilonem super toftum dicti Gilberti et versus australem super viam regiam quod quidem toftum continet in longitudine tres perticatas et sex pedes et in latitudine duas perticatas quelibet earum ex longitudine octodecim pedum. Tenend' et habend' sibi et heredibus suis vel assignatis quibuscumque et ubi illud dare vendere vel legare voluerit sive in prosperitate sive in egritudine libere quiete pacifice et honorifice in feodo et hereditate imperpetuum reddendo inde annuatim domino feodi quatuor denarios ad duos anni terminos videlicet etc. et ad fabricam beate Marie Suthwellie ultimo termino nominato unum denarium pro omni servicio etc.

Margin   *Carta J. de Walur de tofto in Southwell* with *4ᵈ per annum* lower down in right margin in 17ᵗʰ-c. hand.

Date   After **285**.

Note   It is not clear whether the toft mentioned here is the same as that given to John Le Walur in **285**, since the more precise description of its location suggests that the adjacent toft formerly held by Matilda Lefthand in this charter lies on the opposite side to that described in **285**. If it is the same, the description of its bounds has been reversed. It is interesting to note the use of an eighteen-foot perch measurement.

287   *Quitclaim by Augustine, son of William le Bolur of Southwell, to the Fabric of one plot in Southwell*   [late 13ᵗʰ century]

Omnibus Christi fidelibus presens scriptum visuris vel audituris Augustinus filius Willelmi le Bolur de Suthwell' salutem in domino. Noveritis me pro salute anime mee patris et matris parentum amicorum meorum dedisse
p. 165   concessisse et hoc presenti scripto omnino | quietum clamasse Deo et fabrice ecclesie beate Marie Suthwell' totum ius et clameum quod habui vel habere potui vel quod me vel heredes meos contingere possit in una placea in Suthwell' iacente inter toftum thesaurarii Ebor' et toftum quod fuit quondam Matild' Lefthand' et incipit a via regia et se extendit usque toftum quod fuit quondam Gilberti Dande capellani ita quod nec ego Augustinus nec aliquis per me vel pro me nec heredes mei aliquid ius vel clameum umquam de cetero in dicta placea nobis exigere vel vendicare poterimus. In cuius rei testimonium huic scripto sigillum meum apposui. Hiis testibus: Roberto Broun' etc.

Margin   *Carta Aug. filii W. Volur de placea pred* in right margin in 17ᵗʰ-c. hand.

Date   After **286** and Robert Broun witnessed **279** (1296).

Note   This concerns the same plot as **285**.

Suthwell'   **fabrica**

288   *Grant in hereditary fee by William, son of Lecia, daughter of Tirry, to Gilbert of Laxton, chaplain, of part of his toft around his house that he holds of Lecia, daughter of Ranulph of Bradley, widow of William of Rolleston, of the treasurer of York's fee. Also grant of a breadth of ten feet free ingress and egress for one wagon for 8d rent per annum for which he gave 20s*   [1234 × 1249]

Sciant presentes et futuri quod ego Willelmus filius Lecye quondam filie Tyrry de Suthwell' dedi concessi et hac presenti carta mea confirmavi Gilberto de Lexinton' capellano vel cuicumque assignare voluerit pro homagio suo et servicio quamdam partem tofti mei citra domum meam quam teneo de Lecya filia Ranulphi de Bradlege quondam uxore Willelmi de Roldeston' de feodo thesaurarii Ebor' in Suthwell' que quidem pars continet in longitudine usque ad finem tofti versus aquilonem tresdecim perticatas et octo pedes quelibet eorum ex longitudine octodecim pedum et inprincipio primo partis versus austrum quadraginta septem pedes in latitudine sicut se extendit a tofto prebende de Wodeburgh usque ad toftum thesaraurii Ebor'. Dedi eciam et concessi eidem Gilberto vel assignatis latitudine decem pedum a via regia de residuo tofti mei versus orientem iuxta toftum dicti thesaraurii ad liberum introitum et exitum unius quadrige habend' usque ad predictam partem tofti. Tenend' et habend' sibi vel cuicumque assignare dare vendere vel legare voluerit de me et heredibus meis vel assignatis libere quiete et hereditarie reddendo inde annuatim mihi et heredibus meis vel assignatis octo denarios pro omni servicio seculari exaccione vel demanda videlicet quatuor denarios ad festum sancti Martini in yeme et quatuor denarios ad invencionem sancte crucis. Pro hac autem donacione concessione et carte mee confirmacione dedit mihi predictus Gilbertus viginti solidos argenti premanibus nomine de gersumma. Et ego Willelmus et heredes mei vel assignati predicto Gilberto vel cuicumque dictam partem tofti una cum latitudine decem pedum ad liberum introitum et exitum et omnibus aisiamentis assignaverit ut predictum est contra omnes gentes warantizabimus defendemus et acquietabimus. Ut hec mea donacio concessio et carte mee confirmacio rata firma sit et stabilis imperpetuum huic scripto sigillum meum apposui. Hiis testibus: domino Henrico de Mora persona de Ekeryng', Willelmo sacrista et aliis.

Margin   Page heading *fabrica* 17th-c. hand as is *Carta W. filii Lecie de parte tofti* in left margin.

Date   While Henry de Mora was parson of Eakring and before he became a canon.

Note   For the creation of the fee of the treasurer of York in Southwell by William of Rotherfield, which was finally surrendered in 1547, see **Introduction**, p. xcii n. 281 and *Cart. Treas. York*, no. 40, 20 October 1230.

289   *Grant by Gilbert, son of Danda of Laxton, chaplain, to Robert, his brother, chaplain, of one toft with buildings in Southwell that he bought from William le Bolur for 1d rent per annum paid to him during his lifetime and 8d rent per annum to the capital lord for which he gave ten marks*   [mid-13th century]

Sciant presentes et futuri quod ego Gilbertus filius Dande de Lexington' capellanus dedi concessi et hac presenti carta mea confirmavi Roberto fratri meo de Lexington' capellano quoddam toftum in villa Suthwell' cum edificiis desupersitis quod emi de Willelmo le Bolur. Tenend' et habend' sibi et heredibus suis vel assignatis quibuscumque et ubi illud dare vendere vel legare voluerit sive in prosperitate sive in egritudine libere quiete pacifice et honorifice in feodo et hereditate imperpetuum reddendo inde annuatim mihi in vita mea unum denarium infra septimanam Pentecosten et capitali domino feodi octo denarios ad duos anni terminos videlicet ad invencionem sancte crucis quatuor denarios et ad festum beati Martini in yeme quatuor denarios pro omni servicio seculari exaccione consuetudine et demanda. Ego vero Gilbertus predictum toftum cum omnibus edificiis suis et aisiamentis sicut predictum est secundum tenorem principalis carte mee | quam inde habui contra omnes homines in vita mea in omnibus   p. 166 warantizabo et defendam. Pro hac autem donacione concessione et carte mee confirmacione dedit mihi prenominatus Robertus decem marcas pre manibus nomine gersumme. Et ut hec mea donacio concessio et carte mee confirmacio rata et stabilis imposterum permaneat presenti scripto sigillum meum apposui. Hiis testibus: domino Willelmo de Blideworth' et aliis.

Margin *Carta Gilberti de tofto* in left margin with *4ᵈ per annum* below in 17ᵗʰ-c. hand.

Date After **288** and before **290**.

Note Gilbert, son of Danda of Laxton, was probably the son of Ralph or Ranulph of Laxton, who witnessed **96** (1219–21). He may well have been the first (or an early) chaplain of the chantry of St Edmund founded in Laxton church by Sir John of Laxton (d. 1257) or of that founded by Robert of Laxton (d. 1250) in Laxton Moorhouse (www.southwellchurches.history.nottingham.ac.uk under Moorhouse). He granted nine strips of land 'super Prestegrave' in Southwell, which he had also acquired from William le Bolur, to his niece, Alice, who as widow of Thomas of Halam granted the land to John of Southwell, *c.* 1284–90 (BL, Add. Chs 27458–9). Gilbert was apparently dead by 1268 (**285**).

p. 166 **Suthwell'**

290 *Grant by Robert Dande of Laxton, chaplain, to William Dande, his nephew, of one toft with buildings in Southwell that he bought from Gilbert, his brother, chaplain, for 1d rent per annum paid to him and 4d rent per annum paid to the capital lord for which he gave eight marks*
[*c.* 1249 × 1260]

Sciant presentes et futuri quod ego Robertus Dande de Lexinton' capellanus dedi concessi et hac presenti carta mea confirmavi Willelmo Dande nepoti meo unum toftum in villa Suthwell' cum edificiis desuper sitis quod emi de Gilberto fratre meo¹ capellano iacens inter toftum thesaurarii Ebor' ex parte orientali et toftum Matild' Lefthand' ex parte occidentali. Tenend' et habend' sibi et heredibus suis vel assignatis quibuscumque et ubi illud dare vendere vel legare voluerit sive in prosperitate sive in egritudine libere quiete pacifice et honorifice in feodo et hereditate imperpetuum reddendo inde annuatim mihi et heredibus meis vel assignatis meis unum denarium infra septimanam Pentecosten et capitali domino feodi octo denarios ad duos anni terminos videlicet ad invencionem sancte crucis iiii d. et ad festum beati Martini in yeme iiii d. pro omni servicio seculari consuetudine et demanda. Ego vero Robertus predictum toftum cum omnibus edificiis suis et aisiamentis sicut predictum est contra omnes gentes predicto Willelmo et heredibus vel assignatis suis warantizabo acquietabo et defendam imperpetuum. Pro hac autem donacione concessione et carte mee confirmacione dedit mihi predictus Willelmus octo marcas pre manibus nomine gersumme. Et ut hec mea donacio concessio et carte mee confirmacio stabilis imposterum permaneat presenti scripto sigillum meum apposui. Hiis testibus: domino Henrico de Mora et aliis.

¹ MS *me*

Margin *Carta Rob. Dande de tofto predicto* in right margin with *iᵈ per annum* below in 17ᵗʰ-c. hand.

Date   After **289** and while Henry de Mora was a canon.

Note   For later charters concerning this plot, see **285**, **287**, **291** and **292**.

291   *Grant by William, son of Thomas of Halam, to William of Blidworth, chaplain, of one toft with buildings in Southwell that he bought
from Robert Dande, chaplain, for 8d rent per annum paid to the capital
lord for which he gave seven marks*   [1249 × 1260]

Sciant presentes et futuri quod ego Willelmus filius Thome de Halum' dedi
concessi et hac presenti carta mea confirmavi Willelmo de Blithworth'
capellano unum toftum in villa Suthwell' cum edificiis desuper sitis quod
emi de Roberto Dande capellano iacens inter toftum thesaurarii Ebor' ex
parte orientali et toftum Matild' Lefthande ex parte occidentali. Tenend'
et habend' sibi et heredibus suis vel assignatis quibuscumque et ubi illud
dare vendere vel legare voluerit sive in prosperitate sive in egritudine
libere et quiete pacifice et honorifice in feodo et hereditate imperpetuum
reddendo inde annuatim domino feodi octo denarios ad duos anni terminos
videlicet ad invencionem sancte crucis quatuor denarios et ad festum beati
Martini in yeme quatuor denarios pro omni servicio seculari exaccione
consuetudine et demanda. Ego vero Willelmus et heredes vel assignati
mei predictum toftum cum omnibus edificiis et aisiamentis predicto
Willelmo et heredibus vel assignatis suis sicut predictum est contra omnes
gentes warantizabimus acquietabimus et defendemus imperpetuum. Pro
hac autem donacione concessione et carte mee confirmacione dedit mihi
predictus Willelmus septem marcas pre manibus nomine gersumme. Et
ut hec mea donacio et carte mee confirmacio rata et stabilis imperpetuum
permaneat presenti scripto sigillum meum apposui. Hiis testibus: domino
Willelmo de Mora canonico Suthwell' et aliis.

Margin   *Carta W. Hallam de tofto* in right margin with *8ᵈ per annum* below in 17ᵗʰ-c.
hand.

Date   After **290**. As this is the only mention of a William de Mora as canon it may
well be an error for Henry de Mora.

Note   William was probably the son of Thomas of Halam and Alice his wife (**289n**).

292   *Grant and quitclaim by John of the Chamber of Stow to the Fabric
of one plot in Southwell*   [mid-13ᵗʰ century]

Omnibus Christi fidelibus hoc presens scriptum visuris vel audituris
Johannes de la Chaum' de Stouwa salutem in domino. Noveritis nos pro
salute anime mee patris matris parentum et amicorum meorum dedisse
concessisse et hoc presenti scripto quietum clamasse Deo et fabrice ecclesie
beate Marie Suthwell' totum ius et clameum quod habui vel habere potui
vel quod me vel heredes meos contingere possit in una placea in Suthwell'
iacente inter toftum thesaurarii Ebor' et toftum Matild' Lefthand' et incipit
a via regia et se extendit usque toftum Roberti Dande ita quod nec ego
Johannes nec aliquis per me vel pro me nec heredes mei aliquod ius vel
clameum umquam decetero in | dicta placea nobis exigere vel vendicare   p. 167

poterimus salvis mihi et heredibus meis quatuor denarios per annum pro eadem placea. In cuius rei testimonium huic scripto sigillum meum apposui. Hiis testibus: Johanne de Gouverton' et aliis.

Margin *Relax° Jo. de la Cham' de placea predicta* in right margin in 17ᵗʰ-c. hand.

Date After **290**.

SOUTHWELL, EASTHORPE, 293–6

Suthwell' fabrica

293 *Quitclaim by Matilda, daughter of Nicholas, son of Tirry, in her free widowhood to Gilbert of Laxton, chaplain, of part of a toft that he bought from William, son of Lecia Tirry, and nine strips that Gilbert bought from William for which he gave one mark* [1226 × 1249]

Omnibus Christi fidelibus hoc scriptum visuris vel audituris Matild' filia Nicholai filii Tyrry de Suthwell' salutem in domino. Noverit universitas vestra me in libera propria et legia potestate mea et viduitate mea dedisse concessisse quietum clamasse et hac presenti carta mea confirmasse Gilberto de Lexinton' capellano pro una marca argenti quam mihi dedit in magna necessitate mea totum ius et clameum quod habui vel habere potui iure hereditarie in tota parte illius tofti quam emit quondam de Willelmo filio Lecie Tyrry secundum tenorem carte sue a prefato Willelmo illius partis tofti habite et in novem selionibus super Prestgrave iacentibus et in una roda et dimidia terre super Clayhill' quas ipse Gilbertus scilicet a predicto Willelmo emebat cum omnibus pertinenciis suis et aisiamentis infra villam et extra ita quod nec ego Matild' nec heredes mei nec aliquis per nos vel pro nobis in dicta parte tofti nec in dicta terra aliquid iuris vel clamii decetero poterimus exigere vel nobis vendicare nec in dominico nec in servicio. Tenend' et habend' dicto Gilberto et heredibus suis vel assignatis suis vel eorum heredibus in feodo et hereditate libere quiete pacifice et integre imperpetuum faciendo dominis feodi servicium debitum et consuetum ad tantam terram pertinentem. In cuius rei testimonium presenti scripto sigillum meum apposui. Hiis testibus: domino Willelmo de Wydyngton' et aliis.

Margin Page heading as p. 165. *Carta Matildae de parte tofti etc.* in left margin (17ᵗʰ-c.) with *Prestgrave* (medieval) below.

Date After William of Widdington was granted land in Southwell and before his death.

Note See **289n** for the nine strips in *Prestegrave*.

294 *Quitclaim by Matilda, daughter of Nicholas, son of Tirry, in her free widowhood to John, son of Ralph, clerk of Southwell, of one furlong of land and three roods of meadow in Easthorpe for which he gave a half-mark* [mid-13ᵗʰ century]

Omnibus Christi fi[delibus hoc scriptum visuris vel auditur]is¹ Matild' filia

Nicholai filii Tirri de Suwell'[2] salutem in domino. Noverit un[iversitas
vestra me in libera et propria et] ligia potestate mea et viduitate mea
dedisse concessisse[3] quietum clamasse [et hac presenti carta mea confir]
masse Johanni filio Radulphi clerici de Suwell' et heredibus suis vel
[assignatis vel heredibus eorum] pro dimidia marcha argenti quam
michi dedit in magna necessitate m[ea premanibus totum ius . . .][4] et
clameum quod habui vel habere potui iure hereditarie in una cultura
que [appellatur Wodecrofte . . .][4] in teritorio de Estorp' et in tribus rodis
[prati in eodem] teritorio cum omnibus s[uis pertinenciis et aisiamenti]s
infra villam Suwell' et extra, ita quod [nec ego Matild' nec] heredes
mei nec aliquis per nos vel pro [nobis ali]quid iuris vel clamii decetero
in dictis terris [poterimus exigere] vel nobis vendicare nec in dominico
nec in [servicio]. Tenend' et habend' dicto Johanni et heredibus [suis
vel] assignatis et eorum heredibus in feodo et hereditate libere, quiete,
integre et pacifice imperpetuum [. . .] faciendo dominis feodi servicium
et debitum consuetum ad illas terras prenominatas pertinentia. In cuius
rei testimonium presenti[5] scripto sigillum meum apposui. Hiis testibus:
Hugone de Morton', Roberto de Gipismer', Johanne de Guverton', Alano
de Guverton', Ricardo de Guverton', Ricardo de Normanton', Roberto
filio Johannis de Halum, Thoma filio Alexandri de Halum, Roberto de
Barra, Willelmo de Kelum clerico et aliis.

[1] Square brackets indicate missing words in the original   [2] WB lacks *de Suwell'*   [3] WB
concesse   [4] One or two words possibly missing here   [5] *presenti* supplied from original;
huic in MS

Margin   *Carta eiusdem de cultura terre* (17th c.) in left margin with *Wodecrofte* (medieval) below.

Date   See **293**, while most of the witnesses also witnessed another of Matilda's charters
(**530**, 1230 × 1249).

Note   The damaged original is LA, Cragg MS 4/33 (formerly 3/21), formerly sealed
on a double tag through turn-up, which may already have been partially damaged when
transcribed into the WB, where all but the first witness are omitted.

295   *Quitclaim by Hawise, widow of William Bullur of Thurgarton, to
the Fabric, Gilbert Dande, William of Averham and Henry of Upton,
chaplains, Geoffrey son of Sabbe, Matilda Lefthand and Avicia, sister
of Milla, of two bovates of land in Easthorpe that William, her husband,
sometime held and gave to her*   [c. 1249 × 1260]

Omnibus sancte matris ecclesie filiis hoc scriptum visuris vel audituris
Hauwisia quondam uxor Willelmi Bullur' de Thurgarton' salutem in
domino. Noverit universitas vestra me in libera viduitate mea concessisse et
omnino quietum clamasse fabrice ecclesie beate Marie Suthwell' Gilberto
Dande Willelmo de Egrum' Henrico de Upton' capellanis Galfrido filio
Sabbe Matild' Lefthand' et Avicie sorori Mille totum ius et clameum
quod habui vel habere potui vel quod ius contingere possit nomine dotis
in duabus bovatis terre in teritorio de Esthorpp' cum pertinenciis in
toftis et omnibus aliis rebus quas Willelmus le Bulur' quondam vir meus

tenuit et eis vendidit pro quadam summa pecunie quam mihi dederunt ita quod nec ego Hauwisia nec aliquis per me vel pro me aliquod ius vel clameum in dictis duabus bovatis terre cum pertinenciis de cetero nomine dotis habere exigere vel mihi vendicare poterimus renuncians omni impetracioni cavillacioni regie prohibicioni et omni iuris remedio tam civili quam canonici. Ad hanc quietum clamacionem fideliter et sine dolo imperpetuum observandam subieci me iurisdicioni et eciam corporale prestiti sacrosanctum et ad maiorem securitatem presenti scripto sigillum meum apposui. Hiis testibus: domino Henrico de Mora et aliis.

Margin   *Avisia Volur de 2 bovatis terre* (17th c.) in left margin.

Date   See also **283** and while Henry de Mora was a canon.

Suthwell'   **Cimiterium**

296   *Lease in the form of a chirograph by the Chapter to Simon called Brainde, chaplain, of one bovate of land with meadow in Easthorpe that they have of the gift of John de Auger for 18s rent per annum paid to the Fabric*   22 July 1287

Universis presentes inspecturis vel audituris capitulum ecclesie beate Marie Suthwell' eternam in domino salutem. Noveritis nos recepto ex fidedignorum ad hoc deputatorum testimonio ecclesie nostre utilitati uberius fore prospectum si terra eidem adversus ex piis votis defunctorum collata bonis condicionibus aliis ad certam firmam tradatur excolenda quam custodum nostrorum sumptibus excolatur de unanimi fratrum consensu concessisse et dimisisse Symoni dicto Braynd' in Suthwell' capellano unam bovatam terre cum prato et suis pertinenciis in campo de Esthorpp' quam habuimus ex dono pie memorie Johannis de Auger'. Tenend' et habend' dicto Symoni quam diu vixerit libere quiete et pacifice cum omnibus iuribus libertatibus aisiamentis in pratis pascuis pasturis et aliis communis ad tenementa terre infra villam et extra pertinentibus reddendo inde annuatim custodibus fabrice nostre pro omnimodis serviciis singulis annis quibus ipsam tenerint octodecim solidos argenti ad duos anni terminos medietatem scilicet ad Pascha et aliam medietatem in festo sancti Michaelis de quibus primam solucionem faciet in festo Pasche anno domini millesimo cc° octogesimo octavo ita videlicet quod dictus Symon dictam terram in cultura et compostura in eque bono statu quo invenerit seu meliori sustinebit nec licebit sibi dictam terram vel partem ipsius aliis locare vel quocumque alio titulo dimittere suo tempore quod si forte factum fuerit reservamus nobis potestatem illam terram sic dimissam in manus nostras reassumendi et plenam firmam nichilominus exigendi quod si dictus Symon in alicuius termini solucione defecerit quod absit licebit custodibus nostris in ipsum monicione premissa post lapsum decem dierum tanquam pro manifesta offensa maioris excommunicacionis sentenciam usque ad condignam satisfaccionem fulminare ipso vero cedente vel decedente dicta terra sine alicuius reclamacione ad nos pleno iure redibit. In cuius rei testimonium presentibus cirograffatim[1] incisi sigillum nostrum commune parti penes dictum Symonem residenti est appensum dicti Symonis sigillo parti nostre similiter appenso. Datum beate Marie Magdelene anno domini m° cc° octogesimo septimo. Testibus presentibus: magistris Symone de Curtemaiori et Benedicto de Halum et aliis.

¹ MS *sic*

Margin   Page heading, Scribe 4. *Locatio unius bovatae terrae etc. in Esthorpe* in right margin with *18ˢ per annum* below in 17ᵗʰ-c. hand.

Note   This appears to be the earliest mention of Mr Simon de Courmayeur as canon.

SOUTHWELL, CHURCHYARD, 297–8

297   *Lease at farm in the form of a chirograph by the Chapter to Sir Robert of Norwell, chaplain, for his life of a plot in the cemetery with free ingress and egress for 2s rent per annum paid to the Fabric*

24 April 1312

Universis sancte matris ecclesie filiis ad quorum noticiam presens indentura obviam se optulerit intelligend' capitulum ecclesie beate Marie Suthwell' salutem in omni salvatore. Universitas vestre in perpetua reponatur memoria quod nos dictum capitulum in plena convocacione nostra de assensu communi et beneplacito nostro concessimus et ad firmam dimissimus dilecto nobis in Christo domino Roberto de Northwell' capellano quamdam placeam in dicte ecclesie nostre cimiterio prout in longitudine et latitudine extenditur et per divisas includitur inter mansionem domini Roberti dicti Scott capellani ex parte septentrionali et stalarum iuxta domum Johannis Pepercorn' ex parte meridionali continet que xliii pedes in latere occidentali. Habend' et tenend' eidem domino Roberto ad terminum vite sue vel cuicumque infra eundem terminum assignare voluerit libere quiete et integre et cum omnibus assidenciis et commoditatibus quibuscumque eidem placie legitime incidentibus et cum libero introitu et egressu per portam domini Roberti Scott capellani reddendo inde custodibus fabrice ecclesie nostre prelibate duos solidos annuatim ad duos anni terminos videlicet ad festum sancti Martini in yeme xii. et ad festum Pentecosten xii d. pro omni servicio. Et nos dictum capitulum et successores nostri predictam placeam eidem domino Roberto warantizabimus et defendemus. Hoc eciam adiecto quod postquam prefatus dominus Robertus de Northwell' infat' decessit eadem placea penes dominum Robertum dictum Scott capellanum ad totam vitam suam integre remaneat tenend' condicionibus illis et modis omnibus quibus dictus dominus Robertus de Northwell' | eam de nobis primo tenuerat   p. 169 quam eciam prefati dominus Robertus de Northwell' et Robertus Scott in placia illa primo vacante sumptibus propriis edificarint equum reputamus et concedimus pro nobis et successoribus nostris quod iidem domini Robertus de Northwell' et Robertus Scott vel executores eorumdem per nos successores nostros alios ve quoscumque super reparacione domum murorum aut aliorum consimilium dum tamen vendicionem vel vastum spontaneum non fecerint in aliquo non calumpnientur aliquibus vel cohercionibus in quietentur. Et ut hec omnia prescripta testificata et rata perseverent tam nos quam prefatus Robertus de Northwell' sigilla nostra huic cirographo apposuimus. Datum in capitulo nostro die lune proximo ante festum sancti Marci evangeliste anno domini millesimo ccc° xii°. Hiis testibus: magistro Symone de Curtmaiori, magistro Elia de Couton', domino Willelmo de Newerk' canonicis, domino Willelmo de Hokyrton' et Hugone Leuerik' custodibus eiusdem ecclesie et multis aliis.

Margin *Locatio placea* in right margin with *2ˢ per annum* below in 17ᵗʰ-c. hand.

Note Robert Scot was later vicar of Southwell (*Reg. Melton*, v, nos 90, 23 July 1320, and 214, 11 August 1326, when John of Sandale, prebendary of Normanton, was ordered to pay him more).

fabrica

298 *Lease in the form of an indenture by the Chapter to Hugh Quarell of Southwell and John Caue, chaplains and vicars choral, for their lives of one plot built upon in their cemetery in Southwell that Robert de Sandale, canon and one of the prebendaries of Norwell, held for his life for 8s rent per annum paid to the Fabric*	1 June 1361

Sciant presentes et futuri quod nos capitulum ecclesie collegiate beate Marie Suthwell' concessimus et dimisimus Hugoni Quarell' de Suthwell' et Johanni Caue de Suthwell' capellanis ac vicariis in choro ecclesie antedicte unam placeam edificatam cum pertinenciis in Suthwell' in cimiterio dicte ecclesie quam quidem placeam Robertus de Sandale canonicus in eadem ecclesia et prebenda unius prebende de Northwell' tenuit dum vixit. Tenend' et habend' predictam placeam cum pertinenciis predictis Hugoni et Johanni ad totum tempus vite eorumdem seu alterius eorum quem diucius vivere contigerit reddendo inde annuatim nobis capitulo antedicto ad opus fabrice eiusdem ecclesie octo solidos ad duos anni terminos videlicet in festis sancti Martini in yeme et Pentecosten per equales porciones. Et predicti Hugo et Johannes omnia edificia in dicta placea constructa in adeo bono statu sustentabunt que ea receperint vel meliori salvo tamen quod iidem Hugo et Johannes muros lapides dicti cimiterii super quos quadam edificia dicte placee fundata existunt non debeant suis sumptibus sustentare. In cuius rei testimonium partibus huius scripti indentati nos capitulum antedictum ac eciam predicti Hugo et Johannes sigilla nostra alternatim apposuimus. Datum in capitulo nostro Suthwell' die martis proximo post festum sancte Trinitatis anno domini millesimo ccc sexagesimo primo.

Margin *Locatio placeae edificate* in left margin with *8ˢ per annum* below in 17ᵗʰ-c. hand.

Note Robert of Sandal, prebendary of Norwell Tertia Pars (1346–50).

pp. 170–1 These pages are blank.

SOUTHWELL, EASTHORPE, 299–300

Southwell' **Esthorpp'**

299 *Lease in the form of an indenture by the Chapter to Alexander Woodrow, Walter of Ulceby and John of Muskham, chaplains, for their lives of two bovates of land in Southwell that Mr Robert Tanner held of them for his life, for 30s rent per annum paid to the Fabric*

14 June 1373

Noverint universi quod nos capitulum ecclesie beate Marie Suthwell' concessimus dimisimus et hoc presenti scripto indentato confirmavimus Alexandro Woderoue, Waltero de Ulseby et Johanni de Muscham' capellanis duas bovatas terre cum pertinenciis in Suthwell' illas videlicet quas magister Robertus Tanour' clericus de nobis tenuit dum vixit. Habend' et tenend' predictis Alexandro, Waltero et Johanni ad totam vitam eorumdem libere et integre reddendo inde annuatim custodibus operis ecclesie nostre Suthwell' xxx s. ad festos Pentecosten et sancti Martini in yeme per equales porciones. Et nos capitulum supradictum predictas duas bovatas terre cum pertinenciis suis universis predictis Alexandro, Waltero et Johanni ad totam vitam eorumdem sicut predictum est contra omnes gentes warantizabimus acquietabimus et defendemus. In cuius rei testimonium parti huius scripti indentati penes dictos Alexandrum, Walterum et Johannem remanenti sigillum nostrum commune apposuimus parti vero altero scripti indentati penes nos capitulum antedictum remanenti Alexander, Walterus et Johannes sigilla sua apposuerunt. Hiis testibus: magistro Johanne de Crophill', domino Johanne de Kendale, domino Ada de Everyngham', magistro Jacobo de Staunton' et domino Ricardo de Chestrefeld' et aliis. Datum in generali convocacione nostra die martis proximo post festum sancte Trinitatis anno domini millesimo ccc^{mo} septuagesimo tercio.

Margin Page heading, Scribe 4. *Locacio 2 bovatas terre in Southw'* in right margin with *30^s per annum* below in 17th-c. hand.

Note A rare reference to Mr John of Cropwell (cf. **577**); it is not clear whether he held a prebend though his position in the witness list suggests he did. Mr John of Kendal, chaplain of Queen Isabella, granted expectancy as early as 20 April 1353, was certainly prebendary of Normanton by 1377 and was senior residentiary by 1395 (**500**). Mr Adam of Everingham, prebendary of South Muskham (1349–after 14 June 1373); Mr James of Staunton, prebendary of Halloughton (by 1371–after 1395); Mr Richard of Chesterfield, prebendary of Oxton I (1365–70), then Norwell Overhall (1370–1405).

300 *Lease in the form of an indenture by the Chapter to William of Winterington and Richard, his son, for their lives of two bovates of land in Easthorpe for 26s 8d rent per annum paid to the Fabric*

15 June 1400

Hec indentura testatur quod nos capitulum ecclesie collegiate beate Marie Suthwell' concessimus et dimisimus Willelmo de Wyntrington et Ricardo filio suo duas bovatas terre cum pratis pascuis et pasturis ac omnibus aliis pertinenciis suis in campo de Esthorpp iacentes ad terminum vite eorum et diucius viventis. Habend' et tenend' dictas duas bovatas terre cum pertinenciis suis prefatis Willelmo et Ricardo ad terminum vite eorum et diucius viventis reddendo inde annuatim custodibus fabrice ecclesie nostre xxvi s. viii d. ad duos anni terminos per equales porciones videlicet ad festum Pentecosten xiii s. iiii d. et ad festum sancti Martini in yeme xiii s. iiii d. et si contingat dictum redditum ad aliquem terminum durante vita eorum per mensem immediate dictos terminos sequentem a retro existere ex tunc bene licebit nobis capitulo supradicto in dictis bovatis terre distringere et districciones abducere et retinere quousque de predicto redditu cum arreragiis si que fuerint plenarie fuerit satisfactum. Et nos capitulum antedictum predictas duas bovatas terre cum pertinenciis suis universis prefatis Willelmo et Ricardo ad totam vitam eorumdem et diucius viventis sicut predictum est contra omnes gentes warantizabimus acquietabimus et defendemus. In cuius rei testimonium parti predicte alternatim presentibus indenturis indentatis sigilla sua apposuerunt. Hiis testibus: domino Willelmo de Gunthorpp', magistro Willelmo de Cawode etc. Datum in domo nostra capitulari Suthwell' in convocacione generali factam ibidem die martis proximo post festum sancte Trinitatis anno regni regis Henrici quarti post conquestum Anglie primo.

Margin *Locacio 2 bovatas terrae in Esthorpe*, in right margin with *l^li 6^s 8^d per annum* below in 17th-c. hand.

Note This appears to be the last appearance by William of Gunthorpe in the Chapter before his death. Mr William of Cawood, prebendary of Sacrista by 1397, drew up his will on 3 February 1420.

p. 173 This page is blank.

UPTON, 301–4

p. 174 **Upton'**

301 *Grant by Geoffrey le Breton of Upton to John de Auger of a half-acre of meadow* [1244 × 1249]

Sciant presentes et futuri quod ego Galfridus le Breton' de Uptona dedi concessi et presenti carta sigillo meo impressa confirmavi Johanni Augre dimidiam acram prati cum pertinenciis in Grete enge scilicet i rodam iacentem iuxta pratum quod fuit quondam Matild' de Wykes ex parte orientali et i rodam iacentem iuxta pratum capellani de Uptona ex parte occidentali. Tenend' et habend' eidem Johanni de Augre et heredibus vel assignatis suis libere quiete et pacifice cum omnibus pertinenciis libertatibus et aisiamentis ad predictum pratum pertinentibus infra villam et extra. Ego vero Galfridus le Breton' et heredes mei predictum pratum cum pertinenciis Johanni de Augr' et heredibus vel assignatis suis warantizabimus acquietabimus et defendemus in omnibus et contra omnes homines imperpetuum. Hiis testibus: domino Willelmo de Wedyndon', Ricardo de Schireborne et aliis.

Margin   Page heading, Scribe 4.

Date   Richard of Sherburn was instituted to Egmanton 9 June 1244 (*Reg. Gray*, 93–4) and before the death of William of Widdington.

302   *Grant by Geoffrey of Leadenham to John de Auger of three roods of land in Upton for one pair of white gloves worth ½d or ½d rent per annum for which he gave 14s*   [mid-13th century]

Sciant presentes et futuri quod ego Galfridus de Ledenam' dedi concessi et hac presenti carta mea confirmavi Johanni de Augr' vel cuicumque assignare dare vendere vel legare voluerit tres rodas terre arabilis in teritorio de Upton' cum suis pertinenciis videlicet unam rodam et dimidiam versus Normanton' dale buttantem super foreram Galfridi de Ledenam super Blakeland' et i rodam et dimidiam iacentem contra montem de Upton' et buttantem super foreram Hugonis Plumm' de Suthwell' versus orientem et terram domini archiepiscopi Ebor' versus occidentem. Tenend' et habend' dicto Johanni vel cuicumque assignare dare vendere vel legare voluerit sive in prosperitate sive in egritudine de me et heredibus meis imperpetuum libere quiete pacifice integre et hereditarie reddendo inde annuatim mihi et heredibus meis unum par cirotecarum albarum precii unius obuli vel unum obulum infra ebdomadam Pentecosten pro omni servicio seculari exaccione consuetudine secta curie vel demanda ad me vel heredes meos vel quoscumque pertinente. Pro hac autem donacione concessione et carte mee confirmacione dedit mihi predictus Johannes xiiii s. argenti premanibus. Ego vero Galfridus et heredes mei predicto Johanni vel cuicumque tres dictas rodas terre[1] cum pertinenciis donaverit assignaverit vendiderit vel legaverit contra omnes gentes imperpetuum warantizabimus defendemus et acquietabimus. Ut hec mea donacio et carte mee confirmacio firma sit et stabilis imperpetuum huic scripto sigillum meum apposui. Hiis testibus: domino Henrico de Suthwell' clerico et aliis.

[1] MS followed by *d* dotted for deletion

Margin   *Carta Galf. de Ledenham de 3 rod. terre in Upton* in right margin with *par cyrothecarum annum precii unum ob.* below in 17th-c. hand.

Date   Henry of Southwell witnessed 1230–50 (**229–32**).

303   *Grant by Geoffrey of Leadenham to John de Auger of three roods of meadow in Upton for one pair of white gloves worth ½d or ½d rent per annum*   [mid-13th century]

Sciant presentes et futuri quod ego Galfridus de Ledenam dedi concessi et hac presenti carta mea confirmavi Johanni de Aungr' et heredibus eius vel cuicumque assignare dare vendere vel legare voluerit iii rodas prati cum pertinenciis in prato de Upton' quod vocatur Gret enge videlicet dimidiam acram iacentem inter terram Johannis filii Isabelle de Upton' et pratum Henrici filii Agnetis de eadem et i rodam inter pratum Henrici Dodys et pratum Christiane super Hill'. Tenend' et habend' dicto Johanni et heredibus suis vel assignatis libere quiete integre pacifice et hereditarie cum omnibus suis pertinenciis reddendo inde annuatim mihi et heredibus meis unum par cirotecarum albaram precii unius obuli vel unum obulum infra ebdomanam Pentecosten pro omni servicio seculari exaccione consuetudine secta curie p. 175 vel demanda ad me vel heredes meos vel quoscumque pertinente. Pro | hac autem donacione concessione et carte mee confirmacione dedit mihi predictus Johannes xx s. argenti premanibus. Ego vero Galfridus et heredes mei predicto Johanni vel cuicumque dictas iii rodas prati assignare dare vendere vel legare voluerit sive in prosperitate sive in egritudine contra omnes homines et feminas imperpetuum warantizabimus defendemus et acquietabimus. Ut hec mea donacio concessio et carte mee confirmacio firma sit stabilis imperpetuum huic scripto sigillum meum apposui. Hiis testibus: domino Henrico de Suthwell' et aliis. Que terra et pratum dictus Johannes Augr' per cartam suam alibi scriptam dedit fabrice ecclesie etc. in cuius possessione uxoris eius relaxavit in forma consequitur.

Margin *Carta dicti Galfr. de 3 rod. prati* in right margin with *par cyrothecarum annum* below in 17ᵗʰ-c. hand.

Date At about the same time as **302**.

Upton' fabrica

304 *Quitclaim by Agnes de Burbeck, widow of John de Auger, in her free widowhood to the Fabric of five roods of meadow in Upton for which they gave 12s* [mid-13ᵗʰ century]

Sciant presentes et futuri quod ego Agnes de Burbek' quondam uxor Johannis de Augr' in libera viduitate et propria potestate mea dedi concessi et hac presenti carta mea quietum clamavi de me et heredibus meis imperpetuum Deo et fabrice ecclesie beate Marie Suthwell' et custodibus dicte fabrice qui pro tempore fuerint totum ius et clameum quod habui vel habere potui in quinque rodis prati in pratis de Upton'. Tenend' et habend' dictis fabrice et custodibus libere quiete integre et pacifice in feodo et hereditate ita quod nec ego Agnes nec heredes mei nec aliquis pro nobis vel per nos ius vel clameum decetero erga predictum pratum exigere poterimus. Pro hac autem donacione et quieta clamacione dederunt mihi custodes prefate fabrice xii solidos argenti in magna mea necessitate. Et ut hec mea donacio concessio et carte mee confirmacio firmitatem optineat imperpetuum presens scriptum sigilli mei munimine roboravi. Hiis testibus: Hugone de Upton' etc.

Margin Page heading *fabr.*, 17ᵗʰ c. as is *Agn. de Burbecke de 3 rod. prati quieti clamᵒ* in left margin.

Date After **302** and **303**.

Note On 12 June 1263 Hugh of Upton, chaplain, made a final concord with Robert of Oxton and Roesia, his wife, concerning one messuage in Upton (TNA, CP 25/1/183/12 no. 85).

305 *Grant by William Frend of Upton, chaplain, to the Fabric of a half-acre of meadow for ½d rent per annum* [1255 × 1285]

Sciant presentes et futuri quod ego Willelmus Frend de Uptona capellanus dedi concessi et hac presenti carta mea confirmavi Deo et fabrice ecclesie beate Marie Suthwell' dimidiam acram prati in Dersyng' in puram et perpetuam elemosinam pro salute anime mee patris mei et matris mee omnium que fidelium defunctorum iacentem inter pratum Johannis de Dodys ex parte occidentali et pratum beate Marie Suthwell' ex parte orientali et buttantem ad unum caput super Grete et ad aliud caput super le Mylneholm'. Habend' et tenend' fabrice dicte ecclesie libere quiete et pacifice imperpetuum reddendo inde annuatim mihi et heredibus meis vel assignatis meis unum obulum pro omni servicio seculari exaccione et demanda. Et ego eciam Willelmus et heredes mei vel assignati mei dictum pratum predicte fabrice contra omnes gentes warantizabimus et imperpetuum defendemus. In cuius rei testimonium presenti scripto sigillum meum apposui. Hiis testibus: magistro Henrico de Schyptona et aliis.

Margin *Carta W Frende de d. acr' prati in Deersynge* in left margin in 17th-c. hand.

Date While Henry of Skipton was a canon and before he was appointed archdeacon of Nottingham.

MORTON, 306

Normanton'   **fabrica**   p. 176

306 *Grant in free alms by Godfrey the Angevin to Southwell of a rent of 2s 6d received from the toft that Walter of Morton holds, and the toft, and a rent of 10d from Hugh le Lung of Morton, to have one candle daily at the masses said at the altar of St Leonard* [c. 1190 × 1229]

Sciant presentes et futuri quod ego Godfridus Andegaven' dedi concessi et hac presenti carta mea confirmavi Deo et beate Marie et ecclesie de Suthwell' pro salute anime mee et antecessorum meorum redditum duorum solidorum et dimidii percipiend' de tofto que Walterus de Morton' tenet et eciam ipsum toftum et preterea annuum redditum decem denariorum de Hugone le Lung' de Morton' et heredibus suis. Tenend' et habend' de me et heredibus meis in perpetuam elemosinam liberam et quietam ab omni terreno servicio et exaccione. Hanc autem elemosinam dedi prefate ecclesie ad habendum unum cereum cotidie ad missas coram altare sancti Leonardi. Et ego et heredes mei totam prescriptam elemosinam prefate ecclesie contra omnes homines imperpetuum warantizabimus et defendemus. Hiis testibus: Henrico de Roldeston etc. et aliis. In qua villa inveniri debet toftum predictum nescitur. Ideo queratur etc.[1]

[1] MS *In qua ... etc.* in another medieval hand

Margin   Page heading, *fabrica* 17th c. In right margin *Carta de uno cereo ardente coram sancto Leonardo ad missas* (? medieval), with *6d per annum* and *18d per annum* below both 17th c. and *quere melius* (medieval).

Date   While Godfrey the Angevin was active (*Thurgarton*, 233n).

NORMANTON BY SOUTHWELL, 307–11

Normanton'

307   *Grant in hereditary fee by Beatrix de Bella Aqua to Ralph, her son, of three bovates of land in Normanton for 1 lb of cumin rent per annum*
[late 12th century]

Sciant presentes et futuri quod ego Beatrix de Bella Aqua concessi dedi et hac presenti carta mea confirmavi Radulpho filio meo et heredibus suis pro homagio et servicio tres bovatas terre in Normanton' iuxta Suthwell' scilicet duas bovatas que fuerunt Hacun et unam bovatam que fuit Thuka. Tenend' de me et heredibus meis libere quiete in feodo et hereditate reddendo mihi et heredibus meis unam libram cymini annuatim ad festum sancti Johannis Baptiste pro omnibus serviciis mihi et meis pertinentibus salvo forinseco servicio. Hiis testibus: Alano de Pykeryng' et aliis.

Margin   Sub-heading, Scribe 4. *Carta Beatr. de Bella aqa de 3 bovat. terr. in Norm* in right margin, 17th c.

Date   Before **308**. Mr Alan of Pickering witnessed two charters to Rufford in the late 12th c. (*Rufford*, 167, 963).

Note   *Thuka* (*Tukke* in **308**) was the ancestor of the Tuke family of Kelham (*Rufford*, passim).

308   *Grant by Ralph de Bella Aqua to the Fabric of three bovates of land in Normanton next Southwell for 1 lb of cumin rent per annum paid to Adam de Bella Aqua*   [1214 × 1230]

Omnibus sancte matris ecclesie filiis hoc scriptum visuris vel audituris Radulphus de Bella Aqua salutem in vero salvatore. Noveritis me in tuitu Dei et pro salute anime mee et pro animabus antecessorum meorum concessisse dedisse et hac presenti carta mea confirmasse Deo et beate Marie de Suthwell' et fabrice matris ecclesie eiusdem loci iii bovatas terre cum omnibus pertinenciis in Normanton' iuxta Suthwell' scilicet duas bovatas quas Hacun tenuit et unam bovatam quam Tukke tenuit in eadem villa de Normanton', tenendas libere quiete et pacifice de Ada de Bella Aqua et heredibus ipsius reddendo inde annuatim dicto Ade et heredibus suis unam libram cymini ad nativitatem Johannis baptiste pro omni servicio ad predictam terram pertinente salvo forinseco. Et ut hec donacio mea rata firma et stabilis imperpetuum permaneat presenti carte mee sigillum meum apposui. Testibus: capitulo Suthwell' scilicet Hugone decano, T de Wodeburgh', Roberto de Laxington' et aliis etc.

Margin   In right margin *Carta dicti Radulphi de iisdem* (*sic*) 17th c.

Date After Robert of Laxton became a canon and before the death of Hugh the dean.

Note From his position as second witness it appears that T. of Woodborough was a canon.

309 *Confirmation by Adam de Bella Aqua, knight, to the Fabric of three bovates of land in Normanton next Southwell that Ralph de Bella Aqua, his uncle, held of him and gave to Southwell for 1 lb of cumin rent per annum* [1220 × 1230]

Omnibus sancte matris ecclesie filiis hoc scriptum visuris vel audituris Adam de Bella Aqua miles salutem in salutis auctore. Noverit universitas vestra me in tuitu Dei et beate Marie et pro salute anime mee et pro animabus uxoris mee antecessorum et heredum meorum concessisse et presenti carta mea confirmasse Deo et ecclesie sancte Marie de Suthwell' | in promocionem fabrice eiusdem ecclesie iii bovatas terre in Normanton' iuxta Suthwell' cum omnibus pertinenciis suis infra villam de Normanton' et extra scilicet illas easdem bovatas quas Radulphus de Bella Aqua patruus meus tenuit de me in predicta villa et dedit prenominate ecclesie de Suthwell'. Tenend' et habend' ipsi ecclesie imperpetuum de me et heredibus meis libere quiete et pacifice reddendo inde annuatim mihi et heredibus meis unam libram cimini ad nativitatem sancti Johannis baptiste pro omni servicio salvo forinseco. Et ut hec mea concessio et confirmacio firma et stabilis imposterum permaneat eam presenti carte mee attestacione et sigilli mei apposicione dignum duxi roborare. Hiis testibus: Hugone decano et aliis.

p. 177

Margin *Carta Adae de Bella Aqua super iisdem* (17th c.) in right margin.

Date After **308**.

Note Since Adam de Bella Aqua termed Ralph his paternal uncle, then Ralph was another son of William de Bella Aqua and probably brother of Thomas de Bella Aqua of Stallingborough (**416n**). William de Bella Aqua (**119n**) married an unnamed daughter of John fourth baron Deyncourt (*Thurgarton*, lxxix, ccxx), and Beatrix may well be her or a subsequent wife. On the death of William de Bella Aqua in 1196, who held of the archbishop of York and Deyncourt, his heir was a minor (*Chancellor's Roll*, 189; *PR 9 Richard I*, 119). In 1198 and 1199 Hugh Bardolph rendered an account of 100 marks to have the custody of William's lands, his heir and his marriage, and Adam, William's heir, would appear to have come of age in 1201 and certainly by 1204 (*PR 10 Richard I*, 43; *PR 1 John*, 141; *PR 6 John*, 174). William held of Deyncourt in 1166 so his marriage to John fourth baron's daughter had taken place before this time and as his sons Thomas and Ralph were seemingly of age in the late twelfth and early thirteenth centuries, it is suggested that Adam was William's grandson, the son of William's eldest son and heir, whose name is unknown, who had predeceased him. Adam quitclaimed his rights in the chapel of Kirklington (**118**). He made no grants to Rufford but witnessed charters to Rufford in the period 1202–33 (*Rufford*, 39, 163, 181, 183, 187, 190, 726, 771). He witnessed the confirmation of Matilda de Caux to Rufford (*Rufford*, 573), and with her heir, John of Birkin (d. 1227), Alexander, abbot of Selby (1214–21), Richard, abbot of Selby (1195–1215) and Jordan de Landa (**396n**), he witnessed grants to Pontefract priory and Selby abbey (*Pontefract cartulary*, 525, 554–5; *Selby Coucher*, 20, 144). To Selby Adam granted an oak in his wood of Burn (Brayton parish, Yorks.) called *le Fairhac* (*Selby Coucher*, 140). In 1297–8 Adam's grandson, John, held a half fee of the archbishop of York in Burne (*Reg. Romeyn*, ii, 254; *Kirkby's Inquest*, 284). Adam was appointed a justice on 2 December 1227 and 17 June 1229 (*Patent Rolls*, ii, 207, 294). He was dead by 1236 and succeeded by his son Thomas (**412n**).

Normanton'

310 *Quitclaim by Richard, son of Robert of Normanton, to the Fabric of eight strips of land in Normanton* [mid-13th century]

Omnibus Christi fidelibus presens scriptum visuris vel audituris Ricardus filius Roberti de Normanton' salutem in domino. Noveritis me concessisse et omnino quietum clamasse pro salute anime mee et omnium antecessorum meorum Deo et fabrice ecclesie beate Marie Suthwell' totum ius et clameum quod habui vel habere potui vel quod me vel heredes meos contingere posset in octo selionibus terre arabilis in teritorio de Normanton' quorum iii fuerunt ex dono Roberti de Lexington' bone memorie quos idem Robertus habuit de dono Roberti patris mei et iacent in campo occidentali inter terram dicte fabrice et terram Henrici le Tayllur' et buttantes super Grimisdam et quinque ex dono antecessorum meorum in campo aquilonari ex quibus ii seliones iacent super Coliyorne inter terram Henrici le Tayllur' et terram dotis matris mee abuttantes super viam regiam et iii seliones super Bradebusk' abuttantes et iacent propinquiores campo occidentali inter terram dicte fabrice et terram meam cum omnibus pertinenciis. Tenend' et habend' dicte fabrice in liberam puram et perpetuam elemosinam. Et ego Ricardus et heredes mei dicte fabrice dictam terram cum pertinenciis prout supradictum est contra omnes gentes warantizabimus acquietabimus et defendemus imperpetuum. In cuius rei testimonium presenti scripto sigillum meum apposui. Hiis testibus: domino Symone de Gringilthorp milite, Roberto de Barra etc. et aliis.

Margin Page heading, Scribe 4. In left margin *Carta Ricardi de Normanton de 8 selion' terre* (17th c.).

Date After the death of Robert of Laxton (29 May 1250).

Note For Sir Simon of Grimblethorpe see **415n**.

311 *Lease in the form of a chirograph by the Chapter to Sir Richard of Normanton, vicar of the parish of Southwell, John Ben and Matilda, his wife, for their lives of one bovate of land in Normanton of the gift of Ralph de Bella Aqua and four strips of land and the tenement of Richard of Normanton for 10s rent per annum paid to the Fabric* 12 June 1366

Universis presentes inspecturis vel audituris capitulum ecclesie beate Marie Suthwell' eternam in domino salutem. Noveritis nos recepto fidedignorum ad hoc deputatorum testimonio ecclesie nostre utilitati uberius fore prospectum si terra eodem ad usus fabrice nostre ex piis votis defunctorum bonis condicionibus aliis ad firmam certam tradatur excolenda quam custodum nostrorum sumptibus propriis excolatur de unanimi fratrum consensu concessisse et dimisisse domino Ricardo de Normanton' vicario parochiali ecclesie nostre Suthwell' predicte Johanni Ben' et Matild' uxori eiusdem unam bovatam terre cum prato et

suis pertinenciis in campo de Normanton illam videlicet bovatam a sole
remociorem quam quidam dictus Hacun quondam tenuit in eadem villa
nostra quam insuper una cum aliis terris habuimus de dono pie memorie
Radulphi de Bella Aqua et quatuor seliones terre arabilis et tenementum
Ricardi de Normanton'. Tenend' et habend' dictis domino Ricardo Johanni
et Matild' ut premittitur et eorum cuilibet quam diu vixerint vel vixerit
libere quiete et pacifice cum omnibus iuribus libertatibus aisiamentis in
pratis pascuis pasturis et aliis communis ad tantam terram infra villam
et extra pertinentibus reddendo inde annuatim custodibus fabrice nostre
pro omnimodis | serviciis salvo forinseco singulis annis quibus ipsam   p. 178
tenerint vel tenerit decem solidos argenti ad duos anni terminos videlicet
medietatem in festo sancti Martini in yeme et aliam medietatem in
festo Pentecosten de quibus primam solucionem facient in festo sancti
Martini in yeme anno gracie m° ccc^mo sexagesimo sexto et sic deinceps
terminis successivis ita videlicet quod dicti dominus Ricardus Johannes
et Matill' ut premittitur et eorum quilibet qui supervixerit dictam terram
in cultura et compostura in eque bono statu quo invenerint seu meliori
sustinebunt et sustinebit nec licebit ipsis vel eorum alicui dictam terram
vel partem illius aliis locare vel quocumque alio titulo dimittere suo
tempore quod si forte factum fuerit reservamus nobis potestatem illam
terram sic dimissam in manus nostras reassumendi et plenam firmam
nichilominus exigendi quod si dicti dominus Ricardus Johannes et Matill'
vel eorum aliquis qui pro tempore tenerint in aliquo termino defecerint vel
defecerit quod absit licebit custodibus nostris in ipsos et eorum quemlibet
monicione premissa post lapsum decem dierum tanquam pro manifesta
offensa maioris excommunicacionis usque ad condignam satisfaccionem
fulminare ipsis vero cedentibus et decedentibus vel eorum quolibet qui
superfuerit cedente vel decedente dicta terra sine alicuius reclamacione
ad nos pleno iure redibit. In cuius rei testimonium presenti cirografatim
incisis sigillum nostrum commune¹ parti penes dictum Ricardum Johannem
et Matild' residenti est appensum dictorum domini Ricardi Johannis et
Matild' sigillis parti nostre similiter appensis. Datum in domo nostra
capitulari Suthwell' die veneris proximo post festum sancte Trinitatis in
convocacione anno gracie supradicto.

¹ MS followed by *present'* crossed through and dotted for deletion

Margin   In left margin *Locacio terrarum* and *10ˢ per annum* (17ᵗʰ c.). Heading, p. 178
Normanton, Scribe 4.

This page is blank.   p. 179

KIRKLINGTON, 312–16

Kyrtelyngton'

312 *Grant by Thomas of Kirklington to Mr Hugh of Upton of all his land with toft, croft and buildings that he held in Kirklington of the chapel of St Giles of Edingley for 12d rent per annum paid to the chapel for which he gave five and a half marks* [1236 × 1272]

Sciant presentes et futuri quod ego Thomas de Kyrtlingtona dedi concessi et hac presenti carta mea confirmavi magistro Hugoni de Uptona totam terram meam quam habui in teritorio de Kyrlyngton' una cum tofto et crofto que habui in villa de Kytlingtona et edificiis et omnibus pertinenciis ad dictam terram infra villam et extra pertinentibus videlicet illam quam tenui de capella sancti Egidii de Edyngley. Tenend' et habend' predicto Hugoni et heredibus suis vel cuicumque assignare vendere dare vel legare voluerit sive in prosperitate sive in egritudine libere quiete et integre et pacifice reddendo inde annuatim capelle sancti Egidii de Edyngley duodecim denarios tantummodo pro omni servicio seculari exaccione et demanda scilicet sex denarios ad Pentecosten et sex denarios ad festum sancti Martini in yeme. Pro hac autem donacione concessione et carte mee confirmacione dedit mihi predictus Hugo in maxima necessitate mea quinque marcas argenti et dimidiam premanibus. Ego vero Thomas et heredes mei predictam terram cum pertinenciis predicto Hugoni et heredibus suis vel suis assignatis ut predictum est contra omnes homines warantizabimus. In cuius rei testimonium presenti scripto sigillum apposui. Hiis testibus: domino Thoma de Bella Aqua et aliis.

Margin Page heading, Scribe 4. In right top margin in late medieval hand: *reddunt annuatim xii d. capelle sancti Egidii de Edingley. Item xii d. per manus custodis fabrice s.* In right margin in 17th-c. hand: *Carta Tho. de Kirkl' de tofto et crofto*, then *nota tenure* with *12d per annum* below.

Date While Thomas de Bella Aqua was active (**412n**) and before **315**.

313 *Quitclaim by Hugh, son of Richard of Upton, rector of Kneeton, to the Fabric of one toft and all his land in Kirklington for 12d rent per annum paid to the chapel of Edingley* [1236 × 1272]

Sciant presentes et futuri quod ego Hugo filius Ricardi de Upton' rector ecclesie Cnyveton' dedi concessi et hac presenti carta mea confirmavi quietum clamavi Deo et beate Marie ad sustentacionem fabrice ecclesie beate Marie Suthwell' unum toftum et totam terram cum prato quam habui et tenui in villa et teritorio de Kyrtelyngton'. Habend' et tenend' Deo et beate Marie ad sustentacionem dicte fabrice imperpetuum cum omnibus pertinenciis sine aliquo retenemento et cum omnibus libertatibus et aisiamentis infra villam et extra ad dictam terram pertinentibus reddendo inde annuatim capelle de Edyngley per manus custodum dicte fabrice xii d. ad duos anni terminos videlicet mediatatem ad Pentecosten et aliam mediatatem ad festum sancti Martini in yeme pro omnibus serviciis

consuetudinibus sectis et secularibus demandis ita quod nec ego Hugo
nec heredes mei nec aliquis ex parte nostra ius clameum aut calumpniam
aliquo modo in dictis tofto terra et prato cum pertinenciis omnibus aliquo
tempore habere poterimus vel exigere. Et in huius donacionis et quiete
clamacionis mee perpetuum testimonium huic carte sigillum meum
apposui. Hiis testibus: dominis Thoma de Bella Aqua et aliis.

Margin In right margin *Carta Ri. de Upton de eisdem*, with *12^d per annum* in 17th-c.
hand.

Date While Thomas de Bella Aqua was active (**412n**) and after **312**.

Note There is no record of Hugh, son of Richard of Upton, being presented to Kneesall
church. He probably preceded Clement of Kent instituted 22 April 1279 (*Reg. Giffard*,
62). It is unclear if he was the same man as Master Hugh of Upton, chaplain (**304**), but
very likely (cf. **319**).

314 *Quitclaim by Thomas de Bella Aqua, knight, to the Fabric of the
land with toft and croft that Hugh, son of Richard of Upton, rector of
Kneeton, held of the chapel of St Giles of Edingley* [1236 × 1272]

Omnibus Christi fidelibus presens scriptum visuris vel audituris Thomas
de Bella Aqua miles salutem in domino. Noveritis me pro salute anime
mee patris et matris parentum et amicorum meorum dedisse concessisse
et hoc presenti scripto omnino quietum clamasse Deo et fabrice ecclesie
beate Marie Suthwell' totum ius et clameum quod habui vel habere potui
vel quod me vel heredes meos contingere possit in illa terra cum prato
quam Hugo filius Ricardi de Upton' rector ecclesie de Knyvetona habuit
in teritorio de Kyrtlyngton' una cum tofto et crofto illam videlicet quam
tenuit de capella sancti Egidii de Edyngley et dedit Deo et beate Marie
ad sustentacionem fabrice ecclesie beate Marie Suthwell' ita quod nec
ego Thomas nec aliquis per me nec heredes mei aliquod ius vel clameum
decetero in predicta terra cum tofto et crofto nobis exigere vel vendicare
poterimus nec aliquam districcionem eam alicuius secte vel alterius deinde
secularis facere. In cuius rei testimonium huic presenti scripto sigillum
meum apposui. Hiis testibus: Roberto de Sutton et aliis.

Margin *Tho. de Bella Aqua militis de eisdem quieti clam°* in right margin in 17th-c. hand.

Date While Thomas de Bella Aqua was active (**412n**) after **312** and **313** and before
315. Robert of Sutton succeeded his brother in 1268 (*Rufford*, cxi).

Kyrtelyngton p. 181

315 *Lease in the form of a bipartite indenture by the Chapter to Hugh
of Kirklington, clerk, for his life of one toft and croft that they have of
the gift of Mr Hugh of Upton for 6s rent per annum paid to the Fabric*
Southwell, October 1273

Noverint universi quod capitulum ecclesie beate Marie Southwell'
concessit et dimisit Hugoni de Kyrtlyngton' clerico toftum et croftum
in villa de Kyrtlyngton' quod idem capitulum habuit de concessione et

dono magistri Hugonis de Upton'. Tenend' et habend' cum terra et prato et omnibus aliis libertatibus et aisiamentis infra villam et extra ad idem toftum et croftum pertinentibus eidem Hugoni quam diu vixerit pro vi s. argenti annuatim fabrice ecclesie nostre Suthwell' solvend' ad duos anni terminos per porciones equales medietatem scilicet in festo Pentecosten et aliam medietatem in festo sancti Martini in yeme pro omni servicio seculari consuetudine secta curie et demanda ita tamen quod toftum illud et croftum cum ceteris pertinenciis nulli ad perpetuam firmam concedere nec aliquo modo alienare licebit sed post illius decessum toftum illud et croftum cum dictis suis pertinenciis ad predictum capitulum absque clameo alicuius libere revertetur et si contingat dictum Hugonem in aliquo termino a solucione predicte firme deficere licebit procuratori seu procuratoribus fabrice ecclesie Suthwell' tenementum predictum libere ingredi et omnia bona ibi inventa ad manus suas detinere donec de firma retenta et dampnis ac interesse occasione huiusmodi plene fuerit satisfactum. In testimonium autem et evidenciam premissorum sigillum capituli commune et sigillum predicti Hugonis huic scripto bipartito cuius una pars penes dictum capitulum et pars alia penes prefatum Hugonem residet alternatim sunt appensa. Datum in capitulo Suthwell' mense Octobris anno domini m° cc^{mo} septuagesimo tercio.

Margin   Heading, Scribe 4. In left margin *Locatio eorumdem* and *6^s per annum* below in 17th-c. hand.

316   *Lease in the form of a chirograph by the Chapter to William called Study living in Kirklington, Avicia, his sister, and Avicia, his daughter, for their lives of one toft with buildings and a half-bovate of land in Kirklington that Mr Hugh of Upton sometime gave to the Fabric for 6s rent per annum paid to the Fabric*   Southwell, 1322

Universis presentes litteras inspecturis vel audituris capitulum ecclesie beate Marie Suthwell' eternam in domino salutem. Noveritis me[i] de unanimi fratrum nostrorum consensu concessisse et dimisisse Willelmo dicto Study manenti in Kyrtlyngton' Avicie sorori sue et Avicie filie eiusdem Willelmi unum toftum cum edificiis superponitis in villa de Kyrtlyngton' et dimidiam bovatam terre in campo eiusdem ville cum omnibus pertinenciis infra villam et extra que quondam magistrum Hugonem [de] Upton' concessit et dedit Deo et beate Marie ad sustentacionem fabrice ecclesie beate Marie Suthwell'. Tenend' et habend' dictis Willelmo et Avicie sorori sue et Avicie filie eiusdem Willelmi successive prout nomina eorum presentibus inseruntur seratim toto tempore vite sue libere quiete et pacifice sine alicuius impedimento reddendo inde annuatim custodibus fabrice ecclesie nostre predicte sex solidos argenti ad duos anni terminos videlicet ad festos sancti Martini in yeme et Pentecosten per equales porciones pro omni servicio seculari consuetudine secta curie et demanda ita videlicet quod dicti Willelmus Avicia soror eius et Avicia filia eiusdem Willelmi vel unius eorum qui diucius vixerit dictum toftum cum edificiis super ponitis in maeremio et coopertura terra eciam in cultura et compostura in eque bono statu quo eam receperunt vel meliori sustinebunt vel sustinebit nec

licebit eisdem vel eorum alicui dictum toftum terram pratum vel aliquod
ad dictum tenementum pertinens alii vel aliis locare vel quocumque alio
titulo suo tempore dimittere quod si forte factum fuerit reservamus nobis
potestatem dictum toftum terram pratum vel partem eorum sic dimissam
in manus nostras reassumendi et plenam firmam nichilominus exigendi et
si contingat dictos Willelmum Aviciam sororem suam et Aviciam filiam
eiusdem Willelmi vel eorum aliquem in aliquo termino a solucione dicte
firme deficere licebit | custodibus fabrice qui pro tempore fuerint dictum   p. 182
tenementum libere ingredi et omnia bona ibi inventa in manus suas retinere
donec de firma detenta dampnis ac interesse occasione huius plene fuerit
satisfactum ipsis vero successive cedentibus vel decedentibus vel eorum
aliquo qui diucius superfuerit cedente vel decedente dictum toftum cum
terra et prato ac omnibus suis pertinenciis alicuius reclamacione ad nos
pleno iure redibit. In cuius rei testimonium presentibus cirografatim incisis
sigilla parcium alternatim sunt appensa. Actum et datum in domo nostra
Suthwell' anno domini millesimo ccc^{mo} vicesimo secundo.

¹ MS *sic*

Margin   In left margin *Locacio unius tofti et 9 bovat terr* with *6ˢ per annum* below
in 17ᵗʰ-c. hand.

HALAM, 317

Halum'

317   *Lease in the form of a chirograph by the Chapter to Robert Wython,*
chaplain, for his life of one strip of land in Halam for 10d rent per annum
paid to the Fabric   Southwell, 22 July 1288

Universis presentes inspecturis vel audituris capitulum ecclesie beate
Marie Suthwell' eternam in domino salutem. Noveritis nos recepto ex
fidedignorum ad hoc deputatorum testimonio ecclesie nostre utilitati
uberius fore prospectum si terra eidem ad usus fabrice nostre ex piis votis
defunctorum collata bonis condicionibus aliis ad certam firmam dimittatur
excolenda quam custodum nostrorum sumptibus excolatur de unanimi
fratrum consensu concessisse et dimisisse Roberto de Wython' in Suthwell'
capellano i selionem terre arabilis in campo de Halum' iuxta Merthorne
inter terram dicti Roberti et terram Roberti dicti Hasard' de Osmonthorpp'.
Tenend' et habend' dicto Roberto quam diu vixerit libere quiete et pacifice
sine aliquo retenemento reddendo inde annuatim custodibus fabrice
nostre pro omnimodis serviciis decem denarios ad duos anni terminos
medietatem videlicet in festo sancti Michaelis et aliam medietatem in
festo Pentecosten anno domini millesimo cc octogesimo octavo eciam
deinceps terminis successivis ita videlicet quod dictus Robertus dictam
terram in cultura et compostura in eque bono statu quo invenerit seu
meliori sustinebit nec licebit sibi dictam terra aliis locare vel quocumque
alio titulo dimittere suo tempore quod si forte factum fuerit reservamus
nobis potestatem illam terram sic dimissam in manus nostras reassumendi

et plenam firmam nicholominus exigendi quod si predictus Robertus in alicuius termini solucione defecerit quod absit licebit custodibus nostris in ipsam monicione premissa post lapsum decem dierum tanquam pro manifesta offensa maioris excommunicacionis sentenciam usque ad condignam satisfaccionem fulminare ipso vero cedente vel decedente dicta terra sine alicuius reclamacione ad nos pleno iure redibit. In cuius rei testimonium presenti cirografatim incisis sigillum nostrum commune parti penes dictum Robertum residenti est appensum dicti Roberti sigillo parti nostre similiter appenso. Actum et datum die beate Marie Magd' anno domini supradicto etc.

Margin   Heading and sub-heading, Scribe 4. In right margin *Locatio unius selionis*, signum of a hand *nota bene i selio terrae arabilis in campo de Halome fabrice ecclesie spectante* and *10ᵈ per annum* all 17ᵗʰ c.

FLINTHAM, 318–19

p. 182a **Flyntham'** **fabrica** **Eton'**

318 *Acknowledgement by Mr Hugh of Upton that he has received from the Chapter a quitclaim by the Chapter to him of all the land in Flintham that they have of the gift of Thomas of Radcliffe, sometime rector of Flintham* [mid-13ᵗʰ century]

Omnibus Christi fidelibus ad quos presens scriptum pervenerit magister Hugo de Upton salutem in domino. Noveritis me recepisse a capitulo beate Marie Suthwell' cartam de terra de Flyntham' sigillo eius capituli signatam in hiis verbis: Noveritis nos dedisse concessisse et hoc presenti scripto nostro quietum clamasse imperpetuum magistro Hugoni de Upton' et heredibus suis et assignatis totam terram et pratum cum pertinenciis in teritorio de Flyntham' que habemus de dono Thome de Radclyve quondam rectoris ecclesie de Flyntham'. Tenend' et habend' dicto magistro Hugoni et heredibus suis et assignatis suis imperpetuum faciendo inde servicium domini feodi quod ad predictam terram pertinet. In huius rei testimonium sigillum meum apposui. Hiis testibus: domino Roberto de Sutton' et aliis.

Margin   Heading *Flyntham'* and *Eton'*, Scribe 4; *fabrica* 17ᵗʰ c. In left margin *Carta Hug. de Upton reception' scripti testificans* (17ᵗʰ c.).

Date   Probably before **319** and see note. Robert of Sutton, however, succeeded his brother William in 1268 and died in 1286 (*Rufford*, cxi).

Note   The pagination 182a results from a miscounting by the paginator, with the *a* added in a modern hand. There is no record of the institution of Thomas of Radcliffe as rector of Flintham in Archbishop Gray's register. He was presented by Welbeck abbey to Flintham in 1223 (*CRR*, xi, 1217) but Gilbert, parson of Flintham, was fined 1228–9 (*Thurgarton*, 403n). Thomas was the son of Mr Stephen of Radcliffe, rector of Radcliffe on Trent in 1226 who was dead by 1231. Thomas witnessed 1223–8 and Walter, brother of Thomas, parson of Flintham, son of Stephen of Radcliffe, granted land in Flintham to Thurgarton priory *c.* 1231–45 (*Reg. Gray*, 73n; *Thurgarton*, 403n, 404–5). Thomas of Sherburn was instituted to the vicarage of Flintham on 25 September 1278 (*Reg. Giffard*, 71). In its current form the Chapter's quitclaim is very brief, and may well have been abbreviated by the copyist.

319 *Quitclaim by Mr Hugh, son of Richard of Upton, to the Fabric of one bovate of land in Flintham that he holds of the Fabric*
[1255 × 1268]

Omnibus Christi fidelibus hoc scriptum visuris vel audituris magister Hugo filius Ricardi de Upton' salutem in domino. Noveritis me concessisse et hoc presenti scripto quietum clamasse Deo et ecclesie beate Marie Suthwellie ad opus fabrice eiusdem ecclesie totum ius et clameum quod habui vel habere potui vel quod me contingere posset in una bovata terre in Flyntham' quam tenui de fabrica predicte ecclesie cum omnibus pertinenciis in pratis pascuis et omnibus locis imperpetuum ita quod nec ego Hugo nec heredes mei nec aliquis per me vel pro me in predicta bovata terre cum pertinenciis ut predictum est de cetero aliquod ius vel clameum exigere vel vendicare poterimus. Ad hanc quietam clamacionem firmiter et sine dolo imperpetuum observandam presens scriptum sigilli mei impressione roboravi. Hiis testibus: domino Ricardo de Sutton', magistro Henrico de Schipton' canonicis et aliis.

Margin   In left margin *Hug. filii R. de Upton de bovata terre in Flintham quieti clam⁰* (17ᵗʰ c.).

Date   While Henry of Skipton was a canon and before the death of Richard of Sutton.

EATON, 320

320 *Grant by Ralph, son of William, son of Alwri of Eaton, to the Fabric of 3d rent per annum received from Lemnus, son of Hugh de Hascam, for a half-acre of land in Eaton*
[1229 × 1254]

Sciant presentes et futuri quod ego Radulphus filius Willelmi filii Alwri de Eton' dedi concessi et hac presenti carta mea confirmavi fabrice ecclesie beate Marie Suthwell' in puram et perpetuam elemosinam tres denarios quos Lemnus filius Hugonis de Hascam mihi reddere debuit pro dimidia acra terre in teritorio de Eton' que iacet apud Hidecrofte inter terram Henrici carpentarii et totum ius quod mihi de ea possit adquiri solvend' die Pentecosten custodi dicte fabrice ecclesie. Et ego et heredes mei warantizabimus predictam donacionem predicte fabrice contra omnes homines imperpetuum cum omnibus pertinenciis. Hiis testibus: domino Roberto de Wlkric et aliis.

Margin   In left margin *Eton'* (Scribe 4), *Carta de red. 3ᵈ* (17ᵗʰ c.).

Date   While Robert de Wolrington was active (**231n**).

p. 183

Burg'

321 *Grant by William Browning of Southwell to Thomas Ode of Southwell and Agnes, his wife, of one messuage in Southwell*

Southwell, 4 October 1351

Sciant presentes et futuri quod ego Willelmus Brownynge de Suthwell' dedi concessi et hac presenti carta mea confirmavi Thome Ode de Suthwell' et Agneti uxori eius unum mesuagium cum pertinenciis in burgo Suthwell' inter mesuagium quondam Symonis Snowe ex una parte et mesuagium quondam Beatricis de Wellagh' ex altera parte. Tenend' et habend' predictis Thome et Agneti et heredibus ipsius Thome predictum mesuagium cum pertinenciis libere quiete bene et in pace imperpetuum de capitalibus dominis feodi illius per servicia inde debita et consueta. Et ego predictus Willelmus et heredes mei predictum mesuagium cum pertinenciis predictis Thome et Agneti et heredibus ipsius Thome contra omnes gentes warantizabimus imperpetuum. In cuius rei testimonium huic presenti carte mee sigillum meum apposui. Hiis testibus: Roberto Maundvyle de Suthwell', Willelmo de Eton' de Suthwell' et aliis multis. Datum apud Suthwell' die martis proximo post festum sancti Michaelis archangeli anno domini millesimo ccc° quinquegesimo primo.

Margin Heading (and on pp. 184–90) in same hand (Scribe 4). In right margin, a capital *B* (medieval), *Carta W. Browning de mess. in burgo* (17ᵗʰ c.).

Note 321–44 concern three messuages in Southwell (two adjacent to each other) which between the mid-fourteenth and early fifteenth century slowly passed into the hands of the Vicars Choral, providing evidence for complex property dealing between the laity and the Church as well as for trades practised in the town.

322 *Note on missing charter of Thomas Ode*

Margin *Deficit cartam Thome Ode.* (medieval)

Note The missing charter probably related to the messuage mentioned in **321**.

p. 184

Burg'

323 *Grant by Robert Tanner of Southwell to John de Blakemore of one messuage in Southwell*

2 November 1359

Sciant presentes et futuri quod ego Robertus Tanur de Suthwell' dedi concessi et hac presenti carta mea confirmavi Johanni de Blakemore unum mesuagium in burgo Suthwell' iacens inter mesuagium Ricardi de Warsop' ex parte una et mesuagium quod quondam tenuit Ricardus Rofote ex parte altera. Habend' et tenend' cum suis pertinenciis imperpetuum eidem Johanni heredibus et assignatis suis de capitalibus dominis feodi illius per servicia debita et consueta. Et ego dictus Robertus Tanur et heredes mei predictum mesuagium cum pertinenciis suis prefato Johanni heredibus

et assignatis suis warantizabimus imperpetuum. In cuius rei testimonium
huic presenti carte mee sigillum meum apposui. Hiis testibus: Johanne
de Waynflete, Johanne Parker, Roberto Maundevyle et aliis. Datum apud
Suthwell' die sabbati proximo ante festum sanctorum Symonis et Jude
anno incarnacionis domini m° ccc° quinquagesimo nono.

Margin   In left margin *Carta Rob. Tanner de messuagio in Southwell* (17ᵗʰ c.).

324   *Grant by John de Blakemore of Southwell, chaplain, to Alice, his
mother, of one messuage that descended to him in hereditary right after
the death of John Blakemore, his father*   Southwell, 9 September 1375

Sciant presentes et futuri quod ego Johannes de Blakemore de Suthwell'
capellanus dedi concessi et hac presenti carta mea confirmavi Alicie matri
mee heredibus et assignatis suis unum mesuagium cum pertinenciis que
mihi descendebat¹ de iure hereditatis post decessum Johannis Blakemore
patris mei inter tenementum Ricardi Rofote ex una parte et tenementum
Ricardi Warsopp' ex altera parte et abuttat ad unum caput super viam
regiam et aliud caput super culturam domini archiepiscopi. Tenend'
et habend' predictum mesuagium cum suis pertinenciis supradictis
predicte Alicie matri mee heredibus et assignatis [suis] faciendo capitali
domino feodi illius per servicia inde debita et consueta libere quiete
pacifice integre imperpetuum. Et ego dictus Johannes de Blakemore de
Suthwell' capellanus dictum mesuagium cum suis pertinenciis supradictis
prefate Alicie matri mee heredibus et assignatis suis contra omnes gentes
warantizabimus imperpetuum. In cuius rei testimonium huic presenti
carte sigillum meum apposui. Hiis testibus: Johanne de Ferendon' de
Suthwell', Johanne Kyng' de eadem, Johanne Smyth de eadem, Hugone
Swayne et aliis multis. Datum apud Suthwell' die dominica proximo post
festum nativitatis beate Marie virginis anno regni regis Edwardi tercii
post conquestum quadragesimo nono.

¹ MS *descendebant*

Margin   In left margin *Carta Jo. Blackmore de eodem* (17ᵗʰ c.) and signum of hand
nota (17ᵗʰ c.).

325   *Grant by Alice de Blakemore of Southwell to Richard of Darley
of Southwell, draper, and Margaret, his wife, of one messuage in Southwell*   Southwell, 14 October 1375

Sciant presentes et futuri quod ego Alicia de Blakemore de Suthwell'
dedi concessi et hac presenti carta mea confirmavi Ricardo de Derley
de Suthwell' drapure et Margarete uxori sue unum mesuagium cum
pertinenciis suis prout jacet in longitudine et latitudine in burgo de Suthwell'
inter mesuagium Johannis filii Symonis ex una parte et mesuagium
Ricardi de Warsopp' ex altera parte et abbuttat ad unum caput super viam
regiam et ad aliud caput super culturam domini archiepiscopi. Tenend'
et habend' predictum mesuagium cum suis pertinenciis dictis Ricardo
et Margarete heredibus et assignatis eorum de capitalibus dominis feodi

p. 185   illius per servicia inde debita et de | iure consueta imperpetuum. Et ego vero dicta Alicia de Blakemore et heredes mei dictum mesuagium cum pertinenciis prefatis Ricardo et Margarete heredibus et assignatis eorum ut predictum est contra omnes gentes warantizabimus imperpetuum. In cuius rei testimonium huic presenti carte mee sigillum meum apposui. Hiis testibus: Johanne Parkere de Suthwell', Johanne de Farndon' de eadem, Johanne Fissher de eadem et aliis multis. Datum apud Suthwell' die dominica proximo ante festum sancti Dionisii anno regni regis Edwardi tercii post conquestum quadragesimo nono.

Margin   In left margin *Carta Alic Blackmore de eodem* (17ᵗʰ c.).

Burg'

326   *Release and quitclaim by Thomas de Blakemore, son and heir of John Blakemore of Southwell, to Richard Darley of Southwell of one messuage in Southwell*   London, 11 November 1375

Omnibus Christi fidelibus hoc scriptum visuris vel audituris Thomas de Blakomore filius et heres Johannis de Blakomore de Suthwell' salutem in domino sempiternam. Noveritis me remisisse relaxasse et imperpetuum pro me et heredibus meis et assignatis quietum clamasse Ricardo Derley de Suthwell' heredibus et assignatis suis totum ius et clamium quod habeo habui seu quovismodo habere potero in futurum in quoddam mesuagio cum pertinenciis in burgo de Suthwell' antedicto situato inter mesuagium Ricardi Skynner ex una parte et tenementum quondam Ricardi Rofote ex altera quod quidem mesuagium fuit Johannis de Blakomore patris mei ita quod nec ego nec heredes mei nec aliquis alius nomine meo nec nostro aliquid iuris vel clamei in dicto mesuagio exigere vel vendicare potero seu poterint in futurum. In cuius rei testimonium sigillum meum presentibus est appensum. Datum apud London' in festo sancti Martini anno regni regis Edwardi tercii a conquestu Anglie quadragesimo nono.

Margin   In right margin *Tho. Blackmore de eodem quieti clamatio* (17ᵗʰ c.) and *Blakamore* (medieval).

327   *Grant by Richard Darley of Southwell to John Parker of Southwell and Sir William of Cropwell, chaplain and vicar choral, of one messuage in Southwell that Mr Robert Tanner sometime had of the gift of Thomas de Blakemore, chaplain*   Southwell, 23 or 24 February 1384

Sciant presentes et futuri quod ego Ricardus Darley de Suthwell' dedi concessi et hac presenti carta mea confirmavi Johanni Parker de Suthwell' et domino Willelmo de Crophill' capellano et vicario in ecclesia predicta unum mesuagium cum pertinenciis in burgo de Suthwell' situatum inter mesuagium Ricardi Skynner ex una parte et tenementum quondam Ricardi Rofote ex altera parte quod quedam mesuagium quondam fuit magistri Roberti Tanur' habui de dono et feoffamento Thome de Blakomore capellani. Habend' et tenend' predictum mesuagium cum suis pertinenciis predictis Johanni et Willelmo heredibus et assignatis suis imperpetuum de me et heredibus meis libere quiete bene et in pace de capitalibus dominis feodi illius per servicia inde debita et consueta. Et ego vero predictus Ricardus et heredes mei predictum mesuagium cum suis pertinenciis prefatis Johanni et Willelmo heredibus et suis assignatis contra omnes gentes warantizabimus et defendemus imperpetuum. In cuius rei testimonium huic presenti carte sigillum meum apposui. Hiis testibus: Johanne de Euyngton', Johanne de Farndon', Johanne Fyshar, Johanne Smyth' et aliis multis. Datum apud Suthwell' die mercurii in festo sancte Juliane virginis et martiris anno regni regis Ricardi secundi post conquestum septimo.

Margin   In right margin *Carta Ric. Darley de eodem* (17ᵗʰ c.).

Date   1384 was a leap year therefore the feast of St Juliana fell on Tuesday 23 February. Here 1384 is not regarded as a leap year therefore the feast of St Juliana was Wednesday 23 February 1384.

Burg'

p. 186

328   *Grant by John Parker of Southwell and William Crophill of Southwell, chaplain, to Richard Derley of Southwell and Margaret, his wife, of one messuage in Southwell*   Southwell, 6 December 1389

Sciant presentes et futuri quod ego Johannes Parker de Suthwell' et Willelmus Crophill' de eadem capellanus dedimus concessimus et hac presenti carta nostra confirmavimus Ricardo Derley de Suthwell' et Margarete uxori sue unum mesuagium cum pertinenciis in burgo de Suthwell' situatum inter messuagium Ricardi Skynner' ex parte una et tenementum quondam Ricardi Rofote ex altera parte. Tenendum et habendum predictum mesuagium cum suis pertinenciis predictis Ricardo et Margarete uxori sue et heredibus et suis assignatis imperpetuum de capitalibus dominis feodi illius per servicia inde debita et consueta. Et nos vero dicti Johannes et Willelmus et heredes nostri predictum mesuagium cum suis pertinenciis prefatis Ricardo et Margarete heredibus et suis assignatis contra omnes gentes warantizabimus et defendemus imperpetuum. In cuius rei testimonium huic presenti carte sigilla nostra apposuimus. Hiis testibus: Johanne de Euyngton', Johanne Smyth', Johanne de Farndon' et aliis multis. Datum apud Suthwell' in festo sancti Nicholai anno regni regis Ricardi secundi post conquestum tercio decimo.

Margin   In left margin *Carta Jo. Parker de eodem* (17ᵗʰ c).

329   *Grant by Agnes Snowe of Southwell to Richard of Darley of Southwell and Margaret, his wife, of one messuage in Southwell*   Southwell, 22 January 1392

Sciant presentes et futuri quod ego Agnes Snowe de Suthwell' dedi concessi et hac presenti carta mea confirmavi Ricardo de Darley de Suthwell' et Margarete uxori eius heredibus et assignatis suis unum mesuagium cum pertinenciis in burgo Suthwell' inter mesuagium quondam Symonis Snawe ex una parte et mesuagium quondam Beatricis de Wellagh' ex altera parte. Habendum et tenendum predictum mesuagium predicto Ricardo Margarete uxori eius heredibus et assignatis suis libere quiete et [in] pace imperpetuum de capitalibus dominis feodi illius per servicia inde debita et consueta. Et ego predicta Agnes et heredes mei predictum mesuagium cum pertinenciis predictis Ricardo Margarete uxori eius heredibus et assignatis suis contra omnes gentes warantizabimus imperpetuum. In cuius rei testimonium huic presenti carte sigillum meum apposui. Hiis testibus: Johanne de Ledenham de Suthwell', Johanne de Farndon' de eadem, Roberto de Lambley de eadem. Datum apud Suthwell' in festo sancti Vincencii martiris anno regni regis Ricardi secundi quintodecimo.

Margin In left margin *Carta Agnetis de Snaw de eodem* (17ᵗʰ c).

330 *Release and quitclaim by Richard Bunting of Southwell, senior, to Richard of Darley of Southwell of one messuage in Southwell*
Southwell, 25 January 1392

Omnibus hoc scriptum visuris vel audituris Ricardus Buntyng' de Suthwell' senior salutem. Noveritis me remisisse relaxasse et omnino pro me et heredibus meis quietum clamasse Ricardo de Darley de Suthwell' omne ius et clameum quod habeo habui seu quovismodo habere potero in futurum in quoddam mesuagio cum pertinenciis in burgo Suthwell' quod quidem mesuagium iacet inter mesuagium quondam Symonis Snaw ex parte una et mesuagium quondam Beatricis de Wellagh' ex altera parte ita quod nec ego nec heredes mei nec aliquis alius nomine meo aliquod ius vel clameum in dicto mesuagio exigere vel vendicare poterimus sed ab omni accione iuris penitus simus exclusi in futurum per presentes sigillo meo signatos. Hiis testibus: Johanne de Ledenam' de Suthwell', Johanne de Farndon' de eadem et aliis. Datum apud Suthwell' in festo conversionis sancti Pauli apostoli anno regni regis Ricardi secundi post conquestum quintodecimo.

Margin In left margin *Ric. Buntinge de mess. pred. relaxaᵖ* (17ᵗʰ c).

p. 187 **Burg'**

331 *Grant by William of Eaton of Southwell, butcher, to Richard de Warsop of Southwell, skinner, of one messuage in Southwell that William Tredgold of Southwell formerly held*   Southwell, 30 January 1353

Sciant presentes [et futuri quod ego Willelmus]¹ de Eton' de Suthwell' carnifex dedi concessi et hac presenti carta mea confirmavi Ricardo de Warsopp' de Suthwell' pellipario unum mesuagium cum pertinenciis situatum in burgo de Suthwell' inter mesuagium Willelmi Kyng' minoris ex parte una et mesuagium Roberti Tannour ex parte altera quod quidem mesuagium Willelmus Tredgolde de Suthwell' dudum tenuit. Tenendum et habendum predicto Ricardo heredibus et assignatis suis de capitalibus dominis feodi illius per servicia inde debita et consueta libere quiete integre et in pace imperpetuum. Et ego vero predictus Willelmus et heredes mei totum predictum mesuagium cum pertinenciis predicto

Ricardo heredibus et assignatis suis contra omnes gentes warantizabimus imperpetuum. In cuius rei testimonium huic presenti carte mee sigillum meum apposui. Hiis testibus: Johanne de Waynflete de Suthwell' iuniore, Willelmo Brounyng' de Suthwell' et aliis multis. Datum apud Suthwell' die mercurii proximo post festum conversionis sancti Pauli apostoli anno domini m° ccc^{mo} quinquagesimo tercio.

¹ The clerk has omitted the bracketed words in MS which are necessary to the charter

Margin   In right margin *Carta Eton de eod.* (17th c.).

Note   The grant by a butcher to a skinner of a messuage, bordered by a tenement held by a possible tanner, suggests that perhaps these properties lay close to Burbeck or another course of running water.

332   *Release and quitclaim by William of Kirkton of Southwell to William of Eaton of Southwell of one messuage in Southwell*
Southwell, 23 May 1351

Omnibus Christi fidelibus ad quos presens scriptum pervenerit Willelmus de Kirkton' de Suthwell' clericus salutem in domino sempiternam. Noveritis me remisisse relaxasse et omnino pro me et heredibus meis imperpetuum quietum clamasse Willelmo de Eton' de Suthwell' totum ius et clameum quod habui habeo seu quovismodo habere potero in futurum in uno mesuagio situato in burgo de Suthwell' inter mesuagium magistri Roberti Tanour ex una parte et mesuagium Willelmi Kyng' ex altera parte ita videlicet quod nec ego Willelmus de Kirkton' nec heredes mei nec aliquis nomine nostro in predicto mesuagio cum pertinenciis nec in aliqua parte eiusdem aliquod ius vel clameum decetero exigere poterimus vel vendicare sed ab omni accione et iure inde nobis competitura simus exclusi imperpetuum per presentes. Et ego vero dictus Willelmus de Kirkton' et heredes mei totum predictum mesuagium cum omnibus suis pertinenciis predicto Willelmo de Eton' heredibus et assignatis suis contra omnes gentes warantizabimus imperpetuum. In cuius rei testimonium presenti littere quiete clamacionis sigillum meum apposui. Hiis testibus: Willelmo de Rodes de Halum, Willelmo Brounyng', Johanne Parker, Galfrido Barker et aliis. Datum apud Suthwell' die lune proximo ante festum sancti Dunstani archiepiscopi anno regni regis Edwardi¹ tercii a conquestu vicesimo quinto.

¹ MS repeated

Margin   In right margin *W. de Kirkton de eodem quieti clamo* (17th c.).

333   *Grant by Richard of Warsop of Southwell, skinner, to Matilda, daughter of Robert Neucomen of Winkburn, his wife, for her life of one messuage in Southwell that William Tredgold formerly held*
Southwell, 19 March 1358

Omnibus Christi fidelibus ad quos presens scriptum pervenerit Ricardus de Warsopp' de Suthwell' pelliparius salutem in domino. Noveritis me dedisse concessisse et hac presenti carta mea confirmasse Matilde

filie Roberti Neucomen de Wynkborn' uxori mee ad terminum vite sue unum mesuagium cum pertinenciis situatum in burgo de Suthwell' inter
p. 188   mesuagium quondam Willelmi | Kyng' iunioris ex parte una et mesuagium Roberti Tannour' ex altera parte quod quidem mesuagium Willelmus Tredgold de Suthwell' dudum tenuit. Tenendum et habendum predictum mesuagium cum pertinenciis predicte Matilde uxori mee ad terminum vite sue de capitalibus dominis feodi illius per servicia inde debita et de iure consueta libere quiete integre et in pace. Et ego vero predictus Ricardus de Warsopp' et heredes mei predictum mesuagium cum pertinenciis predicte Matilde uxori mee durante termino predicto contra omnes gentes warantizabimus. In cuius rei testimonium huic presenti scripto sigillum meum apposui. Hiis testibus: Willelmo de Eton' de Suthwell', Johanne Parker de eadem, Galfrido Lagh de eadem, Willelmo Philipp' de Wynkborne et aliis. Datum apud Suthwell' die lune proximo ante festum sancti Edmundi regis anno regni regis Edwardi tercii post conquestum tricesimo secundo.

Margin   In right margin *Carta Ric. Warsop de eodem* (17th c.).

Burg'

334   *Grant by Richard of Warsop of Southwell, skinner, to John Sherman of Southwell, chaplain, and John Parker of Southwell of one messuage that William Tredgold sometime held*   [later 14th century]

Sciant presentes et futuri quod ego Ricardus de Warsopp' de Suthwell' pelliparius dedi concessi et hac presenti carta mea confirmavi Roberto Scherman' de Suthwell' capellano et Johanni Parker de eadem unum mesuagium cum pertinenciis situatum in burgo de Suthwell' inter mesuagium quondam Willelmi Kyng' iunioris ex parte una et mesuagium quondam Roberti Tannur' ex altera quod quidem mesuagium Willelmus Tredgold' quondam tenuit. Tenendum et habendum predictis Roberto et Johanni heredibus et assignatis eorum de capitalibus dominis feodi illius per servicia inde debita et consueta libere quiete et in pace imperpetuum. Et ego vero predictus Ricardus et heredes mei totum predictum mesuagium cum pertinenciis predictis [Roberto et] Johanni et heredibus et assignatis eorumdem contra omnes gentes warantizabimus imperpetuum. In cuius rei testimonium huic presenti carte sigillum meum apposui. Hiis testibus: Johanne de Waynflete de Suthwell', Johanne de Farndon' de eadem, Johanne Fyssher de eadem et aliis multis.

Margin   In left margin *Carta Ric. Warsop de eodem* (17th c.).

Date   After **333**?

Note   John Fyssher, senior (cf. **171**), who also occurs as a witness to **325** (1375) and **335** (1391), was one of the leading townsmen of Southwell. In 1395 he and his wife, Margaret, received a messuage, previously belonging to Henry atte Barre, from Thomas Arundel, archbishop of York, on which the Saracen's Head was later located (Thoroton, iii, 85, citing now lost charters *penes* William Wymondfold, esq. of Southwell, then owner of the inn).

335 *Grant by Robert Sherman, vicar choral, of Southwell and John Parker of Southwell to Matilda, widow of Richard of Warsop, skinner, of one messuage in Southwell that William Tredgold sometime held*
Southwell, 29 September 1391

Sciant presentes et futuri quod nos Robertus Scherman vicarius in choro ecclesie de Suthwell' et Johannes Parker de eadem dedimus concessimus et hac presenti carta nostra confirmavimus Matilde quondam uxori Ricardi de Warsopp' pelliparii unum mesuagium cum pertinenciis situatum in burgo de Suthwell' inter mesuagium quondam Willelmi Kyng' iunioris ex una parte et mesuagium quondam Roberti Tanur' ex altera parte quod quidem mesuagium Willelmus Tredgolde quondam tenuit. Habendum et tenendum predictum mesuagium predicte Matilde heredibus et assignatis suis de capitalibus dominis feodi illius per servicia inde debita et consueta libere quiete et in pace imperpetuum. Et nos vero prefati Robertus et Johannes et heredes nostri totum predictum mesuagium cum pertinenciis predictis prefate Matilde heredibus et assignatis suis contra omnes gentes warantizabimus imperpetuum. Hiis testibus: Johanne de Farndon' de Suthwell', Johanne Fyssher de eadem, Johanne Smyth et aliis. Datum apud Suthwell' in festo sancti Michaelis archangeli anno regni regis Ricardi secundi post conquestum quinto.

Margin In left margin *Carta Rob. Sherman et Jo. Parker de eod.* (17th c.).

Burg'

p. 189

336 *Grant by William of Walesby, living in Rufford, and Matilda, his wife, to John Robert of Southwell, chaplain, and Richard of Darley of Southwell of a messuage in Southwell*   Southwell, 24 October 1392

Sciant presentes et futuri quod ego Willelmus de Walesby manens apud Rufford' et Matill' uxor mea dedimus concessimus et hac presenti carta nostra confirmavimus Johanni Robert de Suthwell' capellano et Ricardo de Darley de eadem unum mesuagium cum pertinenciis in Suthwell' situatum in burgo eiusdem ville inter mesuagium quondam Willelmi Kyng' de Suthwell' iunioris ex parte boriali et mesuagium predicti Ricardi de Derley ex parte australi. Tenendum et habendum predictum mesuagium cum pertinenciis prefatis Johanni Robert capellano [et] Ricardo de Darley heredibus et assignatis suis de capitalibus dominis feodi illius per servicia inde debita et consueta imperpetuum. Et ego vero predictus[1] Willelmus de Walesby et Matill' uxor mea et heredes nostri predictum mesuagium cum omnibus suis pertinenciis in forma predicta prefatis Johanni Robert et Ricardo de Derley heredibus et assignatis suis contra omnes gentes warantizabimus imperpetuum et defendemus. In cuius rei testimonium huic presenti carte nostre sigilla nostra apposuimus. Hiis testibus: Johanne de Euyngton' de Suthwell', Johanne de Ledenham', Johanne de Farndon' ballivo in burgo Suthwell' et aliis multis. Datum apud Suthwell' die iovis proximo ante festum sancti Luce evangeliste anno regni regis Ricardi secundi post conquestum Anglie sexto decimo.

[1] MS *sic*

Margin   In right margin *Carta Willelmo Walesby et Matilda ux. eius de eodem* (17ᵗʰ c.).

337   *Release and quitclaim by Richard of Darley of Southwell, draper, to John Robert, vicar choral, of Southwell of a messuage sometime of Richard Warsop of Southwell, skinner*   Southwell, 20 July 1392

Noverint universi per presentes me Ricardum de Derley de Suthwell' draper' remisisse relaxasse et omnino pro me et heredibus meis quietum clamasse Johanni Robert vicario in choro ecclesie Suthwell' totum ius et clameum quod habeo habui vel quovis iuris titulo habere potero a principio mundi usque in diem confeccionis presencium in uno mesuagio cum pertinenciis in burgo Suthwell' quondam Ricardi Warsopp' de Suthwell' skynner' ita quod nec ego dictus Ricardus de Derley nec heredes mei nec aliquis alius nomine nostro aliquod ius vel clameum iuris in dicto mesuagio cum pertinenciis vendicare poterimus in futurum sed ab omni remedio iuris simus exclusi per presentes. In cuius rei testimonium huic scripto meo quiete clamacionis sigillum meum apposui. Hiis testibus: Johanne de Euyngton' de Suthwell', Johanne de Ledenham', Willelmo Helwys et aliis. Datum apud Suthwell' in festo sancte Margarete virginis anno regni regis Ricardi secundi post conquestum sexto decimo.

Margin   In right margin *Ricardi de Derley de mess. praedicto quieti clamatio* (17ᵗʰ c.).

p. 190   **Burg'**

338   *Final concord between John Robert, chaplain, plaintiff, and William of Walesby and Matilda, his wife, defendants, whereby William and Matilda recognised one toft in Southwell to be the right of John that he has of their gift, for which John gave them 100s*
     Westminster, 3 November 1396

Hec est finalis concordia facta in curia domini regis apud Westm' in crastino animarum anno regnorum Ricardi regis Anglie et Francie decimo septimo coram Roberto de Cherlton' Willelmo Thirnyng' Willelmo Rykhill' Johanne Wadham et Ricardo Sydenham justiciariis et aliis domini regis fidelibus tunc ibi presentibus inter Johannem Robert' capellanum querentem et Willelmum de Walesby et Matild' uxorem eius deforciantes de uno mesuagio cum pertinenciis in Suthwell' unde placitum convencionis summonitum fuit inter eos in eadem curia scilicet quod predictus Willelmus et Matill' recognoverunt predictum mesuagium cum pertinenciis¹ esse ius ipsius Johannis ut illud quod idem Johannes habet ex dono predictorum Willelmi et Matill' et illud remiserunt et quieti clamerunt de ipsis Willelmo et Matill' et heredibus ipsius Matill' predicto Johanni et heredibus suis imperpetuum. Et preterea iidem Willelmus et Matill' concesserunt pro se et heredibus ipsius Matill' quod ipsi warantizabunt predicto Johanni \et/ heredibus suis predictum mesuagium cum pertinenciis contra omnes homines imperpetuum. Et pro hac recognicione remissione quieta clamacione warantizacione fine et concordia idem Johannes dedit predictis Willelmo et Matill' centum solidos argenti.

¹ MS *mesuag'*

Margin   In left margin *Finis levatis de eodem* (17ᵗʰ c.).

Note   The foot of the fine is TNA, CP 25/1/186/36, no. 63 [AALT, http://aalt.law.uh.edu/ AALT2/CP25no1/CP25_1_186/IMG_1997.htm]

339   *Grant by John Roberd, chaplain and vicar choral, of Southwell to Richard of Darley of Southwell, draper, and Margaret, his wife, of a messuage in Southwell sometime of Richard Warsop of Southwell, skinner*   Southwell, 14 December 1393

Sciant presentes et futuri quod ego Johannes Roberd' capellanus et vicarius in choro ecclesie beate Marie Suthwell' dedi concessi et hac presenti carta mea confirmavi Ricardo de Darley de Suthwell' draper' et Margarete uxori sue unum mesuagium cum pertinenciis in burgo Suthwell' situatum inter mesuagium quondam Willelmi Kyng' iunioris de Suthwell' ex parte una et mesuagium dicti Ricardi de Derley ex altera parte quod quidem mesuagium quondam fuit Ricardi Warsopp' de Suthwell' skynner'. Habendum et tenendum predictum mesuagium cum suis pertinenciis prefatis Ricardo \de/ Derley et Margarete uxori sue heredibus et assignatis eorum de capitalibus dominis feodi illius per servicia inde debita et antiquitus consueta libere quiete et in pace imperpetuum. Et ego vero dictus Johannes Roberd' et heredes mei predictum mesuagium cum pertinenciis ut predictum est prefatis Ricardo de Derley et Margarete uxori sue heredibus et assignatis suis contra omnes gentes warantizabimus imperpetuum. In cuius rei testimonium huic presenti carte mee sigillum meum apposui. Hiis testibus: Johanne Euyngton' de Suthwell', Johanne Ledenham', Johanne Farndon' ballivo de burgo Suthwell' etc. et aliis etc. Datum apud Suthwell' die dominica in crastino sancte Lucie virginis anno regni regis Ricardi secundi decimo septimo.

Margin   In left margin *Carta Jo. Roberte de eodem* (17ᵗʰ c).

Suthwell'   **Burg'**   p. 191

340   *Grant by Margaret of Darley of Southwell in her widowhood to William Byker, rector of Sutton in the Dale, and Thomas Rolston, vicar choral of Southwell, of three messuages in Southwell*   Southwell, 29 September 1405

Sciant presentes et futuri quod ego Margareta de Darley de Suthwell' in viduitate mea dedi concessi et hac presenti carta mea confirmavi Willelmo Byker' rectori ecclesie de Sutton' in yᵉ Dale et Thome Rolston' uni vicario chori Suthwell' tria mesuagia iacencia in burgo Suthwell' quorum duo mesuagia iacent simul inter mesuagia Willelmi Wyntirton' ex parte australi et mesuagium nuper Willelmi Kyng ex parte boriali quorum unum mesuagium nuper fuit Ricardi Warsopp' et aliud mesuagium quondam fuit Thome Blakomore et tercium mesuagium iacet in dicto burgo inter mesuagium Willelmi Aubyn' ex parte boriali et mesuagium Willelmi Ketyll' ex parte australi. Habend' et tenend' omnia predicta mesuagia cum omnibus suis pertinenciis prefatis Willelmo et Thome heredibus et assignatis suis de capitalibus domini feodi illius per servicia inde debita et de iure consueta. Et ego vero predicta Margareta et heredes mei omnia predicta mesuagia cum omnibus suis pertinenciis prefatis Willelmo et Thome heredibus et assignatis suis contra omnes gentes warantizabimus imperpetuum. In cuius rei testimonium presentibus sigillum meum apposui. Hiis testibus: Willelmo Averham' de Suthwell', Johanne Ledynham', Johanne Warsopp', Johanne Smyth de eadem seniori et multis aliis. Datum apud Suthwell' in festo sancti Michaelis anno regni regis Henrici quarto sexto finiente post conquestum.

Margin   Page heading, Scribe 4. In right margin *Carta Margar. Darley de 3 mess* (17ᵗʰ c.).

Date   Henry IV's regnal years ran from 30 September to 29 September.

341   *Lease in the form of an indenture by William Byker, rector of Sutton in the Dale, and Thomas Roldeston, vicar choral of Southwell, to John of Sutton of Southwell for his life of one messuage and one toft in Southwell for a rent of 2d per annum*   Southwell, 4 April 1406

Hec indentura testatur quod Willelmus Byker rector ecclesie de Sutton' in le Dale et Thomas Roldeston' vicarius choralis ecclesie Suthwell' tradiderunt et dimiserunt Johanni de Sutton' de Suthwell' unum mesuagium iacens in burgo Suthwell' inter mesuagium Willelmi Wyntryngton' ex parte australi et mesuagium vicariorum chori Suthwell' ex parte boriali et unum toftum quod iacet in eodem burgo inter mesuagium Willelmi Ketill' ex parte australi et mesuagium Willelmi Aubyn' ex parte boriali. Habend' et tenend' predicta messuagium et toftum cum suis pertinenciis in villa predicta predicto Johanni ad terminum vite sue de nobis heredibus et assignatis nostris faciendo capitali domino feodi illius servicia inde debita et de iure consueta durante termino predicto reddendo inde annuatim nobis dictis Willelmo et Thome heredibus et assignatis nostris duos denarios argenti ad festa Pentecosten et sancti Martini in yeme per equales porciones. Et si contingat dictum annualem redditum duorum denariorum a retro esse post aliquem terminum predictum non solutum in parte vel in toto quod extunc bene licebit dictis Willelmo et Thome heredibus et assignatis eorum in dictis tenementis distringere et districciones sic capta abducere et asportare et penes se retinere sine contradiccione cuiuscumque quousque de predicto redditu una cum arreragiis si que fuerint plenare fuerit satisfactum. Et predictus Johannes reparabit sustentabit et emendabit quocienscumque opus fuerit durante termino vita sua predicta messuagium et toftum cum suis pertinenciis tam in meremio quam in tectura dawbyng et clausura et defendet erga dominum regem et ecclesiam sumptibus suis propriis. Et si contingat predicta mesuagium et toftum defectum vel ruinosum esse in aliquo premissorum et dictus Johannes monitus per dictos Willelmum Thomam heredes vel assignatos eorum ad emendandum infra spacium quadraginta dierum et non fecerit quod extunc bene licebit prefatis Willelmo et Thome heredibus et assignatis eorum predicta mesuagium et toftum intrare et penes se retinere absque contradiccione aliquali. In cuius rei testimonium sigilla parcium alternatim sunt appensa. Hiis testibus: Edmundo Archer, Waltero de Besthorpp', Johanne de Ledenham', Willelmo

Hudde et Willelmo Schyre et aliis multis. Datum apud Suthwell' in festo
sancti Ambrosii anno regni regis Henrici quarti septimo.

Margin   In right margin *Locacio mesuagii in burgagio*, and *2ᵈ* (both 17ᵗʰ c.).

Burg'   **Suthwell'**   **fabrica**   p. 192

342 *Assignment by William Byker, rector of Sutton in the Dale, and
Thomas Roldeston, vicar choral of Southwell, to Sir Thomas Haxey,
clerk, of the reversion of the lease made to John of Sutton after his death
of one messuage and one toft in Southwell*   Southwell, 25 June 1407

Omnibus Christi fidelibus ad quos presens scriptum pervenerit Willelmus
Byker' rector ecclesie de Sutton' in le Dale et Thomas Roldeston' vicarius
choralis ecclesie Suthwell' salutem. Cum Johannes de Sutton' teneat de
nobis heredibus et assignatis nostris unum mesuagium iacens in burgo de
Suthwell' inter mesuagium Willelmi de Wyntryngton' ex parte australi et
mesuagium vicariorum chori de Suthwell' ex parte boriali et unum toftum
quod iacet in eodem burgo inter mesuagium Willelmi Ketyll' ex parte
australi et mesuagium Willelmi Aubyn' ex parte boriali ad terminum vite sue
prout in quibusdam indenturis inde confectis plenius continetur noveritis
nos dictos Willelmum et Thomam reversionem dictorum tenementorum
cum suis pertinenciis in villa predicta post mortem predicti Johannis de
Sutton' concessisse domino Thome Haxey clerico. Tenend' et habend'
reversionem predictam predicto Thome heredibus et assignatis suis de
capitali domino feodi illius per servicia inde debita et de iure consueta
imperpetuum. Et nos vero dicti Willelmus Thomas et heredes nostri
predicta mesuagium et toftum cum suis pertinenciis in villa predicta
post mortem prefati Johannis cum acciderit prefato Thome heredibus
et assignatis suis contra omnes gentes warantizabimus imperpetuum. In
cuius rei testimonium huic presenti carte nostre sigilla nostra apposuimus.
Hiis testibus: Edmundo Archer, Waltero de Besthorpp', Johanne Alvy et
aliis multis. Datum in crastino nativitatis sancti Johannis Baptiste anno
regni regis Henrici quarti post conquestum Anglie octavo.

Margin   Page heading *Burg'* and *Suthwell'* (Scribe 4), *fabrica* (17ᵗʰ c.). In left margin
Carta W. Byker et Tho. Roldeston de mess. et tofto (17ᵗʰ c.).

Note   Thomas Haxey, prebendary of Rampton (1388–1425), see **141n** for a brief note
on his career, and cf. **Introduction**, pp. ci–cii for his property dealing in Southwell and
eventual endowment of a residence for the Chantry Priests.

343   *Grant by Thomas Haxey, canon of Southwell, to the Fabric of one
messuage and one toft in Southwell*   Southwell, 16 August 1407

Sciant presentes et futuri quod ego Thomas Haxey canonicus ecclesie
collegiate beate Marie Suthwell' per licenciam domini regis ac aliorum
dominorum de quibus tenementa subscripta tenentur dedi concessi et hac
presenti carta mea confirmavi Deo et beate Marie et capitulo ecclesie
collegiate predicte ad opus et proficium fabrice eiusdem ecclesie unum
mesuagium iacens in burgo de Suthwell' inter mesuagium Willelmi

de Wyntryngton' ex parte australi et mesuagium vicariorum chori de Suthwell' ex parte boriali et unum toftum quod iacet in eodem burgo inter mesuagium Willelmi Ketill ex parte australi et mesuagium Willelmi Aubyn' ex parte boriali. Habend' et tenend' predicta mesuagium et toftum cum suis pertinenciis predicto capitulo et successoribus suis ad opus et proficium fabrice ecclesie collegiate beate Marie Suthwellie predicte de capitalibus dominis feodi illius per servicia inde debita et de iure consueta in puram et perpetuam elemosinam imperpetuum. Et ego dictus Thomas et heredes mei predicta mesuagium et toftum cum pertinenciis in burgo predicto prefato capitulo et successoribus suis in forma predicta contra omnes gentes warantizabimus et defendemus imperpetuum. In cuius rei testimonium presenti carte mee sigillum meum apposui. Datum apud Suthwell' xvi° die mensis Augusti anno regni regis Henrici quarti post conquestum Anglie duodecimo.

Margin   In left margin *Carta domini Tho. Haxey de eisdem* and *Memorandum messuagium iacet in burgo nuper in tenura Roberti Franke* (both 17th c.).

BARNBY IN THE WILLOWS, 344

344   *Ordinance by John [Kempe, archbishop of York] about his previous appropriation of the vicarage of Barnby [in-the-Willows] for maintenance of the choristers of Southwell, reserving provision of the vicar to himself and his successors, or during vacancies of the see, to the Chapter of York, but paying ten marks per annum for support of the choristers, while the Chapter of Southwell is to contribute to any future extraordinary costs arising from maintenance of the vicarage, as is the vicar* [1426 × 1452]

p. 193   **In Dei nomine Amen. Universis** sancte matris ecclesie filiis ad quos presentes litere pervenerint, Johannes etc. salutem in synceris amplexibus salvatoris. Noverit universitas vestra quod cum nos nuper ad laudem Dei eiusque gloriose virginis genetricis[1] Marie, ac sui cultus augmentum, nec non uberiorem sustentacionem choristarum in ecclesia nostra collegiata beate Marie Suthwell', in cuius honor dicta ecclesia fundat,[2] Deo devote famulantium: ecclesiam parochialem de Barneby iuxta Newarke, nostre diocesis, dilectis filiis capitulo dicte ecclesie nostre Southwell', ex causis veris et legitimis auctoritate nostra ordinaria et pontificali, de consensu dilectorum filiorum capituli ecclesie nostre Ebor', rite et canonice, appropriavimus et in usus suos proprios concesserimus perpetuo possidendo, reservata, ordinacioni nostre, de ipsius ecclesie fructibus, redditibus et proventibus pro uno vicario in ipsa ecclesia servituro porcione congrua pro ipsius vicarii sustentacione, et supportacione onerum vicarii, qui pro tempore fuerit incumbentem, prout in aliis literis nostris patentibus dicto capitulo super appropriacione huiusmodi confectis plenius continetur: **Nos volentes** prout ex officii nostri debite tenemur pro vicaria in eadem ecclesie de Barneby, canonice ordinando disponere et consultius providere, quantum in Deo poterimus in hoc casu, Dei omnipotentis nomine invocato, ad ordinacionem super vicaria dicte ecclesie auctoritate nostra faciendo et portionibus eidem assignando

perpetuis futuris temporibus duraturo, considerata ipsius ecclesie exilitato modernis temporibus plus solito invalescente, de cuius fructuum, redditum et proventuum, ad ipsam ecclesiam pertinentibus primitus inquiri fecimus diligenter, procedimus in hunc modum: **Inprimis** ordinamus, statuimus, volumus et decernimus in hiis scriptis, quod in dicta ecclesia de Barneby sit unus perpetuus vicarius providus et discretus ac, ad regimen animarum exercendum habilis, idoneus et honestus nobis et successoribus nostris Ebor' archiepiscopis, qui pro tempore fuerint sede plena, et ea vacante, decano et capitulo ecclesie nostre Ebor' antedicte, per dictum capitulum et successores suos, quotiens ipsam vicariam vacare contigerit, presentandus ac per nos et successores nostros sede plena, aut ea vacante per dictum capitulum nostrum Ebor', admittendum et instituendum canonice in eadem, qui curam animarum parochianorum dicte ecclesie gerat, habeat et exerceat, ac personaliter resideat in eadem. Quam quidem vicariam ex hac nostra ordinacione pariter et decreto, consistere volumus in portionibus infrascriptis: Inprimis volumus quod quilibet vicarius, qui pro tempore fuerit, pro manso et inhabitacione sua habeat et teneat, cum competentibus curtilagiis adjacentibus, quas quidem | domos et clausuras   p. 194
vicarius, qui pro tempore fuerit, tam nunc prima vice quam imposterum, quotiens opus fuerit, faciet reparari et emendari suis propriis sumptibus et expensis. **Item volumus** et ordinamus quod dictus vicarius, qui pro tempore fuerit, habeat et percipiat totum alteragium, et etiam omnes decimas majores et minores, obvenciones et alia emolumenta quecunque, ad dictam ecclesiam qualitercunque spectantia seu provenientia, decimis ordei, siliginis, tritici, fabarum et pisarum duntaxat exceptis, quas quidem decimas ordei, siliginis, tritici, fabarum et pisarum assignamus, annuatim prefato capitulo aplicandas, ut ipsi decem marcas choristis dicte ecclesie nostre Southwell' ad sustenacionem eorundem, et tresdecem solidos et quatuor denarios nobis et successoribus nostris Eboracensis archiepiscopis, et capitulo ecclesie nostre Ebor' pro indempnitate ipsius ecclesie nostre Ebor' singulis annis fideliter persolvant, in forma qua in appropriacione prefate ecclesie de Barnebye plenius est expressum. **Item volumus** [et] ordinamus quod vicarius, qui pro tempore fuerit, omnia onera ordinaria dicte ecclesie qualitercunque incumbentia per se subeat, et supportet, et quoad onera extraordinaria cum emerserint, volumus et ordinamus, quod dictum capitulum Suthwell; medietatem omnium huiusmodi onerum extraordinarium, et vicarius qui pro tempore fuerit, alteram medietatem subeat et supportet. Quas quidem domos et porciones suprascriptas pro congrua sustenacione huiusmodi vicarii limitatas, ordinamus, decernimus, volumus et pronunciamus in hiis scriptis pertinere debere ad perpetuum vicarium in dicta ecclesia de Barnby perpetuis futuris temporibus servitur, et ipsas et earum quamlibet exnunc eidem vicario plenarie assignamus, ex quibus volumus quod sit contentus. Hanc autem ordinacionem nostram in omnibus et singulis suis particulis perpetuis futuris temporibus, ratam, firmam et illibatam volumus et precipimus permanere, potestatem corrigendi, augmentandi cum nobis placuerit, et visum fuerit, expediens, ordinacionis premissam, nobis et successoribus specialiter reservimus; juribus, dignitatibus, privilegiis et honore nostris et ecclesie nostre Ebor' in omnibus semper salvis. In quorum omnium

testimonium presentes literas nostras patentes sigilli nostri appensione fecimus communiri. Datum etc.

¹ MS *sic* for *genitricis*   ² MS *sic* for *fundatur*

Margin   Extremely faint foliation *fo. lxxiii* in top right corner. *Barneby vicarie ordinatio* in 17ᵗʰ-c. hand in right margin.

Date   While John Kempe was archbishop (1426–52).

Note   This document was added around 1600 by John Martiall, registrar.

pp. 195–9   These pages are blank.

HENRY VI's CHARTER, 1446, 345

345   *Letters patent of pardon, release and quitclaim by Henry VI to the Chapter of Southwell for offences against statutes concerning cloth, breaking the peace, forest offences, acquisition of lands without mortmain licences before 9 April 1446 and many other possible infringements of laws and statutes before 1 September 1441, specifically exempting from its provisions certain named parties including Eleanor Cobham, John Bolton, bladesmith, of Bolton, William Wyghale, former keeper of Nottingham gaol, and the murderers of Sir Christopher Talbot*

Westminster, 22 July 1446

p. 200   **Carta gracie specialis per Henricum regem sextum concessa capitulo de Suthwell' anno regni sui xxiiiiᵗᵒ de terris ad manus mortuas adquisitis licencia regia non obtenta**

Henricus, Dei gracia rex Anglie et Francie et dominus Hibernie, omnibus ballivis et fidelibus suis ad quos presentes littere pervenerint, salutem. Sciatis quod de gracia nostra speciali, et ex certa sciencia et mero motu nostris, perdonavimus, remisimus et relaxavimus capitulo ecclesie beate Marie Suthwell', alias dicto capitulo ecclesie beate Marie de Southwell' seu quocunque alio nomine conseatur, omnimodos transgressiones, offensas, mesprisiones, contemptus et impeticiones per ipsum capitulum ante nonum diem Aprilis ultimo preteritum contra formam statutorum de liberatis pannorum et capiciorum factos sive perpetratos, unde punicio caderet in finem et redempcionem, aut in alias penas pecuniarias seu imprisonamenta, statutis predictis non obstantibus. Et insuper ex motu et sciencia nostris predictis perdonavimus, remisimus et relaxavimus eidem capitulo sectam pacis nostre que ad nos versus ipsum pertinet pro omnimodis prodicionibus, murdris, raptibus mulierum, rebellionibus, insurrectionibus, feloniis, conspiracionibus, cambipartiis, manutenenciis et imbraciariis ac aliis transgressionibus, offensis, neglicenciis, extorcionibus, mesprisionibus, ignoranciis,¹ contemptibus, concealamentis, forisfacturis et decepcionibus per ipsum capitulum ante dictum nonum diem Aprilis qualitercunque factis sive perpetratis. Ac eciam² utlagere si que in ipsum capitulum hiis occasionibus seu earum aliqua fuerint promulgate et firmam pacem nostram ei inde concedimus. Ita tamen quod stet recto in curia \nostra/ si quis versus eum loqui voluerit de premissis vel aliquo premissorum. Dumtamen idem capitulum proditor de aliqua prodicione personam nostram tangente palam vel occulte non existat. Et ulterius perdonavimus, remisimus et relaxavimus eidem capitulo omnimoda escapia felonum, catalla felonum et fugitivorum, catalla utlagatorum et felonum de se deodanda, vasta, impeticiones ac omnimodos articulos itineris destrucciones et transgressiones de viridi vel venacione, vendicionem boscorum infra forestas et extra et aliarum rerum quarumcunque ante dictum nonum diem Aprilis infra regnum nostrum Anglie et marchiam Wallie emersas et eventas unde punicio caderet in demandam debitam, seu in finem et redempcionem, aut in alias penas pecuniarias, seu in forisfacturam bonorum et catallorum aut imprisonamenta, seu amerciamenta comitatum, villarum vel singularum personarum, vel in oneracionem liberi tenentis eorum qui numquam transgressi fuerunt, ut heredum executorum, vel terre tenencium escaetorum, vicecomitum, coronatorum et aliorum huiusmodi, et omne id quod ad nos versus ipsum capitulum pertinet, seu pertinere possit, ex causis supradictis. Ac eciam perdonavimus, remisimus et relaxavimus eidem capitulo omnimodas donaciones, alienaciones et perquisiciones per ipsum de terris et tenementis de nobis vel progenitoribus nostris quondam regibus Anglie in capite tentis. Ac eciam omnimodas donaciones et perquisiciones ad manum mortuam factas et habendas absque licencia regia, necnon omnimodos intrusiones et ingressus in hereditatem suam in parte vel in toto post mortem antecessorum suorum, absque debita prosecucione eiusdem extra manum regiam ante eundem nonum diem Aprilis factos, una cum exitibus et proficuis inde medio tempore perceptis. Et insuper perdonavimus, remisimus et relaxavimus eidem capitulo omnimodas penas ante dictum nonum diem Aprilis forisfactas coram nobis, seu consilio nostro, cancellario, thesaurario seu aliquo iudicum | nostrorum, pro aliqua causa, et omnes alias penas tam nobis quam carissimo patri nostro defuncto, per ipsum capitulum pro aliqua causa ante eiusdem nonum diem Aprilis forisfactas et ad opus nostrum levandas, ac omnimodas securitates pacis ante eundem nonum diem Aprilis. Similiter forisfactas; ac eciam tercias et terciarum tercias omnimodorum prisonariorum in guerra captorum nobis dicto nono die Aprilis qualitercumque debitas pertinentes seu spectantes per idem capitulum, necnon omnimodas transgressiones, offensas, mesprisiones, contemptus et impeticiones per ipsum capitulum ante eundem nonum diem Aprilis, contra formam tam quorumcunque statutorum, ordinaciorum et provisionum ante dictum nonum diem Aprilis factorum, seu editorum, de perquisicionibus, acceptacionibus, lectionibus, publicacionibus, notificacionibus et execucionibus quibuscumque, quarumcumque litterarum et bullarum apostolicarum ante dictum nonum diem Aprilis, et omnium aliorum statutorum, ordinaciorum et provisionum pretextu quorum aliqua secta versus idem capitulum per billam, vel per brevem, de premuniri facta, seu alio modo quocumque pro aliqua materia ante eundem nonum diem Aprilis fieri valeat, quam quorumcumque aliorum statutorum factos sive perpetratos statutis, ordinacionibus et provisionibus ullis non obstantibus. Ac eciam perdonavimus, remisimus et relaxavimus eidem

p. 201

capitulo omnimodos fines adiudicatos, amerciamenta, exitus, forisfactos, relevia scutagia ac omnimoda debita compota, prestita, arreragia firmarum et compotorum nobis ante primum diem Septembris anno regni nostri vicesimo qualitercumque debita et pertinencia, necnon omnimodas actiones et demandas quas nos solus, vel nos conjunctim, cum aliis personis, vel alia persona, habemus vel habere poterimus versus ipsum capitulum pro aliquibus huiusmodi finibus, amerciamentis, exitibus, releviis, scutagiis, debitis, compotis prefatis et arreragiis ante eundem primum diem Septembris nobis debitis. Ac eciam utlagarias in ipsum capitulum promulgatas pro aliqua causarum supradictarum omnimodis debitis et compotis nobis debitis et pertinentibus que vigore litterarum nostrarum patencium, seu brevium nostrorum de magno, vel privato, sigillo, aut per estallamenta, sive assignaciones respectuata, existunt omnino exceptis. Ita quod presens perdonacio nostra quo ad premissa, vel aliquod premissorum, non cedat in dampnum, preiudicium vel derogacionem alicuius alterius persone, quam personam nostre dumtaxat. Proviso semper quod nulla huiusmodi perdonacio nostra aliquo modo[3] valeat allocetur nec fiat nec aliqualiter se extendat ad Alianorum Cobeham, filiam Reginaldi Cobeham, militis, Johannem Bolton' de Bolton' in comitatu Lancastrie, bladsmyth', Willelmum Wyghale, nuper custodem gaole nostre de Notyngham, nec ad eorum aliquem, neque ad feloniam de morte Christofori Talbot, militis, felonice interfecti nuper perpetratam, nec quod presens perdonacio nostra nec aliqua huiusmodi perdonacio nostra aliqualiter se extendat quo ad aliquas lanas, seu pelles lanutas, seu alias mercandisas de stapula, ad aliquas partes exteras extra regnum nostrum Anglie contra formam statuti in parliamento nostro apud Westmonasterium in crastino sancti Martini anno regni nostri decimo octavo[4] editi, seu aliquorum aliorum statutorum cariatas et traductas, nec ad aliquas forisfacturas nobis in hac parte pertinentes sive spectantes, nec ad exoneraciones sive acquietaciones aliquarum personarum de punicionibus super ipsas fiendas iuxta formam eorundem statutorum pro aliquibus lanis, sive pellibus lanutis, vel aliis

p. 202 mercandisis | de stapulis \ad/ aliquas huiusmodi partes exteras contra formam eorundem statutorum cariatis, sive traductis, nec quod presens perdonacio nostra, nec aliqua huiusmodi perdonacio nostra, ad aliquos magnos computantes nostros, videlicet ad thesaurarios Cales' et hospicii nostri, vitellarios Cales', camerarii Cestrie, Northwallie et Suthwallie, custodes garderobe hospicii nostri aut custodes magne garderobe nostre, aut custodes sive clericos garderobe nostre, clericos operacionum nostrarum, constabularios Burdegal', thesaurarios terre nostre Hibernie et receptores ducatus nostre Lancastrie et ducatus nostre Cornubie, tam generales quam particulares, quo ad aliqua huiusmodi officia sua, seu huiusmodi occupaciones suas aut alicuius eorundem tenencia ullo modo se extendat. In cuius rei testimonium has litteras nostras fieri fecimus patentes. Teste me ipso apud Westmonasterium vicesimo secundo die Julii anno regni [nostri] vicesimo quarto.

[1] Followed by a blank space for a missing word   [2] Here and elsewhere in this document written as *Aceciam*   [3] *modo* repeated   [4] 12 November 1439

Margin Heading in same mid/late 15th-c. hand as text (Scribe 8), extends across full opening of pp. 200–1; p. 200, *Nota bene hanc cartam* and *Nota hic de terris adquisitis ad manum mortuam* in same hand in left margin.

Note   Not enrolled. Although reference is made to several parliamentary statutes, the scribe of this pardon does not in most cases give precise references (perhaps deliberately leaving matters vague, either because he did not know the exact reference, or because it may have better served the purpose of the pardon to leave things as general as possible) so it is difficult to decide which ones he was citing with the probable exception of one concerning the export of cloth in November 1439 (*Statutes of the Realm*, ii, 312–13 (c. xvi)). Edward I had issued his two statutes on mortmain in 1279 (ibid. i, 51) (cf. Sandra Raban, *Mortmain Legislation and the English Church, 1279–1500* (Cambridge 1982)). The Charter of the Forest had been re-issued with Magna Carta in 1297 (*Statutes of the Realm*, i, 114–22) and that relating to the breaking of the peace is probably a reference to the Statute of Winchester (1275) but since the thirteenth century there had been further statutes modifying the original legislation relating both to forest laws and the peace which the scribe may have had in mind (suggestions and references we owe to the kindness of Dr Gwilym Dodd). Eleanor Cobham married Humphrey, duke of Gloucester, as his second wife in 1428 and came to play an important part in court life. In 1441, having procured a horoscope which allegedly predicted a serious illness for Henry VI, she was arrested, accused of treasonable necromancy and heretical practices, probably by enemies jealous of her husband, the king's uncle and heir presumptive. Tried before an ecclesiastical tribunal, she admitted some charges, performed public penance and was eventually forcibly divorced and condemned to perpetual imprisonment (Ralph Griffiths, 'The Trial of Eleanor Cobham : An Episode in the Fall of Duke Humphrey of Gloucester', *Bulletin of the John Rylands Library*, LI (1969), 381–99; *ODNB online*: G. L. Harriss, 'Eleanor [*née* Eleanor Cobham] duchess of Gloucester (*c.* 1400–52), alleged sorcerer': http://www.oxforddnb.com/view/article/5742, accessed 1 February 2016). Sir Christopher Talbot was the second son of John Talbot, first earl of Shrewsbury, by his first wife Maud Neville. A noted jouster, he was killed in suspicious circumstances in 1443 (*ODNB online*: A. J. Pollard, 'Talbot, John, first earl of Shrewsbury and first earl of Waterford (*c.* 1387–1453), soldier': http://www.oxforddnb.com./view/article/26932?-docPos=2, accessed 1 February 2016).

SHERWOOD FOREST, 346

346   *Writ of Edward III to Ralph de Neville, keeper of the forest beyond the Trent, or his lieutenant in Sherwood forest, ordering them to permit the canons of Southwell free carriage of stone from their quarries near Mansfield*   Westminster, 16 October 1337

Licencia domini regis pro cariagio lapidum de lapicio fabrice apud Maunsfeld per forestam de Schyrwode   p. 203

Edwardus, Dei gracia rex Anglie, dominus Hibernie et dux Aquitanie, dilecto et fideli suo Radulpho de Nevyle, custodi foreste sue ultra Trentam, vel eius locum tenenti in foresta de Schyrewode, salutem. Cum de communi consilio regni nostri statutum sit quod nullus forestarius de cetero, qui non sit forestarius de feodo, firmam nobis reddens pro balliva sua, capiat chimnagium[1] aliquod in balliva sua, forestarius autem de feodo, firmam nobis reddens pro balliva sua, capiat chimnagium,[1] videlicet pro carecta per dimidium annum duos denarios, et per alium dimidium annum duos denarios, pro equo, qui portat summagium per dimidium annum, obolum et per alium dimidium annum, obolum, et non nisi de illis qui de extra ballivam suam, tanquam mercatores, veniunt per licenciam suam in ballivam suam, ad buscam, maeremium, corticem vel carbonem emenda, et alias ducenda ad vendendum ubi voluerint, et de nulla alia carecta vel summagio aliquod chimnagium capiatur, et non capiatur chimnagium nisi in locis in quibus antiquitus capi solebat et debuit, ac iam ex parte dilectorum nobis in Christo canonicorum et capituli ecclesie beate Marie Suthwell' nobis sit ostensum quod, cum ipsi quasdam carectas suas pro lapidibus de quarrera sua ad fabri[c]am ecclesie predicte per medium foreste predicte cariandum quandoque miserint, quidam forestariorum in predicta foresta nostra de Schyrewode, et eorum servientes, carectas predictas, cum equis suis, pro huismodi chimnagio eis, contra formam statuti predicti prestandi, sepius arestarunt et indies arestare faciunt, ac eos multipliciter inquietant in ipsorum canonicorum et capituli dampnum non modicum, et ecclesie predicte deterioracionem manifestam. Unde nobis supplicarunt ut eis in premissis de remedio providere velimus. Nos eorum supplicacioni in premissis annuentes, vobis mandamus quod, si ita, tunc predictos forestarios et eorum ac vestros similiter ministros, sive servientes, ab huiusmodi arestacionibus carectarum vel cariagiorum suorum predictorum, et aliis huiusmodi gravaminibus, eis decetero inferendis desistere faciet, ut est iustum, ipsos vel servientes suos seu carectas aut cariagia sua per ministros foreste predicte contra formam statuti predicti nullatenus gravare vel impediri amodo permittentes. Teste me ipso apud Westmonasterium xvi die Octobris anno regni nostri undecimo.

¹ MS *sic* for *chiminagium*

Margin Heading, in bold in same mid-15ᵗʰ-c. hand as main text (Scribe 4), as are 347–54.

Note Pd. in Dickinson, *Southwell*, 345 (correctly attributing it to Edward III, p. 59).

LIBERTIES, 347

347 *Writ of Edward III to Adam of Everingham and other justices of the assizes of bread and ale, weights and measures, in Nottinghamshire, ordering them to respect the privileges of the canons and Chapter as established by William de Herle and his fellow justices in the time of the king's grandfather (sic)* 28 January 1372

p. 204 Edwardus, Dei¹ gracia rex Anglie et Francie, dominus Hibernie, dilectis et fidelibus suis Ade de Everyngham et sociis suis iusticiariis ad assisam panis et cervisie in comitatu Notingham conservandum, necnon ad mensuras et pondera in comitatu predicto, supervidendis assignum, salutem. Quia dilecti nobis in Christo capitulum et canonici ecclesie collegiate beate Marie de Suthwell' clamant habere diversas libertates apud villas de Suthwell', Northwell', Southmuscham, Northmuscham, Calneton', Oxton', Calverton', Wodeburgh, Crophill, Blidworth, Halghton', Bekyngham, Dunham, Halum, Edyngley et Normanton', que quidem libertates eisdem capitulo et canonicis, coram Willelmo de Herle et sociis suis iusticiariis domini Edwardi, nuper regis Anglie, avi nostri, in comitatu predicto itinerantibus allocate fuerunt, sicut per tenorem recordi et processus loquele predicte, quem coram nobis in cancellaria nostra venire, et sub magno sigillo nostro exemplificare fecimus plenius poterit apparere.

Vobis mandamus quod visa exemplificacione tenoris recordi et processus predictorum ipsos capitulum et canonicos omnibus et singulis libertatibus in recordo et processis predictis contentis gaudere permittatis, prout coram prefatis iusticiariis in itinere predicto allocate fuerunt, et prout ipsi libertatibus illis a tempore predicto uti et gaudere consueverunt. Teste etc. xxviii° die Januarii, anno regni nostri Anglie quadragesimo sexto, regni vero nostri Francie tricesimo tercio. Cuius carta que est warantum brevis precedentis intitulata superius folio tercio.

¹ MS *de*

Margin   In left margin *Carta libertatis* (17ᵗʰ c.). Opposite final sentence *nota* in medieval hand; the main text is in hand of Scribe 4.

Note   Not enrolled; cf. **14** and **145–6**. The inquiry by Herle and his colleagues was not made in the reign of Edward I but in 1329.

SHERWOOD FOREST, 348–50

348   *The first lines of another copy of* **106**, *Henry III's forest charter*   p. 205
of 1232, ending with the note Ista quidem carta scribitur superius xxiiii
folio ut patet intuenti.

Margin   Title as heading, in bold, in same late medieval hand as the main text (Scribe 4): *Perambulacio Foreste de Shirwode prima post deafforestacionem factam tempore Regis Henrici secundi filii imperatricis.*

349   *Letters patent of Edward I confirming the perambulation of Sherwood forest by John de Lythgraynes and his fellow justices*
Lincoln, 14 February 1301

Perambulacio foreste predicte secunda¹ facta tempore regis Edwardi filii regis Henrici tercii

Edwardus, Dei gracia rex Anglie, dominus Hibernie, dux Aquitanie, omnibus ad quos presentes littere pervenerint, salutem. Sciatis quod cum communitas regni nostri nobis concesserit quintam decimam omnium bonorum suorum mobilium que habebunt in festo sancti Michaelis proximo futuro extunc taxandorum, que quidem quinta decima post huiusmodi taxacionem colligi debet et levari et fideliter nobis solvi, volumus et concedimus pro nobis et heredibus nostris quod perambulacio facta coram dilecto et fideli nostro Johanne de Lythegraynes et sociis suis ad hoc assignatis per preceptum nostrum de foresta nostra in comitatu Notingham decetero teneatur et observetur per metas et bundas contentas in eadem perambulacione, cuius tenor de verbo ad verbum sequitur in hunc modum:

Perambulacio facta in comitatu Notingham, die veneris proximo post festum sancti Barnabe apostoli, anno regni domini regis Edwardi filii domini regis Henrici vicesimo octavo coram Johanne de Lythgraynes, Johanne Byrun, Michaele de Herteclar', Harusculpho de Cleseby, Ada de Crokdayk' et Ricardo Oysell' ad illam per breve domini regis faciendam assignatis, in presencia Hugonis de Louther, attornati domini Roberti de Clyfford', tunc iusticiarii forestarum domini regis ultra Trentam, per litteras ipsius Roberti patentes, et in presencia forestariorum et viridariorum foreste de Schirewode per sacrosancta Gervasii de Clyfton', Johannis Burdon', Johannis de Leek', Rogeri de Sancto Andrea, Ranulphi de Wandeslay', Thome Malett', Ricardi Pavely, Willelmi de Colewyk', militum, Roberti de
p. 206   Kymverley, Fulconis | de Hovetoft, Petri de Ludeham, Nicholai de Insula, servientum. Qui dicunt super sacrosanctum suum quod perambulacio foreste domini regis de Schirewode incipit ad vadum de Conyngeswath per chiminum quod se extendit usque ad villam de Wellehawe, versus Notingham, ita quod clausum ville de Wellehawe est extra forestam, et sic deinde per idem chiminum quod se extendit inter Wellehawe et Notingham, usque ad quandam particulam bosci qui vocatur Litelhaw, et sic ascendendo per quandam viam versus occidentem inter dictum boscum et boscum abbatis de Rufford' qui vocatur Brunne, et extendit se usque ad Raynwathforth, et deinde divertendo per quandam viam usque orientem inter predictum boscum de Litelhaw, et boscum de Blitheworth, usque ad predictum magnum chiminum quod se extendit de Wellehaw versus Notingham usque ad Bakenstanhaw super illud idem magnum chiminum, et sic deinde per idem chiminum usque ad locum illum ubi rivulus de Doverbek' pertransit predictum chiminum, et deinde sicut rivulus predictus de Doverbek' descendit in aquam que vocatur Trente, et sic in longo per eandem aquam de Trent ascendendo usque ad pontem Notingham.

Incipit eciam perambulacio predicta in eodem comitatu Notingham ad predictum vadum de Conyngeswath ascendendo versus occidentem per aquam que vocatur Medine usque ad villam que vocatur Warsopp', et ad eadem villa ascendendo per eandem aquam usque ad parcum de Pleseley, et deinde ascendendo per ipsam aquam usque ad Haytrebrygge, et deinde divertendo per magnum chiminum de Notingham usque ad pontem de Mulneford', et deinde ascendendo usque Mamesheved, et deinde inter campos de Herdewyk' et moram de Kyrkby usque ad angulum qui vocatur Nonneker' et deinde per assartum Ywayn Breton' usque ad Tarlesty, et deinde usque ad Scolegate, et deinde per magnum chiminum usque subtus vetus castellarium de Anneslay, et ab ipso castellario per magnum chiminum usque ad villam de Lyndeby, et deinde per mediam villam de Lyndeby, usque ad molendinum eiusdem ville, super aquam de Lene, et deinde descendendo per ipsam aquam usque ad villam de Lenton', et deinde sicut ipsa aqua antiquiter currere solebat usque in aquam que dicitur Trent, et sic descendendo per ipsam aquam de Trent usque ad pontem Notingham predictum. Et ita quicquid est infra metas predictas remaneat foresta et quicquid est extra easdem metas extra forestam remaneat.

p. 207   In cuius | rei testimonium tam predicti Johannes de Lethegraynes et socii sui quam prefati perambulatores huic perambulacioni sigilla sua apposuerunt. Ita quod quicquid per istam perambulacionem ponitur extra forestam remaneat extra forestam et residuum remaneat foresta, secundum metas et bundas predictas imperpetuum. In cuius rei testimonium has litteras nostras fieri fecimus patentes. Teste me ipso apud Lincoln'¹ quartodecimo die Februarii, anno regni nostri vicesimo nono.

¹ Followed by *tempore* struck out

Note   For discussion of other copies, editions and translations, but with no reference to this copy, see *Sherwood Book*, 39–41ff. In the spelling of proper names, the present text differs orthographically. For identification of the places, Crook, 'Spigurnels', 50–70; and 'Struggle', 35–45. Of the forest justices, Harsculph de Cleasby was bailiff of the honour of Richmond by 1291, served in the Scottish wars in 1300 and 1301, was a conservator of the peace in the county of York in 1308, but accused of an assault on St Agatha's York in 1310 with Sir John de Cleasby, probably his elder brother (ibid., 211). As Boulton notes (*Sherwood Book*, 40n), all those giving testimony were men of some standing in the county. Sir John Burdon (d. by 1305) and Sir William of Colwick (d. after 1312) were verderers of the forest, and Peter of Lowdham a regarder in Sherwood between 1281 and 1303. Among the other knights involved in this inquiry, in alphabetical order, are: Sir John de Byron, d. after 1316; Sir Robert of Clifford, killed at Bannockburn, 24 June 1314; Sir Gervase of Clifton, d. by 1324; Sir Adam of Crookdake, a justice since at least 1272, d. by 20 March 1305; Sir Hugh of Lowther, d. 21 April 1317; Sir John de Lythegraves, d. 1 November 1303; Sir Thomas Malet, d. *c*. 1315; Sir Richard Oysell, d. after 1 March 1306; Sir Richard Paveley, prior of the Hospital of St John of Jerusalem in England in 1317; Sir Roger de St Andrew, d. after 28 February 1326; Sir Ranulph of Wansley, MP for Nottinghamshire in 1300 and 1301 (Moor, i, 158, 172, 213–14, 226, 254; iii, 51–2, 63–4, 99–100, 293; iv, 16, 169; v, 152).

350   *Memorandum on rights of the archbishop of York and the canons of Southwell in woods in Oxton, Blidworth, Calverton and Woodborough within the forest as affected by the two perambulations of the forest of Sherwood in 1227 (confirmed in 1232) and 1301*   [after 1397]

Sciendum est quod iste due perambulaciones maxime tangunt dominum archiepiscopum Ebor', qui habet boscum infra forestam in quo ipse tenentes et canonici sui Suthwell' habent communia et duos prebendarios de Oxton', qui sunt domini ville de Blithworth, et parcelle ville de Calverton' et parcelle ville de Wodeburgh, que tres ville cum suis pertinenciis stant infra forestam, et racione terrarum eorundem prebendariorum eis pertinencium infra forestam apud Oxton'. Et tangunt prebendarium de Wodeburgh et Eddyngley, qui habent communia infra forestam pro se et tenentibus suis in Wodburgh', qui quidem tres prebendarii habent et de iure habere consueverunt omnes easdem consuetudines de omnibus tenentibus suis nativis \et aliis/ quas habet capitulum ecclesie Suthwell', et que recitantur superius in curia predicti capituli que sic incipiunt: *Prima consuetudo est quod quilibet residens infra dominium capituli etc.*

Margin   The heading of p. 207 is *Prebenda de Oxton*, referring to **351**. *Wodborowe* in later cursive hand in right margin opposite relevant clause.

Date   Between the second perambulation (1301) and the early 15ᵗʰ c. when the latest item (1397, **354**) in the group **348–54** was transcribed.

Note   For the customs enjoyed by the Chapter's tenants see **151**.

Prebenda de Oxton'

351 *Agreement in the form of a bipartite indenture between Mr William of Clifford, canon [and prebendary of Oxton II] and Sir Robert, son of Walter of Strelley, in a dispute over a pond and fishery at Oxton*
Nottingham, 11 December 1280

Concordia Willelmi Clifford clerici et Roberti Strelley super stagno et aliis in Oxton

Anno regni regis Edwardi nono die mercurii proximo post festum sancti Nicholai. Cum motum esset placitum coram dominis Johanne de Vallibus, Johanne de Saham, Johanne de Metyngham et magistro Thoma de Sodynton', domini regis iusticiariis itinerantibus apud Notingham, inter magistrum Willelmum de Clyfford', canonicum ecclesie beate Marie Suwell' ex parte una et dominum Robertum filium Walteri de Straeley ex altera, super exaltacione cuiusdam stagni, obstruccione cuiusdam vie in prato eiusdem domini Roberti, libera piscaria, disseysina commune pasture in Oxton', conquievit dictum placitum inter eosdem finaliter in hunc modum: videlicet, quod predictus magister Willelmus concessit pro se et successoribus suis quod dictus dominus Robertus et heredes sui habeant et teneant predictum stagnum liberum et quietum, una cum piscaria in aqua eiusdem stagni, in eodem statu quo fuit die confeccionis istius cirografi. Concessit eciam dictus magister Willelmus pro se et
p. 208   successoribus suis quod decetero non calumpniabunt | habere aliquam viam in parco¹ supradicto. Et pro hac concessione dictus dominus Robertus dedit et concessit Deo et ecclesie beate Marie Suwell' et predicto magistro Willelmo, canonico dicte ecclesie de prebenda de Oxton', et successoribus suis quatuor seliones continentes tres rodas terre adiacentes curie dicti magistri Willelmi in Oxton' ex parte australi, et extendunt se in longitudine a tofto Ricardi Cesar quantum durat longitudo curie dicti magistri Willelmi versus occidentem. Habendum et tenendum eidem magistro Willelmo et successoribus suis in puram et perpetuam elemosinam imperpetuum. Ita quod dictus magister Willelmus et successores sui predictos quatuor seliones muro, fossato vel haya possuit includere et inclusos tenere in suo separabili imperpetuum prout sibi magis viderit expedire. Et predictus Robertus et heredes sui predictam terram dicto magistro Willelmo et successoribus suis et ecclesie sue predicte contra omnes homines warantizabunt, acquietabunt et defendent imperpetuum, quantum in ipsis est. Et insuper concessit dominus Robertus, pro se et heredibus suis, quod dictus magister Willelmus et successores sui et eorum tenentes habeant quoddam cheminum ultra caput stagni predicti et ultra terram dicti Roberti de Saltreford' ad carectas et animalia sua omni tempore anni in eundo et redeundo versus boscum et de bosco. Et quod dictus magister Willelmus et successores et eorum tenentes habeant communam pasturam² ad omnimoda animalia sua ubicunque in pasturis de Oxton' omni tempore anni et campis et pratis eiusdem tempore aperto

exceptis pasturis dicti Roberti predicto die inclusis. Ita quod si pro defectu unius sufficientis clausure animalia pasturas intrare contigerit, non liceat predicto \Roberto/[3] heredibus suis neque ballivis dicta animalia imparcare sed ea absque imparcamento et dampno racionabiliter refugare. Et quod predictus magister Willelmus et successores sui libere possint piscari in omnibus aquis de Oxton' tam supra stagnum predictum, videlicet extra hayam quam prior de Landa fecit propinquius Rufford' versus boriam quam subtus stagnum extra piscaria in aqua stagni supradicti que libere remanebit dicto domino Roberto et heredibus suis. Preterea concessit dictus Robertus quod faciet prosternere quandam hayam et fossatum que levare fecit iuxta dictum stagnum ex parte dicti stagni versus Oxton'. Ita quod predictus magister Willelmus et successores sui et eorum tenentes libere possint ut communa pasture sue prius per predictam fossatum et hayam inclusa et animalia sua libere absque impedimento predicti Roberti et heredum suorum in dicto stagno adaquare. Et ad maiorem huius rei securitatem, tam dictus magister Willelmus quam dictus Robertus presenti scripto ad modum cirograffi confecto, alternatim sigilla apposuerunt. Hiis testibus: dominis Edmundo de Eyncurt', Radulpho de Crumwell', Johanne de Heriz, Roberto de Wodburgh, Willelmo de Sampson', Waltero de Ludham et Radulpho de Arnhale, militibus, Petro de Ludham, clerico, Hugone de Stapleford' et aliis multis.

[1] Previously the road/path (*via*) was said to be *in prato eiusdem domini* but the readings *prato* and *parco* are clear in the MS   [2] MS *pastura*   [3] Insertion written in another medieval hand

Margin Running head *Prebenda* (p. 208) *de Oxton* (p. 209 and similarly on pp. 210–11) in hand of Scribe 4. Title at head in 17th-c. hand.

Note This agreement, not in the usual form of a final concord, was made at the end of the Nottinghamshire eyre of 1280, which lasted from about 3 November to 9 December, with a separate session for the liberty of Southwell held later at the south door of the Minster on 11 May 1281. An agreement between the same parties is recorded, at Strelley's request, on the Rex plea roll of the eyre among the civil pleas, TNA JUST 1/664, rot. 22 [AALT, http://aalt.law.uh.edu/AALT4/JUST1/JUST1no664/aJUST1no664fronts/IMG_3742.htm], at the end of the Nottinghamshire section, but it differs significantly from this entry in the White Book. It reads: *Robertus filius Walteri de Stredley cognovit quod dedit concessit et carta sua confirmavit Deo et ecclesie sancte Marie de Suwell' et magistro Willelmo de Clifford canonico eiusdem quatuor sellones terre adiacentes curie eiusdem magistri Willelmi in Oxton et petit quod cartam quam ei inde fecit in rotuletur et irrotulatur in hec verba. Sciant presentes et futuri quod ego Robertus filius Walteri de Stredley dedi concessi et hac presenti carta mea confirmavi Deo et ecclesie beate Marie Suwell' et magistro Willelmo de Clyfford canonico eiusdem quatuor sellones terre adiacentes curie eiusdem magistri Willelmi in Oxton ex parte australi continentes tres rodas terre qui se extendunt in longitudi[n]e a tofto Ricardi Cesar quantum iurat longitudo curie predicti magistri Willelmi versus occidentem. Habend' et tenend' predicte ecclesie et predicto magistro Willelmo et successoribus suis in liberam puram et perpetuam elemosinam. Et ego predictus Robertus et heredes mei predictam terram cum pertinenciis predicte ecclesie et predicto magistro Willelmo de Clyfford et successoribus suis contra omnes homines warantizabimus acquietabimus et defendemus inperpetuum. Et ut hoc mea donacione concessio et carte mee confirmatio perpetue firmitatis robur optineat inpositum presentem cartam sigillo in eo consignavi. Hiis testibus dominis Edmundo de Daynecurt, Radulfo de Crumwell', Johanne de Heryz, Radulfo de Wodeburgh, Waltero de Ludham,*

Willelmo Sampson et Radulfo de Arnhale, militibus, Waltero de Stirkelay, Sewallo le Foun, Petro de Venella, Ricardo de Wadeschef, Willelmo de Sancta Cruce et aliis etc.
The list of lay witnesses to the two agreements is an impressive roll-call of leading Nottinghamshire knights: Sir Edmund Deyncourt, eighth baron, 1270–1327 (*Thurgarton*, xcii–xcvii); Sir Ralph of Cromwell died shortly before 18 September 1289; Sir John de Heriz was dead by 27 May 1299; Sir *Ralph* of Woodborough, dead by 1287, whose name has probably been changed to *Robert* by the clerk/s; Sir William de Sampson of Epperstone was dead by 1311; Sir Walter II of Lowdham succeeded his father *c*. 1272 and was still active in 1317; Sir Ralph of Arnold was dead by 28 August 1291 (Moor, i, 21, 255–6; ii, 222; iii, 63; iv, 206–7; v, 206; *Thurgarton*, 485n). Mr William of Clifford, canon by 26 May 1262 (*Thurgarton*, 41) and still on 2 July 1286 but replaced by 3 February 1287 (*Reg. Romeyn*, i, nos 38 and 1040). A series of small ponds still existing on the Oxton Dumble close to the site of Oxton Old Hall before it meets the river Doverbeck may mark the location of the pond.

352 *Grant in the form of a bipartite indenture by Philip of Daventry, canon and prebendary of Oxton and Cropwell, to Richard le Wryght of Oxton and Cecilia, his wife, of one vacant plot in Oxton, for a rent of 3s per annum. Also ratification by the Chapter of this augmentation of the prebend* Oxton, 15 December 1355 and Southwell, 21 June 1356

p. 209 Omnibus Christi fidelibus presens scriptum indentatum visuris vel audituris Philippus de Daventre, canonicus ecclesie collegiate Suthwell' et prebendarius prebende de Oxton' et Crophill' in eadem, salutem in domino sempiternam. Noveritis me pro bono et utilitate prebende mee, dedisse, concessisse et hac presenti scripto \meo/ indentato confirmasse Ricardo le Wryght de Oxton' et Cecilie, uxori eius, unam placeam terre inedificatam¹ in Oxton' quam Thomas le Cok' nuper tenuit, que reddere solebat duodecim denarios per annum, cum duobus selionibus parvis eidem placee adiacentibus et super eandem placeam buttantibus. Habendum et tenendum dictam placeam cum selionibus supradictis Ricardo et Cecilie ac heredibus suis procreatis de suis corporibus de me et successoribus meis prebendariis in eadem prebenda libere, quiete, bene et in pace imperpetuum. Reddendo inde annuatim michi et successoribus meis tres solidos argenti ad festa sancti Martini in yeme et nativitatis sancti Johannis baptiste per equales porciones pro omni servicio preter duos adventus ad magnam curiam nostram per annum. Et prefatus Ricardus placeam antedictam sumptibus suis propriis edificabit prout sibi viderit expedire. Et si contingat ipsos Ricardum et Ceciliam sine heredibus de suis corporibus abire procreatis tunc dicta placea et seliones ad me et successores meos integre revertantur, ac eciam si contingat predictum redditum ad aliquem terminum per quindecim dies a retro esse, quod absit, vel placeam predictam inedificatam esse per duos annos post confeccionem presencium, liceat mihi Philippo de Daventre, prebendario, et successoribus meis predictam placeam cum duobus selionibus intrare et tenere michi et successoribus meis prebendariis imperpetuum. Et ego vero dictus Philippus et successores mei prefatam placeam et seliones prenominatos Ricardo et Cecilie ac heredibus de corporibus suis procreatis contra omnes gentes warantizabimus imperpetuum. In cuius rei testimonium sigillum meum et sigillum dictorum Ricardi et Cecilie partibus huius scripti indentati alternatim sunt appensa. Datum apud Oxton' die mercurii proximo post festum sancti Luce evangeliste, anno domini m° ccc l° quinto, et anno regni regis Edwardi tercii post conquestum vicesimo nono. Hiis testibus: magistro Willelmo de Boston', rectore ecclesie de Cotgrave, Willelmo de Sloswyk', vicario de Oxton', Willelmo de Bulwell' de eadem, Roberto de Bulcot de eadem et aliis multis.

Et quia nos capitulum ecclesie beate Marie Suthwell' comperimus donacionem et concessionem supradictas per augmentum annualis redditus ad utilitatem prebende supradicte fuisse et esse factas ipsas approbamus et ratificamus, ac presentis sigilli nostri apposicione confirmamus. Datum in domo nostra capitulari Suthwell' in generali convocacione confratrum et concanonicorum nostrorum die Martis proximo post festum sancte Trinitatis xi videlicet kalendas Julii anno domini millesimo ccc quinquagesimo sexto.

¹ MS *inedificatum*

Margin *Carta Petri de Coventrie, clerici, de placea terre in Oxton* in right margin in post-1583 hand. *12d per annum* below in same hand.

Note Philip of Daventry had been granted an expectative canonry on 14 August 1328 (*Reg. Melton*, v, no. 267) and was certainly holding Oxton I by 27 September 1337 (ibid., no. 491).

353 *Memorandum that in the court of Mr Nicholas of Oxford held at Oxton on 2 October 1316, the village of Blidworth showed that a tenement held by Peter, son of Ivo of Blidworth, was in the lord's hand because of the outlawry of Peter for various felonies. Roger called* de Galewaye *of Blidworth then appeared and made fine for the messuage according to the customs of the manor of Oxton and was enfeoffed with it as a bond tenant. At the request of Mr Nicholas, the Chapter has attached its seal in confirmation* Southwell, 22 June 1321

Memorandum quod ad magnam curiam magistri Nicholai de Oxon' tentam p. 210 apud Oxton' die sabbati proximo post festum sancti Michaelis, anno regni regis Edwardi filii regis Edwardi decimo, compertum est per villatam de Blidworth quod illa tenementa, videlicet, unum mesuagium et una bovata terre, que Petrus filius Ivonis de Blythworth quondam tenuit, in eadem sunt in manu domini tanquam escaeta sua, pro eo quod predictus Petrus utlagatus est pro diversis feloniis et transgressionibus contra pacem domini regis factis. Postea venit Rogerus dictus de Galewaye de Blithworth et fecit finem cum domino pro dictis mesuagio et bovata terre, cum pertinenciis. Habendum sibi et suis ad tenendum in bondagio imperpetuum secundum consuetudinem manerii de Oxton'. In cuius rei testimonium huic memorande¹ sigillum capituli ecclesie beate Marie Suthwell' ad requisicionem dicti magistri Nicholai prebendarii est appensum. Datum in capitulo nostro Suwell' x. kalendas Julii, anno gracie millesimo ccc^mo vicesimo primo.

¹ MS *sic* for *memorandum*

Margin *Bovata terre in Blidworth escaeta* in post-1583 hand in left margin.

Note Mr Nicholas of Oxford, collated to Oxton II, 22 October 1310 (*BRUO*, ii, 1415), died shortly before 18 January 1327 (*Reg. Melton*, v, no. 228n).

354 *Inspeximus by Richard II of the ratification by Robert [Waldby], archbishop of York, to the Chapter, and confirmation by the Chapter, of the grant in the form of a bipartite indenture by John of Danby, clerk, prebendary of one of the prebends of Oxton and Cropwell, to William of Rothwell and Alice, his wife, of three messuages and two and a half bovates of land in Oxton for 9s rent, other services and two views of frankpledge per annum with reversion to John of Danby, Oxton, 11 September 1396, Westminster, 23 September 1397*

Westminster, 8 October 1397

p. 211 Ricardus, Dei gracia rex Anglie et Francie et dominus Hibernie omnibus ad quos presentes litere pervenerint salutem. Inspeximus literas patentes venerabilis[1] patris Roberti, archiepiscopi Ebor', Anglie primatis, factas in hec verba:

Universis sancte matris ecclesie filiis ad quos presentes litere pervenerint, Robertus, permissione divina Ebor' archiepiscopus, Anglie primas et apostolice sedis legatus salutem in sinceris amplecibus salvatoris. Noverit universitas vestra nos literas approbacionis, ratificacionis et confirmacionis dilectorum filiorum capituli ecclesie nostre collegiate beate Marie Suthwell' super quadam carta per dilectum filium dominum Johannem Danby, nuper canonicum eiusdem ecclesie nostre Suthwell' et prebendarium unius prebendarum de Oxton' et Crophill' in eadem, Willelmo de Rothwell' et Alicie, uxori eiusdem Willelmi, factas sigillo communi dicti capituli consignatas nobis per eundem dominum Johannem Danby presentatas vidisse et inspexisse tenorem qui sequitur per omnia continentes:

Sancte matris ecclesie filiis universis presentes literas inspecturis capitulum ecclesie collegiate beate Marie Suthwell' salutem in eo qui est omnium verus salus. Noverit[2] universitas vestra nos cartam quam dilectus frater et concanonicus noster dominus Johannes de Danby, prebendarius unius prebendarum de Oxton' et Crophill' in ecclesia nostra Suthwell' fecit et tradidit Willelmo de Rothwell' et Alicie, uxori sue, cum diligencia inspexisse, cuius tenor sequitur in hec verba:

Sciant presentes et futuri quod ego Johannes de Danby, clericus et prebendarius alterius prebendarum de Oxton' et Crophill in ecclesia collegiata beate Marie Suthwellie, dedi, concessi et hac presenti carta mea \indentati/ confirmavi Willelmo de Rothwell', servienti meo, et Alicie, uxori sue, unum mesuagium et i bovatam terre cum pertinenciis in Oxton', quondam Willelmi de Bulwell', unam bovatam terre cum pertinenciis in eadem villa, quondam Johannis de Hill', qui quidem bovata terre quondam fuit annexa cuidam mesuagio ad finem gardini mansi prebende mee predicte modo capto in largicionem mansi mei predicti, prout iacet inter grangiam mansi mei predicti et cursum aque ville de Oxton', unum mesuagium et i bovatam terre cum pertinenciis in eadem villa, quondam Ade de Flouburgh', et unum mesuagium et dimidiam bovatam terre cum pertinenciis in eadem villa, quondam Cristiane Rede. Habendum et tenendum predicta tria mesuagia, tres bovatas terre et dimidiam cum omnibus eorum pertinenciis in villa predicta prefatis Willelmo et Alicie et heredibus de corpore ipsius Willelmi exeuntibus de me et successoribus meis pro bono servicio suo michi impenso et amplius mihi impendendo. Reddendo inde annuatim michi et successoribus meis pro mesuagio et bovata terre quondam Willelmi de Bulwell' in villa predicta ad duos anni terminos usuales pro redditu meo tres solidos, pro wodlodes, iii d., pro rompenys et haypenys, ii d., pro una gallina et dimidia tres denarios, pro bovata terre quondam predicti Johannis de Hill' pro redditu meo ii s., pro wodlodes iii d., pro rompenys et haypenys ii d., pro i. gallina et dimidia iii d. Et pro mesuagio et dimidia bovata terre quondam predicte | Cristiane   p. 212 Rede in villa predicta pro redditu meo antiquitus soluto, duos solidos, pro rompeny, haypenys et wodlodes iii d., pro una gallina et dimidia iii d., et pro incremento redditus mei eorundem mesuagii et dimidie bovate terre quolibet anno ad duos anni terminos usuales sex denarios, sic solvendo omnia servicia de dictis tenementis antiquitus debita et consueta, ulterius faciendo duas apparencias quolibet anno, ad duos visus franciplegii mei et successorum meorum apud Oxton' pro omni alio servicio. Et si dictus Willelmus de Rothwell' obierit sine herede de corpore suo exeunte, post decessum dicte Alicie omnia predicta tenementa cum suis pertinenciis in villa predicta mihi et successoribus meis revertentur. In cuius rei testimonium huic parte carte mee indentate penes dictum Willelmum et heredes suos de corpore suo exeuntes remanenti sigillum meum apposui. Alteri vero parti eiusdem carte mee indentate penes capitulum ecclesie beate Marie Suthwell' ad opus meum et proficuum et successorum meorum conservandum remanenti, sigillum eciam meum apposui. Hiis testibus: Nicholao Strelley, Thoma Strelley, Johanne de Oxton', Willelmo Hauberk', vicario de Oxton', Thoma de Bolsom et multis aliis. Datum apud Oxton' die lune proximo post festum nativitatis beate Marie virginis anno regni regis Ricardi secundi vicesimo.

Nos autem capitulum supradictum attendentes predictam concessionem nobis et ecclesie nostre Suthwellie ac predicta prebende utilem esse et in nullo preiudicialem, sicut fidelem inquisicionem coram nobis presentatam et declaratam sumus plenius informati, ipsam concessionem ratam habentes et gratam eam quantum in nobis est approbamus, ratificamus et presenti scripto nostro indentato imperpetuum confirmamus. In cuius rei testimonium parti huius scripti indentate penes predictum Willelmum et Aliciam, uxorem suam, remanenti sigillum nostrum commune fecimus apponi, alteri vero parti eiusdem scripti indentati penes nos capitulum antedictum remanenti, sigillum dicti Willelmi de Rothwell' similiter est appensum. Datum in domo nostra capitulari Suthwell' die lune proximo ante festum sancti Luce evangeliste anno domini millesimo ccc^{mo} nonagesimo sexto.

Post quarum quidem literarum presentacionem nobis ut premittitur factam et receptam earundem fuimus cum instancia requisiti quatinus eandem cartam de dictorum domini Johannis Danby et Willelmi Rothwell' mutuo consensu factam admittere, et ipsam confirmare, corroborare et approbare auctoritate nostra ordinaria dignarentur. Nos igitur Robertus Ebor' archiepiscopus supradictus, attendentes cartam predictam racionabilem deo graciam, ac dicto ecclesie nostre Suthwell' et partibus predictis utilem, ipsam de consensu ipsarum partium expresso robur optinere debere decernimus, ac eam et contenta in eadem in singulis suis partibus auctoritate nostra ordinaria et pontificali autorizamus, ratificamus, approbamus et expresse tenore presencium confirmamus, perpetuis futuris temporibus

p. 213 durature | nostre jurisdiccionis dignitate privilegio et honore nostris et ecclesie nostre predicte in omnibus semper salvis. In quorum omnium testimonium sigillum nostrum fecimus hiis apponi. Datum in hospicio nostro iuxta Westmonasterium xxiii die mensis Septembris anno domini m° ccc^mo nonagesimo septimo et nostre translacionis primo.

Nos autem donacionem, concessionem, approbaciones, autorizacionem, ratificaciones et confirmaciones predictas ac omnia et singula in literis predictis contenta rata habentes et grata ea pro nobis et heredibus nostris quantum in nobis est acceptamus, approbamus et prefato Willelmo, Alicie et heredibus ipsius Willelmi, tenore presencium concedimus et confirmamus prout litere predicte racionabiliter testantur. In cuius rei testimonium has literas nostras fieri fecimus patentes. Teste me ipso apud Westmonasterium octavo die Octobris anno regni nostri vicesimo primo.

¹ MS appears to read *reverabilis*   ² Followed by *vestra* struck out

Margin   p. 211 *Carta Johannis Danby de diversis in Oxton* in post-1583 hand in right margin; *3s nomine wopenyth, 3 Rome nobis etc.* towards the bottom in late medieval hand? p. 213, an erased foliation ?*lxxx°* in top right corner.

Note   John Danby, prebendary of Oxton II and of Bole (York); simply styled 'clerk', he augmented a chantry at Caunton church in 1392, see *Newstead*, 191–8. Robert Waldby, translated from Chichester on 5 October 1396, received his temporalities on 6 March 1397, but died between 29 December 1397 and 6 January 1398. William of Bulwell witnessed **352** (1350).

HENRY VI's CHARTER, 1441, 355

355   *Letters patent of pardon granted by Henry VI to the Chapter for acquiring various lands without licence, recalling that Richard II had granted a licence to William of Gunthorpe, James Staunton and Walter Ulseby, clerks, to acquire a messuage and sixty acres of land with appurtenances in North Carlton to assign to the Chapter for a chaplaincy to celebrate daily mass in the Minster (503, 12 July 1395), and that Henry IV, by his letters patent granted a similar licence to Thomas Haxey, canon of Southwell, to acquire a messuage, 120 acres of land and seven acres of meadow in Bathley, North Muskham and Holme for a similar purpose; that Gunthorpe, Staunton and Ulseby and Haxey, by virtue of these two letters, acquired the lands listed which among others they assigned to the Chapter, and that the Chapter subsequently peacefully held these until by virtue of an inquisition held at Cromwell on 29 October 1439 the Chapter was deprived of possession. The king, moved by the laudable intentions of Gunthorpe, Staunton, Ulseby and Haxey, now confirms the transfer of the lands in question to the Chapter as by his letters patent of 12 May 1440, despite further letters in favour of John Tisyng of 13 May 1440, which are now annulled after proceedings in Chancery at which Tisyng failed to appear*   Westminster, 20 May 1441

Pardonacio Henrici sexti facta capitulo Suthwellie precipue de terris   p. 214
eidem capitulo adquisitis licencia regis prius non optenta anno regni
sui decimo nono

Henricus dei gracia rex Anglie et Francie et dominus Hibernie omnibus
ad quos presentes litere pervenerint salutem. Sciatis quod cum dominus
Ricardus, nuper rex Anglie secundus post conquestum de gracia sua
speciali concesserit et licenciam dedit pro se et heredibus suis quantum
in ipso fuit dilectis sibi Willelmo de Gunthorp', clerico, Jacobo Staunton',
clerico, et Waltero Ulseby, clerico, quod ipsi unum mesuagium et sexaginta
acras terre cum pertinenciis in Northcarleton' que de ipso nuper Rege
non tenebantur inter alia dare possent et assignare dilecto sibi in Christo
capitulo ecclesie beate Marie de Suthwell' habendo sibi et successoribus
suis in subvencionem sustentacionis cuiusdam capellani missam de
beata Maria in ecclesia predicta per notam celebraturam singulis diebus
imperpetuum prout in literis eiusdem nuper regis patentibus inde confectis
plenius continentur. Postmodum que carissimus dominus et avus noster
Henricus, nuper rex Anglie quartus, per literas suas patentes de gracia
sua speciali concesserit et licenciam dederit Thome Haxey, canonico
ecclesie predicte, quod ipse unum mesuagium, centum et viginti acras
terre et septem acras prati cum pertinenciis in Batheley, Northmuskham
et Holme in comitatu Notingham que de ipso avo nostro non tenebantur
inter alia dare posset et assignare capitulo ecclesie predicte, habendum
et tenendum sibi et successoribus suis ad divina servicia et alia pietatis
opera, ibidem iuxta ordinacionem ipsius Thome facienda imperpetuum
prout in eisdem literis plenius continetur, virtute quarum quidem literarum
patentium predicti nuper regis Ricardi predicti Willelmus, Jacobus et
Willelmus per se predicta mesuagium et terram cum pertinenciis in
Northcarleton' ac predictus Thomas per se pretextu predictarum literarum
patentium prefati avi nostri predicta mesuagium, terram et pratum cum
pertinenciis in Batheley, Northmuskham et Holme inter alia dederunt et
assignaverunt predicto capitulo habendum et tenendum sibi et successoribus
suis iuxta vim, formam et effectum literarum dictorum nuper regum
predictarum idem que capitulum et successores sui vigore donacionum
et assignacionum huiusmodi de mesuagio, terra et prato predictis cum
pertinenciis de tali statu continue seisiti fuerunt pacifice et quiete quousque
dilectum nobis in Christo nunc capitulum ecclesie predicte colore cuiusdam
inquisicionis capte apud Cromwell' in crastino apostolorum Symonis et
Jude anno regni nostri xviii° per quam compertum fuit quod Willelmus
de Northwell', clericus, fuit seisitus in dominico suo ut de feodo de uno
mesuagio, centum acris terre et duabus clausuris cum suis pertinenciis
in Batheley et de uno mesuagio et sexaginta acris terre cum pertinenciis
in Northcarleton' et de uno mesuagio et duobus toftis et triginta acris
terre cum pertinenciis in Northwell' et illa cum aliis terris, tenementis et
redditibus cum pertinenciis per finem in curia domini regis Edwardi tercii
apud Ebor' a die Pasche in xv dies anno regni sui duodecimo[1] levatam
dedit Henrico filio Ricardi Grymmyng' de Northwell' et Elizabethe,
uxori eius, et heredibus de corporibus ipsorum Henrici et Elizabethe
exeuntibus. Et si iidem Henricus filius Ricardi Grymmyng' et Elizabetha

obierunt sine herede de corporibus suis exeunte quod tunc post decessum ipsorum Henrici et Elizabethe omnia predicta tenementa \et/ redditus cum pertinenciis ut predictum est integre remanerent Hugoni Rylyng' de Woodhous et Alicie, uxori eius, et heredibus masculis de corporibus ipsorum Hugonis et Alicie exeuntibus. Et si iidem Hugo et Alicia, uxor eius, obierent sine herede masculo de corporibus suis exeunte quod tunc post decessum ipsorum Hugonis et Alicie omnia predicta tenementa et redditus cum pertinenciis integre remanerent Johanni filio Roberti de Holme et Alicie, uxori eius, et heredibus masculis de corporibus ipsorum Johannis et Alicie exeuntibus. Et si iidem Johannes filius Roberti de Holme et Alicia, uxor eius, obierent sine heredibus masculis de corporibus suis exeuntibus quod tunc post decessum ipsorum Johannis et Alicie omnia predicta tenementa et redditus cum suis pertinenciis integre remanerent predicto Edwardo quondam regi Anglie, et heredibus suis imperpetuum. Et quod predictus Henricus filius Ricardi et Elizabetha, uxor eius, fuerunt seisiti et de tenementis et redditibus predictis virtute finis predicti et habuerunt exitum inter se quandam Johannam et obierunt et predicta tenementa et redditus cum pertinenciis descendebant predicte Johanne ut filie et heredi eorundem Henrici filii Ricardi et Elizabethe eo quod iidem Henricus filius Ricardi et Elizabetha obierunt sine herede masculo de corpore suo exeunte et quod eadem Johanna desponsata fuit Roberto Touke et habuerunt exitum inter se Johannem et obierunt et quod idem Johannes obiit die lune proximo post festum assumpcionis beate Marie virginis anno regni nostri decimo septimo[2] sine herede de corpore suo exeunte. Et quod predicti Hugo Rylynge et Alicia, uxor[3] eius, obierunt sine herede masculo de corporibus suis exeunte et predictus Johannes filius Roberti de Holme et Alicia, uxor eius, obierunt sine herede masculo de corporibus suis exeunte de predictis mesuagio, centum acris terre et duabus clausuris cum pertinenciis in Batheley in fine et inquisicione predictis specificatis, que sunt parcelle predictorum mesuagii centum et viginti acrarum terre et septem acrarum prati cum pertinenciis in Batheley, Northmuskham et Holme in predictis literis predicti avi nostri contentorum necnon de predictis mesuagio et sexaginta acris terre cum pertinenciis in Northcarleton' tam in dictis literis predicti nuper regis Ricardi quam in fine et inquisicione predictis similiter contentorum, que una et eadem sunt et non diversa, amotum fuit et expulsum in ipsius

p. 215 capituli | dampnum et dispendium non modica, et divini cultus in ecclesia predicta subtraccionem et diminucionem vehementem, actiones[4] pias et laudabiles intenciones tam predictorum nuper regum quam predictorum Willelmi, Jacobi, Walteri et Thome ceteraque premissa debite ponderantes, et quamquam predicta mesuagium et centum acre terre et due clausure cum pertinenciis in Batheleye predicta ac dicta mesuagia et sexaginta acre terre cum pertinenciis in Northcarleton' in fine et inquisicione predictis specificata ad nox[5] pretextu eorundem finis et inquisicione iure hereditario descenderunt et in manu nostra ea occasione extiterunt. Volentes tamen cum predicto capitulo ut ministri Deo in ecclesia predicta famulantes pro salubri statu nostro dum viximus et pro anima nostra cum ab hac luce migraverimus attentius exorare valerent in hac parte agere graviose duodecimo die Maii anno regni nostri decimo octavo per literas nostras patentes de gracia nostra speciali dederimus et concesserimus predicto capitulo tam predicta mesuagium et centum acras terre et duas clausuras cum pertinenciis in Batheleye quam predicta mesuagium et sexaginta acras terre cum pertinenciis in Northcarleton' in manum nostram vigore inquisicionis predicte seisita habendum et tenendum sibi et successoribus suis in liberam, puram et perpetuam elemosinam in subvencionem sustentacionis capellanorum et aliorum onerum in ecclesia predicta quorum sustentacioni et supportacioni manutendo eadem mesuagia, terre et clausure cum pertinenciis data fureunt et assignata, una cum exitibus et proficuis eorundem a tempore predicte inquisicionis captis qualitercumque perceptis prout in eisdem literis plenius continetur.

Postmodum que ad prosecucionem predicti capituli nobis ostendentis quod licet idem capitulum mesuagia, terram et clausuras predicta cum pertinenciis in Batheleye ac dicta mesuagium et terram cum pertinenciis in Northcarleton' pretextu literarum nostrarum predictarum a predicto duodecimo die Maii obtinuerit et possessionem suam inde continuaverit pacifice et quiete idem tamen capitulum colore quarundem literarum nostrarum patentium cuidam Johanni Tisyng' tercio decimo die Maii tunc proximo sequente de predictis mesuagio, terra et clausura in Batheley per nomina unius mesuagii et ducentarum acrarum terre cum pertinenciis in Batheley ac de dictis mesuagio et terra cum pertinenciis in Northcarleton' per nomina unius mesuagii sexaginta acrarum terre cum pertinenciis in Northcarleton' et unius mesuagii duorum toftorum et triginta acrarum terre cum pertinenciis in Northwell' in comitatu Notyngham a tempore mortis Johannis Touke usque ad finem duodecim annorum ex tunc proximorum sequentium et plenarie completorum sub certa forma in eisdem literis contenta confectorum habendum ab eisdem mesuagio terra et clausura cum pertinenciis in Batheley ac mesuagio et terra cum pertinenciis in Northcarleton' amotum fuit et expulsum nimius iuste in ipsius capituli dampnum et dispendium non modica et nobis supplicantis ut dictas literas nostras prefato Johanni Tisyng' quo ad predicta mesuagium terram et clausuram cum pertinenciis in Northcarleton' sic factas revocari et adnullari ipsumque capitulum ad possessionem suam eorundem mesuagiorum, terrarum et clausurarum una cum exitibus et proficuis inde ab eodem duodecimo die Maii perceptis restitui iubere vellemus et nos volentes in hac parte fieri quod fuit iustum per breve nostrum preciperimus vicecomiti nostro comitatus predicti quod scire faceret prefato Johannis Tysing' quod esset coram nobis in cancellaria nostra ad certum die iam preteritum ubicunque tunc foret ad ostendendum si quid pro nobis aut pro seipso haberet vel dicere sciret quare litere predicte sibi quo ad predicta mesuagium, terram et clausuram cum pertinenciis in Batheley ac dicta mesuagium et terram cum pertinenciis in Northcarleton' ut premittitur facte revocari et adnullari dictumque capitulum ad possessionem suam eorundem mesuagiorum, terre et clausure una cum exitibus et proficuis predictis restitui non deberent et ad faciendum ulterius et percipiendum quod curia nostra consideraret in hac parte. Super quo idem vicecomes nobis in cancellariam nostram predictam retornavit quod scire fecit prefato Johanni Tysing' quod esset coram nobis in cancellaria nostra predicta ad diem predictum ad faciendum quod breve predictum in se exigebat

et requirebat per Willelmum Glosse, Johannem Bower', Johannem
Colyngham et Ricardum Perot, probos et legitimos homines de balliva
sua. Ad quem diem prefatus Johannes Tysyng' in cancellaria predicta
solempniter vocatus non venit per quod de avisamento iusticiarorum et
servientum nostrorum ad legem et alium peritorum de consilio nostro
in eadem cancellaria nostra existentium consideratum fuit tunc ibidem
quod breve predicte prefato Johanni Tysyng' quo ad predicta mesuagium,
terram et clausuram cum pertinenciis in Batheley ac dicta mesuagium \et/
terram cum pertinenciis in Northcarleton' ut premittitur facte revocentur et
adnullentur quod que dictum capitulum ad possessionem suam eorundem
mesuagiorum, terre et clausure cum pertinenciis una cum exitibus et
proficuis predictis restituatur.

Nos volentes consideracionem predictam effectui debito manicipari
dictas literas nostras prefato Johanni Tysyng' quo ad predicta mesuagium,
terram et clausuram cum pertinenciis in Batheley ac dicta mesuagium et
terram cum pertinenciis in Northcarleton' sic factas duximus revocandas
et penitus adnullandas. Et hoc omnibus quorum interest innotescimus
per presentes. In cuius rei testimonium has literas nostras fieri fecimus
patentes. Teste me ipso apud Westmonasterium xx die Maii anno regni
nostri decimo nono.

¹ ?26 April 1338   ² 16 August 1439   ³ *uxor* repeated   ⁴ MS *ac nos*   ⁵ Reading uncertain

Margin The text is in that of an unidentified scribe, who also writes **356** and **357**,
similar to Scribe 6.

Note Thomas Haxey, prebendary of Rampton (1388–1425). William I of Norwell,
prebendary of Norwell Overhall (1333–40). Henry, son of Richard Grymmyng of Norwell,
made a fine in 1338 and he also received a messuage in Middlegate, Newark by grant of
Richard de Galleway on 23 July 1338 (NA, Newark Corporation/Borough Muniments,
T55). His father (a tenant at Willoughby by Norwell, **373**) acquired a messuage, toft,
twenty acres of land and a rent of 7s 3½d in North Muskham, South Muskham, Bathley,
Holme and South (Little) Carlton in 1334–5 for 100 marks (TNA, CP 25/1/185 no. 134)
and another of his sons, William, also acquired no fewer than six messuages, forty-eight
acres of arable, ten acres of meadow and 6s 3½d in rents in North and South Clifton
also in 1335 (ibid., no. 133), together with a messuage in Bathley for ten marks at the
same time (ibid., no. 132). On 1 June 1409, Ralph Lude, son and heir of Thomas Lude
(**487, 488, 495**), released to Thomas Haxey all the lands and services he possessed in
the townships of North and South Muskham, South Carlton, Bathley, Holme and North
and South Clifton, most of which his father, Thomas, had previously transferred to
William of Gunthorpe and others for the endowment of the Vicars Choral (NA, Newark
Corporation/Borough Muniments, F 22/P 45 (150)).

356 *Mandate by Pope Martin V to the prior of Thurgarton to investigate the claims of the Chapter that various persons were withholding or hiding what they owed, and to threaten those who were guilty with excommunication if they failed to deliver by a date to be determined by him*   Rome, 1 June 1429

Martinus[1] episcopus, servus servorum Dei, dilecto filio priori de Thorgaton',   p. 216
Eboracensis diocesis, salutem et apostolicam benedictionem. Significarunt nobis dilecti filii capituli ecclesie de Suthwell', Ebor' diocesis, quod nonnulli iniquitatis filii, quos prorsus ignorant, decimas, redditus, census, fructus, legata, terras, possessiones, domos, casalia, prata, pascua, allodia, silvas, grangias, nemora, foveas, molendina, piscinas, stagna piscarias, auri, argenti, bladi, frumenti, tritici, siliginis, ordei, fabarum, pisarum aliorumque leguminum quantitates, cignos, aucas, oves, porcos, vaccas, boves, parcos, clausos, sepes, gallos, gallinas, anates, vitulos, agnos, equos, pullos, iumentas,[2] pannos, laneos et lineos, vasa aurea, argentea, cupra, enea, pendrea, ferrea, instrumenta publica, literas autenticas, munimenta, calices, libros, vestimenta, ornamenta ecclesiastica, tallias, jura jurisdictiones, pecuniarum summas, domorum, utensilia et nonnulla alia bona ad mensam capitularem ipsius ecclesie spectantia, temere et maliciose occultare et occulte detinere presumunt, non curantes ea prefatis capitulo exhibere in animarum suarum periculum ipsorum que capituli et mense nonmodicum detrimentum, super quo idem[3] capitulum apostolice sedis remedium imploravunt. Quodcirca discrecioni tue per apostolica scripta mandamus quatinus omnes huiusmodi occultas detentores decimarum, redditum, censum, fructum et aliorum bonorum predictorum ex parte nostra publice in ecclesiis coram populo per te, vel alium, moneas ut infra competentem terminum quem eis prefixeris ea prefatis capitulo a se debita restituant et revelent ac de ipsis plenam et debitam satisfactionem impendant, et si id non, adimpleverint infra alium competentem terminum, quem eis ad hoc peremptorie duxeris prefigendum, ex tunc in eos generalem excommunicacionis sentenciam proferas, et eam facias ubi et quando expedire videris usque ad satisfactionem condignam solemniter publicavi. Datum Rome apud sanctos apostolos kalendis Junii pontificatus nostri anno duodecimo.

[1] Followed by *servus servorum Dei* lightly struck out   [2] MS *iunentas*, i.e. mares   [3] MS *iidem*

Note   The name of the prior of Thurgarton in 1429 is uncertain. Permission was given for the election of Robert of Thurgarton in 1416, and Richard Haley occurs as prior in 1435 (*Thurgarton*, ccv).

357 *Sentence, issued in a public instrument under the seal and signature of John of Binbrook, notary public, by Richard Andrew, vicar of the parish church of St Mary's, Southwell, and William Lamley, vicar choral, commissioners appointed by the Chapter, in a dispute concerning the chapels of Darlton and Whimpton between the inhabitants of Darlton and Robert Allerston', vicar of Dunham, who is ordered to provide a suitable chaplain to perform services and administer sacraments at the chapels at his own cost* Southwell, 16 August 1414

Universis sancte matris ecclesie filiis ad quos presentes litere pervenerint Ricardus Andrew, vicarius parochialis ecclesie collegiate beate Marie Suthwell', Ebor' diocesis, et Willelmus Lamley, vicarius in choro eiusdem ecclesie, venerabilium virorum capituli ecclesie memorate commissarii in causa infrascripta, et inter partes infrascriptas legitime deputati, salutem in omni salvatore. Ad universitatis vestre noticiam volumus pervenire quod nos in \quadam/ causa subtraccionis invencionis[1] unius capellani in capellis de Darleton' et Wympton' a prebendali ecclesia de Dunham dicte Ebor' diocesis dependentibus celebraturi prius coram dicto capitulo de inde coram nobis mota inter partes infrascriptas et ad calculandum sentencie diffinitive agitata rite et legitime procedentes sentenciam diffinitivam tulimus sub hac forma:

In dei nomine amen. Auditis et intellectis meritis cause subtraccionis invencionis unius capellani in capellis de Darleton' et Wympton' a prebendali ecclesia de Dunham, Ebor' diocesis dependentibus celebraturi que primo coram venerabilibus viris capitulo ecclesie collegiate beate Marie Suthwell' deinde coram nobis Ricardo Andrew et Willelmo Lamley ipsius capituli commissariis in hac parte legitime deputatis vertebatur inter Gregorium Dunham de Darleton' predicta, Robertum Richardson', Hugonem Barthorp' et Johannem Halum ac alios homines dictam villam de Darleton' inhabitantes partem actricem ex parte una, et dominum Robertum Allerston', vicarium dicte prebendalis ecclesie de Dunham partem ream ex altera. In qua quidem causa oblato libello per partem actricem predictam et per partem ream predictam obtento lite que per partem ream predictam negatias contestata, ad eundem iurata que partibus predictis de calumpnia et de veritate dicenda, testibus que productis rite receptis iuratis et examinatis ac eorum attestacionibus in forma iuris publicatis dato que termino ad dicendum contra huiusmodi testes et eorum dicta. Quo termino adveniente, nichil dicto seu proposito, datus fuit terminus ad proponendum omnia in facto consistencia hinc inde. Quo termino adveniente, perductis et exhibitis per dictam partem actricem quibusdam rotulis visitacionum per capitulum predictum in ecclesia prebendali predicta et capellis predictis ab eadem dependentibus. Factarum quibus rite receptis quia compertum fuit

p. 217 prefatum dominum Robertum Allerston', vicariam predicte | prebendalis ecclesie de Donham ex causa permutacionis facte cum perpetua vicaria ecclesie parochiali de Gryngley dicte diocesis quam dominus Ricardus Atwatyr' nuper obtinebat in manus dicti capituli resignasse et ab eadem vicaria de Donham totaliter recessisse decretum fuit ipsum dominum

Ricardum Atwatyr' successorem predicti domini Roberti Allerston' fore citandum ad diem marcurii[2] proximum post festum apostolorum Philippi et Jacobi proximum tunc sequens ad procedendum procedi vel videndum in dicta causa iuxta formam retroactorum. Quo die adveniente parte actrice predicta per prefatum magistrum Thomam Yngrham ut prius ac prefato domino Ricardo Atwatyr', vicario coram nobis personaliter comparentibus effectu que dicti libelli in presenti causa oblati et totius processus inde habiti coram nobis eidem domino Ricardo Atwatir', vicario exposito et declarato idem dominus Ricardus, vicarius narrata prout narrantur in eodem libello vera esse iudicialiter fatebatur. Et sic de consensu partium in tota causa concluso renunciatis que feriis ob reverentiam hominum introductis datus erat dies iovis proximus post festum assumpcionis beate Marie virginis proximum tunc sequens ad audiendum sentenciam in causa supradicta. Unde nos Ricardus et Willelmus, commissarii antedicti, rimato et investigato toto processu huiusmodi partibus que predictis coram nobis legitime comparentibus et sentenciam ferri cum instancia postulantibus Christi nomine invocato de consilio iuris paritorum nobis in hac parte assidentium ad sentencie nostre huiusmodi prolacionem in hunc modum.

Quia per acta et inactitata producta et exhibita et confessata invenimus predictam partem actricem intenciones suam in predicto libello suo deductam ad plenum fundasse et probasse prefatos Gregorium Donham, Robertum Richardson, Hugonem Barthorp[3] et Johannem Halt ac alios homines dictam villam de Darleton' et Wympton' inhabitantes partem actricem predictam ad statum et possessionem prestinos quibus fuerunt spoliati scilicet ad habendum unum capellanum ydoneum in dicta villa de Darleton' et Wympton' predictis celebrantem ac sacramenta et sacramentalia inhabitantibus easdem villas ministrantes domini Ricardi Atwatir', vicarii suis predicti sumptibus et expensis recedendos, redintegrandos et restituendos fore decernimus ipsos que cum effectu ad statum et possessionem premissos reducimus, redintegramus et restituimus per decretum ac ipsum dominum Ricardum Atwatir', vicarium supradictum, ad subeundum et agniscendum onus invencionis huiusmodi capellani in dictis villis et capellis ut premittitur formaliter et diffinitive adiudicamus et condempnamus in hiis scriptis. In cuius rei testimonium atque fidem presentes literas nostras sentenciam diffinitivam in se continentes ex inde fieri et per magistrum Johannem de Bynbroke, presbyterum et notarium publicum, scribam nostrum in tota causa subscribi et publicavi mandavimus sigilli que dicti capituli ad causas appensione fecimus communiri. Data et acta fuerunt hec prout suprascribuntur et recitantur quo ad predicte sentencie prolacionem sub anno ab incarnacione domini secundum cursum et computacionem ecclesie Anglicane m^o $cccc^{mo}$ xiiii^o, indiccione septima pontificatus serenissimi in Christo patris et domini nostri domini Johannis, divina providencia pape xxiii, anno quinto mensis Augusti die xvi° in domo capitulari ecclesie collegiate supradicte presentibus discretis viris dominis Willelmo Byker' et Roberto Sampson', vicariis in choro ecclesie collegiate memorate et aliis testibus ad premissa vocatis specialiter et rogatis.

Et ego Johannes de Bynbroke, presbyter Lincoln' diocesis, publicus apostolica et imperiali notarius, predicte sentencie prolacioni ceteris que premissis omnibus et singulis dum sic ut premittitur sub anno domini, indiccionis, pontificatus, mense, die et loco suprascriptis agebantur interfui, scripsi, publicavi et ex precepto predictorum commissariorum signum meum solitum et consuetum apposui in fidem et testimonium omnius premissorum.

¹ MS appears to read *nuencionis* but cf. below   ² MS *sic*   ³ MS *Bart*

Margin   *Sentencia pro capellano in capella de Darleton et Wimpton* in post-1583 hand in left margin.

Note   For Binbook see **577n** in volume II.

pp. 218–24   These pages are blank; there are faint foliations in top right corners of p. 215 (?*lxxxvi*), p. 217 (*folio lxxxvij*), p. 219 (*folio lxxxvij*).